Writing for Your Portfolio

Writing for

Your Portfolio

C. Beth Burch

Binghamton University, SUNY

Allyn and Bacon

BOSTON   LONDON   TORONTO   SYDNEY   TOKYO   SINGAPORE

Vice President: Eben W. Ludlow
Series Editorial Assistant: Linda M. D'Angelo
Executive Marketing Manager: Lisa Kimball
Production Editor: Christopher H. Rawlings
Editorial-Production Service: Omegatype Typography, Inc.
Composition and Prepress Buyer: Linda Cox
Manufacturing Buyer: Suzanne Lareau
Cover Administrator: Linda Knowles
Electronic Composition: Omegatype Typography, Inc.

Copyright © 1999 by Allyn & Bacon
A Viacom Company
160 Gould Street
Needham Heights, MA 02494

Internet: www.abacon.com

Library of Congress Cataloging-in-Publication Data

Burch, C. Beth.
   Writing for your portfolio / C. Beth Burch.
      p.   cm.
   Includes index.
   ISBN 0-205-27159-6
   1. English language—Rhetoric.   2. Portfolios in education.
 3. Report writing. I. Title.
 PE1408.B883826   1999
 808'.042—dc21   98-14844
                                   CIP

Credits appear on pages 463–464, which constitute an extension of the copyright page.

Printed in the United States of America
10 9 8 7 6 5 4 3 2 1   03 02 01 00 99 98

For Leonora,
who would have been proud,
and for Paul,
who is.

Writing itself is one of the great, free human activities.
There is scope for individuality, and elation, and discovery
in writing. . . .
Working back and forth between experience and thought,
writers have more than space and time can offer.
They have the whole unexplored realm of human vision.

—*William Stafford*

CONTENTS

CHAPTER **3** Writing What You Live and Know   43

CHAPTER **4** Writing What You Observe and Learn **85**

CHAPTER **5**   Reading, Writing, and Analysis   121

CHAPTER **6**   Writing to Influence   165

CHAPTER **7**   Writing from Investigation and Primary Research   **209**

CHAPTER **8**   Writing from Reading
and Secondary Research   275

CHAPTER **9**   Showing Your Style   **335**

CHAPTER **10** Assembling a Portfolio   357

PREFACE

Writing for Your Portfolio is a book about portfolios and writing. It defines a portfolio adventure that instructors and students can undertake with confidence. Here portfolio pedagogy is realized as the logical conclusion of a writing process. This process—invention, drafting, review, revising, editing, publishing, and the recursiveness of this whole endeavor—takes place in its own unique way for every writer. At the same time, the notion of *writer* is a constructed one: From their earliest encounters with words and texts, writers are shaped by their educational and social environments. Thus, this book provides a structure for learning and teaching writing but allows space within the structure for students and instructors to choose what they want to write (and read) about and to make the writing course their own. Reflection and self-awareness are constant themes, and the book emphasizes writers' increasing sophistication, ability for self-evaluation, independence, and responsibility for their own learning. Indeed, creating writing portfolios can help students prepare for other situations where they will need to show their best work and demonstrate accomplishment and expertise—the search for employment or the process of applying to graduate or professional programs, for instance. I try not to reify the theory or to create what Wendy Bishop has called a "clunk curriculum." The book moves from expressive to analytical writing, reinforcing the personal voice but encouraging that it be heard by wider audiences and in increasingly varied social contexts.

Writing for Your Portfolio is designed to prepare students for general competence in writing, rather than for specific advanced academic writing, which is typically the province of particular courses in students' majors. The book is designed for a first-year composition sequence, for either or both introductory courses; but it is also appropriate for other expository writing courses. You will find ample material for more than one course here, including material on academic writing—writing from primary and secondary research and writing documented essays as well as writing in more narrative and descriptive genres. *Writing for Your Portfolio* presents general principles, for instance, of the two most popular documentation guides, those of the Modern Language Association (MLA) and the American Psychological Association (APA), but does not specifically address writing in such particular or diverse fields as biology, management, history, journalism, or aeronautical engineering. Computer information is similarly introductory and broad; general principles of and tips for using computers in the writing classroom (including research on the World Wide Web) are here, rather than specific word-processing or web-browsing instruction.

Writing for Your Portfolio is unabashedly genre-based. After introductory chapters explaining the concept of *portfolio* and portfolio-related matters, subsequent chapters emphasize genres such as the memoir, the advisory essay, the profile, a study of a place, analysis (including literary analysis), editorial pieces, and position pieces as possible components of a portfolio. Writing and reading in nonfiction genres allows students to create the kinds of pieces that are "out there" in the world in published form. Studying characteristics of genre and form creates a solid understanding of how to uncover form and then create it anew. Working with genres demystifies real-world writing and gives students power and control over their writing. In a genre-based structure, students can choose their topics freely or write within a general theme that the instructor or institution designates, such as "Environmental Choices" or "Problems of Ethnicity." An emphasis on genre also makes it possible for students to give voice to personal concerns and personal ideas and beliefs through personal writing assignments logically related to the major assignments, which emphasize public writing. This book therefore acknowledges and values both personal and public, including academic, writing.

College writing courses are always about more than just writing, and this book tries to reflect that reality: It is addressed to a reading–writing, teaching–learning population that is richly diverse and complex. *Writing for Your Portfolio* includes many widely different kinds of nonfiction reading selections by both student and professional writers, both published and heretofore unpublished. A portmanteau is an old-fashioned suitcase that opens in two halves—and the Portmanteau sections at the end of each chapter display both student and professional writing. These pieces illustrate not only many genres and perspectives but many levels of accomplishment as well. All the essays are provocative; many are stellar. Readers should exercise their critical faculties to determine which pieces come closest to their own standards for excellence. The selections in this book, particularly the student writings, also come from a geographically and ethnically diverse population that will, I hope, reflect its eventual readership.

Please write to me about your experiences with and reactions to this book. You can reach me at Binghamton University, SUNY, Binghamton, NY 13902-6000, or by e-mail at bburch@binghamton.edu.

ACKNOWLEDGMENTS

To many I owe much. This book, long in the writing, has been generously tolerated by family and friends.

The very appearance of this book is owing to Eben Ludlow, editor extraordinary, who had faith in the idea and was willing to take a chance. His considerable expertise, shared with exquisite tact, made the tasks of rethinking and revising palatable—and sometimes even exciting. Linda D'Angelo, editorial assistant, guided me through the details of manuscript submission and publication and lifted my spirits. Tim Barnes at Omegatype shepherded the manuscript through production with a marvelous attention to detail and a precision schedule that kept me on my toes—thanks, Tim! To colleagues who are writers and teachers, Kathleen Yancey, Irwin Weiser, Margaret Rowe, Leslie Field, and Pamela Gay, I am indebted for professional inspiration and for friendship.

And for wise suggestions and recommendations, I am thankful to the readers of the manuscript of this book: Richard Louth, Southeastern Louisiana University; James C. McDonald, University of Southwestern Louisiana; Donna Nelson-Beene, Bowling Green State University; Sue Carter Simmons, Bowling Green State University; Joseph F. Trimmer, Ball State University; and Irwin Weiser, Purdue University. To Julie Quinn and Diane Hinckley, I owe gratitude for endless patience and unflagging assistance.

I am also in debt to my students in West Lafayette, Indiana; Tuscaloosa, Alabama; and Binghamton, New York, whose writing appears throughout these pages: You especially helped to make this book possible, and I thank you.

Warm thanks are due to Stephen Burch for the respite of Orioles games and Bethany Beach, and other kindnesses, and to Larry Burch for expert lawyering. I thank my parents, Harmon and Ellagwyn Saulmon, and my parents-in-law, Jacob and Vivian Burch, for their confidence and encouragement. I couldn't have finished the project without Goire Burch's levity, wit, and attention. But I am most grateful for the love and support from my family: sons Paul Jr., Zachary, and Nathan; daughter-in-law Nena; and sweet Emma, granddaughter. I especially thank my husband, Paul William, who has read all these words countless times and listened to my travails over the text and selections more times even than that, and whose critical eye and ear, patience, and love have always been my mainstay.

Writing with Portfolios

Writing is an unpredictable business.

—John Gardner

When you write, it's like braiding hair. Taking a handful of coarse unruly strands and attempting to bring them unity. Your fingers have still not perfected the task.

—Edwidge Danticat

A writer can be compared to a well. There are as many kinds of wells as there are writers. The important thing is to have good water in the well and it is better to take a regular amount out than to pump the well dry and wait for it to refill.

—Ernest Hemingway

I must say that the portfolio has really worked for me. I never had to force a half-witted idea into a paper; the freedom to rewrite allowed me to ponder until I became comfortable with a subject I wanted to work with. The peer review was very enlightening—it gave me a lot of "second chances" and different points of view.

—Richard Collins, student writer

What is a portfolio? What does a portfolio have to do with writing? What kind of writing goes into a portfolio? How *much* work is supposed to be in a portfolio? How is a portfolio arranged? How is a portfolio graded or evaluated—and by whom? All these questions—and perhaps others—may be going through your mind as you find yourself immersed in a portfolio environment.

Creating a writing portfolio involves collecting, selecting, and reflecting upon writing done over an extended period, such as writing composed throughout a writing course. Not every piece written for the course is included in the final portfolio; and although each piece of writing is read and evaluated by readers, individual pieces are not graded or evaluated. Rather, the evaluation or grade is suspended until you submit the final portfolio. A portfolio showcases your writing talent and in so doing requires you to reflect on your writing accomplishments. The portfolio contains, then, not only writing but writing *about writing.* This writing on writing, or *metawriting,* may be an essay or a letter about why or how you composed the portfolio. Or it can be notes introducing each essay. You'll learn more about metawriting later. In fact, though, this reflection about writing— this thinking about *how you work as a writer and why you make the writing choices you do*— is what distinguishes a portfolio from a writing folder, which is simply a folder storing a quantity of writing.

UNDERSTANDING THE KINDS OF PORTFOLIOS

There are many kinds of writing portfolios, and not all portfolios are associated with classes or with course requirements. You may, for instance, keep a portfolio on your own and for your own purposes, to chronicle your growth as a writer—a personal portfolio. You may keep a portfolio as preparation for securing a job—an employment portfolio. Or you may be required to submit a portfolio as part of an admissions or exit requirement for an academic program. And of course writing portfolios are frequently the culminating project in many writing courses. But even in writing courses there are different kinds of portfolios: You may have a working portfolio that you keep modifying throughout the course; you may submit a miniportfolio after a few weeks to get an idea of what assembling a portfolio feels like; you may eventually submit a final or showcase portfolio.

WRITING IN A PORTFOLIO COURSE

From one portfolio writing course to another, portfolios vary considerably. They especially differ regarding what can or must be included and how many pieces are required. Typically the writer chooses most or all of the pieces. Frequently the writer is asked to include drafts and peer comments. Sometimes the instructor chooses a piece—a sample of in-class writing, for example—to include. Usually the writer is also asked for *metawriting,* writing about the writing. Sometimes a table of contents or specific comments about each piece are added. The physical form of the portfolio is typically the writer's choice; portfolios are housed in all kinds of containers, from large accordion-style envelopes to plastic milk crates to pizza boxes to plain manila folders. Sometimes standard-sized folders are required for the sake of convenience (or necessity) in filing or storing.

Portfolios also differ in the ways and the number of times they are assessed. In many portfolio writing courses, portfolios are evaluated just once—usually near the end of the semester. But your instructor may want you to keep a working portfolio as the course goes along and turn in a final or polished portfolio at the end of the term. Also, keep in mind that the instructor may not be the only person who assesses the portfolio. Another reader (or readers) may evaluate the work. It is up to you to find out exactly how your portfolio will be evaluated. Be sure that you know exactly what is required of you. You can then be thinking of what you can do to make your portfolio successful.

Knowing What the Portfolio Course Requires

Odds are, you already know the requirements for the writing portfolio you will prepare. Be sure, however, that you get these details:

- How many papers are required
- What kinds of papers are required
- Whether additional work may be included
- Whether drafts, peer review comments, or critique sheets should be included
- Whether a certain order or arrangement is required
- How the reflection on the writing (the metawriting) is to be presented
- How the portfolio will be graded and the significance of the portfolio grade
- Who will grade the portfolio
- When and how the portfolio should be submitted
- How feedback on your writing can be obtained before the portfolio is due

When you understand these points, you'll know what is expected of you and more about what you need to do. A suggestion: Mark your calendar or assignment notebook with reminders about due dates.

Portfolios put special demands on writers, but the task of preparing a portfolio also helps you grow as a writer. When you prepare your portfolio, you may find it necessary to approach your writing differently than you have in the past. Consider especially how your writing personality will respond to the requirements of a portfolio.

Computer Writing Tip: Keep a separate file with notes detailing the requirements for the portfolio. This will allow you to refer to those guidelines easily. If your computer center has a scanner, you may even be able to scan your instructor's handout into your file.

Understanding Yourself As a Writer

What kind of writer are you? How do you feel about writing? What are your strengths as a writer? The answers to these questions become especially important in a portfolio writing course because in such a class you take increased responsibility for the pace, selection, and improvement of your work. Some writers don't know their writing habits very well, and this lack of insight causes them problems. Shelley thinks she can revise five essays in one day, so she waits until the day before portfolios are due to tackle the revisions. She pulls out the first paper, sees a lot of things she wants to revise, especially now that the writing is "cold," and gets started. Three hours later, she pulls the first finished draft from the printer. Only four essays to go! The problem, of course, is that at an optimistic three hours per essay, she'll need twelve hours just to finish the revisions, not to mention the time she'll require for arranging the portfolio. If Shelley knew her revising habits better, she could plan her time and perhaps save herself some frustration and lost sleep—and maybe even earn a better grade. It is important to think consciously and honestly about your writing personality and to admit your needs and habits as a writer.

YOUR WRITING PERSONALITY.   Writing is important and useful work. It takes energy, time, and patience. Some writers find writing exhilarating and pleasurable. Others think writing is difficult or frustrating or even humiliating. If, however, you know yourself and your writing attitudes and habits, you can smooth out the writing task.

"I'm a writer, but not, thank heavens, the kind who has to write every day or he gets depressed."

How do you feel about writing and about yourself as a writer? Do you think of yourself as a capable writer? How do you feel when you receive a writing assignment? Jot down truthful answers to the questions that follow:

- What is your favorite or best piece of writing? Describe why you like it and what you can remember about the act of writing it. Was this piece written for a class? Was it graded? Who read it? What have readers said about this piece?
- When you have a writing task, how do you ordinarily approach it? Do you tackle it right away? Do you work on it slowly and gradually? Or do you put writing off until the last possible moment? Do you think about what you are writing in the shower or when you are waiting in your car at red lights? Do you free-associate about your topic? Do you write several drafts? Do you take breaks, writing the paper in chunks, or do you work straight through until a piece is written?
- Think now about the physical act of writing. What time of day do you like to write? Are you a day person or a night person? Do you like company when you write or do you prefer solitude? Do you write to music? If so, what kind and how loud? Do you like the television on in the background? Where do you like to write—on your bed, at your desk, at the kitchen table, sitting on the couch, in a carrel at the library? Do you like to use a certain kind of paper or writing utensil? Do you prefer writing at the computer? Do you like to have a snack, cigarettes, or something to drink handy when you write?
- List two words that describe your attitude toward writing. When did you begin to feel this way? Is any person related to or partly responsible for your attitude? Did anyone ever make you feel especially good or especially bad about your writing? Do you think your attitude might change? How, or under what circumstances?

After responding to these questions, you should now have a great many notes about your writing experience. Keep them in mind as you write an essay about yourself as a writer.

Writing Task:

Write about some aspect of your writing personality or some piece of writing or some person who has influenced your attitude about writing. This piece will help you understand your thinking processes better and may yield insights that will help you be a better writer; it may eventually go into your portfolio.

As you think about how to set up this paper, keep these points in mind:

1. You will probably want to create some kind of dominant impression. In other words, you and other readers should be able to focus on a central idea or attitude.
2. You probably won't use all the data you generated as you answered the questions about your writing personality, and you may find that you'll come up with new information as you write. Select ideas from the information you generated. Emphasize what you think are the most important points about you as a writer. You may focus on your attitude toward writing or perhaps on your writing ritual or even on your most memorable writing experience. You don't, of course, have to limit yourself to these options.

3. Remember to be specific. Show readers one key aspect of what you are like as a writer. Use specific examples and plenty of detail.
4. If you like, look in the Portmanteau section at the end of this chapter to see what other writers have written about themselves and writing.

ANALYZING SOME FEATURES OF YOUR ESSAY.   When you have written a draft, take a few moments to analyze it. What does your written text reveal about you as a writer? What can you learn about your writing style? Make an extra copy of the essay, because you may find yourself marking on the draft. Now answer the following questions:

1. Describe the length of your draft in words. Here's how: Count the number of words in an average-looking line (not the longest or shortest one), then multiply that number times the number of lines in your piece. If an average line has 14 words and you have 24 lines, your essay is approximately 336 words. A typed, double-spaced page with one-inch margins has approximately 250 words, so you can estimate how many typed pages your handwriting will translate to. Make a note to yourself whether most of your essays are longer or shorter than this one, whether this is a typical piece for you. If you are working on a computer, command your word-processing program to do a word count.
2. How many paragraphs are in your paper? How many sentences are in the average paragraph? Where do you characteristically place the topic sentences—at the beginning, the middle, or the end of paragraphs? Here's a paragraph with the topic sentence (the sentence expressing the subject or primary idea of the paragraph) underlined at the beginning:

   It's not easy to get used to contact lenses. A person with new contacts has some adjusting to do. A routine of washing and soaking the lenses has to be established. The contact lens wearer must get in the habit of carrying wetting solution to moisten the lenses for comfortable wearing and sunglasses to protect the eyes from bright sunlight and wind-borne dust particles. Finally, the contact lens wearer must become accustomed to having a foreign object in the eye constantly.

   Here is the same paragraph with the underlined topic sentence moved to the end:

   A person with new contacts has some adjusting to do. A routine of washing and soaking the lenses has to be established. The contact lens wearer must get in the habit of carrying wetting solution to moisten the lenses for comfortable wearing and sunglasses to protect the eyes from bright sunlight and wind-borne dust particles. Finally, the contact lens wearer must become accustomed to having a foreign object in the eye constantly. It's not easy to get used to having contact lenses.

   Do some of your paragraphs lack topic sentences? (This is acceptable—not all paragraphs have them.) Are all your paragraphs about the same length? At what position in the essay are any unusual paragraphs (beginning, end)?
3. Find your longest sentence: How many words are in it? Find your shortest sentence: How many words in this one? Compute the average sentence length by dividing the number of words you found in question 1 by the number of sentences in

your essay. Take further note of your sentences. Do you vary their lengths? Do you use some introductory phrases or clauses? Do you add modification to the end of the sentence, as in this sentence:

> The fruit crop is in danger <u>when the spring nights are damp and the temperature drops unseasonably low.</u>

Or do you like to begin sentences with qualifying phrases or clauses, as in this example:

> <u>When the spring nights are damp and the temperature drops unseasonably low,</u> the fruit crop is in danger.

Do you typically or most frequently combine ideas by compounding (by using *and* kinds of constructions), like this:

> The night was cold, <u>and</u> the moon was yellow, <u>and</u> the leaves came tumbling down.

Or do you combine ideas mostly by making dependent clauses, ones introduced by subordinators like *who, that, which, when, if, although,* or *after* ? Here's an example:

> <u>When</u> the nights are cold and the moon is yellow, the leaves come tumbling down.

Is there a kind of sentence construction you feel most comfortable with? Would you describe your sentences as formal or informal? (A clue: Several semicolons and predominantly long or complex sentences suggest fairly formal sentences; so do lots of multisyllabic or long words.)

4. Now look at your words. What is the average word length? (Check a representative line for average word length.) Do you use mostly short words? Or do you use a lot of multisyllabic words—*utilize* as opposed to *use*, for instance? Do you use slang? Do you consider your word choices mostly formal or informal? For example, are you more likely to write *I'd rather stay home* or *I prefer to remain at my personal abode*? Is the tone staid, loose, easy, carefully structured, balanced—or what?

5. Now look at your essay globally; that is, as a whole. Is your view toward your subject serious, or are you humorous and lighthearted? Does the writing sound like you? Or do you sometimes try out a tone that you don't customarily use, just to sound learned or more sophisticated? Do you think that the essay naturally reflects your writing personality? Are you happy with the result of this essay? Do you see changes you might want to make? Do your feelings about the writing have any relation to the nature of the assignment or the subject itself?

If you answer these questions thoughtfully, by this time you should have some insight into your writing personality and your writing style, at least in this essay. Consider how the requirements for the portfolio will mesh with your personal writing style and habits.

Reflecting on Writing about Writing

Using three sentences, summarize what you have learned about yourself as a writer from writing an essay about writing and from analyzing your essay. What are the results of your analysis?

If you know as much about the requirements for your portfolio as you do about yourself, you are prepared for success.

PURPOSES FOR WRITING: FOR YOURSELF AND FOR OTHERS

Public writing is anything written for someone else, an audience, to read. Any writing course asks you to do public writing, to write with the reader in mind: to write to explain, to classify, to interpret, to analyze, to persuade. A letter to the editor of your local newspaper is certainly public writing; a paper you write for a class is public writing (your instructor and some of your classmates will read it). Most writing is, indeed, public writing.

But this doesn't mean that private writing, writing just for yourself, isn't important, even in a writing class that focuses mostly on public writing. Writing in your journal or writing letters that never get mailed or composing notes to yourself or writing poetry for your eyes only or just doodling—all these are important kinds of private writing. Sometimes this writing helps you focus and find perspective; sometimes you just feel better after you sound off or think on paper. But this kind of personal writing can also profoundly affect your public writing. If you get in the habit of keeping a journal or a writer's notebook, for instance, you'll find that it will become a base or a wellspring for your public writing. It will give you a chance to try out ideas on yourself before you "go public." A journal entry frequently becomes a kind of first draft for a piece, an exploration of an idea. Personal writing tends to be reflective, and reflection is valuable intellectual experience that can be folded into more public writing.

Public writing is occasionally fraught with more anxiety than personal writing, just because you know that someone will definitely read your work and perhaps be affected by something you have written. It's not so easy to put yourself on view for someone to read. Writing can make you vulnerable; it's important to acknowledge that. But a portfolio can minimize this vulnerability. With a portfolio you assume greater control of the presentation of your writing; you have multiple chances for improvement; and you can show your reader/evaluator how much you have accomplished. You'll also feel less vulnerable if you try out most of your pieces on a peer reader or two, even before your instructor reads and comments on them. This means that you'll have a chance for some semipublic readings—by your friends and colleagues—before you have a public reading and/or evaluation.

Computer Writing Tip: Put your journal or writer's notebook on disk with each dated entry in a separate file. For example, you might label a notebook file with a name like jrnl.jan23 for the January 23 entry.

WORKING IN A WRITERS' GROUP

Readers in your writers' group play valuable roles, especially in a portfolio writing class. They respond to your work (and you to theirs) and suggest ways you can improve your writing. They help you find ideas for writing, and they help you listen to your own writing voice better. Writers' groups are typically groups of three to five class members who read and respond to one another's work throughout the course. You may meet with your group to try out ideas for a paper, to respond to drafts, or to proofread. Working well with your group is especially important in a portfolio class. You want thoughtful responses from careful readers that will help you make your writing and therefore your portfolio as good as possible. And you want to be a good responder so that you can help your fellow writers.

How does a writers' group come to run smoothly and work effectively? Here are some tips for helping your group work together well and some ideas for getting and giving feedback.

In your role as a responder, try to follow these guidelines:

1. **Say what works for you as a reader.** Provide at least one positive response when you read a piece of writing. If you like the way a member of your group uses vivid verbs, say so. And be specific about where the vivid verbs work. Everyone likes to know when something goes well.

2. **Suggest specific ways that other writers can improve their writing.** If you think that one of your group should, for instance, state what the electoral college does, explain how such a change may affect readers and suggest how the new material can be integrated into the present writing. In other words, help the writer think about how to make the changes you recommend.

3. If you can't think of anything specific to offer a writer, **respond with a description of how the work makes you feel.** "This piece makes me feel enthusiastic" or "This piece makes me realize how serious the financial aid crisis is" tells a writer that the reader takes the writing seriously and is affected by it. You can also say what you believe the writer's purpose to be: "You seem to be trying to persuade me to form a neighborhood crime watch group." Or you might ask the writer some questions about what is confusing you: "Why did you choose to describe the grandmother as unloving?"

4. **Focus on the writing, not on the writers.** Say "*Your introduction* doesn't give me a clear idea of what your essay is about" instead of "*You* didn't tell me your topic in the introduction." It's better not to put other group members on the defensive.

In your role as a writer in a peer group, consider these suggestions:

1. **Ask your readers specific questions about your writing.** Give them some direction for helping you: "How can I emphasize my feelings about not being admitted to the college I wanted to go to?" and "Do you think my conclusion matches my introduction?" are the kinds of questions that may get the conversation about writing going.

2. **Accept criticism gracefully.** Try not to act angry or defensive if other group members suggest changes in your work that you are not prepared to make or changes with which you disagree. Give your readers the benefit of the doubt and listen carefully to all suggestions. If you react to suggestions by getting angry or defensive, the group members may hesitate to respond honestly because they are reluctant to upset you. Remember: Just because your group suggests changes, you do not have to make them.

3. **Make sure that everyone in the group has a chance to participate.** Some members may be shy; others may be eager to share their work. But everyone needs an audience.

Sometimes when you first begin working with a writers' group, you feel uncomfortable. It takes a while to become confident of your readers and to trust them. It is also sometimes difficult to relinquish your writing, which inevitably has so much of your ego bound up in it, to *any* reader. Think of it this way, though: Each member of the group is in the same position. Each of you needs the help of the others; each of you is presenting unfinished work and hoping for encouragement and guidance.

Writers' Group Task:

Begin working on your group skills by reading the essays about writing written by members of your group. Each writer should read her or his piece aloud while the other group members listen. Then respond to each essay by giving what Peter Elbow has called "movies of your mind." Explain what you see in your mind as each writer reads his or her draft about being a writer. What kinds of scenes and images fleet through your mind? Describe these to the writer.

PORTMANTEAU OF WRITING ABOUT WRITING

To guide you in reflecting about yourself as a writer, this Portmanteau has a selection of writing about writing. Professional writers and student writers are represented here. Both have wisdom to offer. Feel free to imitate strategies and aspects of these essays that feel comfortable to you and are compatible with your writing style. Feel free to criticize the writing here if it doesn't work for you. Feel free to suggest how flaws in the essays can be eliminated or minimized. You may use the student writing, presented first, for your enjoyment, for writers' group practice, for style analysis—or for all three. The student essays are not first drafts, but they are not necessarily finished work either. If you are practicing style analysis, review the guidelines for analyzing style on pages 6–7. If you are practicing peer review in your writers' group, you may want first to write down what you believe to be the qualities of an effective essay about one's writing personality; then you can use those guidelines to evaluate the writing that follows. Try reading the essays aloud, and practice responding constructively. Remember: You do no one a favor by simply offering empty praise or, on the other hand, by being supercritical. Be helpful and sensitive but honest.

In this first essay, Richard Collins writes briefly about his dream to become a writer.

Guts

Richard Collins

I have always had a dream to become a writer. Even though I have never written much outside the classroom, my mind is constantly churning and creating new ideas for stories. How would I do as a writer? I am not sure, but my favorite writers possess some similar characteristics which seem key to writing successfully. These are the ability to be imaginative, to analyze situations, to gain insight into human nature, and to use personal experience to add realism to their work.

If I were to be a writer, developing similar capabilities would be my strong point. This is due, I believe, mainly to my shyness. I am an introverted person; I do not mind being alone and have grown accustomed to keeping things to myself. Although I have few friends, the friends I have are very close. How has this helped me? I think it allowed me to find myself and to find out what true friendship is. I believe my shyness has helped my mechanics, too, in a peculiar way. I am a poor speaker and often break myself off in the middle of a sentence when I think of a better way to get my point across. Although this makes me sound like a bumbling idiot while speaking, it makes me work hard when writing to revise until I have exactly what I want to say down on paper.

So, what is my problem? Why have I not published several books and reaped outrageous profits? Or, more realistically, why have I not just written down one story? I am too chicken to put my thoughts and feelings down on paper. I would hate to look at it after it's all written down and think, "This is the most pathetic excuse for a paper I have ever seen!" And I would definitely hate for anyone else to tell me the same thing. I lack a quality I left off the first list for writers—guts to express myself. I have been working to overcome my shyness and meet new people. I hope that with that effort and this writing class and others to come will come the guts I need to write as boldly as I think.

CONSIDER . . .

1. How would you describe Collins's focus in this essay? That is, on what aspect of his writing experience does he focus?
2. How does Collins's understanding of his personality fit with his understanding of himself as a writer?
3. What else would you like to know that Collins did not tell you here? What suggestions for revision might you offer?

Mark Schlagenhauf describes how he writes best and his ingenious way of coming up with ideas for writing:

Writing Environments

Mark Schlagenhauf

If I know exactly what I want to say and how I want to say it, then I can write almost anywhere. The fewer distractions, of course, the better. Unfortunately, this kind of situation so rarely happens that I am only vaguely aware that it is even possible.

More often than not, I barely know what I need. To help me sort it all out, I need a combination of familiarity and newness. My most common approach is to get a movie I really like but have seen several times and play it on the VCR. The movie provides a familiar background sound with preprogrammed rest breaks. In other words, I look up and watch the good scenes.

This approach works best if I can find a movie that has the same topic or the same "feel" as the paper I want to write. I know the movie already, so I don't have to pay attention to get the jokes. In addition, I usually try to look past the surface and get glimmerings of ideas by comparing my paper to what I don't see in the movie. In other words, I look for hidden relationships that help me focus on what my paper is supposed to say.

The movie also helps to keep me in touch with reality—not that the movie is reality, but that the writing of the movie is a reality. Sometimes when I write I tend to get off track and discuss things which have no bearing on my original topic. When this happens, I quickly review in my mind the sequence of the movie's action. This reminder of how a logical order should be keeps me from writing into my own little world where no one knows what's happening but me.

The second stage of my writing environment is not writing at all. After a while, the walls start closing in and I need to take a walk. On these walks I try to sort through the rough spots in my paper. I have a route I usually follow, but I cut it short or lengthen it, depending if I have anything settled or not. Then I sit back down in the chair and start writing again.

At this point I have about all the ideas I need, so it's off to the word processor. Now comes the hard part: I have to decide what to keep and what to pitch. The trouble is that all my ideas seem to occupy the same level of quality. They are either all good enough or none are worth anything, depending on how critical I am at the time. I usually end up trying to integrate a little of everything, with mixed results.

Since my pen-and-paper brainstorming rarely includes complete sentences, I start from the ground up, using the ideas and outline I have developed. When it's all in the machine, I file my notes somewhere. After that, it's all add, subtract, and rewrite on the computer. I have to print myself a copy every so often; I can't edit well on-screen.

The process ends when I have a finished copy stapled together in a safe place. This usually takes a few tries because I forget to align a paragraph or the page numbering gets messed up. When it is done, I try to forget about it.

For me, organization is harder than creativity.

CONSIDER . . .

1. How does Schlagenhauf reveal that he understands his writing process? What passages suggest to you a self-understanding?
2. In what ways are your writing habits similar to Schlagenhauf's?

3. How would you describe Schlagenhauf as a writer? How does he structure this essay?
4. What does he reveal about his personality and about how his personality influences his writing? What does his vocabulary suggest about him?

In this essay, Heather VanVactor describes her writing rituals and her experience with writer's block.

Writing on Writing

Heather VanVactor

How do I feel about writing?

It's rather a delicate question to answer.

Once upon a time, I loved to write. Many a spare moment I spent scribbling out reams of poetry, or short stories, or essays. Some of which was actually—not bad.

Then one evil day somewhere near the beginning of junior year in high school it happened. I stopped writing. The words somehow were lost in vague, amorphous concepts, and trapped between my brain and my pen, they just would not come out.

A dark and dreary year (and then some) I've spent, suffering acutely under the weight of writer's block. I mechanically cranked out papers for class, but when no grades were involved, I found it difficult even to write letters to friends. Aside from a few brief flashes of inspiration (notably a term paper on Kate Chopin's *The Awakening* and a children's activity book based on Dante's *Inferno*), my writing has been, by my own admission, abysmal.

Nonetheless, there are still certain ritualistic observances I follow, even when slopping out schlock for class.

The writing utensil used to be of primary importance. I found it impossible to believe that any serious writing could be done in any medium other than #2 graphite. Recently, however, I've expanded my horizons, having discovered the joys of the red ballpoint pen. The rationale behind the #2 pencil was that it erases, which I found a necessity since I tend to edit my work as I go along and I had always abhorred cross-outs. But I've overcome my aversion to scratch marks so that I can now revel in the slightly rebellious feeling of doing my writing in red ink. (What was the one color of pen that teachers always forbade?)

With the issue of what to write with becoming less vital to me, the topic of where to write and how to position myself while writing is gaining supremacy. Writing in class is done only in cases of dire emergency; school desks are uncomfortable. I absolutely cannot write while sitting up properly. Most of my writing is done at home, which means that I either sprawl across my bed or curl up in an armchair. This in turn necessitates the wearing of comfortable clothing. Flannel pajamas are the usual uniform. (Optional accessory: pink bunny slippers.) As the weather becomes warmer, the old Chicago Bears T-shirt becomes the apparel of choice.

Since most of my writing is done in the wee hours of the morning the night before the paper in question is due, snack items are occasionally required to keep me awake. Depending on the nature of the writing, said snack might be Oreos and milk (literary analyses and/or anything I'm really interested in), potato chips (boring topics), or carrot and celery sticks (general writing). The food is pretty much optional. One thing I absolutely cannot do without, though, is the large glass of ice water. I usually keep a pitcher somewhere near the writing area, to alleviate the need for frequent trips to the kitchen.

None of these little rituals has ever made writing any easier.

Then again, none of them has ever made it more difficult.

In fact, the process is generally the same, regardless of what class I'm writing for and regardless of whether I've found inspiration. First I have to come up with an outline. I may or may not put it on paper, but I cannot start writing until I've come up with a structure that I think will work. Then comes the main body of the paper; if the outline is good enough, the body will practically write itself. Introductions and conclusions are almost always the most difficult parts of any paper, so I save them for last. Generally, I have to set aside the paper for a bit and go off and do something else (listen to music; play with the dog; sing and dance around the house, reliving great moments on stage—all very quietly of course so as not to wake the other slumber-bound members of the house). Later, I go back and fill in those blank spaces I've left at the beginning and at the end; frequently, introductions and conclusions are scrawled out madly in the seconds before the paper is due.

And that's it.

Like it or not, it's done.

The happy (?) ending: I woke up this morning (Saturday morning, actually, the day I wrote the rough draft for this), and I needed to write. I *wanted* to write. I whipped off five letters and am now drawing near to the close of an essay. Hopefully, my muse hath returned.

And she wrote happily ever after.

CONSIDER . . .

1. On what aspect of her writing experience does VanVactor focus? How does her emphasis differ from Collins's and Schlagenhauf's?
2. Characterize VanVactor's use of paragraphing. Why do you think she makes several one-sentence paragraphs?
3. What adjectives would you use to describe VanVactor's style?

In the opening pages of her autobiography *One Writer's Beginnings*, Eudora Welty introduces us to some childhood experiences that, she realizes upon reflection, influenced her writing.

From *One Writer's Beginnings*

E U D O R A   W E L T Y

In our house on North Congress Street in Jackson, Mississippi, where I was born, the oldest of three children, in 1909, we grew up to the striking of clocks. There was a mission-style oak grandfather clock standing in the hall, which sent its gong-like strokes through the living room, dining room, kitchen, and pantry, and up the sounding board of the stairwell. Through the night, it could find its way into our ears; sometimes, even on the sleeping porch, midnight could wake us up. My parents' bedroom had a smaller striking clock that answered it. Though the kitchen clock did nothing but show the time, the dining room clock was a cuckoo clock with weights on long chains, on one of which my baby brother, after climbing on a chair to the top of the china closet, once succeeded in suspending the cat for a moment. I don't know whether or not my father's Ohio family, in having been Swiss back in the 1700s before the first three Welty brothers came to America, had anything to do with this; but we all of us have been time-minded all our lives. This was good at least for a future fiction writer, being able to learn so penetratingly, and almost first of all, about chronology. It was one of a good many things I learned almost without knowing it; it would be there when I needed it.

My father loved all instruments that would instruct and fascinate. His place to keep things was the drawer in the "library table" where lying on top of his folded maps was a telescope with brass extensions to find the moon and the Big Dipper after supper in our front yard, and to keep appointments with eclipses. There was a folding Kodak that was brought out for Christmas, birthdays, and trips. In the back of the drawer you could find a magnifying glass, a kaleidoscope, and a gyroscope kept in a black buckram box, which he would set dancing for us on a string pulled tight. He had also supplied himself with an assortment of puzzles composed of metal rings and intersecting links and keys chained together, impossible for the rest of us, however patiently shown, to take apart; he had an almost childlike love of the ingenious.

In time, a barometer was added to our dining room wall; but we didn't really need it. My father had the country boy's accurate knowledge of the weather and its skies. He went out and stood on our front steps first thing in the morning and took a look at it and a sniff. He was a pretty good weather prophet.

"Well, I'm *not*," my mother would say with enormous self-satisfaction.

He told us children what to do if we were lost in a strange country. "Look for where the sky is brightest along the horizon," he said. "That reflects the nearest river. Strike out for a river and you will find habitation." Eventualities were much on his mind. In his care for us children he cautioned us to take measures against such things as being struck by lightning. He drew us away from the windows during the severe electrical storms that are common where we live. My mother stood apart, scoffing at caution as a character failing. "Why, I always loved a storm! High winds never bothered me in West Virginia! Just listen at that! I wasn't a bit afraid of a little lightning and thunder! I'd go out on the mountain and spread my arms wide and *run* in a good big storm!"

So I developed a strong meteorological sensibility. In years ahead when I wrote stories, atmosphere took its influential role from the start. Commotion in the weather and the inner feelings aroused by such a hovering disturbance emerged connected in dramatic form. (I tried a tornado first, in a story called "The Winds.")

From our earliest Christmas times, Santa Claus brought us toys that instruct boys and girls (separately) how to build things—stone blocks cut to the castle-building style, Tinker Toys, and Erector sets. Daddy made for us himself elaborate kites that needed to be taken miles out of town to a pasture long enough (and my father was not afraid of horses and cows watching) for him to run with and get up on a long cord to which my mother held the spindle, and then we children were given it to hold, tugging like something alive at our hands. They were beautiful, sound, shapely box kites, smelling deliciously of office glue for their entire short lives. And of course, as soon as the boys attained anywhere near the right age, there was an electric train, the engine with its pea-sized working headlight, its line of cars, tracks equipped with switches, semaphores, its station, its bridges, and its tunnel, which blocked off all other traffic in the upstairs hall. Even from downstairs, and through the cries of excited children, the elegant rush and click of the train could be heard through the ceiling, running around and around its figure eight.

All of this, but especially the train, represents my father's fondest beliefs—in progress, in the future. With these gifts, he was preparing his children.

CONSIDER . . .

1. One of Welty's purposes is perhaps to show how her writing was shaped by events in her childhood and by her parents. In this excerpt, what specific influences does she describe?
2. Notice how Welty associates an object with a story or a specific memory. Can you find an example of this technique? How does she manage to bring the memory into line with the purpose of the writing, to show how these events influenced her writing?
3. What is your favorite bit of detail in this passage? Find a sentence or two that you like particularly and explain why you think the detail "works."

---

2 Writing Processes: What Happens When We Write

Writing is not like painting where you add. It is not what you put on the canvas that the writer sees. Writing is more like a sculpture where you remove, you eliminate in order to make the work visible.

—Elie Wiesel

When I was a freshman in college, I began typing all my assignments. My writing speed decreased. Writing became a struggle. In high school I had been able to handwrite ten- and twenty-page papers in little more than an hour— and I never revised what I wrote. A college essay took me several nights to prepare. Suddenly everything I wrote seemed in need of revision. I became a self-conscious writer. A stylist. The change, I suspect, was the result of seeing my words ordered by the even, impersonal, anonymous typewriter print. As arranged by a machine, the words that I typed no longer seemed mine. I was able to see them with a new appreciation for how my reader would see them.

—Richard Rodriguez

I sometimes write a thousand pages of notes for a 200-page novel.

—John Gardner

Everyone has written about everything; you're not going to come up with some new topic to write about. So I always tried to come up with some kind of form for the piece that would be intrinsic to what I was saying. I like restrictions when I write. I don't understand people who want more freedom. The terrifying thing about writing is freedom, when people say, "But you can do anything."

—Fran Lebowitz

By now in your career as a writer, you may have heard a considerable amount of talk about how writing happens, especially about "the writing process." No such thing actually exists. Rather there are many personal writing processes, many ways that writers approach writing. Yes, researchers have found similarities in the ways that writers work; but now more than ever before, the individual and idiosyncratic nature of writing is also understood. Rather than thinking of the writing process as a progression of mandatory steps, let's consider the act of producing a written text as a series of stages through which *most* writers work at *differing* speeds. The process that you enact or that you put yourself through when you write is unique. Of course, your process may *resemble* the ways that other writers work, but it is truly your own. This chapter gives you ways to think about and examine your writing process and strategies for enhancing it. It will help you become conscious of your process. This consciousness is vital to the reflection necessary for your portfolio.

For most writers, a good bit of *recursiveness* exists between and among the stages of the writing experience, whether what is being composed is a grocery list or an entire portfolio. That is, the movement of producing a text (an exam answer, a letter to the editor, or a novel) is usually not linear, smooth, or straightforward; there is instead a lot of backtracking, rereading, rewriting, rethinking—in general, a lot of shifting between the stages. That's recursiveness. And you haven't heard the last of it.

This recursiveness becomes especially evident and important in a portfolio writing class because submitting your work in a portfolio gives you the opportunity to exploit the available time. You have time to let drafts cool, to ask for (and get) help from other readers, to revise and rewrite. Assembling a portfolio actually encourages you to return to a piece of writing many times for a deepening of the text. This recursiveness also produces a paper trail; and you should keep *all* this paper for your portfolio. Remember that you may be required to submit all the documents associated with your writing, including planning notes, writers' group comments, and drafts. Don't throw anything away!

How does writing generally happen? What do writers typically do when they write? What do you typically do when you write?

Computer Writing Tip: If you consistently date and name files, you can distinguish among different versions of an essay.

INVENTION: DISCOVERING WHAT TO WRITE

The invention phase of the writing process is the stage in which a writer finds or discovers or understands a topic. *Invention* refers to the task of finding and selecting the ideas to be treated in a piece of writing—and also to the process of developing those ideas. In this broad stage the writer invents or formulates the piece. The writer may also combine or search among familiar elements to create something new, but *invention* does not refer to a thing or a product as much as it describes the notion of *coming to new insights or understandings.* In this part of the writing process, a writer casts about for an idea, settles on something to pursue, then explores it in such a way as to discover or uncover a way to think or write about it.

In the invention stage of writing, you may find that you already know a great deal about your subject. When you answered the questions in Chapter 1 about how you write, you were gathering your knowledge about a topic you already know very well but may not have thought about much—yourself as a writer. As soon as you begin assembling the content of the essay, you typically begin shaping or planning how you will write it. You may do this without touching pen to paper or hand to keyboard. Some writers carry ideas and fragments of papers around in their heads for days or weeks before they actually begin to write. If you have lain awake at night mentally writing an

WHERE EARL GETS HIS IDEAS

introduction to an essay or thought about the conclusion of a paper as you were listening to a lecture or carried on an internal debate about what you could title a paper as you waited in line at a store, you have actually been *incubating* an idea. This incubation is important to the writing process. If you have to be in a certain "mood" to write, what that may truly mean is that your idea has to reach a certain stage of incubation before you can produce words on paper. You have to be ready to write.

Fortunately, you can help yourself get ready to write by using some conscious and deliberate exploring techniques. The kind and the depth of exploring that writers do vary according to the writer and the nature of the writing. Some writers are casual about invention; they explore a subject by talking about it with friends or classmates or by making simple word or phrase outlines. But other writers have more success with more formal strategies. Below are a few formal exploring strategies that you may try. Some of them may fit your writing personality better than others. If you don't have much luck with one strategy, try another.

Brainstorming

Simple *brainstorming* is probably the most common way to explore or discover ideas. You can brainstorm or force ideas alone or with a group of people; sometimes group brainstorms yield more ideas because one good idea begets another and then a chain reaction produces ideas quickly, like popcorn popping. When you brainstorm, try writing down or recording on audiotape as many ideas as you can. If you have access to a video camera, you might also try videotaping a brainstorming session. Whatever recording method you use, try to put down *all* the ideas that leap into consciousness, no matter how weird or how inappropriate they may seem: Sometimes your subconscious is trying to tell you something, trying to produce analogies or comparisons. When the brainstorm subsides, analyze your notes or your tapes to look for ideas that you repeat, patterns of thinking, or simply something interesting that you'd like to pursue.

Freewriting and Looping

Freewriting is a variation of brainstorming usually done under a time constraint. You can do freewriting in a classroom or alone. You need some clean sheets of paper and a writing utensil. A timer or an alarm on your wristwatch, something with which to time yourself, is useful. Write the subject you want to explore at the top of the page, set the timer for five minutes, then begin writing. Do not lift your pen or pencil from the paper except between words. Regardless of what you find yourself thinking, keep writing. Don't worry about spelling, correctness, or coherence. You are exploring ideas, taking a metaphorical walk through your brain. If you lose direction or can't think of anything to write, simply write something like "Can't think, can't think, can't think" until you *do* think of something to write. When the timer signals the end of five minutes, stop writing, flex your tensed fingers, and read what you have written.

Now skip a line from the bottom of the freewriting and write one sentence that summarizes or describes the main idea or essence of the freewriting. Then set the clock for five minutes more and begin writing again, taking as your point of departure the summary you just wrote. When the time is up, stop, reread your second freewriting excerpt, then summarize or describe this section of text. What you are now doing is called *looping* because you are drawing together disparate ideas with the loops of summary. When you explore a subject, you may do as many loops as you want or need. Here is an example of freewriting and looping on the subject of spiders. The writer was asked to freewrite about something from the natural world that was frightening.

Spiders

I'm not too crazy about spiders. They remind me of a fear I have carried over from childhood. I remember being warned about playing in the attic or garage where there might be black widow spiders (shiny with a red spot on their globular bellies) and fiddlebacks or brown recluses. I would never stick my hand into any dark unknown area in a closet or garage. Are spiders afraid of us? Who knows? Can't think. Can't think. Also: one memory of a tarantula on our western Oklahoma driveway—where did it come from? It was black, seemed as big as a hand, furry. Dad smashed it with a shovel. Must have been a lot of squisssshhst. I have also dreamed about spiders and been terrified of them in my dreams. Can't believe some people have tarantulas for pets. Fear and loathing.

<u>I seem preoccupied with a fear of spiders.</u>

This fear of spiders may be pretty much universal. Think of how this is emphasized in movies. When I was a kid, I saw "jungle" movies where a dangerous-looking spider lurked near a heroine's pillow. How about *Home Alone,* that tarantula on the robber's chest? And *Arachnophobia,* which really exploited the fear of spiders. Both movies also have a considerable amount of comedy. Arachne. Great story, great myth. Spiders aren't actually insects; they have eight legs, not six. Yet we call all of them bugs. We are pretty ignorant of the complex world of "bugs." Maybe that's why we fear them and they generally disgust us (or at least me).

<u>I wrote about spiders in movies and stories, among other things.</u>

Computer Writing Tip: If you freewrite at the computer, designate your invention files with a suffix like *.in* for invention. And if you have e-mail or access to a program that lets you communicate on-line simultaneously with other writers (Daedalus Interchange, for example), try a brainstorming conversation on-line.

Clustering or Webbing

Besides freewriting and looping, you can try other exploring techniques. In *clustering or webbing*, you draw a diagram or graphic representation that roughly shows the relationships among ideas. Figure 2.1 shows a cluster on the same subject, spiders, done

Figure 2.1   A cluster diagram for the topic "spiders"

when the instructor asked the class to look at the topic of spiders in a different way. Notice how *spider* is literally the central, thus primary and most general, idea and how the other ideas derive from a response to that central idea.

Among the subtopics in the *spider* cluster are *movies and stories, environment, Arachne, "seem to be in humans' way,"* and *webs*. A subtopic is a part of the main topic, a part that also has a small cluster of ideas surrounding it. Several ways to write about spiders emerge from this clustering exercise: The writer could write about spiders in movies (or maybe books or legends), about the role of spiders or of one particular kind of spider in the environment, about how spiders seem to be where humans don't want them to be, about how spiders came to be called *arachnids*, or about the kind of webs spiders make or how webs are made.

Using the Topics

Still another formal way of exploring a topic is to move through a series of six ordered guidelines based loosely on Aristotle's *topoi*, or *topics.* Working with these guidelines allows you to explore different aspects or perspectives of a subject. Here is a sample topic exploration, again on the subject of spiders. The writer did this exploration outside class, using the library and other resources, and working systematically through the *topics* guidelines.

■ **Define your topic.** Consider etymology, synonyms, and changes in the meaning of the topic over time.

> A spider, the dictionary says, is an "arachnid that has eight legs, a body divided into a cephalothorax and an abdomen, and several spinnerets that produce silk used to make nests, cocoons, or webs for trapping insects" (*AHD*). It comes from the Middle English *spither,* which derives from the Old English *spithra.* The word has been in our language for a long time. The *Oxford English Dictionary* gives other meanings of *spider,* among them several negative ones, including *spider* as a term of opprobrium and vituperation and *spiders* meaning "goes bankrupt."

■ **Compare and contrast** your topic to itself and to other similar topics. Consider whether your subject and people's attitudes about your subject have changed over time and what your topic most resembles.

> Spiders are a lot like insects. In fact, many people consider spiders and insects as one huge group of creatures and lump them all together as bugs. But in reality spiders are quite different from insects. Spiders have eight legs instead of six. Their bodies are divided into two parts, instead of the insect's three, for example.
>
> Spiders and scorpions have evolved from a common arachnid ancestor, thought to have arisen from a simple segmented worm sometime before the Cambrian Period about 570 million years ago. Some arachnids were water creatures; others were land creatures, but several physical changes had to occur before arachnids were really suited to terrestrial life. One feature of arachnid evolution, *Encyclopedia Britannica* tells us, is that segments were lost or fused. Primitive spider families had as many as twelve segments; today, spiders have two segments. Spiders are more highly evolved than scorpions.
>
> Attitudes about spiders (and about almost all living creatures) are probably changing now. In the past we have regarded spiders as intruders into our cozy warm houses, bugs to be destroyed. But I think that many people are becoming more aware of the role of each individual species in the good of the whole.

■ **Classify your subject** by putting it in a class and then describing the class. Consider how your subject differs from other items in its class.

> Spiders are themselves a class—*Arachnida*—all by themselves. They are different from other creatures with which we lump them (insects, bugs) because of the number

of their legs and the number of segments in their bodies. Also, spiders have a highly developed use of silk. Spiders are predators, carnivores; not all insects are.

There are also special kinds of spiders, particular species. Tarantulas interest me particularly. I could also classify spiders according to the kinds of webs they build (orb, flat, bolas) or according to the kinds of prey they pursue. Maybe spiders have different reproduction cycles and rituals; some females eat the males during and after mating. Spiders also have different ways of stalking or catching their prey (spitting spiders, stalking spiders).

■ **Present some examples or illustrations** of your subject.

Some examples of spiders are the tarantulas, brown recluse, black widow. There are common grass and garden spiders. Grandaddy Longlegs. Sometimes spiders come into the house more often when the days turn cool.

Spiders can be used to tell the weather.

Spiders can be used in agriculture—in apple orchards in Israel and rice fields in China.

■ **Explain causes and effects** associated with your subject. Consider whether we can understand the consequences of the subject.

It's easier and more useful to look at the effects of spiders. People are generally afraid of spiders. We associate them with dark places, uninhabited places, Halloween, the "Dark Side," a vampire's castle. But spiders do have some interesting effects in nature: They can be used to control the insect population and therefore put to work in agriculture.

Spiders, especially spider bites, are associated with certain consequences. Spiders bite humans who happen into their environment or territory. These bites have certain consequences, in turn; they can sometimes be swollen, red, and painful. Bites from a brown recluse or fiddleback spider can cause actual death of the flesh immediately surrounding the bite, and bites from other kinds of spiders might make a victim ill or even cause death in rare circumstances.

■ **Describe a process** associated with the subject. Consider whether the subject (or some aspect of the subject) can be thought of as happening in stages or whether a sequence or series of steps can be understood in relation to the subject.

The sequences of web making and of the spider's trapping its prey can be described and arranged into chronologically ordered processes. Other processes associated with spiders are how silk is made and how mating occurs.

Several possible aspects of the subject of spiders emerge from this exploration with the six topics. This writer discovers many possible angles from which to think about the subject: an explanation of how spiders make webs or catch their prey; an essay re-counting a personal experience with spiders; a comparison of two different species of spiders, perhaps two poisonous spiders or two that build their webs differently; a paper about kinds of webs; the story of the connection between the term *Arachnid* and the Greek myth starring Arachne. Clearly, the possibilities arising from exploring a subject with the topics are many—and not all of them are listed here. Can you think of other avenues for writing about spiders?

Computer Writing Tip: If using the topics works for you, type or scan the six guide-lines into a file and save them to use with your next writing task. You can call the file topics.tem for *topics template*, for instance.

Using the Library to Explore Ideas

Using the topics to explore a subject from different perspectives helps you think delib-erately, but there are also other ways to explore a general idea to find something to write about or an angle to explore.

Another approach: Go to the library! Your university or community library is a wonderful source of *ideas* as well as *information*. When you think of a topic you'd like to write on, first go to an encyclopedia (like *Britannica or Americana*) and read the general article on your topic just to get a sense of its depth and range. If you look up *Arachnids* in *Britannica*, for instance, you'll find information on their general features (size, diver-sity of structure, distribution, and importance); their natural history (reproduction and life cycle, ecology and habitats, locomotion, food and feeding, and associations); their form and function (general features, external features, internal features); their evolution and paleontology; their classification. Beyond that article on arachnids, you'll also find comparable articles on spiders, scorpions, mites, and so forth. This is how encyclope-dias are meant to be used: as excellent sources of general, reliable information. Armed with information from the encyclopedia, you can then go to more specific sources, if you need to do so; or you can effectively refine your subject to something within your experience and knowledge.

Here's another way to explore a subject if you can't get a fix on how to think about writing on it: Look it up in the *Library of Congress Subject Headings*, a large, red several-volume reference work found near the card catalog and online catalog. This book shows how topics are arranged, ordered, and labeled by the Library of Congress and thus by all American libraries. *Library of Congress Subject Headings* is the standard for card cata-logs and on-line catalogs all across the country. Figure 2.2 is a sample page from the *Sub-ject Headings*; notice how *spider* is referenced. As you can see, the *Subject Headings* can give you still other ideas for writing about spiders. You can write about different kinds of spi-ders, about poisonous spiders and jumping spiders and trap-door spiders and tarantu-las; about spiderwebs; about spiders in folklore and mythology; about fictitious characters based on spiders (like Spider-Man); about spider venom and spider fossils; about wasps that prey on spiders. Even if you don't actually investigate all the sources listed, this book is a wealth of related ideas and subtopics for almost any subject.

Spider, Black widow
  USE Black widow spider
Spider, Water
  USE Water spider
Spider (Fictitious character)
  (Not Subd Geog)
  UF Richard Wentworth (Fictitious
      character)
      Wentworth, Richard (Fictitious
      character)
Spider (Game)
  [GV1511.S7]
  BT Games
Spider beetles
  USE Ptinidae
Spider fingers (Disease)
  USE Marfan syndrome
Spider flowers (Grevillea)
  USE Grevillea
Spider-hunting wasps
  USE Spider wasps
Spider-Man (Fictitious character)
  (Not Subd Geog)
  UF Parker, Peter (Fictitious character)
      Peter Parker (Fictitious character)
      Spiderman (Fictitious character)
      Spidey (Fictitious character)
Spider mite, Carmine
  USE Tetranychus cinnabarinus
Spider mites
  USE Tetranychidae
Spider mites, False
  USE False spider mites
Spider monkeys *(May Subd Geog)*
  [QL737.P9]
  BT Cebidae
  NT Black spider monkey
      Central American spider monkey
Spider monkeys as pets *(May Subd Geog)*
  [SF459.M6]
  BT Pets
Spider populations *(May Subd Geog)*
  BT Arthropod populations
Spider venom
  USE Spiders—Venom
Spider wasps *(May Subd Geog)*
  [QL568.P6]
  UF Ceropalidae
      Pompilidae *[Former heading]*
      Psammocharidae

Spider-hunting wasps
  BT Hymenoptera
      Solitary wasps
  NT Anoplius
      Atopopompilus
      Pepsis
      Pompilus
      Simotocyphus
Spider web animals *(May Subd Geog)*
  UF Spider web fauna
      [Former heading]
  BT Animals
Spider web fauna
  USE Spider web animals
Spider webs
  [QL459]
  BT Spiders
Spiderflower, Brazilian
  USE Tibouchina
Spiderman (Fictitious character)
  USE Spider-Man (Fictitious character)
Spiders *(May Subd Geog)*
  [QL458.4–QL458.42]
  UF Araneae
      Araneida *[Former heading]*
  BT Arachnida
  NT Actinopodidae
      Agelenidae
      Amaurobiidae
      Anapidae
      Antrodiaetidae
      Anyphaenidae
      Araneidae
      Argyronetidae
      Atypidae
      Caponiidae
      Clubionidae
      Crab spiders
      Desidae
      Dictynidae
      Dinopidae
      Dipluridae
      Dysderidae
      Gnaphosidae
      Hahniidae
      Hersiliidae
      Heteropodidae
      Hypochilidae
      Jumping spiders
      Linyphiidae

      Liocranidae
      Loxoscelidae
      Microstigmatidae
      Mimetidae
      Mysmenidae
      Nemesiidae
      Nesticidae
      Oecobiidae
      Oonopidae
      Oxyopidae
      Pacullidae
      Palpimanidae
      Philodromidae
      Pimoidae
      Pisauridae
      Pycnothelidae
      Spider webs
      Symphytognathidae
      Tarantulas
      Tengellidae
      Tetrabiemmidae
      Theridiidae
      Theridiosomatidae
      Thomisidae
      Trap-door spiders
      Uloboridae
      Wolf spiders
  —Anatomy
    NT Spinneret (Anatomy)
  —Folklore
    UF Spiders (in religion, folk-lore, etc.)
        [Former heading]
    NT Anansi (Legendary character)
  —Mythology
    UF Spiders (in religion, folk-lore, etc.)
        [Former heading]
  —Venom   *(May Subd Geog)*
    [QP941.S66]
    UF Spider venom
Spiders, Fossil *(May Subd Geog)*
  BT Arachnida, Fossil
Spiders (in religion, folk-lore, etc.)
  USE Spiders—Folklore
       Spiders—Mythology

UF	Used For
BT	Broader Topic
RT	Related Topic
SA	See also
NT	Narrower Topic

Figure 2.2 Library of Congress subject headings for "spider"

Computer Writing Tip: Your library probably has on-line databases that provide reference information. You may be able to access the databases from outside the library—from your dorm or a computer center, for instance. Check with the reference librarian for help.

Exploring the Internet and the World Wide Web

If you have a computer and Web access, browsing the World Wide Web can also yield rich invention material. Use your Web browser or search engine (such as Yahoo, for instance) to search for information on your subject. Type in your subject or topic as a keyword and let your browser find some sites for you to explore—and from which you can also download information (or copy it to your computer). If you don't have a computer with which you can access the Web, go to your university library and use the computers there. Your reference librarians are skilled Web users and can help you become a first-class Web navigator.

Invention Task:

Begin with a topic you choose—or select one from the list that follows. Try at least three invention strategies for exploring the topic. Then write a list of at least five different approaches for writing about this subject. Keep all these explorations for possible use later and for your portfolio. (You may designate a special *Ideas for Future Writing* section in your working portfolio.)

You might compare your findings with those of other members of your writers' group and get ideas from them. Talking about your writing and exchanging ideas for topics and subjects is an excellent invention strategy.

A favorite place	Procrastination	Danger
Makeup	Cemeteries	Chauvinism
Soap operas	Moving	Waterloo and Watergate
Sharks	Vanity	Interesting relatives
Elections	Inventions	Jazz
Student government	Racism	Ethics
Crime shows	Slang	Etymology of a word
Remote control	Killer bees	Dreams
Divorce	Superstitions	Vikings
Gossip	Pollution	Hunters
Fingerprints	Icebergs	Money

Computer Writing Tip: Create an *Ideas* file for storing ideas for future writing.

FINDING A THESIS, ARTICULATING A PURPOSE

When you feel reasonably confident that you have gathered enough material to begin writing, you should consider what you want the piece of writing to accomplish. You need to determine your purpose for writing, then to craft a *thesis statement*. A *thesis* or *purpose statement* is a road map for your essay: It tells your readers where your ideas are taking them (and helps keep you on track during the writing, as well).

A thesis or a purpose statement is not a statement of fact. Writing a fact doesn't give you much else to say: "Yellow mixed with blue creates the color green," "Thomas

Jefferson was the primary author of the Declaration of Independence," "Houston is about three hours from San Antonio by car." A thesis is, rather, a statement with an edge, a statement that establishes what your piece of writing must demonstrate, show, or establish (not *prove*; *proof* is for legal matters and geometrical theorems). The thesis typically occurs early in the essay, frequently near the end of the first or second paragraph. Putting the thesis too far into the piece of writing diminishes its psychological effect: If you drive nearly all the way to your destination and only then look at the road map, you may already be lost. So put the thesis early enough in the essay to help your reader.

Here are a few theses or purpose statements for you to examine. Try to predict the content of the essay that might be developed from each thesis.

1. "The scientists considered the structure of webs spun by spiders under the influence of marijuana, benzedrine, chloral hydrate (a sedative), and caffeine." ("Oh, What a Tangled Web," *New Yorker*, 5 June 1995, 34.)
2. "Whatever the practical necessity that may have led him to take up the short story, Faulkner turned it to his artistic advantage, for it became his opportunity to make a distinctive contribution to the short story form." (Donald Kartiganer, "An Introduction to the Last Great Short Story," *Oxford American*, June 1995, 51).
3. "I found what I can only term my perfect holiday retreat last fall when I embarked upon a walking tour in Vermont with the appropriately named Walking Tours of Southern Vermont." (Sharon A. Cohen, "Travelscope," *AAA Today*, Summer 1995, 9.)
4. "Now as never before, exotic plants and creatures are traversing the world, borne on the swelling tide of human traffic to places to where nature never intended them to be." (Alan Burdick, "It's Not the Only Alien Invader," *New York Times Magazine*, 13 November 1994, 50.)
5. "I decided that the best approach would involve placing myself in the wolves' path, so to speak, as they made the rounds of their territory." (Jim Brandenburg, "In the Company of Wolves," *National Wildlife*, December–January 1995, 6.)

One type of thesis simply presents a general idea to be addressed in the essay: how Faulkner made a distinctive contribution to the short-story form, why/how walking in southern Vermont is a perfect holiday retreat, how exotic but unwelcome plants and creatures are showing up in unexpected places in the world, and what happens when one places oneself in the path of wolves. The other type of thesis presents a general idea and then a program for developing the thesis. Statement 1 above and the essay from which it is drawn present and carry out such a program: a discussion of web structures spun by spiders under four types of chemical influence. You can use either kind of thesis. Writing a thesis with a program can help you plot the course of an essay. But, a caution: Followed rigidly and mechanically and word-for-word, a thesis-plus-program statement can make an essay sound predictable and formulaic.

Some kinds of essays (reviews, informative research reports, expository essays) frequently call for a more deliberate statement to the reader, a purpose statement. Here are some excerpts from essay introductions, with purpose statements underlined:

1. "Our Virginia tour took us past many preserved Civil War battlefields. <u>Here are notes on four of them.</u>" (Ken Gross, "This Hallowed Ground," *Automobile*, Special Issue 1995, 67.)

2. "In the end, Foster's merits as a physician and educator were unfairly eclipsed by the White House's inept handling of a politically incendiary issue—abortion. <u>Here's the diary of a Washington disaster.</u>" (Bill Turque and Bob Bohn, "Foster Follies," *Newsweek*, 20 February 1995, 26.)
3. "A round of applause, please, for the humble onion. Except for salt, and perhaps pepper, onions may be used in more recipes worldwide than any other ingredient. Americans, for example, annually consume about 16 pounds of the vegetable per person. <u>Here's the story behind one of our true culinary stars.</u>" (Fred and Linda Griffith, "All About Onions," *Food and Wine*, June 1995, 26.)
4. "<u>The purpose of this paper is to open a discussion of what happens to the published literature on composition in these new contexts</u> [universities in Kenya, Tanzania, Zaire, and the United Kingdom]." (Mary N. Muchiri et al., "Importing Composition: Teaching and Researching Academic Writing Beyond North America," *College Composition and Communication* 46.2, May 1995, 176.)

Writers' Group Task:

In your group, discuss and evaluate each of the following sentences as a potential thesis. Which ones have an edge? Which ones assert something to be demonstrated, explained? Which ones are primarily statements of fact and thus unsuitable for use as theses? Which ones might open the way to ideas or information that you would want to read (or write) about?

1. The first polyester suit was manufactured in 1953.
2. Americans are dressing more casually than ever—and this is not a positive fashion development.
3. The court system conspires against the very children that it is designed to protect.
4. Attention deficit disorder (ADD) is a neurological syndrome whose classic defining triad of symptoms includes impulsivity, distractibility, and hyperactivity or excess energy.
5. Being a parent means being able to meet the emotional and psychological needs of a child for at least twenty years.
6. Wankel engines are very efficient but not very durable.
7. My uncle is a clergyman.
8. Marijuana ought to be legalized for some purposes.
9. Some crack babies have strokes before they are born.
10. Crack is cocaine that has been mixed with baking soda and water and then boiled.
11. Deinstitutionalization of the mentally ill was not even remotely popular until the middle of the 1960s.
12. In 1954 the Supreme Court outlawed segregation in the public schools with *Brown v. Board of Education.*
13. Bringing a sexual harassment case is very much like bringing a rape case.
14. Eric the Red sailed from Iceland to Greenland in the tenth century.
15. Helping the poor will strengthen families.

After you draft a thesis or a purpose statement, you can use that to guide your drafting process. But your thesis does not have to be cemented in. If you start drafting and your essay turns out differently than your thesis intended, then you should reexamine both. Does the draft improve on the thesis you originally wrote? Did new and better ideas come to you as you started to write? If the answers to these questions are yes, then you should revise your thesis.

One more thing about theses: In some essays, particularly narratives and descriptions, the thesis may be implied rather than stated outright. In a short story, for example, an explicit thesis might seem too obvious. In most other kinds of writing, however, an explicit thesis is helpful, almost obligatory. You will learn more about theses, *explicit* and *implicit* ones, as you prepare pieces for your portfolio.

DRAFTING A PIECE OF WRITING

Once you conceptualize a thesis, you'll want to begin putting pen to paper. Or perhaps your thesis will emerge as you draft: You don't have to have a thesis in hand before you start drafting. Regardless, you know when it is time to start writing. You itch to write down your ideas, your planning reaches a critical mass, or maybe the draft of the paper is due the next day. At some times for all writers, getting started can be difficult. You may resort to all sorts of unconscious delaying tactics: You can't write unless your desktop is cleared; you can't write without taking a long, hot bath; you can't write unless all your other work is done; you can't write until you phone your closest friends for sympathy. If any of these behaviors sounds like yours, be aware of what you are doing, and don't kid yourself. Do you really need to call your friends or get your grocery shopping done? If you don't, start writing. Gather your invention notes, your references, your materials, and your snacks, and just settle in to the work.

Some writers get bogged down in drafting because they insist on getting each sentence "just right" before they go on to the next one. If the floor around your writing space becomes littered with crumpled-up pages of false starts and discarded introductions, you might try leaving the introduction until later in your writing process. Or if individual word choices stall your progress, underline the word or highlight it and make a mental note to return later and insert a better word. The author John Gardner claimed that when he was at a loss for just the right word, he would write a nonsense word—*ba-da-da*—and hope that the right word would come to him later. It doesn't matter what you tell yourself or what tricks you use to start writing and keep writing until you have a more or less complete draft. It does matter that you understand your writing habits and needs so that you can satisfy the needs and manage the habits long enough to produce the draft. Don't worry about correct spelling and punctuation when you draft.

Once you have a complete draft, read it through to make sure that you *can* read it. A draft needs to be legible and comprehensible. This is especially important if you draft in longhand. "Cold" writing (longhand reread after some time has passed) is sometimes illegible; make sure your handwriting will be decipherable once you have had time to forget what those squiggles in the margin are supposed to say. Then put the essay away for several days—or for as much time as you can spare. Time will fade the initial flush of excitement that comes with finishing a writing project. Time increases your objectivity and makes you a more dispassionate reader of your writing.

REVIEWING AND REVISING THE DRAFT: SELF-REVIEW AND WRITERS' GROUP REVIEW

After your work has cooled as long as possible, look at it again. Consider how well the piece accomplishes what you intended. Think about its strengths and weaknesses. Read it aloud to yourself and then have someone read it aloud to you. Present your writing to be read in your writers' group. This oral reading of your written text is important. You need to hear your words as they were put down on paper. If a reader hesitates at a word or intones incorrectly, you may infer problems with your logic, transitions, word choice, or punctuation; so listen not only to your words but to how easily your reader processes and reads those words. As soon as the reading is over, ask for more specific feedback.

If you are not in a writers' group, ask a friend or roommate to be a serious reader for you. Note all readers' observations and suggestions. You will appreciate some of the suggestions and disagree with others, but if the same suggestions recur several times, you may find a clue to a writing problem there. Ultimately, though, *you* choose which suggestions to act on. The writing belongs to *you*.

You don't have to *take* all the writing advice you get, but you should *weigh* the advice as you reconsider your draft. You may have the help of several readers as you work on your draft. You may have a review partner or a writers' group. Your instructor or perhaps a tutor at a writing center may give you feedback. As you evaluate the advice you get from all these readers, don't forget to put the writing to your own test too. (Revising is also recursive.) From time to time, reread the essay, trying as you do so to imagine yourself as a reader. Think globally, about the large issues of the paper. Do not, absolutely not, start correcting spelling or mechanics. It is counterproductive to spend time editing text or correcting errors before you are satisfied with the content of the piece. Why spend time editing a section that you may later decide to discard? Ask yourself these questions:

🖥 *Computer Writing Tip:* Type the questions that follow into a template file to be used again with other writing projects.

1. How clear is my focus? What point or idea do I want to make in this essay? Is that point expressed in my thesis? If my thesis is implicit, are there enough linguistic markers in the text so that my readers know what I am getting at? How well does the essay address the thesis? Where might the essay falter? Where might the reader get off the track?

2. How thorough is my development? Have I explained enough to satisfy my readers' expectations? Have I assumed that my readers know more than they do? Are some points less developed than others, and is there a reason why? Have I been lazy in showing or explaining? Do I know enough about my subject to develop it well? What else do I need to learn?

3. How good is my beginning? My ending? Does my opening sufficiently forecast the remainder of the essay? Have I earned the right to draw the conclusions I make in the ending? Do these parts of the essay appeal to the reader—and if not, why?

As you evaluate your writing in light of readers' comments, change what you know needs to be changed and what you are capable of changing. Then write down your questions about areas where you feel insecure. If you think a passage is choppy, make a note like "How can this passage be smoother?" If a word doesn't sound right, make a note: "What word will work better in this spot?" If you want to make a passage tighter, but you aren't sure how to do it, make a note: "How can this passage become less wordy?" You should then address these questions to your instructor, either in a conference or in a note accompanying your draft. For specific problems with regard to style or usage, you can look at the advice in Chapter 9.

At this point you may find yourself going back to the notes you made during the invention stage. Sometimes it's a good idea to examine the writing choices you did *not* make; that way, the choices you made seem clearer, more defined. Your invention notes may also remind you of an idea that you intended to include but somehow neglected. And sometimes, if an essay just isn't working for you at all, you may find inspiration or a new perspective on your topic just by reviewing those notes. You are your own best and most reliable resource.

⚠ *Remember:* Keep all notes and drafts for your portfolio.

EDITING AND POLISHING: MAKING THE WRITING SHINE

By this time in the process, your drafts have probably been reviewed by several readers; and you have been over the writing countless times yourself, tinkering and changing, revising, rethinking, and rewriting. Once you feel comfortable with the paper, with what it says and how thoroughly you have developed your ideas, you are ready to edit and polish it. Editing and polishing means getting the rough edges off and going over the text until it shines, reflecting *your* brilliance. The way you edit may differ from essay to essay, depending on what you are writing, but some considerations will remain the same. When you polish your writing, ask your writers' group to help you think about these questions in relation to your text:

1. Are my sentences varied in length and style? Can I combine any sentences for smoothness?
2. Are any sections of my paper redundant? Do I use passive voice and begin sentences with expletives *(there is, there are)* appropriately?
3. Is the level of my language consistent and appropriate for my audience (either mostly formal or mostly informal)? Do I use slang and/or technical language judiciously? Are my word choices good?
4. Is my punctuation correct? Are there any misspelled words? (For proofreading, use the spell-checker on your word processor or find a reader who is a capable speller. Remember that the spell-checker won't catch all the words that may be misspelled; it will, for example, skip right over *new* written for *knew*.)
5. Have I presented my writing in an appealing way? Does my paper look neat? Is the print dark? Are the margins adequate and even? Did I include a title for the paper— and the date it was written? Have I satisfied my instructor's requirements for format?

BEGINNING AGAIN

Even after you think a paper is finished—after you have handed it in, gotten readers' comments, revised, edited, and polished it—even after all this work, you may not be entirely happy with the result. You may want to, yes, begin again. It's not so uncommon among writers to throw material away. Indeed, to be able to say to yourself, "This is not the best I can do" and then to start over is a sign of maturity. So if you are starting over, don't despair. Instead, rejoice that you have the strength to begin again. To find out where your essay may have gone astray, go back over all your material, starting from the invention stage. Perhaps there's a usable idea there, one you rejected the first time around. Maybe you can salvage something from your notes.

You know where to start and what you can do.

 ## PORTMANTEAU OF INTERVIEWS ABOUT WRITING

Regardless of what you write, you express something of who you are in—and with—your writing. Writing is a unique, individual act. This Portmanteau section contains writing about individual writers' processes and about how individual writers solve writing problems. Here you will find excerpts from interviews that focus on writing. You may hear echoes of your writing process in these writers' accounts. As you read, think about what you do, or want you want to learn to do better, when you write.

In this first piece, James Scarcelli reports on a series of interviews with writers in his home town.

Writing Habits
James Scarcelli

As I sit here trying to organize my interviews with five writers, I have to chuckle. The variety and nature of responses I received have surprised me in ways (and in other ways they haven't). The most interesting responses to my questions about writing came from my little brother, who is eight years old. This little guy has four older brothers and sisters and doesn't see himself as the youngest. He acts very grownup and is also very self-centered (probably from sibling competition). Another interesting interviewee was my father, a professor in Creative Arts and, as he put it, someone who "lets [his] art do [his] writing," meaning that he puts his ideas into his art work and not into writing. He dreads writing and almost never writes. The friends I interviewed responded in similar ways to my questions; they are students who write mostly notes and assigned essays. The last person I interviewed was an administrator who does quite a lot of writing and enjoys it.

Well, now that you have some background of the interviewees, here are my questions and summaries of the responses I heard.

Does your profession involve a lot of writing?

All the responses to this question were "yes" except for the artist's "no." The administrator said that she writes two to three hours a day, and my friends said they write two to three times a week. The eight-year-old writes a couple of times a day. It seems that everyone has his or her own definition of how much "a lot" is.

Do you enjoy writing?

In response to this question I received two *yes,* two *sometimes,* and one *no* answer. Again, the *no* was from the artist, who dislikes writing because he finds it hard to organize his thoughts on paper. The two respondents who said *sometimes* like to write when they like the subject but dislike writing tasks that take "too much time." The persons who answered *yes* like to write because they enjoy putting their ideas down on paper. They like to convey and clarify their thoughts through writing.

Do you do any personal writing?

Only the artist and one of my friends do no personal writing. Everyone else does personal writing by writing at least letters to friends and relatives. Most people don't write for themselves very often, though—maybe about once every week.

Where do your ideas for writing come from?

Most of the interviewees said their ideas come from their personal experiences. They observe people around them and how they act and react. The professional person said that her ideas for writing came from her job; the eight-year-old said, "The ideas come from myself" and reported that he has all kinds of ideas he made up that he is keeping in his head.

What is your favorite atmosphere for writing?

Everyone interviewed here agreed that they like a quiet, relaxed atmosphere. The two friends like to write on their beds in their rooms at home. The administrator likes to write at her computer in her office. The eight-year-old likes to write at the big dining room table, and the artist doesn't like to write anywhere. All interviewees said they like their special place because it was comfortable and peaceful.

Only two people said they like to have music on when they write. The type of music was either classical or slow, easy rock. One interesting note is that only one person (one of the students) likes to have the television on when he writes. He said that when he gets stuck and needs an idea, he looks up and watches the television until he gets one. Also the administrator likes to have something to drink (preferably a cherry Coke) when she works.

What kind of preparation for writing do you go through?

Three of the people said that most of the time they conduct research before they write, but ultimately even that depends on what they are writing. The eight-year-old said he "just got right at it." The artist goes through agony in preparation for writing, but he declined to describe the nature of it.

What kind of problems do you have when you write?

All the answers to this question were different. One student said he had trouble with grammar, spelling, and the opening paragraph. The other student has trouble getting stuck with the idea and with getting bored. Getting started is the trouble the eight-year-old has. The administrator has trouble reworking her ideas and finding ways to say the same thing without sounding redundant. But the artist has the most difficulty. He said that he has trouble "getting started, continuing, and finishing."

Do you procrastinate soon after a writing task is presented to you?

All the writers said they procrastinate sometimes, depending on how important the assignment is and how much time they have. They also all said that they write well under pressure. Another interesting note is that responses to a question about writing well under pressure brought forth the artist's only "yes" answer during the whole interview. He said he writes well under pressure because he has to write very concisely.

Has your writing style changed as you have grown older?

All said that their styles have changed except the artist. The administrator and one of the students said that their writing has become more precise. The other student said that his writing has gotten better structurally. The eight-year-old said that he has gotten more creative. All agreed that their writing has improved as they have grown older.

What writers do you think are best?

No one had any specific writers whom they like best. But in response to the question of who influenced their writing, all answered that teachers have been the biggest influence. The administrator said that her college composition teacher and her friend, a professional writer, have influenced her writing most. The artist and two students said it was their high school English teachers. The eight-year-old said it was his grade school teacher, his mom, and his dad—"if Mom isn't around." Everyone said that the reason for the teachers' significant influence was suggestions which helped to improve their styles of writing.

It seems that all these interviewees enjoyed writing some of the time. Everyone has his or her own place and atmosphere that is best for writing, but for a variety of reasons (time, outside interests) most people don't write unless they find it necessary to do a report or an assignment. What was especially interesting was that the responses of the eight-year-old were amazingly similar to those of older writers!

CONSIDER . . .

1. To what parts of the writing process do Scarcelli's interviewees refer most frequently?
2. What problems do these particular writers encounter most often?
3. Can you think of some ways that these writers can begin to solve their writing problems by improving their individual writing processes? Make some recommendations.
4. Can you think of any questions you'd like to ask that Scarcelli omitted?

Here Ann Molter describes what she learned from surveying several writers:

A Survey of Writers, Writing
Ann Molter

A writer's appeal is determined through such factors as style and general attitudes toward his or her writing, attitudes reflected in the work. I have gathered from four writers from a sixth-grader to a scholar of French history information on their personal writing backgrounds. Studying the style of others helps us understand our own styles and attitudes about writing.

Tom is a sixth-grader at Happy Hollow Elementary School. Although he is just eleven years old, he has some strong opinions about writing. Through school, Tom is exposed to writing daily, spending up to fifty percent of his class time writing. He tells me that he doesn't enjoy writing, for he runs into difficulties when he writes. Tom believes that he is a poor speller, and he hopes someday to develop better penmanship. Because of these difficulties, Tom avoids personal writing of any kind; he thinks it involves too much work to make it worthwhile. These obstacles also make it easy for him to delay starting writing assignments until the last minute. His subject matter is usually preselected for him, but if he is given a choice of topic, he writes about the Civil War, a favorite topic. "I like being able to write about something that I didn't even get to see," Tom says. He adds, "I wish I could enjoy writing more because it's important to be able to write well when you're older. If you can't write well, you can't show other people your ideas."

Todd is a senior in high school. Sixty percent of his class time is spent writing, with other writing in homework assignments and personal writing. Todd doesn't really enjoy writing, but he still finds time to write for a club newsletter nevertheless. Ideas for his work come easily and are usually presented in a "thesis statement" format. Topics are derived from either personal experience or specific researched information. Most school papers are done from assigned topics which relate very little to his personal writing or experience.

In preparation for writing, Todd will look over an assignment "to see what it is I'm actually supposed to be doing" and will start writing, usually on the floor of his room. He usually starts a writing project about halfway in between the given and due dates but produces a final copy very close to the due date. Pressure makes Todd write faster, but as with any writer, pressure magnifies the obstacles present even in everyday writing. Todd believes that openings are especially difficult to write because establishing an idea is tricky. This may explain why his final copies are so late: getting started is difficult for Todd. Despite a few persistent writing problems, though, Todd thinks that his writing has improved over the past few years: "My writing is more fluent and descriptive, more constructed."

Mary is a working mother with a position in development in the school of humanities at a university. Despite a seemingly airtight schedule, she spends around fifty percent of each day writing, for work and for personal reasons. Mary enjoys writing and explains that she "likes to construct smooth, flowing prose." Her personal writing includes family history and research on French colonial history. She has published two books and currently has plans for two more.

Mary finds her ideas for writing mainly from research in primary documents and oral recordings, but she also brainstorms to discover what she knows or thinks about a subject. After settling on ideas, she lets them "gestate" while carrying on with everyday life. A few notes, an outline perhaps, and Mary is ready to write.

A quiet atmosphere of a bedroom or living room "along with a cup of tea, of course," helps Mary with any problems she may have while writing. She finds it most frustrating when a precise word is hard to come by and occasionally has difficulty bridging ideas. She writes well under pressure but likes to finish a piece at least twenty-four hours before a deadline. She feels her writing has become more terse, with fewer fancy phrases and complex comparisons than she used several years ago. Her style has been influenced by such authors as Hemingway, Bradbury, Frost, and Bruce Catton. She also enjoys works by Dorothy Parker and African poetry. "There's nothing like being able to write 'Your skin is as smooth as a piece of fresh liver,' " Mary quipped, joking about poetic license.

Evelin is a native of China attending college in the Midwest. She has studied English for the past four years, two years before coming to the United States. She enjoys writing, despite her difficulties with English, and hopes to make her work appear "more literate." Her classes involve quite a bit of writing through extensive notes and assignments, but she believes this pressure helps her develop speed and accuracy. She finds it frustrating when she is unable to correct her work grammatically, but continues sharpening her English skills to improve her usage and spelling.

Evelin tells me she does a lot of personal writing in Chinese. She writes weekly to her family and composes an occasional short story or poem. [For assignments] she usually chooses topics from the vast history of her country, but she also develops ideas through her observation of human behavior. Preparation is kept to a minimum, and Evelin starts her work immediately after it is assigned. She hopes to see her writing improve structurally and objectively in the future and wishes to be more secure about what she has written: "I hope to become more relaxed when I write, for it carries over into my work and makes it more enjoyable to read and comprehend."

After talking with these writers, I compared some of their traits to my own and found several similarities. It is most interesting that all of us seem to have very unique writing habits and styles. Our writing is like our fingerprints: it is individual, personal, and yet absolutely self-identifying.

CONSIDER . . .

1. Compare the processes these writers describe with the writers' problems James Scarcelli refers to. List some points of commonality.
2. What seem to be the most frequent stumbling blocks for these writers? Recommend help.
3. Compare the way Molter structures her paper with the way that Scarcelli sets up his essay.

In a summer 1993 *Paris Review* interview with James Linville, Fran Lebowitz talks about her ambivalent feelings about writing. This is an excerpt from that interview; Linville has just inquired what Lebowitz did during a five-year interval between books, when she had writer's block:

From a *Paris Review* Interview with Fran Lebowitz

JAMES LINVILLE

Lebowitz: I sulked. Sulking is a big effort. So is not writing. I only realized that when I did start writing. When I started getting real work done, I realized how much easier it is to write than not to write. Not writing is probably the most exhausting profession I've ever encountered. It takes it out of you. It's very psychically wearing not to write—I mean if you're supposed to be writing.

Linville: Is that because the ideas come streaming along and you feel like you should put them down and you don't?

Lebowitz: Not writing is more of a psychological problem than a writing problem. All the time I'm not writing I feel like a criminal. Actually, I suppose that's probably an outmoded phrase, because I don't think criminals feel like criminals anymore. I feel like criminals used to feel when they felt guilty about being criminals, when they regretted their crimes. It's horrible to feel felonious every second of the day. Especially when it goes on for years. It's much more relaxing actually to work. Although I might not strike you as languid, I'm much more relaxed than when I wasn't writing. I'm much cheerier, I'm definitely much happier.

Still, I don't get nearly the amount of work done that I read other people do. This is what most interests me in those interviews you do. If I could meet Shakespeare, I would ask, "What time do you get up? Do you write at night?" That is the reason I think these interviews are so great; but they're only interesting to writers. If you're not a writer, why would you care? I'm not interested in the thoughts or ideas of these people, I only want to know how many pages a day they wrote. I don't know many writers. I don't have many friends who are writers. But as soon as I meet any, as soon as I can figure out that it's not too intimate a question to ask them, which is about six seconds after I meet them, I say, "How many words do you write a day?"

Linville: Why do you want to know that?

Lebowitz: So I can compare myself to them.

Linville: Hemingway used to write down the number every day and post it on a piece of cardboard on top of his bureau.

Lebowitz: I count my words too. I was once at Sotheby's looking at some furniture. Just looking. This guy whom I knew came over and asked if I'd like to look at a Twain manuscript that was going to be for sale. I constantly have to disabuse people of the notion that I can afford things like Twain manuscripts. I said I'd love to look at it, but I can't afford it. He said, "Oh, no, no, no, that's okay."

They think you're lying. It's amazing. You usually think of people bragging about being richer than they are. But people always assume that I'm lying when I say I can't afford something. I have to explain this to the Good Humor man, let alone the Sotheby's man with a Twain manuscript. He showed it to me. A short story. He was telling me about the manuscript and where they found it and everything.

He said, "I'm pretty knowledgeable about Twain but there's one thing we don't understand. We've called in a Twain scholar."

I said, "What is that?"

He said, "See these little numbers? There are these little numbers every so often. We just don't know what those are."

I said, "I do. I happen not to be a Twain scholar but I happen to be a scholar of little numbers written all over the place. He was counting the words."

The Sotheby's man said, "What are you talking about? That's ridiculous."

I said, "I bet you anything. Count. I don't want to touch it, smudge up this manuscript." You know, like the sign says, you break it, it's yours.

He counted the words and saw I was right. He said, "Twain must've been paid by the word."

I said, "It may have nothing to do with being paid by the word." Twain might have told himself he had to write this many words each day, and he would wonder, am I there yet? Like a little kid in the back of a car: are we there yet?

Truman Capote wrote many short stories and novels, including *In Cold Blood*, the first "nonfiction novel." This excerpt from an interview with Truman Capote is also taken from the *Paris Review Writers at Work* series:

From a *Paris Review* Interview with Truman Capote

Interviewer: What are some of your writing habits? Do you use a desk? Do you write on a machine?

Capote: I am a completely horizontal author. I can't think unless I'm lying down, either in bed or stretched on a couch and with a cigarette and coffee handy. I've got to be puffing and sipping. As the afternoon wears on, I shift from coffee to mint tea to sherry to martinis. No, I don't use a typewriter. Not in the beginning. I write my first version in longhand (pencil). Then I do a complete revision, also in longhand. Essentially I think of myself as a stylist, and stylists can become notoriously obsessed with the placing of a comma, the weight of a semicolon. Obsessions of this sort, and the time I take over them, irritate me beyond endurance.

Interviewer: What happens next [after the longhand draft]?

Capote: Let's see, that was second draft. Then I type a third draft on yellow paper, a very special certain kind of yellow paper. No, I don't get out of bed to do this. I balance the machine on my knees. Sure, it works fine; I can manage a hundred words a minute. Well, when the yellow draft is finished, I put the manuscript away for a while, a week, a month, sometimes longer. When I take it out again, I read it as coldly as possible, then read it aloud to a friend or two, and decide what changes I want to make and whether or not I want to publish it. I've thrown away rather a few short stories, an entire novel, and half of another. But if all goes well, I type the final version on white paper and that's that.

Interviewer: Is the book organized completely in your head before you begin it or does it unfold, surprising you as you go along?

Capote: Both. I invariably have the illusion that the whole play of a story, its start and middle and finish, occur in my mind simultaneously—that I'm seeing it in one flash.

But in the working-out, the writing-out, infinite surprises happen. Thank God, because the surprise, the twist, the phrase that comes at the right moment out of nowhere, is the unexpected dividend, that joyful little push that keeps a writer going.

CONSIDER . . .

1. Are any parts of your writing process like what Capote does when he writes?
2. Have you ever experienced that "unexpected dividend" of the exactly right word or idea that comes out of nowhere when you are writing? How would you explain the source of such words?

3

Writing What You Live and Know

The point of a notebook is to jump-start the mind.

—John Gregory Dunne

I may start a piece, find it obstructive, lack a way out, and not complete the thing for a year, or years, am thrifty. I salvage anything promising and set it down in a small notebook.

—Marianne Moore

Advice, hmm. It plays an important role in people's lives. I tend to ask for advice before I do a lot of things. A lot of people may be timid in asking for advice because doing so exposes them, makes them vulnerable. People who feel this way miss out on a lot of information they could receive from their peers.

—Ari Toll

Experience is the surest teacher. Its lessons are thorough, enduring, rarely forgettable. Observation is a deep seeing of the world, an attention to detail, nuance, motive, consequence. This chapter suggests some ways to draw upon your experience and observation by using a writer's notebook to record and filter your experiences and observations and to respond to the writing tasks you are doing in preparation for your portfolio. It explores ways to draw on experience in the writing of a memoir and an essay of advice. All these pieces focus on you and what you have learned and are learning in living. For some writers, writing about personal experience is pleasurable, even enlightening and rewarding. For others, it is sometimes difficult to focus so unrelentingly and to reflect so consciously on the self. However you feel about doing it, though, writing that originates in your experience is a valuable part of your portfolio; you will want to have at least one sample of this kind of writing in there.

PERSONAL WRITING: KEEPING A WRITING NOTEBOOK

A writing notebook is a good place to record your experiences and observations, a good place to write ideas so that you can gain perspective on them. It is a place for writing anything for anyone, but mostly for yourself—because you must be outside something, as Fran Lebowitz has noted, truly to see it. The notebook can help you create that distance so as to see more clearly. Sometimes a writing notebook is required for a class, but you can always keep a writing notebook or journal on your own. A writing notebook may be an end in itself, as a record of experience and observation; or it may be a source of concepts, lines, or words for essays: an idea bank. You may even find yourself using whole journal entries as essays.

The writing notebook is not a unified, edited, revised work. Rather it is a compilation, an assemblage of pieces with uneven lengths, varying voices, and a multiplicity of subjects. A writing notebook or journal is honest. It is not false or written in a phony persona. It is not meant to impress or to be a record for posterity. It is a working document, a piece always in progress. Mistakes don't count. Dumb ideas don't count. What matters is the writing. Just the writing.

A writing notebook should have regular but not necessarily daily entries. Arrange or design a writing notebook any way that makes you comfortable. Some writers like small portable notebooks for recording ideas or details. Others prefer large spiral or loose-leaf notebooks. Others like to jot notes or observations on cards they always carry with them. Loose-leaf notebooks are a bit easier to handle; you can add in more pages if you like for clippings or photocopies. Regardless of how you constitute the notebook, however, you should always think of it as yours. You choose what to put in; you determine whether to edit and select something from the journal. Do not let anyone else edit your writing notebook or journal.

Writing Task:

Keep a writer's notebook for a month. You can write on paper or note cards or you can keep your notebook on the computer. Just remember to save each entry in its own dated file. You'll also find that if you give a title to each entry, whether it is in a notebook or in a computer file, you'll be able to find or refer to individual ideas more quickly.

Ideas for a Writing Notebook

Here are some suggestions for what you can do in your writing notebook. You may try all or none of them in any order you like. After a while you will think of many other ideas for your writing notebook.

1. Keep a running commentary on what you are reading for class (any class, not just your composition class) or for pleasure. A commentary is not a summary; it is an opinion on and a response to what is on the pages that you are reading. You can record your amazement at something in your biology or political science or psychology texts as well as your enjoyment or dislike of a character in a novel or movie.

2. Record quotations or favorite sayings that you see in print or elsewhere. Sometimes writers keep a special section of the notebook for quotations.

3. Write down snatches of conversation, heard and overheard. A funny or trenchant line from a conversation may find its way into a later essay or story or poem.

4. Copy poems or song lyrics or passages of prose that interest you. Many writers keep examples of writing that they especially like. You may want to write an imitation of someone's writing—or even a parody.

5. Make lists. List interesting or favorite names of people, cars, shampoos, streets. List places you have visited or those you would like to see. List restaurants where you have eaten. List things you despise. List anything that interests you.

6. Describe a specific place or setting: your favorite booth in the student union, the interior of your car, your garden, your favorite fishing spot, your grandmother's living room. Recall as many details as you can.

7. Write about your position on a controversial national issue. What do you think about capital punishment? About term limits for congresspeople? About welfare reform? About educational reform?

8. Clip an article or a cartoon from a newspaper or magazine. Put it in your notebook.

9. Record notes from a conversation with a child. How old is the child? What did you talk about? What interesting remark did the child make? What is your impression of the child?

10. Freewrite about a specific word. This may be a word you use frequently or one you don't know at all. Then photocopy a definition of the word from a dictionary or an etymology of the word from the *Oxford English Dictionary* (available in your university library) and put it in your notebook next to your writing about the word.

11. Write about a recent meal. What did you eat? How was the food prepared and served? Where did you eat it? In what manner did you consume the food?

12. Think back about five minutes ago. What were you thinking about? Where did that thought lead? Write down a stream of your consciousness that draws on a very brief and very recent time of thinking.

13. Make lists of characters who might inhabit a story you would write.

14. Write a letter to yourself about something you want to remember in five years.

15. Write a love letter (you don't have to send it).

16. Write a complaint (you don't have to send this either).

17. Write a fan letter to someone whose work or prowess you admire. (You could send this if you like.)

18. Design your perfect house. Would it have a gourmet kitchen? A room for your drums? An office? A mud room? A sewing room? A game room?

19. Write a prayer.

20. List substitutes for *said*.

21. Write from the consciousness of an animal as you imagine it. What might your cat think when she hears your car in the driveway? What does your bird think and do

when you let her out of the cage? What might your dog feel when a baby is allowed to pull his ears?

22. Make up a product that you would like to see sold in stores.
23. Watch two different news programs on the same evening. List the stories each presents and their order of appearance. Compare lineups for the two shows. What do you learn?
24. Don't put anything into words: Sketch a picture or a cartoon or insert a photograph that you took.
25. Recall a childhood experience. How old were you? Where were you? Who was involved in the experience besides you? What happened? Why do you think you remember this so clearly?
26. Record details about a dream you recently experienced.
27. Write about your favorite article of clothing. What does it look like? Feel like? Smell like? How does it make you feel?
28. Describe your most pressing current problem.
29. Write about your most hated enemy. Why do you despise this person?
30. Choose a notebook entry that you've already written and sharpen it. Revise it for another reader.
31. Describe a memorable wedding or funeral.
32. Describe the next thing you plan to buy, no matter how small, and why you are buying it.
33. Read a favorite notebook entry aloud to a classmate or a friend.
34. Write about your favorite television program, explaining why you like to watch it.
35. Explain what you would do with one million dollars.
36. Tell about something you might or could do to make money.
37. Write about the two best movies you have seen.
38. Go to a public place—a library, municipal office building, restaurant, hospital lobby—and record what you see.
39. Write about a course you would like to take just for the sheer pleasure of learning about the subject.
40. Write about an appliance in your house or apartment. What does the specific appliance do? What does it look like? If it could talk, what would it say?
41. Write about a theological or spiritual question you have. You don't have to answer the question—just articulate it clearly.
42. What person from the past would you like to meet? Write how, why, and where you would like to meet this person.
43. Observe something very ordinary and write about what you see. Flush a toilet and watch what happens—which direction does the water swirl in the bowl? Boil water and record the changes that seem to occur as the water comes to a steady boil.
44. Write about a game that children play. What are the beauties of this game? What lessons about life can be learned from this game?
45. Describe your favorite kind of weather. Do you like sunshine or clouds or snow or wind? Why?
46. Catalog your morning ritual, then analyze it.

47. Do you collect something? Rocks, bells, art, baseball cards, antique glass, restaurant menus? Coins? Signed letters? Write about your collection and why you like it; explain how you got started as a collector.
48. Make a list of states you have been in and countries that you have traveled to. Write about where you'd like to go next.
49. Write a secret.
50. Articulate your goals: what you want to accomplish and when.

Things to Do with Your Writing Notebook

How does a writer use a writing notebook? In many ways. Use your notebook as a source of ideas for essays or research. If you are assigned to write a position piece on a controversial issue, page through your notebook to find places where you expressed your thoughts and feelings on a controversial issue. If you are asked to review a movie, book, or product, look through your notebook to remind yourself what you have recently read, seen, or purchased. Sometimes you can lift whole passages or entries from your writing notebook and transplant them into a larger piece. (This is particularly easy if you do your writing notebook on a computer.) There is also an intensely personal use for your notebook: It provides a record of your intellectual growth and development and as such can help you remember and understand how you have grown. A writing notebook can be an excellent place to reflect on your pieces of writing. This reflection is especially valuable when you assemble your portfolio.

On Keeping a Writing Notebook

In this article, which originally appeared in *Esquire*, John Gregory Dunne describes how he uses his writer's notebook.

Sweet Liberty

JOHN GREGORY DUNNE

I am at liberty. A writer at liberty is a writer without anything to do, and no real idea of what he is next going to do. Of course I am not totally at liberty. I have this column. For one week every month I sit in front of my typewriter pounding it out, trying not to think of the three weeks after I finish when I will be at liberty until the next deadline rolls around. I have a file that says COLUMN IDEAS. I want to do a column about baseball books, but it is 23 degrees outside and my heart is really not into Keith Hernandez and his ghost. I want to do a column about Paul Scott and *The Raj Quartet,* but every time I mention it to my editor her eyes glaze over and she mumbles something like, "Wouldn't you rather do the literary scene in Indianapolis?"

I think a writer never works harder, or more desperately, than when he is at liberty. There is a constant omnivorous trolling for material. *In Search of a Character,* Graham Greene called the notebooks he published recounting two trips to Africa, one in 1941, the other in 1959; the character he finally found was Querry in *A Burnt-Out Case.* When I am at liberty, I start keeping notebooks, which I never do when I am in the middle of a project. The notebooks a writer keeps when he is at liberty are proof that time has not been misspent. On a shelf in my office, there are a dozen three-ring binders, each holding some three hundred typed single-spaced pages of the notes I have made and transcribed between books. Twice I have started a diary, and each time I have abandoned it within a week. Keeping a diary the way Harold Nicolson or John Colville did, with a seemingly effortless congruence of great events and vanity fair, simply takes up too much time. Nor do I find an account of the social ramble all that interesting. To write down "Cocktail party for Brian Moore—David Rieff brought Joseph Brodsky and Derek Walcott—Edna O'Brien & Harrison Ford, etc." is an invitation for ridicule if publication is contemplated. If you doubt me, just read the critical hammering Stephen Spender received last year when he published his diaries, which to his detractors seemed only a chronicle of a lifetime spent lunching or dining out, and not the musings of the man who wrote, "I think continually of those who were truly great."

The point of a notebook is to jump-start the mind. I am always jotting down first lines: "Billy Rutland was getting laid that night, which is how I happened to get the case." That is from a novel I might like to read but know I will never write, an echo (I realize now) of one of my favorite first lines: "I came up out of Central America, traveling fast." That one comes from a paperback original I once read on an airplane; the title and the author elude me, but the sentence has the kind of panache—Cyrano as a merc—that I sometimes wish were more indigenous to my own work. My prevailing disposition tends more toward the metaphorically gloomy: "The S.S. *American Dream* slipped out of San Pedro harbor at midnight, with a cargo of death heads." And promptly ran aground before I could arrive at the second sentence.

I look through my binders and find endless lists of Irish names. The people in a novel are people the author is going to live with for two years or more. He is going to sleep with them, love them, hate them, betray and perhaps even murder them, and he must be comfortable with the names he gives them. "Hercules Finnigan, Mouse McKenna, Wendell Gaffney, Bones Brady, Dougie Doyle, D'arcy Degrian." None ever used, but I can tell by the alliteration and by the nicknames the kind of character I had in mind, a minor character, an assistant commissioner in the Department of Sanitation or the toastmaster at the annual communion breakfast held by the Knights of Columbus in St. Finbar's parish hall. I find a short dissertation: "First the name. An Irish name, of course. Not Sullivan or Meenan. Something more vague. Or less common. Which lets out the O's and the Mc's. O'Malley and O'Neill, McGuire and McDermott. Dunne is good, but out of the question for obvious reasons. Hackett. Not bad, but a touch bloodless. Fair, Flood, and Clare. The same. Something more muscular but still ethnic. Mackey. Too heavy on the mick. Broderick. Getting warm." I finally used Broderick, but admit a hint of dissimulation in the entry. What I was actually trying out was an opening in the manner of Trollope (*The Way We Live Now* was the novel I had in mind), one I fortunately abandoned.

The entries multiply, with neither rhyme nor reason. "For George Will piece: In 1230, the Florentines, who were warring with Siena, catapulted dead donkeys and excrement over the walls in hopes of starting a plague." I wrote that in Siena but have no memory as to how it applied to George Will, except that I sometimes think his column would fit nicely into a Florentine catapult.

Newspapers and magazines are continuing suppliers. From *Soldier of Fortune* I note how to kill a man with a pistol, preferably an H&K P9S 45 cal. ACP, with a polygon barrel for increased accuracy. "The objective is a no-reflex kill." The objective is therefore to cut the medulla oblongata. Or the motor nerves in the pelvic girdle. From a diocesan newspaper (my reading is eclectic) I copy a personal: "38 year old mature male wishes to meet a Catholic female who has a strong faith in the Sacred Heart and the Immaculate Heart of Mary. Not fanatical." Sheila Mulvihill is a good candidate, devoted to the Sacred Heart but not Nutsy Fagan about it, just the kind of Catholic female for Bart Hoolehan or John Murrihy, Vincent Cusick or Aloysius Kenna. A United flight makes an emergency landing in Denver because a casket in the cargo compartment has ruptured its seal, sending the noxious fumes of the late lamented into the passenger cabin. Why would I possibly clip that? Perhaps because Walter Hackett had not planned to stop in Denver, and as a result of that and a number of other equally unforeseen coincidences ended up booking passage on the S.S. *American Dream* with Sheila Mulvihill, having established before sailing that the best way to cut the medulla oblongata (all parts of the head not being equal) is by firing into the open mouth toward the center of the skull, the proof of the pudding being several of those death heads in the cargo hold.

This is what I mean by jump-starting the mind. Sooner or later the mind starts making connections. Of course, not all the entries are so grisly; I just have a weakness for the grotesque and its impact on the mundane. There is also The Scene. The writer is essentially a professional shut-in and the restaurant his dining room. Whenever I am at liberty, I never refuse an invitation; if a writer is interested in manners, he must go out. There is always the chance he will overhear someone say, as I once did, "Women are to tennis pros what tips are to a waiter." Or a female agent's evaluation of another female executive: "She fucked her way to the middle." Admittedly this is a buzzard's scavenging; my only answer is that there is no copyright on repartee.

The cocktail party, the small dinner, the black-tie benefit—this is work, the source of combat stories from the social battlefield. "Paint peeling on ceiling over coromandel screen; empty roll of toilet paper in the bathroom": an apartment is locked into place. I remember another particularly odious evening redeemed only by an introduction to a woman who had been exposed to most of the famous and powerful men of several generations. What struck me immediately about her was the way she spoke, in a peculiarly dated slang, as if she had been cloistered in a nunnery for the nearly twenty-five years she had in fact been in public life. She said she was "having a ball"; she asked a waiter for "a weak Scotch highball"; she said of the world-class philanderer that he was "a make-out artist." In my notebook I also wrote: "She grew up in a world in which not much was expected of women and married into one in which everything was demanded, in which she was expected to move on an international scale, and she was found wanting." I rather liked her, but the cold-blooded professional bottom line was that her situation was too obvious. I did, however, ultimately use her slang, putting it, appropriately enough, in the mouth of an ex-nun who had jumped over the wall after twenty years in the convent.

Sometimes I just noodle: "We had a postcoital discussion of the ablative case." And then again: "The mark of a truly sadistic school system is one that teaches *The Mill on the Floss.*" True enough, but I wonder what provoked me to write it down, other than my own inability to finish *The Mill on the Floss,* not to mention *Felix Holt, The Radical* or anything else by George Eliot. I think I just recognized a line with latent possibilities, a wild card. "Prepare yourself for *quenelles.*" That was my wife, on our way to dinner at the home of a woman who serves spectacularly bad expensive food, the kind so labor intensive that only the very rich could afford the kitchen staff necessary to prepare it. "The U.S. should never get too tight with any country whose leaders wear sunglasses at night." Another wild card, one I could fit into a conversation with "Sartre said revolution was seeing each other a lot." The fact is, I don't know if Sartre ever did say that, but the kind of character I have in mind would have intuited that not many others would know if Sartre had said it either, and be smart enough not to say it in company where he thought someone might call him on it.

I haunt courthouses when I am at liberty. There is a drama in every courtroom—always a plus for someone who has difficulty with plot—and a rancid view of human behavior that I find absolutely invigorating; there is entirely too much humanism around. "Crime is the cottage industry of the underprivileged; whites make bail." "Moral exhaustion is the AIDS of the criminal attorney." My notebooks are crammed with such entries. I notice "Condoms in the stairwell, glassine envelopes and blood-flecked disposable needles in the can"; "the Indian who runs the newsstand in the lobby is making book." " I don't do that anymore," a habitual offender whines to his lawyer. "You don't do it any less, either," the lawyer replies. Another attorney: "My guy only sticks up things beginning with the letter *a*—*a* gas station, *a* liquor store, *a* delicatessen."

The appeal of the courthouse is not parochial. I have, in fact, watched murder trials in London and Paris, in Cartagena and Bogotá, in Singapore and Kuala Lumpur. For the writer at liberty, travel is always broadening. Unless he is Flaubert in Egypt, however, or Henry James in Italy, he is not so much interested in learning anything substantive about the country he is visiting as he is in establishing an attitude a character might have toward it. "Have you ever noticed how the English shake hands? They shake hands as if they're tipping a headwaiter. There is a slight backhand action, palm low and pointed out, as if to conceal a bill." I wrote this down after a dinner party on Thurloe Square in London. Another guest had recently published a new translation of Proust. He was so full of himself that I began needling him. I said I found it odd that a Proust scholar could not locate the Buttes de Chaumont in Paris. His response was to ask our hostess if I were perhaps a tennis pro.

The real trick for the writer abroad is getting to those parts of the world where he would never dream of going unless someone else paid his way. Here is where the USIA comes in; a Ph.D. dissertation wants to be written on the number of American novels that show the spoor of the USIA trip. Think of John Updike's two Bech books (*Bech: A Book* and *Bech Is Back*) and Henry Bech's adventures both in the heart of darkness and in Sofia with the Bulgarian poetess. Under the auspices of the USIA, I have had dinner with the director-general of the Indonesian Humor Institute, who asked me, face abeam with good humor, "Why so many dirty words in American movies? Shit, piss, son of a bitch." And spent an afternoon in El Salvador with the counterpart of Henry Bech's Sofia siren; this is how she appeared in the final text, from the point of view of a Vegas comic in-country judging an international beauty contest: "Buddy Seville could not take his eyes off the remaining guest, Dra. Lourdes Abauza, the most prominent poet in Cristo Rey, a woman in her sixties with a moustache and a generous assortment of moles on the breasts that seemed to be cantilevered out of her parrot green silk dress. 'Now I know who that chick looks like,' Buddy Seville whispered. 'Don Ameche.' "

So: I once was able to make connections. I look at the notes I have made since I have been at liberty and wonder if I will ever again be able to jump-start my mind. There is one that I have retyped on a card and pinned to my bulletin board: "Her first priority has always been the maintenance of her own interests."

Perhaps that is where I will attach the jumper cables next.

CONSIDER . . .

1. Describe two ways that Dunne uses his writing notebook for further writing.
2. How does Dunne physically keep his notebooks? In what form?
3. Select a short passage from Dunne's article to copy into your writing notebook.

PUBLIC WRITING: THE MEMOIR

A memoir explores an event or a series of related events that remain lodged in memory. A memoir describes the events and then shows, either directly or indirectly, *why* they are significant—or, in short, *why* you continue to remember them. The memoir is focused in time; it does not try to cover a great span of years (that's what autobiographies are for). It centers on a problem or focuses on a conflict and its resolution—and on the understanding of why and how the resolution is significant in your life. Memoirs are frequently published in magazines and literary journals; they have become so popular that recently the *New York Times* called ours "The Age of the Literary Memoir."

 Writing Task:

Write a memoir that draws on one event or a series of related events in your life. Help the reader understand the significance of those events.

Invention Ideas

To begin exploring subjects for a memoir, try imagining a series of snapshots of yourself. What would a typical snapshot of you at age five or six look like? Who would be in the photo with you? Where would you be? What would you be doing? Freewrite on this subject for five minutes and see what emerges.

Next, turn to another page in your imaginary photo album, one with pictures of you in high school, those years of adolescent turmoil. Now what picture emerges? What are you doing in the photo? Is anyone in the picture with you? Does this picture represent a typical experience? How? Freewrite about this snapshot for five minutes.

Take one more look now, at a recent picture of you, one taken within the last year. What has the photographer captured? Was this a typical moment? Is anyone in the picture with you? What are you doing? Freewrite about this for five minutes.

Does one of your snapshots suggest an event that you might write about? Connie visualized the photograph that you see here, a picture of her at about age five, standing with her arm around her younger sister, both dressed in spring finery and holding their hats against the wind. They are smiling and dressed alike. This image led her to explore her role as "big sister" in the freewriting exercise and eventually to write an essay about how looking after her younger sister helped to shape her personality and, eventually, her career. At the center of the essay were two separate but thematically related "big sister"

incidents recalled in the freewriting exercise. Connie did not write an essay about the photograph but used the ideas generated by the photo and the freewriting to conceptualize her memoir.

If freewriting does not yield any suitable writing material, try another invention strategy (see Chapter 2 for some ideas). If you try clustering, use a time or an activity (playing basketball, drama club, the senior prom, a recent job, a current intellectual challenge) as the centerpiece. You may also want to try clustering *after* you have a subject or topic, as a way of generating material.

Drafting a Memoir

Once you know what you want to write about, articulate the dominant impression you want the essay to create. This dominant impression may be expressed in a thesis or it may be implicit. Do you want to create an impression that your parents' divorce changed your life and eventually made you a stronger person? That your inability to pass geometry ultimately affected your academic confidence and college career? That your childhood love of music helped you weather a difficult personal experience? Try to say what impression you want your narrative to create, even if you decide not to use an explicit thesis but simply to imply the dominant impression.

Now, dominant impression in the back of your mind, plan your essay by chunking it. *Chunking* a paper means dividing it into its most important parts or events. Table 3.1 shows an example of the substance of an essay, represented in chunks.

Computer Writing Tip: Learn how to use the Columns feature in your word-processing program and set up columns for chunking.

Table 3.1 An example of chunking

Chunk 1	Chunk 2	Chunk 3	Chunk 4	Chunk 5	Chunk 6
A football player gets a scholarship to a major university.	He finds out that big-time college football is not so easy, that the game and the coaches are very demanding.	He starts to use steroids in imitation of older teammates who use an assortment of drugs.	As the size of his doses increases, he experiences serious personality and physical changes.	A tumor on his hand is removed and he lives through a wild weekend; he quits the team temporarily.	He has anxiety attacks and becomes suicidal. His father rescues him from school. He is hospitalized and begins to improve.

When you chunk an essay, you can see its parts—and manipulate them to create the effect you want. If you want the story to appear straightforward and simple, tell it in a straight narrative order. Write Chunk 1 first, Chunk 2 second, and so on straight through the material: 1, 2, 3, 4, 5, 6.

Or, to emphasize the desperation of the football player, begin the essay with Chunk 5 and describe the fear that leads him to quit the team. This will draw the reader into the turmoil of the situation very quickly. After you tell the events of Chunk 5, do a simple flashback to Chunk 1 to show the reader how the situation developed, then continue through to Chunk 6 to conclude the story: 5, 1, 2, 3, 4, 5, 6.

To frame the story and create a sense of closure and completion, begin and end with Chunk 6. Recount the events of Chunk 6, beginning perhaps with his rescue and recovery; then flash back to the beginning of the story, following through all the chunks in sequence, reiterating briefly for emphasis the football player's recovery: 6, 1, 2, 3, 4, 5, 6.

Once you decide on the order you want, start drafting. Set down a draft as quickly as you can. Actually, you may want to try several different versions of the essay to see which one best achieves your intentions. Don't worry about style or correctness at this point.

Looking at a Memoir

Here is a memoir to examine. Notice how the writer, Mylese Tucker, structures the essay around a series of related events and how the essay does more than simply tell a story. It is a story with a purpose, a story with insight and reflection. The writer understands the significance of the events related here.

A Cinematic Diary of the Tucker Children
Mylese Tucker

Home movies. They are as American as apple pie and as psychologically important as any necessity. Every family needs at least one movie for visiting friends, relatives, and neighbors. What better way for parents to show off their adorable children and their many talents than in home movies?

My dad, who had a severe movie camera habit all during our growing-up days, was rarely seen without his photographic paraphernalia. He didn't carry the compact video camera of today, but a bulky 8mm movie camera with four extra rows of floodlights. In his worn Kodak shoulder bag he toted a light meter, emergency replacement bulbs, lens cleaner, and twelve extra rolls of film. He had the entire, outrageous outfit.

An ideal camera event for Dad was the annual family trip to Yellowstone National Park. Year after year, he began by panning the entire area, always ending with Old Faithful, the famous geyser. Satisfied with his opening shots, he would then start diffusing us kids into the scene—one at a time, two at a time, sometimes all five of us together. This process would go on for the entire day or until the film ran out. Sometimes

I wondered if we went to Yellowstone to see the sights or just to take movies. It was hard to tell.

Picnics were another movie-time favorite for my dad. He could never sit through an entire meal without pulling out the camera, floodlights, and shoulder bag for more cine-matography. Shawna eating, Kerstin drinking, and Stacy spilling were all common fac-tors in the picnic movies. He would film the various stages of the meal, from the fried chicken to the cole slaw and down to the Twinkies. I always wondered how Dad could eat his whole lunch and never miss a shot! He was amazing when it came to that 8mm camera.

Along with the Yellowstone and picnic epics were the ever-popular bathtub scenes (which in later years turned out to be quite embarrassing), swimming scenes taken at the YMCA pool, baseball games, dance concerts, piano recitals, and anything else that involved my sisters and me. Dad was an absolute fanatic! Our basement is filled with boxes and boxes of home movies, stacked in rows and labelled carefully with little white stickers in alphabetical order, allowing for easy access.

Of these many movies, everyone agrees that Dad's greatest masterpieces were taken at Christmas. Christmas morning was an exciting event in my house, and Dad captured it on film every year. The day would always begin with Stacy, the early riser, waking up at 4:00 A.M. yelling, "It's Christmas, it's Christmas, it's Christmas!" Not long after, everyone in the house was up and ready to see what treasures Santa Claus had left during the night.

All of us girls would line up in the hallway while Mom combed our slept-on heads of hair. After our grooming, we couldn't run into the living room until Dad was finished with his opening shots, the panning of the area. He would go up the tree, down the tree, around the tree, over to the fireplace, back to the tree, over to the piano, and then back to the tree again for a finish. We were very impatient until we heard his authoritative, "OK. Let's go!"

Kerstin, the oldest, usually came out first, and I, as the youngest, brought up the rear. We each pulled a present from under the tree, opened it, and held up a Spirograph or an Etch-a-Sketch for my dad to record on film. One by one the presents would dis-appear from under the tree until we were all sitting in front of the camera, surrounded by our unwrapped gifts from Santa, happy and smiling.

Every year was different, yet every year was the same. Poor Travis never went through a Christmas morning without receiving a broken toy. Kerstin, the tomboy of the family, got a basketball every single year. (I wonder what happened to all those basket-balls!) Stacy and I could never get through a Christmas morning without fighting over something, and Mom would have to enter the picture to settle our dispute.

So this was all captured on sixteen years of film. Watching these movies is a favorite pastime of my family when we are all together. There is a special closeness when we sit down and watch ourselves grow up again. I guess my dad had a pretty good idea when he decided to buy that old 8mm movie camera.

CONSIDER . . .

1. What *kinds* of events does Tucker describe?
2. How does she arrange the events? What kind of order does she use? What do you consider the dominant impression of the essay?
3. What details of the essay are especially memorable to you?
4. What is the significance of these events to Tucker? How do you know? Tucker writes that home movies are "psychologically important"; how well does she develop this idea? How could she pursue this notion more fully? Give her specific advice.
5. Where could Tucker add details to create more effective images?

Writers' Group: Rethinking the Memoir

Now that you have a complete draft of a memoir, get some feedback and response from your writers' group. Your group might begin with an oral reading of each member's paper by a reader other than the author. If so, listen carefully as your piece is being read. If a reader hesitates at a line or misreads what you *think* you wrote, this is a clue for you: You may need to clarify the wording or change the punctuation to make a section more readable. Remember that while peer readers offer you responses and suggestions, the writing remains yours, and you decide what to do with those peer reactions.

After each memoir is read, the members of the group can respond to these questions in a brief discussion:

1. What dominant impression or main idea do you hear in this essay? Would you say this essay has a thesis? Is the thesis stated or implied?
2. Recall two details that reinforce the dominant impression.
3. From memory, chunk the memoir as it is plotted. Then consider this: Is there another way that the writer can think about arranging or constructing this essay?
4. Does the writer use effective transitions between chunks? Find an instance of effective transitions.
5. What other suggestions do you have for one another as you prepare to revise?

Now return to your memoir yourself for another critical look. The key to an effective memoir is the subtlety with which you present the significance of the event or events. If you baldly tell the reader up front that "I learned to be careful when I drive" and then relate the series of events surrounding an auto accident, you state the obvious and the trite. If, however, you allow the importance of the story to unfold in its telling—if you *show* your reader the significance of the events—your essay is more effective. The best way to infuse this kind of subtlety into an essay is first to understand the event thoroughly. *Think* hard about it. When you ponder a personal event consciously, asking yourself why the event persists in your memory and why it is important, you acquire an understanding of the event that shows itself in your word choices and in the way that you relate what happened.

Think about the significance of your memoir. Will a reader who doesn't know you understand you better after reading the memoir? Will your motive for writing the essay be understood? Will a reader be able to discern how this event shaped you?

Think about the events you relate. Have you written about the most important ones? Sometimes memoirs and other narratives get cluttered with trivial events that are ultimately unnecessary to an understanding of the point of the memoir. Of course, you need to present enough background or detail so that your reader can comprehend how the situation arose. But you may not want or need to tell the reader *every* detail about the subject. Telescope events to focus on a few main occurrences; that way, you are less likely to lose the reader along the way. Be selective; tell events that will move the story along. Your writers' group can be especially useful in helping you eliminate excess details.

Think about your transitions. In a narrative piece, one that relates a sequence of events, you often need many transitions of time: *first, next, then, later, eventually, after that, finally*. Make sure that you use enough transitions to guide your reader through the time chunks of your narrative. And don't forget that you can effect transitions by repeating a key word or part of a phrase or by using synonyms. Find some transitions in "A Cinematic Diary of the Tucker Children."

Computer Writing Tip: When you finish drafting your essay, search it, putting all transitions in bold type or in a larger font to make them more visible. This will allow you to see which sections are missing transitions.

As you polish and rewrite this essay, remember that a well-written memoir

- creates a dominant impression of the event(s);
- focuses on the meaning or significance of the event;
- demonstrates the conflict that creates the significance of the event;
- uses detail to create credibility;
- uses some logical time order; and
- summarizes less important events to keep the action moving.

Reflecting on and Presenting the Memoir

When you are satisfied with the substance of your memoir, consider how it might appear in your portfolio. Does the essay have an intriguing title? Is it formatted neatly and appropriately, with maximum readability? Are all the words spelled correctly? Is the punctuation appropriate?

As soon as you finish the essay, write a few notes about the writing of it; reflect. You might put your notes in your writing notebook. Mention how you came up with the title; record any special problems that presented themselves along the way and how you solved them. Write about what you learned when you wrote this piece. When you assemble your portfolio, you will need this reflective writing later for the overview memo or reflective piece or perhaps for an individual reflection. Also, consider giving a copy of this piece to someone who was mentioned or who was involved in the events of the essay—your brother or mother, perhaps, or a friend or colleague.

PUBLIC WRITING: AN ESSAY OF ADVICE

Giving advice is a natural human trait. We all enjoy offering our opinions when they are asked for—and sometimes even when they aren't. You may believe that only "experts" are truly qualified to give advice. If so, reconsider your definition of *expert*. Everyone is an expert at something. You may be an expert driver, baker of bread, closet cleaner, batter, burger flipper, studier, shoe buyer, or dog trainer. Or you may be an expert in ending relationships, talking on the telephone, making speeches, drawing cartoons, or getting along with your in-laws. Just living gives you enough experience to know how to do many things well. The essay of advice draws on your accumulated expertise in something.

Writing Task:

Write an essay that gives advice in some area where you are an expert. You may give advice to a very narrow audience interested in some quite specific subject (like tying fishing lures or changing the desktop pattern on a Macintosh computer), or you may write to a general audience of your peers. You should give advice on how to *do* something, how to *make* something, or how to *be* something.

Invention Ideas

If you are unaware of the depth of your expertise, this list-making *heuristic*, or problem-solving strategy, will help you discover your talents. Try to respond to all these requests for lists, then decide which list yields the most fruit for writing.

- List five things you can prepare (a great salad? a term paper?).
- List five things you can fix or repair (a broken fingernail? a VCR? a 1965 Mustang?).
- List five things you can operate (a forklift? a copy machine? a microwave?).
- List five things you can construct (a birdhouse? a Lego fire truck? a piñata?).
- List five things you can appreciate (horror movies? opera? Cajun cuisine?).
- List five things you can do around the house (polish silver? take out trash? mow grass?).
- List five of your academic strengths (solving quadratic equations? diagramming sentences? analyzing the players in a political movement?).
- List five of your talents in getting along with your family (making children laugh? getting money from your parents? helping to care for a handicapped family member?).

- List five of your abilities for getting along with your friends (bumming gas money? doing favors? helping people move?).
- List five of your strengths in getting along with the opposite sex (turning down a date request? handling blind dates? starting a conversation?).

Drafting an Advisory Piece

When you have chosen a subject on which you want to give advice, begin thinking about how you would like to present the advice. Decide what your thesis should emphasize about the process: *"Collecting baseball cards can be a lucrative and enjoyable hobby, if it's done right."* Or decide whether you simply want to use a purpose statement such as *"Here are four ways to impress members of the opposite sex."* Early on, you may also want to think about how you will establish your authority as an expert. You can do so *directly* (by simply making a claim such as "I have been very successful at growing orchids" or "I have trained as a cross-country runner for five years now") or *indirectly* (through the cumulative force of your details and special knowledge and your tone of confidence)—or both. You may also want to consider the main points of your advice. If you are advising your reader how to *do* or *make* something, you may present the advice in a series of steps. If you are giving advice as tips on how to *be* better at something (conversation, friendship, library research), you may need to order the advice another way (least important to most important tip, for instance). Working from an outline or sketch of your essay-to-be may be helpful. As soon as you figure out how to frame your thesis or purpose statement, how you will establish your authority, and how you will order your advice, begin drafting. As usual, write as quickly as you can to get a draft that you can later shape and revise.

Looking at an Essay of Advice

Here is an advisory essay for you to read and ponder. (You can read a reflection about the writing of this essay in the Portmanteau section.) Julie Hunt is a competitive swimmer. Notice how she establishes authority, how the essay is structured, and how the parts of the essay are held together.

How to Put On a Swim Cap Easily
Julie Hunt

Most of you female competitive swimmers with semi-long or long hair often find it somewhat difficult to stuff all your hair into a tiny, tight swim cap. The tugging and pulling can get to be a hassle. To make putting on your cap a little easier and to prevent wear and tear on your scalp and hair, follow the tips listed below for putting on a swim cap.

The most important step before you even begin to put on your cap is to "powder" it. Before someone told me about "powdering" my cap, I found it a struggle to put my cap on without pulling my hair in all different directions. To powder your cap, take a bottle of any brand of baby powder. Hold your cap open in one hand and in the other hold the powder and sprinkle your cap lightly. Using the powder that you sprinkled into the cap, gently rub together the two sides of the cap, making sure to get all the way to the top of the edges. Your cap should now have a very light film of powder on the inside of it. If you have any excess powder inside, then dump it out into the trash can.

After you have powdered your cap, you are ready to tackle putting it on. If you don't already have your hair pulled back, then you will need to put your hair behind your ears. This will prevent you from having to do this after you have your cap on. It is much easier to do it before rather than after you put it on. Now put your cap on the way you usually do, just pull it onto your head with a front-to-back movement. I'm sure that the powder you put on earlier made the cap slip on much more easily than before.

The next step is to stuff your hair into the cap. The first thing you need to do is put your bangs, if you have them, into the cap. Split your bangs into two sections. Gently lift up the front of the cap and put one section of bangs under the cap. Then do the same with the other section. Since you have already slid your hair behind your ears, the second part of stuffing your hair in should be fairly easy.

To finish stuffing the remaining hair into the cap, separate the hair—which should all be at the back of your head, behind your ears—into two parts. Choose one section and twist it loosely. Then stuff that twisted section underneath the cap. Twisting the hair is important because twisted hair doesn't pull out as easily as untwisted hair. Now do the same thing with the other section of hair.

Following these simple tips can make putting on your swimming cap much easier and save you needless frustration before a swim meet. Remember that the most important aspect of putting on your cap with relative ease is the powder. This ensures that no matter how you stuff your hair into the cap, it should slide in fairly well, with not much pulling. These are the steps that I have been following for years, and I have found this method to work!

CONSIDER . . .

1. What is Hunt's purpose for giving advice? What part of the text presents this purpose? Describe the location within the essay of this purpose/thesis statement.
2. Hunt assumes that most female competitive swimmers wear caps. As a reader, do you agree with this assumption? Should she explain why caps are useful for competitive swimmers—or do you think that doing so is unnecessary?
3. One of the most difficult aspects of writing an essay of advice is that to the expert, some aspects of the subject seem natural, even self-explanatory. Does Hunt fall into this trap? Are there some parts of the essay that would benefit from additional detail or explanation? Would it help readers to know, for instance, why a powdered cap goes on more easily than one without powder?

4. How does Hunt establish her authority to give advice? Rate the effectiveness with which she does this: Is the essay *barely credible, credible,* or *very credible?* If you believe that the voice lacks credibility and authority, suggest how the advice can be made more credible.

Writers' Group: Rethinking the Essay of Advice

Readers are especially important with the essay of advice because they can help keep writers on track. The essay of advice is essentially a piece by an expert written for an inexpert audience. As such, it must be clear; in other words, readers should be able to follow your advice. Readers in your writers' group might listen to you read the piece, then try to repeat back to you the major parts of the advice strategy. If your readers express difficulty repeating or understanding the advice, you should definitely consider that response important and revise the essay for clarity.

After your readers respond generally, ask for specific recommendations. Write down three questions you would like a peer reader to address—and be sure to make them questions about the substance of the essay. (It's not time to worry about spelling or mechanics yet.) Then ask your reader to respond in writing to your questions. Finally, evaluate the responses from your readers: Do you think readers have read carefully? Do you think readers have been critical enough—or too critical? Do you *believe* readers' comments?

When you are satisfied with the substance of your essay, edit and polish it carefully. If you like, use the guidelines for polishing on page 32. Remember that an essay of advice

- presents logically ordered advice;
- establishes the credibility and authority of the writer; and
- explains terms or concepts that may be unfamiliar to the reader.

Reflecting on and Presenting the Essay of Advice

When you present an essay of advice—in your portfolio and/or to the public—consider how you format the paper. If you have steps for the reader to follow, would subheadings, numbered or unnumbered, help the reader follow the advice? Would an illustration or a diagram help? Sometimes visuals or graphic devices help readers follow instructions.

 # PORTMANTEAU OF WRITING FROM EXPERIENCE AND OBSERVATION

In this Portmanteau you'll find some excerpts from writers' notebooks to give you an idea of the kinds of work that other writers do in their notebooks or journals. You will also find more examples of memoirs and advisory writing, by both student writers and professional writers. Maybe these pieces will inspire you or give you ideas about how you can frame your essays. Perhaps you will want to discuss or analyze these essays with your writers' group, your class, or your instructor.

Excerpts from Writers' Notebooks

In the following passages from their notebooks, writers reflect on various stages of the process of preparing an advisory essay.

Reflections on Writing an Essay of Advice

I had a hard time coming up with a topic for my advisory essay. In fact, I changed my topic three times. I would find a topic and then find it very hard to articulate exactly what I was trying to give advice about. Then the night before it was due, my brother (I am lucky to live at home) asked me how I put on my swimming cap without ripping all of my hair out. As I was telling him how, my mom interrupted and said that I was describing it very well and that I should write my essay on it (she knew I was having trouble). As I got rolling on my topic, I found it much easier to write. I think that since I had

just given the advice and it was fresh in my mind that it made it easier to write. I had a lot of fun writing this essay once I found a topic.

—Julie Hunt

I have wanted to write an article like this for a long time. I have been backpacking since I was 11, and it is one of the few things I am good at. Over the years I have built up a good deal of experience about how to go simply and cheaply and it is nice to be able to share this knowledge.

—M. Adam Jacob

I am thinking of giving advice on tutoring. This topic is going to be directed to those who have a certain intelligence on a certain topic. They must *want* to help others, but not necessarily know how. They may have tried but not succeeded. Tutoring takes a certain type of person who has *a lot* of patience. People will also be able to decide whether or not they are eligible to tutor after reading this article.

—Karen Schwingendorf

As for advice, I love to give it. It makes me feel as if I am needed. I think I give pretty good advice. My only problem is that sometimes I get too critical with it and that tends to offend others. The other bad thing is that I don't follow my own advice. It's somewhat hypocritical. . . . I'm having some trouble with my advisory piece. I have many ideas but I need something I can get into at length.

—Teddy Coleman, via e-mail

Hi, everyone! I am sitting in the CIW library now and this girl is complaining really loudly to a friend (I looked over; it's none of you!) about her love life, so I decided now was the time to add my 2 cents about giving and receiving advice. Asking for advice is a very personal thing—certain people will ask anyone for it, others are intensely private. A lot of people feel better unloading their problems and aren't necessarily seeking advice, though. A lot of times I'll tell someone what's on my mind not because I want to hear another angle on it, but because by telling a problem it seems less overwhelming, like someone is "sharing" the burden. This may sound egocentric, but if I look deep enough, I know what I really want to do.

Getting back to our topic, I am having a lot of trouble with my paper. I am going to start over. I wrote about hummus just like I told everyone I would, but it ended up being a little commentary on what a great food it is. I feel really uncomfortable telling anyone how life should be lived.

—Rachel R., via e-mail

The next two excerpts capture details from memorable experiences.

Saddle's Heavy
Joe Merrick

Saddle's heavy. Everyone stares, whispers. Stewardess smiles as I get on, smiles but looks strangely at my saddle; slides it in a baggage compartment. Careful while she's bent over to keep her dress just right. I bet she thinks everyone's watching her all the time. Chairs are too soft. No one looks anyone else in the eye; I guess they've all got something they want to hide. You look at them and they look down—it's fun. The guy's beside you, but he doesn't touch you or look at you; people are nutty. I bet if I hollered boo! he'd land in the aisle. Need to go to the john. Blue stuff in the water, real noisy. Everything's written twice, maybe three times, English, Spanish, French. Assembly-line sweet roll with coffee, tea, or me. They smile all the time, bugs in their teeth. They aren't so happy though. One time a guy got sucked out of one of these windows. Fasten seat belts, we are beginning our descent, ping.

Dove Hunting
Mike Luckett

Three or four boys pull up to the river in a pickup, then pull their shotguns out of the back and look at the sky to check the weather. When they reach their favorite hunting spot, a couple of them load their guns and you can hear receivers slamming, the wind blowing, voices murmuring, and boots stomping weeds down for a place to hide. A few stray birds fly by and the voices of hunters yelling out their position to others can be heard. One boy takes a chew, then yells to another, "It's 6:30, prime time, and they're leaving the feed patch." Then after that the guns roar like they were defending their owners.

CONSIDER . . .

1. What does the Calvin and Hobbes cartoon (page 62) imply about the nature of being a writer? What qualities might Bill Watterson think that writers possess?
2. What kinds of struggles were the students having with their essays of advice? In your experience, are these typical writing problems?
3. The short sketches about the cowboy on the airplane and about dove hunting suggest another kind of writing that can appear in a notebook. How might each of these pieces lead to longer pieces of writing? What kind of essays might each sketch lead to?

Several Memoirs

In this memoir Ting Hung, a student, describes her memories of her first days in America.

Stranger in a Strange Land

Ting Hung

America, the renowned "melting pot," became my new home in 1974. America meant a new beginning for me, whether I wanted one or not, and at first I didn't. Joining my parents in the states forced me to leave behind everything in Thailand that was familiar. To the seven-year-old I was at the time, the prospect of moving to a new country with a dramatically different culture was more alarming than exciting.

I noticed the difference between the others and me as soon as I stepped off the plane at O'Hare airport. The others, virtually everyone around me, were not Asian. I had never seen a black or white person before then. But I soon realized that black people and white people were not different, I was. *I* was the minority! When I saw my parents for the first time in four years, however, my preoccupation with racial differences was soon forgotten. They had left me behind and had gone to the U.S. to study for their medical licenses when I was a baby. Now they were virtually strangers too.

My parents took me home to a two-story house in the Indiana suburbs not far from Chicago. As I look back now, *culture shock* is the only expression I know to describe how I felt during those first few days. From the looks of things in Indiana, it seemed that the industrial revolution had not yet reached Thailand. The television, the flush toilets, the stereo, the telephone, and many other things were so unfamiliar to me that moving to the U.S. was like moving to the twilight zone. I was scared to touch anything for fear of the consequences. If I touched the toilet, the water might come out, I feared. The ringing telephone was at first terrifying. But the surprises weren't over yet: some of the surprises were good, and the best surprise came last. I finally got to sleep alone on my own bed. I remember thinking that things were looking better and better!

Gradually I adapted to living in the U.S. I would say that my total acclimation took about two years, but by the time I had been in this country two months, I was no longer uncomfortable. Modern conveniences had become a regular part of life, and my parents and I became a family again. Normality apparently returned to my life. Then school started and insecurity once more became very real. The first day of school was a disaster. There were racial differences and a language barrier to contend with on that first day. And there was more—I was forced to wear shoes, forced to eat American food, and worst of all, I was stared at constantly as if I were the main attraction in some sideshow. The other students had apparently never seen an Asian before. I even got put back two years so that I could be with other students of the same age. The result of all this turmoil was that I never felt comfortable at school. For me, academic life was miserable.

My social life was not much better. Some kids tried to be friends, but their friendly overtures never went beyond a smile of acknowledgement. Now I realize that it could not have been otherwise. Friends need to communicate, and because of the language differences in those early months, we could not. Unfortunately, not everyone was even kind. I never knew what the unkind ones said exactly, but I knew what they meant when they glanced at me and whispered. *Boat people* became a regular word in my vocabulary—and I have never grown used to it. I felt very different.

Those early days of culture shock are long over now, but I can still remember the terrible insecurity and uncertainty I felt. Those were probably the worst days in my life. The obstacles to adjusting seemed insurmountable at the time. After overcoming one, I was always faced with another. It was like a never-ending cycle, but I survived it all. I eventually learned to take for granted the modern conveniences that seemed so revolutionary at the beginning. I even learned to speak and to write English and began to make friends with willing people. The others, I learned to ignore. I do not feel like an outsider any more, but I still have that pervasive sense of being a stranger.

CONSIDER . . .

1. The events in this essay cover several years. Explain how Ting Hung keeps the order of events clear.
2. What is the significance of the events she describes? What is the dominant impression that you are left with?
3. What advice would you give Hung for revising this draft? What more would you like to know? Where might she tell readers more and create more interest?

In this memoir Margaret Shoyinka explores a memory that leads her to insights about her identity. As you read, notice how she links the memory to the insights.

Best of Both Worlds
Margaret Shoyinka

When I was six years old, my family and I vacationed in Jamaica. I remember the trip only vaguely, since my childhood consisted of so many journeys to distant countries. But on one particular cloudless afternoon on this beautiful island, I distinctly recall being at play on the beach. I was with two other children, slightly older than myself, attempting to create the largest sand castle ever constructed. During our endeavor my mother came to call me for lunch. Noticing our determination, she allowed me another thirty minutes of play; then I would have to tear myself away from my undertaking and join my family for a meal. I agreed to this compromise and she left me with my newly found friends. As my mother walked away, one of the little girls made a comment that utterly perplexed me. She gestured to my mother and asserted, "*Oh,* so you are adopted." At that time I am not even sure that I understood the full meaning of the word. But at six years old I did recognize that there was a visible distinction between my mother and me. She was white and I was black.

Although I was born in the United States, I spent the first five years of my life in Nigeria. Since the time my family and I moved to New York City, I have made annual trips back to the country that I consider home. My father, Layiwola Shoyinka, is a Yoruba chief educated in the United States. My mother, Mary Winifred Smith, is the first generation of her family born in the United States. Both her parents migrated here from Ireland. My parents met in New York City while my father was employed in a civil engineering firm in Manhattan. Three years later they married and moved to Lagos, Nigeria.

It is not uncommon in Nigeria for a man educated in the West to bring home an American wife. In fact I can recall three or four other families living within close vicinity of my Nigerian home that were biracial. Yes, there I was not peculiar. There, people understood why my mother had blue eyes and I didn't. There, little girls would never inquire if I was adopted.

But once I step out of that great continent, Africa, society feels the necessity to categorize me into a certain race. It is now a strange, odd, bizarre situation seeing a little kinky-haired seven-year-old girl sitting on her white mother's lap on the six train going uptown. A simple walk to the grocery store, my mother's pushing my younger brother in his carriage and my holding on to my mom's arm, was punctuated by double takes by passersby.

As I get older and grow better able to communicate my "uncommon" situation, I am still faced with a whole other set of questions. "Well, then what do you consider yourself?" "But, you're black, right?" Most of the time, I choose to avoid getting asked these questions, and it's just assumed that I am an African American. But when I allow this to happen, doesn't it seem like I'm denying my Irish ethnicity and, more importantly, the woman who raised me, my mother? Aren't I allowing myself to be labeled something that I am not?

A month ago I filled out a form for jury duty. One question that was asked of me was my race. This particular form did not have an "other" category. Furthermore, it was stated that if a question was left unanswered, I could be required to appear in some office somewhere and be fined. This policy of the United States judicial system is compelling me to choose "black" as my race. This form, which I left uncompleted, mirrors society's need to classify me. In this "land of the free," I do not have the choice to define myself.

This story may seem to emphasize negatively the hardships that children of biracial couples face. I don't mean to feed into the separatist argument that is often voiced on talk shows. Instead, I call into question the forces in this society that perpetuate divisions between races. For instance, a 1988 study conducted by the Council for Biracial Children demonstrated that these children are the first to be victims of racism in classroom settings. Some scholars argue that racism is directed earlier toward biracial children because the culprits feel that they must place their victims in a role of inferiority as being "borderline black." Racists take these actions so that biracial children will recognize their inequality in society from an early age. This sort of practice needs to be illuminated in order for schools to prevent it from occurring.

My being brings together two races that historically maintain deep cleavages. What a perfect plan to begin breaking down walls that have been constructed for purposes of creating an underclass. I view neither people of the African diaspora nor people of European descent as different from myself. I can relate to both races and refuse to accept stereotypes that breed division. I can recollect my mother always explaining to my brother and me as children that we were the best of both worlds. But what comfort does this bring me, when in this country I am prohibited from defining myself?

CONSIDER . . .

1. What dominant impression does Shoyinka create in this memoir?
2. What is the base memory from which the piece springs?
3. What suggestions do you have for enriching this essay?

This essay by the professional writer Joseph Monninger appeared in *Sports Illustrated*. As you read, consider what you think is the significance of the memory being described.

When Youth Has Been Stolen

JOSEPH MONNINGER

Somebody stole my high school football jacket last summer. I was fishing in the Great Smoky Mountains and I left it in the tent while I waded downriver after trout. When I returned after a day on the water, the jacket was gone. Also gone were my sleeping bag, two six-packs of beer, a Walkman and a supermarket bag filled with Ritz crackers and Skippy peanut butter.

I suppose I was stupid to leave the stuff in my tent, but there's a limit to the precautions you can take in life. Camping in the woods without anyone else around—or so you think—seems the right time to let down your defenses and go fishing a quarter of a mile away without worrying about burglars. Besides, you can't lock a tent. Short of loading everything into the trunk of my car, which was parked in a turnoff a good distance from my campsite, I didn't have any alternative.

That night, naturally, I slept with visions of the movie *Deliverance* dancing in my head. I found a stout, knotted piece of oak and kept it close to my side through the darkness.

I left the next morning, cutting my fishing trip short by three days. I regretted missing time on the river and was angry that I would have to spring for a new sleeping bag and radio. But the loss of the football jacket burned me most.

What got me was the thought of some guy walking around in my jacket, without any idea of what it signified to me. I pictured him wearing it to the local 7-Eleven or bopping in to a pizza parlor, thinking that the jacket was a tremendous joke. As teenagers my friends and I had done the same thing, borrowing clothes from our fathers or buying old bowling shirts bearing logos—ECHO TAVERN PIN-MEN, BOYLE MIDWAY BULLETS—from thrift shops. We never considered that some guy named Benny or Frank had actually earned the shirt by maintaining a high pin average for a season. I knew what the punk wearing my jacket would say to his buddies: "Hey, I'm number 14 for the Blue Devils! Look at the name . . . Joe! Quarterback . . . State champs . . . Whoa, big *deal-l-l-l!*"

I probably deserved the ridicule. Like a fallen Hell's Angel, I had lost my colors through my own fault. Not just anyone could wear a football jacket at Westfield (NJ) High School. You had to earn it by playing in a minimum of 19 of the 36 quarters that made up our nine-game regular season. Being in one play gave you credit for a quarter; it didn't matter if you held the ball for extra points or were an all-state fullback. Theoretically it was possible to "letter" by mixing it up in 19 plays, which is more or less what my classmate Lee Batzel—I've changed his name in case I run into him at our class reunion—did in our sophomore year.

For that entire season, I watched the varsity play without bothering to keep track of the score. What I monitored, although I'm still ashamed to admit it, was the playing opportunities afforded Batzel. He was on the punt and kickoff teams, primarily because of his speed, and thereby got credit toward a letter no matter what the team happened to do. Fourth-and-15? In came Batzel. Touchdown for our side? Batzel trots onto the field. One for their side? Here come the return team and Batzel again.

On the opening kickoff of our next to last game that year, against Hillside, Batzel lettered. The s.o.b. knew it, too, because as he jogged off the field, I saw him slap five with a senior, then point to his chest and wave at his father sitting up in the grandstand.

There were profound reasons for wanting a varsity football letter jacket. It was the Cadillac of jackets, a distinct trade-up from the windbreakers jayvee players were entitled to wear. The jacket was lined with silver quilting, and it fit over a crew-neck sweater as if it had been tailored on Savile Row. The jacket tapered in close at the waist and puffed out at the shoulders, making its wearer look like an All-America linebacker. And, God love it, the jacket had a collar meant to be worn—no matter what the weather—turned up in the back. I'm not sure what the manufacturers put in the collar, but once turned up, it never came down. Bela Lugosi's Dracula cowl looked limp in comparison.

I earned my jacket the following year, when I was a junior. The very Saturday that I played my 19th quarter I quickly showered after the game, rushed to the sporting goods store before it closed and ordered it. I was the first-string quarterback for the Blue Devils by then, and I took at least half an hour to decide whether I wanted JOE or JOSEPH embroidered in script over my left breast. Joe was the name I went by, but Joseph sounded faintly mythic. I decided, finally, on Joe.

The jacket was delivered to my house a couple of weeks later. I tore through the plastic wrapping and picked the jacket up without really looking at it. I put it on, and closing my eyes, walked to the large mirror in the living room.

When I opened my eyes, I saw that I had been transformed. Although I was starting that year, I had never, in my heart, really considered myself the Varsity Quarterback. But the jacket changed things: QB was on one sleeve, 14 on the other; BLUE DEVILS was spelled out in nubby lettering, and a stylized devil, pitchfork and all, was sewn on the back. The jacket gave me a thin waist and wide shoulders. It also gave me an identity.

Due to an adolescent quirk, however, I didn't wear it very much until I turned 30. When my parents saw the jacket, they assumed they were spared buying a coat for me for two or three years, but I was reluctant to appear to be a show-off. There are strange currents in the deep waters of high school life, and one jumps in at his peril. I chose not to make the leap this time, so I continued to wear a shabby brown mackinaw my mother detested.

"Why someone would want to catch cold when he has a perfectly fine jacket hanging in the closet, I'll never understand," she said almost every night. I didn't understand my decision either, but I knew it was the right one for me.

So that was the jacket that was stolen. The logical thing to do, of course, was to replace it. But the thought of going to a sporting goods store at the age of 33 to pick through football jacket catalogs was daunting. Another option was to call my high school coach and find out where the kids ordered their jackets these days. When I thought about explaining my problem to a smirking salesclerk, or to Coach, the idea soured. I was also put off by the thought of the jacket's appearing brand new. Wasn't this somewhat juvenile? Where was I going to wear it? To the teen canteen?

For a while, I studied the football jackets today's kids are wearing. I also browsed through sporting goods stores around New York City, pretending to look at skis or socks but invariably ending up at the jacket rack. I noticed that the quality of jackets had declined. Instead of silver quilting, these jackets were lined with some inexpensive, tacky material. They also whistled when you put them on because they had lost weight and bulk. The manufacturers still put the white piping at the waistband and along the pockets of most of the jackets, but the thickness, the heft of the jacket was gone. If hit by a snowball, the old jacket made a sound like someone beating a rug hung over a clothesline. I'm sure the new jackets just sound rubbery and cheap when they are plunked.

The collar was also missing, and the collar was 90% of my old high school jacket. You turned it up, preferably just high enough to let a little tail of hair hang over the back; that made the wearer look somewhat hoody, while still informing the world that he was a football player. It wasn't enough to say: JOE . . . 14 . . . BLUE DEVILS. The turned-up collar also said that Joe was one badass; he would as soon rip the transmission out of your car with his bare hands as look at you.

There was also the lettering. What, if anything, could a 33-year-old man have inscribed on the sleeves and back of his jacket? My big worry was having the wrong thing put on my jacket and then finding myself in a fight with a bunch of 18-year-olds the next time I went to a Pizza Hut. Nor did I want to wear the emblem of any pro team. I had seen too many fights in grandstands to ignore the risk of wearing the wrong allegiance on my sleeves. I also faced the bleak realization that I wasn't a guy who could have L.A. LAW arcing across his back and carry the pose off with much conviction.

After two or three months of procrastination, I finally settled on a plain black jacket with white leather sleeves. The body of my new jacket is made of flannel with a texture not unlike the felt backing on old tabletop radios. Velcro sticks to it without much problem.

The jacket snaps up the front and rides high on my hips. It doesn't have a collar, but I've found that my old jacket habits have returned: I like to stand leaning against things, my hands in my chest pockets, the jacket tight around me. Because of the bomber-jacket cut, my shoulders look pretty big and my gut—which over the years has changed from washboard to junior Maytag—has a comfortable pouch all its own. I love the smell of the jacket because it is exactly the same as that of my old high school jacket. It smells of model train sets and overheated transformers.

I can't kid myself, though. I don't look like a player any longer. This new jacket is something old jocks wear. It's what dads wear as they step up to the card tables at Little League sign-ups. It's a Saturday touch football jacket. Sometimes I wonder if I should wear a jacket at all. I'm pretty sure the guy who coached the comic book characters *Archie* and *Moose* wore a jacket just like the one I bought. And that some rip-off artist is wearing the one I earned.

CONSIDER . . .

1. Why is the high school letter jacket important to Monninger? What does the loss of the jacket mean to him?
2. What strategies does Monninger use to help you "see" the events of the narrative?
3. Within this narrative is a flashback to an earlier time. Find where the flashback begins and ends, and note how Monninger separates this section from the main narrative.
4. What are for you the most vivid details or images in this essay? Without looking back, think of what you remember most from the essay.

In "Flower Childhood" (from the *New York Times Magazine*), Lisa Michaels remembers her childhood during the 1960s and considers how her parents' politics shaped her life and experience.

Flower Childhood

LISA MICHAELS

In 1969, my father was arrested for his part in organizing an antiwar protest in Boston and was sentenced to a two-year prison term. (He and my mother had split up a few years earlier, but they had remained close, sharing the child-rearing duties and trying to forge a new kind of divorce, one that was in keeping with their progressive politics.) It would take me many years before I would understand the times in which this event took place. I'm still trying, and failing, to understand. But before I knew anything of politics, or war, or social movements, I knew my father's enveloping presence. He was more than six feet tall, with huge hands and a laugh that rippled through his chest when he carried me. He crooned me to sleep, twirled me in his arms, and then—without warning—he was gone.

My father began serving his time not long after his 28th birthday. I was 3 years old. Shortly after he went to prison, my mother took me to see him. He had written her a letter asking for books and a new pair of tennis shoes; he was playing a lot of pickup basketball in the yard to keep his head clear. On the ride out to the prison, I clutched a box of black Converse high-tops in my lap, my head bubbling with important things to tell him.

I remember very little of our lives then, but that visit has the etched clarity and foggy blanks of a fever dream. We pulled into the broad prison parking lot and stepped out to face the gray facade, punctured by a grid of tiny windows. Mother lifted her hand against the glare, then pointed to a figure in one of the barred openings. Was it my father? She hoisted me onto the roof of the car, and I held the shoe box over my head and shook it up and down. I thought I saw the man wave back.

In the waiting room, the guard called our names in flat tones, never looking us in the eye. He led us through a series of thick hydraulic doors and down long corridors to the visiting room. Once we were inside, I saw something soften in his face. "Sit right here, missy," he said. Mother lifted me into a plastic chair and my feet jutted straight out. I stared at the toes of my tennis shoes, printed with directives in block letters: left, right.

I sat still until a door on the far wall opened and a flood of men filed in. Out of the mass of bulky shapes, my father stepped forward, the details of his face reassuring in their particulars. He grinned and reached for me across the tabletop scribbled with names and dates, and despite the no-touching rule, the guard said nothing. When he took my hand, every manic bit of news I had rehearsed in the car flew out of me. I was stunned by the dry warmth of his skin, his white teeth, the way he cleared his throat in two beats before speaking.

Our conversation was simple. He read to me from a book of stories that my mother had brought along, his voice roving from bass to falsetto as he acted out the dialogue. I told him what I had eaten for lunch, and in the silence that followed I remembered the tennis shoes, flushed with relief to have something to give him. "Look what we got you," I said, and then tore the box open myself. I beamed and bunched my skirt between my knees while he admired them. "All Stars!" he said. "I'm gonna tear up the court."

At the end of the hour, the guard rested one hand on his gun, tipped back on his heels, and called the time. Panic closed my throat. I looked to my father for a sign—he would tell the man we weren't ready—but his eyes were wet and the corners of his mouth twitched down. I turned to the stranger by the wall and flashed a saccharine smile. "Daddy," I asked, leaning my cheek on the table and looking at the guard, "is that the nice man you told me about?"

The guard squinched his face at me, in what passed for kindness in that place, then turned away slowly and gave us a few extra minutes. Once they were granted, we could think of nothing more to say. It was a relief when the guard said, "Time's up."

In the clamor of chair legs and murmured goodbyes, we could speak again. "Hey, what do you want for Christmas?" my father asked. I stopped in the doorway and stared at his dark bulk. I wanted *him*. But his voice was filled with a sudden expansiveness, and I knew I should ask for something he could give.

"Something purple," I told him. It was my favorite color then.

I still have a letter he wrote me that night from his cell: "It may take a long time, but I'll try to get you a purple thing. Here's a pretend one for now." At the bottom of the page is a necklace with a carefully drawn purple star.

This was the first of many letters he wrote me, each with a drawing in colored pencil. "Darling Lisa—Hello, Hello, Hello. I am very happy tonight. I got a guitar yesterday and am learning to play it. I am on a diet so I won't be fat at all—not even a little bit." Then half the page taken up by an abstract drawing: a grid filled with tangled clots of scribbling, a black anvil shape, a downward arrow, the symbol for infinity. "I call this picture, Being in Jail: JAIL. I love you darling, Your Father."

At first his absence was a plangent note, always sounding in the background, but it became muffled as the months passed. In time, I had trouble recalling his face.

My mother made several visits to prison, but gradually she began to cut ties. My father had become increasingly focused on his political work in the months leading up to the demonstration, and now his arrest meant she had no help in caring for me, no one to consult with, no air.

She was furious at him, and fury made her feel free. We would move to Mexico and buy a piece of land. She would become a potter, maybe look for work teaching English. I would wear embroidered dresses and turn brown in the tropical sun.

In the flush of her newfound independence, Mother went to a Postal Service auction and bought herself a used mail truck. She parked it outside our three-story walk-up and gave me a tour. With a tuneup, she said, it would get us south of the border. The cab had one high leather seat and a long lever that worked the emergency brake. A sliding door led back into a cold metal vault, bare but for a few mail shelves. "This is going to be our cozy rolling home," Mother said, her voice echoing off the walls.

For the next few months, my mother worked as a waitress and took steps to make the mail truck roadworthy. The first rains of autumn had revealed a couple of leaks in the side of the van, so she spent a weekend driving around Cambridge in search of sheet metal for patching.

On a narrow side street, she spotted a promising sign: Earth Guild. We Have Everything.

She stopped in and asked the cashier if they had any sheet metal. The store was a kind of counterculture supermarket, stocked with incense, bolts of cotton, paraffin, books on homesteading, yarn and looms. But it seemed that everything didn't include sheet metal.

"What do you want it for?" the woman asked. It was a slow day in the store. Had there been a line of customers, impatient to buy beeswax and clay, our lives might have taken a different turn.

"I need to patch a hole in the side of my mail truck," my mother said.

"Well," the woman offered, "we don't have sheet metal, but we have Jim, and he has a mail truck, too." She yelled toward the back room, and out loped my future stepfather, a lanky man in square-toed Frye boots, smiling an easy smile.

Jim went out to the curb and looked over the rust spots. He and Mother talked about their vans, how much they'd paid at auction, where they were headed. Jim also had his eye on Mexico. And at the very moment my mother dropped by, he had been building a kiln in the back of the store for the Earth Guild's pottery studio. It seems she had stumbled on the perfect partner, a man who could help her turn her schemes into brick and wood. By the time they finished talking, the sun was low in the sky and they had a date to change their oil together.

Jim wore hand-painted ties, listened to the Stones and collected Op Art. When he met my mother, he was living in a commune in Harvard Square called the Grateful Union.

Mother and Jim soon made plans to head across the country under the same roof. We would take his truck, since it was considerably cozier than my mother's. A platform bed stretched across the width of the van, and a hinged half-moon table folded down from one side. We ate sitting cross-legged on the mattress. The walls were lined with bookcases, fitted with bungee cords to hold the books in place. On a shelf just behind the cab was our kitchen: a two-burner propane cooking stove, a tiny cutting board and a 10-gallon water jug. Jim covered the floor with Persian rugs.

Before we set out, Jim bought a small wood stove and bolted it to the floor near the back. The smokestack jutted out the side of the truck, the hole weather-sealed with the fringe from a tin pie plate. One of Jim's friends from the Grateful Union wired a stereo system into the van, and Mother sewed heavy denim curtains that attached to the windshield and side windows with Velcro, so we could have privacy at night. The engine on the snub-nosed truck bulged into the cab and was housed by a metal shell that served as a shelf for bags of mail. Jim cut a piece of thick foam just the shape of the engine cover, which would be my bed.

In the spring of 1970, we packed up our essential belongings and set out on a year-long journey across the country, down the Eastern Seaboard and then across the low belly of the continent to California. The thrill of traveling sustained me for a while, but it was a difficult age to be rootless. I played with other kids for a day or two at a campground or a city park, and then we drove on.

After a day on the road, Mother tucked me in on my foam pad, warmed from below by the engine's heat. In the foot well below me was a small chamber pot we used during the night, and so I drifted off to the smell of urine and the tick of the cooling engine. Now and then, when we were parked on some dark residential street, I would wake to the knock of a policeman, asking us to move along.

And move along we did, until our funds started to run thin, and Mother and Jim began to search for a piece of land—"our pie in the sky," as Jim called it. Mother was browsing through a copy of Mother Earth News when she saw a classified ad listing land for sale. It was the summer of 1971. She located the town, which had a population of 2,000 and was marked with the tiniest speck the map allowed, and we drove up through San Francisco headed for that dot.

We ended up buying a clapboard house in the heart of this costal valley town, a half-acre plot that came with a stucco duplex—two apartments end to end. Later, Mother would say that you had to call the people who lived in those buildings home-less. Only two of the four toilets worked. The ceiling plaster bloomed with stains. There were a handful of ramshackle sheds on the property and a line of rusted cars in the driveway. The yard was nothing but thistle and dry grass. My mother and Jim dickered with the landlord a little and agreed to buy the place for $18,000.

Our new address was 10000 Main Street. Apparently the town's founders had been anticipating an explosive growth period that never arrived. Just past our house, the only sidewalk in town ceased abruptly, the last slab jutting out toward the cow pastures and orchards down Powerhouse Road. We would hold down the end of the main drag, on about an acre of good river valley soil gone hard from neglect.

The apartments were full when we took title to the place, so we lived in the mail truck for a while. The front half of the clapboard house was rented by a man named Floyd Root, an old woodcutter who sat around in his undershirt drinking gin. He took two or three newspapers a day, so Jim considered him an intellectual.

When he heard we were living in the truck, Floyd called my mother to his porch. "I'm going to die soon," he said, "and then there will be a place for you folks."

Mother brushed this off, but a week later, Floyd invited his logging buddies over and made a great show of giving away his chainsaws. The next morning, Jim saw Floyd's newspapers untouched on the porch and went in to find the man lying cold in his bed, three empty gin bottles lined up on the floor.

It took us a week of scrubbing to make that place fit to live in. There was stand-ing water in the sink that the neighbor told us hadn't been drained for six months. Mother made batik curtains for the windows and lined the musty drawers with butcher paper. In the bedroom, the wallpaper hung in thick tatters, a yellowed flow-ery print laced with ribbons. We pulled that down and found a layer of cheesecloth tacked beneath it, and when that was stripped away, solid foot-wide redwood planks, rough-planed from trees that must have been 500 years old.

I was given Floyd's bedroom. Mother and Jim slept in the living room on a sofa bed. I was not yet 5, and it was summer, so I was sent to bed before the sun went down, which felt like exile from the world of light. I would press my face against my bedroom window and watch the older neighborhood kids playing kickball in the street or straddling their bikes on the corner. One evening not long after we had moved into the house, my mother and Jim came to tuck me in, and the two of them lingered for a moment. Mother sat on the edge of my bed and sang to me. Jim stood in the middle of the room with his hands in his pockets, looking out the western window at the torn-up yard, the bristle of cattails in the ditch and the corrugated roof of Mel's welding garage across the street, where he went every afternoon to buy glass bottles of Coke from the vending machine.

The novelty of the two of them tucking me in together in my very own bedroom set me humming with pleasure, and I wanted to say something in honor of this, but I didn't dare break their reverie. Even as I lay there, mute with happiness, I was conscious of the fragility of the scene: two parents, one child, pausing for a few moments together under one roof at the day's end.

It would be years before I would understand that my father would have loved to have had his own such moments with me, to have been a source of stability and comfort. But after he was released from prison, my mother kept him at bay. I saw him only intermittently during the next four years. He would have to fight his way back into my life.

Late in the summer of 1971, when my father got out of prison, friends of his were living on a commune in Oregon; they had invited him to come west and sort himself out. As soon as he was free, he came to California to pick me up.

It must have been a shock to see him again, for I have no memory of our first hours together. I know we took a bus up to Eugene, and a friend from the commune picked us up and drove us out to the property—acres of dry grass and scrub oak. There, my memories become clearer. The commune members were roughing it—no running water, no electricity, just a few dilapidated houses at the end of a long dirt road.

My father's attempt to unwind in the woods was a disaster. The sudden move from a cell to the wilderness seemed to leave him nervous and unsettled. The first day he tried to play the hip nudist and got a terrible sunburn. Then he drank some "fresh" spring water and spent three days heaving in the outhouse. I stayed indoors with him while he recovered, making him tell me stories. "Me and nature never got along," he said.

But as the days drifted on, we settled into the place. My father taught me to use a BB gun in the field beside the commune's main house. Arms around me from behind, he cheered when we shot the faded beer cans off the stump. "Sock it to me," he would say, holding out his enormous, olive-colored palm. We ate homemade bread and black beans and swam naked in the creek flowing through the property.

One day we wandered into one of the many rough-framed buildings on the property to take shelter from the midday heat. The walls were lined with bookshelves made of cinder blocks and knotty pine boards. A sink and countertop unit salvaged from a remodeled kitchen shored up one wall. There was no running water; spider webs stretched from the tap to the drain. A propane stove sat on the drain board, and beneath it, on the floor, were jugs of cooking fuel and water.

My father moved to the open door, raised his arms up to the door frame and stretched like a cat. He was there in body—a body honed by hours in the weight room, on the courts playing ball with the other prisoners—but in another way he was fitfully absent. He circled the room slowly, traced a pattern in the countertop's dust, not pent up, but aimless, as if he had lost something and didn't know where to search. I squatted near the sink, playing with a set of plastic measuring cups, and watched him closely. He moved through the doorway—for a moment framed by light, a dark cutout of a man—then passed out of view.

I was thirsty and decided to make a tea party. I went outside to see if my father wanted to play, and found him sprawled under a large oak tree near the door. He was staring up at the leaves, his hand spread open in the air above him, and he didn't answer at first.

"Do you want some tea?"

He raised his head and his eyes slowly focused, placing me. "No thanks, honey."

I went back into the shack and filled two of the cups from a jug on the floor. I pretended to have a partner for my tea and chatted with him awhile before drinking from my cup, thumb and forefinger on the short handle, my pinkie raised high.

From the first sip I could tell something was wrong. The water burned my tongue, and when I opened my mouth to scream all the air in the room was gone. I spat out what I could and yelled, feeling a white heat unfurl down my throat. My father dashed in, smelled my breath and the spilled gas and scooped me up from the floor. He ran with me toward the spring and over his shoulder I watched the shack jiggling smaller and smaller in the field. It seemed lonely, canted off to one side on its foundation like a child's drawing of a house. The dry summer hay swayed like the sea, and I heard his breathing, ragged as surf.

When we reached the spring, a bearded man was there filling a green wine bottle. Water spilled down a rock face into a pool bounded by ferns and moss. My father gasped out the story and together they hovered over me, making me drink from the bottle again and again. "That's good," they said. "You're doing really good." My father stroked my hair. And though I wanted to stop, I tipped my head back and drank for him.

That night we stayed in the main house. My lips and throat were chapped and burning. I began to have visions. A crowd of ghosts led by a goateed figure marched with torches through the room. I told this to the grownups and they seemed alarmed. Some of the other people staying at the house lighted extra kerosene lanterns to soothe me, but I could still see the figures. The leader looked furious, driven, his whole body straining forward toward some unknown mission.

My father moved with me to a bedroom upstairs and held me in a worn corduroy armchair, talking softly, telling me stories of what we would do together when it was light. The vagueness I felt in him during the day had disappeared. He was dense, focused, his legs pressed long against the side of the chair, his arms around me heavy and still. I sat in his lap, leaning into the rise and fall of his chest. In my delirium, I closed my eyes and saw his body supporting me like a chair, the long, still bones, and under him the real chair, fabric stretched over wood, and all of this 20 feet above the ground, on the upper floor of the house, held up by the beams and foundation, and beyond that the quiet fields, silver under the moon, alive with animals, the punctured cans lying still by the stump. I saw us perched in the center of this, neither safe nor doomed, and in this unbounded space I fell asleep.

CONSIDER . . .

1. What was the effect on you as a reader of Michaels's opening sentence: "In 1969, my father was arrested for his part in organizing an antiwar protest in Boston and was sentenced to a two-year prison term"?
2. In a sentence, write what you believe is the dominant impression of this piece.
3. What is your feeling about the way that Michaels concludes this piece? What would have been the effect of a more obvious, "summing-up" ending?

Some Essays of Advice

In this essay of advice, Sara Ubelhor shares her experience and her expertise with other young people who work in fast-food restaurants.

Surviving the Fast-Food Job
Sara Ubelhor

The first job held by many teenagers is working as a cashier or grill person at a fast-food restaurant. Working at a fast-food restaurant myself for two years, I frequently saw employees quit after a couple of months or even during the first week. After all, fast-food jobs are boring, stressful, and unpleasant unless, like a veteran employee, you learn how to deal with the management, customers, and responsibilities with the proper attitude.

The key to surviving is learning your job well. Concentrate when you are being trained, and if you do not understand the logic in performing a procedure in a certain manner, ask the manager. Some policies must be followed for your own safety, and you will not mind the extra inconvenience if you realize this.

Working as a cashier, you will have to deal face-to-face with customers. No matter how grumpy customers look, always greet them politely with a smile. Your smiling not only pleases your boss, but your smile may just cheer the customer up who is simply having a bad day. If you are friendly, you may have some interesting conversations with total strangers. If, however, you are being treated rudely by a customer, you can use subtle methods to get even—methods that will not get you fired. For example, do not go out of your way to offer the crabby customer cream or sugar for coffee as you ordinarily would.

Or if a customer unpleasantly demands ketchup instead of asking for it politely, give that person only one or two packets so that returning for more will be necessary. These strategies may sound juvenile, but they provide an important psychological function by reducing your feelings of resentment and frustration.

Perhaps the worst fast-food employees are people who get flustered easily. You have to remain calm and work through the daily crises. Ice cream machines break down on the hottest days of summer, and little kids love to spill cokes during lunch rush; you simply must take time to mop up the drink spills and explain to the customers why you cannot serve ice cream, whatever the particular case may be. Because mishaps such as these are unavoidable, you must realize that they are not life-and-death situations and not become unduly stressed.

Above all, remember that you are being paid, so make sure that your first priority at work is doing your job well. But this does not mean that you have to be serious all the time. You should become friends with the other employees; then you can tell jokes to lighten the mood. Or try singing "Stand By Your Grill" or the old favorite "Beverly Hillbillies' Theme Song," to see how many people you can get to join in or give some sort of reaction. You will find that spontaneous people are fun to work with.

Fast-food restaurants hire many teenagers who want to make some spending money, so you will have no difficulty in finding a job. You will enjoy your job and stay with it longer if you can handle routine tasks and maintain a good working relationship with the management and customers. If you do a good job and build up your seniority, most companies will reward you with a raise, making it more worthwhile for you to work in the fast-food industry, at least until you have put yourself through school.

CONSIDER . . .

1. How does Ubelhor arrange the advice? What organizational strategies does she use?
2. Explain how Ubelhor demonstrates her authority and asserts her credibility.
3. Point out an instance where Ubelhor gives an example to illustrate a point.

In this advisory piece, Tara LeMaistre gives readers advice about making special gift albums. Notice how she draws on her expert knowledge.

Untitled

Tara LeMaistre

The sweetness of spring and the spice of summer allow me to savor their delicacies for only a second. May marches into June which jumps into July which jets to the arrival of August. August is one of the most beautiful months of the year, yet I can never fully enjoy it because September lurks near. September means books and rent; therefore August means job.

This summer I decided not to torture myself by working as a telemarketer. I had worked as a telemarketer for two previous summers, and I had discovered that telemarketing does some serious damage to your brain cells. I was determined to find a job that allowed for creativity and the use of your imagination, not the recital of a script to people who the last thing they want is for you to try and sell them something over the phone that they don't and won't ever need.

My mother suggested that I work with my aunt, who runs a business out of her apartment making everything from floral arrangements to decorative baskets. My mother knew that I had a talent as well as a love for making albums, so she proposed the idea of making albums, which my aunt could sell for me out of her apartment as well as at the flea market. I became thrilled at the thought of making money for something that I would gladly do for free. Because the flea market has many people who sell beautiful albums, I knew that my success would depend not only on the quantity but the quality of my creations.

The first step to making an album is knowing who you are creating the album for. A wedding album would require white or ivory material with matching lace. A baby's album could be blue, or pink, or yellow if the sex isn't known. Albums don't have to be made to honor a special occasion. If you know the demographics of your buyers' market, then you can specialize albums according to what you think can sell. For example, I knew that the shoppers at the flea market my aunt frequented were mainly blacks and Latinos. For the black people I created an album out of kente cloth which I adorned with various African beads. The Latino people loved the "busy" albums, so when I made albums with them in mind I made sure that there was an abundance of lace, beads, and flowers. I call it "The Works."

After you establish whom you are making the album for, the next step is to acquire all the materials required to make the album. You will need an album (any size according to your preference); batting, which is some sort of fiber that provides the cushiness of the album (enough to cover your album); a piece of oaktag, which will be cut to fit the inside of the album; material of any style/color/texture (the material must be about an inch longer than your album, and you must also buy enough to cover the oaktag on the inside of the album); and decorations (dig deep into your imagination and see what you can find).

After you assemble all your materials, apply the batting to the album. The batting is applied by first cutting it the same size as your album, then gluing it on with a glue gun. The thicker the batting the better. Even if an album is empty, it seems inviting if it is thick and plush.

The next step is to cover the album with the material you've selected. This is done by cutting the material about one inch longer than the album and gluing down all of the edges with a glue gun. The inside of the album will expose all of the glued edges, which will next have to be covered with a piece of oaktag sized to fit the insides of the front and back of the album. The pieces of oaktag will have to be covered in your chosen material.

After the body of your album is finished, all that is left to do is the decorating on the cover of the album. For me this is the part where I become entranced. I never know how I am going to decorate an album. I like to surround myself with any objects that can be used for decorating. Flowers, pearls, beads, lace, buttons, ribbon, miniature toys—the possibilities are endless. I try to make each album a unique creation, a work of art.

One of my greatest works of art is an album that I made for my mother for her birthday. I approached this album as if I were writing a biography or a memoir. Yet the wonder of an album is that all the details of her life could be explicitly stated without a word. The pain of her pregnancy or the joy of her college graduation didn't have to be surrounded by prose. Vivid images became the author of a timeless story.

I decorated my mother's album with a dress she wore for her graduation. I cut the dress to provide me with the material I needed to cover the album and then I affixed the buttons from the dress on the album. Out of the lining of the dress I created bows and ribbon to further adorn her album. When my mother saw that all of her pictures had been transported from an old shoe box to an album solely made for her and her memories, she began to cry, noting that now she will never be forgotten.

Making albums for me is a very soothing and healing process. For hours at a time I could be working on my albums, and after I finish feel invigorated and refreshed. The creative process transports me away from the confinements of life. When I am making albums, I have no restrictions: I am free.

The best thing about making albums is knowing that you have created a safe place for memories to be saved. My mother was an avid photographer when I was a child; however, I have some friends that have only two pictures of their entire childhood. I like to think that if they had had one of my albums, they couldn't have stood seeing it empty, so they would have filled the album with pictures to grant it the life it deserves.

CONSIDER . . .

1. Why do you think LeMaistre tells the story about not working as a telemarketer to introduce this essay?
2. This piece has especially strong transitions that connect the different parts or steps; point out several of them.
3. How does LeMaistre convey the importance and the pleasure of making albums?
4. LeMaistre did not give this piece a title. This is your job: What should the title be?

This piece of advice on saying thank you originally appeared in *Esquire* magazine.

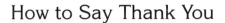

How to Say Thank You

ROY HOFFMAN

Most of us will acknowledge that saying thank you is a gesture of decency—and survival—for anyone wandering a foreign realm. What educated American, no matter how parochial, doesn't know *gracias, danke,* and *merci*? Curiously, though, when the time comes to say thank you to someone in our own land, many of us fall mute. When the kid at the gas station washes our windshield, our office colleague covers a blunder, or our sweetheart serves us a dinner of rump roast and claret, we tend to suffer selective amnesia.

Of course, there are a thousand ways to say thank you. And there are times when the spoken word is not enough.

When someone sends you a gift, a thank-you note acts both as a thank-you and as a kind of receipt. It is also called for when someone has you in his home who usually doesn't; when someone entertains you for a weekend; when someone does you a special favor; or when you know deep in your bones that if you don't send a note you'll be prickled by guilt whenever you see the person you didn't thank. Of course, you can always thank someone by phone, but unless you know the person well or see him or her frequently, a note is more intimate. As with birthday greetings and congratulations, the phone has a way of taking some of the fizz out of thank-yous.

As a literary form, thank-you notes are rather like haiku. How can you cram into only three lines a description of a vegetable dicer, your sentiment about it, and a touch of gratitude that you'll never have to chop onions again? Actually, the note need not be terse, but it should be brief. It should also be personal, mentioning some specific virtue of the gift, like the ideal spacing of teeth in the moustache comb. Above all, the note should be prompt and should never begin, "I'm sorry for not writing sooner," since it's obvious you should have written sooner. My mother always contended that it was never too late to send a thank-you note, but, like all gracious gals of her generation, she never tarried more than a few days anyway. It's my feeling that a thank-you note sent within a week or two of a gift or event is okay, a month pushing it. If I've let two months slip by and still haven't buckled down, I usually let it slide and resign myself to being thought of forever as an ungrateful slob.

Caveat emptor: Card companies still presume that only teenage girls send thank-you notes; they adorn them with baskets of flowers, bounding squirrels, or tinselly rivers. Another style of commercial card—plain and white, with THANK YOU stamped on the front—is fine to send only if you're thanking somebody for bar mitzvah cufflinks. My own preference is for blank notepaper or, for chummier thank-yous, cards or postcards with catchy pictures on the front.

A thank-you gift is classier by far than a thank-you note, but it's also trickier, since gifts cost money and money, of course, can be counted. The thank-you gift is appropriate when someone's done you a huge favor or has shown you extended hospitality. Like any gift, it is best when it has a personal signature—if you're from New Orleans, pralines; from Vermont, maple syrup. You can combine the thank-you gift with the house present, showing up with a bottle of Scotch at your friends' beach house, then sending a note after your visit. But sending a gift after your stay still means more than showing up with it—it means you're still with your friends in spirit.

Thank-you gifts should never be too lavish, though. Since a thank-you is, when you get down to it, a way of paying off a debt, the object is not to put the other person in your debt. If a friend takes you skiing a few times and you reciprocate by sending him a new down jacket, he'll love the jacket but probably be uncomfortable at now being in debt to you. He'll feel forced to take you skiing again and will resent you for it.

When it comes to a business thank-you, think long and hard before sending a gift. I've heard embarrassing tales of movie directors and magazine editors receiving expensive wallets, bunches of roses, and baskets of gourmet food after throwing the smallest amount of work the way of some poor actor or writer. This is gratitude's dirty side—a thank-you as buttering up or bribe. Unless an employer helps you a great deal with your work, avoid sending a thank-you gift and go with the note—one that tells your boss why you've enjoyed working with him (or her). If you do send a gift, don't make it too personal. In my opinion, tickets to a ball game or a play are better than a shirt or a hat. You're not romancing, just thanking.

If you're a boss, giving thank-you gifts to your employees, except on special occasions, might seem like an effort to hush them with trinkets. Thank an employee verbally, with a memo that other employees will see, or, best of all, by giving him an afternoon off. A lunch or dinner is often just the right way to say thank you—and not only in business relationships.

Saying thank you is such a simple act that it's surprising it's not as common as saying good morning or nodding hello. Certainly, it's an act that we need more of—one that will help us all get through the day a little more easily, even a little less selfishly.

CONSIDER . . .

1. How does Hoffman establish his authority in this arena? Do you believe his advice? Why?
2. Describe how this essay is structured or organized.
3. What would you say is the tone of this piece? How does Hoffman create the tone? Point to some words or phrases that typify the tone.

4 Writing What You Observe and Learn

All my senses were very keen; things came to me through my eyes, through all my pores. Everything hit me at once, you know.

—Katherine Anne Porter

A writer needs three things, experience, observation, and imagination, any two of which, at times any one of which, can supply the lack of the others.

—William Faulkner

Every observer brings to his or her own science a unique perspective, and I am no exception.

—Geerat Vermeij, blind evolutionary biologist

This chapter emphasizes writing that draws heavily upon what you observe and learn through observation. Not all your writing comes directly from your past, your experience, your personal fund of accumulated knowledge. You also write from your observations in primarily the present: what you see and hear and reflect on. Of course, the distinction between what you experience and what you observe is artificial—because observation becomes transmuted into experience. The pieces that you may write in this section are, however, somewhat different from the ones in the chapter on writing from experience: They do not depend on your personal experience as the heart of the writing, and they do not focus so entirely on what has happened to you or what you have done. The kinds of writing in this chapter—the learning log, the profile, the study of a place—invite you to look carefully at the world around you and to describe what you observe. Your final, finished portfolio should probably include at least one of these kinds of essays.

PERSONAL WRITING: KEEPING A LEARNING LOG

A learning log is a journal or notebook with a specific purpose: to record observations, insights, and understanding as you progress through a learning project. It is primarily personal writing, undertaken for personal purposes, but it may sometimes be excerpted in more public papers (for course work, for example). A learning log may be assigned by an instructor or undertaken personally in a spirit of reflection and responsibility for one's own learning. The log, typically with dated chronological entries, focuses on documenting experiences, observations, and sensations to provide evidence that a learning task was accomplished. Learning logs, valuable sources of details and facts, are frequently excerpted in reports of internship experiences of all kinds or are themselves required for some courses.

Tips for Keeping a Learning Log

You can ensure the potential usefulness of your learning log by following these tips:

1. **Date each entry and record how much time you spend** on the project. You may have to show that you spent a required number of hours at an internship or in performing a certain task. The specific data you record in your log will help you establish credibility.
2. **Label each entry with a descriptive title.** If you need to find the section in your log where you wrote about observing a patient in an emergency room, you can find it more easily if it is titled.
3. **Write down lots of details,** even if you think they are superfluous. Go overboard on details because you may have to rely on the details later to recreate some activities or accomplishments. Specific details can help you remember long after an event is past.
4. **Pause occasionally to reflect and summarize.** Ask yourself periodically, "What exactly am I learning?" "What is the significance of these events or occurrences?" "How are my views and opinions changing?" "How is this experience affecting me?" Include these reflections and assessments in your log.

Reading a Learning Log

As a classroom project, Marie Sulit spent twenty-plus hours observing in two middle school classrooms. As part of the course requirement, she kept a learning log describing and reflecting upon her experience. Notice how she records details and then how she thinks about what she has seen in an attempt to make sense of it.

Excerpts from a Learning Log
Marie Sulit

From *February 21: Getting Acquainted with Students*

On this visit I worked with Brad and Al, who has since been moved to another special education class because he has fallen so far behind. (Will Brad suffer this fate too?) During third period we worked on vocabulary words. Brad started with a lot of resistance and "I don't knows," but as the period went on, things got smoother. Brad knows more than he lets on and through oral education or what he hears quickly picks up information. He seems very shy and self-conscious about his reading disabilities; when the study hall became occasionally quiet, he would quickly shut up and regress to saying, "I don't know." I did not push, but in fourth period, I worked with both of them on their vocabulary words. Both of them have to be read to when they are tested for their basic skills. They also tend to lose focus rather easily, so constant discipline and many "Pay attentions" are needed. Yet overall, things went pretty well.

From *March 14: Aesthetics of a Science Classroom*

I hadn't noticed before how overcrowded this class is. A skeleton stands in the front of the class, and a makeshift greenhouse illuminates the back left side of the classroom. All the way in the back of the room lie overturned and broken desks, while about 15 microscopes find their niches on top of an already cluttered lab table. There are 28 students sitting sideways or with their backs toward the teacher because all the seats in standard front-to-back line form have been taken up by other students. The students will be taking a test today.

Can anyone take a test *comfortably,* sitting at a table that is already littered with various books? These students need space to take a test.

From *March 28: A Disciplinary Atmosphere*

In this school, even the physical space is a vehicle for instruction. The arrows on the main set of stairs, just beyond the main office, indicate the flow of traffic—more ways to give and instill some discipline to grades and ages that are not so regimented. The bathrooms and hallways are relatively clean, no graffiti, which sometimes marred my junior high school, Kakiat. But then I notice, ironically, a red-smeared "Fuck you" displayed prominently on a hallway door, probably the custodian's closet. Some things never change.

From *April 4: A Pep Talk from Nancy, Special Education Teacher*

Today Nancy gave a kind of pep talk/reprimand speech to the students because a new marking period began. She told them that she was proud of them for the most part, but that some students really need to work. She said that she was very happy with the results of their grades overall. Only 3/13 students failed miserably; science proved to be the worst subject with 5/13 students failing. I admire the way Nancy balances the encouragement with the reproach when she speaks to and with the students. She has their confidence. In general, they seem to respect her, certainly enough to confide in her. Yet I wonder if she feels that she knows too much of their lives. And how do you know when it is too much? Does she ever get burnt out? I have also noticed that before classes, she quickly talks to the teachers to set up meetings (e.g., parent conferences, progress reports, course work, detentions, etc.). A great amount of patience, frustration, anxiety, concern, understanding, and knowledge round out Nancy.

CONSIDER . . .

1. Point out some specific details that Sulit includes; explain why these details might have stuck in her memory.
2. Find a place where Sulit reflects, questions, or thinks about the meaning of what she has observed.
3. What themes emerge from the entries excerpted here? What ideas and issues might Sulit want to emphasize if she were considering writing a report on these observations?

PUBLIC WRITING: PROFILE

You know what a profile looks like if it's a photograph or a painting: It's a view from one side that distinctly shows the outline of a face. A written profile is much the same: a view of one aspect of a person's life, perhaps a view of someone's school experiences or work as a stockbroker. Maybe it's a view of a person revealed through a hobby such as collecting coins or constructing model railroads. Maybe it's an outline of one aspect of a person's experience—someone's experiences as a mother or a teacher or a marine biologist. A frequent structure for a profile essay is the "day in the life of" arrangement. Whatever the subject, the profile emphasizes *a single perspective* on a person's life rather than a summary of an entire life experience.

 Writing Task:

Write a profile piece about one aspect of a person's life or experiences. Be sure to limit your focus to one dominant perspective on this person's life.

Invention Ideas

You can approach your planning for the profile in at least two ways. You can think of a person (or *maybe* an animal) that you would like to feature. Or you can think of a topic that you are interested in and find a person whose work or hobby is connected to that topic. To think of a good topic, try making three lists. At the top of a sheet of paper, write headings for three columns: *people, occupations,* and *hobbies.* You are going to brainstorm as many interesting people, occupations, and hobbies as you can. Now set your timer for five minutes and see how many items you can list under each heading.

When your lists are full, put asterisks by the most promising topics and ask yourself these questions about each:

- How much do I care about this topic?
- How much do I already know about this topic?
- Who will want to read about this topic?
- What will my readers want to know about this topic?
- How will I find out what I need to know to write a fully developed essay?

And consider these questions, too:

- Will I need to conduct an interview with my subject? (Probably!)
- Will I need to interview any other people who can tell me more about my subject/person or topic?
- Will I need to read about my topic in an encyclopedia or a book or magazine?

Think about all these questions as you plan and think about your profile essay.

Once you choose an attractive topic, brainstorm a list of facts and ideas that you already have about this subject. You may also want to use the topics guidelines or webbing (Chapter 2) as ways of discovering what you already know about your topic. If you plan to conduct an interview, first read the guide to interviewing (pages 218–222). If you read to gather information, take careful notes in your own words. (If you copy word for word from any source, you may accidentally plagiarize.)

If you gather information from a direct observation, be sure to address those famous five W's—who, what, when, why, where—and how. If you write about a person, observe what the person looks like, both facial features and dress, and what the person does. Observe and take notes on what the person says and how he/she speaks. Jot down your impressions and intuitions, too; they may come in handy when you draft your piece.

Drafting a Profile

When you feel comfortable and knowledgeable about your topic, you are ready to start writing. Begin with a thesis that previews the main idea that you want to express about your subject or that expresses the *dominant impression* that you want to create about your subject. The dominant impression highlights the single perspective through which you want your reader to understand your subject. As usual, draft your essay as quickly as possible, in one sitting if you can. Get what you know onto paper expeditiously. Then review what you have written, clarifying whatever seems unclear at first glance. Remember that a profile takes one view of its subject, describes that view fully, and draws on a variety of structures. Your profile may combine description and narration. It may use definition or comparison and contrast. You may also include dialogue in the profile;

you may write not only what the subject says, but also what someone else says about the subject.

Once you have what feels like a complete draft, put it aside for a while and look at the profiles in this chapter. Maybe you'll get even more ideas for your profile.

Looking at Some Profiles

Profiles are common pieces in popular magazines because readers like to read about interesting people and places. In a profile from *Esquire*, Mike Lupica portrays the boxer Riddick Bowe and, using an interesting rhetorical strategy, compares Bowe's experience to that of another famous boxer, Mike Tyson. As you read, think about the view of Bowe emphasized by Lupica.

The Other Kid from Brownsville

MIKE LUPICA

He stood at the end of Maher Drive in Fort Washington, Maryland, his huge boxing hands pointing all over the empty lot, quick and busy as jabs. "This is my property," he said. There was nothing to see, really, just red ribbons attached to trees, marking the start of the five acres he had bought before he beat Evander Holyfield to become the heavyweight champion of the world.

Riddick Bowe saw plenty, though. He pointed with his great left hand and said the gym would be over there. On the other side of the house, he would build a garage big enough to fit his Jeep Cherokee, a red BMW, and *eight* other cars. The whole complex would sit behind an ornate gate with BOWE FAMILY written across the front.

He stood patiently in front of the black Cherokee and showed me what until now had been only a landmark of imagination. After a while, he reached into the Jeep and pulled out the blueprints. He showed me the master bedroom—with two television sets, a Jacuzzi, and even a small kitchen—and the master bathroom, which on paper looks more like the site of the 1994 Super Bowl.

"Long way from eleven o'clock in the night on Lott Avenue," he said, tracing in his mind the route he had taken from Brownsville, Brooklyn, to the end of Maher Drive.

Bowe is twenty-five years old, the twelfth of thirteen children. His mother worked the midnight-to-eight shift as a machine operator at a place called Admiral Plastics on Avenue D, a twenty-minute walk away. On weeknights when Bowe was a teenager, she would wake him at 10:30 and he would walk her to work.

"I didn't want to get out of bed some nights," he said. "I didn't have much, but I had that warm bed.

"The scary part was getting out of the building. The elevator didn't work and we had to walk down six flights. It seemed like there was a drug deal going on on every landing. Which meant an automatic weapon on every landing. Every night, I'd be afraid of the same thing: Somebody'd mistake us for the police and we'd be shot for nothin'.'"

He looked out at the empty lot and the trees beyond it. The car windows were down and you could hear Phil Collins on the tape player. Riddick Bowe tried to remember all of the old geography, the geography that took one of his sisters—a mother of four, stabbed to death for a welfare check.

"New Lott Avenue to Rockaway Avenue," he said. "Then left on Rockaway Parkway to Avenue D and maybe another quarter-mile from there. Back to our building and up those stairs. They'd hear me on the landing and I'd say, 'Not a cop, not a cop. Riddick Bowe from the sixth floor.' I was trying not to be a damn statistic."

His new geography is worlds away. To get to this spot, Bowe had driven past well-tended houses with fancy red brick made to look old, past streets with suburban names like Ambrose Lane and Sero Estates. A pair of miniature boxing gloves bounced from the Jeep's rearview mirror. Phil Collins screamed from the cassette deck.

I can feel it coming in the air tonight.

"That's the song I used going to the ring," Bowe said, singing along.

I've been waiting for this moment all my life.

Kareem Muhammed, his training-camp coordinator, nodded in agreement from the backseat, his eyes closed.

Growing up in Brownsville with crack cocaine, guns, and death all around him, Riddick Bowe had always lived large in his dreams. Today, the undisputed heavyweight champion of the world, he could see mansions reaching to the sky.

I first met him in South Korea, in a section of Seoul known as Itaewon. All the Olympic athletes went there for the shopping deals. Bowe was just a big New York kid with a smile, charming and all mouth.

"I'm a businessman," he told me then. "I'm in the business of doing all the right things to be champion of the world."

Now his manager, Rock Newman, runs the heavyweight division, which for as long as your man wins is the same as owning the hottest studio in Hollywood.

Newman comes out of northwest Washington, D.C. He once sold cars and did some radio before entering the boxing business. He became Bowe's manager in 1988 after Bowe lost to Lennox Lewis in Seoul. A lot of people had given up on him then. Rock Newman saw a six-five kid who had made it to the gold-medal fight with a bad hand and a bad foot, not long after his sister was killed. He went to Brownsville, walked up those six flights of stairs, and told Bowe he wanted to represent him.

"I didn't have any idea what I was getting myself into," he says. "I drove over there in my brand-new BMW. There was this gate outside his building, and I saw a couple of guys sitting there. I gave them each ten dollars and told them there was more where that came from if the BMW was still there when I came out."

Newman swears he told Bowe that very day, in December 1988, that he would get him a title shot in September 1992. He delivered Holyfield to Bowe on November 13. "So I was off by a couple of months," he says. "Sue me." It took skill and moxie, but Newman was ready for anything. One night, when fighter Elijah Tillery started kicking Bowe after the bell, Newman jumped into the ring, put a headlock on him, and tossed him over the ropes. After the decision in the Holyfield bout, he was involved in a brawl with an Associated Press photographer.

Newman's scrappiness and persistence paid off when Bowe was declared champ after one of the best heavyweight title fights in years. If Mike Tyson hadn't been convicted of rape, things might have worked out differently. But Tyson was in prison when Bowe and Holyfield produced the brutal majesty of the unforgettable tenth round, and unless something happens on appeal, he is there a long time.

"We went to the same school for about six months," Bowe tells me. "P.S. 396, on Chester Street in Brownsville."

He is always concerned with the geography of things.

"A long time after that, a friend said, 'You remember a guy named Mike Tyson?' I didn't remember anybody by that name. 'He's a boxer now,' he said, 'starting to knock out guys twenty-three, twenty-four years old.' I still said no. Then my friend said, 'They called him Bummy Ike. That's when I knew who he was."

On the morning of the Holyfield fight, the biggest day of Riddick Bowe's life, Tyson called from prison to wish him well. Afterward, Bowe took some postfight hits for dedicating part of his win to Tyson.

"People can come from the same place but be made different," Bowe says. "All I'm saying is, I know where he's coming from. Doesn't mean I want to turn out like he did."

Right now, Riddick Bowe is living in a modest house in Fort Washington, on a street called Lourdes, like the town in France known for miracles. There is a painting of the Last Supper on his dining-room wall, framed color photographs of his wedding, and pictures of the children. Bowe sits in the cool basement—a few miles from the empty lot where he will build his dream house—and talks about the first day he ever got into the ring.

He was in the seventh grade. "Skinny little nothing," he says. But he had beat up this kid at school because he dared to bad-mouth Muhammed Ali. The school principal told Bowe about a gym in the Bedford–Stuyvesant section of Brooklyn. She suggested that he try fighting under supervision. Bowe took the bus over there, walked up to the first trainer he saw—all this Ali in him—and announced that he could whup anybody in the place. Before the afternoon was out, he was given headgear and a mouthpiece and sent into the ring.

"The other kid's name was Willie," Bowe says. "He beat the hell out of me. But I stayed around. They gave me some pointers, and the next day I beat the hell out of Willie. Then they put me in with another kid. Beat the hell out of me. Day after that, I beat the hell out of *him.*"

Before long, Bowe was getting up in the morning to run in Betsy Head Park. After school he'd go to the gym. Then he'd return home, go to sleep, and wait for his mother to wake him.

"Ali's my idol," he tells you. "My mother's my hero."

"She told me a lot of things," he says. "Told me that Ali had finished high school and that I was gonna finish, too. She told me I was gonna use my head for something other than being a greaseball. And she told me this: 'If you ever go to jail you can cancel Christmas.' That meant she wasn't ever gonna visit me."

Dorothy Bowe retired from Admiral Plastics two years ago. Riddick moved her to Coney Island. She now lives in a small apartment, third floor, in an area with pleasant-sounding street names like Neptune and Mermaid.

"Riddick always told me that someday he was going to make so much money I wasn't gonna have to do nothin'," she says.

Dorothy Bowe's youngest son likes to show you what success has brought him, too: the black Jeep he calls *Old Betsy;* the BMW he calls *The Show;* twenty-five thousand dollars' worth of exercise equipment in the basement; and the video arcade for his son and two daughters.

In his backyard, there is a small blue Everlast heavy bag for Riddick junior. "I watch him get going on that thing sometimes and it lights up my whole day," the father says. "Maybe 'cause I see myself in him."

He throws a neat left hand into the small bag now and you can feel the neighborhood move. Bowe smiles.

He says he wants to be champion long enough to fight Mike Tyson, and who knows if things will work out that way? That is his dream, though, and Riddick Bowe has always been a champion in that area.

"Let's go see where the new house is gonna go," he says, leading the way to the Jeep. Kareem Muhammed tosses him the keys. The heavyweight champion gets in and wrestles with the antitheft bar on the steering wheel.

"You sure you got the right key, Bowe?" Muhammed says cautiously.

Riddick is all business. "I got the right key," he says.

"You want me to help?" Muhammed asks.

"I'll get it," Bowe says.

The key turns finally. Bowe puts on the Phil Collins tape and steers the Jeep toward the future.

"You're from Brownsville and you can't handle an antitheft device?" I say.

Riddick Bowe, dead serious, eyes straight ahead, as always, replies, "I never stole anything."

He earned his way to the end of Maher Drive.

CONSIDER . . .

1. What would you say is the dominant impression of Riddick Bowe created in Lupica's essay?

2. Without looking back at the essay, jot down a few memorable details about Bowe. What do these details suggest about Bowe's personality?

3. Find a place where Lupica reveals something about Bowe's past. How does this information contribute to the dominant impression of Bowe?

Barbara Jordan was a person who was listened to. Read this *New York Times Magazine* profile of her by columnist Molly Ivins for the dominant impression.

She Sounded Like God

MOLLY IVINS

Finding Barbara Jordan in the directory of distinguished Americans is easy. She was always a First and an Only.

First woman, only black; in the Texas Senate, in the Texas Congressional delegation, from the entire South. She served on the Judiciary Committee during the decision on Richard Nixon's impeachment. Her great bass voice rolled forth: "My faith in the Con-sti-tu-tion is whole, it is com-plete, it is to-tal." She sounded like the Lord God Almighty, and her implacable legal logic caught the attention of the entire nation.

The degree of prejudice she had to overcome by intelligence and sheer force of personality is impossible to overestimate. She wasn't just black and female: she was homely, she was heavy and she was dark black. When she first came to the Texas Senate, it was considered a great joke to bring racist friends to the gallery when B.J. was due to speak. They would no sooner gasp, "Who is that nigger?" than she would open her mouth and out would roll language Lincoln would have appreciated. Her personal dignity was so substantial even admirers hesitated to approach her. No one will ever know how lonely she was at the beginning.

Her friend Representative Eleanor Holmes Norton justly reminds us that B.J. was not effective solely because she sounded like God. Born and raised in the fifth ward of Houston, the biggest black ghetto in the biggest state, she graduated magna cum laude from Texas Southern University and went on to Boston University law school. Jordan was so smart it almost hurt. Lord, she was a good legislator, never wasted a minute on a hopeless cause. Ask those cornered-cottonmouth, mean-as-hell-with-the-hide-off conservatives. Fought her on the floor in head-up debate, fought her in the back room over Article 53, Subsection C, Part II: Jordan always knew what she was talking about, and almost always won. She traded some public suck-up with the Texas Democratic establishment—Lyndon Johnson, Ben Barnes— and got the first black Congressional district drawn in Texas. Smart trade.

As it happened, the night B.J. spoke to Congress in favor of impeaching Richard Nixon was also the last night of the Texas legislative session. Came B.J.'s turn to speak and everyone back in Austin—legislators, aides, janitors, maids— gathered around television sets to hear this black woman speak on national television. And they cheered for her as though they were watching the University of Texas pound hell out of Notre Dame in the Cotton Bowl.

She cut her Congressional career short; it seems likely that she knew she had multiple sclerosis. Of course, she wanted a seat on the Supreme Court. If there is one thing I would ask you to accept on faith, it is that Barbara Jordan had Judicial Temperament. Her faith in the Con-sti-tu-tion was whole, it was complete, it was total. I consulted her about appointments from Robert Bork to Clarence Thomas and never found her less than fair. George Bush the Elder will tell you the same.

In the last 14 years of her life, B.J. was a magnificent teacher, at the L.B.J. School of Public Affairs. The only way to get into her classes at the University of Texas was to win a place in a lottery. For many students, she was the inspiration for a life in public service. No perks, no frills, no self-righteousness: just a solid commitment to using government to help achieve liberty and justice for all. Her role as a role model may well have been her most important. One little black girl used to walk by Jordan's house every day on her way to school and think, "Barbara Jordan grew up right here, too." Today Ruth Simmons is president of Smith College.

Jordan was a helluva poker player. And before M.S. twisted her poor hands so badly, she loved to play guitar. It was like God singing the blues. "St. James Infirmary"—Let her go, *Looord,* let her go.

But let's not let her go without remembering that the Woman Who Sounded Like God had a very dry sense of humor. One time, she invited Ann Richards, then a mere county commissioner, over for dinner. Jordan lived down a dirt road and had a troublesome neighbor who kept locking the gates on it. Jordan, never one to miss an opportunity to Make Government Work, asked the Commissioner to do something. Richards made some phone calls, to no avail.

Time went by and Jordan again invited Richards, by then Governor of Texas, to dinner. Richards inquired idly: "Barbara, whatever happened to that dreadful neighbor of yours? Did she ever quit lockin' the gates?"

Jordan said: "I am pleased to report that the woman in question has since died. And gone to hell."

Today Barbara Jordan is the first and only black woman resting in the Texas State Cemetery.

CONSIDER . . .

1. How does Ivins prepare you for the dominant impression of Jordan from the beginning, even from the title of the profile?
2. Find a sentence that might be the thesis of this piece; copy it. Is the idea in the thesis reiterated throughout the profile? Is the dominant impression articulated in the thesis?
3. What other points about Jordan does Ivins emphasize? How does she tie these points to the dominant impression?
4. What is one memorable detail from this piece?

In the next profile student Rob Goldman emphasizes one aspect of his roommate's chess-playing ability. As you read, notice how Goldman creates and sustains a dominant impression of Noble Murphy.

Checks

Rob Goldman

Noble Lycester Biddinger Murphy, my roommate, pushed his piece up one square and sat back, pleased. Snatching the piece with my knight, I looked up, expecting to see an expression of disgust and regret at the loss of a piece so early in the game. Instead, Noble gave me only a disturbing look of amusement.

"If you take that piece," he said, "you'll lose the game in seventeen moves."

"What?!" was all that I could respond with.

He sat back and shrugged as if the logic spoke for itself. One of those parental "You've made your decision, now you're going to have to live with it" looks on his face.

"You play much chess?" A fair question for me to ask, although a bit late.

"You mean I didn't mention that I am the state high school champion?"

I glanced across the board to see his eyes darting from piece to piece, square to square . . . obviously considering the best way to orchestrate this alleged seventeen-move blitzkrieg.

"You have unwittingly fallen victim to my king side attack turbines," he said, smiling coyly.

His face was calm. His body reclined, and the fingertips of his right hand gently touched those of his left, making a sort of tent shape in the middle of his chest.

Noble casually sat up and snapped off a move. Sinking back into his chair, he said "Check." I defended the king with the only available piece . . . my queen. Noble nodded as if I had come up with the "correct" move, and he again looked down at the board. He was the master puppeteer, and all the pieces were his puppets . . . mine included. He smiled warmly, and slammed my now vulnerable queen off of the board.

As it turns out, Noble learned to play chess at a relatively late age . . . fifteen. With only three years of tournament experience, Noble has obtained a rating of 2176, only 24 points away from master status. Experience isn't the only key to winning, however. According to Noble, a great chess player is a complex blend of book knowledge, positional maturity, and, of course, analytical and tactical thinking, clearly qualities that I lack. Apparently book knowledge is the real meat of a good player's game. Positional strategies and higher thinking are much like McDonald's special sauce, adding only stylistic flair and personal character.

"You see, every six months all of the grand masters publish their games in a book. It's called the *Sahovski Informator* . . . that's where I pick up most of the stuff I use."

Still skeptical of the idea that anyone could memorize every move of even one chess game, much less hundreds, I challenged Noble to show me quickly how our game would have ended.

"It's funny that you mention that, actually," he lectured. "This game is really very famous. It was first played by Mikhail Tal and Victor Korchnoi. . . . I'll show you the way their game worked out."

Moving his fingers as the pieces, he quickly dictated the remaining moves.

"Your knight moves here, my pawn defends, rook takes, knight takes, queen takes, check. Now watch, this is really elegant! I move my king here, threatening your pawn and your knight; you defend with your rook, and I move bishop here . . . check mate."

His fingers were in a tangle somewhere in the middle of the board, his face smirking at the "beauty" of the game that he had played out. I hadn't followed a single word. But no matter, because all the time he was talking I had been carefully assessing the best move. Reaching out, I "accidentally" knocked the board off of the table.

Noble looked down at the board, then up at me, a distracted look on his face, and began to replace the pieces from memory.

CONSIDER . . .

1. What would you say is the dominant impression of Noble Murphy?
2. How do you think Goldman obtained the information for this essay?
3. What part of Noble's background does Goldman integrate into the essay? Is this information in keeping with the dominant impression?
4. How does Goldman use dialogue or speech to characterize Noble?
5. Can you think of other kinds of information you would like to know about Noble? How would you advise Goldman to revise?

Writers' Group: Rethinking the Profile

Look again at the draft of your profile essay and ask yourself these hard questions:

- Does my profile clearly have a dominant impression? Am I emphasizing one view of my subject? And have I made that view clear to my reader?
- Do I use dialogue and description adequately? Have I *shown* enough? Have I used enough detail? Are there places where I could add dialogue and/or description and help the reader?
- Are there questions about my subject that I have not addressed? Do I need to add information? Where? What else might my reader like to know?

Revise your essay accordingly. This revision may mean you have to do more observation and thinking, or you may need to speak to your subject again and ask some follow-through questions.

When you are satisfied with your draft, ask your writers' group to give you a reading. Try listing three questions you'd like answers to on a blank sheet of paper and asking your readers to respond to those questions. When you get your readers' responses back, consider them and revise your essay as you see fit. Then proofread to eliminate mechanical errors.

Reflecting on and Presenting the Profile

When you prepare this essay for your portfolio, consider including a photograph of the subject of your profile. In magazines, profile essays are frequently accompanied by photographs.

Consider, too, giving a copy of your profile to the subject of your essay. Most people are delighted to read about themselves, and the finished essay plus a short note of thanks will not only be courteous but will pave the way for future cordial relationships.

Finally, don't forget to reflect on the experience of writing the profile in your writing notebook. What was easy about this essay? What was difficult about the process? Was anyone especially helpful to you? What surprised you about this experience? What did you learn through this writing experience?

PUBLIC WRITING: STUDY OF A PLACE

A study of a place is actually a profile of a place. Writing about a place is a particularly good way to heighten your powers of observation and to increase your awareness of your surroundings. Profiling a place makes you more alert to the whole notion of context, a useful concept in academic as well as personal situations. A profile of a place creates a dominant impression of a place, just as a profile essay attempts to create a dominant impression of a person. To create this dominant impression, you will need to observe and select specific details to craft a view of the place that emphasizes what you think is its most important feature.

    Writing Task:

Write a description, a detailed study, of a place. Focus on creating a dominant impression of the place.

Invention Ideas

First, find a place to write about. You don't have to look far, and you don't have to choose an exotic place. In fact, some of the most interesting spots are right before us and require only the appropriate attention—which you will provide—to be noticed. You might want to write about a local cemetery that has always fascinated you, or a hardware store, or a doll repair business. You might want to study the nature preserve on your campus, the laundry room in your dormitory, or the tree house you built in your back yard during your childhood. You could write about your grandmother's attic or your favorite diner. You might write about the law office where you worked during the summer or the headquarters of the painting business that your brother-in-law operates.

To begin crafting a study of a place, do some careful but active observation. Take notes. Consider the appearance of the place, the location of the place, the purpose of the place (if one exists), the activities that happen in or at the place, the inhabitants of the place, and the emotions evoked by the place. Taking an abundance of notes is very important, for these notes are likely to emerge in one form or another in the finished piece. Be sure to notice the size of the place (see if you can compare its size to something familiar, like a basketball court); its dominant colors; its furnishings (whether these are buckets and bales of hay in an old barn or purple art deco chairs in a Manhattan loft); its arrangement (what goes where); its history (you can observe it or ask about it or research it). You might even jot this information in a chart, as in Figure 4.1. In the figure, notice how the writer gathers details about her favorite place in the house, a screened-in back porch, in preparation for writing.

When you have collected what seem to be enough details, study them carefully to determine what dominant or principal impression of the place they create. When you add up the details, what kind of place emerges? If you have a clear notion of the way you want to portray the place, you are ready to begin drafting.

Today's date _9/16/97_

Notes about _My back porch_

Time of day _2:00 p.m._

Location	Size	Colors	Arrangement	Mood	History
At northeast corner of my house, off kitchen and near dining room. This is the back of the house, facing toward the back yard.	About 15' x 10' but seems bigger because two walls are open and screened; one wall is all glass windows looking in to the kitchen.	White (clapboard from original outside of house); beige (carpet and chairs and file cabinet); green (Rubbermaid tote boxes storing family stuff).	Door from house at SW side; door to outside at NW side; stacks of Rubbermaid tote boxes beside file cabinet and against house wall; wicker chair and table across, near screen; table covered with rag rug in corner, for dog grooming.	Peaceful. Sounds of birds, crickets, light traffic from street in summer. Breeze blowing through. Wind chimes. Occasional bark of neighborhood dogs.	Added onto 1901 Victorian house when previous owners extended kitchen in about 1985.

Figure 4.1 Organizing details gathered through observation

Drafting a Study of a Place

To begin drafting the study of a place, begin by writing the dominant impression (or the thesis you want to reinforce) at the top of the page. This thesis/impression may not necessarily remain in the final draft of the paper, but if it is always at the top of the page, you will find it easier to ensure that what you write about the place contributes to it. With the thesis at the top of the paper and always physically before you, begin drafting. You might begin by sketching some visual details so that the reader has a sense of the appearance of the place as the piece goes on. Or you might imagine that you are in the place and try to re-create for the reader the feeling of being there. As usual, draft as quickly as possible. Remember that you are not trying to tell everything about the place but selectively re-creating an impression of the place for the reader. Don't be concerned about mechanical problems as you draft; you can address those later.

Looking at a Study of a Place

Consider this study of a place by Macy Hueckel, who re-creates from memory her favorite high school classroom, the drafting room, where she spent many pleasant hours. As you read, think consciously about the impressions you are forming of the place.

Room 121
Macy Hueckel

To some, it looks like just another door in the maze of rooms and hallways and floors of West Lafayette High School. But to others, the door marked "Room 121" can be the door to a magical place. At least that is how I remember it, for the time I spent there was enchanted.

Room 121 is the drafting room, the home of drafting students. This is where they work and laugh and are taught. During a typical school week, Mr. Florence, the ever patient drafting teacher and leader, usually introduces a new technique on Monday. He uses an overhead projector and draws diagrams and sketches on it, explaining as he goes. Then after the introduction, he leaves the students to themselves, and the rest of the week is devoted to practicing that new technique in the form of worksheets and textbook assignments. For that is the only way to learn drafting—to learn by doing.

But students are not expected to master the new concept all at once or all by themselves. Mr. Florence is always around in class to help. Or students can consult other students. The whole atmosphere of the drafting room is alive and relaxed. The radio plays popular songs, some people sing along, others bicker good-naturedly about which station to play. The room is full of busy conversation; everywhere there are students comparing their work, redrawing, helping, collaborating, teaching others and themselves.

But a non-drafting student isn't part of that. A non-drafter doesn't see the room when it is alive with activity; she sees it only after everyone has gone. She peers in the window at the straight, stiff metal desks with slanted tops and weird contraptions attached. She sees tall, cold, uncomfortable-looking metal stools, rows upon rows of assignments and page numbers on the chalkboard, the printing straight and uniform, like soldiers standing at attention. Locked drawers—what's hiding inside? And why are the drawers locked up so tightly? The place seems so barren, unyielding to a non-drafter.

But a drafting student sees something entirely different. The drafter sees a bright, well-lit room that is always warm inside, no matter how cold the rest of the school is in the winter. The lights are always on, making it an inviting, welcoming place. The door is always open—students can come in any time to work. It's like a beacon of comforting, familiar light shining out into the darkened hall.

The drafter walks through the door, into this magical place. She sees those same tall desks the non-drafter sees, only in the drafter's eyes the desks are strong and sturdy, with the tops slanted back at just the right angle so she doesn't get a sore back leaning over the drawing. To the slanted tops are attached the so-called "weird contraptions." Except to a drafter they are the familiar, supportive mechanical arms and parallel bars, which slide up and down and around freely, enabling her to draw a perfectly straight line anywhere on the page.

The drafter digs deep in a pocket and produces the key to those seemingly forbidding locked metal drawers. She unlocks the drawers, and with them the mystery of what is inside. The drafter knows what's inside—all the reference books, tools, and other equipment helpful in producing a good drawing. There are textbooks to refer to, books that explain, diagram, and demonstrate anything anyone ever needs to know about drafting and different drawing techniques. The instructions are step-by-step and easy to follow; it's as if in the height of a student's confusion and ignorance, the book simply, calmly takes her by the hand and shows her exactly what she needs to know.

In the drawers also is a vast array of instruments—compasses to construct arcs with, dividers to copy lines, and eraser shields to carefully erase small parts of the most intricate drawing. There are protractors to measure angles with, circle templates to help one trace out perfect circles of every imaginable size, and masking tape to affix the paper firmly in place while working on a drawing.

The drafter sits, and prepares to draw. But first she glances up at the chalkboard at the neat, organized rows of "challenges," for that is what they are rightly called; they are not simply dull "assignments." Then she settles down into the comfortable, familiar routine and begins to draft.

The drafter is all alone now, working steadily. But she doesn't feel alone. For she is in a magical place, and the warm, relaxing atmosphere of Room 121 closes in around her, shielding her from all else. She is perfectly happy to be left to her work in the drafting room.

CONSIDER . . .

1. What details used in the essay might Hueckel have noted first in her invention work?
2. What is the dominant impression of room 121 you get from this study?
3. What adjectives would you use to characterize this room? What words in the essay suggest or reinforce this impression?
4. Describe an effective rhetorical strategy that Hueckel uses.
5. Suggest some considerations for revision: What could Hueckel do to make this an even better piece?

Writers' Group: Rethinking the Study of a Place

Ask the members of your writers' group to read your essay, then to write two adjectives that describe the dominant impression of the place you profiled. Compare the adjectives: Are the lists similar? Do the adjectives match the impression you were trying to create? If not, ask the members of your group and your instructor how you can create a more solid impression.

After the readers have given you a reading, scrutinize your piece by yourself. Ask yourself these questions:

- Will more details solidify the dominant impression I am trying to create? (Cumulative detail is the most powerful way to create an impression.)
- Do my details draw on imagery from several senses? (If you have only visual imagery, for instance, you may fail to appeal to some readers' most powerful sense.)
- Have I eliminated extraneous details that do not contribute to the dominant impression?
- Is there some logical structure to the presentation of the details? That is, if I am describing a place, does the description move from inside out, outside in, right to left, left to right, down to up, far to near—or some other sensible structure that will help the reader process the information clearly?

Reflecting on and Presenting the Study of a Place

When your study of a place sounds the way you want it to, take some time to proofread and edit for readers. You might try this trick when you proofread: Read your essay backward, from end to beginning. This will force you to attend to each individual word, and you will be less likely to overlook the misspelled word or the misplaced comma.

If you are artistic, you can add a photograph or a drawing to your essay. Many published studies of places are accompanied by sketches or photographs. Make sure that your artwork complements your writing, that both contribute to the same dominant impression of the place.

When you finish the piece, don't forget to jot down a few notes about the process of writing this piece—to reflect on the writing. What did you do to prepare yourself for this essay? What problems or successes did you have when you were writing it? Who helped you? What do you like best about the work?

PORTMANTEAU OF WRITING WHAT YOU SEE AND STUDY

This Portmanteau section contains additional examples of writing from observation, published and unpublished—more learning logs, profiles, and studies of places. The first three excerpts from learning logs show how different students approach the same task: being in a middle school classroom as observers for an extended time.

Excerpts from Learning Logs

Lunchroom Politics
Joseph Robinson

One of my greatest learning experiences took place in the faculty dining room today. I listened while career teachers debated what was important to them: State budget cuts, children's behavior problems, and the goings-on in their classrooms. Doom and Gloom dominated these interchanges from time to time. The system seemed to the teachers like a bureaucracy operating for its own interests.

Hope lived, too. Teachers identified what good goes/went on, either in their own classrooms, those of the people they knew, or relating to people they had read or heard about. Good seemed always pitted against evil in these little dramas, as with the story of the Boston schoolteacher who was a dedicated runner and always had competed in the Boston Marathon. Because the race fell on a school day, she would be seriously penalized or fired (I can't remember which) if she used a sick day. Understandably, this noble teacher submitted her resignation, ran the race, and took a job with a more reasonable, less senselessly bureaucratic district. The teacher who related this story told of the victory of high ideals and good teaching while the "bad guys" clearly lost big.

Conversations were generally friendly and open, as the teachers and other personnel invited me into the conversation too. I got the impression that I was sitting around some pretty good, dedicated teachers, and I instinctively compared and contrasted myself to them. I thought quite a bit about how I'd do things similarly or differently from them. How would I handle myself? How would I be able to "live" in the middle school?

Politics was the name of the game as power struggles went on all around me. While I include this theme under "lunchroom," these discussions went on more in the teachers' lounge between classes and in other rooms, where only a few teachers would confide honest opinions to each other (and me) and trusted colleagues. Some issues: tension between those pushers of the "Middle School Philosophy" and the more conventional teachers who clung to traditional ways; infighting among cliques of teachers on the same team (who was good and who was downright awful); and general school policy. . . .

The Characters
Patricia Foley

. . . Indeed, it has been years since I have stepped into an eighth grade classroom. Despite the fact that I now sit at a different desk and play a different role, things, especially the students (or characters in this drama), do not appear to have changed that drastically. Students still have the same concerns: members of the opposite sex, dances, class trips, gossip. Alas, classes remain a secondary (pardon the pun) concern to teenagers at this point in their educations. Hormones are raging, and settling the students into their seats and quieting them down usually steals the first few minutes of a lesson. Additionally, it remains true that kids say the darnedest things. In one section Mrs. C. made reference to a student in another section and something this student had done positively with his paper. Upon hearing the name of this student, someone in the class offered the information that this other student had told him that he regularly masturbates.

Having heard the previous comment, I was delighted to remember that I am now a peer of the teachers. All of the teachers that I met were sincerely warm and dedicated people. They lacked a good deal of the cynicism that I have seen in other members of our profession. The teachers at East Middle School work in blocks. In other words, the teachers of the different subjects share the same students. Once a week the five teachers in the block meet and discuss concerns they may be having with any student or group of students. In addition to knowing their subject matter, the teachers make it a point to familiarize themselves with issues that directly affect their students. For example, over seventy percent of the students at this school qualify for free lunches. . . .

A Lesson in Mathematics
Juliet Smith

. . . The students' desks are precisely aligned in equal rows all facing the blackboard. The teachers' desk is set off to the side. Mrs. W. stands at the board working through a problem to find the mean of 99, 256, and 1789. Students raise their hands anxiously wanting to be called upon, even if they do not know the answer. Mrs. W. has all the knowledge and authority, and the students are left to figure out the answers and vie for the teacher's validations.

This is not to suggest that Mrs. W. does not care for her students nor that she wishes them to fail. Mrs. W. is a concerned teacher who likes her students and insists upon mutual respect in her classroom. She wants her students to be active participants and encourages questions. Yet she always knows the answers; there are no gray areas where her class is concerned. Perhaps one would argue that math is a neutral, apolitical subject. Yet numbers do have a tremendous effect on individuals' lives, and they signify something far greater than marks on the number line.

For instance, one day Mrs. W. had the students make bar graphs indicating the number of barrels of oil spilled in various offshore drilling disasters. This material was supposed to be cross-disciplinary. The science teacher in Mrs. W.'s block, Mrs. S., covered a section on the environment, but unfortunately Mrs. S. had completed this material two months prior. Furthermore, the enormity of these catastrophes did not seem to register with the students: they were simply shading in the correct number of squares. Mrs. W. did not engage in any kind of discussion on what these numbers meant in real-life terms: what does it mean to have 245,000 barrels spill in Prince William Sound, or 21,000 barrels off the coast of France? How much oil is contained in a barrel? What is the distance between these places and Binghamton, New York? How far does the oil spread? These are all questions that involve numbers, and they all begin to indicate the ramifications of these ecological catastrophes for Mrs. W.'s students. The students do not live in a vacuum, and they need to become increasingly aware of the world around them, to work towards some kind of critical consciousness even at the age of 12. Active engagement should mean more than being picked to go to the overhead and write in the answer with a red marker.

CONSIDER . . .

1. What do all the learning log excerpts have in common? How do all the writers draw on their observations to find something to write?
2. Consider the titles. Evaluate how well they reflect the dominant impressions of the excerpts. Suggest alternate titles if you like.
3. What details are particularly memorable to you in these excerpts? Why do you think you remember them so easily? How can you make a similar impression on your readers?

Three Profiles

These profiles by professional and student writers illustrate how you can write profiles about subjects that are not human as well as the more typical profiles of human subjects. Adrian Polit's "Indomitable Misha" is a portrait of a cat. A very different kind of profile, Stefan Kanfer's "Protean Penman" from *Time*, characterizes the famous and prolific scientific writer Isaac Asimov. "Uncle Chul Gets Rich" by Chang-rae Lee, from the *New York Times Magazine*, is a profile of an interesting relative.

Indomitable Misha
Adrian Polit

Reaching the bottom of the stairs, I turn into the dining room and head toward the kitchen to break my fast. Curled in a semicircle on one of the chairs is Misha, one of my two cats. Her white chest and paws stand out in contrast to the yellow–orange coat and fat tail tucked along her side. On the small side, as cats go, and compact rather than long and lanky, Misha has an overall appearance of neatness, enhanced by her thick, well-groomed fur. Her head is already raised from napping because, of course, she sensed me well before I encountered her. She greets me with an affable "myaa," which she extends right into a yawn. Giving her a quick pat as I go by, I continue into the kitchen for my morning fuel-up.

Being the last out of the house in the morning, I am charged with putting the cats out before I leave. The other one, Alex, shoos right out, but Misha is loath to leave her comfortable chair. After a few indignant "rrrauws," she trots out the door, needing no further herding once her mind is made up. Thrust into the outdoor environment, she stands a moment, tail whipping back and forth, as she absorbs the rush of sights, sounds, and smells.

When I arrive home from school, the cats appear at the sound of the door and gallop in ahead of me. After a few crunches of food and laps of water, Misha settles down to stare out the back door. Turning my attention to the mail, I sit down at the table and slit open envelopes. A low, warning growl prompts me to look up again; the cats have spotted an intruding dog. While Alex heads for the underside of the couch, Misha presses up against the door. As I slide it open, she slithers out onto the back porch. Her tail puffs up like a balloon, her hackles stand on end, and she stalks forward. Head down low and tail straight back, she hisses like a fierce gas leak. As the imbecilic dog snuffles closer, nine-pound Misha raises the pitch of her growl and redoubles her imitation of an aerosol can. Suddenly she jumps forward and swipes at the dog's snout. Curiosity suddenly forgotten, Fido dodges away and canter-scampers off. After sniffing the scene of action and giving one last sputter, Misha the Great stalks back in and heads for a spot to sleep.

About 5:30 she gets up and joins Alex, who by now has emerged from under the couch, in the kitchen. In between dodging heavy feet, they lobby for some supper with a polite but insistent "mraaa." Every time Misha catches my eye, she reminds me that it is suppertime, emboldened by hunger and knowing she is right. Growing impatient at the delay and perhaps a little frustrated, she halfheartedly cuffs Alex, who swats her in return. For all her effort to get the supper, when it is finally dished up she only eats half of it and relinquishes the rest to Alex, who happily obliges.

In her desire to sleep in a variety of places, Misha invariably trespasses on the forbidden territory of the upstairs. This night is no exception. Within a half hour she comes hurtling down the stairs with a bellowing Father close behind and a flying slipper even closer. As I hold the door open, she shoots outside and skids around the corner.

Misha is banished for a whole twenty minutes, until I smuggle her in the front door. This time she heads to where I am sitting at the table and hops aboard, having forgiven me for having expelled her this morning.

CONSIDER . . .

1. Polit writes the profile of Misha in present tense. What effect does this create on the reader?
2. What dominant impression do you have of Misha? What specific details contribute to this impression?
3. What is the most memorable detail of the essay for you?

The Protean Penman

STEFAN KANFER

By the end of this year the Library of Congress will have received the 403rd book in a unique collection. Some of the volumes are composed of bawdy limericks: "There is something about satyriasis/ That arouses psychiatrists' biases,/ But we're both very pleased/ We're in this way diseased/ As the damsel who's waiting to try us is." Others are concerned with nuclear physics and organic chemistry: "It is the electron that is mobile and the proton that is relatively stationary . . . Benjamin Franklin had a fifty–fifty chance of guessing right, and he muffed it. Too bad." Some are science fiction—excursions out in the galactic void or deep within the vessels and sinews of the human body: " 'Watch what's coming.' All eyes turned ahead. A blue-green corpuscle was bumping along ahead of them." Some follow the adventures of Sherlock Holmes in outer space; some track the steps of Albert Einstein in his Princeton office: "He could not believe that the universe would be so entirely in the grip of chance. 'God may be subtle,' he once said. 'But he is not malicious.' "

In addition, there are mystery novels, short stories and a two-volume, 1,500-page autobiography: "I did a Dick Cavett segment on June 3. It was my fourth time with him. This time I was publicizing *The Sensuous Dirty Old Man,* so I came out with a bra over my eyes . . . It was the silliest thing I ever did on television, and I was sorry I had agreed to do it even as I stepped out onto the stage."

And this is only a partial register. Scores of additional works are listed under such disparate categories as the solar system, the meaning of the Greek myths, the shaping of England, the birth of the U.S. and secular explanations of the Old Testament: "If the Biblical account [of Jericho] is taken literally, this is a miracle, but . . . while the defenders watched in fascination at the slow parading about the city, and listened to the awesome sound of the trumpets, they might not have had time to see and hear the very mundane activity of Joshua's sappers slowly undermining the city's walls."

At first glance, these volumes would seem to have nothing in common. In fact, they are closely related. Every one of them was written by the same man.

"The *Guinness Book of World Records* says that mystery writer John Creasey in England published more than 500 books," says Isaac Asimov. "But it seems fair to say that no one has written more books on more subjects than I." The vertical pronoun frequently occurs in the author's conversation, but there is as much self-concealment as self-promotion in his talk. As he approaches his 70th year, for example, Asimov has come to see himself merely as a "born explainer." Yet explaining implies understanding, and there is very little in this world that Asimov does not understand. If something stumps him, he goes out and buys a book on the subject. Then he stays in and writes a book on the subject. Usually, the volume he reads is full of recondite information. Typically, the one with his name on the cover is a model of clarity, making difficult subjects accessible to the common reader.

By performing this alchemy for four decades, Isaac Asimov has become an oracle, particularly in the world of science. These are, after all, the Years When the Earth Talked Back, and long before the politicians, he was listening. Today readers search works like *The Intelligent Man's Guide to Science* and *Today and Tomorrow and . . .* for advice on space programs and the greenhouse effect. Many of them go directly to the source with their questions. If Asimov has respect for the interrogators, he answers thoughtfully, in detail. If not, he has a habit of assuming an abstracted, extraterrestrial manner, as if he had a lunch date on the other side of time.

Asimov is all too frequently barraged by those who confuse Shirley MacLaine's utterances with thought. The interrogations have to do with UFOs, alien visitors, astrological predictions and the healing power of crystals. "Cab drivers mostly," he says, "and passersby. I guess these are what causes them to recognize me." The term these refers to a pair of voluminous sideburns, and they make it impossible to mistake the wearer for anyone else, except possibly Martin Van Buren, the eighth President of the U.S. New Age inquisitors remain one of the few puzzles Asimov is unable to crack: "I have never found a way to convince them. They tell me there is 'absolute proof' of aliens landing on this planet. They read it with their own eyes. It turns out they read it at the supermarket checkout counter, trying to escape from reality."

This impatience with pseudo science began some 60 years ago, when little Isaac fell in love with facts. He was introduced to the world of information in his parents' Brooklyn candy store. The Asimovs were culturally ambitious Jewish immigrants from Russia, where their son was born, and the boy made a habit of devouring magazines as soon as they were put in the rack. "So that the publications could be sold later without looking used," he recalls, "I read them with a very light hand. When I was through, they would close as neatly as though they had never been read. To this day I read the *New York Times* that way. When I am through, you will not be able to tell that it has been in any way disturbed."

The same light hand is evident in the thousands of books that fill his apartment near Central Park. From his 33rd-floor aerie, he and his second wife Janet, a retired psychiatrist, overlook the city they seldom leave. The proof of Asimov's immobility lies in the terrace situated some 40 ft. from his study. Janet tends the little garden. Incredibly, he has never set foot on the terrace, for the man whose *Foundation Trilogy* centers on a Galactic Empire and interplanetary voyages is terrified of heights. He has flown only once: "It was in the Army, and to refuse meant a court-martial." Acrophobia has its drawbacks: he does not visit foreign cities, or even many domestic ones. Fourteen honorary degrees have come his way; he has turned down many others because he hates to travel to any college or university beyond a 400-mile limit from New York City. But this unwillingness to venture far from the word processor also gives the explainaholic a few benefits: more work hours and more books. "My pace has increased through the years," he says."In the decade from 1950 to 1960, I wrote 32 books. From 1960 to 1970, I wrote 70; from 1970 to 1980, 109 books; and in the current decade, I wrote 192."

The first of those works was a futuristic novel called *Pebble in the Sky,* in 1950. "I presented a copy to my father," Asimov remembers. "I think it was then that he finally forgave me my failure to get into medical school ten years before." Actually, he *was* in medical school—Boston University School of Medicine—but as an instructor in biochemistry. The meager salary, plus payments for occasional sci-fi short stories, supported Asimov, his first wife and their son and daughter for ten years. It was then that he decided to break for New York City and a freelance career. But he retained his academic title, and he never really stopped being professorial. As he sees it, the unexamined life is not worth loving: "The moons of Saturn, the Bard of Avon, the mysteries of sex, the behavior of ancient societies—all have to be analyzed before they can be appreciated." Besides, Professor Asimov has a vision: "I believe that if there's such a thing as God's word, it's rationality, and I have the call to spread it."

Rationality means turning away from the siren lure of mysticism and confronting beautiful theories with ungainly facts. "The so-called New Age," he maintains, "is really a throwback to the early times when we believed in ogres and devils and monsters and evil fairies. We knew so little about the world that it seemed filled with intelligences superior to our own. Naturally, we lived in terror. But now we know so much about the whole universe. Now we can concentrate on real evils."

Such evils, for example, as the assumption that nations are separate unto themselves. Today all countries are interconnected despite their territorial claims, he argues, and "saying that the Japanese have a pollution problem is like saying there's a bad leak in your end of the boat." Of course, hundreds of futurists share that insight. Some of them, when pressed hard enough, may even present a solution or two. That is the Asimov difference: without prompting, he offers remedies by the ream. The man who predicted assembly-line robotics in 1939, coined the term *psychohistory*—"the prediction of future trends in history through mathematical analysis"—in 1941, and foresaw the computer revolution in 1950 not only faces tomorrow, he also embraces it.

An aging population? No problem. Put senior citizens back in college: "Under such conditions, accustomed to lifelong learning, why shouldn't they remain creative and innovative to very nearly the end of their lives?"

Dirty air? Look outside the window. There stands the most efficient antipollution device ever made: trees. "They absorb carbon monoxide and carbon dioxide and give out oxygen. What could be more desirable? And they look good in the bargain. Stop chopping down the rain forests and plant more saplings, and we're on our way."

The teeming earth? Simplicity itself: "Colonize the moon. Build space stations. Then go on to populate Mars and the other planets. There is unlimited solar energy out there, and a plethora of minerals and acres of land. Going into the galaxy is not nearly so fantastic as it seems. We are already more informed about outer space than the early explorers ever were about oceans they sailed on or the lands they discovered."

Ebullience does not mean blindness. Asimov is alarmed by overpopulation, with its insatiable demand for natural resources. He is not sanguine about the medical establishment's inability to find a cure for AIDS: "It may just burn itself out the way the bubonic plague did in the London of 1665. But this tragic disease moves much more slowly. It might take a century to disappear." And wars and weapons continually remind him about the fragility of Spaceship Earth. But in the Asimovian view, that fragility is an echo of his personal history. He was felled by a heart attack in 1977 and underwent a triple coronary bypass in 1983. Manners and habits changed overnight. Although he had a great appetite for high-cholesterol foods and no taste for exercise, he bought a machine that demands the efforts of cross-country skiing. Week by week, he worked himself into shape. En route he totally altered his diet and dropped 50 lbs. If he could overcome his nearly fatal difficulties, Asimov reasons, why can't the world do the same? Solipsistic, perhaps, but plausible. "A hundred years ago," he reminds skeptics, "95% of the labor force was involved in food production or distribution. Experts predicted that once the farms went, the world would be put out of work. If you had told them that in the next century their descendants would be, say, flight attendants or television cameramen, they would have thought you were crazy. The future is full of impossible possibilities. The irony is, those who predict it best are the historians."

So those are the ones Isaac Asimov is currently studying, seated at his TRS 80, beginning the long trek to Opus 500. Working in his customary routine from 7 A.M. to evening, he will pursue a science fiction novel, provisionally titled *Nemesis;* a "rather large history of science"; a collection of columns for *Fantasy & Science Fiction* magazine; and a collaboration with wife Janet on a children's book about Norby, the friendly robot. Every so often, he and Janet will saunter downtown for a look at some Fifth Avenue shopwindows. Royalties and lecture fees bring in a high-six-figure income; the Asimovs can indulge themselves. "And we will," Isaac says, taking his wife's hand. "We've done enough work for now. Today we'll try something different. Today we'll charge into Doubleday's and buy somebody else's books."

CONSIDER . . .

1. What does *protean* mean? How does this word in Kanfer's title set the view or establish the dominant impression of Isaac Asimov?
2. Find other words or word clusters that relate to *protean.* Circle or highlight them. How would you describe the function of these words and phrases? How do they help to keep the dominant impression before the reader?
3. Find a place where Kanfer backtracks or gives historical background on Asimov. Why does Kanfer include this background? How does he integrate it with the dominant impression he is creating?
4. Can you find a place where Kanfer seems to diverge from the dominant impression? Why do you think he chooses to include this information?

Uncle Chul Gets Rich

CHANG-RAE LEE

My father's youngest brother, Uncle Chul, shared the Lees' famously bad reaction to liquor, which was to turn beet-red in the face, grow dizzy and finally get sick. In spite of this, he was always happy to stay up late at family gatherings. After a few Scotches he would really loosen up, and, with the notable exception of my mother, we all appreciated his rough language and racy stories. Only when Mother came in from the kitchen would his talk soften, for he knew he had always fallen short in her eyes. If they were ever alone together, say in the kitchen, after dinner, he would use the most decorous voice in asking for a glass or a fresh bucket of ice, and even offer to help load the dishwasher or run an errand to the store.

On one of those nights we sped off, both happy for a break in the long evening. He asked me about school, what sports I was playing, but the conversation inevitably turned toward my parents, and particularly my mother—how much she had invested in me, that I was her great hope. I thought it was odd that he was speaking this way, like my other relatives, and I answered with some criticism of her—that she was too anxious and overbearing. He stared at me and, with a hard solemnity I had not heard from him before, said that my mother was one of the finest people one could ever know. He kept a grip on the wheel and in the ensuing quiet of the drive I could sense how he must have both admired and despised her. In many respects, my mother was an unrelenting woman. She tended to measure people by the mark of a few principles of conduct: ask no help from anyone, always plan for the long run and practice (her own variation of) the golden rule, which was to treat others much better than oneself.

In her mind, Uncle Chul sorely lacked on all these accounts. In the weeks following our drive, my father would be deciding whether to lend him $10,000 to start a business. As always after dinner, my parents sat in the kitchen (the scent of sesame oil and pickled vegetables still in the air) and spoke in Korean, under the light of a fluorescent ring. My mother, in many ways the director of the family, questioned my uncle's character and will. Hadn't he performed poorly in school, failed to finish college? Hadn't he spent most of his youth perfecting his skills as a black belt in taekwondo and his billiards game? Wasn't he a gambler in spirit?

My father could defend him only weakly. Uncle Chul had a history of working hard only when reward was well within sight, like cash piled high on the end of a pool table. His older brothers were all respected professionals and academics. My father was a doctor, a psychiatrist who had taught himself English in order to practice in America. Uncle Chul had left Korea after a series of failed ventures and odd jobs, and found himself broke with a wife and new baby. How valuable were his taekwondo trophies now? What could he possibly do in this country?

My parents argued fiercely and my father left the kitchen. But as was my mother's way, she kept on pushing her side of the issue, thinking aloud. My father was throwing away his hard-earned money on the naïve wish that his little brother had magically changed. Uncle Chul was a poor risk and even now was complaining about his present job, hauling and cleaning produce for a greengrocer in Flushing. He would get to the store at 4 A.M. to prepare vegetables for the day's selling. While he shared a sofa bed with his nephew in his older brother's tiny apartment, his wife and infant daughter were still in Seoul, waiting for him to make enough money to send for them.

But his wages were only $250 a week for 70 hours of work and he loathed the job, the brutal effort that went into clearing a few cents a carrot, a quarter a soda, the niggling, daily accrual. The owners themselves would toil like slaves to see a till full of tattered ones and fives at day's end.

I knew Uncle Chul craved the big score, the quick hit, a rain of cash. For the very reasons my mother had so little faith in him—his brashness, his flagrant ambitions—I admired him. Over Scotch and rice crackers, he would tell my father about the millions he was going to make by moving merchandise wholesale, in bigger-ticket items with decent margins. He would never touch another orange again. I remember my father absently nodding his head at each vague and grandiose idea, probably hearing my mother's harangues.

The other men in my father's family were thick-lensed scribblers who worked through their days from A to Z, assiduously removing uncertainty by paying close attention to the thousand details of each passing hour. My father worked long days at the hospital, and spent weekends poring over volumes of Freud and Rank and Erikson in his second language, to "catch up" with the American doctors. When my father decided to lend Uncle Chul the $10,000, making it clear that no further discussion was needed, my mother transferred her worrying energy squarely onto me. It seemed no accident that her latest criticism was that I was "always looking for the easy way." I had, in fact, been feeling moody and rebellious, weary of being a good student and a good boy. I was in the eighth grade, and my friends were beginning to drink beer and smoke pot. I secretly resolved to join them.

I was also taking solo train trips from Pleasantville, N.Y., down to the city to visit my older cousins on the weekends, prompting questions from my mother about what kind of fun we were having. I didn't tell her that what thrilled me most was riding the elevated trains between Flushing and Grand Central, shuttling back and forth with the multitude. My newcomer's heart was fearful and enthralled, and I naïvely thought Uncle Chul felt the same way. He had quit working for the greengrocer after getting the money, and brought over his wife and child. He was busy scouting out stores for his first business in America.

But Uncle Chul found that the leases for even the smallest stores were $4,000 a month, and he seemed tense and even a little scared. I felt a strange pang of guilt because of the extra pressure on him—the $10,000 and the tenuous faith behind it. The only thing worse than losing the money was what my mother would never have to mention again: that he started working a little too late.

But he did find a store, in the Bronx, and we drove down one Sunday to see it in all its new glory. It seemed as if half the tenement buildings on the block were burned out or deserted, and the sidewalks were littered with garbage, broken glass and the rubble of bricks and mortar. My father pulled up behind Uncle Chul's car and we peered out to see if we had the right address. The shop couldn't have been more than eight feet wide. A single foot-wide corridor running its length was lined with accessories, odd-lot handbags and tie clips and lighters; the stuff hung on plastic grids on the walls and overhead. In the back, there was a hot plate on the floor, two stools and a carton of instant ramen noodles.

Uncle Chul proudly showed us the merchandise and, from a glass display box, gave me a watch; my sister got a faux-pearl necklace. A customer peered in but waved her hand and scurried away. My mother said that we were disturbing the business, and after a rush of bows and goodbyes we were in the car, heading back to Westchester.

Uncle Chul had no choice but to be in that neighborhood, in that quarter-size store, with the risk of crime and no insurance. The trade-off was the low rent, and it soon became clear that he had made an excellent choice. With little competition on the block, the money started coming in, and soon he moved to a larger store nearby, and then moved again. His volume and cash flow surged, and after selling each successive business, he staked his profit on the next store.

We didn't see him much during this time, but when we did he made sure to show off his success to my parents. My aunt wore designer clothes, and Uncle Chul sported a fat gold Rolex. If we were out somewhere, he would casually pull out a rolled wad of $100's when a check arrived, proclaiming affably to his brothers that it was his turn to pay.

But I noticed, too, that he and my aunt looked haggard and pressed. They spoke hurriedly and ate as quickly as they could. My mother would say something like, "You've developed such expensive tastes," and tell him that he was still frittering away his money on useless luxuries.

When Uncle Chul amassed the war chest he needed to open the wholesale business he had hoped for, he moved away from New York. He had heard of opportunities in Texas, where goods could be imported across the border and sold at big profits. Within a few years he had more than 50 people working for him, selling, by containers and truckloads, the same purses and belts he started with years before.

He bought a sprawling ranch house, brand-new and fitted with jet-action bathtubs and wide-screen televisions. He hired a team of Mexican maids to keep the place running. He traded in his Cadillacs for BMW's and sent his daughters to private school. One summer he paid my sister outrageous wages to sit in his air-conditioned office and practice her Spanish with the retailers. The business was on automatic pilot—effortless. Uncle Chul was now a millionaire several times over, richer than all his brothers combined.

I spent time with him again years later, when my mother became terminally ill. He visited regularly, always bearing gifts for the family. To me, he simply gave money. He knew I had quit my first job to become a writer, which meant little to him, except that I would be poor forever. Maybe, someday, my name would be famous, and he invested in that possibility, slipping me a couple of $100's when my mother wasn't looking. He did this naturally, with an ease and power in his grip full of cash. His money was like a weight outside his body, which he could press upon others, like me. But in my mother's presence, his swagger vanished, and he was just Uncle Chul again, prodigal and bereft.

He was especially solemn on the day of her funeral. Of the many people who made their way to the cemetery and later to the house, I suspect Uncle Chul knew he was among those she would be most closely watching. My mother's friends had brought food and electric rice cookers and the men were in the living room, drinking companionably, speaking in low voices. My mother had been dying for nearly two years, and now that it was over waves of exhaustion and relief were washing over everyone in the house.

I remember Uncle Chul padding softly about the house, wary of disturbing even the layer of dust on her furniture. He was speaking in a soft register, his voice faltering, like a nervous young minister on his first encounter with the bereaved. He was nodding and bowing, even helping the ladies gather cups and plates, exercising until the last visitor left a younger brother's respect and obedience to the family and the dead.

In the Korean tradition, mourners brought offerings of money, all token amounts, except for Uncle Chul's fat envelope, which held thousands of dollars. He would have given more, he said, but his wholesale business wasn't doing so well anymore. I knew that wasn't the real reason. He must have known what my mother would have said, perhaps was telling him now—that he couldn't help but be the flashy one again.

CONSIDER . . .

1. What is the dominant impression you get of Uncle Chul? When does Lee begin to establish this impression?
2. What aspect of Chul's life would you say is being profiled?
3. What seems to be the source of the writer's fascination with the character of his uncle? Cite details to support your response.

Three Studies of Places

These three pieces focus on places. "Vanished" is William Finnegan's *New Yorker* study of Port Arthur, Texas and one of its most famous former residents, Janis Joplin. Cesni Gulen's "Istanbul Covered Market" describes the ebullience and energy of an exotic place, and "A Day at O'Rear's" by Julie Franzmeier chronicles a day in the life of a bakery.

Vanished

WILLIAM FINNEGAN

A lot of people seem to come from Port Arthur, Texas—Robert Rauschenberg, Janis Joplin, Johnny Winter, Tex Ritter, just to name some of the best known. Traffic in the other direction must have been mighty sparse. That was our first thought, anyway, when we rolled into downtown Port Arthur recently. It was the middle of a sunny Friday afternoon, and the city was totally deserted. For block after silent, crumbling block, we saw no man, beast, or going concern. The stoplights would have made as much sense blinking in the Sahara. To call downtown Port Arthur depressed would be like calling the surface of the sun warm. Our destination was a former industrial laundry where we had heard that a sculptor named Doug Clark lived and worked. The address turned out to be an oasis, with a great Chinese tallow tree and bright, thriving grass behind an ancient iron fence, and half a dozen people welding and sandblasting and puttering in the shadowy depths of a foundry. Doug Clark himself— an affable, sturdy-shouldered man of about forty—claimed to be happy to show a visitor around. Of the neighborhood he said, "Some people think I'm nuts to be here, but, really, at night it's like being way, way out in the country."

Mr. Clark grew up on a Gulf Coast rice farm, and later had his own rice farm, until a couple of shifts in the Department of Agriculture's attitude toward domestic rice production effectively deeded his farm to the government. "But that's O.K.," he said evenly. "Art is better, ultimately." He usually works on commission, he ex- plained, so he didn't have much finished sculpture around. But he had a lot of pieces in progress, from tiny clay maquettes to monumental bronze figures, ranged like preoccupied hosts along the route of our tour through the foundry.

It would be an exaggeration to say that we understood everything Mr. Clark told us about wax molds, crucibles, sprues, sand, and the mineralogical qualities of bronze. But we did begin to grasp some of the economics of making art in Port Arthur after he mentioned that he had bought a pleasant, four-bedroom house near downtown for forty-five hundred dollars. He wasn't able yet to earn a living from his sculpture, he said, and still had to work for a local shipyard. But the shipyard's owner, as luck would have it, liked his work and had become his patron, and that had freed him to spend most of his time sculpting. And the commissions were rolling in. His big project of the moment was a nineteen-foot alligator for the local Museum of the Gulf Coast. It was supposed to be a replica of the largest Gulf Coast gator on record. Mr. Clark had somebody out looking for models, and as we were finishing our tour that person appeared. It was Patrick Lowry, Mr. Clark's foundryman, back from his researches. He'd found an alligator farm that was perfect, he said. There were lots of live gators, and a sixteen-foot stuffed gator with a ten-point buck in his mouth. Mr. Clark's eyes glittered.

To see the Janis Joplin Memorial, one of Mr. Clark's more celebrated pieces, we had to go over to the Port Arthur public library. Riding through the city in his van, we were stunned again by Port Arthur's emptiness. A few public buildings—a school, the library—stood surrounded by acres of space. The buildings looked like restored ruins from a vanished civilization. Some downtown blocks were still cov- ered with abandoned buildings or rubble—Mr. Clark pointed out a large commercial building in fairly good condition and said, "They'd be happy to get ten thousand dol- lars for that"—but other blocks looked like pristine parkland. There wasn't even any litter. "Nothing to throw away, and nobody to throw it," Mr. Clark said. The Janis Joplin Memorial turned out to be a group of five busts of the singer; in the largest, she is belting her lungs out, head thrown back, microphone in hand. Her husk of a home town, we thought, was like the remains of some world-ending binge.

What happened? White flight from school integration. The crash of the oil business. A major blow, Mr. Clark said, came with the election of a Baptist sheriff, who shut down one of the city's few flourishing industries: a red-light district that catered to sailors and roughnecks and oilmen. Mr. Clark offered to show us Sabine Pass, a small town south of Port Arthur. We drove through a ramshackle neighborhood, and then through a vast oil refinery, and then through wide salt marshes, where egrets perched on fence posts. At Sabine Pass, we found a fleet of shrimp boats—nearly all of them now owned by Vietnamese, Mr. Clark said—and a regiment of offshore oil rigs, standing mothballed in the shallows of the Sabine River. Looking up at the silent, rusting rigs from the riverbank, we felt as if we had wandered into a graveyard for sci-fi monsters. The rigs were gargantuan. They are also fantastically expensive, Mr. Clark told us. And when there was no immediate prospect of their operating profitably their owners often had them cut up for scrap. "Which is what a lot of them are doing right now," he added.

We wanted a postcard. Mr. Clark thought awhile, then drove us back to Port Arthur and deposited us before what he said was probably the only cache of picture postcards still locally available. It was a revolving rack full of small, stiff, yellowing cards showing a sunny, sleepy, well-built city prowled by dark-green Chevrolets. The cards were being sold by a tall, slim Vietnamese man with a graying ponytail, who sat behind a counter smoking a cigarette through a holder. His shop was huge, dusty, and bare. On long pea-green shelves single copies of pornographic magazines were placed every few feet, their covers curling. We bought postcards showing the library, the high school, and three laughing women on water skis.

There was one more thing we had to see, Mr. Clark said: the Pompeiian Villa, the pride of the Port Arthur Historical Society. Built in 1900 by a barbed-wire tycoon from Illinois, the villa is a careful copy of a typical pre-cataclysm Pompeiian home. It has eleven rooms, which form a U around a three-sided courtyard, or peristyle. Mary Crowder, an exuberant woman in her early sixties, was on hand to show us around. The barbed-wire tycoon had brought his wife down from Illinois, Ms. Crowder told us, but when they arrived she refused to get out of her carriage. "She refused *twice*," Ms. Crowder said. "She was afraid of mosquitoes. So she never set foot in the house, and her husband turned it into a hunting lodge." We were invited to admire paintings, chandeliers, an eighteenth-century diamond-dust mirror, a Hepplewhite chest of drawers, and a magnificent old Scottish piano. The single most valuable furnishing in the villa, Ms. Crowder said, was the antique Kashan rug in the living room. "Supposedly, it has a flaw," she said. "So that's what we do on rainy days: look for the flaw."

CONSIDER . . .

1. What notes do you think the writer might have made to prepare for drafting this piece? Point out several very specific details that could have been in the invention notes for this piece.
2. What is the dominant impression of Port Arthur, Texas, in this essay?
3. How does the title help to create the dominant impression?

4. Cite at least five specific words or phrases that contribute to the dominant impression and create coherence.
5. What connections do you see between the way Port Arthur is characterized and Janis Joplin?

Istanbul Covered Market

Cesni Gulen

Everyone has undoubtedly wondered about the mystery and adventure the Istanbul Covered Market has to offer. Internationally famous, this bazaar offers everything money can buy. Continually bustling, noisy and aggressive, the Istanbul Covered Market is a sensation.

The main area of entrance to the Market is near a big mosque continually surrounded by pigeons and people feeding them. Around these pigeons are men and boys selling trinkets, tops, lighters, gum, nuts, water, miniature mosques—you name it. Proceeding through these ambulatory vendors are the narrow, entwined streets typical of the bazaar. Tables of fruits and vegetables of all kinds such as figs, peaches, strawberries, berries, peppers, eggplant etc. are lined up right next to each other. The merchants try to deceive the customers by putting the ripest fruit for show but selling the rotten ones to them. The competition is fierce: Price wars, yelling wars and display wars can make or break a business. This section is full of lost-looking tourists and old holy men wearing white robes, carrying canes and sporting long grey and white unkempt beards. Conservative village women wearing baggy cotton print pants and scarves about their heads shop side by side with the wealthy city women wearing Western clothes and a lot of gold. Young children, full of the life of the bazaar, run around laughing. Teenagers on mopeds, horses and even a lost taxi or two beep and push their way through the market. Every imaginable type of person is found in the outdoor fruit and vegetable areas.

Closer to the market, the brick roads elevate and divide to create a complex maze of roads which all lead to other sections of the market. A visitor is struck by the vastness and history of the place. The bazaar has been around for a couple of centuries—one can tell this from the feeling of age in the air, the ancient columns, the mosaic tiles and writings, the simple dirt floors. It is a very great feeling knowing that the market has such a history.

On both sides of the indoor market are stores, some no larger than a closet, that are set *right* next to each other. Each store displays their wares by hanging them on the door or walls, anything from cheap shoes and dresses to expensive pottery, jewelry, purses, bronze and silver vases. Owners sit outside their stores, sipping tea and watching the crowd. One thing characteristic of all owners is their vocal advertisements: "Come, this is the store you need to look" in broken English, or "Welcome, Madame" in

French, German and English. There is absolutely *no* end to being pestered by these overambitious, aggressive merchants. No outwitting them, either.

Men carry bundles so huge, wide and heavy that they are bent over and barely can be seen under their enormous load. They just walk to their usual destination, beeping with their mouths, never bothering to look ahead on their path. Managing to jump out of their way on the crowded compact streets leads only to an inevitable spiel by a store owner who desperately tries to sell his items. Men carry huge, traditional canisters, with bells on them and brightly colored beads and stones to ward off evil; these often four-foot water canisters are a sight. Dirty, hunched, poorly clothed in ragged clothes, poverty-stricken women meekly saunter up to tourists and beg them to buy a fan from them. Foreign tourists get caught up in the emotional aspects of a poor woman who desperately needs money and the aggressive owners who continually eye them. Nevertheless, tourists enjoy the scene.

The true essence of the bazaar still awaits, for all the scenes previously described have taken place outdoors. The lighting decreases dramatically as the halls of the covered part are entered. The ceilings are extremely high, the lighting hazy yellow–white. The bazaar has many entrances; this particular one happens to be the spice area. The comforting, pleasing scents of calm chamomile, pecan, cashew, spices of all kinds float enticingly about. The stores have piled colorful green, red and yellow spices into perfect pyramids in their big barrels. Past the spices, the market turns in four directions. One of the paths leads into an area with beautiful walls covered with ancient tiles with Arabic writing. A fountain, shaped like a circle with layers on top of each other, offers water for the thirsty and religious cleansing for the devout who must wash up before their prayers. Jewelry is the main item in this section. Windows display rich gold and silver earrings, bracelets, necklaces, belts, vases—some hundreds of years old! The jewelry is over-priced, as are all the products in the bazaar. Experienced Turkish shoppers know the market is overpriced and dicker with the store owners and bargain with them over the price of something. Price bargaining is really a popular "sport" in the market and Turkey.

Storekeepers yell out "Come in, please!" or "May I help you?!" and smile innocently. There is a beautiful area that sells expensive, buttery-soft, exquisitely colored leathers: shoes, slippers, clothes, coats, designer accessories. The clothes section is an array of extremely diverse and well-supplied stores. The constant movement of tourists, messengers and tea boys adds to the initial confusion of where to look first.

Carpets, those oriental flying carpets. Beautiful, painstakingly detailed by hand, the carpets are rolled out and left on the ground or hung up on the walls to show off their incredible beauty. Some of these carpets are extremely large, while others are small as doormats. Bronze, copper and mosaic pots, each shined to its brightest, are hung from the ceiling in the stores that are selling them. Ancient samovars (teapots) are on display, shelf after shelf, side by side, in many different colors, shapes and sizes. The scene is quite overwhelming and breathtaking. There is a very deep and ancestral air in these parts. Due to this fact of culture, fast-food places are not common in the market—it's purely traditional.

Once filled with all the images the bazaar has to offer, one is definitely captivated by the ancient world. There is a tug at the heart for all the beautiful merchandise left behind. Outside of the market, though through a different exit, are innumerable stores selling perfumes, spoons, yarns, glasses, buttons. The Istanbul Covered Market has no borders, and will always overwhelm the shopper.

The Turkish Bazaar and Covered Market in Istanbul is an adventurer's dream. The bazaar is the meeting point of thousands of years of Turkish tradition and the modern world. This time-machine element of the market is what makes it so fascinating and a must to see.

CONSIDER . . .

1. What details stand out in your mind about the covered market? How do these details contribute to the dominant impression?
2. What two adjectives characterize the Istanbul market?
3. Suggest how Gulen might consider revising this piece.

A Day at O'Rear's
Julie Franzmeier

When most businesses close at five in the afternoon, there are no people working in them until nine the next morning—but not at O'Rear's Pastry Shop! At O'Rear's, work goes on at all hours; it takes a long time and quite a few people doing quite a few tasks to make pastries and breads.

At about midnight, every midnight before a business day, the bakers come in. "Ah . . . some day I'll git used to workin' nights and sleepin' daytimes," moans Skinner, who is over 70 years old and has been employed at O'Rear's for more than 25 years. "Now Dave, he's so young he can git used to anything," he continues as Dave walks in, wide awake of course because his friends have just dropped him off from their usual night on the town. Round-faced Kathy (the half-owner with her husband Mike) looks down at her list of pastries that need to be prepared and reads off, "Make half again as many glazed, blueberry, and chocolate doughnuts. We have so many orders and it's a football Saturday." Then she turns around to start the ovens and get the mixers ready for the cake ingredients that Nathan has quietly been getting ready. Shoulder steady and hips swaying, Nathan brings his already weighed and measured ingredients to the mixers. These mixers are not like everyday kitchen mixers; they stand over five feet tall, and the bowls are so big that you can't fit your arms around them. Efficiently yet with a flourish, Nathan pours in his ingredients and looks pleased after doing so. And so it goes until four o'clock. The four pastry bakers work systematically, then they clock out without wasting time; they want to get home and get a good day's sleep.

O'Rear's is quiet for about an hour and a half. At five-thirty, Mike, Betty, and Susanna walk in, turn on the lights, and start to get things ready for the early morning customers. "Susanna honey, will you run downstairs to get me some extra trays? Your legs are so much younger than mine," Betty whines while just standing around. Betty is only about fifty, but she's really old at heart, and her heaviness really cripples her. New at the job, Susanna doesn't answer; she just does what she is told. At six o'clock, O'Rear's opens and Betty and Susanna wait on the early morning customers—as Mike keeps things going in the back, baking doughnuts and applying glazes and toppings.

Wilma and Mary Lou come in around eight o'clock to start decorating cakes. "Let's put on some good ole country music," Wilma says in her usual cheery voice.

"How many orders we got today, Mike?" Mary Lou asks.

"Oh, about the usual—you won't have to be here much past noon."

"Hey, that's what we like to hear, idn't it, Wilma?" They start to decorate cakes while comparing what they grow in their gardens. This crew works hard until about noon.

At twelve, Leslie, Storie, and I go in. "The Saturday Afternoon Girls are here; we can go home now," Betty says as she's clocking out. Everyone else stays to help clean up the morning mess before they leave us with the bakery all to ourselves.

"We're leaving now; you girls can change the radio station," Wilma laughs. Even though there is a generation gap between the two groups of workers, we enjoy each other's company for the half-hour that we need to be together. The three of us wait on customers, clean up, and close about 6:00. O'Rear's is quiet, but only until midnight.

CONSIDER . . .

1. How does Franzmeier arrange the description of the place? What is the organizing principle? What categories do you think her invention chart might have used?
2. What is the dominant impression of O'Rear's?
3. How do the descriptions of the employees of O'Rear's contribute to the dominant impression?

5

Reading, Writing, and Analysis

Creativity requires a continuity of concern, an intense awareness of one's active inner life combined with sensitivity to the external world.

—Vera John-Steiner

The real academic job is to absorb an idea, to put it into perspective along with other ideas, not to dilute it to lingo.

—Robert Penn Warren

Writing comes from many places—from our experiences, our observations, our imaginations, our readings and conversations. Analytic essays draw on all these sources to explain why something happens, to account for *causes* or *effects* of some phenomenon. This chapter gives you experience in working with three kinds or genres of analytic writing: a dialogue journal, an analysis, and a literary study.

PERSONAL WRITING: DIALOGUE JOURNAL

A dialogue journal is a two-sided, two-voiced journal where writers exchange ideas, impressions, and opinions and reflect on the meaning of a shared experience, whether that is a book both writers have read, a play both have attended, or a class or internship both have taken. The key is dialogue: more than one voice. These voices may be your voice and that of a classmate, friend, or instructor. Frequently dialogue journals are personal writing, voluntarily undertaken to explore an experience. Sometimes dialogue journals are assigned as a way of encouraging the exploration of a text or a subject. When the dialogue journal is assigned, your instructor may get you going with a prompt—a provocative question or topic. You will find that once you and your dialogue partner begin thinking and writing together, you will have plenty of your own ideas.

Advice for Your Dialogue Journal

The dialogue journal can be a rich exploration that can provide fertile ground for writing larger, more formal pieces. It may be an important prologue to a deepening of your intellectual growth and development. It can give you an opportunity to explore ideas, to experience genuine and thoughtful dialogue, and to try out different voices and attitudes on paper. And the suggestions that follow may make your experience with a dialogue journal more worthwhile.

- **Focus on ideas** rather than on expression. Because you are conscious of another immediate reader, you may be distracted by a desire to make your style and your presentation cleaner or more elegant than if you were writing just for yourself. Don't be. Remember that ideas are the important thing. Time to correct spelling errors or smooth a phrase may steal valuable thinking time. Consult with your writing partner. Agree to be decidedly casual in your presentations. Agree that spelling errors, sentence fragments, and ill-formed sentences *are not* important. Agree that good ideas and an easy exchange *are* important.
- **Be honest.** If you are struggling with a text or don't understand a certain passage or cannot figure out why a novel is set in Rangoon, say so. Part of the purpose of a dialogue journal is to enhance your problem-solving skills; but if you never admit to encountering problems, you will never improve your problem-solving abilities. The intellectual conversation may indeed help you work through some difficult issues or concepts. Or you and your partner may have widely differing abilities—and in that case, each of you can help the other over the rough spots.
- **Be sincere.** Offer opinions and ideas that originate in your true feelings. Don't write what you think will flatter your partner, your instructor, or the author(s) of the works you are studying. The authors will probably never know what you really think and are likely to be impervious to readers' opinions anyway. Your instructor knows that intellectual discourse thrives on healthy differences of opinion and fosters that discourse with dialogue journals and discussions. Tolerate others' ideas; give them space and serious consideration. In the end you don't, of course, have to accept the ideas of others; but it can't hurt to consider them.
- **Allow time** for this endeavor. You and your partner should agree on a time limit for responding to one another. Provide enough time for thought and reflection but not so much that your exchange loses spontaneity and freshness. Factor in class requirements. Determine how and how often you will exchange the journal—unless of course you are keeping an electronic dialogue journal via e-mail.

Here are some ideas for ways to respond to fiction, nonfiction, film, or discussion.

- Write about what pleases you, or irritates you, and why.
- Write about the emotions you experience, how you feel as you read.

- Write about the counterfactual—what could or might have happened but did not—and about what is revealed by examining the counterfactual.
- Write about what you think of the characters (or of any feature of the text)—which ones you like, which ones you despise, which ones you just don't understand.
- Write about what you think of the author's style.
- Write about what you observe about yourself as a reader—how you read.
- Write about issues in the text that are unresolved and questions you would like to ask the author.

Reading a Dialogue Journal

Here is an excerpt from Erin Wilson's dialogue journal. Wilson's class had been studying *Hamlet*, and the instructor posed the question, "What have you learned that is useful for your life from reading *Hamlet?*" Wilson's correspondent is one of her classmates, Passie Hinden.

Excerpts from Dialogue Journal

Erin Wilson	Passie Hinden
Whether reading silently in the quiet recess of my room or in a heated and chaotic discussion in class, I have found that my study of *Hamlet* has taught me many things. It has given me insights into the world around me and insights into myself and those I am directly involved with regularly as well as insights into the text itself.	
Many themes from *Hamlet* apply not only to Shakespeare's world but to our world today. The vagueness of any distinction between sanity and insanity is certainly apparent in the current judicial system where thousands of cases a year are judged "not guilty by reason of insanity" and many more accused criminals plead such. Another theme our society shares with Elizabethan society is the conflict between social mores and education. In 1.2.46–47 Hamlet says "For there is nothing either good or bad but thinking makes it so." Not only does thinking "make it so," but it can	I've always felt weird about the insanity plea. If you are killed by an insane person, you are as dead as if you had been killed by a sane person. I think insanity ought to be a plea made at sentencing and that a trial should determine simply guilt or innocence. Insanity would then affect sentencing. What do you think?

also change it. Is it wrong to kill a man who has killed twelve others? Education in the form of philosophy throws a wrench in the smooth machinery of morals. A third theme that is especially apparent in our world is the reaction to the fall of our heroes. Seth Weingram mentioned this in class the other day.

This is a hard question. How do I know what I would do? I am for the death penalty myself. If you kill somebody, you should also lose your right to be alive.

In the world around me, I learned more about human nature and its quirks. *Hamlet* emphasizes that, in interpretations, as in life, there is no black or white, only slightly variant shades of gray. I was, though, surprised to learn of the magnitude of "ego types" who insisted—backed by no evidence—that Ophelia had "wronged" Hamlet.

I know! Isn't it incredible how some people can be blind to what seems so obvious to others? We know the truth—a truth, I mean! Is there one? What did you really get out of this play?

I'm not sure if there is a truth, but the most important thing I learned goes under education in the traditional sense of the word. I learned to read carefully and slowly to get more than a plot from my time. I found beautiful imagery such as the garden imagery and the many references to corruption. I found deeper meaning such as the double (sexual) connotations of many words. I found real beauty in the text.

Every time I read Shakespeare I find more, too. *That* is the genius of Shakespeare. Have you read *Lear* yet?

In the next installment, Wilson and Hinden may pick up this discussion and continue to reflect on *Hamlet.* Or they may shift to an entirely new topic.

CONSIDER . . .

1. What kinds of things does Wilson write about/respond to?
2. What is the nature of Hinden's responses? How would you describe them? Would you respond differently to Wilson? What kinds of things would you key in on in Wilson's commentary?

Examining an E-Mail Conversation

Another kind of thoughtful conversation frequently occurs in cyberspace, in listserv communication. A *listserv* or electronic study group (ESG) is a group of conversants, electronically connected; if you post a message to the list, it goes out to many people—perhaps, in the case of large lists, thousands of people. Your instructor may arrange for you to be part of an ESG. The ESG functions like a conversation. Someone (frequently the instructor, to begin) posts a prompt that continues a class discussion or that prepares the class for something to come. Then the recipients of the post or message respond to the prompt and carry on a conversation via e-mail.

Here is an expanded dialogue journal, an ESG conversation that took place at all times of the day and night during the course of a week. The first message is the prompt from the instructor; after that, the students take over.

Writing As Free Fall

Date: Mon, 21 Oct 199- 20: 53: 03
From: Beth Burch <bburch@BINGHAMTON.EDU>
Reply-To: RHE-L Electronic Study Group
Subject: Writing As Free Fall

I've been thinking a lot this week about writing and editing and rewriting, so I share this from Allan Gurganus with you.

"Writing is a kind of free fall that you write, then go back and edit and shape. I think the best things that I've ever got as a writer come frequently all in a burst. You don't ask too many questions at the outset. You can analyze belatedly and retrospectively, but there's a kind of physiological sensation that happens when you are really on the trail of a story. When I'm working well, I wear a moving man's zip-up uniform because I perspire so freely that I sweat my way through the fiction. Finally the body is the ultimate testing ground of what works and what doesn't on the page."

Granted, not all of us may have the same kind of response to the act of writing as does Gurganus, but I find this very interesting. It suggests (actually, Gurganus is not suggesting but is quite explicit about this) that there is a very physical response to "cooking" as you write. Has anyone else ever experienced anything like this? What do you think about what Gurganus said?

Date: Mon, 21 Oct 199- 23: 47: 02
From: JelliFli <be17408@BINGHAMTON. EDU>
To: Beth Burch <bburch@BINGHAMTON. EDU>
Subject: Re: Writing As Free Fall

I agree with Gurganus that shaping and forming comes later. I think it is better to get everything out first; then it is simpler to go back and rearrange, correct, or delete part of what you wrote. But I do not wear a uniform that is specifically used for perspiring in.   —Pam

---

Date: Tue, 22 Oct 199- 08: 51: 58
From: bc709913@BINGHAMTON. EDU
To: Beth Burch <bburch@BINGHAMTON. EDU>
Subject: Re: Writing As Free Fall

I think Gurganus is entitled to his opinion. I have never tried to write a paper as "a kind of free fall" because to me that would be counterproductive. What happens when I "go back and edit and shape" the "free fall" and find out it's not what I want, then what? What did I accomplish by "free falling"? If you have the time to waste (spend) or if that method works for you, then you should go ahead and do it, but we should remember that what works for that writer might not work for every writer.

. . . . .From Trevor

Date: Tue, 22 Oct 199- 13: 03: 52
From: bd305521@BINGHAMTON. EDU
To: Beth Burch <bburch@BINGHAMTON. EDU>
Subject: Re: Writing As Free Fall

Hello, group.

Well, I do kind of "cook" as I write, but I've never sweated over it or worn a special jump-suit. I actually think wearing a writing "uniform" like that is a bit strange—but hey, whatever floats his boat.

I prefer a tee shirt, sweat pants, and warm slippers, as a general rule.

Have a wonderful day.

Rachel E

Date: Tue, 22 Oct 199- 15: 18: 09
From: bf20053@BINGHAMTON. EDU
To: Beth Burch <bburch@BINGHAMTON. EDU>
Subject: Re: Writing As Free Fall

hi there . . .

I can relate to the almost "physiological sensation" that Allan speaks of during writing—I don't sweat it out, however, but I think sometimes my pen does—you know when you've been writing for a long time really fast and you get that dent in your finger from the pen, and then the pen begins to ooze some gooey ink all over the page smearing the words? Well, anyway. . . . I agree with the process of getting it all out in one large draft, and then editing later on. I don't think it's a waste of time, I think the best, most natural and honest writing comes in one huge wave, and then you work on it from there.

I wonder who does his laundry.

Jessica

....

Date: Tue, 22 Oct 199- 20: 53: 03
From: scotty <br18111@BINGHAMTON. EDU>
To: Beth Burch <bburch@BINGHAMTON. EDU>
Subject: Re: Writing As Free Fall

Writing is like sex. (See me through this—I'll try not to be too blunt.) Starting off a writing project involves parts of nervousness, excitement, and anticipation. How will this turn out; will it be great; will I do well? In the process, a rhythm evolves. Sureness settles in and our confidence increases as we progress in our endeavor. As we reach the end of the event, our energies are focusing. Conclusion will be reached. Then the final moment. The last period is put on the page.

For some of us, reflection of our recent activity must occur immediately. Review, analysis, understanding. Once we have done this, then can we feel complete about our evening's action.

....

Date: Thu, 24 Oct 199- 00: 16: 40
From: Jelli Fli <be17408@BINGHAMTON. EDU
To: Beth Burch <bburch@BINGHAMTON. EDU>
Subject: Re: Writing As Free Fall

When I think of free-fall, I think of bungee jumping and it's scary to think that my writing is only being supported by a bungee cord. I would like to have more control over things than that. So now I'm not sure if I agree anymore.   —Pam

....

Date: Thu, 24 Oct 199- 01: 27: 38
From: Tracee Beroza <TraceeLB@BINGHAMTON. EDU>
To: Beth Burch <bburch@BINGHAMTON. EDU>
Subject: Re: Writing As Free Fall

I think if we are going to compare writing to a free fall, we have to remember that a free fall is a dangerous chance . . . for me, anything I write down is a dangerous chance.

There is never any true right or wrong, therefore chance takes a great part in the writing process. Since we have begun to make some silly parallels here, why not try the writing is a lot like streaking comparison? Think about it:

1. you set a goal/spot you will attempt to reach
2. you run naked . . . hence, you are vulnerable and completely exposed
3. you hope it will be a quick, painless and hopefully not too embarrassing an effort
4. you attempt to do it with grace and ease to get it over with. Also you hope not to trip!
5. upon reaching your goal, you may find a new meaning for life OR you may feel really stupid

Mind you, I don't ACTUALLY speak from experience here. Yes, I write but NO, I have not streaked. I just think they would be a lot alike. If any of you wants to try it, feel free and let me know if it really was like writing a paper :)

tracee

PS—if you will notice there would be no need for a "special writing suit" in this case! :)

....

Date: Thu, 24 Oct 199- 10: 50: 29
From: be613933@BINGHAMTON. EDU
To: Beth Burch <bburch@BINGHAMTON. EDU>
Subject: Re: Writing As Free Fall

I think Gurganus has serious problems. Yet the feeling of satisfaction I experience after writing something I am proud of could be equated with his experience. (Just on a different scale.) Responses of borderline heart attacks may require him to see a doctor.

Margaret Shoyinka

hey, did anyone read my letter in the *Pipe Dream*???? comment please (but only if you liked it, I'm sensitive)

....

Date: Thu, 24 Oct 199- 09: 54: 28
From: Rachel Rosen <be72940@BINGHAMTON. EDU>
To: Beth Burch <bburch@BINGHAMTON. EDU>
Subject: Re: Writing As Free Fall

hello

Writing is EXACTLY like free fall, but that's not the issue anymore—we've beaten that one to death. The issue now is our analysis papers. I think I'm going to try to answer

"Why are the weather and movies the standard topic for small talk?" What are you all writing about?

Good job Scott and Tracee for saying something bold—I appreciate it.

Rachel

****

CONSIDER . . .

1. Describe the initial responses to the Gurganus quotation. What specific parts of the Gurganus piece draw the most attention?
2. What are two or three important beliefs about writing that emerge from this conversation?
3. Respond to the prompt or to any posting in the conversation.

PUBLIC WRITING: ANALYSIS

An analysis draws on a variety of strategies (definition, comparison, contrast, narration) for a very precise purpose: An analysis answers the questions *why?* and *how?* It may begin with a situation and analyze how and why the situation occurred, or it may look at an event and speculate or predict what the effects of the event may be. The analytic essay concerns, above all, the notions of *cause and effect.*

Invention Ideas

To choose a subject for the analysis, ask yourself *why* and *how.* Why did the Civil War begin? Why have CDs become popular? Why did Chrysler Corporation develop the Stealth automobile? Why do dogs bark? All these questions invite you to explore *causes,* but you can also write an analysis that explores *effects* by asking yourself *how:* How has Project Head Start affected the educational system? How does the rain benefit crops? How does a water faucet work? You may also find that reading will help pique your imagination and give you ideas for writing.

Once you choose a question you would like to write about, brainstorm or freewrite to find out what you already know about the subject. When you have a clutch of notes reflecting what you know, organize your material before you draft; an analysis is by nature logical and well organized. Some writers find full formal outlines useful, but others feel constrained by them; do what makes you feel comfortable. At least, though, *think* about an order for your arguments. If you are explaining the causes why something is the way it is, begin with the effect or result first and then move to the causes. You may present causes in several different ways, but one very effective way is from least to most important cause or from minor to major causes or from least to most inclusive causes. In other words, you will be most effective if you end with your most important cause. Thus, an essay explaining how your friend got elected president of the student government association might be roughly outlined like this:

Cause 1: Jim is smart and thoughtful; he can make wise decisions.
Cause 2: Jim gets along well with peers and older adults (faculty, administration).
Cause 3: Jim had a good campaign manager and effective campaign ads.
Cause 4: Jim had the support and influence of his fraternity—and consequently, of the whole Greek system.

If you reason in the opposite direction and write about the effects of a given action or event, begin with the cause and then list the effects. The same principles apply with this ordering: You should arrange the list of effects so that they will have an impact on the reader. If you discuss the most important effect first, your reader may lose interest by the end of the essay. Here's a rough outline of how you might organize a cause–effect essay:

Cause: You lose your backpack and in it, your notebook and textbook.
Effect: You have to buy a new backpack at $35.95 because you don't have anything to carry your books in. This costs half an hour of your free time.
Effect: You have to buy new notebooks at $4.50 each and a new physics textbook, which alone costs $67.50. This takes half an hour.
Effect: You have to copy class notes from a classmate; this costs $7.70 in Xerox money and takes you one and a half hours.
Effect: You have to get a new university ID, which costs $5.00 and a twenty-five-minute wait.
Effect: You have to call the phone company to find out how much your bill (which was in your backpack) was and when it is due. This requires fifteen minutes.
Effect: You spent three hours ten minutes and $120.65 replacing your backpack and the items in it. This makes a significant dent in your budget, and either you have to call your parents to ask them to spring for your phone bill and electric bill, or you have to work more hours at your work–study job—and you need this time for studying.

Drafting an Analysis

No matter whether you write to explain the cause of some event or to explore the effects of some action, remember that an effect can become a cause—and vice versa. That you have to work extra hours to earn enough money to recoup the loss of your backpack (an *effect*) can become a *cause* for lower grades.

Once you conceptualize your analysis piece, draft it as quickly as you can, in one sitting if possible. The important thing to remember is to get the essay from inside your head onto the paper. Then you can let it cool for a while and eventually take another look at it.

As you draft and revise this analysis, remember the power of reading. You may be very knowledgeable about your subject, but even experts read and investigate their areas of expertise constantly to keep up to date. If your analysis feels thin and unsatisfying, satisfy your hunger for more information by reading and doing research (see Chapter 8 for help with doing research).

Keep in mind also that analysis can be a minefield, booby-trapped with all sorts of errors in logic that can destroy your essay. Here are some tips for avoiding the buried mines of logical errors:

1. **Look for more than one cause.** A terrorist may be motivated by more than political injustice; such other motives as anger against a father, loss of employment, gross personal insecurity, or desire for publicity may incite a person to terrorist acts.
2. **Don't confuse remote causes and immediate causes.** Some causes are so remote as to have no bearing on the problem being analyzed. If you are thinking about why you got measles at college, you could blame your illness on coming to college (after all, this event put you in the environment where you became ill)—but more immediate causes might be poor diet, lack of sleep, stress, and lack of immunization, as well as exposure to the measles virus.
3. **Be sure that the cause–effect link is actually possible.** If two people were home when a crystal vase was broken and one of them is a baby two months old, then it is not possible for the baby to grasp and drop the vase.
4. **Recognize time connections as different from causal ones.** If two events happen close in time, one is not necessarily caused by the other; indeed, there may be no relationship at all between them. If your brother moved to Los Angeles and then shortly thereafter divorced his wife, you might conclude that the move was a cause of the breakup. In reality, though, the two events may be totally unconnected.

Looking at Some Analytic Essays

In "Roots of Genocide," from *Time*, Andrew Purvis analyzes and explains why the Hutu and Tutsi peoples cannot live in peace in Africa. Notice how he explains the causes for their conflict both chronologically and historically.

Roots of Genocide

A N D R E W   P U R V I S

Images of women and children with their heads split open, of babies stacked in heaps, of limp corpses sprawled in doorways have become almost routine in this part of the world [Bujumbura, Burundi] in the past two years. The July 20 massacre of 330 Tutsi civilians in Burundi and subsequent Tutsi-led army coup are just the latest turns in a horrifying spiral of violence that has engulfed Rwanda, Burundi and eastern Zaïre in a conflict that often seems to defy explanation. Yet, like most wars, the struggle between Hutu and Tutsi is the product of unique influences that beat in the heart of each combatant as he sets about his deadly work.

When Belgium assumed control of the region in 1916, it was called Ruanda–Urundi, two kingdoms of similar ethnic makeup—some 85% Hutu, 14% Tutsi and 1% Twa. Under the rule of a godlike Tutsi King, unquestioned by all ethnic groups, each nation had achieved a measure of cohesion rare in Africa at the time. While Tutsi dominated society, intermarriage was common, Hutu and Tutsi spoke the same language, and each fought side by side in wars against neighboring kingdoms.

Like other colonists in Africa, the Belgians singled out one group to serve as their proxy. By independence, they had not only installed the Tutsi as an administrative over-class but also, thanks to the pseudoscientific theories favored at the time in the West, led them to believe they were biologically superior as well. This engendered a level of resentment previously unseen in the region. "Tutsi and Hutu have killed each other more to upbraid [sic] a vision they have of themselves and the others than for material interests," historian Gérard Prunier wrote in his account of the 1994 Rwandan holocaust. "That is what makes the killing so relentless."

Independence ushered in a new, bloodier era. With the dissolution of the monarchies and removal of an external Belgian military force, the struggle for power became more overtly ethnic at all levels of society. At this point, Rwanda and Burundi took different paths. In 1959 Rwandan Hutu launched a murderous uprising and forced the creation of a majority-controlled republic, which survived until 1994. In Burundi, by contrast, the Tutsi remained in control. Both armies were dominated by the ruling tribe and did not hesitate to suppress uprisings by the opposing ethnic group. Peasant revolts in Burundi in 1965, 1972 and 1988 were ruthlessly put down, in one case leading to the loss of 200,000 lives.

Ironically, diplomatic intervention in both countries in the early 1990s triggered the bloodiest massacres to date. A U.N.-backed campaign to secure power sharing for Rwanda's Tutsi minority provoked Hutu extremist politicians to conceive a plan that would rid the country of all Tutsi, even the young. To incite peasants into murdering their neighbors, Hutu leaders played on historical fears of a return to Tutsi hegemony and capitalized on a uniquely hierarchical social structure, in which peasants obey their chiefs however chilling the command. Competition for land in what has traditionally been Africa's most densely populated region further egged on the would-be killers. In three months of 1994, nearly a million civilians were butchered.

Burundi's current war has similarly tragic origins. In June 1993, the Tutsi government acceded to international pressure and held the country's first multiparty presidential elections. Hutu turned out in force and elected their first head of state, Melchior Ndadaye. Four months later, elements of the Tutsi military reacted by launching a coup, killing Ndadaye and triggering a bloodbath in which some 50,000 Hutu and Tutsi were slain.

The lesson learned throughout the region from the staggering death tolls, sums up one senior U.S. diplomat, is "if you don't strike first, you risk annihilation." That belief led to last week's military coup in Burundi. When the coalition government designed to protect the interests of both sides invited foreign military intervention last month to impose security as a prelude to all party talks, government figures were denounced as traitors at home by Hutu and Tutsi extremists alike. Both groups feared that the outside forces would help their enemies to victory and endanger their very existence.

Given those sentiments, the cycle of Hutu–Tutsi massacre and revenge seems unbreakable. Perhaps in time separate homelands can be created or power-sharing negotiations can once again take place. Until then, so long as Hutu and Tutsi are left to themselves, the killing will continue.

CONSIDER . . .

1. Early in the essay, how does Purvis dramatize the seriousness of the phenomenon he will analyze?
2. Chunk the major parts of the analysis. Use the transitions of time to help you find the major sections.

Now examine an analysis written by Zachary Armstrong, a thoroughbred horse trainer—and a student writer.

The Effects of Navicular Disease
Zachary Armstrong

Navicular disease in horses is one of the most serious problems facing horse owners today. This disease of the feet claims thousands of horses each year. Navicular disease affects the navicular bone, a tiny bone in the coffin joint of the ankle, which rests on a deep flexor tendon. Navicules will often begin as bursitis, or the drying of the bursa (fluid-filled sac) that lies between the navicular bone and the deep flexor tendon. This drying causes the navicular bone to deform. When weight is put on the deformed bone, great pain results.

Navicular disease affects a horse in a couple of different ways, the first being temporary spells of lameness. Inexplicably, the affected horse will appear fine one day and extremely lame the next. This sign is often seen in horses that have just developed the condition.

Another effect of the disease is that the horse will tend to favor the affected leg. This causes many problems for the horse and rider alike. The first problem to the rider will be the horse's sideways, shuffling, and often lazy or stumbling gait; this is caused by the horse's attempts to favor the affected leg.

This favoring of the affected heel will cause the feet to change shape. When the disease has reached this state, the heels will begin to contract and bruise. At this point the toes will start to grow in short, severe developments. When this condition is attained, the only thing left to do is to lay the horse up or rest the horse in a pasture where it can move about freely until the disease subsides.

Navicular disease had plagued horses and horsemen forever, but now there is an end in sight. Though no drugs or techniques have been put on the market, promising research is being done in the areas of esoxuprine hydrochloride, synovid, fluid transfers, and corrective shoeing. Maybe someday soon the memory of the number one cause of equine lameness will be left behind.

CONSIDER . . .

1. What is the cause that Armstrong will explore? How does he make the cause seem important?
2. What is the principle governing the presentation of effects in the essay?
3. Describe the intended audience for this essay.
4. Is there anything more you'd like to know about navicular disease? If so, suggest how Armstrong might revise.

Writers' Group: Rethinking the Analysis

It's time now to take another look at your draft analysis. Analyze your analysis: Have you made your purpose clear early in the essay? Have you cited a sufficient number of causes or effects so that your analysis seems credible? Have you arranged your points logically? Do you have a conclusion that reinforces your strongest arguments? When you are satisfied with your draft, read it aloud to your peer group, then ask your colleagues to write down your purpose and your strongest argument. Compare their responses with your intentions; revise if you think you need to.

Reflecting on and Presenting the Analysis

When you eventually prepare your analysis for your portfolio, consider using graphs or tables to help make your points. For example, to show how the number of businesses in a downtown area has declined over a period of years, use a line or bar graph.

Finally, remember to reflect on and write about your experiences in writing the analysis. Consider how the whole process went and how you made it through. Record your successful moments and your trying times.

PUBLIC WRITING: LITERARY STUDY

In the analysis paper you presented your analysis of a given situation: Essentially, you took a position and explained why you held that position. Your essay thus inevitably assumed a persuasive aspect, even though your intention may not have been to persuade a reader to accept your point of view. The literary study has much the same subtly persuasive purpose. In this kind of essay you are saying to a reader, "This is something interesting that I perceived in this literary work; this is why I think my reading works; this is what the significance of my reading is; and this is the evidence for my interpretation—the reasons I read the piece as I do." Regardless of whether the topic for a literary analysis is assigned or whether you have to originate it, a literary analysis is a personal reading of a piece of literature—a poem, story, novel, or play. When the analysis succeeds, it focuses on a small topic or narrow perspective and explores that discrete focused area very thoroughly by means of a compelling and careful engagement with the text. It shows how that finite perspective can illuminate the entire text.

Invention Ideas

An effective literary study begins with a thorough reading of the text. Thorough reading usually means more than one careful reading; three or four readings may be necessary. Thorough reading also means looking up the meanings of unfamiliar words or phrases. Thorough reading means addressing these questions:

1. Who is telling the story or saying the poem?
2. What actually happens in the story, poem, or play? What does the narrative tell me?
3. Why are these events or this story or these thoughts worth sharing?
4. What doesn't happen that could have happened?
5. How could the story, poem, or play be different if it were told from the point of view of another character or speaker?

The literary study is frequently an assignment. Your professor may say, "Write a ten-page paper on _____." If you must respond to a topic you've been given, one of the best strategies for invention is to imagine the counterfactual. If the topic or question asks you, for example, to address the significance of the older generation in Shakespeare's *The Taming of the Shrew*, try imagining a counterfactual scenario: *Taming* without the older generation. How would the play be different? What would be missing? What can you learn, then, about the reason for the older generation's being in the play? It is fair to assume that in a work of art all detail is significant; that nothing is gratuitous, just stuck in the story or the poem to fill up space. Therefore, possible meaning resides in all details of a piece of literature.

But if thinking about the counterfactual isn't producing all the ideas you need for writing, try freewriting. Sometimes the freewriting helps your ideas to surface. To find something useful to write about, ask yourself first what you remember most about the text. Make these lists:

1. List five memorable details about the text—without looking back.
2. List as many characters or voices as you can recall.
3. Describe what you remember about the setting or places and times where the story takes place.
4. List as many conflicts as you can recall.
5. Sketch five main plot events or narrative incidents, including the beginning situation and the conclusion or ending.
6. List as many symbols or unusual items—objects—from the text as you can remember.

7. Write down as many unresolved questions as you can think of.
8. Write down alternative endings—other ways the ending of the story or poem could have been articulated or presented. (Sometimes it's what the author does *not* say that is most revealing; sometimes the best clues are mute.)

Look over your lists to find a topic about which you feel most knowledgeable. Once you select a topic, make sure it's as narrow as you can make it. Instead of writing about the female characters in Faulkner's *The Unvanquished*, a very broad topic, write about *one* aspect of *one* character: how Drusilla's bitterness drives her actions, for example. This is a very specific and manageable topic. After you determine your topic, go back to the text and highlight or copy (by hand or by machine) all the passages mentioning your topic or relating directly to it. It is important that each passage be on an individual card or sheet of paper. This is an important step, because these passages will form the groundwork for the supporting text of your arguments. As you plan your essay, you can lay out the cards with the supporting passages in the order that you want to use them and rehearse the essay aloud—talk it out.

Drafting a Literary Study

When you have an idea about what and how you want to write, assemble your notes, sit down, and write without stopping. *Consider that you are writing to someone who has read the literary text* and is also interested in the insight you will bring to it; therefore, you do not need to summarize the plot or tell what happens. You may occasionally need to remind readers who a particular character is or what happened in Act 3, but you should assume that when prompted, readers of your piece will recall their reading of the original. Don't worry about making your argument complete in this first draft: Just write down your rough reasons for your interpretation. When you finish the draft, put asterisks where you need substantiation; that is, where you need to support your interpretation with summary, description, or quotations from the text. Later you will go back to the copy and weave in the textual support, complete with page numbers, inserted parenthetically. When you have a draft complete with asterisks and inserts, put it aside.

Reading Published Literary Criticism

After you draft your literary analysis, you may find it useful to read what other critics have published about the text. In fact, your instructor may request that you consult the critical literature. It would be wise, however, to determine exact requirements here—because some professors may prefer that you not read the criticism. If you do look at what critics have written, be sure to take careful notes on the points of similarity between your arguments and theirs. You must cite others' comments and points very carefully to avoid plagiarism (see page 299 for more information). And if you argue against a critic's interpretation of a text, you will want to be specific in constructing your analysis *against* the published one. Indeed, this kind of analysis can be quite exciting—like an intellectual duel.

If you are searching for literary criticism, the best place to look is the *Modern Language Association (MLA) Index*, located in the reference section of your university library or perhaps in an on-line database. To use the *MLA Index* efficiently, you will need to know how to categorize the literature you are critiquing by country, literary period, and author. In some cases you may also find books or articles by searching under a particular theme, such as animal imagery, female protagonists, or the poetry of witness. For help in using the *MLA Index*, read the introductory information at the beginning of the first volume; or ask your reference librarian or instructor for help. Remember that the *MLA Index* and other indexes provide you with citations or references to specific books and journal articles; you must record the citation carefully, then look up the actual article in the specific publication.

Looking at a Literary Study

The more literary criticism you read, the more you will realize the diverse forms it can take. Some literary criticism is very personal, the critic's voice very present. Other literary writing is much more self-effacing and impersonal. Some literary essays trace a small theme through broad territory, maybe even through a writer's entire *oeuvre* or works; other essays focus on a single image in a single work. Some essays focus on the writer's adherence to some philosophy; some, on style; some, on relationships between or among characters. Some literary essays are highly structured, logical formal analyses; others are reflective, associational, and informal. Regardless of the kind of analysis you write, however, you must ground your arguments in the text and use the text in supporting your point. A sound literary analysis bases its conclusions on specific details in the text. Listen carefully to the suggestions your instructor gives you about this kind of writing and about his or her criteria for a successful literary analysis.

Here are some examples of effective and strikingly different ways of writing about literature. The first essay is a brief piece (called a *note*) from *Massachusettes Studies in English* about a single character in a Faulkner novel, *The Unvanquished.*

Rosa Millard and the Railroad: A Note on William Faulkner's *The Unvanquished*

BETH BURCH

Most critics of William Faulkner's *The Unvanquished* agree that one of its most prominent themes is the corruption of Rosa Millard, Granny, under wartime duress.[1] As the Civil War continues, the destruction of Southern property and the erosion of values occur simultaneously. One of the most potent symbols of this ruin is the wreckage of the railroad near Hawkhurst.[2] The fate of the railroad and that of Rosa

Millard are closely linked; the railroad may be read as a metaphor for Granny's morality.

Bayard recalls the railroad as it existed when Denny was so small that Jingus had to carry him out to the tracks:

> It was the straightest thing I ever saw, running straight and empty and quiet through a long empty gash cut through the trees, and the ground, too, and full of sunlight like water in a river, only straighter than any river, with the crossties cut off even and smooth and neat, and the light shining on the rails like on two spider threads, running straight on to where you couldn't even see that far. It looked clean and neat, like the yard behind Louvinia's cabin after she had swept it on a Saturday morning, with those two little threads that didn't look strong enough for anything to run on running straight and fast and light, like they were getting up speed to jump clean off the world.[3]

As the railroad is a slash of light through the dark trees, so Granny's moral–religious sense is a beacon illuminating her direct path through a world of uncertainty and sin. Throughout *The Unvanquished,* Bayard's memories of Granny's frequent praying and Bible reading reinforce an impression of her staunch religiosity. In "Ambuscade" and most of "Retreat," Rosa Millard's convictions appear absolute—as neat, categorical, and predetermined as the length and spacing of the crossties of the railroad tracks—and she disciplines the boys according to the sureness of her sense of right and wrong. Ringo's predictable and repeated "Git the soap" illustrates the certainty of her displeasure with cursing, and Bayard tells us that Granny would punish him and Ringo "even when it wasn't a told lie, but just keeping quiet" (32). Moreover, Faulkner has Bayard describe Granny and the railroad in similar terms indicating precision, firmness, and strength. Granny is "rigidly erect" (48), "strong and thin and light" (p. 84), "bolt upright" (117), and even wears her bonnet on the "exact top" of her head (43). The railroad tracks are "straight," "even," "smooth," "neat," "fast," and "light."

The advent of the war changes Granny just as the presence of the enemy wrests the traditional supports from life in the Old South. Soldiers and scavengers loot the countryside, burn buildings and crops, confiscate livestock, and shoot to kill. Both the Sartoris and Hawkhurst plantations are ravaged, and when Ringo finally gets a look at the railroad, he discovers

> something that looked like piles of black straws heaped up every few yards . . . they had dug the ties up and piled them and set them on fire . . . it looked like four or five men had taken each rail and tied it around a tree like you knot a green cornstalk around a wagon stake.   (100)

The destruction of the railroad foreshadows what happens to Granny. Like the rails wound around the tree trunks, her values become twisted and blackened. As the rails of steel are manipulated by men and fire, so Granny's morals are altered by the necessity of adopting a wartime mentality. Indeed, both Rosa Millard's corruption and the destruction of the railroad are associated with the coming of Union troops. When Granny sees the blue coats ride by the window and hears the boots and spurs on the porch at Sartoris, her face looks "like she had died" and her once-strong voice sounds "like she had died too" (31). From this point, the survival of her family and herself becomes more important to Rosa Millard than strict adherence to any moral or religious code. While Bayard and Ringo hide beneath her voluminous skirts, she boldly lies to the rude sergeant who familiarly calls her "Grandma": "You are mistaken. . . . There are no children in this house nor on this place" (32). Later she repudiates ownership of the musket. She also "borrows" two horses after Yankees seize her mules right out of the traces. Eventually she acquiesces to something like the lie of "just keeping quiet"; when the Union orderly makes gross errors in the requisition order, she accepts, though reluctantly, the unexpected bounty, attributing it to "the hand of God" (128). Finally, she allies herself with Ab Snopes, with whom she would never traffic in ordinary times and circumstances, and from that point her corruption is swift and terrible. Yet as long as she is swindling the Yankees for altruistic purposes—to feed and clothe the people of the ravaged countryside—there is something redeeming in her deceit. It is when she turns to thievery for more selfish reasons—the final $1500 will be for the Sartorises—that her end becomes inevitable, and for her final lie there is no opportunity to kneel and ask forgiveness.

Thus Faulkner uses the metaphor of the railroad to imply early in the novel what the fruits of Granny's improbity will be. As the railroad is uprooted and wrecked by the Union soldiers, so too are Granny's values dislocated and confused: during wartime, morality bows to expediency and necessity. Eventually Rosa Millard's corruption and her religion become entwined, like the railroad ties wound around the trees. She distributes the stolen goods in the church and equates the Confederacy with a "holy cause" (167). It is this kind of disoriented and fallacious thinking—she later relies on Grumby to act the Southerner and the gentleman—that leads to her violent death.

Notes

[1] Among others, see Melville Backman, *Faulkner, The Major Years: A Critical Study* (Bloomington: Indiana Univ. Press, 1966), p. 124; John Lewis Longley, Jr., *The Tragic Mask: A Study of Faulkner's Heroes* (Chapel Hill: Univ. of North Carolina Press, 1957), p. 179; Hyatt H. Waggoner, *William Faulkner: From Jefferson to the World* (Univ. of Kentucky Press, 1959), pp. 173–78.

[2] Elizabeth M. Kerr, *Yoknapatawpha: Faulkner's "Little Postage Stamp of Native Soil"* (New York: Fordham Univ. Press, 1969), p. 96, notes that the description and account of the railroad "prepares for the activities of Colonel John Sartoris after the war," but no critic has remarked on the railroad as related to Granny.

[3] William Faulkner, *The Unvanquished* (New York: Random House, 1938), p. 99. Further citations from this novel will be noted parenthetically in the text.

CONSIDER . . .

1. What is the thesis of this article? What point does Burch want to get across to the audience?
2. What specific details from the novel support the thesis?

3. Notice how Burch opens the essay. How extensive is the introduction? Does it concern all of Faulkner's themes? All the ideas in this book? One particular thread in this book?

4. How do you know that Burch looked at the criticism before she finished this draft?

Now turn to some different kinds of literary analyses. The first, a brief essay Daniel Margrave wrote after reading the opening pages of a Dickens novel, is a prediction about what the novel will hold. Notice how closely Margrave attends to the details in the text. The second essay, by Elizabeth Foley, is a longer analysis of the protagonist in William Kennedy's novel *Ironweed*.

Dombey's Son's Son
Daniel Margrave

Authors usually try to give a general introduction to the main characters of their novels in the opening sections. *Dombey and Son* (Dickens) introduces three characters: Mr. Dombey (Paul Dombey II), "Son" (Paul Dombey III, a newborn infant), and Mrs. Dombey. It seems that Dombey and Son will be the most important characters, from the amount of time spent on them, and Mrs. Dombey incidental. Dombey is portrayed as a rather self-centered, pompous business owner. Mrs. Dombey is a weak-willed, dependent creature. The son is, as yet, nothing, but the narrator indicates his similarity to Dombey. The focus of the novel may well be on Dombey's influence on his son.

The most obvious imagery centers on the similarities between the middle-aged Dombey and his son. Both are bald and red, good-looking with a couple of faults, and creased: Dombey wrinkled by Time and his son by Time's absence. That Dombey intends to exert influence on his son is made clear in the last paragraph: he thinks that Heaven and Earth were created to aid their *common* interests.

Hints about the thoughts of the characters are revealed in small actions. Dombey is unused to calling his wife "my dear," and her "flush of faint surprise" indicates a pleasure seldom received. Mr. Dombey's emphasis on "Dombey and Son," and his reference to the name of his father as *Paul,* indicates that *his* father and he had a relationship similar to the one he intends for the son.

Finally, small details add emphasis to certain points. The scene is initiated in darkness with the light focused on the son; he will be the focus of Dombey. Dombey's "phosphorescent" buttons and gold watch-chain indicate his love of possessions. And the mention of the infant's tiny fists seems an indication of the uselessness of any resistance on his part.

CONSIDER . . .

1. What is the focus in Margrave's prediction about *Dombey and Son*? Where is the reader cued to Margrave's intention?

2. What imagery does Margrave find significant? Do you think his analysis is credible? Why?
3. How does Margrave incorporate the text into his prediction—and why?
4. Can Margrave strengthen his suppositions and arguments about the text? If so, what suggestions would you make for his revision?

Part Beast, Part Man: William Kennedy's Francis Phelan
Elizabeth Foley

In some ways, William Kennedy's *Ironweed* answers perfectly to the description of a 1980s naturalistic novel. Francis Phelan, its fifty-eight-year-old hobo protagonist, has certainly led his life in the naturalistic vein. The events that have scarred his existence seem to have been imposed on him by some antagonistic outside force, or even by fate. Why his life has taken the direction it has is a mystery perhaps eternally beyond his understanding. And he has definitely run the gamut of animalistic behavior: he has killed, both accidentally and with intense purposefulness; he has slept around enough to have become something of a sexual connoisseur; he has been dirty, sick, and hungry; he has taken wild flight from his attackers like a hunted animal. Yet Kennedy's portrayal of his hero clashes with the naturalistic model in that his stand where Francis is concerned is sympathetically righteous and deeply sensitive, rather than distant and matter-of-fact. Kennedy could be called a naturalistic author who, instead of objectively presenting man as an animalistic, victimized exhibit in a cage, connects those animal urges and psychological struggles to himself and all men and is drawn to the intense humanness of that condition.

In a sense it's possible to label Francis a passive victim, a man to whom things happen and who then lives by reacting to those things. The path of his life has been irreversibly shaped by people and events out of his control: his half-accidental murder of a trolley scab; his mother's cold-hearted rejection of his new wife Annie; his accidental killing of his own baby son Gerald by dropping him and breaking his neck; his near-seduction as a very impressionable seventeen-year-old by an erotic older woman; and even, near the novel's end, his murder, in self-defense, of a raider. At wits' end to trace the origins of these circumstances and his violent reactions to most of them, Francis wonders at one point whether his hands, the perpetrators of so many bloody deeds, are somehow possessed by evil spirits which cut them off from the wiser instincts of his mind:

> Francis' hands, as he looked at them now, seemed to be messengers from some outlaw corner of his psyche, artificers of some involuntary doom element in his life . . . no one else he knew of in his family had ever lived as violently as he. And yet he had never sought that kind of life. (145)[1]

Similarly mysterious to Francis are his seemingly inborn instinct for flight and its contradiction in his eventual return home. He does manage to find some answers, but they are vague and ephemeral. In his thoughts concerning his urge to run from justice, family, fear, anything, he asks himself:

> What and who were again separating Francis from these people [his family] after he'd found them? It was a force whose name did not matter . . . but whose effect was devastating. He knew a larger fate had moved him westward and shaped in him all that he was to become; and that moving and shaping was what Francis had not understood, for he perceived the fugitive thrust that had come to be so much a part of his own spirit. (205)

Even more cryptically, Francis breaks his pattern of flight just long enough to visit his family after twenty-two years' absence. He says of this momentous visit:

> There was no way he could reveal all that had brought him here. It would have meant the recapitulation not only of all his sins but of all his fugitive and fallen dreams, all his random movement across the country and back, all his returns to this city only to leave again without ever coming to see . . . them, without ever knowing why he didn't. . . . Everything was easier than coming home, even reducing yourself to the level of social maggot, streetside slug. (160)

Something more of an answer comes with a mental image Francis conjures up of himself as a trolley car in which two kings are fighting for power,

> . . . neither in control, each driving the car, a careening thing, wild, anarchaic, dangerous to all else, and then Billy [his son] leaps aboard and grabs the power handle and the kings instantly yield control to the wizard. (164)

But when forced to step back and pinpoint the central causes of the half-rational instincts that have fatally shaped his existence as a whole, Francis is at a loss. He does know by this time that there is something intrinsic about his being that he can never and will never comprehend, and probably is not meant to. The following paragraph is as close as Francis comes to a general, cohesive self-analysis.

> Francis was now certain only that he could never arrive at any conclusions about himself that had their origin in reason. . . . He believed that he was a creature of unknown and unknowable qualities, a man in whom there would never be an equanimity of both impulsive and premeditated action. Yet after every admission that he was a lost and distorted soul, Francis asserted his own private wisdom and purpose: he had fled the folks because he was too profane a being to live among them; he had humbled himself willfully through the years to counter a fearful pride in his

own ability to manufacture the glory from which grace would flow. What he was was, yes, a warrior, protecting a belief that no man could ever articulate, especially himself. (216)

Depending upon one's interpretation of the ending of the novel, the conclusion can be made either to support the interpretation of the book as on the whole naturalistic or not to support that idea. The most logical and believable and, perhaps more importantly, the most conclusive way to explain the ending is to assert that both Helen and Francis die, and that Francis' apparent return home is one in a succession of pre- or post-death visions or remembrances. In this case, Francis is a naturalistic model in death as well as in life. While he is not described as being in pain near the novel's end, he presumably dies from a fairly brutal wound received in his fight with the raider, not exactly a peaceful and complacent way to go. At the time of his death, little has been resolved: he has been back to see his family, but wasn't psychologically able to stay and doesn't really understand what any of it means; his friend/lover Helen has died, but this is a forced conclusion to her life, not a natural resolution of anything; and he is still in the dark about the essence of his being. In the naturalist mode of thinking, "life is a cruel game," a notion whose truth is revealed here by the fact that death is almost a welcome thing for these characters: nothing can provide conclusive answers to their struggles and soul-searching, so one must settle for the next best thing—interruption of those struggles, and forced resolution of them, through death.

William Kennedy, however, throws a wrench into the machinery of this not-so-easily-classified-as-naturalistic novel, and that is his attitude toward Francis and his tragic misadventures. Naturalistic writers, by definition, are supposed to approach their characters' lives in a cool, aloof, matter-of-fact way; they are supposed to shock their audiences by refusing to cling to any coherent set of values or to support or condemn their protagonists on the basis of those values; they are supposed to describe man's surrender to his primitive, passionate anger (fighting, sex, fear) with no more passion than they would use in describing the weather.

Kennedy breaks most of these rules. While his portrayal of Francis is devoid of any ostentatious, melodramatic pity (a great temptation, since Francis' whole life is an excellent target for pity), it shows a deep and consistent sympathy, even empathy, toward the bum's lot. It is impossible to claim that Kennedy does not feel deeply involved in Francis' plight; if he doesn't, why does he include so many sensitive, pensive passages in which he muses at length about why Francis lives as he does, almost as if he were trying to help Francis reach a conclusion? Kennedy obviously doesn't view Francis' dabblings in murder and casual sex and his evasion of the law with a clinical eye, either. Take, as an outstanding example, Kennedy's treatment of the increasingly romantic and sexual relationship between Francis and Katrina Daugherty. Francis' guilty yearning for the love/lust relationship he can never achieve is one of the book's most exquisite and acutely painful moments. Kennedy describes it like this:

> [Francis'] . . . swollen member rose to offer [Katrina] the enduring, erubescent gift of retributive sin. And then this woman interposed herself in his life, hiding herself in the deepest center of the flames, smiling at him with all the lewd beauty of her dreams; and she awakened in him the urge for a love of his own . . . a love he would never have to share with any other man, or boy, like himself. (115–16)

Hardly an emotionally detached point of view. And while Kennedy never, ever passes judgment on any of Francis' "sins," his approach to them can't be called amoral. He is simply questioning, in a quiet way, all established value systems which would stereotype Francis as a no-good bum without a conscience or moral code—and also those value systems which would view Francis solely as an object on which to fling pity, tears, and bewailments over what a terrible world it is that can produce a tragic case like his. Kennedy chucks value systems out the window because it is not his purpose to measure Francis' worth, but to make his readers see that whatever standard we measure him by, we will also be measuring ourselves. We are all a lot like Francis. His hobo lifestyle is, in the end, inconsequential except in that the traits of humanity seem more exposed and extreme in him and are therefore easier to present to the reader. Francis is a human being who just happens to be a bum; it is this common bond of humanity that draws Kennedy to him. For these reasons, Kennedy is not really a naturalistic writer; instead, he is a nonjudgmental humanitarian who uses naturalistic backdrops to bring out mankind's human qualities with especial force.

[1]Quoted passages are from *Ironweed* (New York: Penguin, 1984).

_____

CONSIDER . . .

1. What is Foley's focus in her *Ironweed* analysis? Where does she cue the reader to her purpose/thesis?
2. What do you think about the amount of Foley's quoting? Is the quoting appropriate to the demands of her analysis? Would summary work as well as the quoting?
3. How does Foley's conclusion help the reader to shape an understanding of the novel? Does she succeed in adhering to her thesis/purpose?

_____

Writers' Group: Rethinking the Literary Study

By now you've had a chance to see how some other writers have handled writing about literature. Reread your draft literary study. Then skim through the work of literature that you wrote about. Then read your draft again. What do you think? Has your interpretation of the work changed? Do you see other arguments you'd like to add? Do you need to soften some of your claims? Have you claimed too much importance for your thesis? It's not advisable to claim, for example, that your interpretation *proves* a point. Proof is appropriate for the legal brief, not for the literary study. Have you supported your interpretation by clear references to the text?

When you are ready to have a reader respond to your essay, choose someone who has read the literary work you are addressing. That way your reader will be able to give you more accurate feedback. Ask your reader to fill out this brief questionnaire:

1. The thesis of this essay is _____

    _____.

2. I remember these ideas from the essay: _____

    _____

    _____.

3. I would like to know more about _____

    _____.

Finally, remember that there is no *one* way to read a text, no absolutely correct interpretation. Some readings are, however, better than others because they correspond better to the possibilities within a text, explain a text more completely, and are more fully supported by textual evidence.

Reflecting on and Presenting the Literary Study

You may find that the paragraphs in your literary essay look long. They may indeed be longer than your usual paragraphs—because you frequently have to blend considerable textual evidence into your paragraphs to develop them. Also, when you quote a passage longer than four lines, you must handle the quoted material as block quotation or extract—as Elizabeth Foley handles the passages from *Ironweed*. Double indent (ten spaces) each quoted line, but keep the right margin and the spacing the same as in the rest of the text. In these longer passages, eliminate quotation marks: Indentation signals the reader that the passage is quoted.

If you are working with a relatively short literary work—a short story, a poem, or a one-act play—consider including a photocopy of the work in your portfolio. Your reader may appreciate being able to refer to the entire text.

Don't forget to reflect on and write about your experience in writing the literary study. Writing about literature is not likely to be a neutral experience, so be sure to record how you felt and what you thought as you went through this process. What did you do well?

 ## PORTMANTEAU OF ANALYTICAL WRITING

Here you will find further examples of analytical writing, published and unpublished: dialogue journals, more formal analytic pieces, and two literary studies.

Excerpts from Dialogue Journals

Nathan Jericho and Ahmad Tobon

Nathan Jericho	Ahmad Tobon

Of the characters we have met so far this semester, I think Tess's life had the best implicit advice for living. I chose Tess because of the way she had acted or just the way she was. I think she was a bit weak on what she wanted, though I liked the way she loved Claire. She loved him so much that she didn't really care for herself; she just wanted him to be happy. I think her love showed most when she wanted her sister to be with him. And I hated when Claire was treating her like s*?# in the D'Urberville mansion on their honeymoon. He had done the same thing she had done—actually he had done his wrong more willingly than she had. But she loved him so much that she was willing to hurt herself for his happiness. I think that Tess deserved someone better than Claire because a real man who truly loved her would not have treated her like that; he would have let bygones be bygones. If everyone would love like Tess did, everybody would be happier, more faithful, and honest.

Tess was very weak! She couldn't stand up for herself at all; actually she made me angry—I wanted her to quit being such a doormat. I'm not really sure I believe her unselfishness; is she for real?

I hate to admit it, but this is that double standard we were talking about in class. I think this general attitude is still alive today. It's OK for us guys to be be sexual, but girls can't be sexual and still be "nice." (Too bad for girls!)

This is easier said than done, though. It's hard to *forgive* somebody for hurting you, but it's even harder to *forget* what they did, especially if you felt betrayed by someone near and dear to you. You're a real Pollyanna, aren't you? I don't think that a lot of love would save the world.

Elizabeth Foley and Emma Armstrong

Elizabeth Foley	Emma Armstrong

I think that to accurately say what I've learned from *Hamlet,* I need to divide my response into (a) what I learned from actually reading *Hamlet* and (b) what I learned from watching other people (and probably myself too) become petty and opinionated over the thematic intricacies of *Hamlet*. The thing that struck me the most about Hamlet and his contemporaries was that they were just as interested in and aware of sex (and sometimes as sexually perverted) as people are nowadays, so I chose that topic as the subject of my *Hamlet* paper. I could stretch that idea a little further and say that it was interesting and rather comforting to see that all kinds of corruption (and not just sexual corruption) did exist in the 1500s, in the same forms and with the same ends that they have in the 1990s. *Hamlet* also reinforces the impression I've gotten from reading *Romeo and Juliet* and *Macbeth* (in high school) that Shakespeare, in direct contrast to the picture many people have of him as an overly intellectual, overly profound bard, was probably an extremely wise but intensely human guy who knew exactly what was true and relevant, who could condemn people's values without sounding stern and moralistic, and who had a very clever, pertinent sense of humor. Somehow with Shakespeare, poetic language is not something haughty and frilly and artsy, but something so eloquent and hard-hitting that you wish you had had the savvy to say it that way.

I have also concluded from our class discussion that there are certain aspects of Hamlet that will probably never be figured out, that are maybe purposely fuzzy and ambiguous. Nevertheless, some people will take up the most minor points in discussing it.

Yeah, I guess you are right about this. I remember some pretty loud discussions about Hamlet and Ophelia. I don't understand why we can't just admit that there are many ways to read the play (or any play or piece of literature) and be done with it. Why do some people in class always want to argue and debate? I guess it can can be useful to debate, but I get really tired of the arguments (I don't like conflict, either in words or any other way) over whose interpretation is better. Who cares? Those people are just sucking up to the instructor.

Do you think that he really loved his wife Anne Hathaway or that they had a whatchamacallit—marriage of convenience? Isn't it strange that so few documents and personal records exist about Shakespeare? I wonder what my life's paper trail is so far!

I liked the low characters and their humor best. Some of the humor is too verbal and pointed—I can't get it.

During the discussion I felt like I was beating my head against a wall and I came out of the class thinking that nothing had really been accomplished at all. This could be partly due to feelings of inferiority I have at not being as glib as other individuals in the class, but I really felt that our discussions often obscured what was relevant about the play instead of making it clearer.

I guess that I like talking in class more than you do. I remember that you didn't have much to say in the group discussions. I like the discussions, though, because I can talk better than I can write. Also I come from a family that's kind of loud: I come from a pretty big household.

I disagree with you. I think our discussions helped me understand the play better. I know more because of them.

More Analyses

In the first piece in this section, Alissa Perrucci examines the reasons why she believes that many females are prone to eating disorders. In the second, an article from *Time*, Michael Lemonick analyzes the effects of famine. And finally, in excerpts from *A Distant Mirror*, Barbara Tuchman explains the causes, both real and imagined, of the Black Death, the plague that decimated Europe during the fourteenth century—and the effects of the Black Death on the population.

How Our Society Affects Women and Their Weight
Alissa Perrucci

When we think of the sex symbols of history, we think of the Venus figure with her fleshy thighs, hips and stomach, and her large bust. This look of motherhood and maturity was considered the ideal look at the time when sources of food were scarce. However, with the coming of the flapper era and models such as Twiggy, societies' views on the perfect weight have changed drastically. Our obsession with weight has given rise to the "eating disorder," now affecting one percent of females between the ages of twelve and twenty-five. What are the reasons for the great number of victims of these disorders? How is society putting the pressure on women?

The greatest source for our obsession with weight is the media: mainly television and magazines. Our models are perfect—they have not an ounce of superfluous flesh on them; long, slender legs, flat stomachs, narrow hips and nonexistent waists. The females who see these models think they can be like that, too. What they don't know is that these women are probably on semistarvation diets and are not having menstrual periods—a condition which can seriously harm them in later life. New fashions in clothes are being tailored down to fit only the superthin. Girls who are conscious of wearing the "in" things may be persuaded to drop those "extra" pounds to get into the clothes. They see the models on TV and in magazines do it, and assume that they can, too. Why can't these girls just ignore what it is they're seeing around them? we ask. It is because these looks are glamorized, and everyone is made to think that "thin" is the best.

The word "thin" has become a synonym for beauty and loveliness. Women are told they can only be loved if they are thin. As the quest for zero population growth grew, physical development was no longer necessary and thus slowly became an unpopular quality. The nonreproductive, neutered image took its place and became the image of beauty. Obesity in women has come as far as suggesting inferiority because it con-traindicates beauty. Fat men are thought of as "big men." Sometimes they are even given positive images such as "jolly" or even "strong." Such positive images do not ex-ist for fat women; they are only failures for not keeping up with what society expects of them.

Even thinness and success have blended together. Thin means self-control and hard work. A thin person has sacrificed all other needs to make it to the top. The fat woman lacks self-control; she has no self-discipline. We connect thin with the upper class and obesity with the lower class. "You can never be too rich or too thin," exclaimed the Duchess of Windsor. Because we have connected thin with status, eating disorders have become the disease of the well-off, who are surrounded by plenty. They no longer need to show their wealth in the food they eat, but quite the contrary—in the food they can keep themselves from eating.

If society is ever to stop discriminating on the basis of weight, women need to as-sure themselves that they will be accepted as who they are, not how much they weigh. Appearance must not be used as a source of power; rather it needs to be thought of as a trivial detail. As women become increasingly successful, they will find themselves in increasingly important roles, and they will make it known that exterior beauty does not count.

CONSIDER . . .

1. State Perrucci's thesis or purpose for writing in your own words.
2. What are the causes of women's obsession with thinness, according to Perrucci?
3. What questions would you like to ask Perrucci? Are there confusing places in the essay? Would you like to know where or how she got her information? Are there places in the essay where more explanation would be helpful? Are there sections of the essay that you especially like?

It Takes More Than Food to Cure Starvation

MICHAEL D. LEMONICK

An alarming sight greeted American health officials visiting the town of Hoddur in Somalia. Relief workers had distributed unmilled wheat to starving villagers, and scores of living skeletons were pounding the wheat by hand in order to make an edible mush. To the casual witness, the rhythmic thuds might have seemed the music of deliverance, but to those familiar with the grim calculus of starvation, they formed a dirge. The energy expended in grinding the wheat vastly exceeded the nutritional benefit of the mush. Relief supplies were killing the starving.

The tale underscores the difficulties of helping people who are dangerously malnourished. Starvation is a complex biological process; the more advanced it is, the dicier the treatment. During the famine in Somalia, perhaps the worst ever recorded, average food intake for adults has dwindled from a satisfactory 1,700 calories a day in 1988 to a hopelessly inadequate 200. A majority of children under the age of five have already died in some regions. "The mortality is higher than that of the Irish potato famine," says Daniel Miller of the U.S. Centers for Disease Control and Prevention. "It's the worst nightmare you could think of."

Children are affected more severely than adults by famine. The reasons are tied to the biochemistry of starvation, which has been documented both in the fields of human tragedy and in labs with fasting volunteers. In essence, the starving body consumes itself, devouring its own fat and muscle while shutting off less important systems to keep the brain and the rest of the central nervous system operating. Children simply have less fat and muscle to consume.

The first, mild stage of starvation begins within hours after food intake stops. The body quickly burns through its reserves of sugars in the blood and starches stored in the liver and muscles. It then begins raiding fat deposits for triglycerides, compounds that can be broken down into fatty acids that the body can use for fuel. After days or weeks, depending on how meager the rations, these raids result in a condition known as marasmus. Without fat to support it, the skin begins to lose elasticity and sag. Loss of fat around the eyes gives them a sunken look, and the face starts to wrinkle in what starvation experts call the old-man syndrome. The other principal form of starvation, kwashiorkor, is largely a protein–vitamin–mineral deficiency. Its most common symptom: swollen legs and ankles, caused by fluid leaking from blood vessels into the body.

If people could survive on stored fat alone, those who are well padded could survive quite some time. But human metabolism is not so simple. The brain, consumer of about 20% of the body's energy, cannot burn fatty acids. It needs glucose, a form of sugar. And the major source of glucose in a starving body is protein. The first proteins to go are digestive enzymes in the stomach, pancreas and small intestine and nutrient-processing enzymes in the liver, no longer of much use anyway. Then the muscles begin to wither away, giving limbs a sticklike appearance.

As starvation advances, the body tries to conserve energy by limiting all but the most vital processes. Cell division slows drastically. Even hair stops growing. Reduced fuel burning drives body temperature down; that, combined with the loss of insulating fat, can lead to death from hypothermia—a threat on a cool Somalian evening. The shutting down of the intestines can lead to the paradox of death by diarrhea. Reduced production of white blood cells weakens the immune system, a kind of starvation-induced AIDS that turns diseases like measles into killers. Eventually the body begins burning muscle tissue wholesale: victims become too weak even to move, and the heart muscle begins to shrink. By then death is almost inevitable.

Because starving bodies are so severely disrupted, it takes more than good meals to restore them. In fact, too much food too suddenly can kill victims by triggering shock. The process of refeeding, which in Somalia will take place mainly in huge feeding camps, usually starts with fluids to counter dehydration. Then comes a high-calorie, high-protein mixture such as the U.S. government's Unimix, made of ground beans, ground rice or corn, sugar and vegetable oil. This is given in frequent, small meals so that the out-of-practice digestive tract can handle it. Severely malnourished children may require hourly feedings. "They are hard to rehabilitate because they are lethargic and lose their appetite. They turn their head when spoon-fed," says Dr. Graeme Clugston, chief of the World Health Organization's nutrition program.

Within weeks after refeeding begins, even those adults who were on the verge of death will have largely recovered. But children, especially those under five, can carry the scars for life. They can go blind from lack of vitamin A. They may never achieve their full height. Girls may never be able to safely bear children because of malformed pelvises. And mental function is often impaired. "Even when they are fed and back on their feet, you'll have a generation of kids with a considerable degree of retardation," says Michael D'Adamo of Catholic Relief Services.

The feeding camps will operate until the Somalis regain enough strength to start producing their own food again. Herds of cows, goats and camels and stores of seeds, all long since eaten, will have to be replaced. After that, Somalia has a chance to be self-sufficient once again—as long as social and political stability are restored.

—Reported by Farah Nayeri/Paris and Dick Thompson/Washington

CONSIDER . . .

1. What is Lemonick's purpose in writing this essay? What is he analyzing?
2. Does this essay focus more on causes or effects?
3. Find a place in the essay where Lemonick traces the steps in a process.

Causes of the Black Death

BARBARA TUCHMAN

Ignorance of the cause [of the Black Death] augmented the sense of horror. Of the real carriers, rats and fleas, the 14th century had no suspicion, perhaps because they were so familiar. Fleas, though a common household nuisance, are not once mentioned in contemporary plague writings, and rats only incidentally, although folklore commonly associated them with pestilence. The legend of the Pied Piper arose from an outbreak of 1284. The actual plague bacillus, *Pasturella pestis,* remained undiscovered for another 500 years. Living alternately in the stomach of the flea and the bloodstream of the rat who was the flea's host, the bacillus in its bubonic form was transferred to humans and animals by the bite of either rat or flea. It traveled by virtue of *Rattus rattus,* the small medieval black rat that lived on ships, as well as by the heavier brown or sewer rat. What precipitated the turn of the bacillus from innocuous to virulent form is unknown, but the occurrence is now believed to have taken place not in China but somewhere in central Asia and to have spread along the caravan routes. Chinese origin was a mistaken notion of the 14th century based on real but belated reports of huge death tolls in China from drought, famine, and pestilence which have since been traced to the 1330s, too soon to be responsible for the plague that appeared in India in 1346.

The phantom enemy had no name. Called the Black Death only in later recurrences, it was known during the first epidemic simply as the Pestilence or Great Mortality. Reports from the East, swollen by fearful imaginings, told of strange tempests and "sheets of fire" mingled with huge hailstones that "slew almost all," or a "vast rain of fire" that burned up men, beasts, stones, trees, villages, and cities. In another version, "foul blasts of wind" from the fires carried the infection to Europe "and now as some suspect it cometh round the seacoast." Accurate observation in this case could not make the mental jump to ships and rats because no idea of animal- or insect-borne contagion existed.

The earthquake was blamed for releasing sulfurous and foul fumes from the earth's interior, or as evidence of a titanic struggle of planets and oceans causing waters to rise and vaporize until fish died in masses and corrupted the air. All these explanations had in common a factor of poisoned air, of miasmas and thick, stinking mists traced to every kind of natural or imagined agency from stagnant lakes to malign conjunction of the planets, from the hand of the Evil One to the wrath of God. Medical thinking, trapped in the theory of astral influences, stressed air as the communicator of disease, ignoring sanitation or visible carriers. The existence of two carriers confused the trail, the more so because the flea could live and travel independently of the rat for as long as a month and, if infected by the particularly virulent septicemic form of the bacillus, could infect humans without reinfecting itself from the rat. The simultaneous presence of the pneumonic form of the disease, which was indeed communicated through the air, blurred the problem further.

The mystery of the contagion was "the most terrible of all the terrors," as an anonymous Flemish cleric in Avignon wrote to a correspondent in Bruges. Plagues had been known before, from the plague of Athens (believed to have been typhus) to the prolonged epidemic of the 6th century A.D., to the recurrence of sporadic outbreaks in the 12th and 13th centuries, but they had left no accumulated store of understanding. That the infection came from contact with the sick or with their houses, clothes, or corpses was quickly observed but not comprehended. Gentile da Foligno, renowned physician of Perugia and doctor of medicine at the universities of Bologna and Padua, came close to respiratory infection when he surmised that poisonous material was "communicated by means of air breathed out and in." Having no idea of microscopic carriers, he had to assume that the air was corrupted by planetary influences. Planets, however, could not explain the ongoing contagion. The agonized search for an answer gave rise to such theories as transference by sight. People fell ill, wrote Guy de Chauliac, not only by remaining with the sick but "even by looking at them." Three hundred years later Joshua Barnes, the 17th century biographer of Edward III, could write that the power of infection had entered into beams of light and "darted death from the eyes."

Doctors struggling with the evidence could not break away from the terms of astrology, to which they believed all human physiology was subject. Medicine was the one aspect of medieval life, perhaps because of its links with the Arabs, not shaped by Christian doctrine. Clerics detested astrology, but could not dislodge its influence. Guy de Chauliac, physician to three popes in succession, practiced in obedience to the zodiac. While his *Cirurgia* was the major treatise on surgery of its time, while he understood the use of anesthesia made from the juice of opium, mandrake, or hemlock, he nevertheless prescribed bleeding and purgatives by the planets and divided chronic from acute diseases on the basis of one being under the rule of the sun and the other of the moon.

In October 1348 Philip VI asked the medical faculty of the University of Paris for a report on the affliction that seemed to threaten human survival. With careful thesis, antithesis, and proofs, the doctors ascribed it to a triple conjunction of Saturn, Jupiter, and Mars in the 40th degree of Aquarius said to have occurred on March 20, 1345. They acknowledged, however, effects "whose cause is hidden from even the most highly trained intellects." The verdict of the masters of Paris became the official version. Borrowed, copied by scribes, carried abroad, translated from Latin into various vernaculars, it was everywhere accepted, even by the Arab physicians of Cordova and Granada, as the scientific if not the popular answer. Because of the terrible interest of the subject, the translations of the plague tracts stimulated use of national languages. In that one respect, life came from death.

To the people at large there could be but one explanation—the wrath of God. Planets might satisfy the learned doctors, but God was closer to the average man. A scourge so sweeping and unsparing without any visible cause could only be seen as Divine punishment upon mankind for its sins. It might even be God's terminal disappointment in his creature. Matteo Villani compared the plague to the Flood in ultimate purpose and believed he was recording "the extermination of mankind."

Efforts to appease Divine wrath took many forms, as when the city of Rouen ordered that everything that could anger God, such as gambling, cursing, and drinking, must be stopped. More general were the penitent processions authorized at first by the Pope, some lasting as long as three days, some attended by as many as 2,000, which everywhere accompanied the plague and helped to spread it.

Barefoot in sackcloth, sprinkled with ashes, weeping, praying, tearing their hair, carrying candles and relics, sometimes with ropes around their necks or beating themselves with whips, the penitents wound through the streets, imploring the mercy of the Virgin and saints at their shrines. In a vivid illustration for the *Très Riches Heures* of the Duc de Berry, the Pope is shown in a penitent procession attended by four cardinals in scarlet from hat to hem. He raises both arms in supplication to the angel on top of the Castel Sant'Angelo, while white-robed priests bearing banners and relics in golden cases turn to look as one of their number, stricken by the plague, falls to the ground, his face contorted with anxiety. In the rear, a gray-clad monk falls beside another victim already on the ground as the townspeople gaze in horror. (Nominally the illustration represents a 6th century plague in the time of Pope Gregory the Great, but as medieval artists made no distinction between past and present, the scene is shown as the artist would have seen it in the 14th century.) When it became evident that these processions were sources of infection, Clement VI had to prohibit them.

In Messina, where the plague first appeared, the people begged the Archbishop of neighboring Catania to lend them the relics of St. Agatha. When the Catanians refused to let the relics go, the Archbishop dipped them in holy water and took the water himself to Messina, where he carried it in a procession with prayers and litanies through the streets. The demonic, which shared the medieval cosmos with God, appeared as "demons in the shape of dogs" to terrify the people. "A black dog with a drawn sword in his paws appeared among them, gnashing his teeth and rushing upon them and breaking all the silver vessels and lamps and candlesticks on the altars and casting them hither and thither. . . . So the people of Messina, terrified by this prodigious vision, were all strangely overcome by fear."

The apparent absence of earthly cause gave the plague a supernatural and sinister quality. Scandinavians believed that a Pest Maiden emerged from the mouth of the dead in the form of a blue flame and flew through the air to infect the next house. In Lithuania the Maiden was said to wave a red scarf through the door or window to let in the pest. One brave man, according to legend, deliberately waited at his open window with drawn sword and, at the fluttering of the scarf, chopped off the hand. He died of his deed, but his village was spared and the scarf long preserved as a relic in the local church.

Beyond demons and superstition the final hand was God's. The Pope acknowledged it in a Bull of September 1348, speaking of the "pestilence with which God is afflicting the Christian people." To the Emperor John Cantacuzene it was manifest that a malady of such horrors, stenches, and agonies, and especially one bringing the dismal despair that settled upon its victims before they died, was not a plague "natural" to mankind but "a chastisement from Heaven." To Piers Plowman "these pestilences were for pure sin."

The general acceptance of this view created an expanded sense of guilt, for if the plague were punishment there had to be terrible sin to have occasioned it. What sins were on the 14th century conscience? Primarily greed, the sin of avarice, followed by usury, worldliness, adultery, blasphemy, falsehood, luxury, irreligion. Giovanni Villani, attempting to account for the cascade of calamity that had fallen upon Florence, concluded that it was retribution for the sins of avarice and usury that oppressed the poor. Pity and anger about the condition of the poor, especially victimization of the peasantry in war, was often expressed by writers of the time and was certainly on the conscience of the century. Beneath it all was the daily condition of medieval life, in which hardly an act or thought, sexual, mercantile, or military, did not contravene the dictates of the Church. Mere failure to fast or attend mass was sin. The result was an underground lake of guilt in the soul that the plague now tapped.

That the mortality was accepted as God's punishment may explain in part the vacuum of comment that followed the Black Death. An investigator has noticed that in the archives of Périgord references to the war are innumerable, to the plague few. Froissart mentions the great death but once, Chaucer gives it barely a glance. Divine anger so great that it contemplated the extermination of man did not bear close examination.

CONSIDER . . .

1. Tuchman announces the purpose of this analysis with a key word in the first sentence of the selection. What is that key word?
2. Make a note about the content/purpose of each paragraph. Try to reconstruct Tuchman's thinking. How would you describe the order of the passage? What were the apparent causes of the plague?
3. Tuchman's explanations are made rich by an abundance of detail. Which details are most memorable for you? Why?
4. Find a place where Tuchman explains a concept or idea or where she identifies a person who may be unknown to the reader. How would you describe her strategies for defining?

In this same chapter about the plague in her book *A Distant Mirror*, Barbara Tuchman explains some of the *effects* of the plague: what happened to the population as a result of the ravaging epidemic. Examine this excerpt from the chapter to see how she handles an analysis of the *effects* of the plague.

Effects of the Plague

BARBARA TUCHMAN

What was the human condition after the plague? Exhausted by deaths and sorrows and the morbid excesses of fear and hate, it ought to have shown some profound effects, but no radical change was immediately visible. The persistence of the normal

is strong. While dying of the plague, the tenants of Bruton Priory in England continued to pay the heriot owed to the lord at death with such obedient regularity that fifty
oxen and cattle were received by the priory within a few months. Social change was
to come invisibly with time; immediate effects were many but not uniform. Simon
de Covino believed the plague had a baneful effect upon morals, "lowering virtue
throughout the world." Gilles li Muisis, on the other hand, thought there had been an
improvement in public morals because many people formerly living in concubinage
had now married (as a result of town ordinances), and swearing and gambling had
so diminished that manufacturers of dice were turning their product into beads for
telling paternosters.

The marriage rate undoubtedly rose, though not for love. So many adventurers
took advantage of orphans to obtain rich dowries that the oligarchy of Siena forbade
the marriage of female orphans without their kinsmen's consent. In England, Piers
Plowman deplored the many pairs "since the pestilence" who had married "for greed
of goods and against natural feeling," with result, according to him, in "guilt and
grief . . . jealousy, joylessness and jangling in private"—and no children. It suited
Piers as a moralist that such marriages should be barren. Jean de Venette, on the
other hand, says of the marriages that followed the plague that many twins, sometimes triplets, were born and that few women were barren. Perhaps he in turn reflected a desperate need to believe that nature would make up the loss, and in fact
men and women married immediately afterward in unusual numbers.

Unlike the dice transformed into prayer beads, people did not improve, although it had been expected, according to Matteo Villani, that the experience of
God's wrath would have left them "better men, humble, virtuous and Catholic." Instead, "They forgot the past as though it had never been and gave themselves up
to a more disordered and shameful life than they had led before." With a glut of merchandise on the shelves for too few customers, prices at first plunged and survivors
indulged in a wild orgy of spending. The poor moved into empty houses, slept on
beds, and ate off silver. Peasants acquired unclaimed tools and livestock, even a
wine press, forge, or mill left without owners, and other possessions they never had
before. Commerce was depressed, but the amount of currency was in greater supply because there were fewer people to share it.

Behavior grew more reckless and callous, as it often does after a period of violence and suffering. It was blamed on parvenus and the newly rich who pushed up
from below. Siena renewed its sumptuary laws in 1349 because many persons were
pretending to higher position than belonged to them by birth or occupation. But, on
the whole, local studies of tax rolls indicate that while the population may have been
halved, its social proportions remained about the same.

Because of intestate deaths, property without heirs, and disputed title to land
and houses, a fury of litigation arose, made chaotic by the shortage of notaries.
Sometimes squatters, sometimes the Church, took over emptied property. Fraud
and extortion practiced upon orphans by their appointed guardians became a scandal. In Orvieto brawls kept breaking out; bands of homeless and starving brigands
roamed the countryside and pillaged up to the very gates of the city. People were
arrested for carrying arms and for acts of vandalism, especially on vineyards. The

commune had to enact new regulations against "certain rascals, sons of iniquity" who robbed and burned the premises of shopkeepers and craftsmen, and also against increased prostitution. On March 12, 1350, the commune reminded citizens of the severe penalty in store for sexual relations between Christian and Jew: the woman involved would be beheaded or burned alive.

Education suffered from losses among the clergy. In France, according to Jean de Venette, "few were found in houses, villas and castles who were able and willing to instruct boys in grammar"—a situation that could have touched the life of Enguerrand VII. To fill vacant benefices the Church ordained priests in batches, many of them men who had lost their wives or families in the plague and flocked to holy orders as a refuge. Many were barely literate, "as it were mere lay folk" who might read a little but without understanding. Priests who survived the plague, declared the Archbishop of Canterbury in 1350, had become "infected by insatiable avarice," charging excessive fees and neglecting souls.

By a contrary trend, education was stimulated by concern for the survival of learning, which led to a spurt in the founding of universities. Notably the Emperor Charles IV, an intellectual, felt keenly the cause of "precious knowledge which the mad rage of pestilential death has stifled throughout the wide realms of the world." He founded the University of Prague in the plague year of 1348 and issued imperial accreditation to five other universities—Orange, Perugia, Siena, Pavia, and Lucca—in the next five years. In the same five years three new colleges were founded at Cambridge—Trinity, Corpus Christi, and Clare—although love of learning, like love in marriage, was not always the motive. Corpus Christi was founded in 1352 because fees for celebrating masses for the dead were so inflated after the plague that two guilds of Cambridge decided to establish a college whose scholars, as clerics, would be required to pray for their deceased members.

Under the circumstances, education did not everywhere flourish. Dwindling attendance at Oxford was deplored in sermons by the masters. At the University of Bologna, mourned Petrarch twenty years later (in a series of letters called "Of Senile Things"), where once there was "nothing more joyous, nothing more free in the world," hardly one of all the former great lecturers was left, and in the place of so many great geniuses, "a universal ignorance has seized the city." But pestilence was not alone responsible; wars and other troubles had added their scars.

The obvious and immediate result of the Black Death was, of course, a shrunken population, which, owing to wars, brigandage, and recurrence of the plague, declined even further by the end of the 14th century. The plague laid a curse on the century in the form of its own bacillus. Lodged in the vectors, it was to break out again six times over the next six decades in various localities at varying intervals of ten to fifteen years. After killing off most of those susceptible, with increasing mortality of children in the later phases, it eventually receded, leaving Europe with a population reduced by about 40 percent in 1380 and by nearly 50 percent at the end of the century. The city of Béziers in southern France, which had 14,000 inhabitants in 1304, numbered 4,000 a century later. The fishing port of Jonquières near Marseille, which once had 354 taxable hearths, was reduced to 135. The flourishing cities of Carcassonne and Montpellier shrank to shadows of their former prosperity, as did Rouen, Arras, Laon, and Reims in the north. The vanishing of taxable material caused rulers to raise rates of taxation, arousing resentment that was to explode in repeated outbreaks in coming decades.

As between landowner and peasant, the balance of impoverishment and enrichment caused by the plague on the whole favored the peasant, although what was true in one place often had an equal and opposite reaction somewhere else. The relative values of land and labor were turned upside down. Peasants found their rents reduced and even relinquished for one or more years by landowners desperate to keep their fields in cultivation. Better no revenue at all than that cleared land should be retaken by the wilderness. But with fewer hands to work, cultivated land necessarily shrank. The archives of the Abbey of Ramsay in England show that thirty years after the plague the acreage sowed in grain was less than half what it had been before. Five plows owned by the abbey in 1307 were reduced to one a century later, and twenty-eight oxen to five.

Hill farms and sections of poor soil were let go or tamed to pasture for sheep, which required less labor. Villages weakened by depopulation and unable to resist the enclosure of land for sheep were deserted in increasing numbers. Property boundaries vanished when fields reverted to wasteland. If claimed by someone who was able to cultivate them, former owners or their heirs could not collect rent. Landowners impoverished by these factors sank out of sight or let castles and manors decay while they entered the military brigandage that was to be the curse of the following decades.

When death slowed production, goods became scarce and prices soared. In France the price of wheat increased fourfold by 1350. At the same time the shortage of labor brought the plague's greatest social disruption—a concerted demand for higher wages. Peasants as well as artisans, craftsmen, clerks, and priests discovered the lever of their own scarcity. Within a year after the plague had passed through northern France, the textile workers of St. Omer near Amiens had gained three successive wage increases. In many guilds artisans struck for higher pay and shorter hours. In an age when social conditions were regarded as fixed, such action was revolutionary.

The response of rulers was instant repression. In the effort to hold wages at preplague levels, the English issued an ordinance in 1349 requiring everyone to work for the same pay as in 1347. Penalties were established for refusal to work, for leaving a place of employment to seek higher pay, and for the offer of higher pay by employers. Proclaimed when Parliament was not sitting, the ordinance was reissued in 1351 as the Statute of Laborers. It denounced not only laborers who demanded higher wages but particularly those who chose "rather to beg in idleness than to earn their bread in labor." Idleness of the worker was a crime against society, for the medieval system rested on his obligation to work. The Statute of Laborers was not simply a reactionary dream but an effort to maintain the system. It provided that every able-bodied person under sixty with no means of subsistence must work for whoever required him, that no alms could be given to able-bodied beggars, that a vagrant serf could be forced to work for anyone who claimed him. Down to the 20th century this statute was to serve as the basis for "conspiracy" laws against labor in the long struggle to prevent unionization.

A more realistic French statute of 1351, applying only to the region of Paris, allowed a rise in wages not to exceed one third of the former level. Prices were fixed and profits of middlemen were regulated. To increase production, guilds were required to loosen their restrictions on the number of apprentices and shorten the period before they could become masters.

In both countries, as shown by repeated renewals of the laws with rising penalties, the statutes were unenforceable. Violations cited by the English Parliament in 1352 show workers demanding and employers paying wages at double and treble the pre-plague rate. Stocks were ordered set up in every town for punishment of offenders. In 1360 imprisonment replaced fines as the penalty and fugitive laborers were declared outlaws. If caught, they were to be branded on the forehead with F for "fugitive" (or possibly for "falsity"). New laws were enacted twice more in the 1360s, breeding the resistance that was to come to a head in the great outbreak of 1381.

The sense of sin induced by the plague found surcease in the plenary indulgence offered by the Jubilee Year of 1350 to all who in that year made the pilgrimage to Rome. Originally established by Boniface VIII in 1300, the Jubilee was intended to make an indulgence available to all repentant and confessed sinners free of charge—that is, if they could afford the journey to Rome. Boniface intended the Jubilee Year as a centennial event, but the first one had been such an enormous success, attracting a reported two million visitors to Rome in the course of the year, that the city, impoverished by the loss of the papacy to Avignon, petitioned Clement VI to shorten the interval to fifty years. The Pope of the joyous murals operated on the amiable principle that "a pontiff should make his subjects happy." He complied with Rome's request in a Bull of 1343.

Momentously for the Church, Clement formulated in the same Bull the theory of indulgences, and fixed its fatal equation with money. The sacrifice of Christ's blood, he stated, together with the merit added by the Virgin and saints, had established an inexhaustible treasury for the use of pardons. By contributing sums to the Church, anyone could buy a share in the Treasury of Merit. What the Church gained in revenue by this arrangement was matched in the end by loss in respect.

CONSIDER . . .

1. What is the purpose of Tuchman's question at the beginning of this excerpt?
2. List the major effects of the plague in the order that Tuchman discusses them here. Do you see any particular design to this arrangement?
3. Find and highlight some examples of transitions.

A Pair of Literary Studies

Tracy Lucas analyzes Hemingway's use of Spanish in *For Whom the Bell Tolls* in the first selection here. In the second, Ingrid Eagly analyzes Matthew Arnold's "Dover Beach" by comparing it to Joni Mitchell's song "Woodstock."

***LaGuerra* Means War:**

The Use of Spanish in *For Whom the Bell Tolls*

Tracy Lucas

Throughout Ernest Hemingway's *For Whom the Bell Tolls* there is an overwhelming reminder that the novel takes place in Spain. No important action is even mentioned in the book unless it is directly related to Spain. In fact, there is very little mention of the outside world. The dialogue itself seems to be translated to English for the benefit of the reader. Blanche Gelfant, in "Language As Moral Code in *Farewell to Arms*," suggests that Hemingway "held purity of language as his esthetic standard, pursued clarity of vision as his moral commitment. For such a writer the relationship between the experience and the word was of utmost concern."

Hemingway continues this commitment to proper word choice in *For Whom the Bell Tolls,* even going so far as to include a number of Spanish words and phrases in the text. This device is used to draw the reader into closer contact with the minds of the Spanish characters, by introducing the actual words spoken by the character rather than a secondhand "translation."

The use of what, to the American reader, seems a confused word order is actually the use of vocabulary and sentence structure which imitate Spanish (Moses, 65). First meeting Robert Jordan, Pablo asks "What have you in the packs?" (10). The American reader finds this sentence structure slightly disconcerting and old-fashioned. He would be more comfortable with "What do you have in the packs?" which retains the slight formality that is associated with Pablo. His actual words would have probably been *"Que tiene Ud. en los paguetos?"*—a word-for-word translation. The *guerrillero* uses a formal address to denote that Jordan knows more than himself. But by *demanding* to know what is in the knapsacks, his formality is undercut by irony and mockingly sarcastic. Throughout the novel Pablo treats Jordan with a certain distant and laughing respect, knowing that the foreigner has a job which he plans to do well—even though the chore may be distasteful and dangerous. This underlying current is actually voiced to Jordan before the band blows the bridge: " 'I do not hold this of the bridge against thee, Ingles,' Pablo said. 'I see a successful termination for it' " (404). Pablo's old-fashioned, disillusioned outlook on life is enhanced by the use of Spanish words and sentence structure in his dialogue.

Hemingway uses many Spanish words throughout the novel, some of them to the exclusion of their English equivalents. Some examples of these are *nada, hombre, queva,* and *Ingles.* The word "nothing" is used, in dialogue, almost only in conjunction with the Spanish *nada.* The English slang word "man" is used several times, but *hombre* is by far the more frequently used. *Queva* is never even given an English translation. Its meaning is so elusive that the American reader must pull it out of the context. And although *Ingles* is translated by both Pilar and Jordan, "Englishman" is never used in its place. These few Spanish words are sprinkled from the beginning to the end of the novel to remind the reader that the book is written from the point of view of citizens of another nation.

Other words that are given in Spanish, if at all, are the curses. George Monteiro suggests, in *Not Hemingway but Spain,* that Hemingway uses Spanish to cover up curses and Christian blasphemies. For precisely this reason there has never been a translation of *For Whom the Bell Tolls* into Spanish, although there have been translations of many of Hemingway's other novels. Monteiro says that "the reason is entirely understandable. . . . If this novel were given to a Spanish translator, huge liberties would be taken with the history and politics of the *querilleros,* especially with Pilar's account of the executions in her village." In the novel, Pablo is called both *cobarde* and *cabron* when he refuses to rise to the taunts of Agustin and Jordan. But Pablo does not seem to mind being called a coward or a fool, because he is *muy borracho*—very drunk. Pilar even goes so far as to call her man a homosexual, a *maricon* (212–216). Never are the truly coarse words mentioned in English. They may be omitted from the dialogue (30) or written in Spanish. The use of *joder, cogar,* and *mierda,* instead, gives these words a deeper sense of mystery and danger. It is more fun for a child to say *fuck* or *shit* when he has to guess the meaning than it is when he can visualize the concepts in his mind. Carole Moses feels that "there is no language so filthy as Spanish. There are words for all the vile words in English and there are other words and expressions that are used only in countries where blasphemy keeps pace with the austerity of religion." Hemingway capitalizes on this wonderfully.

Hemingway's main reason for including Spanish in *For Whom the Bell Tolls* seems to be to enhance the meaning of his chosen word. These shades of meaning are noticed only by Robert Jordan, as the primary bilingual character. Jordan admits that although he speaks Spanish fluently, he still thinks in English. Jordan develops a habit of capitalizing on this difference. When Maria asks him about his family, he tells her that his father is a Republican. He offers no explanation, although he realizes that Maria thinks that his father's political affiliation makes him an active revolutionary, when of course an American Republican is a conservative.

Spanish is not the only language used to further impress upon the reader the differences in the characters. Andre Marty speaks French to Karkov (424). French seems to be even more patronizing and sarcastic: " 'I did not read it,' Andre Marty said. 'Et maintenant fiche moi la paix' " (426). Andre Marty did not find it necessary to waste his time reading Jordan's dispatch. And now he wants to be left alone. The reader senses Marty's air of petulance because French fits his character perfectly as he forces his twisted ideas of righteous warfare practices onto the Spanish Republicans. Language is undoubtedly used to help establish the identities of the characters and their atmosphere in the mountains of Spain in Hemingway's world.

Works Cited

Gelfant, Blanche. "Language As Moral Code in *Farewell to Arms.*" *Modern Fiction Studies* 9: 173–76.

Monteiro, George. "Not Hemingway but Spain." *Fitzgerald–Hemingway Annual* (1971): 304.

Moses, Carole. "Language As Theme in *For Whom the Bell Tolls.*" *Fitzgerald–Hemingway Annual* (1971): 215.

CONSIDER . . .

1. Lucas focuses on a very narrow topic. What does she say about Hemingway's use of Spanish in the novel? What point about the novel is she making? What then is her thesis?
2. How many examples support Lucas's thesis? In your opinion, are these sufficient examples?
3. Notice that Lucas refers to the work of other critics in her essay. What is the effect of this research on readers? Describe how the "Works Cited" list is constructed and organized. Do you have all the information you need to retrieve the articles she cites?

The Quest for Peace

Ingrid Eagly

Matthew Arnold's poem "Dover Beach" and Joni Mitchell's poem "Woodstock" both contain quite similar themes, despite differing time frames and historical subject matter. In addition, the two poems possess contrasting structures. I will compare these poems on both a structural and thematic level.

"Dover Beach" has quite a varied structure. The most dominant beat is the dactyl; however, Arnold does not use the dactyl consistently throughout the poem. The variations in the beat of the poem are due to the different lengths of the lines of the poems. Throughout most of the poem, Arnold uses a combination of long and short lines. The varied line length reinforces the images of the poem. As he discusses the "draw back and fling" of the waves and the "ebb and flow" of human misery, the reader imagines the rising and falling of the tides. The sound of the poem not only creates one similar to the roar and hush of the ocean, but it also creates a graphic design on the page which brings to mind the eternal rise and fall of the tides. The first stanza of Arnold's poem is rather long, 14 lines to be exact. This lengthy stanza provides an emphasis on Arnold's theme, "the *eternal* note of sadness." The stanzas that follow are all shorter (6, 8, 4, and 5 lines). Each stanza continues the imagery of the sea. Arnold has been able to brilliantly use different lengths of stanzas to once again create a rhythm parallel to that of the sea.

Structurally, Mitchell's poem is quite different from Arnold's. Mitchell has chosen a much more rigid pattern. She has a four-line refrain, repeated three times in the poem.

Mitchell's poem is written, like Arnold's, with a predominantly dactylic rhythm. In addition, both poets use varying lengths of lines. However, Mitchell's stanzas begin with shorter lines which grow until the third line. Then the line length continues to decrease until the refrain. The refrain, too, repeats this pattern of a crescendo at the center (the third of four lines). Although Mitchell's pattern is not the same as Arnold's, she does use structure to reinforce the poem's images, as does Arnold. As each of Mitchell's stanzas builds to the longest line, the optimism builds.

The reader almost can't help but begin to read faster as Mitchell gains confidence and feels herself "to be a cog in something turning." As the lines get shorter, the optimism dies out and Mitchell admits that maybe "I don't know who I am."

Despite varying structure, Mitchell and Arnold both convey similar themes in their poems. Arnold's poem was written in 1851. The scene is Dover Beach, only 20 miles from the French coast. Historically, this period in England was one of social and political unrest. The people, especially the middle and lower classes, were dissatisfied with wages and working conditions. England was losing its prominence in the world with the successes of the French and American Revolutions. Arnold's poem refers to the people's dissatisfaction as he speaks of "the eternal note of sadness," "human misery," and "confused alarms of struggle and flight." In contrast, Mitchell's poem was written in 1969 and refers to the Woodstock concert that took place in America. As in Arnold's poem, "Woodstock" reflects a great deal of social and political unrest. People were angered by the American government and especially by U.S. involvement in Vietnam. Mitchell says that "we've got to get ourselves back to the garden." Here she is using a biblical allusion to demonstrate the need for peace in America, to return to the innocence of the Garden of Eden. The narrator follows the "child of God" to try to "get my soul free," continuing the religious reference and the notion that a purging is needed to cleanse us of the hatred and war in our nation.

Although "Woodstock" and "Dover Beach" have different structures and were written in different time frames by different authors in different countries, they both contain a universal theme—peace. Arnold complains of "ignorant armies" that "clash by night," and Mitchell wishes that she could get rid of "the bombers riding shotgun in the sky." They may be speaking of different wars; however, they are both condemning the human vice of hatred and evil that leads us to war. Arnold pleads "Ah, love, let us be true." He feels lost in a world that is lacking joy, love, light, certitude, peace, and help for pain. Mitchell wants to "lose the smog," rejoice in "song and celebration," and watch the bombers turn into golden butterflies. In the modern world, peace is still something that we all long for. After all, without war, we will be able fully to appreciate our world which is "like a land of dreams, so various, so beautiful, so new."

6 Writing to Influence

> *There are two levers for moving men—interest and fear.*
>
> —Napoleon Bonaparte

> *One often contradicts an opinion when what is uncongenial is really the tone in which it was conveyed.*
>
> —Friedrich Nietzsche

> *The best emotions to write out of are anger and fear or dread. . . . The least energizing emotion to write out of is admiration. It is very difficult to write out of because the basic feeling that goes with admiration is a passive contemplative mood.*
>
> —Susan Sontag

When you write a letter to a tire company maintaining that your year-old, prematurely worn tires should be replaced under warranty; when you write a note to your younger cousin persuading her to take a scholarship to a small arts college far from her home; when you pen a request to a professor for a grade appeal—when you do all these kinds of writing, you are writing to influence or to persuade. You are writing to change a person's mind, to affect opinion or thought.

In many ways, most writing is meant to persuade, to convince a reader that a given thesis or idea is a valid perspective on a topic. You want your reader to understand that learning to use a computer requires a certain emotional state and willingness, so you write about that. You conduct a survey and learn that only 7 percent of eleventh-grade students read a newspaper every day—and you use this finding as one cornerstone in a descriptive piece about the dearth of time people under twenty spend reading. Persuasion is a common strategy in much writing and so is important throughout this book; but the explicit and overriding purpose of this chapter is to help you persuade readers to accept, or at least to entertain, a particular point of view.

Persuasion is a subset of formal argument. When you refer to "arguing a point" to persuade a reader, you invoke a general sense of *argue*, meaning *to trade opinions or facts in an effort to convince one's audience or to find the truth.* But there is a difference between formal argument and persuasion, one residing chiefly in their slightly different purposes. The purpose of formal argument is truth-seeking through exploration of reasonable causes and effects. In a strictly formal argument you might explore the causes of the high price of medical care and attempt to understand the issue without particularly trying to persuade the reader of your views; your purpose would be to explore ideas and come to comprehension. You have been practicing argument throughout this book as you sought, brainstormed, and ranked ideas; you have been trying to find reason and truth with each topic you explored, discussed, drafted, revised, and edited. But persuasion has narrower purposes: to change opinion, to affect thinking, to dispose an audience to agree with you. Your specific purpose in writing persuasively is to marshal ideas, facts, and information to change a person's thinking on a given topic, one in which you genuinely believe. This chapter explores the process of writing persuasively through problem finding, the writing of editorial pieces, and the preparation of a position paper.

PERSONAL WRITING: FINDING AND EXPLORING PROBLEMS

The idea of finding problems may initially seem a bit bizarre. After all, problems typically have a way of finding us—or so we think. In reality, though, problems exist everywhere in the world around us, and those who perceive problems and work to address them are those who frequently turn out to be leaders. Being able to detect and think constructively about problems is a valuable skill for academic experience as well as for life beyond academe.

Problems originate in *disequilibrium* and *incongruities:* in imbalances within systems and situations and in the differences between what exists and what we expect to exist. If you need $227 to purchase chemistry textbooks and you have only $173, then you have a problem, a disequilibrium between cost and available money; there is a gap between what exists and what you expected to exist. If you expect that a killing frost will not arrive until late October and fail to prepare your garden accordingly, and the frost happens in mid-September, then you also have a problem. These are everyday, ordinary problems, but in them you can recognize the key notions of *disequilibrium* and *incongruity.*

Problems come to consciousness when you experience *cognitive dissonance*. It is cognitive dissonance—the perception of imbalance or incongruity, of something just not right, of an internal clash between two phenomena or ideas in the writer's mind—that helps a writer begin to realize that a problem exists. When you experience cognitive dissonance, you know that you are realizing the existence of a problem. Most persuasive writing originates here, with a problem a writer believes needs attention: Too few parking places exist on campus, the English curriculum places too little emphasis on American literature, the price of textbooks creates a financial burden for many students, students' health care is inadequate—and so on. What kinds of problems do you see around you? What is troubling you? What incongruities do you notice in your environment? Consider primarily local and immediate problems; understanding and then writing about national and international problems with true authority may require more time, expertise, study, and attention than you can devote now.

Brainstorm a list of problems. When you have a sizable list, compare your list with the lists of your peer group members, then enlarge your list and your thinking about problems. Choose one problem to explore by working through the questions in the problem-exploring rubric that follows. (Your writers' group may prefer exploring a problem together.)

Computer Writing Tip: Use the Internet to find problems. If you join a chat group or participate in a listserv (ESG), you will soon hear of others' problems. Sometimes listening in on conversations gives you a perspective on what other readers and writers find problematic.

Exploring a Problem

A. Write a statement here of what you perceive the problem to be:

B. Now answer these questions about the problem to the best of your knowledge. If you can't answer the question, write a note to yourself.

1. How do you know that the problem really is a problem?
2. How long has this problem existed?
3. How long have you known about the problem?
4. Who is involved in this problem? Be as specific as you can.
5. Who is affected by this problem? Again, be as specific as you can.
6. Are there stages or parts to this problem? If so, describe them.
7. How did the problem begin? What is its history?
8. What are probable causes of the problem?
9. What has been done to solve this problem? What were the costs of the attempted solutions?
10. What were the results of the attempted solutions?

12. What can be done to solve this problem?
13. What would these solutions cost?
14. What may happen if this problem is not addressed or solved?

A Sample Problem Exploration

Here is Jacob Nathan's exploration of the problem of the lack of a recycling program at his college.

Exploring a Problem

A. Write a statement here of what you perceive the problem to be:

> *State College has no recycling program in dormitories and classroom buildings, so many recyclable items end up in the trash and potential income is not realized.*

B. Now answer these questions about the problem:

1. How do you know that the problem really is a problem?

    A survey of the dumpster near any dormitory on campus will yield countless aluminum cans; plastic bottles with 1, 2, and 4 recycling codes; newspapers; and office paper. Last week I checked the dumpster by my dorm one day after a regular garbage pickup, and a friend and I counted 73 soda cans, 21 plastic bottles, and a pile of newspapers about one foot tall. Of course, this is an informal counting, but I think it is revealing. Another part of the problem is that the residence manager tells me that tipping fees (what the university has to pay to dump garbage in the local landfill) are going up $5.00 a ton by July 1 of next year. That's certainly going to increase the university's expenses.

2. How long has this problem existed?

    I don't think this was a problem until recycling became so popular across the country (or until some laws mandating recycling were passed). It has also been more of a problem since landfills began to fill up. So I guess it started becoming a problem in the mid-80s. (I'll have to check on this date: <u>research problem</u>.)

3. How long have you known about the problem?

    I've known about this problem since I moved into the dorm this year. At home we have curbside recycling, and we recycle newspapers, office paper, aluminum, cardboard, and certain plastics. But there is no mechanism in place here at college for keeping up my good habits of recycling.

4. Who is involved in this problem? Be as specific as you can.

    The people primarily involved in the problem are those generating the trash (students, staff, faculty) and those handling the trash, mostly people who work at the Physical Plant. Other key players involved would be people who make decisions about university policy and expenditures—residence hall managers and so forth.

5. Who is affected by this problem? Again, be as specific as you can.

   Those who are involved are also affected by the problem, but the circle of effect is really even wider. If garbage is not recycled, it is not reclaimed for reuse. This wastes resources, which affects all citizens. And citizens are. also affected by increasing costs for dumping and by the fact that landfills are filling up and no one want his/her community to be the location for the next one.

6. Are there stages or parts to this problem? If so, describe them.

   Parts. There is the part of the problem that is concerned with diminishing resources. And there is a part of the problem that has to do with finances. And there is part of the problem that is about citizenship and stewardship.

7. How did the problem begin? What is its history?

   The problem began because resources were perceived to be infinite and the public did not have any consciousness about recycling. No one ever used to worry about soil and water contamination from landfills either, so landfills weren't seen so negatively by the community. Also, a market for recycled material had to develop: In the beginning, no one would buy tons of recycled newspaper, and no one knew how to recycle certain kinds of plastics. See item #3.

8. What are probable causes of the problem?

   The current problem is probably caused by the ignorance of consumers, who don't realize how easy recycling is, and by some reluctance of campus leaders, who may not want to invest the time and effort needed to find buyers for the recyclables or to educate faculty, staff, and students about how to recycle. The university also may own its own landfill area so may not see the need to recycle. (I'd better see if I can find out more about this.)

9. What has been done to solve this problem? What were the costs of the attempted solutions?

   It's amazing, but on this campus no one has ever addressed this problem. I looked in the archives of the student newspaper and found no articles or references anywhere to recycling. I also talked to the manager at the Physical Plant, and she said that the issue had never been perceived as a problem, that they never had any requests or complaints.

10. What were the results of the attempted solutions?

    See #9.

12. What can be done to solve this problem?

    First, we might use existing governing structures among faculty and students to devise an educational consciousness-raising plan and to figure out how to furnish recycling receptacles. We also need to find buyers for the recyclables. I estimate the receptacles would cost about $5.30 apiece; we would need three for each floor of each building on campus. Someone will have to figure this out exactly, but there are 32 buildings on campus with an average height of 3 stories: 32 × 3 = 96 × 3 receptacles per floor = 278 receptacles @ $5.30 apiece = $1423.40 as a minimal start-up estimate for materials. There would be no specific costs for the educational effort, but that would require a commitment of time and paper, etc. (Great project for fraternities, sororities, and service clubs.) I can tell I'm going to have to do some more specific investigation on this part of the problem.

13. What would these solutions cost?

    Included in #12 above.

14. What may happen if this problem is not addressed or solved?

    If this problem is not solved, the landfills will fill up more quickly and the cost of dumping garbage will continue to increase. The university will lose money that could be earned from selling recyclables. The students and staff will fail to develop a consciousness of waste and an understanding of husbandry of resources.

Reflecting on the Problem Exploration

After you work through a problem exploration of your own, consider these questions: What additional information would you need to gather if you wanted to write about this problem? Whom would you want or need to talk to? Are you still interested enough in the problem to write about it? Are you more interested in it than you used to be, or less? Do you still care about the problem?

Retain your notes and your list of problems. You may want to go back to the list later as you pursue a subject for a persuasive piece.

PUBLIC WRITING: AN EDITORIAL PIECE

You can find the editorial piece, a fairly brief persuasive piece, most easily on the editorial page of any newspaper and perhaps less easily as a special feature in many magazines. The newspaper editorial page is home to several kinds of editorial pieces, all written on timely and recent topics of public discourse and concern: formal editorial essays by editorial staff of the publication, regular columns from syndicated writers, and letters to the editor from readers. The purpose of all editorial pieces is to persuade others of one's ideas or opinions on a matter of social or political concern. Sometimes, though, letters to the editor are more like vehicles for venting emotions than carefully reasoned pieces of persuasion; these letters aren't as effective as they might be if their writers added reason and explanation.

Reading Persuasion

An editorial piece typically reacts to an issue current in the community of readers or to something happening in the news or to a piece previously published in the editorial space. It is like one voice in a conversation where many voices insinuate themselves. Listen to these voices; learn to be a good reader of persuasion. Being a good reader of persuasion will help you also to be a good writer of persuasion. So here is a four-part strategy for reading persuasion:

1. **Read slowly and actively.** To understand the points made and to think carefully about the logic of the points presented, read comprehensively and analytically rather than speedily. You are not reading fiction, and you'll need to pay careful attention to the text. While you read, write notes in the margins or on a note card. Resist the urge to underline or highlight important ideas; underscoring and highlighting require little thought and help you less than writing.

2. **Understand what you read.** Use the dictionary to look up unfamiliar words. Read aloud. Stop periodically and ask yourself, "What did I just read?" If you can't give yourself a decent answer, take a break and try rereading. Ask another reader for help if the piece doesn't make sense, or try reading in concert with a friend or colleague so that you can talk about the reading every paragraph or so.

3. **Think rhetorically.** As you read, try to determine the rhetorical situation that produced the piece. Ask yourself these questions: What can I know or figure out about this author? What is the audience like? What kinds of readers are also reading this piece? How may they respond to it? What seems to be the author's purpose? Was this piece written to respond to a particular situation? What kinds of points does the author make? What can I say about the thinking of the author, as revealed in the way the piece is constructed?

4. **React to the reading.** Think about how you are responding to the writer's points. Think about your views on the issues. Pretend that you are talking back to the writer; write down your ideas.

Here are two letters to the editor, both expressing similar sentiments on the subject of normalizing diplomatic relations with Vietnam, relations which had been severed since the Vietnam War. The first letter appeared in the *New York Times;* the second was written by a veteran of the war. Practice the four-part reading strategy on each letter. When you finish a careful reading of each letter, jot down the points that the writer makes, then flesh out the other side of the argument as well.

"The War Is Over.
Life Goes On."

WILLIAM BROYLES JR.

Representative Randy Cunningham burst into tears last week at a Congressional hearing on the recognition of Vietnam. Mr. Cunningham, a California Republican who had been shot down as a Navy pilot in Vietnam, was so overcome with emotion describing the deaths of his comrades that he could not go on. When he recovered, he charged that President Clinton was morally wrong to recognize the former enemy.

Any one of us who fought in Vietnam knows the emotions Randy Cunningham must have felt: the deep grief and anger, the sense of loss, the pride, the whole confusing mess. I have wept, been to the wall on the Capitol Mall, traced the names of the fallen, sought out my old comrades, worked with troubled vets, helped build memorials and led parades.

I feel for the families of the 2,000 or so Americans still unaccounted for. But Randy Cunningham's tears leave me cold. The grief we veterans share should be above partisan politics. It is purer, more honorable and lasting. And it is personal. Tears and emotion in politics fuel partisan suspicions and revenge.

Public emotion has turned Vietnam into a haunting specter that has often sapped our military will. Bosnia is our greatest failure of collective security since Munich because we are afraid of repeating the mistakes of Vietnam. But Nazi aggression had little to do with the postcolonial war in Vietnam, which in turn has little to do with Bosnia. The Balkan tragedy does, however, have a lot to do with Munich. Because our memories are so faint and our emotions so vivid, we persist in applying the lessons of the wrong wars. We must put Vietnam behind us.

The Vietnam veterans who support recognition have impeccable credentials: Senator John McCain, Republican of Arizona, was a P.O.W.; Senator John Kerry, Democrat of Massachusetts, won the Navy Cross; Senator Bob Kerrey, Democrat of Nebraska, won the Medal of Honor and left part of a leg in Vietnam. Does their support for recognition mean they are betraying their comrades who are still missing?

That is the hardest question, because the deep, uncompromising rule of the soldier is not to leave your comrades on the battlefield. But the fighting has been over for 20 years. Our battlefields are rice paddies now, tilled by men and women not even born when the guns fell silent. There were more M.I.A.'s in World War II than the total number of Americans killed in Vietnam. Thousands remain unaccounted for after the Korean War. We should continue to try to account for everyone. But the time has come to do so in cooperation with our old enemies.

The reason why is in the mirror. Look at us. Our hair is gray, what little there is. Some of us are grandfathers now. Many of us went to war 30 years ago. Thirty years! That's the time between the start of World War I and the end of World War II. In those earlier 30 years, more than 100 million people died. Millions perished in death camps. Millions more died and were never found. Tens of millions were homeless. The maps of Europe and Asia were redrawn. Whole countries disappeared.

In comparison, Vietnam is a footnote. Yet we can't get beyond it—supposedly because we lost. But our countryside wasn't ripped with bombs, our forests defoliated, our cities pulverized, our people herded into camps. We had casualties, but we did not have millions of refugees and more than a million dead. We weren't thrown into the sea as the British were at Dunkirk.

I never felt defeated. I just felt wasted. I would have fought in World War II. I would fight today in Bosnia. But where I fought was in Vietnam.

And by now the only true response by a soldier should be this: tough. As we said in Vietnam, it don't mean nothing. Which meant, it means everything, but what can you do? In war people die. Sometimes the best people die. We want there to be a reason. Sometimes there is, sometimes there isn't. War is messy and unfair. That's why it needs a clear purpose. There was no clear purpose in Vietnam. There is one in Bosnia.

Ten years ago, I visited the site of the base where I had been a Marine lieutenant, just west of Da Nang. I went with a man named Hien, who had been a company commander in the Vietcong. We had fought each other up and down the rice paddies, mountains and in the jungles. Almost all his comrades were dead or missing.

It was hard not to respect our enemies. They had been bombed by B-52's, bombarded with shells hurled from battleships, incinerated by napalm and white phosphorous, drenched in defoliants. They had no R & R and no Medivacs. They lived in tunnels and caves, never going home and getting no letters for as many as 10 years.

Hien and I met a woman whose husband had been killed where I had fought. She never found his body. Most likely we bulldozed him into a mass grave. That's what we did. We incinerated them, buried them alive, pushed them from helicopters. And they did their best to kill us. That's what happens in a war. What should happen after a war is what the woman said after we had talked long enough to realize her husband had been killed by my platoon, possibly by me. "That was long ago," she told me. "The war is over. Life goes on."

The Vietnamese have hundreds of thousands of M.I.A.'s. Soldiers trying to find the bodies of their lost comrades is a constant theme in Vietnamese novels and films. Their families grieve no less than ours. They know better than anyone the pain we feel. We should all search together for the answers that would help families on both sides finally end this.

I loved the men I fought beside. I feel pride in their courage and unselfishness. But the time has come to say to all my buddies who are missing, as we say to those names on the wall, rest in peace. You did your best. We miss you terribly.

We fought to make Vietnam free and independent. Today it is independent. And if we engage its leaders diplomatically with the same will we showed against the Soviet Union, it will become more free. To recognize Vietnam is not to dishonor the memory of our fallen or missing comrades. It is to recognize the truth: The war is over.

To the Editors
Paul William Burch

I get up in the morning and the pain is there. Unapologetic. It is the residue of my late adolescence—the war in Vietnam. My knees hurt and my right ankle is stiff and achy. It's no big deal. I can't run very long, or fast or hard. But I can keep up with my ten-year-old; and my two older sons, now in their twenties, know me for all my weaknesses and still love me. So does my wife. I'm damn lucky. It's more than twenty-seven years since I was there. So many others have not been so lucky. I know this. I will never forget it. It's personal. Like my aches it remains—unamended by adult reasoning. I can live with it. And I can live with Clinton's actions with regard to Vietnam.

CONSIDER . . .

1. What points do both writers address? Where are the major points of agreement?
2. Part of the rhetorical context for these pieces is that both arose as a response to President Bill Clinton's reestablishing ties to Vietnam. Another part of the rhetorical context involves the authors: What seems to be each author's point of view here? Compare the use and purpose of personal experience and narrative in each piece.

Writing Task:

Choose your role—member of editorial staff or reader—and write a piece for an editorial page or section. Your goal is to persuade other readers at least to entertain your ideas and at most to act on them.

The editorial piece does not have to address an issue of local or national significance, even though many editorial pieces do. It should, however, offer an opinion on an issue or idea that matters to you and to the other readers whose conversation you are joining, whether they are readers of your local newspaper or of *Men's Journal, National Review, Photography Today, Sports Illustrated, American Historical Quarterly,* or *Journal of the American Medical Association.* Typically an editorial piece originates in a response to a specific situation. It may conclude with a general principle that undergirds the specific response, but it almost always begins in specificity. The editorial piece should be a serious piece that you will submit for publication. It will demonstrate to readers of your portfolio that you are a reader and writer of substance, one who can participate in a conversation about ideas; and it will reveal your ability to marshal arguments and information in support of your thesis or point of contention.

Invention Ideas

Consider first if any problems or issues have recently presented themselves, especially in publications you have been reading. Then consider whether you have experienced cognitive dissonance with regard to anything specific lately: Is anything bothering you? Has anything struck you as unfair, out of balance? Think of your immediate environment and interests within it first; then consider state and local issues. Make a list of problems that trouble you. Star the most promising problems. Then choose one and begin.

BRAINSTORMING YOUR ARGUMENTS.   Persuading readers requires care and preparation, so you will find that invention and preparation for drafting this piece involve several stages. Here's the first: Before you draft, try brainstorming your arguments—both your own arguments *for* your position and your opponents' probable arguments *against* your position. Put two columns down a large page, as in Figure 6.1.

Statement of Problem:

My problem is that _____

_____

Points FOR My Argument	**Points AGAINST My Argument**

Figure 6.1   A useful format for brainstorming about an argument

Computer Writing Tip: As part of your invention strategy for the editorial, you might try an e-mail response to a newspaper or magazine article. Most newspapers and magazines have e-mail addresses for readers' responses.

REEVALUATING YOUR STANCE.   After you finish brainstorming points, reevaluate your initial position. Do you still believe in your first ideas? If so, number the points as you believe they should be arranged so that the brainstorming list can serve as a sketchy outline of what to include. If you no longer believe in your topic or if you have lost your fervor for it, begin again. Caring about what you write, believing in what you have to say, is important when you are trying to persuade others.

ANALYZING AUDIENCE.   Jot brief responses to the questions that follow to gain a better understanding of your audience, who you imagine your readers to be. Considering audience is especially important in persuasion because your purpose is to affect your readers.

1. Exactly who is your audience? Are you writing to a specific person on a specific topic? Are you writing to a large, general audience that has one or a few beliefs or circumstances in common—like political persuasion, religion, region of the country, interest in sports or decorating or guns?
2. What do you, the writer, have in common with the audience? Are you one of the audience or an outsider? With what issues in your writing will the audience probably agree? How close a fit exists between you and the audience in terms of education, socioeconomic background, experience, and ideology?
3. Where are the potential points of conflict in the essay between you and the audience? What do you need to understand or realize to attract this segment of the audience?

Now ask your writers' group to answer these same questions from their perspective, and keep their recommendations in mind as you consider how to reach your audience more effectively.

REVIEWING STRUCTURE.   Another important aspect of preparing to write the initial draft is planning its structure. Formal persuasion typically has several identifiable parts:

Claim: The thesis or point the writer wishes to argue on behalf of.
Stated reason(s): A reason for supporting the claim, frequently expressed in *because* clauses or sentences.
Warrant or **unstated assumptions:** Points (beliefs, principles, values, ideas) that the writer assumes the audience will accede to.

Examine William Broyles's persuasive piece "The War Is Over" (p. 172) again. Here are the claim, the stated reasons, and the warrant:

Claim: We must put Vietnam behind us (paragraph 4).
Stated reasons: Twenty years have passed (paragraph 5).
The battlefields are rice paddies, tilled by people not even born when the Vietnam War ended (paragraph 5).
World War II produced more men missing in action than were killed in total in Vietnam (paragraph 5).

Thousands of Americans are still unaccounted for after the Korean War (paragraph 5).

American veterans of Vietnam are now old (paragraph 6).

Warrant: The passage of time cannot change the outcome of the past. It is good to accept what we cannot change and put it behind us.

Taken together, the claim, stated reasons, and warrant constitute what Aristotle called the *enthymeme*. Try to build this skeleton of the persuasive piece into your essay.

A skeletal enthymeme must be fleshed out, though, if it is to present a lively editorial piece that will persuade a reader. To make your piece work, you will need to add what philosopher Stephen Toulmin calls *grounds* and *backing*. *Grounds* are supporting evidence for the enthymeme: facts, statistics, examples, data. *Backing* is the support behind the warrant (or unstated assumptions). If the warrant for Broyles's piece is that *it is good to accept what we cannot change and put it behind us*, backing addresses the question *Why is it good to accept what we cannot change?* Describe what constitutes the grounds and backing in Broyles's piece.

Fill in the chart shown in Figure 6.2 to ensure that you have a claim, stated reasons and grounds, and warrant and backing.

Structuring an Argument

A. My claim is that _____

_____

B. These reasons support my claim (fill in as many as you need):

1. _____

2. _____

3. _____

4. _____

5. _____

C. The warrant for my argument is that _____

_____

[When you complete item C, you have outlined the enthymeme.]

D. The backing for the warrant is that _____

_____

E. The grounds or evidence (facts, statistics, data, examples) for my argument are these (again, use as many as you need):

1. _____

2. _____

3. _____

4. _____

[When you finish item E, you have outlined information for the body of your essay.]

Figure 6.2 Outlining an enthymeme, grounds, and backing for a persuasive essay

Computer Writing Tip: Copy or scan this heuristic (Figure 6.2) into your computer so that you can reuse it whenever you want to plan an argument.

Drafting the Editorial Piece

Notice how your finished chart is actually an outline of most of the information you'll use in your paper. Now you are ready to draft. As usual, write as quickly as you can, disregarding concerns for correctness and word choice and spelling. Don't worry, either, about emotional or off-the-wall expressions revealing your feelings about the subject. You can evaluate the need for emotion later. Don't be overly concerned about form at this point either; you will have an opportunity to revise that later too. Now it is important to get the ideas from your head to the page.

Once you have a draft, let it cool for a few days. Then take it to your writers' group.

Writers' Group: Rethinking the Editorial Piece

Your writers' group will test your ideas. You can evaluate the persuasiveness of your piece in an informal debate on your topic. If you are writing in favor of term limits for senators and members of the House of Representatives, for instance, ask your writers' group to marshal all the arguments against term limits and fire them at you. This process will help you detect weaknesses in your argument so you can bolster your case. Finally, revise the piece to underscore your capable argument. You may want to go through the writers' group review and the revision process more than once.

Presenting the Editorial Piece

You have invested significant thinking and writing time in your editorial piece. When you have polished the piece, submit it for publication in an appropriate college or community newspaper or in a magazine whose audience will care about what you have to say. Using formal business-letter format, prepare a very brief cover letter for your piece. Address the letter to the editor of the publication by name. Say simply that you are submitting the enclosed piece for possible publication and that the piece has not been submitted elsewhere.

Reflecting on the Editorial Piece

What did you find most satisfying about the process of writing the opinion piece? What worked well? What did you learn from this experience? Reflect on the experience in your writing notebook.

PUBLIC WRITING: POSITION PAPER

A position paper stakes out a more formal position than an editorial piece. An editorial piece is typically a response to some event or happening in a given community, even to another piece of writing. A position paper frequently initiates or sets forth a position or a belief on the part of the writer and may not be immediately related to a specific or current event or issue. A position paper is also likely to be philosophical in nature. Typically a position piece assumes a problem/solution structure, one emphasizing either the problem or the solution to the problem. The piece may examine a problem, then state the writer's position on it. Or the piece may briefly sketch a problem, then propose a solution—again, the writer's solution. Or the position paper may combine problem and solution in a statement of the writer's position. The preferred way to manage this kind of piece to prevent it from becoming unwieldy, however, is to give dominant emphasis to either the problem or the solution.

Writing Task:

Write a position paper setting forth your position on an issue or problem. The issue may, but does not have to be, of current interest.

Invention Ideas

What problems exist in your family or personal relationships (that you feel comfortable writing about)? At your work? In your classes? In teams or organizations to which you belong? In student government at your school? In local or state government? What is your position regarding these problems? What solutions do you offer to these problems? What is your position regarding the solutions?

To increase your awareness of problems, listen with an attentive ear and read with a careful eye for a few days. Be especially aware of what is said at meetings, on the radio, or on the television news; read carefully newspapers, newsletters, and magazines. Give yourself a few days, and a topic/problem should present itself to you.

Drafting the Position Paper

Before you draft your paper, sketch an outline of the claim; then state reasons to support the claim and the grounds for them; finally, lay out the warrant (unstated assumptions) and the backing for it. Then write a brief audience analysis.

Then, having prepared the heart of the paper, draft the entire position piece. Draft as quickly as possible, being mindful of your outline. When you have a complete draft, put it aside while you look at some examples of position papers.

Looking at Some Position Papers

College sports provide a lot of matter for conversation and reading. In these two pieces about college sports, two writers take positions regarding college athletes. Each writer identifies a problem, then establishes a position vis-à-vis the problem.

The Shame of College Sports
Nick Deets

The Associated Press has estimated that as many as 40% of major sports schools cheat in a big way. The shame and the problems within the system can be defined in all too many unpleasant contexts. It is fiscal: football and basketball are big business for most schools. It is educational: when a kid is cheated out of all chance of learning, the institution is also cheated out of its reason for being. The fact is that less than one-third of the athletes in revenue-producing sports graduate from college. It is social and racial: many victims of the "dumb jock" syndrome, 1990s version, are black or from minorities and from underprivileged or so-called "ghetto" neighborhoods. But most of all, it is moral. In the quest for victory, the vast majority of fans, alumni, and even coaches and administrators have accepted the notion that a winner may have to cheat.

Suggest almost any cure, from keeping freshmen off varsity teams to an NCAA clearinghouse where high-school and junior-college transfer athletes would be evaluated and approved, and you will probably be proposing an improvement in the dismal system of college athletics. Political, financial, and administrative obstacles, however, make many reform measures unfeasible. Based on conversations with various coaches and a lot of reading on the subject, here are some suggestions which, together or in part, might help turn college athletics in a sensible and realistic direction.

Athletic scholarships should be frozen over a five-year period. That is, if an athlete had not received his degree after five years, his scholarship could not automatically be awarded to an incoming student. In fact, that same scholarship could not be used for a period of three years. This procedure would motivate coaches to get players to class. It would not eliminate efforts to railroad kids through easy courses toward degrees, but that abuse can be controlled by the next remedy.

Every school should be required to appoint a faculty committee to oversee academic performance by athletes. It would report to the college president and, if necessary, to the NCAA on ludicrous course loads or lack of attendance. Makeup sessions would be available and required when athletes missed classes due to game schedules. Even the most "jock-oriented" schools have some faculty members who are skeptical about the athletic program. They should be given a voice as a check and balance. At the same time, athletic department "advisors" should submit their planned academic advice to the faculty committee for approval.

Coaches should be redefined as teachers and athletes as students. If either breaches his responsibility to foster education, he should be disciplined as would a disrupter of a classroom. Anyone caught undermining the educational system by cheating should be placed on the same probation as the school—unable to coach or play until the punishment is served.

The large sums of money awarded to schools appearing in post-season bowls or tournaments should be reallocated. Under the current method, a mere appearance in the NCAA basketball tournament can thrust a shaky program into the black. An appearance in the final round can be worth millions of dollars. At those prices, it is often worth it for a coach to risk probation in pursuit of the money. A team's share should be limited to expenses plus a bonus of perhaps 10% of the game's net profit, and the remainder distributed throughout the entire network of NCAA members.

The crux of the solution seems to be that the penalties for cheating need to be increased so that the impact on offenders is significant. Colleges should have to pay dearly for infractions of NCAA regulations. Then school officials would have a serious incentive for controlling their boosters as well as their athletic staff. The revenue loss from probation could drive a reluctant administration to take action. As for individual coaches, they would be more cautious if they faced the possibility that their future employment would be jeopardized by probation. On a second offense, a school should not merely be deprived of TV revenues and bowl bids, but should have its schedule suspended until it had satisfied all requirements. It is very possible that boosters without ball games might reform in a great hurry.

Indiana basketball coach Bobby Knight places this sick and sleazy atmosphere in a suitably sleazy context. "Cheating in college athletics is like messing around with another guy's wife," he says. "It's not bad until you get caught. But you might think twice if you knew that the guy who finally caught you was sure to have a gun."

CONSIDER . . .

1. What claim does Deets make about college sports and athletes?
2. What grounds does Deets state for his claim?
3. What is the warrant of Deets's piece? In your opinion, does he do a sufficient job of backing his warrant?
4. Does this piece try to persuade the reader that the problem needs addressing or that Deets's solutions are the best remedies for the problem?
5. If you were writing this piece, what changes might you make in the next version of it?

In a piece from *U.S. News & World Report*, John Leo, too, writes about a problem related to varsity sports. Notice especially how Leo eases the reader into a statement of the problem and then how he defines the problem and establishes his position on how to address it.

Should Stars Get Dunked?

JOHN LEO

We are deep into another cycle of celebrated redemption cases, ranging from Mike Tyson, unrepentant heavyweight rapist, to Gina Grant, manipulative matricide and Harvard reject.

In all these cases, it is understood that the media have the job of either conferring instant rehabilitation or, if the public balks, suggesting that it's surely time to offer the perpetrator a second chance—or, as in the cases of New York Yankee career screw-ups Steve Howe and Darryl Strawberry, a seventh or eighth chance.

But the changing cultural climate has started to alter the way these stories play out, as the Richie Parker case shows.

Parker is a blue-chip high-school basketball star and a sex felon. One January morning last year, Parker, then 17, and a friend forced a 15-year-old girl to perform oral sex on them in a stairwell at their New York City high school. He was charged with felony first-degree sodomy, which could have meant two to six years in prison. But he plea-bargained to a reduced charge of felony sex abuse and he was sentenced to five years of supervised probation.

This meant that Parker could go on to play college ball as if nothing had happened. Seton Hall was the first university to recruit him. According to Parker's lawyer, Seton Hall promised a scholarship even if he pleaded guilty to the sex felony—an interesting reflection of the moral priorities at this Roman Catholic basketball school.

When New York newspapers hammered away at the story, public outrage forced Seton Hall to back down and withdraw. The same thing happened at George Washington University, with Washington media taking the lead. GWU, apparently in an attempt to disinfect its recruitment of a newly convicted sex abuser, offered a scholarship to his victim as well.

"This will haunt him." In between the media onslaughts at Seton Hall and GWU, Parker had a crack at a school in a lesser media market. He was recruited by the University of Utah. Whatever chance he had there disappeared when the school's head coach and an assistant coach flew to New York and suggested to the media that Parker's victim might be lying. "This girl could have damaged Parker for life," explained the assistant Utah coach. "Five years from now, this will haunt him." After the predictable uproar, Utah's assistant coach apologized and was put on probation by the university. This may have been a historic first: a college coach disciplined for blaming a jock's female accuser.

In all redemption cases—and Parker's is no exception—someone is bound to suggest that the perpetrator is the real victim. Even in the Susan Smith case, sympathy for the accused as a victim of sexual and emotional abuse is snaking its way through the media. But public tolerance is low these days for conventional descriptions of the perp as victim.

A stronger case can be made for Parker under the heading of "second chance." It goes like this: He is a youngster with a clean record before and after this ugly crime. He comes from an intact, protective family that has tried to push decent values and upward mobility—both of Parker's older sisters made it to college. Parker has apologized to his victim, and her lawyer says he believes Parker is sincerely sorry. In return for her dropping her lawsuit, Parker agreed to give the victim a significant percentage of any money he makes as a pro basketball player. Almost everybody who knows Parker seems to say nice things about him. Since the crime, he has worked hard at school and graduated with a flurry of A's and B's.

Since one act does not define a life, doesn't Parker deserve another chance? Sure, but not now, with the prize of a basketball scholarship to a big-time school. It violates a sense of justice that a sex abuser should continue a glittering basketball career without missing a beat while the victim has had to flee to a second high school, then to a third because fans and friends of Parker harassed her at the second school.

The "second chance" argument for Parker is taking place amid great cynicism about college athletic departments, some of which would apparently be willing to recruit serial killers if it meant filling the arenas for every game and making it to the Final Four.

It's a disgrace that all three universities backed away only because of bad publicity, not because of any concern over the moral message they would have sent by welcoming a serious sex offender to four free years on campus. "With society unraveling at such a breakneck pace, the signals we send as institutions are very important," said Richard Lapchick, director of Northeastern University's Center for the Study of Sport in Society.

In addition, rape charges against college basketball and football stars have been a persistent problem over the years at many colleges. Traditionally, these charges tend to fade away without many expulsions or indictments. That's changing. But if the colleges are serious about the problem, it makes no sense to start importing well-known and unrehabilitated sex offenders. Some sports columnists think Parker should head for an obscure community college, put his life together there, then switch to a Division 1 school when he has a longer record of good behavior. Good idea. Right now he's not ready for prime-time hoops.

CONSIDER . . .

1. Leo's essay attempts to persuade readers that a problem exists. Are you convinced that this situation is a problem as Leo writes about it? Do you believe that Leo succeeds in the intent to persuade?
2. What exactly is Leo's claim—and what are the grounds for this claim?
3. Put Leo's warrant into your own words. Are you satisfied with the backing for this warrant?

University life is a popular topic. In an article from *Newsweek*, Kurt Wiesenfeld, a physicist and professor at Georgia Tech, addresses a problem in the academic aspect of college life.

Making the Grade

KURT WIESENFELD

It was a rookie error. After 10 years I should have known better, but I went to my office the day after final grades were posted. There was a tentative knock on the door. "Professor Wiesenfeld? I took your Physics 2121 class? I flunked it? I wonder if there's anything I can do to improve my grade?" I thought: "Why are you asking me? Isn't it too late to worry about it? Do you dislike making declarative statements?"

After the student gave his tale of woe and left, the phone rang. "I got a D in your class. Is there any way you can change it to 'Incomplete'?" Then the e-mail assault began: "I'm shy about coming in to talk to you, but I'm not shy about asking for a better grade. Anyway, it's worth a try." The next day I had three phone messages from students asking *me* to call *them*. I didn't.

Time was, when you received a grade, that was it. You might groan and moan, but you accepted it as the outcome of your efforts or lack thereof (and, yes, sometimes a tough grader). In the last few years, however, some students have developed a disgruntled-consumer approach. If they don't like their grade, they go to the "return" counter to trade it in for something better.

What alarms me is their indifference toward grades as an indication of personal effort and performance. Many, when pressed about why they think they deserve a better grade, admit they don't deserve one but would like one anyway. Having been raised on gold stars for effort and smiley faces for self-esteem, they've learned that they can get by without hard work and real talent if they can talk the professor into giving them a break. This attitude is beyond cynicism. There's a weird innocence to the assumption that one expects (even deserves) a better grade simply by begging for it. With that outlook, I guess I shouldn't be as flabbergasted as I was that 12 students asked me to change their grades *after* final grades were posted.

That's 10 percent of my class who let three months of midterms, quizzes and lab reports slide until long past remedy. My graduate student calls it hyperrational thinking: if effort and intelligence don't matter, why should deadlines? What matters is getting a better grade through an unearned bonus, the academic equivalent of a freebie T-shirt or toaster giveaway. Rewards are disconnected from the quality of one's work. An act and its consequences are unrelated, random events.

Their arguments for wheedling better grades often ignore academic performance. Perhaps they feel it's not relevant. "If my grade isn't raised to a D I'll lose my scholarship." "If you don't give me a C, I'll flunk out." One sincerely overwrought student pleaded, "If I don't pass, my life is over." This is tough stuff to deal with. Apparently, I'm responsible for someone's losing a scholarship, flunking out or deciding whether life has meaning. Perhaps these students see me as a commodities broker with something they want—a grade. Though intrinsically worthless, grades, if properly manipulated, can be traded for what has value: a degree, which means a job, which means money. The one thing college actually offers—a chance to learn—is considered irrelevant, even less than worthless, because of the long hours and hard work required.

In a society saturated with surface values, love of knowledge for its own sake does sound eccentric. The benefits of fame and wealth are more obvious. So is it right to blame students for reflecting the superficial values saturating our society?

Yes, of course it's right. These guys had better take themselves seriously now, because our country will be forced to take them seriously later, when the stakes are much higher. They must recognize that their attitude is not only self-destructive, but socially destructive. The erosion of quality control—giving appropriate grades for actual accomplishments—is a major concern in my department. One colleague noted that a physics major could obtain a degree without ever answering a written exam question completely. How? By pulling in enough partial credit and extra credit. And by getting breaks on grades.

But what happens once she or he graduates and gets a job? That's when the misfortunes of eroding academic standards multiply. We lament that schoolchildren get "kicked upstairs" until they graduate from high school despite being illiterate and mathematically inept, but we seem unconcerned with college graduates, whose less blatant deficiencies are far more harmful if their accreditation exceeds their qualifications.

Most of my students are science and engineering majors. If they're good at getting partial credit but not at getting the answer right, then the new bridge breaks or the new drug doesn't work. One finds examples here in Atlanta. Last year a light tower in the Olympic Stadium collapsed, killing a worker. It collapsed because an engineer miscalculated how much weight it could hold. A new 12-story dormitory could develop dangerous cracks due to a foundation that's uneven by more than six inches. The error resulted from incorrect data being fed into a computer. I drive past that dorm daily on my way to work, wondering if a foundation crushed under kilotons of weight is repairable or if this structure will have to be demolished. Two 10,000-pound steel beams at the new natatorium collapsed in March, crashing into the student athletic complex. (Should we give partial credit since no one was hurt?) Those are real-world consequences of errors and lack of expertise.

But the lesson is lost on the grade-grousing 10 percent. Say that you won't (not can't, but won't) change the grade they deserve to what they want, and they're frequently bewildered or angry. They don't think it's fair that they're judged according to their performance, not their desires or "potential." They don't think it's fair that they should jeopardize their scholarships or be in danger of flunking out simply because they could not or did not do their work. But it's more than fair; it's necessary to help preserve a minimum standard of quality that our society needs to maintain safety and integrity. I don't know if the 13th-hour students will learn that lesson, but I've learned mine. From now on, after final grades are posted, I'll lie low until the next quarter starts.

CONSIDER . . .

1. What was the immediate problem that prompted Wiesenfeld to write this piece?
2. What is the larger problem—the way of conceptualizing academic performance—that Wiesenfeld calls to the readers' attention?
3. What is Wiesenfeld's point, his position, with regard to the larger problem?

Writers' Group: Rethinking the Position Paper

Now reconsider your draft position paper, then ask your group to examine the piece. In addition to ensuring that your claim and grounds, warrant, and backing are clear and sound, you and your group may want to review the writing for the seven deadliest logical fallacies, errors in thinking that can creep into anyone's writing. Here they are:

- **Bandwagon appeal:** An appeal for everyone to join the latest fad. For example: Everyone likes tax cuts; therefore, tax cuts are good and you should agree with the proposal to cut taxes.
- *Ad hominem* **appeal:** An attack against the person *(hominem)* rather than the idea. For example, rather than attack a senator's ideas, a political columnist attacks the senator herself.
- **Red herring:** A distraction ploy. Instead of addressing a critical issue, the writer throws out a "red herring," or less relevant issue, as a distraction. In an interview, an interviewee asked a difficult question may simply ignore it and provide an unrelated response.
- **Begging the question:** Supporting a claim with a statement that simply restates the claim instead of offering support for it: "Imports are good for the American economy because they offer real economic benefits."
- **Either–or fallacy:** Making a complicated issue seem simple by setting up two possible solutions and creating a binary opposition, even though there may be many possible subtle solutions: "Sandy's financial situation can be solved only if she takes a better-paying job or sells her house." There are probably many ways that Sandy can affect her financial situation without having to resort to two such drastic solutions.
- *Post hoc, ergo propter hoc* **fallacy:** Literally, the "after this, therefore because of this" fallacy. This fallacy confuses simultaneity with cause: If two things happen near one another in time, one is believed to cause the other. For instance, "I wore my lucky yellow shirt, and I won the tennis tournament; therefore, I won because I wore my lucky yellow shirt."
- **Hasty generalization:** Use of a small bit of evidence to support a wide generalization: "Everyone in my study group is having trouble with punctuating complex sentences; therefore, complex sentences are too hard for undergraduates to understand."

Computer Writing Tip: You may find it useful to make a file of these common errors in logic so that you can check your persuasive pieces against them in the future.

Publishing the Position Paper

The position paper is frequently quite effective as an oral presentation. Consider presenting your position piece as a speech before your classmates. Doing so would give you yet another chance for feedback before you include it in the portfolio.

Another possibility is that the position piece can and should be a documented essay (see Chapter 8). At any rate, the position piece is an excellent candidate for inclusion in your portfolio.

Reflecting on the Position Paper

Compare your process in writing the position paper to that in writing the editorial piece. Which seemed easier? Which was more enjoyable?

What particular problems presented themselves during the writing of the position paper? How might you prevent those problems in future writing experiences?

Are you hoping to publish either of these pieces? Write about how you chose a publication to submit your persuasive piece(s) to.

Write about these ideas in your writing notebook.

PORTMANTEAU OF WRITING TO INFLUENCE

The following Pormanteau selections give you a chance to explore other examples of persuasive writing.

First you will find some editorial pieces, several of which cluster around the specific event of the bombing of the Alfred P. Murrah Building in Oklahoma City in April 1995. In the May 1, 1995, issue of *The New Yorker*, Mark Singer writes "Them and Us" in the editorial section ("Talk of the Town"). A week later, also in the editorial sections of the magazine, appear Adam Gopnik's "Violence As Style" and Joyce Carol Oates's "American Gothic." In the June 12 issue, letters responding to all those pieces appear under the heading "Whose Fault Is It?" in the "mail" section.

Them and Us

M A R K   S I N G E R

The true cliché that was uttered so frequently in the immediate aftermath of the murderous explosion last week at the Alfred P. Murrah Federal Building, in Oklahoma City—"It's not supposed to happen here"—contained multiple shades of meaning. Implicit was the shock of recognition colliding with the shock of unrecognition. "It," of course, referred to the mass slaughter of innocents—an image previously beamed in from places where horror was routinely drained of its meaning by the application of the modifier "war-torn," another true cliché. "Here" was a synonym for balmier abstractions: "the heartland" and "Middle America." To make bigger headlines, you would have to blow up Hannibal, Missouri.

The world that I knew growing up in Oklahoma was a place of simple distinctions—them and us. When I studied United States history in high school, there were two assigned texts: a survey book and J. Edgar Hoover's "Masters of Deceit." When I studied Oklahoma history—a requirement—I recognized a protesting-too-much quality about the endeavor. "We know we belong to the land, and the land we belong to is grand," Rodgers and Hammerstein wrote, but until they came along we didn't have an official state song, perhaps because we didn't have much history to sing about. An accurate time line would start with Francisco de Coronado in 1541, skip to the Trail of Tears in 1838, and then to the land rush in 1889. Most of the settlers had been run off from someplace else, and disenfranchisement must have felt like a birthright. Statehood didn't come until 1907.

Oklahoma City became the capital three years later, a tribute to its central location rather than its indigenous charm. For a while, the big oil and gas discoveries seemed to be occurring everywhere else, but finally, in 1928, the Oklahoma City Field erupted. It was so prolific that three times during the nineteen-thirties the Oklahoma National Guard was called out to curtail production. By then, as well, drought and the Depression and armies of Joad families had become reality.

After Steinbeck published "The Grapes of Wrath," decades ticked by during which little happened that gave events in Oklahoma a wider resonance. For restless adolescents, that fact of life felt like a conspiracy—the fear that nothing would ever happen existed in counterpoise with our parents' anxiety that something actually would.

Last week, something finally did happen. The dust literally had not settled before fingers pointed, reflexively, in the direction of the Middle East—a vast, amorphous "them." Scattered throughout the Middle East are people with whom Oklahomans, especially, have a complicated relationship. The oil-and-gas boom of the nineteen-seventies and early eighties came courtesy of OPEC and the Islamic fundamentalists who brought about the fall of the Shah of Iran. When the bubble burst in 1982, it left a dual legacy—an Oklahoma economy that has never recovered and a confusion about the boundaries between "them" and "us." The startling news, last Friday afternoon, of the arrest of one white American suspect and the questioning of another deepened that confusion. Now the enemies seemed to be homegrown haters, not swarthy foreigners.

What has happened in Oklahoma is another history lesson, one that dawned in a heartbeat, and it bears a message that the rest of America now finally understands: all terrorism is local.

Violence As Style

ADAM GOPNIK

"TERROR STRIKES THE HEARTLAND," read one headline, echoing a note widely sounded in the immediate aftermath of the Oklahoma City bombing. But, even before the revelation that this particular atrocity had been as homegrown as a bushel of wheat, the alibi of foreign infection already seemed evasive. For the heartland was in many ways where terror began. The practice of political terrorism has been refined in

Europe and the Middle East, but its theory—the understanding that in an age of instant communications killing can be a kind of symbolic speech, a form of show business, engaged in for its publicity value—was pioneered by Americans. It was out West, among the frontier outposts, that the vigilante groups of the mid-nineteenth century—Bald Knobbers, White Caps, and Regulators—developed the practice of killing people in order to send a message. Lynch somebody in New Mexico and they'll get the word in Oregon. Unlike the city-bred (and usually foreign-born) anarchists of a generation or two later, the vigilantes had no interest in notions of universal brotherhood. They saw themselves as personifying an authentic, organic Americanism, the very opposite of the procedural Americanism of laws and legislators and United States marshals. Last week's bombers in Oklahoma City fit all too well into that bloody tradition, and are all too faithful to its code: Stop thinking of the other person as a person and start thinking of him as an occasion—a blank slate on which to inscribe a Thought for the Day.

The vigilantes were always a weird mixture of fraternal lodge and Murder, Inc., and so are the militias of today. Blood lust shares time with the lure of the secret handshake. The years of the founding of the American West marked the advent of a peculiarly American confusion, from which America has never really emerged: the intertwining of real violence and its romance. Violence gets so tangled up with group symbolism that it becomes a demotic idiom, even a kind of slang. Until the moment when the bullet strikes home or the bomb goes off, it all looks disarmingly like Culture. Wild Bill Hickok killed people, and then went on Broadway to show how it was done. Jesse James was a bank robber and a killer, but within seven weeks of his death his wife and his mother had a book ghostwritten explaining that he was just misunderstood—all he was trying to do was make a point on behalf of Confederate war veterans.

Anyone who has spent time reading—"monitoring" is the term of art—the literature of the militias and the survivalists might be forgiven for assuming that they, too, have been engaged in a cultural charade, a game, something like a hobby. For instance, the April issue of *American Survival Guide,* the consumer magazine of the militia movement, doesn't seem very different in its ingenuous tone and style from an issue of *All Chevy* or *Classic Trucks,* which its publisher, McMullen & Yee, also puts out. An article on raising emus (a kind of ostrich) for fun and profit runs several pages after the column "On Reality," where you can read about the Clinton Administration's "abhorrence for the American people" ("They"—the Clinton gang —"must be stopped, if not for us then for our children and for their children"). On one page you can find an ad for a closeout on the 1995 Women & Weaponry Calendar, which features hot-looking babes wearing bandoliers as halter tops, and on the next you can send away for a claymore mine and a bazooka accurate to three hundred yards. In the personals, a lonely guy from Texas announces that he is forming a group "to take action against the up and coming demise of our country," and adds, "The weak hearted need not reply." But another fellow, from Spokane, just wishes to survive "the turmoil of the immature, ignorant and irrational," and is seeking a "survivalist/warrioress/philosopher." The wild nuts tend to turn pretty quickly into pathetic nuts, even likeable nuts: in the letters section, a now chilling question asking "Would it be possible for you to advise me as to how I might contact any lo-cal militia units in the Midwest?" follows one that hints at the damp reality of Sur-vivalist Weekend Training: "What is the best way to clean/freshen-up a down bag?"

If violence in America leads a kind of double life, as both folk culture and real killing, that double life has produced the peculiarly American overlap of style with action, rhetoric with reality. We are all implicated in this: the intellectual writing for the *Times* who pretends that gangsta rap is part of a continuum with Baptist preach-ing; the *frisson*-seeking movie critic who wants his "Pulp Fiction" and cannot see that having it might help explain why he cannot allow children out after five o'clock in the afternoon; and the right-wing thinkers and politicians who have spent fifteen years inventing a demonic abstract enemy called the federal government and now have to explain that they never meant to be taken literally.

Our readiness to explain away violence as style might be called the Anthropo-logical Temptation: everything becomes a hobby, a bit of Americana, a colorful sub-culture in the pluralistic kaleidoscope. But what happens when the people you patronizingly encouraged, because you thought they were engaged in style and metaphor, turn out to have meant exactly what they said? The American left is fa-miliar with this problem, because it was the left's trendily succumbing to the ro-mance of violence that, more than any other one thing, did it in in the late sixties and early seventies as a serious political force. In those days, the idea that violence was redemptive in itself led Norman Mailer to praise two kids for killing a candy-store owner, and led New Leftists like Peter Collier and David Horowitz (then the ed-itors of *Ramparts*) to become infatuated with the thuggery of the Black Panthers. It wasn't that the left loved violence, exactly, but that the left—or, anyway, too much of it—liked the thrill of seeing its musty intellectual beliefs acted out as dashing cul-tural theatre. (The left's bombs, though, were often duds, unlike the right's—the dif-ference between the kids who paid attention in social studies and the ones who paid attention in shop.)

In the first couple of days after the Oklahoma City horror, conservative com-mentators clamored to make clear that they, at least, were able to see that you can't separate inflammatory rhetoric from violent acts—that ideas have consequences. Just after the bombing, when it seemed likely that Islamic militants had done it, Ru-pert Murdoch's New York flagship, the *Post,* was prepared to throw the book not only at the presumed terrorists but at their whole network of ideological support and encouragement—what the *Post* called, scarily, their "terror links." One headline read, "TERROR-LINK GROUPS MET REGULARLY IN OKLAHOMA CITY," and the story described militant Muslim groups as meeting for "jihad conventions," in which various sheikhs say things like "Attend shooting practice. There is nothing greater than the shot." Of course, the right quickly found itself obliged to pull a one-eighty, leaving skid marks and the smell of burning rubber all over the information highway. By Sunday morning—four days after the explosion—George Will and Robert Novak were mak-ing delicate civil-libertarian noises about guilt by association and how climates of opinion shouldn't be construed as chains of causal connection. Will followed up with a column on the subject for the Washington *Post,* conceding that ideas produce actions but dismissing the past two years as a cool technocratic debate about "the duties and capacities of government." At the same time, in a *Newsweek* column, evidently written before the Oklahoma City revelations, Will fêted the right-wing congressional fruitcake Robert Dornan (who routinely calls anyone to the left of Bob Dole a traitor), chortling at Dornan's flair for "verbal napalm" and promising that his presence in the Presidential race would make the Republican campaign "more fun than a food fight." Some fun. And by Monday afternoon Rush Limbaugh himself was mocking the phrase "right-wing extremists" and rounding up the usual suspects: the fault, he explained, lay with the liberals, who, back in the sixties and seventies, had tied the hands of the F.B.I. A couple of months earlier, discussing supposed environmental tramplings on property rights, he predicted, "The second violent American revolution is just about—I got my fingers about a quarter of an inch apart—is just about that far away. Because these people are sick and tired of a bunch of bureaucrats in Washington driving into town and telling them what they can and can't do with their land."

The point, of course, isn't that Limbaugh or Pat Robertson or G. Gordon Liddy caused the killing. It is that they seemed never to have given a moment's thought, as they addressed their audiences, to the consequences of stuffing so much flammable resentment into such tiny bottles. Conservatives are generally clearheaded about the connection between rhetoric and action when it comes to people who are not conservatives. A generation ago, conservatives had no trouble associating "revolutionary" sloganeering of the "by any means necessary" variety with the bomb that shattered the math building at the University of Wisconsin. And when it comes to Leonard Jeffries or Louis Farrakhan today, it is not hard for George Will or Murdoch's *Post* to insist, against the grain of liberal indulgence, that if you daily inject hatred into the bloodstream someone might get sick.

That's a fair point. Timothy McVeigh may be a nut, but nuts don't fall far from the tree. Fifty years from now, historians are unlikely to write, "In the mid-nineties, politicians and talk-show radio hosts created an atmosphere of poisonous hatred against the national government. Also, in a completely unrelated development, somebody blew up the federal office building in Oklahoma City." What they will write is more apt to be something like "In the mid-nineties, an atmosphere of poisonous hatred of the national government was allowed to grow in America; a few right-wing extremists even went as far as to bomb a federal building." The problem is not that the militias have been mysteriously infiltrated by extremists but that the federal government has, especially in the past two years, been inflated into an imaginary hate-object big enough for a nut. That's happened with the enthusiastic help of "mainstream" right-wing paranoia: Bill Clinton is an illegitimate President; liberals are the enemies of normal Americans; gun control is a conspiracy to tyrannize the populace; a New World Order is being put in place by foreign bankers. These are the ideas of Pat Robertson and Pat Buchanan and the N.R.A.—ideas, in other words, that a section of the "responsible" right in this country has spent the last few years legitimating and circulating. It is no great exaggeration to say that *American Survival Guide* is just *The American Spectator* with bazooka ads.

Of course, the difference is that the militia right comes armed with ideas and guns, whereas the mainstream far right comes armed only with ideas. Not a meaningless difference but not a decisive one, either, as we discover when the ideas being promoted are the kind whose logical consequence is to make somebody else want to go pick up a gun. It turns out that there isn't one world of cultural theatre and another world of real acts. The terrorists, though, had come to believe they weren't bombing a building full of people but obliterating an abstract object of hate. The "grievances" that are said to have moved them seem, on examination, curiously bloodless—things seen on television and in "instructional" videos rather than actually experienced. The people who had helped teach them to view the world as a set of easy abstractions, rather than as intricate arrangements made by human beings and inhabited by them, are under no obligation to take the blame for what happened. But it would be nice to see a little remorse.

American Gothic

JOYCE CAROL OATES

Timothy James McVeigh, the chief suspect in the recent bombing in Oklahoma City, grew up in the western corner of New York state, in Pendleton, a rural community of small farms and suburban homes twenty miles north of Buffalo and five miles southwest of Lockport. Pendleton is barely even a town, lacking its own post office, commercial center, and coherent identity. It's more a region than a community, farmland interspersed with ranch houses of modest dimensions, often with flagpoles in the front yards (as in front of the McVeigh family's home). Here and there are the remains of old, weatherworn farmhouses, perhaps an old, rotted barn, coop, or silo—relics of an era so seemingly remote in 1995 that they might be from another century. Pendleton, like nearby Millersport, Rapids, Wrights Corners, and Cambria Center, is a place of such minimal visual identity that one suspects that lives here are intensely inward—in the way, that is, of contemporary "inwardness," a function not of the inner self, or soul, but of the media. If you seek identity in such places, you will take it from stylized, generic, action-oriented television or film images, not from the community. There is no community. By tradition, western New York state has been a region of hunters, fishermen, "sportsmen." Now that wildlife has been severely depleted, and hunting strictly regulated, gun lovers are often obliged to travel some distance to use their guns both passionately and legally.

In the mythos of the surrounding countryside, Lockport, with its twenty-five thousand inhabitants, is *the* city. When Timothy McVeigh spent time there, he would have been identified as "from the country"—the vague, just slightly pejorative designation given such boys and girls, as if identity might be a matter of geography and distance. Until April 22nd, Lockport's most notable citizens were, arguably, the late William E. Miller (Barry Goldwater's running mate in the 1964 election), the late William G. Morgan, inventor of volleyball, and lately Dominic (Mike) Cuzzacrea, world-record holder for marathon running while flipping a pancake. It's a city of vertiginously steep hills built on the banks of the Erie Barge Canal—Lockport's predominant feature—which cuts through it in a deep swath and divides it approximately in two. (The well-to-do sector is generally south of the canal, sloping upward; Lowertown, steeply downhill, has always been working-class, semi-industrial, relatively undeveloped.) Uptown are elegant mansions and walled "estates" dating as far back as the eighteen-fifties. Within its city limits, Lockport his changed very little since the nineteen-fifties, a decade of local prosperity. As soon as you cross the city limits, however, you're in Lockport Mall—Fast Food–Gas Station Hell, U.S.A.

Shabby not only at its edges, Lockport still exudes an air of romance. It might have been imagined in a more innocent time by Thornton Wilder or Edward Hopper, appropriated now by David Lynch. In the canal area, it seems to possess on even the sunniest days a faint sepia cast, as in an old photograph. Downtown Main Street has a look of malnourished "urban renewal"—reasonably new buildings juxtaposed with aged buildings, structures under perennial renovation. For Sale/For Lease signs, vacant lots in what would seem to be prime real-estate territory. It is the Barge Canal that draws one's attention, though. To walk along the canal's high banks, on cracked and littered pavement, gazing down at the foaming, black water below, is mesmerizing. Framed by dizzyingly steep, stark stone walls, the canal has the look of a nightmare domesticated by frequent viewings, like German woodcuts in an edition of the Grimms' fairy tales.

In Pendleton, at Star Point Central High School, Timothy McVeigh is said to have had an undistinguished, virtually anonymous career. The iconographic image of the fanatic, the madman, the lover of guns and explosion fantasies, the coolly plotting terrorist, is difficult to derive from such a modest, homogeneous American background. D.H. Lawrence described the essential American soul as "hard, isolate, stoic, and a killer," but this seems a romantic exaggeration in our media-processed time. To grow up in Pendleton, New York, is to know oneself distinctly marginal; wherever the fountainheads of significance, let alone power, they are surely not here, nor are they even within easy driving distance. The way to the marginal personality, like Timothy McVeigh's, must be through identification with power. When not isolates, such men (yes, they are nearly always men) join paramilitary groups or para-religious cults, for which they are often willing to die. In these groups, one is both nowhere and at the very center of power: the "power," at least, to destroy.

To visit such wholly American places as Pendleton and Lockport is to be granted a revelation: how little where we have lived, with whom we have lived, and of whom we are born has any longer to do, in the public sense, with who we are. What connection is there between place of origin and destiny? Where Timothy McVeigh came from is of relatively little significance set beside where, as a young man, he went: into the United States Army and the Gulf War, to a semi-rural paramilitary organization called the Michigan Militia, and, it now appears, to Oklahoma City and the Alfred P. Murrah Federal Building, with a crude homemade bomb, on April 19,1995. Where we come from in America no longer signifies—it's where we go, and what we do when we get there, that tells us who we are.

Whose Fault Is It?

Mark Singer's article in The Talk of the Town (May 1st) about the bombing in Oklahoma City aptly described what we Oklahomans were feeling after the April 19th bombing as "the shock of recognition colliding with the shock of unrecognition." But his implication that it was some ingrained prejudice that made us look eastward for the culprit is wrong. The bombing felt like an act of war, and during wars you are wary of enemies, not friends. Our innocence and naïveté prevented us from even thinking that hundreds of people could be killed by a neighbor's hand. Oklahoma City is fairly small, and everyone was touched by the bombing; we were wounded in a way that might not be possible in a larger, more sophisticated metropolis. Don't make us ashamed of our innocence.

JAN CARRILLO-JONES
Bethany, Okla.

Thanks to Adam Gopnik for saying so well and so civilly that ideas do lead to action (Comment, May 8th). We live according to that assumption when we teach or preach, and when we advertise or campaign. As Gopnik points out, the idea of Americanism today does seem to reflect a mythologized American West, a culture that none of us have ever experienced, but one that was marked by ignorance, injustice, and danger. We seem to be revelling in a similar incivility in our streets, on our airwaves, and in our publications now.

K. ROOT
Hutchinson, Kans.

I believe we breed villains like those in Oklahoma when we take boys to whom we devoted years of prayer, education, and law, and then send them off to war.

Counsellors, psychiatrists, and clergy poured into Oklahoma to help the survivors of the bombing. We recognize the trauma of their tragedy. Yet young men plucked out of cozy homes to prepare for the horror of war come back to nothing. I don't know how to shoot a gun. Nor do I have the faintest notion how to build a bomb. I can't imagine dressing up in combat fatigues and spending my weekends playing war games in the woods. That is because I have never had to prepare for war. Perhaps we need to think about the tragedy of sending our children off to become animals without providing them a better way to become human again.

DONNA M. ZUBERT
Bloomington, Minn.

When Joyce Carol Oates claimed, in her article on Timothy McVeigh's home town (Talk of the Town, May 8th), that "there is no community," and that the only way McVeigh could establish his marginalized identity was "through identification with power . . . the 'power,' at least, to destroy," I felt sad.

Perhaps the estrangement Oates describes is one reason that fewer than forty percent of Americans voted in recent federal elections. Living in a country where it is not unusual for seventy percent of the eligible population to vote, I have come to believe that this disparity in enfranchisement is based on the way each population uses the power of talk. Rather than inflaming the destructive passions of individualism, talk, in my experience, actually encourages the spirit of community by creating a means for orderly interaction among citizens.

HEINZ SENGER
Langley, B.C.

CONSIDER . . .

1. Describe how Singer, Gopnik, and Oates go at the topic of the bombing from different perspectives. Then comment on any similarities you observe in their pieces, despite the different emphases in each piece.
2. What are Singer's claim and stated reasons? Gopnik's? Oates's?
3. What warrants are shared by all three writers? Or do you think that there is very little consensus on warrants?
4. How do the writers of the letters respond to the articles? Would you say that they write to agree with various points made, to add points overlooked or purposely not included by the writers, or to criticize the writers' points?
5. Write a letter to the editor responding to any one of the editorial pieces by Singer, Gopnik, or Oates. Compare your letter (its claims and grounds, warrant and backing) to other letters written by members of your peer group.

Here are two additional editorial pieces for you to scrutinize. One is a piece by lawyer David Helfant, published in the "Commentary" section of *Billboard* magazine; the others are four letters that appeared in a small-city newspaper on Wednesday, 4 August 1997.

Corporations Must Decide
Own Philosophies

DAVID HELFANT

In today's complex and challenging times, the morality and political sensibilities of the public influence the goals and directives of corporate America. In the recording industry, how does one balance the ever-changing moralities of society against the desire to make money and provide an open forum for artists to creatively express themselves?

This difficult and controversial issue is a constant balancing test for record companies. On one hand, labels want to promote an open forum for creative recording artists to affirmatively and, at times, aggressively take positions on issues that may not be popular or embraced by the masses. In fact, many cutting-edge artists have been catalysts in the evolution of the music industry, among them the Doors, Jimi Hendrix, Bob Dylan, Jane's Addiction, 2 Live Crew, Ice-T, and Nine Inch Nails. These artists, in turn, attract new acts to their labels.

Juxtaposed with this creative balance of artistic freedom and First Amendment expression is the practical reality that every record company is running a business, the success or failure of which rests upon the record-buying public and its perception of the label's image and artist roster. When parents decide to buy an album released on Walt Disney Records, they have a good idea of what the substance of the material will be. Should the public be allowed to force Disney to put out gangster rap because it feels that Disney's product is too juvenile and clean? The answer is obvious.

However, the answer becomes less obvious when politicians and influential public figures apply pressure to a record company by requesting that it stop distributing product that is potentially offensive to a portion of society. Naturally, adults can make objective decisions about the content of the music that they want to listen to or purchase. The lines are blurred when the record buyer is young, naive, or not knowledgeable about the content of the record. Who should be socially responsible for our children? Is it the obligation of corporate America, the government, or the children's parents?

These threshold issues have taxed the minds of brilliant thinkers for years without resolution. The forefathers of our country encouraged free speech to such an extent that the First Amendment is a brick in the foundation of our existence as a democratic society. Yet the courts have carved out certain exceptions to the First Amendment, usually utilizing a larger public policy rationale; for example, the decision that screaming words in a crowd in order to incite a riot is not protected speech.

Frankly, I do not believe that the First Amendment is the real issue. When politicians and public figures approach a corporation with complaints or criticisms about the content of its products, free speech is not being challenged. Since there is no pending legislation regulating the lyrical content of records, this issue is really about the public's ability to influence or attempt to control the type of product released by corporate America. The issue is free enterprise versus social responsibility.

In a free market economy, every company must independently determine the direction of its entrepreneurial intuition. Gangster rappers sell a tremendous volume of records today; however, so do children's artists. Since each corporation determines its own philosophies, ideals, and directives, the decision to sign artists who may be perceived as controversial is up to the particular record company. But the bottom line is still *selling* records.

If there were no market for gangster rap or children's records, the companies that sell these types of product would be out of business or would discontinue the sale of these albums.

The president of a major record company in Los Angeles told me, "If the records do not sell, the label will change the scope and direction of its artist roster. It's that simple!" The executive went on to state that "the public at large should not tell a record company what type of product it can or should release." I surmise that the opinion of most record company presidents is identical. In fact, some would undoubtedly be angered by the suggestion that a sector of the public is trying to dictate the lyrical content of its product or the A&R direction for his or her label.

This debate continues to invoke a passionate response from many people today. Certain individuals or interest groups want to dictate policy and influence corporate America. Conversely, corporate America simply wants to engage in free enterprise.

If a segment of society wishes to affect the policies of Corporate America, its members should voice their opinion by boycotting the product or products perceived to be offensive. In that regard, each corporation should independently decide whether the product it intends to release will alienate or enhance its share of the marketplace.

Letters to the Editor

Don't House "Predators" with the Mentally Ill

The recently passed state Senate Bill 751, sponsored by Assemblywoman Katz and Assemblyman Sweeney as A.8441, provides for the retention of sexually violent predators. This would be an appropriate measure to protect children and adults from the horrible crimes committed by these individuals if it were not for a procedure in the bill that would have them retained in psychiatric centers.

The mingling of these criminals with mentally ill patients in psychiatric centers is wrong and dangerous.

The language of the bill appears to stretch the concept of a Kansas law upheld by the U.S. Supreme Court this June on sexual predators. This bill operationally redefines mental illness in criminal terms, thereby fitting its purpose, namely that this abhorrent criminal behavior is a form of mental illness.

Mentally ill people are not criminals. They should not be made vulnerable to sexual predators either inside psychiatric centers or outside on the grounds of these centers. Sexual predators must be housed in secure facilities geographically separated from those that house and serve for the treatment of the mentally ill.

It would be shameful for this bill to allow violent sexual predators to be warehoused in psychiatric centers, thereby using funding already inadequate for serving mentally ill people in New York. The risk of mentally ill patients housed in proximity to criminals would only create more problems.

We of the Otsego Alliance for the Mentally Ill strongly urge the Assembly Codes Committee to strike from this bill any procedure that allows sexual predators to be commingled with the mentally ill. If rules do not permit revising the terms of the bill, then it should be rejected and re-introduced devoid of the procedure in question.

JOE FODERO
Action Chairman
Otsego Alliance for the Mentally Ill

Teens need love, care

Mary Franzonello should have her way. If she objects to her children receiving sexuality education in school, she should have the option to exclude them.

However, most parents welcome help in this area, and they should have their way, too. Comprehensive sexuality education provides information most teens will need at some point in their life.

As a mother of three teen-agers and a sexuality educator for seven years, my message strongly emphasizes the benefits of postponing sexual involvement. If they choose to have sex (despite my advice) I hope that they do it safely, responsibly and with love and respect for their partner. And if they find themselves in trouble, I hope that they turn to me. I may not like what I hear, I may be initially upset, but I would be there for them no matter what.

Young people take risks, they make mistakes, but mostly they need caring adults in their lives to turn to in time of need.

ANDREA LIVINGSTON
Oxford

Who needs new cells?

Here's a simple and relatively inexpensive solution to a problem Gov. George Pataki has placed before the people of New York. He is looking to build more prisons, 7,500 new cells I believe, to take care of the increased number of those convicted of crimes.

Why not take advantage of the efforts of the HMOs to reduce the use of hospitals by not allowing people to stay there but insisting on outpatient treatment for all ailments and injuries? Keep the existing prisons for violent offenders and put steel wire mesh over the windows of the hospitals to convert them to those 7,500 (or more) cells for minor offenses, whatever a minor offense is.

The buildings are already there, emergency lighting systems installed, cafeteria services available, nurses stations for the guards' use, so locks on the room doors are about all that would be needed. All that would really be required would be to legislate that the HMOs build their own facilities for treatment and (ha-ha) care of their patients, leaving the hospitals free for the state's use.

REV. L. ELMO SNEDAKER
Endicott

CONSIDER . . .

1. Write a rebuttal response to Helfant *or* to the writer of one of the Letters to the Editor. What flaws do you find in the pieces and in their writers' thinking? What is the other side of the argument that isn't being addressed in each piece? What else may the audience be thinking or wondering about each issue?
2. Analyze the audiences who probably read these pieces. *Billboard* is a national publication for people in the music industry. The other pieces come from the Binghamton, New York, *Press and Sun–Bulletin*, a small-city newspaper with a readership of about 205,000.

Position Papers

The remaining pieces in this Portmanteau are position papers on a variety of topics that resurface periodically in American discourse: a paper on trade restrictions and trade bills; a piece on animal experimentation; a *Newsweek* column concerning prayer in schools; and an essay from *Automobile* magazine about "smart" highways.

The Problem with Trade Restrictions
Stacey Bourland

It's human nature to want security. When a person is in a safe, comfortable position, he or she doesn't want anything to jeopardize this. For example, a person who is employed doesn't want to lose her or his job. As a result, employers and executives in companies that are in danger of going bankrupt sometimes ask the U.S. government to protect their workers' jobs. The government often helps these companies by imposing trade restrictions, protecting the company from foreign competition. With the help of trade barriers, the company stays in business, and the employees and executives keep their jobs and their comfortable incomes. Trade restrictions seem like a very good deal, but are they really helpful to America as a whole? Actually, trade barriers have several disadvantages which are often overlooked.

One problem with trade restrictions is that they make the protected product more expensive to the consumer. Tariffs, for example, or taxes on imported goods, obviously raise the price of the imported goods because the consumer must pay the price of the product plus the tariff. Of course, the consumer may buy the same product made in America, which is the whole point of the tariff. But although the American product may be cheaper than the imported one, it will be more expensive than it would have been without the tariff. This is because the American producer can now raise the price of its product without worrying about being undersold by a foreign producer. Of course, the American producer wants to make the greatest profit possible, so it does raise the price and the consumer pays more. The list of products under the protection of trade barriers in America is very long, so that much of what we buy is artificially expensive in this way. This means that the consumer can buy less with the money he or she earns, and America's standard of living is lowered.

Another disadvantage of trade barriers is that they take resources from their most productive uses and put them to less productive uses. If an industry needs government protection to survive, it is not operating as efficiently as an industry that doesn't require government support. When we protect the weak industry through trade restrictions, we allow our resources to be used in that inefficient activity when they could be used in a more productive industry. Our total output is reduced, and our standard of living drops even more.

Trade barriers also prevent our economy from growing and developing. If we had imposed strict trade restrictions when our country was mostly an agricultural society, most of us would still live on the farm and we wouldn't have all the planes, automobiles, and computers that are so common today. As our economy grows, our basic industries change, becoming more advanced. Old industries, such as agriculture, become less important as we use more of our resources to build new products such as computers. If we protect the old industries with trade restrictions so that they will always remain our basic industries, our economy will cease to develop.

Unfortunately, just as workers and business executives are comfortable with their jobs and salaries and as they don't want to risk losing them, so our whole country has a mindset that we have to preserve our economy the way it is. We assume that any industry going out of business must be bad for the economy, so we are willing to sacrifice free trade to protect all of our industries. Unfortunately, the sacrifice we make is great. When we impose trade restrictions, we lower our standard of living by reducing the amount we can afford to buy and by reducing the amount we produce to be bought. We restrain the growth and advancement of our economy by trying to hold on to outdated industries. In the end, although they do provide security for the few people in the protected industries, trade restrictions can do nothing for the economy as a whole but hold us back.

CONSIDER . . .

1. How does Bourland support her claim regarding trade restrictions?
2. What warrant does Bourland posit? How would you describe the audience being addressed in her piece?
3. See if you can think of evidence to refute points made by Bourland. Find logical places in the essay where she could address your points in a subsequent draft of the paper.

The Sadistic Games of Animal Experimentation
Mike J. Lim

Animal experimentation is designed for the good of mankind. However, the good intentions of experimentation on animals (vivisection) do not always achieve their desired effect. In fact, the negative effects of animal experimentation far outweigh the advantages.

First, consider the number of animals sacrificed for the selfish purposes of man. The authors of *Animals in a Research Laboratory*, a book issued by the Humane Society of the United States, estimates the number of vivisected animals in the U.S. alone to be somewhere between fifty million and five hundred million per year. This includes warm-blooded vertebrates such as dogs, cats, monkeys, and rabbits. In Great Britain, the only country obliged by law to release such figures, ninety percent of the experiments are performed without anesthesia. The animals suffer.

Second, the animals go through sheer torture during the many cruel experiments done on them. The Draize Test, a common test for sensitivity, involves placing a granule of the substance to be tested into a rabbit's eye (the substance is often makeup) and observing the results closely. The rabbit must endure the pain for up to 72 hours—and a rabbit's eye is much more sensitive than a human's. All this pain just to see if the new Maybelline eyeliner is suitable.

Hans Ruesch, author of the book *Slaughter of the Innocent,* describes a test for frostbite:

> Using ten dogs, they [the researchers] placed the dogs up to the hocks in a freezing mixture of ether chilled by solid carbon dioxide. With both hind legs frozen solid, each dog was returned to its cage to experience how it feels to have the frozen legs begin to thaw out and swell. In some dogs, the swelling tore the skin apart. . . . All the legs were badly injured. Some of them actually fell off.

What did these researchers derive from this? The fact that freezing dogs' legs, then thawing them out will cause injury? If there were some real point to these experiments, they might seem a bit more justifiable. But these are just a few of the sadistic games those who experiment on animals play.

Vivisection is not always reliable, and the results can be lethal. Different animal species can react very differently to a drug, as evidenced by the tragic thalidomide case. In testing for the safety of the tranquilizer thalidomide, animal tests failed to reveal any danger whatsoever. So the drug was put on the market for pregnant mothers to use. Advertised as "the most harmless tranquilizer in the history of modern therapeutics," thalidomide was nevertheless the furthest thing from harmless. Over 10,000 children were born severely deformed, some with stunted or missing limbs, others with finlike hands grown on the shoulder, and still others with other horrible deformities. The pregnant mothers trusted the scientists and paid dearly for it.

Finally, animal experimentation cannot be condoned when there are accurate alternative methods of research. Tissue and organ cultures obtained from deceased humans give results which are undeniably applicable to man, and the computer can logically and accurately predict the results of a test. Lower life forms, such as protozoa and eggs, can also be used to test drugs. Using chick embryos, a Turkish researcher discovered within weeks the danger that thalidomide represented.

The senseless slaughter of innocent animals must be stopped. Claude Bernard, considered the father of the vivisection method, suffered from manic depression and schizophrenia. Professor Blanchard, his colleague, went insane and kept seeing the eyes of the cats he had tortured. Vivisectors such as these two, who direct their sadism toward animals, are called scientists. But those who direct their sadism toward humans are called psychotic.

CONSIDER . . .

1. Restate Lim's claim.
2. What warrant underlies Lim's claim?
3. Characterize Lim's audience. What advice can you offer Lim in terms of thinking about the audience for this piece?
4. Should this paper be documented? Do you find Lim's claims credible as they are written here? Or would you like to see more information on his sources?

Opposing Prefab Prayer

GEORGE WILL

I stand foursquare with the English ethicist who declared: "I am fully convinced that the highest life can only be lived on a foundation of Christian belief—or some substitute for it." But President Reagan's constitutional amendment concerning prayer in public schools is a mistake.

His proposal reads: "Nothing in this Constitution shall be construed to prohibit individual or group prayer in public schools or other public institutions. No person shall be required by the United States or by any state to participate in prayer." This would restore the status quo ante the 1962 Supreme Court ruling that public-school prayers violate the ban on "establishment" of religion. The amendment would not settle the argument about prayer; it would relocate the argument. All 50 states, or perhaps all 3,041 county governments, or all 16,214 school districts would have to decide whether to have "voluntary" prayers. But the issue is not really voluntary prayers for individuals. The issue is organized prayers for groups of pupils subject to compulsory school-attendance laws. In a 1980 resolution opposing "government authored or sponsored religious exercises in public schools," the Southern Baptist Convention noted that "the Supreme Court has not held that it is illegal for any individual to pray or read his or her Bible in public schools."

The Question: This nation is even more litigious than religious, and the school-prayer issue has prompted more, and more sophisticated, arguments about constitutional law than about the nature of prayer. But fortunately Sen. Jack Danforth is an ordained Episcopal priest and is the only person ever to receive degrees from the Yale Law School and the Yale Divinity School on the same day. Danforth is too polite to pose the question quite this pointedly, but the question is: is public-school prayer apt to serve authentic religion, or is it apt to be mere attitudinizing, a thin gruel of vague religious vocabulary? Religious exercises should arise from a rich tradition, and reflect that richness. Prayer, properly understood, arises from the context of the praying person's particular faith. So, Danforth argues, "for those within a religious tradition, it simply is not true that one prayer is as good as any other."

One person's prayer may not be any sort of prayer to another person whose devotion is to a different tradition. To children from certain kinds of Christian families, a "nondenominational" prayer that makes no mention of Jesus Christ would be incoherent. The differences between Christian and Jewish expressions of piety are obvious; the differences between Protestants and Roman Catholics regarding, for example, Mary and the saints are less obvious, but they are not trivial to serious religious sensibilities. And as Danforth says, a lowest-common-denominator prayer would offend all devout persons. "Prayer that is so general and so diluted as not to offend those of most faiths is not prayer at all. True prayer is robust prayer. It is bold prayer. It is almost by definition sectarian prayer."

Liturgical reform in the Roman Catholic and Episcopal churches has occasioned fierce controversies that seem disproportionate, if not unintelligible, to persons who are ignorant of or indifferent about those particular religious traditions. But liturgy is a high art and a serious business because it is designed to help turn minds from worldly distractions, toward transcendent things. Collective prayer should express a shared inner state, one that does not occur easily and spontaneously. A homogenized religious recitation, perfunctorily rendered by children who have just tumbled in from a bus or playground, is not apt to arise from the individual wills, as real prayer must.

Buddhists are among the almost 90 religious organizations in America that have at least 50,000 members. Imagine, Danforth urges, the Vietnamese Buddhist in a fourth-grade class in, say, Mississippi. How does that child deal with a "voluntary" prayer that is satisfactory to the local Baptists? Or imagine a child from America's growing number of Muslims, for whom prayer involves turning toward Mecca and prostrating oneself. Muslim prayer is adoration of Allah; it involves no requests and asks no blessing, as most Christian prayers do. Reagan says: "No one will ever convince me that a moment of voluntary prayer will harm a child. . . ." Danforth asks: how is America—or religion—served by the embarrassment of children who must choose between insincere compliance with, or conscientious abstention from, a ritual?

A Suggestion: In a nation where millions of adults (biologically speaking) affect the Jordache look or whatever designer's whim is *de rigueur*, peer pressure on children is not a trivial matter. Supporters of Reagan's amendment argue that a 9-year-old is "free" to absent himself or otherwise abstain from a "voluntary" prayer—an activity involving his classmates and led by that formidable authority figure, his teacher. But that argument is akin to one heard a century ago from persons who said child-labor laws infringed the precious freedom of children to contract to work ten-hour days in coal mines.

To combat the trivializing of religion and the coercion of children who take their own religious traditions seriously, Danforth suggests enacting the following distinction: "The term 'voluntary prayer' shall not include any prayer composed, prescribed, directed, supervised, or organized by an official or employee of a state or local government agency, including public school principals and teachers." When religion suffers the direct assistance of nervous politicians, the result is apt to confirm the judgment of the child who prayed not to God but for God because "if anything happens to him, we're properly sunk."

It is, to say no more, curious that, according to some polls, more Americans favor prayers in schools than regularly pray in church. Supermarkets sell processed cheese and instant mashed potatoes, so many Americans must like bland substitutes for real things. But it is one thing for the nation's palate to tolerate frozen waffles; it is another and more serious thing for the nation's soul to be satisfied with add-water-and-stir instant religiosity. When government acts as liturgist for a pluralistic society, the result is bound to be a purée that is tasteless, in several senses.

CONSIDER . . .

1. Will's piece, written in 1982, addresses a problem that refuses to leave the American political conversation. What is the problem?
2. What is Will's claim with regard to the problem?
3. What unstated assumptions (warrants) are present in this piece?
4. What points can be made in opposition to Will's case?

Give Me a Road with an IQ of Zero

RICH CEPPOS

Ann Arbor—News flash! The *Automobile Magazine* Department of Oxymorons reports that it has just unearthed another deliciously amusing example of that form of verbal juxtaposition. Since good ones come along so rarely, it deserves a proper introduction. Please allow me:

Ladies and gentlemen, it is with sweet sadness that I bring to your attention a new oxymoron, a phrase for the ages, one that deserves a place in that cruelly kind pantheon of silly speech next to such gems as "efficient government," "near miss," and "Bosnian peace plan." Please put your hands together in thunderous silence and give a warm welcome to a really funny couple of words . . . "intelligent highway."

You know, *intelligent highway,* where a computer located miles away drives your car for you through a roadside communication network, so you can sit there like a couch potato, hands off the controls, doing crossword puzzles or stuffing your face with an Egg McMuffin or watching talk shows ("This week: Women who love men who love waxing their cars in the nude!"). Maybe you'll explore the information superhighway during your free time on the freeway.

Don't laugh; they're working on it full time down at the National Automated Highway Systems Consortium. I know: I saw it on TV! Actually, I saw it on video (big screen) at a rah-rah presentation at this year's North American International Auto Show. It was the Buick Motor Division that pulled back the curtain on the future, in conjunction with the introduction of its new XP2000 concept car. The XP2000 is loaded with enough computing power to do Donald Trump's taxes, hence the connection with the intelligent highway network.

Buick's video-production number showed its new experimental model in pretend action in a playlet about an executive on a business trip. He's trying to get home in time for a father–daughter softball game he promised to attend. Next thing we know, he's easing his sleek XP2000 onto the nearest intelligent highway (an empty two-lane conveniently located mere feet from his last business call) and—presto!—he's cruising hands-off at 150 mph. (One hundred fifty! You gotta *love* the guys who came up with that one.)

Safe in the hands of the traffic-control computer, Mr. Dad, thoroughly relaxed, leans back in his seat, tunes in a movie, and later fires up the cellular TV-phone for some video conferencing that solves a major business problem on the way home. And of course he makes it to the big game in time. His family life is saved!

Yeah, right!

This is the wowie-zowie vision of the future we see on *Star Trek,* where everyone wears identical no-wrinkle jumpsuits and life is uniformly neat, ordered, and antiseptically clean. Hey, wake up! We're talking about smart highways in the middle of cities like New York and Los Angeles. Cities with hundreds of miles of concrete arteries clogged cholesterol-like with automobiles. Flaring tempers. Overheating radiators. People with guns.

The whole reason for automated highways is to pack as many cars as possible, running as close as possible, into special rapid-transit lanes—automated versions of the carpool or bus lanes already in use on major arterial routes. *Just* what we need. (Actually, the guys with the guns will appreciate intelligent highways; they'll have both hands free to aim now.)

After the Buick presentation, I talked with Jim Rillings, and Bill Spreitzer, two high-level executives from the National Automated Highway Systems Consortium, the corporate and government research group that is trying to invent the high-IQ highway system. They said that the plan is to have cars zipping along nearly bumper to bumper—steered, braked, and throttled by computer—in about ten years or so. A city might receive forty to sixty miles of such roads covering the busiest routes. The first prototype test on a real road is expected sometime in 1997. More thorough testing could be under way by 2001.

The smart highway is one of those things that sounds good on paper and looks great in video presentations but is going to go haywire in real life. In real life, the possibilities for computer-controlled mayhem boggle my RAM and jump up and byte me in the hard drive. I mean, can you imagine what's really going to happen when we have special "computer commuter" lanes?

How about illegal-lane immigrants? *Those people.* They're the ones who currently dive into carpool lanes in order to make better time even though they're alone (a few of them have been known to strap one of those cute blow-up dolls into the passenger's seat, hoping to fool the police). In the intelligent-highway future, you'll see them slipping into the computer lane without the benefit of the on-board electronics necessary for hands-off cruising,

Imagine: You're in the smart lane, moving briskly, when suddenly a clapped-out ten-year-old Toyota Corolla wobbles into the gap ahead of you. The driver is white-knuckling it, grimly trying to keep his car two feet off the bumper of the car in front of him. Then he reaches down to adjust the radio, and . . . nooooo!

And speaking of pileups, how many times have you been told that "the computer's down"? It happens so often, it's just a part of daily living: The computer's down at the travel agency—sorry, no reservations. At the mall. (It'll take a few moments to authorize your credit card, sir.) On your own desktop. (Sorry about that story being late, boss—my computer bombed. *Really.*)

These are minor inconveniences compared with what will happen when the Amazing Infallible All-Knowing Highway Control Computer hiccups with, say, 35,000 cars moving nose to tail at 65 mph. It'll give new meaning to the phrase "computer crash." Can you say "10,000-car pileup"?

And don't forget the hackers, who wreak electronic havoc for fun and profit. If they can break into the government's high-security computers, then what's to keep them from messing with highway-control circuits? Maybe we'll get lucky, and one of them will crank up the travel speed to 100 mph. But one wrong keystroke, and the lot of us will be in good hands with Allstate. I'm telling you, it's not funny.

Then again, we might not be as close to driving this expressway to hell as the scientists would have us believe. This past summer, I witnessed some smart-road technology live. Chrysler is developing a driverless-car roadway at its Chelsea, Michigan, proving ground to test the durability of new models. The electronics firm designing the control system showed us a prototype set-up; it consisted of guide cable lying on the surface of a half-mile circular test track and a Dodge Intrepid sagging under the weight of computer gear.

An engineer rode along in the back seat for safety reasons—and a good thing it was, too. At the touch of a button, the car headed off, its driver's seat unoccupied. The first fifty feet were *great.* But then—*Houston Control, we have a problem.* The Intrepid veered into the grass, and the emergency braking system brought it to an ignominious lurching stop. Bad dog! After three tries with the same result, they gave it a rest.

Folks, don't we have better things to do with our tax dollars? Not even the National Automated Highway Systems Consortium knows how much smart highways will actually cost (billions, no doubt), and we can't even maintain the roads we already have. Besides, even if computer-brained road systems were free, we'd run into what you might call buyer resistance. Who's going to be the first to drive one? Me? You? Where are you when we need you, Evel Knievel?

Somehow, computer-smart roads cross a line we didn't even know existed. It concerns a personal freedom we never had to worry about before: steering. Steering is an inalienable human right. It's natural to want directional control of your own individual transportation system—be it your feet, a moped, or a Mercedes. It's pure physiology. We human beings plain like to steer for ourselves, and it is with reluctance that we allow someone else to do it for us—let alone an absentee-driver computer. As the next century dawns, I sincerely hope we come to our senses. The dumbest thing in the world is a road with a high IQ.

CONSIDER . . .

1. Point out a sentence that seems to summarize Ceppos's claim effectively.
2. Find a place where Ceppos anticipates points that the reader may raise against his case.
3. How do you think Ceppos regards or imagines his audience? Explain why you believe this.

7 Writing from Investigation and Primary Research

Most people don't see what's going on around them. That's my principal message to writers: For Godsake, keep your <u>eyes</u> open. Notice what's going on around you.

—William Burroughs

You may think that what makes or breaks an interview is how fascinating the interview subject is. But the key, finally, is your interest in your subject. If you are truly interested, you will convey that to the person, and it will show in the written version too.

—David Marc Fisher

Making sure you are prepared for the interview is very important. Even if you don't ask all your questions or follow your outline, make sure to go in with questions ahead of time. And don't be afraid to ask questions not on your list. These might be the ones you use most in your interview report.

—Amy Peterson

In this chapter you will read, read about, and write pieces based on investigation. Of course, investigation or research can be necessary for any kind of writing. You may have to do research to write an analysis or persuasive piece with convincing detail, for instance. The pieces in this section, however, depend especially on investigation for their content. Writing these pieces depends, in fact, on *primary research:* research where an investigator comes into direct contact with information. (When you go to the library and read what someone else has written about a subject, you are doing *secondary research*.) To write a review, you read a book, see a movie, attend a ballet or play or concert, or test a product. To write an interview report, you interview someone who interests you. To write a survey report, you conduct a survey and interpret the results. So in this chapter you learn about conducting investigations as well as about writing the essays that grow out of the primary research.

PUBLIC WRITING: REVIEWS

A review evaluates a publication, performance, or product. Consumers must choose from among an often bewildering array of products, books, movies, and plays, and reviews help them choose wisely. A reviewer evaluates a subject carefully and writes a clear recommendation, *not* an evenhanded description. Your job as a reviewer is not to be objective, but to help readers by offering solid reasons—evidence and examples—for endorsing or rejecting the item under review.

Writing Task:

Review a publication, performance, or product. Decide beforehand the criteria for excellence for the item under review, measure the item against the criteria, and write about your findings.

Invention Ideas

Begin by finding something to review. Are you reading or planning to read a book? Are you assigned to read a book for a course? Do you have a favorite mystery novel or children's book? Are you planning to see a movie soon? Or have you planned to see an opera or attend a concert or a play? Do you have plans to try out a new restaurant? Perhaps you just bought a new CD or tape, or you are going to purchase something interesting—anything from pizza to Band-Aids to a hair dryer. Any of these topics could eventually yield an interesting review essay.

Once you choose a subject, something to review, you need to gather some information—by reading the book, viewing the performance, or testing the product. Before you actually begin the review, jot down answers to this question (this forces you to articulate the criteria for your review):

- What qualities do I value in this kind of item, and what qualities will my reader value? That is, what makes a good spy thriller book, documentary film, shampoo, and so on?

Then, as you view the performance, reread the book, or use the product that you'll review, take notes to use when you draft. You'll need to note responses to these questions:

- What are the outstanding positive features of this item? What things do I really like? What features work especially well? How does this item meet my expectations?
- What are the outstanding negative features of this item? What things do I really *not* like? What features of the product do not work well? What aspects of the item fail to meet my expectations?
- How do my observations match up with or fit the criteria that I defined before I got started?
- Do I endorse this item? For whom and in what circumstances? Do I want to qualify my recommendation or rejection of the item?

Be sure to take enough notes so that your draft can have ample detail.

Computer Writing Tip: Copy this heuristic (the previous list of questions) into a template file to use when you want to evaluate a product or performance.

Drafting a Review

Here is a standard structure for a review. A review is, you'll remember, written to inform and evaluate. Begin drafting by writing down your expectations for a good movie, book, or whatever you are reviewing. Then describe what your movie (or other item being reviewed) does and how it does it. Compare your movie (for instance) to your expectations for a good movie of its genre: psychological thriller, horror, Western, comedy, or other genre. Then make your recommendations, specifying the intended appropriate audience for the performance or the book or user for the product. In short,

1. List your expectations for the genre, or kind, of work of art or product. These expectations may be implicit in your criticisms and evaluation of the art or product.
2. Say *what* the performance, book, or product does.
3. Say *how* the performance, book, or product does what it does.
4. Compare the reality of the item to your expectations for the genre or product.
5. Recommend or don't recommend the item. This sentence is the thesis or purpose of your review: It's the bottom line.

You may of course order these elements of your review differently, but you should include them all to produce an effective review. Once you internalize these elements of the review, draft it as quickly as possible. Then lay it aside while you examine some reviews written by professionals and students.

One caution: Don't overdo the summary of the performance or book or go overboard describing the product. It is your *evaluation* of the item that matters. Your audience wants to know how exciting the thriller movie feels, how intricately choreographed the ballet was, how well the antiskip feature on the CD player works. Lean toward less summary and more analysis and evaluation.

Looking at Some Reviews

Here are two professional reviews—one a restaurant review from *Food & Wine* magazine, the other an *Automobile* magazine commentary on the Harley-Davidson motorcycle. Read them and consider what they have in common.

Eating Out: Brasserie Le Coze, Coconut Grove

JOHN MARIANI

Having made a big splash in New York when they opened the deluxe seafood restaurant Le Bernardin in 1986, Gilbert and Maguy Le Coze have achieved much the same impact on the Miami dining scene with the debut of **Brasserie Le Coze,** a very chic but convivial homage to Paris's grand brasseries.

The decor is immediately reminiscent of classic Parisian brasseries—butter-yellow walls, big tilted mirrors, a long zinc bar, brown banquettes, frosted glass and rattan chairs—yet this is a fresh-looking, stylish place and a welcome relief from the pink and aqua Art Deco that has glutted the current Miami restaurant landscape.

The short menu includes many of the cherished staples of bistro–brasserie fare, starting with platters of glistening shellfish (also served at a raw bar as you enter). The rib eye with béarnaise (for two) is full of beefy flavor, and the *frites* are near perfect. There is even a hearty leg of chicken stuffed with mushrooms and herbs that's roasted to a succulent turn and served in a reduction of herbs with a tomato Provençal garnish.

But the Le Cozes are best known for their imaginative seafood dishes, and you'll find out why here. Seviche of grouper with olive oil, dill and a touch of jalapeño gets the appetite going, and the same fish with potatoes in a light saffron aioli is a satisfying entrée. Codfish with white beans, tomato and basil–garlic pistou makes for elevated comfort food.

Every dessert is memorable, especially the rich, smooth crème brûlée, the frozen melon sorbet and the Le Cozes' famous chocolate soufflé cake with vanilla ice cream.

Brasserie Le Coze has really upped the ante for exciting dining in Coconut Grove and may well start a rage for the French bourgeois cooking this town has too long been lacking. *[Brasserie Le Coze, 2901 Florida Ave., Coconut Grove, FL; 305-444-9697. Dinner entrées $14 to $19.50.]*

Harley-Davidson Sportster

J . M .

Finesse has never been a part of the Sportster's repertoire. Even back in the late Sixties, when I wanted one so badly my teeth hurt, I had no illusions about its abilities. Handling and braking didn't rank in my list of priorities; all I wanted was that lusty V-twin. With its huge engine, tiny gas tank, and loping idle, the XLCH looked and sounded as if it had been forged in God's own foundry.

By that time, the Harley's styling and reputation were well established. Based on the K-model, a four-speed, flathead V-twin brought out in 1952, the 883cc XL-series Sportster was introduced in 1957. The CH, for "competition hot," XL came out a year later, designed as a lightweight off-road model, and with it came the famous 2.2-gallon "peanut" tank that has been a Sportster trademark ever since.

But the XLCH made its mark as a street model during the 1960s. Brutally fast for its day, the CH was capable of thirteen-second quarter-miles at a time when anything approaching fifteen seconds was considered quick. And, if that wasn't good enough, an entire industry devoted to hot-rod XL parts was willing to take your money and help out.

By the early 1970s, the Sportster had been surpassed as a front-line sprinter by Japanese in-line fours that became more and more powerful. The bike grew to 998cc in 1972; other Seventies updates included disc brakes and electric starting. An unsuccessful shot at the growing sport market, the 1977–78 XLCR Cafe Racer, turned H-D away from sport bikes. The Sportster was groomed as an entry level Harley custom, designed primarily for urban use. Its pullback handlebar and pseudochopper styling became the Sportster's calling card.

During this period, H-D's owner, American Machine and Foundry (AMF), had let the product line stagnate and kept improvements to a minimum. Quality plummeted, and so did the company's reputation. In 1981, a group of H-D executives, led by board chairman Vaughn Beals, bought the company from AMF.

The new management introduced a bare-bones model, the XLX61, in 1983. Priced under $4000, the stripped XL sold like popcorn at a matinee. The same year, H-D accused the Japanese manufacturers of "dumping" cut-rate models in the United States. It applied for, and won, a temporary tariff from the International Trade Commission on imported motorcycles larger than 700cc.

In 1987, with its own sales running strong, Harley-Davidson asked that the tariff be lifted one year ahead of schedule, making the company lots of public relations hay.

Further investment paid off with two new Sportsters, introduced in late 1985. Both versions sported aluminum heads and cylinder barrels to replace the cast iron pieces, with hydraulic tappets and all-new crankcases and engine covers. Using the XLX chassis, the smaller XL marked a return to the original 883cc displacement. It was joined by a larger (1101cc) model. For 1988, both XLs received a stouter front fork, and the larger engine was bumped to 1204cc.

In thirty-one years. H-D has sold more than 300,000 Sportsters, making it Harley's most popular model. And my teeth still hurt when I look at one.

Harley-Davidson Sportster XLH883
Base price/price as tested $3995/$3995

General:
1-passenger motorcycle

Powertrain:
OHV V-twin, 54 cu in (883cc)
Power SAE net 55 bhp @ 6000 rpm
4-speed manual transmission

Chassis:
Damper-fork front, pivoted swingarm rear suspension
11.5-in front disc, 11.5-in rear disc brakes
MJ90-19 front, MT90-16 rear Dunlop K181 tires

Measurements:
Wheelbase 60.0 in
Dry Weight 463 lb
Fuel capacity 2.25 gal

CONSIDER . . .

1. Each reviewer subtly lets you know what the expectations for the restaurant or the motorcycle are. What are the standards against which the Brasserie Le Coze and the Harley are matched?
2. Notice also that each review has a significant amount of detail. Why is the detail useful for the reader? What particular details stick in your mind?
3. Look at each review again. About what percentage is summary or description? Point to words, phrases, or passages that indicate evaluation.
4. Most published book reviews begin with a heading that includes the title of the book being reviewed, the author, the publisher, the date and place of publication, the cost of the book, and notations to tell the reader if the book has illustrations, maps, charts, or graphs. What equivalent "product information" do you find in these reviews?

Here is a book review written by a student for a history class. What features does it have in common with the restaurant and motorcycle reviews?

What's Good about *Good Wives*
Ashley Forrester

Good Wives: Image and Reality in the Lives of Women in Northern New England. 1650–1750. By Laurel Thatcher Ulrich. New York, 1980. 296 pp. Index, historical maps, illustrations, photographs, and bibliographic essay. $11.00, paper.

Laurel Thatcher Ulrich earned the Pulitzer Prize, the Bancroft Prize, and the American Historical Association's John Kelly and John H. Dunning Prize for 1990 for *A Midwife's Tale: The Life of Martha Ballard, Based on her Diary, 1785–1812.* Her other nonfiction book, *Good Wives,* also looks at colonial women as it attempts to find a place for women in history by examining the daily lives and tribulations of New England women.

Intending *Good Wives* to be a "study in role definition" (10), Ulrich provides a glimpse into the lives of ordinary women who lived in New England between 1650 and 1750. She sheds light on an important, though often forgotten, part of the population. Because of their social status, women had to work behind the scenes, so they did not gain recognition from society. For this reason, Ulrich focuses on the ordinary to reveal the contributions that women made. She divides the duties of these women into eight categories: housewife, deputy husband, consort, mother, mistress, neighbor, Christian, and heroine. These duties fall under larger roles which Ulrich bases on the lives of three Biblical women—Bathsheba, Eve, and Jael. Devoting a section of her book to each of these roles, Ulrich explores the ordinary and extraordinary events which marked women's lives.

The first section of *Good Wives* compares the role of New England women to the prototype wife Bathsheba from the book of 2 Samuel. The Puritans considered Bathsheba the epitome of a good wife, able to incorporate the demanding duties of housewife, deputy husband, mistress, neighbor, and Christian. According to Ulrich, a Puritan woman always had to run her household efficiently, and in her husband's absence, she often had to fulfill his obligations as well. She might have found herself shouldering traditionally male duties like running a business and conducting financial transactions—without the training and experience that men benefited from. A woman's duty as mistress included her social relationships to her servants and to her husband. Her duty as a good neighbor required that a woman uphold community standards and support other women, but it also gave her the power to condemn other women for not fulfilling their own duties. In addition, women had to lead a good Christian life. To fulfill the role of Bathsheba, women had to behave in a way that reflected well on their status and on their husbands.

The next section of *Good Wives* examines the role of women as Eve, whom God created to be a "helpmeet" (87) and consort for Adam. According to Ulrich, women had to learn to balance sexuality and virtue. Affability could not translate into accessibility, because female chastity remained the property of men. Ulrich's accounts of scandals make this section lively and exciting, and they prove that the role of Eve challenged some women. The case of a young wife, Mary Rolfe, illustrates the difficulty of appearing virtuous and appealing at the same time. While Mary's husband was away, a charming if roguish gentleman physician, Harry Greenland, began to flirt harmlessly with Mary.

One night, in a scene that could have taken place on a modern-day soap or comedy, Greenland crossed the line of socially acceptable flirting. Peeling off his clothes, Greenland climbed into Mary's bed. Mary fainted; her attendant screamed, and the result was gossip and scandal.

Ulrich emphasizes the importance of women's relationships with one another in fulfilling the role of Eve when she describes the support women gave one another during crises. Forming a type of support group, Puritan women banded together to face traumas such as childbirth and abuse from husbands. As the "mother of all living" (88), the role of Eve also involves the duties of motherhood. Motherhood granted women their most distinguished recognition, because loyal children honored their mothers by naming descendants after them. As Eve, women had to reconcile sex and reproduction with chastity, and they had to be good mothers.

The third section of the book concerns the role of Jael. A woman who combines violence and femininity, aggression and Christianity, Jael embodies the New England woman's experiences as an Indian captive, heroine, and virago. Ulrich uses the famous example of Mary Rowlandson and other less well known women such as Hannah Duston who were the hostages of Indians. Women like Rowlandson and Duston received great acclaim as "defenders of Zion" (183) for having triumphed over their ordeals—and for bringing back a few Indian scalps—and thereby glorifying God. Ulrich further explains the role of Jael by examining the participation of women in religious developments and the relationships between women and others in their community. Women played an important part in establishing new churches, and church membership offered women "one of the few public distinctions available to [them]" (216). Ulrich points out, however, that churches still endorsed traditional views of women's roles.

Another aspect of Jael includes violence in relationships with other community members. When family squabbles or neighborly quarrels escalated into violence, Ulrich reveals, women transformed into viragos, and their violence followed distinct, often purposeful patterns, including authoritarian violence, disorderly violence, defensive violence, and demonstrative violence. Most dramatic were disorderly violence and demonstrative violence. Elizabeth Fanning, a woman who both "fascinated and horrified her neighbors" (191), displayed disorderly violence when she threw bricks at a man, chased another man with a hatchet, and even beat her own husband. A particularly bloody instance of demonstrative violence occurred in Salem shortly after Metacom's Rebellion. Two Indian prisoners, destined for Boston courts, came ashore with their captors. A crowd of women rushed the men and killed the Indians. Leaving the Indians "'with their heads off and gone, and their flesh in a manner pulled from their bones'" (194), the women escaped prosecution because no witness was willing to identify them. Ulrich argues that colonial women fulfilled the role of Jael by combining aggression with virtue and violence with religious fervor.

Ulrich presents a sensitive, practical assessment of the lives of New England women in the colonial period. Because lengthy entries about women do not appear in most historical accounts, Ulrich encountered difficulty in locating information. As she writes, "The record of women's lives is there, but it is largely uncatalogued and undefined" (279). For this reason, *Good Wives* draws heavily from primary documents which Ulrich lists as court records, probate records, family papers, diaries, and church records. These sources strengthen Ulrich's arguments because they do not have the bias inherent in secondary sources. Additionally, the fact that Ulrich uses examples of actual women makes the book more interesting and insightful; the lively accounts of scandals and illicit affairs help *Good Wives* make colonial women seem more real to the modern reader. These examples, however, have a drawback. Although they add to the effect of *Good Wives,* the numerous assortment of names sometimes slows down the flow of the book; Ulrich seems to digress from her thesis at times as she lists example after example.

Ulrich offers particular insight as she reveals the way many women achieved some degree of power and authority without directly challenging the patriarchal New England society. The ability to influence their husbands and to control their families gave women their greatest tool for gaining power. Operating behind the scenes, women did not achieve formal recognition nor independence, but their contributions were significant, nonetheless.

By comparing the roles of colonial women to the roles of Biblical women, Ulrich suggests the far-reaching influence of religion in New England. Puritan ministers urged women to strive to be as industrious and godly as Bathsheba, as seductive and productive as Eve, and as violently righteous and courageous as Jael. Surprisingly, women did wield power and influence over their lives and communities. Yet society constantly reminded women of their inferiority and subservience to men—an idea hopefully unacceptable to modern men and women. As Ulrich writes, "Colonial women might appear to be independent, even aggressive, yet still have derived their status primarily from their relationships to their husbands" (42). Ulrich's view of Puritan women is a refreshing departure from the traditional history—these women are not mousy, unemotional creatures. Rather, Puritan women loved deeply and acted passionately. Any reader interested in American history and/or women's studies will agree that *Good Wives* successfully re-places women in the formal history of colonial America.

CONSIDER . . .

1. Identify the elements in Forrester's heading. How does this heading compare to the product information in the restaurant review and motorcycle review?
2. Occasionally Forrester quotes fragments of the text, as in her description of how the women left the murdered Indians "with their heads off and gone." How does this quoting affect you as a reader?

3. Point out places where Forrester indicates her evaluation of the book. How do she and other reviewers personalize their reviews?

4. About what percentage of the review would you characterize as summary? How much would you describe as evaluation?

Computer Writing Tip: Find other reviews, especially book reviews and software reviews, on the Internet. Use your searching program and type in keywords that describe the topic or even the specific review that you are looking for.

Writers' Group: Rethinking the Review

Are there any strategies from the sample reviews that might be effective in your review? Go back to your review; reconsider its structure and its special features (quoting or providing "flavor," personalizing, etc.); and revise anything that you think needs to be changed. When you are ready, let your group evaluate your review. Ask them to make three trenchant observations about your review and then to weigh the relative amounts of summary and evaluation. Afterward, consider their comments carefully and revise further if you think it is necessary. Then polish your draft.

Reflecting on and Presenting the Review

If you review a product, think about including a photograph of the product. Before you publish the review in your portfolio, you should also check all your "product information," especially prices and specifications and names of authors, actors, producers. Incorrect information may not only confuse your reader but even make finding the book or product difficult for a prospective reader, concertgoer, or consumer. You will also want to format the product specifications neatly. You could arrange material in columns or lists, for instance, or set it off in a box somewhere in your review.

Computer Writing Tip: Use the graphic, line drawing, or border functions in your word processing program to draw boxes around text, including columns, or to create tables. You can even shade the interior of boxes with varying hues of gray. Experiment with ways to make the bibliographic data or the specifications more accessible to your readers.

Don't forget to write a page or two of reflection in your writer's notebook about how you fared with this assignment. What was difficult? What worked especially well?

PUBLIC WRITING: INTERVIEW REPORT

The interview report has become a very popular genre. Pick up any *People*, *Time*, or *Sports Illustrated*, and you will find an interview with a famous actor, athlete, or political figure. There are interviews in *Ebony* and *Publishers Weekly* and in scholarly journals as well. Why do readers like interviews? Perhaps because interviews have an immediacy—readers can feel as if they are chatting personally with the person being interviewed—and because interviews seem credible: The words appear to come directly from the interviewee.

Learning to conduct interviews and to write reports on them is a valuable experience because interviews are excellent research tools. Also, interviewing an expert on a subject in which you are interested gives you not only information but a contact, an introduction to a person who may be helpful to you now or in the future.

Writing Task:

Interview a person who interests you, and write a report on that interview for an audience that you specify or for an audience of your university peers.

Invention Ideas

Preparing to write the interview report involves several separate processes: finding a subject, setting up the interview, planning the interview, conducting the interview, and following through after the interview.

FINDING AN INTERVIEW SUBJECT.   To discover a good interview subject, begin by making some short lists.

- List three interesting people you are acquainted with.
- List three careers or occupations interesting to you.
- List three social problems that concern or interest you.
- List three questions (on any subject) that you'd like to have answered.
- List three organizations you'd like to know more about.

Which list was easiest to make? Which list has the most intriguing results? Choose the most promising list, then the most promising subject from that list. If you find that a person from the first list is your most promising subject, you are now ready to pursue that subject. But if you have chosen a subject from one of the other lists, you must now find a person to interview, someone who can address that issue or who is an expert in a particular area. Luckily, a college campus is populated with a variety of experts in different fields, so an interviewee is probably nearby. Your instructor can help you identify possible interviewees, but you will probably also have to dig in and investigate your possibilities. If, for example, you are interested in becoming a veterinarian and you want to interview someone about how to become one, you might find a practicing veterinarian in the community or a student, professor, or advisor in the veterinary school who will talk to you. You might begin by talking to a secretary in the veterinary school and asking for names of people you might approach for an interview. Most people are delighted to be interviewed and pleased that you consider them a valuable resource, so you should anticipate cooperation.

SETTING UP THE INTERVIEW.   Once you identify a potential interview subject, you are ready to set up the interview. This too requires planning. If you are not prepared, you may make a bad impression on your subject and prejudice the tone and quality of your interview from the outset. So, even before you phone your subject, rehearse what you will say and identify several convenient times when you would like to conduct the interview. That way, if your interviewee asks you to name a time, you will be prepared. Here are some other tips for setting up the interview:

1. Determine several times when you'll be available, and have your calendar and a pen ready.
2. Phone or visit the person at work. Don't phone too late in the day.
3. Identify yourself and your purpose for calling right away.
4. Request a thirty-minute interview at the interviewee's convenience and at his or her choice of locations.
5. If you plan to record the interview, ask the interviewee's permission now, not when you show up for the interview.
6. Once you establish a time and place for the interview, make a note on your calendar and repeat aloud the date, time, and place to the interviewee—with your thanks.

PLANNING INTERVIEW QUESTIONS.   Planning the interview is the next step. First, brainstorm a list of questions for the interview. Remember that your goal is to get your interviewee to respond to you by talking; and remember that certain kinds of questions elicit fuller answers than others. Which question, for example, is more likely to engender a full response:

Do you like collecting baseball cards?

Or

What is fun about collecting baseball cards?

The first question inspires either *yes* or *no* for an answer; whereas the second, open-ended question invites the interviewee to explain and even perhaps tell a story. So when you plan your questions, write open-ended ones that produce full answers. Plan at least ten questions; the more, the better. You may find it useful to write these interview questions on five-by-eight-inch cards: That way, you can rearrange questions until you find a logical order, and you can also write responses on the fronts and backs of the cards. When you arrange your questions, put the most innocuous ones first so that your interviewee will feel comfortable and so that the interview will begin smoothly. If you want to ask some controversial or difficult questions, save them for last. If the interviewee balks and the situation turns awkward at the end of the interview, at least you already have answers to most of your questions.

As another part of your planning, make sure that your tape recorder functions properly. Have a standby set of batteries ready and a fresh extra tape. If you are not recording the interview, take several pens that you like to write with. Avoid using pencils; the writing often smears, and leads break easily. Once you plot the questions and check your equipment, you are ready to conduct the interview.

CONDUCTING THE INTERVIEW.   Necessary to a good interview is professionalism on your part. If you act professional, responsible, and serious, your interviewee will be more confident, comfortable, and responsive. If your interviewee is more responsive, you will have more material and ultimately a fuller interview report. So show up on time and ask your questions with courtesy and respect.

You might think of an interview as a planned conversation. It should be organized but comfortable, without formal rigidity. You will get better responses from the interviewee if you can relax and rely on your notes and planned questions to ensure that you ask everything you want to know. Be sure to listen carefully, too—and to follow through when the interviewee says something interesting but unexpected. During the interview you may discover something so totally different from what you had anticipated that your planned agenda is thoroughly derailed. That's OK. In fact, that's usually quite exciting. Don't feel that just because you have a certain number of questions planned, you are obligated to ask them all. Your planned questions are, after all, simply a guide to what you anticipate may happen, to what you think the interviewee may say.

If you have a difference of opinion with the interviewee, it's best not to insist on your beliefs during the interview. If you argue with the interviewee or even express your perspective inadvertently through grimaces or other facial expressions or body language, the interviewee may sense your hostility and not talk freely. Remember that your purpose is to gather information rather than to convert the interviewee to your views.

During the interview, watch the time and be careful not to overstay your welcome. Thirty minutes should be ample time for an interview; but if the interviewee starts shifting in his or her seat or glancing at the clock, you should take your cue, say good-bye, and leave. A reluctant or bored interviewee will not give you much good copy.

Occasionally even the best-planned interview can go awry: The interviewee may not feel well, may have a family crisis, or may be unexpectedly busy. Or the chemistry between you may simply not be right. The interviewee may be shy or may not really have wanted to do the interview in the first place. Some people don't know how to say no gracefully. If your interview doesn't go well, perhaps for any of these reasons, chalk the failure up to experience; don't blame yourself (after all, you planned the interview and conducted yourself professionally); and find another interview subject.

Computer Writing Tip: It is also possible to do an "interview" via e-mail, perhaps even in real time. So when you plan your interview, you may not have to meet face-to-face with the interviewee. If you do an e-mail interview, follow all the protocol for personal interviews, including the thank-you note.

FOLLOWING THROUGH AFTER THE INTERVIEW.   After the interview you have two tasks to do right away. First you need to write a thank-you note to the person you interviewed. This courtesy is important because it acknowledges the value of the interviewee's time. A brief note of thanks also smooths the way if later you need to phone and ask a question or two that you forgot.

Your second task after the interview is to jot down your impressions of the interview itself—what the setting was like; what the interviewee looked like; how he/she spoke, gestured, sat, or acted. Go over your notes and make sure that you can read your handwriting (a cold manuscript can be unreadable). Check your tape to make sure it is audible and intelligible. Take time to transcribe your tape as soon as possible so that you have a text to work with.

Drafting the Interview Report

Once you have a transcript of the interview, you have a draft of the report, a draft that you must, however, edit. So now it's time to switch roles from interviewer to editor. How do you edit an interview report? Here are some considerations for editors of interviews.

- Leave the material in a question-and-answer format. Although your interview report will look quite different from a typical essay, you will be formatting it as interview reports are almost always presented.
- You may reorder or rearrange the questions to make the interview read more smoothly. You may also want to combine some of the questions. A recorded conversation may bounce from topic to topic, but a written one should progress logically and smoothly from one topic to another. If you rearrange your material, be sure to keep the appropriate questions with their answers to preserve their context.
- You may also cut parts of the interview. It is wise to cut sections that are truly irrelevant to the focus of your dominant impression or those that are way off the subject. But be careful not to cut so much that you remove the context or change the impact of what the interviewee says. You *must* honestly report the content and intent of the interview.
- You may correct minor speech errors made by the interviewee to preserve consistency of tone or voice. All speakers sometimes make errors in conversation without realizing it. Correcting a minor error is perfectly legitimate. If an interviewee characteristically and consistently uses colloquialisms, unusual dialectical pronunciation, or nonstandard usage, however, you may be acting dishonestly if you make so many corrections that you alter the interviewee's voice. Tread this ground carefully. Consider your purpose for reporting the interview; consider what thesis or dominant impression emerges from your interview (what does the interviewee say about the subject that you want especially to convey to the reader?); and consider what your editing accomplishes on behalf of that thesis.
- You'll have to decide where to begin sentences and paragraphs. If you transcribe from a tape, listen carefully for stops or pauses. Your ear will tell you where sentences should begin and end. Begin a new paragraph when the subject shifts or if an answer grows inordinately long.

When you finish editing the text, write an introduction to the interview. You will be very familiar with the content of the interview by then, so this part should be fairly easy. In the introduction, your job is to create a context, to prepare the reader for what's coming in the interview—maybe even to tell the reader that what's coming *is* an interview. Interview introductions usually announce who is going to be interviewed and why; and frequently the introduction also describes the background or setting of the interview. The introduction is typically two or three paragraphs.

Typically, there is no formal conclusion to the interview. Rather, it closes on a response that sounds final, broad, and/or conclusive. This allows the interviewee to have the last word. If you feel more comfortable adding a closing sentence or two, you may, but don't overdo it.

When you finish your draft, share it with your writers' group. Ask your group to describe the best answer in the interview and the weakest one, and ask them to provide one or two additional questions they would like the interviewee to answer.

Looking at Some Interview Reports

While your interview cools, read some interviews by other writers. This first interview, from *People* magazine, is actually a spoof of an interview; but like all good spoofs or parodies, it follows interview form perfectly. Notice the interaction between the interviewer and Piggy and Kermit—and observe how the introduction prepares you for the exchange that follows.

A Marriage Made in Hog Heaven Unites Miss Piggy and Her Reluctant Frog-Prince

FRED BERNSTEIN

Call it animal attraction. Since their paths first crossed eight years ago, Miss Piggy has been frog-wild over Kermit. And if he was never head over flippers for her, so what? This time Piggy used feminine guile—and, when necessary, a pork chop to the jaw—to win her little green-dyed monster. Her object? Matrimony.

While filming their just-released *The Muppets Take Manhattan,* their third big-screen collaboration, the two superstars finally became frog and wife, but not without the help of a few porcuitous plot twists. After inducing Kermit to marry her in a play-within-the-movie, wiggly Piggly substituted a real preacher for the Muppet who was supposed to play the part. Kermit realized he was trapped, and when it was time to say "I do," he froze. For a moment Piggy wondered if there was a throat in her frog. But he finally croaked the words, and Piggy was on cloud *neuf.*

For Kermit it's more like the dismal swamp. That's one reason Hollywood wags are already saying the marriage won't work. And there are other problems. Both bride and groom have yet to tell their families (including Kermit's 17,000 siblings). They have to mix family life with busy careers (professional commitments keep them hopping between London and L.A.). And they must get away from Muppet-meisters Frank Oz and Jim Henson, who, Miss Piggy snorts, "are always hanging around." Last week Miss Piggy took time off from monogramming towels at the couple's posh Manhattan town house to tell Assistant Editor Fred Bernstein—and her Kermit—how she plans to make their marriage more enduring than mere puppet love.

Miss Piggy, congratulations.

Piggy: Thank you. But we've always been married in our heart of hearts. This only makes it *officiel.*

Kermit: This makes it *nothing.* We're not married.

Piggy: We *are.*

Kermit: We're *not.* I was playing a part. The script said, "Kermit says, 'I do,' " so I did. Do you think if you commit a crime in a movie, they put you in jail?

Wait a minute, are you comparing being married to Miss Piggy to being in jail?

Kermit: You said that, not me.

Piggy: I want you to know that Kermit does not speak like this in private. In private he is a very romantic frog. This is a public facade. You have to understand frogs.

What other wildly romantic couples would you compare with you and Kermit?

Piggy: Fred Astaire and Ginger Rogers.

Kermit: Roy Rogers and Trigger.

Piggy: This is not something to be funny about. This is not funny at all. This is *moi's* life.

Miss Piggy, when did you first realize your prince would turn out to be a frog?

Piggy: The moment we met, at a beauty contest I was in years ago. Naturally, *moi* won.

Did you think then that you would someday be betrothed?

Piggy: I didn't *think.* A woman *knows.*

Kermit: I'm sorry, I missed that. Were you talking about marriage again?

I know you've been busy. But what kind of honeymoon do you plan?

Piggy: A small cozy cottage, a roaring fire, a warm blanket over us. And just a few photographers.

What kind of parents will you be?

Piggy: Loving, desperately caring, but at the same time respectful of the children's feelings. Smothering but respectful.

Kermit: Our children might be little green pigs. Or big pink frogs. It's hard for me to conceive of us having babies, if you'll excuse that phrase, which is one of the reasons I wasn't ready to get married.

Miss Piggy, do you think you may retire now that you're married?

Piggy: I don't know. I'm at a point in my career where I have to decide what's more important to me, whether I should continue that mad, dashing pace of being a superstar or just stay at home waiting for my frog.

If you do stop working, do you think Kermit will have to find other leading ladies—say, Elizabeth Taylor?

Piggy: I suppose you think I'm going to be jealous now. Well. I'm not. I understand a professional relationship. I understand an actor's need to express himself.

Miss Piggy, can you imagine Kermit ever leaving you for another pig?

Piggy: Why should he, when he can have everything he's ever wanted in this body?

Kermit: There certainly is a lot there.

Have you picked out a ring?

Kermit: A ring? That reminds me. I don't think you can be legally married without a ring.

Piggy: Of course you can. All you *need* is a tuxedo.

Kermit: And a blood test. You can't be married without a blood test!

Piggy: Who ever heard of a pig and a frog having a blood test?

Kermit: It's the law.

Piggy: Laws can be waived. *Moi* waived it.

CONSIDER . . .

1. What specific information in the introduction helped set the stage for the interview?
2. Characterize the interviewer's opening remarks. What is their purpose?
3. Find a place where the interviewer listens carefully and follows through by framing a question from a response.
4. Describe how you can distinguish the different voices by the way the interview is formatted.

This student interview report describes an interview with an instructor who was a child in Europe during World War II. The subject, Madame Kleine-Ahlbrandt, is a good conversationalist, but notice particularly how Macy Hueckel asks questions that invite her to respond.

Wartime Memories: An Interview with Kay Kleine-Ahlbrandt
Macy Hueckel

Most of us know her as simply "Madame." She has been affectionately termed at various times as the "Tasmanian Devil" or a "whirling dervish." *Whirling* is just the word to describe her—always in a rush.

And this is how she came to the interview—rushed, her thoughts scattered. But when she sat down and began to speak of her childhood, a whole new person emerged. There was a quietness about Kay Kleine-Ahlbrandt that I have rarely seen in all the time I have known her. There was a calm feeling, as if she took a time out from all her to-ing and fro-ing to tell me about this other part of her. The usual rapid fire of words that she speaks in everyday conversation was now slower, broken up in places by pauses and silences. Sentences trailed off, to be replaced with the start of new ones. It was obvious that the words were more difficult in coming—they didn't flow as freely as normal. At times her voice became low and full of feeling as she struggled to get the words out.

But even in her faltering speech, she conveyed a message that is invaluable. She showed a side of herself, an undeniable part of her, that few ever see. She spoke of her experiences as she was growing up in the Netherlands during World War II, a topic she had mentioned in passing but had never dwelled on until now, when she was specifically asked to.

Sitting in the foreign language office one afternoon, she brought this little-known side of her out of hiding for just a brief moment. But that moment was enough to at least catch a fleeting glimpse of what shaped the beliefs and opinions she has today. But soon the moment was gone, as quickly as it had come, and she was on her way again, rushing once more, coping with the stresses and joys of daily life. The war stories had gone back to their place inside for now, only to be drawn out again later, perhaps, by another curious person.

But in that one brief moment, there was much information brought to light, uncovered by these questions:

Where were you living at the time World War II started?
In my home, in the Netherlands, in a big house close to the sea, on the coast of the Atlantic Ocean.

How old were you at this time?
Three and a half years old. . . . I was born in '36, December '36, and the war started in May, 1940.

How old were your brothers and sister at the time?
My sister was two years old, and my brother was four years older [than I was], and my other brother was two years younger [than I].

At what point did the war begin to affect your life . . . the first significant event . . .
Well, it affected us right away, because we were thrown out of our house; we had to go and live somewhere else, and we had to leave in a rather precipitous fashion . . . we had to run out. My father was driving the car, he didn't usually drive, and we killed somebody

on the way because there was this soldier who was driving, was riding on a motorcycle without a light because it was blackout time, and we didn't have any lights on our car. My father smashed into him and killed him.

And we got back into our house after the war had started. When we got back into our house later, the soldiers had smashed a lot of rooms in our house up. Took a lot of work to get it back.

Why were you thrown out of the house? Who threw you out?
Because the Dutch soldiers took it over as an outpost; they made a bunker out of it, and then we were in it for a little while, then the Germans took it after they were in our country (. . . they were in the Netherlands), the Germans took it over, and they used it as a bunker until the very end of the war. It was a fortified bunker. There were passages underneath, and, oh, God, it was a mess. After the war we never moved back into it.

Where did you live after you were driven out of your house?
We were given another house; it was further inland, in the city, not close to the sea. And that's the house where I lived all through the war. We never did go back into the other one, the house by the sea.

How did you get that second house?
Oh, the Dutch would give priority to people with certain kinds of jobs. My father was a lawyer, so he was allowed to live in The Hague. Other people were sent out to other cities. We really had no free choice in that, but we were kind of lucky to have gotten a house. It was very small, but. . . .

In retrospect, we would have been better off in one of the other provinces in the countryside; there would have been more food, but what the hey, we were in The Hague, and that's where we stayed.

Do you remember the war at all, even though you were only 3 years old when it started?
Yeah. I remember when the war started. My mother took me out of the house and showed me soldiers falling out of the sky. Parachutists.

But it didn't make much sense to you then, did it?
Well, I was scared, and she, you know, she said, "Look, those are the bad guys, falling down . . . " you know, ". . . those are the people that are invading us, they're the bad guys." And of course, *ex post facto,* it makes a lot more sense now than it did then.

How did the war change your daily existence, your way of living?
Well, there was never any food, towards the end of the war, 1944, '45, when the Allies had invaded France, but they had gotten stuck in southern Netherlands, by Armhan. So, a lot, a good part of Europe was liberated, but the northern part of the Netherlands

wasn't. And there was absolutely no food that last winter. We ate everything we could get our hands on; it was very very bad. And so, the war affects you, because there's nothing to eat. I have bad teeth and bad bones, because I didn't have the proper calcium and vitamins and stuff when I was growing up.

So we had to make do with whatever food we could find. I didn't go scavenging, but my mother did. She went scavenging for food with her friends. Like she used to take her dresses and stuff, and walk into the countryside, and trade her dresses for food. I know she once went with this beautiful, long, yellow, gold lamé gown, and she came back with one little loaf of bread. And I don't know what was in it; it didn't taste like bread, but, boy, that little loaf lasted forever. She used to come back with cheese and stuff because Dutch farmers, some Dutch farmers made a fortune, because they took advantage of the war. There was a thriving black market. Because the Germans took all the food and sent it to their own, in Germany; but of course then the farmers held back, and then they would sell it at incredible prices to the Dutch—barter, because money had very little value. These fat farmers' wives, with dresses of my mother's that they would never get themselves into, you know, mother was real small. Very small.

A lot of the food was requisitioned for the army, but you know, the Dutch farmers grew it themselves, so they were able to hold back, keep some back, and that's what they bartered with, and that's what they fed themselves with. The city people starved. The people living in the countryside did a lot better, for obvious reasons: they were close to the food supply. They were able to hoard. But it just didn't filter down to the cities.

Are there any results of the war, any memories, that stand out?
Well, yeah. There was this Jewish family we hid underground. A father and a mother and their son. And they actually made it; they lived in our coal hole, under our dining room, and we were . . . we were told that they'd been given away, that it had gotten out. And I don't know how, because I didn't tell any of my friends; I was scared to death. But anyway, somebody talked. And we got them out of there just in time. We'd been checked out before; you know, the Germans used to come from house to house and check, to see if you were using electricity that you weren't supposed to and stuff, and you know, you could always tell when somebody stepped on that coal hole—it made a different kind of sound. I could always tell, you know, that it was a loose part of the floor, but of course they never did; they never realized.

But that one day, then, they walked in and they went right to the place and they pulled up the linoleum and they went right in there, and of course we'd gone through it with a fine-tooth comb—not a crumb of bread, nothing was left. You couldn't tell somebody had lived there. So the people got away, and we didn't get . . . you know, we'd be executed, we'd be sent to a labor camp, or killed for keeping people, you know, Jewish people. So I was really scared that . . . I never talked, and I know my brothers and my sister didn't, either. Our best friends didn't know. It was just a very well-kept secret, and somehow it did get out, and we did not get hurt because of it. And the family—the most important thing is that the family did survive.

Do you know how the family got out, or where the family went?
No, they went to somebody else; of course I don't know where, because the underground never told. You know, they just crawled out one night late at night, out the back door, and I never saw them again.

How did you happen to have these people living in your basement?
Because my mother was active in the underground. So she knew them, and took them in.

Did your family and the people close to you survive the war?
Oh, no, no, I lost a lot of friends. Oh, no, no . . . no, there was a bombardment where a bomb fell in the block right next to me, kind of behind me in the corner, and my best friend got it. Went to look for her, and had a hard time finding her. And our maid lost her daughter, little baby. A shell took her head off, in another bombardment. Oh no, I know lots of people who were . . . killed, but gosh, uh huh, oh no.

You said you had a maid?
Yeah, we had a maid. We had a maid, and we had a chauffeur. . . .

How did you have enough money to hire help?
Well, we were a wealthy family; my father had money.

As to your immediate family, did they survive the war?
Well, my father died, indirectly from suffering during the war. They put him in jail, and he had a stomach ulcer, and it started to bleed and he never really got well again.

Why did they put him in jail?
Because he was there, and he was . . . they didn't trust him, the Germans didn't trust him. . . . Towards the end of the war, they didn't ask questions; they'd just come and take you away.

What did the rest of your family do while your father was in jail?
Survived as well as we could.

Were you allowed to communicate with him at all?
Yeah, my mother used to go visit him. And then, we were in school, you see, until the last year of the war when they stopped school because there was no heat, there was no light, there was no electricity, there was no nothing. We ended up with school in the basement, with candles, and that just got to be too much, so there was no school the last year of the war. . . .

I was home, mostly, and I was very weak because I was hungry a lot, so I didn't, you know, we didn't do much. You know, after the war when we started to get fed again, I'd like to roller skate, and I'd jump rope, and I'd run, and, you know, hell around, but there was no such thing during the war because I was just too weak; I didn't have any energy. And you know, I didn't have shoes; I walked around with rags around my feet and wooden soles, because there was no leather and there were no shoes. My mother made my winter coat from an old curtain; I mean . . . but, we were badly off, but we survived—were lucky; a lot of people didn't.

Did you have to hide from the Germans?
No. We just carried on; the Germans were just there. They were a real invasive presence.

So they didn't antagonize you much?
Well, you know, I'd go shopping with my mother, shopping for to find some food somewhere, and we were walking along, and I remember there was a German parade, you know, they came walking by singing their crummy songs, and my mother took my hand and we stood and we turned, looking the other way into a shop window, and this German came by and he gave her a lecture and she . . . I don't know what she said to him . . . she said something like "I forgot all my German on May 5th," and he hit her, and then he kicked her. So she had to turn around, and I turned around fast, man, because I was just a kid—I didn't care, you know, but she was just furious. So that's that presence, you know; it was an invasive presence.

Do you remember the exact day the war ended? What did you do? How did you hear the news?
Yes, my brother was out. They had said that the Allies were breaking through, and my brother was out with his friends celebrating, and then the fire started; they were, they were firing. The shooting started; they were firing on people, and my mother was scared to death because here we had survived the bloody war and here at the end of the war, my brother Theo was going to get hit. Right, so we were all waiting in the house, lights out, and we had all our orange ready, you know; we had this orange curtain we were going to hang out the window, because orange is the color of the House of Orange, the Queen. We were all ready to be, to be liberated, and . . . but then they started shooting and a lot of people were killed, because the Germans got mad because they did not want to lose; they were mad because they were losing the war, and my brother came crawling home on all fours. He was really scared; he didn't get hurt, but he. . . .

He almost got hurt before, because he used to go to the minefields to get wood for fire, firewood, and my mom found out that he went to the minefield, and she was pretty unhappy about it, and she kind of lectured him and stuff, and he didn't go again. But, she only found out because his best friend blew up. They went to the minefield together to get wood, and he stepped, his best friend stepped on a mine, so my brother came home, kind of covered with his best friend's blood and stuff, and brains—it was awful; he was a mess. He was very shaken, so after that he didn't go back in the minefields to get wood again, and we were pretty cold because we had no more wood to burn. It was weird; it was really weird.

How did you receive news that the war was over? Did someone come and tell you?
No, what happened was . . . we weren't allowed to listen to the radio, you know, and of course we always did; it was called Radio Orange, and we'd put it on very softly; we'd turn it on. And of course, you had to black out all the windows and stuff, so, you know, one of us would listen very carefully, and when the Germans came, we all had a job to do when the Germans came to check the houses. And my job was to take this red cloth and put it up against this light, because you weren't allowed to use the electricity, but my brother fiddled around with the meter, you know . . . so, we were listening to Radio Orange and we were hearing that, you know, the end was near; liberation was near.

And then the Swedish Red Cross had a dropping of bread and butter. They went, and they flew over The Hague—The Hague was . . . the people in The Hague were very hungry; the people in Amsterdam—they were starving. They flew over The Hague with these aircraft, and they dropped food. And then we knew the end was near. I don't actually know whether it was before or after liberation.

I know that at liberation, we had a lot of Canadians who gave us food. Canadian soldiers liberated The Hague. And they came in these tanks that chewed up the streets . . . and they gave us chocolate bars, and all sorts of foods that I'd never seen. Bananas . . . I ate a banana with a peel on it; I was sick as a dog. And fresh foods that you open up the can and eat it, like stew and stuff. I'd never seen that kind of food, you know. I was too little when the war started, and by the time I would remember it, it just wasn't there. Stew was made with meat . . . soup, we always had watery soup with crap in it . . . yuck.

Do you remember what you did right after the war officially ended?
I don't remember. I remember getting food, taking it to my mother, and getting cigarettes and taking them to my mother, because mother was so weak she could hardly walk. And my mother said, "No, no. No cigarettes," and she went and bartered cigarettes for food. She was afraid to start smoking again after all those years, you know—she was too weak. I don't remember, at all. What I remember is the wartime, the postwar time. I remember having a lot of stomach aches, because I wasn't used to the food I was getting. And school started again—kind of a drag.

Are there any lasting effects that this exposure to the war has had on you?
Yes—a complete disgust for people who make racial slurs, or who despise minorities, like Jews, who always have to somehow defend themselves being Jewish. Because I saw what it does when it's pushed to the extreme—they were herded up like animals. I

saw a seven-year-old Jewish boy, with a red wig on his head, beaten along the street, and he expired in about two blocks, two and a half blocks. That's what happens when people hate people because of the way they are, what they are; you can't deny what you are . . . whether you're black or Jewish or Chinese or Japanese or whatever, and that's because I saw what happens. I really am very violent against people who make racial slurs and stuff; that just bothers the hell out of me. That's how the war has affected me.

CONSIDER . . .

1. What is the interviewer's relationship to Madame? How do you know?
2. How would you describe the focus of this interview? What aspect of Madame's life does it treat?
3. How does the introduction affect your perception of the interview?
4. Find a place where Hueckel listens carefully and follows through to construct a question from one of Madame's responses.
5. Describe how Hueckel distinguishes her voice from Madame's.

Writers' Group: Revising Your Interview Report

Have you learned any strategy from reading Hueckel's interview that you would like to incorporate into your interview report? Look at your interview now and consider whether you would like to make any changes. Have you established the context adequately? Is your interview focused on one subject or issue? Did you provide a thesis, implicit or explicit, or a dominant impression of the interviewee? Have you asked enough questions to satisfy your audience? If your interview is too short or if you know your interview lacks vital information, get in touch with your interviewee again. It's not too late to get additional substantial information.

Ask your writers' group for help too. You'll want to ask them if your interview is focused and developed, if there is a thesis or purpose evident in the essay/report. If you want to incorporate suggestions from your peer group, do it now. Then proofread. You may find that it is helpful to check your punctuation as you proofread: Remember that *you* set the sentence boundaries; make sure they are accurate.

Reflecting on and Presenting Your Interview Report

As you think about how you will present your interview in your portfolio, consider formatting it in two columns. The questions and answers often seem denser and the whole interview takes on a different look. Also pay attention to how you format the questions and answers and to how you designate speakers. Some writers like the Q & A format; others prefer using only surnames as labels for the speakers; still others like to designate speakers by initials. Another popular format includes putting questions in boldface type and responses in regular or italic type. Editors at *The New Yorker* typically frame interview questions indirectly in short paragraphs, then begin new paragraphs for responses. (See "Playground Person" in the Portmanteau section of this chapter.) How you format the interview is not, however, as important as the result: a clear, easy-to-read essay where the speakers' voices are easily distinguishable.

When you finish the interview report, write about the experience of interviewing and writing up the interview. What did you do that particularly succeeded? Did anything unexpected happen? What advice would you give someone who was preparing to do an interview and write about it? Reflect on these writing experiences.

PUBLIC WRITING: THE SURVEY REPORT

The survey report is closely related to the interview. Both entail talking to people to gather primary information. When you conduct an interview, you usually talk to one person for the purpose of gathering a significant amount of detail: You are interested in the *individual* view. But when you conduct a survey and then write a survey report about the information you gleaned, you usually gather information from a larger number of people: You are interested in the *collective* view.

You will find at least two different types of surveys: *broad-based surveys*, in which questionnaires are administered to a large number of people, usually at least fifty; and *in-depth surveys*, in which identical interview questions are posed to four to six respondents.

Writing Task:

Consider a question that you'd like to have answered or a topic that you are curious about. Design a survey instrument and decide whom you want to survey; then administer the survey, evaluate the results, and write a report about what you learned.

Invention Ideas

Your first task in writing a survey report is to find a survey population and a subject about which you are curious. You may find it easier to think first about the populations to which you have access: your classmates (would your colleagues in some of your classes be available to help you?); the people in your dorm or apartment building; the members of a club or organization to which you belong; the members of a religious group; the employees where you work; your friends or acquaintances, here at school or perhaps even in your home town. If you select a population first, you automatically narrow the topic possibilities.

FINDING A TOPIC AND A POPULATION.   Now look around you for a population and a topic. If you work in a fast-food place, you may be able you enlist the help of all the shift workers; but their primary common interest will be what goes on at the restaurant. You could survey the shift workers on their attitudes about working at the restaurant, on ways to improve customer satisfaction, on how work schedules might be improved, or on rapidity of promotion. If you live in a dorm, you will have relatively easy access to all the people living on your floor, and you might ascertain their opinions about life in the dorm—or (because all are university students) about almost any aspect of university life, from participation in intramural sports to the topic of cheating on exams. Of course, if you live in an exclusively male or exclusively female dorm, you will get just one gender's view of the situation; additionally, your findings may be valid only for a certain age group (ages seventeen to twenty-two), but you can discuss those demographic variables in your survey report. Because finding a perfectly balanced survey population is extremely difficult, you will almost always have to limit your claims about the importance of your results in light of the limits of your survey population. If you want to do an in-depth survey, you'll need a population that is smaller but more keenly interested in your subject and willing to give you more time. Instead of all the shift workers at the restaurant where you work, for example, you might choose only four—male and female workers from different shifts and of varying ages.

So begin by making a list of all the populations you believe you have reasonable access to. Then choose the population you find most interesting. Then list at least five topics that that population may know or have opinions about. Your survey questions will most likely develop from these topics. Finally, determine a promising topic from your list.

CREATING A QUESTIONNAIRE.   Next create a questionnaire or a list of interview questions. Construct a list of interview questions for an *in-depth survey* using the same strategies as for the interview report (see pages 219–220 in this chapter). You will need at least ten open-ended questions arranged from least to most difficult to answer. For the in-depth survey, you will ask all your subjects the same questions, if possible, and in approximately the same order. You should see a similarity in the structures of the interviews even before editing.

To prepare a questionnaire suitable for a *broad-based survey* requires a bit more work. Some general guidelines: First try to restrict the length of the questionnaire to the front and back of one sheet of paper (two pages of text). Second, make sure that your respondents will find completing the questionnaire a quick and simple process; keep to a minimum the actual writing they must do. Checking boxes or circling words is easier than writing sentences. And finally, organize your survey questions from the simple to the most complex or from the innocuous to the threatening. That way, if a respondent gets irritated or insulted at your questions, he or she will probably already have answered several items, so your questionnaire will not be a total loss.

Begin your questionnaire with a short paragraph introducing your purpose for the survey and enlisting the respondent's help. For instance, if you are doing the survey as part of the requirements for a course, say so. If you want to learn more about the extent to which underclassmen are planning public-service careers, say so. This statement of purpose is important. Few people are willing to leap into a questionnaire without knowing how their responses will be used. You may also find it useful here to promise your respondents anonymity; after all, surveys generally do not have spaces for respondents to indicate their names, and the purpose of a survey is to determine the aggregate, not the individual, response. Finally, you should also include in the introduction to your questionnaire directions on how to return the survey and a date by which you need the questionnaire. Sometimes this information is reprinted at the very end of the questionnaire, too, as a reminder for the respondent. Provide enough time for respondents to complete and return the questionnaires, but not so much that they put the questionnaire sheets away to "do them later" and then forget. Anywhere from two to seven days should be plenty of time. Be sure to announce the specific due date clearly. To sum up: Your introduction to the questionnaire should include your purpose; information about anonymity; and notice about how, when, and where to return the completed questionnaire.

Look at the introduction to a questionnaire by Kevin Miles, who went back to his high school and administered this survey to fifty seniors. His former English teacher collected the completed surveys, which Kevin picked up at a specified time. Kevin originally intended to survey teenagers, mothers, and fathers, but he had to rely on the students to take home the parents' part of the survey and then return it. As you might imagine, this part of the project did not work out well. As you read Miles's introduction, however, consider its effectiveness on other points.

Parent–Teen Relations Questionnaire

Hello! I am conducting a survey as an attempt to discover some of the reasons for today's parent–teen conflicts. I know that parents can be a big problem for teens. By taking a couple of minutes to fill this out you can help me discover why parents can be such a burden. Your answers will be completely confidential. After you have completed your part of the survey, please take home the questionnaire and have your father fill out the "Father's Part" and your mother fill out the "Mother's Part." If you only live with one parent, leave the appropriate part blank. Please stress the confidentiality on their part of the survey. Your participation is greatly appreciated. Please give the completed survey to your English teacher by _____.

Thank you,
Kevin Miles

Please circle, check, or otherwise indicate your desired response.

1. Sex?   M   F

2. Do you live with two parents?   Y   N

3. How much "relaxed" time do you spend with one or both of your parents a day? (Relaxed time is time spent with no apparent goal in mind. Meals, for instance, are not included in relaxed time.)

   a. none
   b. almost none
   c. 5–10 mins
   d. 10–15 mins
   e. more than 15 mins

4. If you answered "yes" to question #2, which of the two you live with do you have more problems with?

    a. father
    b. mother
    c. stepfather
    d. stepmother

5. What is the biggest problem you have with your parents?

    a. the car
    b. money
    c. your grades
    d. your chores
    e. curfew
    f. punishment
    g. clothes/haircut
    h. your friends
    i. other

6. How often does this problem come up?

    a. every day
    b. three times a week
    c. once a week
    d. twice a month
    e. once a month
    f. other

7. What do you consider to be the biggest stress on your life?

    a. grades
    b. sports/activities
    c. being accepted
    d. girlfriend/boyfriend
    e. parents
    f. money
    g. other

8. Do you feel that you could go to your parents about this stress?   Y   N

9. Would you?   Y   N

10. Do you think you would be better off on your own?   Y   N

PLEASE RETURN THE COMPLETED SURVEY TO YOUR ENGLISH TEACHER.

CONSIDER . . .

1. What is Miles's purpose for preparing and administering the survey?
2. Comment on the effectiveness of Miles's directions for completing and returning the survey.
3. Describe the tone of Miles's introduction. Is it formal, informal, friendly, cold?

Once you have written the introduction to your questionnaire, it's time to launch into the actual questionnaire items. You may find that drafting each item on a separate index card makes it easier to arrange the questions later. Most questionnaires begin with *demographic* questions, ones that establish the variables for your research. Demographic information may include such items as age, grade or achievement level, gender, income, experience, and so on. Look at two demographic questions that Miles wrote. He wanted to know whether males or females have more trouble with their parents and whether young adults have more conflicts with parents if they live with a single parent or with both of them. Can you think of other demographic questions that Miles might have asked? For example, he might have asked the student's exact age (in years and months), the approximate annual family income, or the parents' level of education. All these items are variables; that is, they may have an influence on the ways that students and parents respond.

When you finish writing demographic questions, begin constructing the major questions in the questionnaire. Prepare questions that are *valid* and *reliable*. A question's *validity* is its effectiveness in getting at the subject under investigation. If you were investigating a local health problem, for example, you might consider asking questions about absenteeism from work, thinking that health problems sometimes result in workers' calling in sick. The answers to these questions, however, might reflect a problem with morale on the job rather than with health. A valid question obtains information on only the subject being investigated. A question's *reliability* is its ability to elicit the same answer from the same person in repeated tests. For example, could a respondent interpret a question one way today, choosing one answer, but a different way next week, choosing a different answer? If so, your question is not very reliable. Make questions unambiguous to maximize reliability. Here are some tips for writing these items:

1. **Avoid slanting the questions** or you may get biased results. Compare, for instance, these two items:

    Why do you think the decision to build yet another bridge across the river is ill-advised?
    And

    How do you feel about the decision to build another bridge across the river?

    The first item can yield only reasons against building the bridge. A respondent who thinks the bridge will be useful will have to leave this item blank. The second, less slanted item provides more opportunities for a range of responses and will yield less bias.

2. **Provide a variety and true range of responses.** In response to the question *How do you feel about the decision to build another bridge across the river?*, you could offer these possible responses:

    (a) happy
    (b) disappointed

    But if you provided more response options, you could more accurately describe your respondents' feelings. Consider these responses describing attitudes toward the bridge:

    (a) happy and pleased
    (b) disappointed
    (c) frustrated
    (d) angry
    (e) hopeful

3. **Consider how easy tabulating the results will be.** If your directions ask respondents to choose the best response or the response that most accurately describes their feelings or attitudes, and if you ask for only one answer per item (the *best* answer), tabulation will be easier than if you allow for multiple responses.

4. **Choose the question format that suits your needs best.** *Multiple-choice items* are probably the most common kind of survey item because they do a good job of delineating possible responses. Here is an example:

Which items best describe your favorite types of reading?
(a) historical romance
(b) biography
(c) travel
(d) classical literature
(e) science fiction
(f) spy or detective thrillers
(g) mysteries
(h) how-to books
(i) inspirational
(j) other _____

Sliding scale items allow respondents to rate items or statements: they look like this:

Judge the fit of each kind of jeans in the experiment. For best fit, use 1; for worst fit, use 5.

	Best			Worst	
Levis	1	2	3	4	5
Lees	1	2	3	4	5
Guess	1	2	3	4	5
Girbaud	1	2	3	4	5
Pepe	1	2	3	4	5
Boss	1	2	3	4	5
Calvin Klein	1	2	3	4	5
Eddie Bauer	1	2	3	4	5

Agree or disagree items usually present a list of opinions and allow you to evaluate the extent of agreement and disagreement. Here is an example:

	Disagree				Agree		
The university should provide more parking for undergrads.	3	2	1	0	1	2	3

5. **Use predominantly closed questions** to save respondents' time. Closed questions require true/false, yes/no, multiple choice, ranking, or other short answers. Closed questions make the questionnaire easier to respond to (for respondents) and easier to analyze (for you). If you want to ask an open-ended question, save it until the end—just in case the respondent runs out of time or energy. The end of the questionnaire is the best place to invite your respondents to tell you more specifically what they think.

Here are some examples of flawed survey questions. Can you spot the problems?

a. If someone offered you a great salary, would you work inside a nuclear power plant?

b. Did you receive p.r.n. Med stats?

c. What kind of car do you think gets the best city mileage?

 1. Compact

 2. Subcompact

3. Diesel

4. Sport utility

5. American-made car

6. Foreign-made car

d. Should we continue to spend taxpayers' dollars needlessly on trying to revive down-town?

Now look at the following roommates questionnaire and determine how it can be improved. Is the introduction adequate? Are the questions in the best possible order? Can the questions be phrased more clearly or with less bias? Can you think of additional options that should be added to any questions? Working with your writers' group, revise the questionnaire to create an improved survey instrument. Then test it in your class and see how your classmates/respondents feel about working through it.

This is a survey to determine the attitudes of college students toward living in an apartment. Answer the following questions very honestly to help you determine if you like living in an apartment or not . . .

1. What year of school are you in?   Fresh   Soph   Jr   Sr   Grad

2. Have you ever lived in a dorm?   Yes   No

3. If you answered yes to #2, why did you leave the dorm?

_____ Too small

_____ Did not like to have quiet hours

_____ Did not like to share the bathroom

_____ Did not like the inability to party at your place

_____ Other, explain

4. When did you move into your apartment?

5. Why did you choose to live in an apartment?

_____ More roommates

_____ More parties

_____ Bigger rooms, more rooms

_____ Your own bathroom, kitchen

_____ Other, explain

6. How many people do you live with?   1–2   3–4   5–6

7. How long have you known each of your roommates?

8. Do you feel comfortable living there?   Yes   No

Why or why not?

9. Describe the over all appearance of your apartment.

	Filthy	Messy	Neat	Clean	Spotless
Kitchen	_____	_____	_____	_____	_____
Bedroom	_____	_____	_____	_____	_____
Bathroom	_____	_____	_____	_____	_____
Living room	_____	_____	_____	_____	_____

10. How do the chores get done?

_____ Do not get done

_____ I end up doing them

_____ We share the responsibility

11. How do you take care of the bills?

_____ In one person's name, we give him/her the money

_____ Each person is responsible for a certain utility

_____ Whoever has enough money in their checking pays and we repay him/her

_____ Do not get paid

_____ Other, explain

12. Are your study habits . . .

_____ Excellent

_____ Good

_____ Average

_____ Bad

_____ Would be better in a dorm

13. Describe your social life.

_____ Less than one party per week

_____ More than one party per week

_____ Party on weekends only

_____ Party on any weeknight

_____ Go out to party

14. What do you like most about living in an apartment?

Least?

15. Do you want to live with these same people next fall?   Yes   No

Why or why not?

16. Do you have any advice for those considering moving into an apartment?

ADMINISTERING THE QUESTIONNAIRES.   Administering the questionnaires is worth doing well because you need a high percentage of returns to produce a good study. If you can, administer the questionnaires yourself. Allow about five minutes for the respondents to complete the questionnaires and then retrieve them. This method produces the optimum response because it is the easiest way for respondents to do questionnaires: They have to spend, send, or deliver absolutely nothing. If, on the other hand, your respondents are out of town, you may find it cheaper and easier to mail the questionnaires. If you mail out questionnaires to be completed, remember to supply return postage and a self-addressed envelope; respondents may not care enough about your research to purchase stamps and mail your questionnaire. As you can imagine, this method of distribution can become expensive quickly.

Another way to handle the questionnaires is to distribute them yourself, then have respondents return them to boxes at convenient designated spots (near entrances or exits to major buildings, for example). This method of capturing completed question-naires is not, however, as reliable as having respondents fill them out while you wait. If you do not retrieve completed questionnaires immediately or if you have to mail them out and wait to have them returned, you will do well to get 30 to 35 percent of them back—and that's frustrating.

TABULATING AND EVALUATING THE RESULTS.   One way to tabulate results of your survey is to use a blank questionnaire sheet clearly marked *Results* on which to tally re-sponses. Some researchers prefer to use a special handmade grid for tallies. No matter how you decide to record the results of your questionnaires, though, be sure to devise a way to mark all tallied questionnaire sheets so that you record the results of each sheet only once. Once you get simple tallies, convert them to percentages, which are more understandable to your readers. For example, consider which of the following makes a clearer point:

> *12 of 96 respondents characterized their kitchens as spotless.*

> or

> *12.5 percent of respondents characterized their kitchens as spotless.*

You may find that tallying results and converting raw numbers to percentages consumes quite a bit of time. This step is, however, a vitally important part of the preparation for actually writing up the results of your survey in a report.

Computer Writing Tip: If you have a large survey population, you may find a spread-sheet program helpful for tabulating the results of your survey.

Now the serious analysis begins, for now you must consider the significance of your results. What story do your numbers tell? What generalizations can you draw from the results of your survey? Work through each item in your survey, summarizing the num-bers and writing notes to yourself about what the results seem to mean at this point. (When you have a chance to consider *all* figures together, your interpretation may change.) Speculate about *why* the results may have occurred. Remember that you are not committed to this interpretation of the importance of your numbers: You are just trying out different possibilities, attempting to make sense and create enough coherence to answer the questions from which this research project arose.

If you have time, put your results aside for a few days and let them cool.

Drafting the Survey Report

Now it's time to begin writing a report of your findings. It's a good idea to start, as usual, with an introduction that tells your reader about the major finding (expressed in a the-sis) of your survey, about the questions that drove your research, about the research population, and about how you administered the questionnaire. This important section helps establish your credibility; it gives your reader reasons to believe in your results and your interpretation. The introduction may be more than one paragraph.

Next, present results. The easiest way to show results may be to group similar or related questions and explain not only the results but their significance. How should you order or arrange the material? A least-to-most-important order is common, but you may find that the order in which you structured the questionnaire may also be workable—least-to-most-difficult questions or least-to-most-controversial items. In a few cases, chronological or earliest-to-latest order may fit some questionnaire results. Although there is no absolute rule about ordering results, you should choose some organizing principle. If you don't, your reader will find it difficult to make sense of your study. *It is your job to make the information clear.*

As you write, be sure to match claims to data. If 51 percent of your research population believes that the best pizza in town comes from Bruno's Pizzeria, saying that "an overwhelming majority of those surveyed preferred Bruno's" is stretching your results and exaggerating your claims. It is better to understate the significance of your data or to qualify your claims than to claim too much. Phrases such as "For this population, the results suggest that . . ." are more judicious than "These results surely prove that. . . ."

When you have presented all your information and interpretation, conclude with a generalization that addresses the research project as a whole. The conclusion is also a good place to speculate about why the results turned out as they did; again, though, make it clear that you are generalizing on the basis of your research, not presenting hard claims about reasons. This subtler tone does not impugn your research or make it less valuable; rather, it enhances your credibility.

Drafting this report may require more time than drafting some other kinds of writing. The results may be complex, and thinking through the writing may go more slowly than usual. Do not be alarmed if you cannot maintain your usual drafting pace. Just be kind to yourself and allow yourself enough time to do a good job. Then let your draft lie for a while.

Looking at Some Survey Reports

While you give yourself some perspective on your survey report, look at some ways that other writers have done this writing task. First, from *American Film* magazine, is a 1990 poll of eighty movie critics, rating the films of that year.

Can 80 Critics Be Wrong?

PATRICK MCGILLIGAN AND MARK ROWLAND

For once, American film critics agree on something. The Man of the Year is Martin Scorsese, director of that scary–funny descent into mobsterdom, *GoodFellas*. If the other Oscar nominees for **Best Director** of 1990 have any sense at all, they'll practice their good-natured losers' smiles.

Scorsese's decisive win in the *American Film* critics poll completes a grand slam that includes best-picture and best-director awards from the Los Angeles Film Critics Association, the New York Film Critics Circle and the National Society of Film Critics. It marks the first time in a decade of these surveys that a film and its director have received such unanimous acclaim.

Among the 80 critics writing on film for newspapers, magazines, television and radio polled for our annual alternative to the you-know-whats, there is little doubt that Scorsese is the best director of 1990. "In a year that had many first-rate directors on the job—Francis Coppola, Bernardo Bertolucci, Stephen Frears, David Lynch, Robert Altman, Tim Burton and Woody Allen—Scorsese was working closest to the top of his form," observes *Rolling Stone*'s Peter Travers.

But beneath that apparently united front lurk a number of caveats regarding Scorsese's uncompromising depiction of the criminal element, and his *film,* with 34 votes, could not rouse a majority among this year's poll participants. Indeed, many critics split their ballots, giving Scorsese the nod for directing (45 votes) while supporting a film other than *GoodFellas* for **Best Picture.** "Scorsese is obviously the ultimate director," explains Joan Bunke of the *Des Moines Register.* "But I'm unwilling to go on record saying that such a violent and foul-mouthed film is the best of the year."

If history is any indicator, that's just the sort of reservation that could cost *Good-Fellas* the Best Picture Oscar in favor of a more uplifting social drama, something on the order of *Dances With Wolves,* for instance. Directed by Kevin Costner, the screen adaptation of Michael Blake's novel revives the Western with cinematic grandeur while spinning a fable unusually sympathetic to Indian culture, complete with Lakota dialogue.

Wolves, the only movie to provide *GoodFellas* with competition of any sort, places a respectable if distant second (16 votes) in the Best Picture category. For Best Director, Costner receives only 12 votes; however, this total may be diluted by the votes he received in such far-flung categories as Best Actor, Rookie of the Year and Producer's Trophy.

In a year with few controversial films, *Dances With Wolves,* a feel-good movie made by a handsome, nice-guy, novice director, sparks, surprisingly enough, the most arguments among critics. Its admirers tend to cluster west of the Mississippi and in smaller burgs (*GoodFellas* reigns supreme among urban scribes, which may account in part for its domination of awards from the big-city critics' associations). "They should have called it 'Saves the Whales'," the *Chicago Tribune*'s Dave Kehr dourly observes of *Wolves.* He nominates it for 1990's Worst Film. At the other end of the spectrum is the *Richmond Times-Dispatch*'s Carole Kass, who chooses *Wolves* for Best Film and Costner for Best Director and Best Actor, noting, "Costner has shown himself adept with both a large canvas and small, intimate moments."

Another critical consensus—one not unrelated to Scorsese's overwhelming triumph—posits 1990 as a year of slim pickings, with many good films but few, if any, great ones. Some 11th-hour releases that promise satisfaction, like Woody Allen's fantastical *Alice* or Bertolucci's film of Paul Bowles' allegorical novel, *The Sheltering Sky,* were not shown in most markets, so few critics queried got a chance to see them. Those movies will likely show up on year-end lists for 1991.

Excepting *GoodFellas* and *Dances With Wolves,* no movie in this survey received more than five votes for Best Picture. No director besides Scorsese and Costner received more than four.

Three of *American Film*'s acting awards go to portrayals of characters on the shady side of the law. Jeremy Irons earned best-actor honors from the National Society of Film Critics, the Los Angeles Film Critics Association and the foreign press' Golden Globe award for his arch portrayal of Claus Von Bulow in *Reversal of Fortune,* Barbet Schroeder's examination of the notorious attempted-murder trial. Irons sweeps our **Best Actor** poll as well, with a whopping 40 votes, easily outdistancing New York Film Critics Circle winner Robert De Niro, and runners-up Al Pacino and Gérard Depardieu. "He plays Von Bulow as though he were Count Dracula—a dapper bloodsucker," enthuses Carrie Rickey of the *Philadelphia Inquirer.*

The **Best Actress** race turned into a classic heat between two past Academy Award winners. Early balloting favored Joanne Woodward (17 votes), whose subtle turn as the unfulfilled Kansas City housewife of *Mr. and Mrs. Bridge* is viewed by many as the capstone of a remarkable career. But Woodward's tally ultimately trails Anjelica Huston's (22 votes). Huston's two dissimilar but striking performances, as a madcap witch and a vulnerable but ruthless petty criminal, couldn't be topped. "She was spectacular in *The Witches,* but compelling and real in *The Grifters,*" writes Robert Denerstein of the *Rocky Mountain News.* Placing a solid third (11 votes) is screen newcomer Kathy Bates (*Misery*).

Looking over the field for **Best Supporting Actor,** *Newsweek*'s David Ansen comments, "This is the strong category this year—too many good people." His peers agree, and their votes are divided among 25 candidates. Nonetheless, Joe Pesci's performance as the hair-trigger lowlife of *GoodFellas* elicits 34 of them. "You loved him and hated him," opines Jack Mathews of the *Los Angeles Times,* "which was just the idea." Taking second, with 17 votes, is Bruce Davison, who brought home the human drama of AIDS in *Longtime Companion.* Sneaking in third is old smoothie Marlon Brando (6 votes) for his droll send-up of Don Corleone in Andrew Bergman's comedy *The Freshman.*

Best Supporting Actress produced the wildest scramble in our poll, with just one vote preventing a five-way tie between Jennifer Jason Leigh, for her sensual turns in *Miami Blues* and *Last Exit to Brooklyn;* Dianne Wiest, the beatific Avon Lady of *Edward Scissorhands;* Billie Whitelaw, *The Krays'* smothering mother; and Lorraine Bracco, riding the ups and downs of a mobster's wife in *GoodFellas.* The winner—barely!—is Uma Thurman, the sexual muse at the center of Philip Kaufman's *Henry & June* (8 votes). The remaining votes are scattered among 27 other performers.

Best Original Script ends in a tie for the writer–directors of decidedly different tales: on the one side are the Coen brothers, Ethan and Joel, for their mordant saga of '20s gangland love and death, *Miller's Crossing;* and on the other is Charles Burnett for *To Sleep With Anger,* about a family thrown into tumult by the visit of a mysterious guest. Each receives 20 votes. Like last year's Original Script winner, Woody Allen (for *Crimes and Misdemeanors*), none placed in any other category.

On the other hand, lest anyone think Jeremy Irons' performance in *Reversal of Fortune* trancends the film's other merits, Nicholas Kazan has formidable support for **Best Adapted Script** (30 votes). His screenplay drew from an account of the case by Von Bulow's renowned attorney, Alan Dershowitz. Donald E. Westlake's script of Jim Thompson's *The Grifters,* one of three adaptations of the late pulp novelist's work brought to the screen this year, shares runner-up honors (10 votes) with Michael Blake's *Dances With Wolves* (9 votes).

There are other surprises in the distribution of awards in the crafts and technical categories.

Best Cinematographer: For the spacious beauty of *Dances With Wolves,* 19 votes went to Australian Dean Semler (*Mad Max*). Last year's winner (for *The Fabulous Baker Boys*), Michael Ballhaus, is runner-up (14 votes) for *GoodFellas.*

Best Editor: Thelma Schoonmaker's career spans almost 30 years and encompasses director Martin Scorsese's earliest features. She scores more votes—50—than anyone else in any category! Her cutting of *GoodFellas* was crucial to the impact of the film and is "at times a reflection of the actors' paranoiac state," observes Sheila Benson of the *Los Angeles Times.*

Best Production Designer: This is where overmarketed cartoon-character movies generally receive acknowledgment. Last year, *Batman's* Anton Furst received that film's only kudos in our survey; this year's best goes—where else?—to Richard Sylbert (27 votes) for the otherwise disappointing *Dick Tracy.* It's gotta be the cars!

Best Special Effects: Upon its release, critics tended to dismiss *Total Recall,* otherwise known as Arnold Schwarzenegger Goes to Mars. But the spectacular effects are fondly recalled by enough scribes (18 votes) for Paul Verhoeven's film adaptation of the Phillip K. Dick short story to best the charming, whimsical *Edward Scissorhands* (9 votes).

Best Musical Score: Last year, the score for *Batman* lost this category by one vote. This year, the ubiquitous Danny Elfman takes no chances, racking up tallies for three films: *Edward Scissorhands, Dick Tracy* and *Darkman.* That hat trick is enough for Elfman to pull several votes (19) ahead of veteran John Barry (15), whose rousing score for *Dances With Wolves* adds to a distinguished career dating back to James Bond films of the '60s. In the spirit of fairness—three scores versus one—we declare a tie.

Best Foreign Language Film: A big year for films from French directors, at least among U.S. critics. Three of them nearly finish in a dead heat here: *Cyrano de Bergerac* (11 votes), Jean-Paul Rappeneau's cinematic adaptation of Rostand's classic play; Bernard Tavernier's ambitious meditation on the spoils of war, *Life and Nothing But* (12 votes); and the surprise winner, Patrice Leconte's *Monsieur Hire* (13 votes), a psychological/political thriller about a man falsely accused of murder based on a Georges Simenon novel.

Best Documentary: Picking 1990's best documentary is a problem for some heartland critics: "They don't show those here," deadpans Douglas Armstrong of the *Milwaukee Journal.* Well, they don't show too many of them anywhere else, either, so it's not surprising that this year's victor (16 votes) is the one documentary everyone saw, Ken Burns' epochal re-creation *The Civil War,* broadcast on PBS. Harper Barnes of the *St. Louis Post Dispatch* commends the "unprecedented achievement of bringing drama and motion to a historical era without any corny dramatic reconstruction." The nearest rival is Mark Kitchell's flashback, *Berkeley in the Six-ties* (13 votes).

Our **Rookie of the Year** award honors two debuts, *Dances With Wolves'* pro-ducer–director Kevin Costner, and producer–director–writer Whit Stillman, whose droll peek at the smug life of upper-crusters in Manhattan turned *Metropolitan* into a cult and critical success. Both receive 17 votes. *Sweetie's* Australian director, Jane Campion, places third, with 10.

Our **Producer's Trophy** (for the producer, studio executive, production com-pany or studio showing meritorious acumen) also goes to Costner, along with fel-low *Wolves* producer Jim Wilson and Orion (13 votes). Honorable mention (10 votes) goes to the Weinstein brothers, Harvey and Bob, whose feisty Miramax con-tinues to produce and distribute films of uncommon quality and, in 1990, helped to force revision of the X rating in the process.

This year we decided to eliminate the category of Best Children's Movie—now go to bed!—and replace it with a topic dear to any critical curmudgeon's heart: **Worst Movie** of the year. No contest: Brian De Palma's *The Bonfire of the Vanities*. "Absolutely unwatchable," marvels Merrill Shindler of *Los Angeles* magazine, "made by people who had apparently read only the dust jacket of the book."

One book that warrants reading—beyond the dust jacket, that is—is our **Best Movie Book** of the year. Actually, there are several. *Francois Truffaut: Correspon-dence, 1945–1984* (12 votes), the collected letters of the late and lamented French New Wave director, tallies just behind *Preston Sturges,* edited by Sandy Sturges (16 votes). This year's winner is Kevin Brownlow's investigation of movies of social con-science in the era of silent films, *Behind the Mask of Innocence* (18 votes). Along with Ava Gardner's autobiography and *Produced and Abandoned,* a collection of essays about neglected movies edited by Michael Sragow, there are enough worthy tomes around for one critic to call 1990 a better year for books about film than for movies themselves.

Film historian Brownlow and the influential *auteurist* Andrew Sarris were the re-cipients last year of *American Film's* **Special Career Achievement Award,** honoring a deserving film critic, historian or institution with a praiseworthy body of work pre-serving or illuminating American film. For 1990, film critics again choose to pay tribute to one of their own, with a flood of votes for Pauline Kael. With four decades of stylish and trenchant commentaries for *The New Yorker,* collections of reviews and essays, and a groundbreaking book about *Citizen Kane,* the doyenne of Amer-ican film critics continues to influence the way we observe, think and write about motion pictures.

"She's the best film critic we have," says Joe Meyers of the *Bridgeport Post,* "go-ing strong after nearly 40 years in a brain-numbing trade."

Well, people in lots of trades lose their minds, but, after Kael, film critics can proudly boast of having lost theirs at the movies.

Patrick McGilligan's biography of Robert Altman, Altman: Jumping Off the Cliff, *is now avail-able in paperback from St. Martin's Press. Mark Rowland is West Coast editor of* Musician *mag-azine and a frequent contributor to* American Film.

The Critics

David Ansen, *Newsweek;* Douglas Armstrong, *Milwaukee Journal/WKTI;* Gary Arnold, *Washington Times;* Joe Baltake, *Sacramento Bee;* Harper Barnes, *St. Louis Post-Dispatch;* Sheila Benson, *Los Angeles Times;* Ed Blank, *Pittsburgh Press;* Joan Bunke, *Des Moines Register;* Robert W. Butler, *Kansas City Star;* Duane Byrge, *Hollywood Reporter;* Jay Carr, *Boston Globe;* Kathleen Carroll, *New York Daily News;* David Crumpler, *Florida Times-Union;* Bill Cosford, *Miami Herald/WPBT-Ch.2;* Jim Delmont, *Omaha World-Herald;* Robert Denerstein, *Rocky Mountain News;* Steve Dollar, *Atlanta Journal Constitution;* Duane Dudek, *Milwaukee Sentinel;* Rob Edelman, *Schenectady Gazette;* David Ehrenstein, *The Advocate;* David Elliot, *San Diego Union;* Jim Emerson, *Orange County Register;* Frank Gabrenya, *Columbus Dispatch;* Jack Garner, *Gannett News Service;* Gary Giddins, *Village Voice;* Owen Gleiberman, *Entertainment Weekly;* Edward Guthmann, *San Francisco Chronicle;* John Hartl, *Seattle Times;* Molly Haskell, author of *From Reverence to Rape;* George Hatza, *Reading Eagle-Times;* Cathy Huffhines, *Detroit Free Press;* Stephen C. Hunter, *Baltimore Sun;* Richard Jameson, *Film Comment;* Michael Janusonis, *Providence Journal-Bulletin;* Carole Kass, *Richmond Times-Dispatch;* Dave Kehr, *Chicago Tribune;* Rita Kempley, *Washington Post;* Peter Keough, *Boston Phoenix;* David Kronke, *Dallas Times Herald;* Shawn Levy, *American Film;* Joe Leydon, *Houston Post;* Glenn Lovell, *San Jose Mercury-News;* Tony Lucia, *Reading Eagle-Times;* Mick Martin, *Sacramento Union,* coauthor, *Video Movie Guide 1991;* Jack Mathews, *Los Angeles Times;* Todd McCarthy, *Variety;* Michael Medved, *Sneak Previews;* Joe Meyers, *Bridgeport Post;* Howie Movshovitz, *Denver Post;* Martin Moynihan, *Albany Times-Union;* Terry Orme, *Salt Lake Tribune;* Lloyd Paseman, *Register Guard;* Danny Peary, *Cult Movies;* Gerald Peary, *Boston Review;* John Powers, *L.A. Weekly;* Michael H. Price, *Fort Worth Star-Telegram;* Peter Rainer, *Los Angeles Times;* Carrie Rickey, *Philadelphia Inquirer;* Candice Russell, *Fort Lauderdale Sun-Sentinel;* Andrew Sarris, author of *The American Cinema;* Stephen Schiff, *Vanity Fair, National Public Radio;* Wolf Schneider, *American Film;* Nat Segaloff, *Boston Herald;* Merrill Shindler, *Los Angeles;* Jeff Simon, *Buffalo News;* Michael Sragow, *San Francisco Examiner;* Susan Stark, *Detroit News;* David Sterritt, *Christian Science Monitor;* Judy Stone, *San Francisco Chronicle;* Bob Strauss, *L.A. Daily News;* Jeff Strickler, *Minneapolis Star Tribune;* Ella Taylor, *L.A. Weekly;* David Thomson, author of *A Biographical Dictionary of Film;* Peter Travers, *Rolling Stone;* Kenneth Turan, *Buzz;* Joan Vadeboncoeur, *Herald-Journal* and *Herald-American;* Candice Van Dyke, *Wyoming Eagle-Tribune;* James Verniere, *Boston Herald;* Michael Wilmington, *Los Angeles Times;* Josef Woodard, *Santa Barbara Independent.*

CONSIDER . . .

1. Who constitutes the population for this survey? Where do you find this information in the report?
2. Explain the writers' strategy in opening the essay with the news about Scorsese.
3. Describe the organizing principle for this essay–report.

This student-written essay is an in-depth look at the world of night workers. Judy Vestre interviews four people who work at night to learn more about how they accommodate their lives to their work schedules.

Nightworkers
Judy Vestre

When one of the first space shuttles was launched from Cape Canaveral, some attention was focused on the astronauts and how they were adjusting their circadian rhythms in order to work more efficiently in outer space. That was my first acquaintance with the words "circadian rhythm," the dominant cycle of day and night produced by the rotation of the earth on its polar axis. It has been found to be the most powerful influence on biological rhythms and affects us all.

Science, at last, is investigating the effects of biological rhythms on ordinary people, and several studies are now being initiated to find ways to reduce problems incurred by people who work during the night. A recent study, for example, found that productivity in a Western salt mine was markedly reduced during the night, and as a result some methods were devised to help the employees cope better with their adjustments. It was an important landmark study since the population that works at night is increasing dramatically.

Almost every segment of the workforce works at night now. Hospitals, police stations, and a few motels and gas stations used to be the only establishments open during these hours. Now, due to increased consumer demand, factories churn out products twenty-four hours a day. As a result, peripheral enterprises such as drugstores, restaurants, supermarkets, and even the occasional retail outlet stay open around the clock. The interstate highways are constantly rumbling with semitrailers whose drivers prefer to travel at night to avoid losing any time in delivering their goods.

I've long been curious how people who work at night feel about their lives since I worked those hours for five years myself. I remember the special camaraderie that developed among my colleagues and the usually relaxed atmosphere created by the absence of bosses and administrators. I also remember the chronic fatigue that I developed, especially after working a long sequence of nights and spending a large portion of my days off just recovering. My sleep time during the day was as precious as any jewel to me, and I guarded it as such by taking the phone off the hook. Friends and relatives were instructed not to bother me during the day while I slept.

People who work at night are usually very willing to discuss their work and their feelings about it. Recently I talked at length with four of them—two women, two men. The women both work in the same unit of a local hospital, but for different reasons and at different capacities. One of the men is a local policeman, and the other is a miner. They all work full time, eight hours a shift, forty hours in total a week, and have been at the same occupation and place at least four years.

Lisa K. is a registered nurse, presently working in an obstetrical unit. She has been employed there for four years, on the night shift:

"I'm a crab when I work nights. I fall asleep anywhere. Today, for example, the telephone woke me up at 2 P.M. and then again at 2:30 P.M. I don't want to unplug the phone in case there's an emergency, but these calls were dumb ones! You know—people selling something or other. Anyway, I couldn't get back to sleep, so I got up and lolled around in a stupor for the rest of the day. Bob, my husband, cooked supper for the two of us, and then, before I knew it, it was time to shower and get ready for work. Tomorrow will be just the same.

"I'm the breadwinner of the family right now while Bob's in school. The area of the hospital I work is my favorite, and I just don't have any interest in working anyplace else, even if there was an opportunity to work days. The staff on the day shift is pretty stable.

The last time there was a position on that shift was three and a half years ago, and there's a long waiting list.

"There are some advantages to working nights, though. I don't have to miss out on important events. I'll do without sleep to attend them. For instance, if I've got a wedding to go to on a Saturday and I have to work the previous Friday night, I'll stay awake to attend it. Mind you, I'm pretty tired by Saturday evening!

"It's also quieter at night, because there are fewer doctors, visitors, and other people around. I like that!

"We also get a good bonus on this shift, and the two of us can sure use the extra money.

"I plan to work only about two more years on this shift. That's when Bob, hopefully, will be finished university, and by that time I will have had my fill of working nights.

"One last thing I don't like about nights is not being able to sleep with my husband. When I first started working this shift, I used to make Bob stay in bed with me in the morning until I fell asleep. I don't do that anymore, but it's something I do regret."

Susan S. is a divorced mother of two teenagers. She works the same unit of the hospital Lisa does. She has worked the eleven-to-seven shift there for eight years now:

"I assist in the delivery of babies and help care for patients in labor and recovery. It's an interesting job, and I can't imagine working in another area right now.

"I was trained as an operating room technician, and if I was employed in that capacity now, I would be working days. At the time I graduated from training, my children were in elementary school, and since I was divorced, I wanted to be at home during the day in case they needed me. My mother babysat for me at night. It was an important priority for me to be at home, especially when the kids returned from school. If I had worked days then, I wouldn't have been able to do that.

"The kids are in high school now, so don't need me to greet them at the door every day. However, now I'm locked into this shift because there are no jobs for me on this unit during the day. I don't want to work the evening shift because then I'll have no time with my children.

"The thing I like best about nights is loyalty that develops among us who work at night here. We have a common bond of being a forgotten shift. The people who work days and evenings—they seem to forget that there's a job to do at night too.

"I hate the physical effects, though. The exhaustion! The messed-up biorhythms! Your whole system goes out of whack. I become more impatient because I'm constantly tired. Sometimes it seems like I am living for my days off just so I can sleep at night.

"Someday, I'll work the day shift, but as it stands now, I'm going to have to bump somebody off in order to do that. I'm only joking, of course!"

Peter W. is a young police officer and has worked nights for four years. He refers to the night shift as the "graveyard shift," as do people in many other occupations, excluding hospitals for obvious reasons. He revealed a problem unique to his profession that other night workers don't commonly encounter. Daytime and nighttime police work are two very different jobs:

"A new cop on the force usually starts out either working evenings or nights, and then every year gets to bid for the day shift if he wants; and if there's an opening, I hope to get on days in about two years. Presently, I'm the low man on the totem pole.

"My job begins at midnight when we report at the station and then get our assignments. The first half of the night is busiest and mostly involves picking up and arresting drunks, thieves, and mischief-makers. It can be dangerous, and you always have to be on guard in case someone is armed. The drunks don't handle guns with the greatest care. It's usually quiet by 4 A.M., and then I'll go back to the station and do my paperwork.

"I get home about 8 A.M., eat breakfast, go to sleep 'til 4 P.M. or 5 P.M. My wife's an emergency-room technician and works the same shift I do. We've been lucky to be able to arrange our schedules so that we get the same days off together.

"Even though I get eight or nine hours' sleep a day, I never seem to feel completely rested. It takes me the first full day off to recover from a set of graveyards. So, I guess you could say, out of two days off, we only have one to enjoy.

"I think I'm slowly getting burned out working this shift, dealing with the type of people I do. But the light at the end of my tunnel is changing to days in a couple of years. Police work during the day is mostly public relations. You get to meet the nice, ordinary people. That will be a welcome change!"

The previous three people all liked their chosen occupations but experienced difficulty especially with the physical aspects of working nights. There are very few people, I've discovered, who enjoy working this shift just because it is at night. The only one I could think of was my brother-in-law, whom I called long-distance to get his point of view.

Elwood A. has worked in a potash mine in a western province of Canada for almost twenty years, all the time on the night shift. Potash is a mineral used in the manufacture of fertilizer and is in demand all over the world:

"The mine stays open 24 hours a day because it's too expensive to shut down the machinery and start it up again every day. The wages are good. I've got only a high school education, so I probably wouldn't find a better-paying job anywhere else. Besides, I've got lots of seniority, so I'm usually in no danger of being laid off.

"The actual job I have isn't very difficult. I start at midnight by taking the elevator down to almost a mile below the surface. It's hot down there—almost 90 degrees even in the winter. All I do is sit and watch the cars carrying the potash to the surface and make sure that they're on the track and all that. It's very monotonous, but I'm allowed to read to keep alert, so I've probably read hundreds of books and magazines over the years.

"I've never thought about working days. It doesn't make any difference when you're a mile underground whether it's night or day.

"I get home about 8 A.M. and go straight to bed and sleep anywhere until 2 to 4 P.M. I've got part of the afternoon and all of the evening to do odd jobs around the house and go out in the evening if I want. I've got more time to do what I like when I work this shift. Besides, I've worked with the same crew at the mine for years and wouldn't feel right leaving them just to work days."

CONSIDER . . .

1. Describe the kinds of people Vestre interviews. Do you think she provides for enough diversity among the people interviewed?
2. Vestre names her interviewees by first name and surname initial. Why do you think she does not use the entire surname? Do you think this naming strategy is useful?
3. Vestre's introduction is very informative and fairly long. Do you like this strategy? What might Vestre's purpose be in creating such a lengthy introduction?
4. How does Vestre show you where her words end and the interviewee's words begin?

Look now at Kevin Miles's survey report, which describes the results of his research into relationships between teenage children and their parents. You saw Miles's questionnaire earlier.

Parents, Teenagers, and the Fight
Kevin Miles

It seems that all you ever hear about today is all the terrible problems of our society. There are this many murders in New York, X million new AIDS cases in California, and every teenager in Miami is hooked on drugs and headed for jail. I'm sure all these statistics and records must be true, but to me here in West Lafayette, Indiana, the problems are more ordinary. We have different problems here, average problems that almost everyone faces. So when I was assigned to do a survey for my composition class, I decided to try to find out more about the clash between parents and teenagers, a problem that affects almost everyone at some time.

I gave questionnaires to fifty English students at my old high school, hoping that since I knew many of them I would get good responses. Each questionnaire consisted of three parts: a student's part, mother's part, and father's part. I asked the students to take the surveys home and have their parents fill out the appropriate part. This was a mistake. I only got fifteen people to return surveys, and of these fifteen only ten took them home to be filled out by their parents. Maybe this display of forgetfulness (or whatever the problem was) is a reason why some parents have so many problems with their kids, maybe not. Either way, I needed more sources than just fifteen partially completed questionnaires, so I interviewed some of my former classmates to try to find some more information. What I learned was interesting because it didn't support my predictions.

When I wrote the questionnaire, I had those predictions in mind. I thought there would be a connection between the amount of time a family spends together and the frequency of its conflicts, for example, so I asked for the amount of time the family spends together doing fun, relaxed activities. I thought that the less time a family spent together, the more disputes they would have. I just assumed that a lot of families spend almost no time together on a daily basis. Apparently this is not the case at all because nearly every family surveyed indicated that they spent at least a little time together every day. Another of my predictions was that the parents who didn't know their kids very well would have more problems, so I asked the parents several of the same questions that I asked the teenagers. In every case the parent marked the same responses as the teen did on the questions dealing with the nature and frequency of the conflicts; this reveals that both sides agree on what the problem is. I also asked the parents to name the biggest stress on their son or daughter, and although there were a few inconsistencies, an overwhelming majority did respond the same way their teenager did. Since I didn't get what I expected regarding family time and since the parents seemed to know their kids pretty well, I couldn't conclude that this or that family has more problems based on either one of these factors. The only thing that I can conclude is that the type and frequency of a family's problem cannot be predicted on the basis of a statistic but is determined by the individual personalities of a mother, a father, and their offspring.

Even though the data I collected were not what I had hoped for, there were a few interesting facts that turned up. All six females who returned the questionnaire had taken it home to their parents to complete while only four boys returned it completed; but nine boys returned at least a partially completed survey, compared to only six girls. All nine boys indicated that they had more problems with their mother, and only four of the six girls responded the same way. I suspect that more problems exist with Mom because of the nature of the problems themselves. In many households Dad is not to be bothered with minor squabbles. Because minor squabbles occur almost every day, it naturally seems to the teen that he has more problems with Mom. There was one other interesting little trend that I noticed. Of the nine males who participated in the survey, six reported that their biggest stress concerned their girlfriends. Five of those six guys didn't feel that they could go to their parents about this stress. It doesn't take a genius to figure out that there is a problem here. Two-thirds of the males picked the same response out of seven possible choices. This means that this is by far the most common stress on a young man, and yet almost none of them feels he can go to his parents about it. Obviously, better communication needs to exist between parents and teens. First the teen needs to let the parents know that there is a problem; then the parents need to let the teen know that they want him to come to them when he has a problem, be it little or big.

If a teen is made to understand that his or her parents are on his side, he will be more willing to accept his parents as authority figures; and this ultimately will help resolve most conflicts.

CONSIDER . . .

1. Describe Miles's survey population and his means for administering the survey.
2. Miles uses the first person—"when I was assigned to do a survey"—extensively. As a reader, what do you think of the first-person style here?
3. Miles shares his predictions about the results of the survey and compares his predictions to the actual results. What is the effect on the reader of knowing this information?
4. How does Miles arrange his findings? What is the organizing principle of his report?
5. Look back at the questionnaire that Miles used (page 235). Mothers and fathers had virtually identical versions of this questionnaire. Are there other results or findings that Miles might have written about?
6. Help Miles rethink this entire project, from the questionnaire to the report. What is your overall advice for him?

Writers' Group: Rethinking the Survey Report

Now it's time to rethink and possibly revise your survey report. Did you glean any writing strategies from the sample reports, strategies that might be useful in your own survey report? Are your data correct? Now is the time to double-check all the numbers. Have you truly explained your results and interpreted them for your readers? Have you speculated about why the results occurred? Have you answered—or addressed, at least—the questions that prompted the survey project in the first place?

When you feel comfortable with your draft, invite your writers' group to review it. Write three questions you'd like to have answered about your draft and request responses to those questions from your readers. After you receive your readers' comments, decide whether you want to act upon their recommendations. Remember that this is your writing; but if your readers unanimously have difficulty with the same features of your essay, you may have a problem that needs attention.

Reflecting on and Presenting the Survey Report

Charts and graphs that show some of your relevant findings are especially appropriate with a survey report. If you format your paper in two or three columns, you may also find that pull-quotes, vivid quotations pulled from the text, can effectively break up the linear look that columns can acquire. The film critics' survey report from *American Film* (pages 267–268) may suggest some formatting devices.

You may want to present an oral report of your survey findings to your class. Be sure to show your classmates the questionnaire or the list of interview questions you used.

(You might put the survey on a transparency.) Your colleagues may enjoy comparing their private responses to those of your survey population.

Finally, reflect on and write about your experience in conducting the survey and writing up the results. What was rewarding? What was frustrating? What do you like best about the results?

PORTMANTEAU OF WRITING FROM INVESTIGATION AND PRIMARY RESEARCH

Following are more essays and reports based on investigation and primary research. You'll find reviews, interview reports, and survey reports in this collection.

Reviews

Read these reviews, then consider the questions that follow. You'll find a review of the condensed Bible (from *Time* magazine) and a review of a performance of *Hamlet* (from *The New Yorker*). Also in this part of the portmanteau are a book review of Jonathan Kozol's *Illiterate America* and a review of Monty Python's film *Life of Brian*.

Bringing Down the Bible

TIME, 4 OCTOBER 1982

Were God and his inspired scriptural writers unforgivably long-winded? Could they have benefitted, like other authors, from a dose of tough-minded, unworshipful editing? Verily, saith the Reader's Digest, and last week it brought forth the *Reader's Digest Bible*. Priced at $16.95, it is 320,000 words (or 40%) shorter than the Protestant text of the Revised Standard Version on which it is based. The Old Testament has been cut down by half and the New by one-fourth. Alas, less in this instance is not more.

The project began in 1976 when the Digest won the approval of the National Council of Churches, which holds copyright to the Revised Standard Version. As general editor, the Digest recruited the Rev. Bruce M. Metzger of Princeton Theological Seminary, a distinguished Bible expert, to supervise the work of nine staff condensers. Despite the inevitable jokes to come about the Six Commandments or the 4.2 Days of Creation, the team wisely left unshrunk the best-known passages, like the 23rd Psalm. Instead they applied the scissors to parallel accounts, such as the dozens of stories concerning Jesus Christ that appear in more than one of the four Gospels. Whole narrative passages are squeezed to a minimum. God's words to Moses out of the burning bush are boiled down by two-fifths.

The editors also eliminated entire sentences, like *Matthew 4:25:* "And great crowds followed (Jesus) from Galilee and the Decapolis and Jerusalem and Judea and from beyond the Jordan." This moves the action along briskly, but at the sacrifice of historical detail. Many complicated sections are cut altogether, such as those Old Testament family trees and lists of kings and much of the ritual law in *Leviticus.*

In the poetic books, chapter after chapter is hacked away. Gone is fully half of the book of *Psalms,* which might now be better retitled *David's Greatest Hits.* The prophets are especially victimized. Besides large chunks, telling phrases are lost. Consider the felicitous line from *Jeremiah:* "The heart is deceitful above all things, and desperately corrupt." Snip out the last three words. Or this passage from *Isaiah,* immortalized in Handel's *Messiah:* "He was wounded for our transgressions, he was bruised for our iniquities." Away with the second phrase, on grounds of redundancy. So much for poetry.

Also omitted are the chapter and verse numbers. Ostensibly this is to aid readability, though other modern editions avoid clutter by including unobtrusive numbers in the lines or at the margins. The Digest's Bible leaves the reader with no idea what is missing.

What justifies such a venture? Metzger hopes that once people have been lured into his 60% rendition, "a sizable proportion who have never cracked the cover of a Bible will go on to read the whole thing." The Digest contends that the Bible is all too little read, because many sections are rough going for the typical reader. Undoubtedly so, but such people could use one of the readable modern translations of the real thing (such as the *Good News Bible* or *New International Version*) and skip the slow parts.

The Digest Bible comes with ringing publicity hosannas from the likes of Norman Vincent Peale, Oral Roberts, Pat Boone (an "authentic Bible feast"), Executive Director John Mostert of the conservative American Association of Bible Colleges, and President Donald Shriver of New York City's liberal Union Theological Seminary ("an important new addition to the life of Christians, the churches and the world . . ."). So far, only cranky Fundamentalists seem to be offended. They argue that Christians must take the Bible straight, the way God gave it. Warns the *Christian Beacon:* "The Reader's Digest has done a good job for Satan."

A bit much, to be sure, but even the Digesters must have entertained the thought that not everybody was going to be pleased. Why else would they have dropped some of the climactic words from the last book in the Bible, *Revelations?* The [excised] passage threatens eternal damnation if anyone takes away from the words of the book of this prophecy.

Hamlet

REVIEW BY MIMI KRAMER

"Die, you creep!" called a woman toward the back of the theatre on the night I went to see Ingmar Bergman's "Hamlet" at the Brooklyn Academy of Music—presumably an outraged feminist, angered by Hamlet's treatment of Ophelia. The cry came during Hamlet's dying speech, and it was loud enough for the actors to hear. (You watched it register on the faces of the actors playing Hamlet and Horatio.) More startling than the moment itself, though, was the realization that nothing quite so shocking had happened in the theatre all evening. The stage had been filled with breaches of decorum—carnal, bloody, and unnatural acts visited by Claudius upon Gertrude and the Player Queen, and by Hamlet upon Ophelia. (One could sympathize with the outraged feminist, even if one could not applaud her manners.) Claudius had mounted Gertrude from behind before the entire Danish court, and had performed the confession scene while alternately manhandling and fondling the Player Queen. Hamlet had forced himself on Ophelia after spitting in her face, and had hacked Polonius to death after stabbing him in the eye through the arras.

That none of these images had the power to jolt us out of our seats as that disembodied voice did says something, I think, about where we have arrived in our dealings with this play. Owing partly to Tom Stoppard and partly to the high premium that New York, as a culture, places on the idea of innovative Shakespeare, we have reached a point where nothing one could possibly think of doing to or with "Hamlet" could reasonably hope to suprise us. As a collective audience, we have no preconceptions left—beyond the preconception that someone will do something unconventional. Thus, even if one has not actually seen a production in which the Ambassador from England carries a ghetto blaster, and Fortinbras, got up like a Cuban revolutionary, has Horatio hauled offstage and murdered, one *feels* that one has.

"I can't die without having made 'Hamlet,' " Bergman recently told a reporter from the *Times*. In a sense, though, Bergman had already given us his version of "Hamlet"—in *Fanny and Alexander,* the movie about the little boy who keeps seeing his father's ghost. "Don't act Hamlet, my son," the Widow Ekdahl says to the ten-year-old who is sulking over her second marriage. "I am not Gertrude and the Bishop is not Claudius. This is not Elsinore Castle, even if it does look gloomy." But the Bishop turns out to be a lot worse than Claudius, from a child's point of view, and Mrs. Ekdahl has to have Fanny and Alexander spirited away before they, and she, can return to the bosom of their father's warm theatrical family. *Fanny and Alexander* is like a child's rewriting of the Hamlet story in which Gertrude deserts Claudius, taking Hamlet and Ophelia with her.

In *Fanny and Alexander,* in order to make us care more viscerally about the Hamlet–Gertrude–Claudius relationship, Bergman shows us, as it were, life at Elsinore before the old king dies. "Look here upon this picture, and on this," he says to the audience. But the values have been reversed: a satyr to Hyperion. It is the bawdy, permissive Ekdahl household, full of farting and fornication, that we're meant to approve of and set against the austere palace of the Bishop. In Bergman's "Hamlet," there was no such reversal. Up until the last moment, when Fortinbras did indeed seem to burst on the scene in the person of Che Guevara, nothing in the production seemed to tamper with the values of the play. On the contrary, the images of violence and carnality seemed calculated to heighten or reaffirm the conventional moral reading. The "scene of sexual violation between King Claudius and Queen Gertrude that takes place before the entire court" (I quote from the press release issued by BAM) was not, like the fun-loving bed-hopping in *Fanny and Alexander,* meant to amuse us. Despite what the press release implied, it wasn't even to be taken literally. It was simply a stark, theatrical image of the Danish court's willingness to sanction Gertrude and Claudius's behavior.

Throughout the production, characters roamed about the stage or lingered in the background—much like the ghost of Oscar Ekdahl in *Fanny and Alexander.* During the brutal murder of Polonius, Ophelia was right there onstage, not—as the press release maintained—as an actual witness but as a spiritual presence. The ghost was forever popping up where he shouldn't be, and, in a brilliant touch, he took hold of Claudius and held him still, forcing Hamlet to administer the death blow. But, though much in the production was haunting or thought-provoking, nothing seemed wildly unconventional: not the music-hall turn that Ulf Johanson did as the gravedigger, not Pernilla Östergren's gutsy, earthy Ophelia, not the suggestion of homosexual love between Hamlet (Peter Stormare) and Horatio (Jan Waldekranz), not the progressively more contemporary costumes, not the liberties taken with the text, not even a Hamlet who at first is not in control but gains dignity and stature. (I resist this reading, but it is familiar.)

The audience for Bergman's "Hamlet" seems to have been heir to a series of fortunate ironies. To begin with, BAM had thought to import this foreign-language production—a good idea not in itself but in view of how well we know this particular play. Then, having come up with a felicitous idea, BAM—being BAM—had tried to hype the event with intimations of avant-gardism. In the end, owing to Bergman's particular genius (the last five minutes notwithstanding), what the production amounted to was a chance to see Shakespeare straightforwardly performed by a first-rate company of European classical actors. Can we have reached a point in our jadedness about "Hamlet" where the only thing that might seem innovative is inspired traditionalism of this kind?

Illiterate America

Demorah Hayes

Illiterate America. By Jonathon Kozol. 223 pp. New York: Plume, $9.95.

If you are a white American comfortably tucked away in a middle-class enclave or the hallowed halls of academia or the White House, Jonathan Kozol has a message for you. The crusader for literacy has spoken again, with a dire warning and a call to arms. *Illiterate America* puts to rest once and for all any notion that we have eradicated illiteracy in the United States. With fact after fact, statistic after statistic, Kozol brings home the awful truth that illiteracy is alive and well, and is in fact a growing problem. The numbers are frightening, and he makes no attempt to spare us as he delivers a barrage of data. But he also gives faces to the illiterate with personal stories drawn from his many years of activism in the literacy movement. They are testimonies that won't be easily shrugged off and forgotten by the reader, no doubt Kozol's intent.

Kozol goes to great lengths to show us that illiteracy is everybody's problem. He gives a numerical value to the costs of social problems, such as crime and welfare dependency, that can be linked to the inability to read and write. But he also raises the ethical and humanitarian dilemmas involved in illiteracy. Indeed, perhaps his strongest argument is that we have a moral obligation to end the oppression of illiteracy. Kozol draws on poets and philosophers to remind us that "we are one nation." He warns us that if we continue to condemn millions of people to the hopelessness of illiteracy, we must be prepared to endure the eruption of their rage.

Illiterate America is a scathing indictment of the economic, political, and social conventions which tolerate and even promote illiteracy. No group is left out: industry, government, the Army, misdirected humanitarian groups, the average person on the street—all are held responsible for this national tragedy. Even our great universities, dedicated to learning and scholarship, are condemned by their inaction.

The most interesting aspect of Kozol's treatise—and the most important—is his plan of action. Although he does call on the federal government to pump money into literacy campaigns, as the state governments are too financially strapped to do so, he insists that old-fashioned grass-roots activism is the only way to erase illiteracy. He proposes a massive mobilization of individuals, especially students, to make literacy programs accessible and unintimidating to impoverished neighborhoods. He maintains that these programs will be successful only if they are designed and promoted by people already within these neighborhoods. In fact his ideal literacy program resembles a neighborhood barbecue more than a class. If this plan sounds vaguely utopian, perhaps it is because Kozol is a product of the '60s and the romantic social activism that marked that decade. But he supports his proposal with solid evidence that this method works and is the only way to get the job done.

Illiterate America is a passionate plea for justice. Kozol speaks on behalf of those who cannot be heard, and does so eloquently. Although the stream of numbers is intimidating, the figures tell a tragic story and may be the only way to reach a society that wants the bottom line and wants it yesterday. This is a book that will cost the reader sleep, and that is exactly as Kozol wants it. Every American should read this book and consider Kozol's warning. And every reader should remember that one out of every three American adults could never hope to read this book.

Monty Python's *Life of Brian*
Mike Wright

Film directed by Terry Jones and produced by George Harrison. Released in 1979. Screenplay by Graham Chapman, John Cleese, Terry Gilliam, Eric Idle, Terry Jones, and Michael Palin.

In the town of Bethlehem, the Three Wise Men, bearing their gifts of gold, frankincense, and myrrh, enter the dwelling of a child lying in a manger. The Kings are greeted by the child's mother, who screeches "What do you want?" They explain that they have come from afar to bring gifts to the Holy Child. The mother has no idea what they are talking about, but after she learns that one of the gifts is gold, she accepts the presents. The Wise Men depart, but a minute later they barge back in, knock the mother to the ground, and grab the gifts back. They leave, and the camera swings around to show the abode of the child the Three Kings really seek: Jesus Christ. Thus begins the life of Brian.

Monty Python's *Life of Brian* is essentially a biographical account of Brian, played by Graham Chapman. Born just down the alley from Jesus, Brian grows up to be continually mistaken for the Messiah. He begins his escapade by joining the Judean Peoples Front, a revolutionary group dedicated to overthrowing the Romans. Later, he is chased and apprehended by the Romans during a raid on Governor Pilate's palace. Brian escapes and poses as a prophet to elude recapture. His prophesying attracts a large group of religious fanatics who take him as their savior. He is again captured by Pilate, and this time sentenced to crucifixion. The movie ends with this crucifixion scene.

So goes the Python troupe's second attempt at a feature film. This time they have hit the mark dead center. *Brian* is an amazingly smooth-flowing story, considering their earlier movie *Monty Python and the Holy Grail,* which was slightly choppy to say the least. They are no longer attempting to string together their skits to form a ninety-minute film. The jokes and gags successfully advance the plot rather than delay it. For example, when Brian is brought before Pilate the first time, Pilate's continuous references to his close friend Bigger Dickus render his guards useless because of uncontrollable laughter, thereby providing Brian a means of escape. This is only one example of the many memorable scenes in the movie. The script can also become very crude in places. As Brian becomes fed up with the horde of harassing followers, he says "Fuck off." To which they reply, "Tell us, Lord, how shall we fuck off?" Scenes such as these have evoked some religions to declare the movie blasphemous. But at worst, *Brian* can be accused of being in bad taste. It does not poke fun at God; rather it is a spoof on people and society. Judea is merely the setting for the movie which conveys its satire. *Life of Brian* is a splendid movie that is a must for anyone who enjoys Monty Python's style of humor and even for those who like to watch a good comedy.

CONSIDER . . .

1. In what ways are the openings of these reviews similar? How would you describe the writers' various opening strategies?
2. Which review seems most favorable toward its subject? Which seems least favorable? Find at least two *evaluative phrases* in each review.

3. Find examples of the reviewer's giving the reader a sample or flavor of the item being reviewed. This might be a quotation from a book or a characteristic line from a movie or performance.
4. Two of these reviews lack informational headings. Discuss the merits and disadvantages of each typical review ingredient or stylistic feature.

Interviews

As you read the following interviews from professional and student writers, consider their common features. You will find here a *New Yorker* interview with Iona Opie, who with her husband Peter Opie wrote *The Lore and Language of Schoolchildren*. And you'll also read student interviews with a counselor in a crisis center and with an expert seamstress.

Playground Person

ADAM GOPNIK

Iona Opie, the Marie Curie of hopscotch and skip rope, came to New York for the first time in her life last week. She is sixty-five years old and lives in Hampshire, and she will talk to perfect strangers in hotel lobbies about the nature of play, the architectural origins of evil, the absurdity of games instruction, and where in the human body grief resides. Forty years ago, when intellectuals were speculating on the Nature of Play, and the Psychological Origins of Play, and the Dubious Future of Play, she and her husband, the late Peter Opie, decided that one good way to find out about playing was to go to a playground and watch. The result of their years of research, *The Lore and Language of Schoolchildren,* was published in 1959, and it remains a classic of anthropology and a book rich in the contagious joy of finding things out. The Opies discovered, for instance, that a children's rhyme took only a few months to travel from its starting point in, say, London to the most distant playgrounds in Britain. Iona and Peter Opie also edited scholarly collections of Mother Goose rhymes and children's games, among much else. Mrs. Opie is one of the very few experts on anything whom we have ever wanted to interrogate, and when we found out that she was in New York we rushed over to the lobby of her hotel and begin to pepper her with questions.

First, we asked something that we have wanted to ask an expert since ninth-grade English class: Would kids on an island *really* act the way the kids do in *Lord of the Flies*?

"Do you know, it's very odd that you ask that," she said happily. "That's a question that Peter and I debated for quite a long time. Peter thought that children in such a situation would be entirely just. I'm more cynical perhaps. It seemed to me that they might become like animals in a zoo, tearing each other to pieces. But it's nothing to do with human nature or sin. I really believe that it's a function of the geography of playing. In playgrounds, if there's a place apart, a kind of refuge, where people can get away from bullies, then on the whole there is no bullying. Everyone in a playground knows that the best thing to do about a bully is just to go away. Now, those children were on a small island, weren't they? I'm sure I sound a bit simple, but it's my experience that big questions about good and evil sometimes come down to the question Have you anywhere else to go? There's one playground in Leeds, for example, that's a nightmare. It's rather like a bullring—a big pit with high buildings all around. I'd hate to base a theory of good and evil on what one saw children do *there!* So often psychological problems have architectural solutions. Is there a place for people to play in quiet? Is there somewhere else to go?"

We asked Mrs. Opie if she thought that discoveries about the creativity of children were generally true about all human creativity.

"Well, children aren't really creative," she said gently. "Not, anyway, in the sentimental sense that people normally use when they swoon about the untrammelled creativity of children. Children invent nothing. They adapt things. It's fascinating to see what they will adapt and what they feel has to remain constant. There's that famous and very old counting-out rhyme, for instance—'eeny, meeny, miney,' and so on—which used to have that terrible word right in its middle. Well, that became a forbidden word, so it was changed to 'tigger,' as a rhyme. Then children changed it to 'tiger,' in order to make sense of the rhyme. And once it became plain that you could change one word without losing the meaning of the rhyme—well, the word was freed! It could become any two-syllable animal—'spaniel' or 'donkey' or 'budgie.' Children create only in that sense. They are Tories of the whole and anarchists of the particular."

Next, we asked Mrs. Opie if she agreed that television was killing off playground culture.

"Oh dear!" she said. "Do you mean Children Nowadays Do Not Have the Fun That They Used To? You know, that itself is part of the lore of *older* children. At about thirteen or fourteen, when a child stops playing, he will tell you that all the playing has gone right out of the world. It's the beastly superiority of the adolescent to the child, and we never outgrow it. Just recently, we had quite a terrible furor at home. Some educationists went to a playground and didn't see any children skipping rope. They noticed a Lack of Skipping. A Disturbing Failure to Skip! So they published a little pamphlet, 'Lets All Skip!,' and distributed it in the playgrounds. Well, of course, the children *were* skipping. They simply happened not to be skipping right where the grownups happened to be. They were down the street or around the corner—or perhaps it wasn't the skipping season. What's so hard for many people who care about children's play to understand is that children don't play. One of my favorite remarks came from a child who, when I asked him what he was playing, told me *very* severely, 'I never play.' I watched him for weeks, and found that he led most of the games. I was puzzled, and so I described to him what I had seen and asked him why he had told me that he never played. 'I *never* play,' he repeated. 'That's just what I *do.*' "

We asked Mrs. Opie how she had coped with the death of her husband, in 1982, and what she had been doing and writing since.

"When Peter died, my grief was intense, and lasted for three years," she said softly. "But at the same time I realized that I had become the only remaining member of Opie & Opie. We were in the middle of two projects—*The Oxford Book of Narrative Verse* and *The Singing Game*—and I knew I had to finish them. I couldn't let him down. I was writing the preface to 'Narrative Verse' an hour after he died. Grief is so strange. It's located right here." She pointed to a spot just to the right of, and about six inches above, her navel. "My own grief became another playground—a thing to observe. There were sudden rushes of happiness in the worst moments. You live so *intensely* in grief. It's a mysterious pain. I lived so intensely for three years while I was grieving that now I find myself grieving for my grief. But since the pain left I've been very happy. It was only after his death that I realized that Peter and I worked very differently. Peter was a Puritan, and for him work had to be painful. I try to make my work into a kind of play. When we were reading proofs, which is really the most tedious and time-consuming process, I would grow bored and read them out in a Scots accent or an Irish brogue. Peter thought it really very dreadful.

"I decided next to take a holiday from childhood and to edit a dictionary of superstitions. But now that's done, and I'm back to the playgrounds. The old routine—stand at the side of the playground and ask the children what they're doing. Posing as the village idiot. They teach me how to play marbles. They teach me *terribly* vulgar stories, or children's versions of those stories, which tend to be a little vague, as they don't quite understand them. When we originally published our book, we weren't allowed to publish even slightly sexy rhymes. So now I shall. I have a title for the new book. May I tell it to you? It is *The People in the Playground. People,* you know, because children *never* refer to themselves as children. They say, 'You need four people for this game' or 'Some people say that rhyme differently.' "

Finally, we asked Mrs. Opie the question we ought to have begun with: What were her favorite books as a child?

"Well, I loved *Beauty and the Beast* and *The Frog Prince,* because they suggested a strong, not a sentimental, compassion. They faced reality. They are stories about the good consequences of accepting ugly things for themselves. Of course, I don't doubt that they have other themes—sexual themes—within them. But I think that what remains with us in children's literature is not what is invisible but what is most apparent—the beauty of compassion and courage and loyalty. Do you know, as a child I could never *abide* Lewis Carroll. The 'Alice' books seemed so obviously written for someone older than I was. But when I knew that, finally, I was going to come to America I decided to bring along *Through the Looking Glass* to read on the airplane and to keep with me here. Well, do you know what the White Queen says about trying to believe six impossible things each day? That's very good advice for New York. In my two days here, I've been blissfully astonished the whole time. So now I find myself living according to Carroll."

Dealing with Crisis: An Interview with Cathy Buksar
Wayne Bischoff

What do you do when you are faced with a problem and need some advice? One option is calling the Lafayette Crisis Center, an establishment for those who have no one to turn to. Cathy Buksar has volunteered at the Center for several months while studying at Purdue University and she informed me in an interview about the training, problems, and people someone working at the Crisis Center encounters.

As I talked with her, Cathy energetically tossed out various aids the Center has given her on how to handle phone situations. She displayed her schedule, her call sheets, her color stress scale, her list of thesaurus key words in case she got "stuck" without the right word to say, and her training book: all given to her by the Crisis Center and necessary for smooth and beneficial work with telephone callers. As the interview went on, I quickly realized the amount of work and dedication it takes to voluntarily help people with problems.

Q: How did you get interested in this job?
A: In high school, I was the one my friends always dumped all their problems on. And I thought, why am I wasting all this on my friends? I could do this for other people for hours. When I got here (Purdue), I thought maybe I could do that here, because I needed to get in volunteer hours for Teacher Education. So I called them up, and I said, "Hey, why don't you train me in this?" and they had a training class coming up in two weeks, so here I am.

Q: How long have you been doing this, then?
A: I started training in late August and early September, and I've been doing it continuously up to now.

Q: What are your hours at the Crisis Center?
A: The hours of the Crisis Center are 24 hours a day, 365 days a year. Shifts run normally four hours apiece, except the only one that's longer is midnight to eight in the morning. That's the longest one. I usually work eight to midnight, four in the afternoon to eight, or sometimes from midnight to eight in the morning.

Q: How many people do you work with?
A: Midnight to eight and four to eight, there's only one person on duty. And then eight to twelve, there's two people, because it's the busiest, because it's right after work, and that's when most things happen.

Q: What are most of the callers looking for from you?
A: A lot of them are just looking for someone to listen to them, or they're looking for someone to solve their problems for them, which we are not allowed to do. We try to get them to figure out [their problem] by themselves.

Q: How do you approach someone with a problem?
A: It really depends on what they're asking. I always start with, "Crisis Center, can I help you?" But you want to get them to talk to you, because there's some reason why they called you up in the first place. It's different for every [caller]. The Center doesn't have one certain way you're supposed to answer.

Q: Can you give me some examples of problems you face?
A: I'm ready for that question. This manual is like my Bible. [She opens her training manual.] I need this a lot. We get just about anything you can imagine. We get people who have broken up with their boyfriend or girlfriend, their husband or wife's left them,

divorces, bankruptcies, people who've lost their jobs, people who are just lonely or who are failing their classes, and some emergencies. We get 35,000 calls a year, and ten percent of those are emergencies.

Q: While we have this training manual open, what training did you receive before working at the Crisis Center?
A: You go for three weeks on Tuesday, Thursday, and one Sunday; in all, you get about forty hours of training. And each time you go, you get one speaker, who talks on one subject in the book. Then after the talk, you split up into little groups of three trainees, two trainers, and you do role playing . . . and then they evaluate you, and then you talk about what you did and how you can improve yourself.

Q: What is the most common problem you face?
A: We don't really have a most common problem, they're all different. But if I had to say which is the most common, I'd have to say people who don't have anyone to talk to. They just want somebody to listen to them and say, "That's okay."

Q: What situation was the most rewarding for yourself?
A: There was this girl who was all upset because she was doing really, really bad in her classes. This was her first year in graduate school, and she had started really enthusiastically, but she found out her classes were really hard, and she was new to the state, and just couldn't get it together. And I told her, "Listen, honey, I'm a transfer student, too. I understand." And we just hit it off, and we talked for an hour, and when she hung up, she felt a lot better. And I was really happy, because for her there was someone else who had transferred and who had done really bad. And for me, it was, "Wow! Even grad students run into this." It went really great, so I was happy about that.

Sewing for Success: An Interview with Gracie Smith
Susan Buchman

I walked up to the back door—the door that Mrs. Smith's customers enter through—and knocked. A few minutes later, she appeared at the door with a tape measure around her neck, having come up from her basement workplace to let me in. She welcomed me into her "shop" on 23rd Street and asked me to have a seat while she finished with her client. As I waited, I looked around the room and noticed several machines, numerous spools of thread, pattern books, and dress forms. Mrs. Gracie Smith, a 55-year-old dress designer, seamstress, and tailor, was very warm and friendly to me and interestingly answered all my questions.

Q: Obviously, you enjoy sewing, as you have been at it for many years. When did you first become interested in sewing?
A: Oh, that was a long time ago! I was in elementary school. I'd say around the age of eight.

Q: How did you learn to sew?

A: My mother and grandmother were both seamstresses, and I watched them. My mother worked as a consultant in a boutique, so there was always beautiful fabric lying around. My sister and I always thought what pretty things we could make from the scrap material, and so we would watch our mother and learned to make doll clothes and eventually our own clothes. I was a 4–H member for 10 years and learned a lot about sewing from this experience. During my senior year, I designed a dress that was the grand champion at the Indiana State Fair in 1950. From 1955 to 1958, I attended the National School of Dress Design in Chicago where I learned professional pattern making, fitting, and sewing techniques.

Q: When did you first make something for someone else?

A: Oh, at least by the time I was in high school.

Q: When did you go public with your sewing?

A: Between 1958 and 1965, I ran a sewing business as a part-time hobby to give me extra spending money. But I guess I would say I went public in 1965 after my divorce.

Q: Do you advertise for your business?

A: No! I *did* advertise foolishly once, though, and I got too swamped with customers, so I decided never to do that again! No, I prefer referral, word-of-mouth customers.

Q: How much time do you spend sewing daily?

A: I can't really say. I don't know how much time I actually spend at the machine each day. It's so intertwined; customers come in, I work with them, and then I sew. I don't really know.

Q: Then how many hours do you spend on the total job each day?

A: At least 17 hours. I usually work late, so I don't get up early. I tell customers to come after noon.

Q: How late will you see a customer?

A: Oh, they usually don't come much later than 8:00 P.M., but I've had a couple come as late as 10:00 P.M. Some find it hard to come at convenient times for me, so I just work around their schedules.

Q: What types of things can and do you make for people?

A: Oh, anything—they can have anything. I've made a tent and even a pig hammock!

Q: What is your favorite type of thing to sew?

A: I really enjoy suits. I'm more tailor-oriented. I do make frilly things, but I prefer more tailored sewing.

Q: You've been sewing for many years, but do you ever mess up (make a mistake)? How do you handle this with your customers?

A: Yes! Everyone makes mistakes, and with sewing, it's just a matter of covering them up so no one but you knows it. No, if I mess something up, I tell my clients and they are always very understanding. Once, I cut out the sleeve of an Ultrasuede suit on the wrong nap and it turned out that the customer just loved the way I fixed it up—she said I couldn't have made anything she could have liked better! Some of my neatest and most unique garments have been results of a mistake.

Q: How do you get inspiration for new styles or new ways of doing things?
A: I used to actually dream up outfits during my sleep, so for a while, I kept a sketch pad in which I would sketch my ideas. But the way my business runs, I don't really have time to make up original things to sell. I just have too much work with my clients. When a person comes in to have me make something for the first time, and they don't really know exactly what they want, I have them look through the pattern books so that I can see what type of person they are. Then we go from there and I can follow a pattern, change a pattern, or design a pattern if need be. So many people come to me because they want to be different and because they can't find what they want in the stores.

Q: Do you find clothes in the stores of poorer quality than the things you make? Do you ever feel that you could have made a garment of higher quality than one in the store?
A: Sure, I know I could make it better. I'm really into matching plaids, and it really makes me quite upset when they fail to do so in the stores and then charge an outrageous price.

Q: What kind of machine do you use?
A: I use Elena equipment, just because it's what I'm used to.

Q: What do you find to be the hardest thing in sewing for other people?
A: People's physiques. Some bodies are difficult to fit.

Q: What is the most unusual fitting problem you've ever had?
A: That's an interesting question. I once had to fit someone with a curvature of the spine. Oh, I know! I used to make pants for a man who had been wounded in the war and had one very swollen leg. I had to make his pant legs different—one for the normal leg, and one for his injured leg, which was swollen 25 inches!

Q: Mrs. Smith, you have devoted yourself to being an excellent seamstress. Do you ever get tired of sewing?
A: Every day is a new day. I get tired physically; but mentally, my mind just keeps going. The completed garment fascinates me, and I work for that outcome. My philosophy is that the good Lord gave me a talent, and I had better make the most of it!

CONSIDER . . .

1. The interview with Iona Opie is formatted differently than most interviews. Explain how the writer distinguishes the interviewer's questions from Opie's responses.

2. Find a place in each interview where the interviewer, listening carefully, follows through with a question based on the interviewee's previous response.
3. Choose one interview report, read it carefully, and construct three additional questions that the interviewer *could* ask.

Survey Reports

Here are some survey reports and some questionnaires for you to examine. You'll find a reader questionnaire about the best movies for 1990 from *American Film* (you read the survey report for this questionnaire earlier in the chapter) and a student questionnaire about geography knowledge. There are also a survey of customers' satisfaction with their cars (from the 1991 *Power Report*) and a student's in-depth survey of attitudes about the minimum wage.

American Film 1990 Readers' Poll

THE MOVIES

After a year's worth of film-going, film-talking and film-fighting, surely you've formed a few opinions. We'd like to know what they are. Here's your chance to choose the best of 1990 in each of the following categories.

Best Film _____

Best Director _____

Best Actor _____

Best Actress _____

Best Supporting Actor _____

Best Supporting Actress _____

Best Original Screenplay _____

Best Adapted Screenplay _____

Best Foreign Film _____

Brightest Newcomer of 1990 _____

THE CRITICS

We're always listening to what they think, but what do we think of them? Here's your chance to speak up and reveal your opinions of the opinion-molders.

Do you read, watch or listen to film critics?   Yes _____   No _____

Are your opinions of films influenced by critics?

Always _____ Often _____ Sometimes _____ Rarely _____ Never _____

Who is your favorite film critic? _____

Why? _____

_____

Who is your least favorite critic? _____

Why? _____

_____

What makes you decide whether or not to see a film? (Rank them in order from 1 to 5, with 5 being the least influential.)

Reviews _____   Trailers _____
Advertising _____   Word of mouth _____
Other (specify) _____

Name (optional) _____
Profession (optional) _____
City _____ State _____
Did you subscribe to this magazine primarily because (choose one):
You wanted the magazine? _____   You wanted to join the AFI? _____

Please use this sheet to mail or FAX your responses by January 5, 1991. Results will be published in *American Film*'s Second Annual Critics Poll, which will appear in our April 1991 issue.

MAIL	FAX
Readers Poll	(213) 962–1352
American Film	ATTN: Readers Poll
6671 Sunset Blvd.	
Suite 1514	
Hollywood, CA 90028	

Geography Survey
Larry A. Crozier

The purpose of this questionnaire is to determine how various factors influence basic geography skills. This questionnaire is anonymous, so do not sign your name. Circle the answer that is most appropriate for questions 1 through 7. The second page is a map of the United States. Fill in the name of each state in the space provided. Don't worry about filling in every state, and don't use any reference material. All questions should be answered with general knowledge. Your response to this survey is important to my study. Thank you for assisting me in my research.

1. What is your sex?
    Male   Female

2. What is your age?
    10–12   13–15   16–18   19–22   23–29   30–39   40 and up

3. How many different states have you visited?
    1–5   6–15   16–30   31–50

4. What is the highest level of education that you have completed?

Grade school	4	5	6	7	8
High school	9	10	11	12	
College/trade school	13	14	15	16	17 and up

5. How many semesters have you completed in geography? (Include all courses from grade school to college.)

   0   1–2   3–4   5–6   7–8   9–10

6. Do you think more attention should be given to geography in school?

   Yes   No   Don't know

7. On a scale of one to ten, how important is geography to you? (One is the lowest, and ten is the highest.)

   1   2   3   4   5   6   7   8   9   10

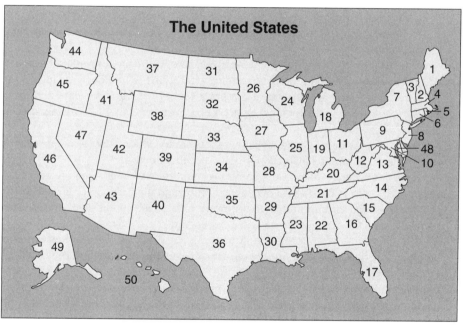

1. _____	13. _____	25. _____	37. _____
2. _____	14. _____	26. _____	38. _____
3. _____	15. _____	27. _____	39. _____
4. _____	16. _____	28. _____	40. _____
5. _____	17. _____	29. _____	41. _____
6. _____	18. _____	30. _____	42. _____
7. _____	19. _____	31. _____	43. _____
8. _____	20. _____	32. _____	44. _____
9. _____	21. _____	33. _____	45. _____
10. _____	22. _____	34. _____	46. _____
11. _____	23. _____	35. _____	47. _____
12. _____	24. _____	36. _____	48. _____
			49. _____
			50. _____

Measuring Customer Satisfaction with New Cars

In their first year in the race for top ranking in the J.D. Power and Associates Car Customer Satisfaction Index[SM] (CSI), Infiniti and Lexus led the charge that finally achieved what nameplates have been trying to do for the past four years—catch Acura. The two new Japanese luxury marques displaced Acura at the top of the CSI rankings in a dead heat, each with a potent 170 CSI index.

The dynamic automotive duo helped raise the jump bar for CSI excellence far above what it was just a year ago. Manufacturers may have caught up and in some cases surpassed Acura's performance, but there is clearly more room to raise the jump bar even higher.

In 3rd place was Mercedes-Benz, which recorded a CSI of 147. Acura tied with its sister division Honda for 4th place with a CSI of 146.

The Customer Satisfaction Survey was calculated on responses by nearly 23,000 owners of 1990 model-year cars purchased in the first quarter of last year.

The survey looks at aspects of owners' experiences with their cars during the first 12 to 14 months of ownership, with an emphasis on customer satisfaction with service.

The CSI provides a single, objective measure by which people can judge relative levels of customer satisfaction among owners of new cars.

This year's study follows the same procedures used every year since its last major revision in 1986. The 23 questions comprising the Customer Satisfaction Index are weighted for importance to represent a balanced synthesis of owner experiences during the first year of new-car ownership.

The measures of performance—Customer Handling and Vehicle Repair/Reliability—help explain the dynamics behind the CSI. Of the 23 questions that make up the overall CSI, 10 are summarized by the Customer Handling measure and six by the Vehicle Repair/Reliability measure. The remaining seven CSI items are not included in these two measures, but they are still important and are included in the calculation of the overall CSI.

Fourteen nameplates exceeded the industry CSI average of 127 this year, compared with 18 last year, when the industry average was 122. The total CSI of all models falling below average this year was 114, three index points better than last year's.

By origin, the Europeans and Domestics are still slowly but steadily cutting into the Asians' CSI lead, but the latter import group still outperforms its Western competitors in most cases.

This year, Asian nameplates had a total CSI of 137, two index points better than last year. Europeans notched an industry-tying 127 CSI, an increase of three index points over 1990's results (when they were above the industry average).

Domestic manufacturers, while still trailing this year with a CSI of 121, nevertheless gained the most—their finish was 5 index points better than in 1990.

The top-finishing Domestic in the 1991 study was Cadillac, in 8th place with a CSI of 139. Last Year, Cadillac also led the Domestics, finished in 4th place with a CSI of 142.

Other Domestics exceeding the industry average were Buick, finishing in 9th place with a CSI of 137 versus last year's 130 CSI and 7th-place finish; and Oldsmobile, a real success story in this year's study.

Oldsmobile jumped seven places in the rankings, finishing this year in a tie for 12th with a CSI of 128, versus a 19th-place, and below-average, finish in 1990.

Last year, five Domestics exceeded or matched the industry average but Plymouth and Mercury—both above average in 1990—and Lincoln just barely fell below average this year.

The Europeans were well represented in 1990, with Mercedes-Benz, Porsche, BMW, Audi, Volvo, and Volkswagen all exceeding the industry average.

This year, however, only Mercedes, Audi, and BMW enjoyed that distinction. Last year, Audi and BMW tied for 10th place, each with a CSI of 127. In 1991, Audi owners gave their makes a CSI of 140 and 7th place. BMW owners gave their nameplate a CSI of 132, good for 10th place.

In order of finish, the remaining above-average nameplates in 1991 included Honda (up six CSI points from last year); Toyota (unchanged); Subaru (down one CSI point); Mazda (up one CSI index point); and Nissan (down seven CSI points).

Regarding the two performance measures, the industry Customer Handling CSI of 129 this year is seven index points above last year's finish.

In 1991, the industry Vehicle Repair/Reliability measure was 118, compared to 116 in last year's study.

The top five finishers by nameplate in the Customer Handling measure were, in order, Infiniti (a Customer Handling CSI of 187); Lexus (183); Mercedes-Benz (157); Audi (155); and Cadillac (155).

On the Vehicle Repair/Reliability measure, the top five makes included Lexus (with a CSI of 144); Infiniti (142); Toyota (135); Mercedes-Benz (134); and Honda (132).

1991 Customer Satisfaction Leaders

Rank	Make	CSI Score
1	Infiniti	170
1	Lexus	170
3	Mercedes	147
4	Acura	146
4	Honda	146
6	Toyota	144
7	Audi	140
8	Cadillac	139
9	Buick	137
10	BMW	132
11	Subaru	129
12	Mazda	128
12	Nissan	128
12	Oldsmobile	128
Total Industry		127
Average of Remaining Makes		114

Source: *The Power Report,* July 1991.

Minimum Wage

Stacey Bourland

The minimum wage act was originally passed in 1938 as a way to protect workers from being exploited. The law says that no employee may be paid less than a certain hourly wage rate. The original minimum wage was 25 cents an hour, and it has since risen to the present rate of $5.15 an hour. Is this a reasonable minimum wage, and does it effectively protect workers? To learn about the public's opinion of the minimum wage law, I talked with several people who have jobs or are presently seeking employment. Two of the people I spoke with are unemployed, one is an employed member of a labor union, one is employed but does not belong to a union, one is an employed teenager, and one is a professional.

Susan K. is one of the unemployed people I interviewed. She has recently been laid off from a management position.

Susan said that she'd like to see the minimum wage moved up to $7.00 an hour. "But I don't worry about it—I just do the best I can with the law as it is now. I don't think the minimum wage law has any effect on me personally, because I'm past that point. I don't have to settle for a minimum wage job. I'm used to a management salary. Besides, I don't think we have much choice about what the minimum wage is. It's the government that decides." Even if the minimum wage were raised to $7.00 an hour, Susan is afraid it might have a negative effect on the economy: "Prices would go up, so it might be a bad idea. I think what we really need to do is steady the economy."

When I asked Susan whether she would take a job for minimum wage if one were offered to her, she said it would depend on how badly she needed work: "I'd take it if I were desperate and starving, but right now I couldn't afford to take it. It wouldn't meet my expenses."

Pete G. is also unemployed. If he were offered a job at minimum wage, he said he's not sure whether he'd take it or not. "It would depend on where the job was," he said. "I'd take it if it were in my home town, but it wouldn't be worth driving out of town for a minimum wage job." Like Susan, Pete thinks that the minimum wage should be raised. Unlike Susan, though, he does not think that this increase would cause an increase in prices. "The way the price of everything is going up anyway, it wouldn't make a difference," he added.

Charles S. is employed and is a member of a labor union. When I asked Charles whether he thinks $5.15 an hour is a reasonable minimum wage, he said that this rate is too low and that increases in the minimum wage have not kept up with the rising cost of living. "It would have to be $8.00 an hour to be equivalent to the original level. Five dollars and fifteen cents an hour isn't even above the poverty level. Why have a job if you can't make ends meet?"

He continued, "Some people say that an increase in the minimum wage would cause an increase in unemployment because an employer would hire only one or two people instead of four. I don't think this would ever happen. An increase in the minimum wage wouldn't hurt high school students either because many businesses that hire these students aren't governed by the minimum wage law."

Charles thinks that the low minimum wage rate hurts him personally in two ways: "I'm paid more than minimum wage, and my employer is less willing to raise my salary when he knows that other people are working for only $5.15 an hour. I'm also hurt as a taxpayer because I pay for the government benefits that people earning minimum wage need to survive."

Dennis L. has a steady job with a construction company during the summer and finds temporary work each winter. He is not a member of a labor union.

Dennis feels that the minimum wage should be raised higher than anyone else I interviewed wants it raised. He would like to see it increased to $9.00 an hour. Although he predicts a possible negative effect of this increase on America's economy, he thinks that this could be avoided. "Prices would rise tremendously, but this could be prevented if whoever was hiring didn't have to make such a profit," he maintained.

When I asked Dennis if he'd be willing to work for the minimum wage, his immediate response was an emphatic "No!" He explained, "I couldn't even afford to drive anywhere. By the time I paid the gas cost to get to work and back, I'd have too little money left. I might as well just sit at home and draw unemployment."

Abigail R. is employed, but she is different from anyone else I interviewed because she is a teenager. Her opinion about whether $5.15 an hour is a reasonable minimum wage is also different from the opinions of anyone else I talked to. "Yes, I do think it's pretty fair in most situations," she said. Abigail went on to explain, "Everyone has to start at some level, and most people can work their way up to get a raise. If the minimum wage were higher, there might be less opportunity for a raise and therefore less incentive to work hard to get that raise."

Abigail's answer to my question about whether she'd work for minimum wage was also different from anyone else's response. "It depends on how old I am and how much education I have," she replied: "Now I would, but if I were a college graduate, there'd be no way."

Abigail believes that she is personally helped by the minimum wage law. "It helps me want to work harder and harder to get a raise so I can say that I don't work for minimum wage any more," she said.

Although she finds the law so helpful to herself, Abigail thinks that the low rate might hinder other people: "Some people say that $5.15 an hour is way too low, and they refuse to work for it. This hurts them because they don't take jobs."

The opinions of the last person I interviewed were surprisingly different from those expressed by any of the other people I talked with. Barbara B., a physician, feels that there should be no regulated minimum wage at all. "A fair minimum wage is that wage which an individual is willing to accept to perform the duties requested by the employer. This is not regulated by the government. If there were no minimum wage law, more currently unemployable, unemployed, low-skill workers would find jobs," she argued.

When I asked Barbara if she would accept a minimum wage job if she were unemployed, her immediate answer was yes. "I would much rather work," she said, "and have the opportunity to improve my skills and my lot in life, which any job would give me at any wage, than receive welfare or sit around on my duff and starve. In fact, early in my career I did work for much less than the minimum wage!"

"There is a class of people," she went on, "which the minimum wage helps very much: the medium-skilled workers who are paid well above the minimum wage but who do not have competition from lower-skilled workers who are effectively kept out of the job market by the minimum wage. The law hurts lower-skilled workers (the very ones it is intended to help), who are basically kept out of the job market. They can't get experience, so they can't climb onto the 'lowest rungs of the ladder.' "

CONSIDER . . .

1. Identify the survey populations for each questionnaire. Who would be a good population for Larry Crozier's geography survey?
2. What methods of information retrieval were probably used for the survey results in these reports? What do you think of *American Film*'s suggestion that results be faxed in?
3. Consider the use of graphics in some of the survey reports. Is the graphic in "Measuring Customer Satisfaction with New Cars" effective and appropriate? Can you think of information in other reports that might be highlighted with a chart, graph, illustration, or pull-quote?
4. How would you describe the difference in tone between an in-depth survey such as Bourland's "Minimum Wage" and a broad-based survey such as "Measuring Customer Satisfaction with New Cars"?

8 Writing from Reading and Secondary Research

I believe that a writer owes a debt of authenticity to his readers.... You do not have a right to mislead people. Now I do a lot of research in books, and I read a lot of old diaries. There's an enormous amount of material available if one will take the time to get it.

—Louis L'Amour, on how he makes his Western adventures realistic

One element of my world was history, and that is why I read and reread so many medieval chronicles; and as I read them I realized that the novel had to include things that, in the beginning, had never crossed my mind, such as the debate over poverty and the Inquisitions's hostility toward the Fraticelli—an offshoot of the Franciscan order.

—Umberto Eco, on how he wrote *The Name of the Rose*

Whether they spin stories or write reports on governmental policy, writers have always done research by reading. This is especially true for writing in college, which frequently and typically means writing from research. In this chapter you will work first with summarizing articles, a necessary skill for reporting on your research. Then you will focus on other aspects of academic writing: specifically, summaries, essay exams, documented essays, and annotated bibliographies.

If your instructor doesn't require you to submit a documented essay or an annotated bibliography in your portfolio, you may still wish to document an essay that you will be submitting anyway. Many pieces of persuasion, analysis, information, and advice need to be documented. Also, documented essays lend depth and gravity to your collection of writing. They reveal your research skills and testify to your quest for credibility. They strengthen the body of your work—and they make you look good.

SUMMARIZING ARTICLES

One of the most important skills for writing from research is the ability to summarize. Effective writers can express in their own words the ideas that they read; they can study an article, sort the important from the unimportant information, and translate that knowledge in a way that readers can understand.

Drafting a Three-Sentence Summary

How is a summary written? A good summary begins with careful reading. Read the article to be summarized quickly, but with a focused attitude: Try to get an overview, a dominant impression of what the article is about. On the first reading, resist the urge to use your pen to underline, highlight, or write notes in the margins; leave the pen alone. On the second reading, pick up the pen if you want. This time through, read to see if you can pick out a thesis or a purpose statement and two or three supporting details. Make checks in the margin, underline ideas you want to note, or write down points to remember. You are looking for the big ideas—and although details may be interesting and relevant to the larger concepts, you must focus on the essence of the piece.

To write a summary, imagine that you are telling your roommate or best friend what the article is about. And you are providing this information *in your own words*. (This distinguishes a summary from a précis, in which the words are the author's.) Get ready to write a formal summary by looking over this outline:

1. This article is about _____.
2. The author wants me to remember these two things about the subject:
   (a) _____ and
   (b) _____.
3. Important supplementary points are these:
   (a) _____
   (b) _____
   (c) _____

Now take a moment to read the article and, afterward, your notes. Do the notes represent the main and supplementary points accurately? If not, revise them.

Finally, cast your notes and outline into a tight summary, following the heuristic above. Three sentences will typically be all you need. Write the main idea in the first sentence, then put the two supplementary or supporting ideas in the second and third sentences. Add the details you need in phrases and subordinate clauses. Thus you match rhetorical importance with grammatical structure.

Looking at Summaries

Read "Nature's Time Capsules" (about pack-rat middens), from *Time* magazine, and the summary of it that follows. As you read, think about the author's thesis and supplementary points.

Nature's Time Capsules

LEON JAROFF

Part way up we came to a high cliff and in its face were niches . . . and in some of them we found balls of a glistening substance looking like pieces of variegated candy . . . it was evidently food of some sort, and we found it sweet but sickish, and those who were hungry, making a good meal of it, were a little troubled with nausea afterwards.

—from the diary of a lost prospector in the Gold Rush of 1849

Nausea? Little wonder. The glistening balls mistaken for a snack that day in Nevada were later identified as pack-rat middens—globs of crystallized pack-rat urine containing sticks, plant fragments, bones and animal dung. Still, while the middens failed to make the grade as cuisine, they have begun to excel in another role—as a kind of natural time capsule.

From the well-preserved contents of middens, scientists using radiocarbon dating can peer thousands of years into the past to discern when climates changed, why civilizations withered and how plants and animals migrated.

Pack-rat middens are found in arid regions of North and Central America and take shape when the acquisitive rodent, like its human namesake, collects and carries home virtually all the trash it can find. It piles the debris in its den, where it becomes saturated with urine. As the urine evaporates in the dry climate, it crystallizes, gradually enveloping the collection and forming a large, hard clump. Protected from the elements, the pack rat's trophies, like insects entombed in amber, are preserved for millenniums.

"A pack-rat midden is a snapshot of the flora and fauna existing within about 50 m [164 ft.] of the midden at the time it was accumulating," explains Peter Wigand, a paleoecologist at the University of Nevada's Desert Research Institute. Scientists can pin down the approximate time the snapshot was taken by radiocarbon dating of a preserved twig or fecal pellet; the technique can date specimens that are more than 40,000 years old. And by studying middens of different vintages in the same area, researchers can in effect create a movie from a sequence of snapshots, showing changes in local ecosystems.

The analysis of middens is emerging as a distinct scientific specialty. Its handful of practitioners have already published a 472-page tome on the subject (*Packrat*

Middens; University of Arizona) and have considered naming the specialty pale-onidology, which roughly translated means "study of old nests."

By whatever name, the investigation of middens is paying off with a host of new insights about the past. Using midden evidence of tree growth and distribution in the Mojave Desert, botanist W. Geoffrey Spaulding of the University of Washington determined that average desert temperatures during the height of the last Ice Age, about 18,000 years ago, were 6°C (11°F) colder than they are today.

In a midden study covering 11,000 years of vegetation change in New Mexico's Chaco Canyon, Julio Betancourt of the U.S. Geological Survey and Thomas Van Devender of the Arizona–Sonora Desert Museum found evidence that could explain why a once thriving Anasazi Indian community was abandoned 800 years ago. Simply stated, the Indians eventually used all the surrounding pine trees for their dwellings and firewood, depleting the woodland and eroding the farmland vital to the tribe's survival.

Middens made by hyraxes—rodents found in Africa and the Middle East—have provided similar evidence that human clearing of surrounding forests and shrubbery led to the sudden collapse in A.D. 900 of the ancient metropolis of Petra, in what is now Jordan.

Middens can reveal changes in the heavens as well as on earth. That was demonstrated by hydrologist Fred Phillips of the New Mexico Institute of Mining and Technology, who checked an ancient pack-rat midden for evidence of cosmic-ray bombardment of the earth. He knew that highly energetic cosmic-ray particles create the radioisotope chlorine 36 when they strike argon atoms in the atmosphere, and that the isotope finds its way into plants and the urine of mammals, including the pack rat.

With the aid of radiochemist Pankaj Sharma of the University of Rochester, he compared the amount of the isotope in the midden urine with contemporary values, and concluded that cosmic-ray bombardment was 41% more intense 21,000 years ago than it is now. This suggests that the earth's magnetic field, which acts as a partial barrier to cosmic rays, was then considerably weaker. One implication: terrestrial life had been—and could someday again be—exposed to higher doses of dangerous radiation from space.

Researchers are gleaning other secrets from plant leaves preserved in the middens. At the end of the last Ice Age, for example, plant structures called stomata, which are used to process carbon dioxide, were far denser than they are today. This suggests that the ancient atmosphere contained much less carbon dioxide. Middens have even more to reveal. The well-preserved plant and animal DNA in midden specimens promises to be a bonanza for genetic researchers.

History does not record if the band of nauseated Forty-Niners eventually reached California or how they fared in their quest. Yet on that day long ago in Nevada, they had already struck gold.

One outline for a summary of the pack-rat article looked like this:

1. This article is about pack-rat middens.
2. The author wants me to remember two main things about the subject: (a) a pack-rat midden consists of items from the pack rat's past, preserved in a glob of crystallized

urine; and (b) the midden reflects the flora and fauna of the pack rat's ecosystem and is therefore valuable to scientists studying the past.

3. Important supplementary points are (a) midden analysis is becoming a scientific specialty; (b) midden analysis of the radioisotope chlorine 36 in the urine suggests that the earth's magnetic field is much stronger now than it was 21,000 years ago; and (c) scientists have also learned from middens that the atmosphere at the end of the Ice Age contained much less carbon dioxide than today's atmosphere.

Here is the three-sentence summary based on that outline:

Scientists are studying pack-rat middens—odds and ends accumulated by pack rats and bound together and preserved in globs of crystallized pack-rat urine—to learn more about the plants and animals of ages past. Midden analysis is becoming a scientific specialty that is yielding important information about the past. For example, through analyzing the radioisotope chlorine 36 in the crystallized urine, scientists have learned that the earth's magnetic field is much stronger than it was 21,000 years ago; other researchers have learned that today's atmosphere contains more carbon dioxide than the atmosphere during the Ice Age.

CONSIDER . . .

1. How thoroughly does this writer address the major points of the pack-rat essay?
2. Point out the sentence in the summary that contains the main idea or thesis of the article.
3. Show where the writer has included supplementary details. Was anything important omitted?

Read the following essay from *The Atlantic Monthly,* Cullen Murphy's "The Lay of the Language," and work with your peer group to collaborate on drafting a summary of it. Follow the outline procedure before you draft the actual summary.

The Lay of the Language

CULLEN MURPHY

The year was 842. The occasion was a meeting in Strasbourg between two grandsons of Charlemagne, Louis the German and Charles the Bald, to form an alliance against a third grandson, Lothar I. That alliance was embodied in what are known today as the Strasbourg Oaths, and for linguistic reasons these oaths remain significant. The scribe, fluent in Latin, wrote out copies of the oaths in two languages, the

German spoken by Louis and the Latinate tongue spoken by Charles. The language of Charles looks odd (it is written out phonetically according to Latin rules of spelling), but it is unmistakably the language that is now called French. Here is why it is important: the French version of the Strasbourg Oaths is the earliest extant written evidence that classical Latin, once a standardized international language, had evolved into several vernaculars.

In thinking about the probable successors to the English language, I have often wondered what form their equivalents of the Strasbourg Oaths might take. An MTV video? An FBI wiretap transcript? Inevitably, I have also wondered when these new vernaculars will come into existence. Do candidates already exist somewhere? Certainly, as John Platt and his colleagues document in their book *The New Englishes,* distinctive variants of the mother tongue have by now emerged in India, Southeast Asia, Africa, and the Philippines, though in each case the speech so far remains recognizably English. Most of us would acknowledge, I think, that a certain drifting from the anchorage of standards has been taking place, too, among native speakers of English, and even among those who would consider themselves members of the elite.

I don't mean to be schoolmarmish about this. I want simply to note a phenomenon, and perhaps take the long view. A few years ago, in his inaugural lecture as occupant of the Chair of Latin at the University of Newcastle upon Tyne, Professor J. G. F. Powell took such a view of both Latin and English, drawing instructive parallels. The English written by his students, he said, "reminds me forcibly of some of the Latin written during the Dark Ages, after the collapse of the Western Empire and of the old Roman education." And Powell observed that although the emergence of the Romance vernaculars was a long and gradual process, subtle signs of it can be found with the benefit of hindsight even in the classical period. The spelling and grammar in papyrus letters written by an imperial soldier named Claudius Terentianus "already in some ways foreshadows modern Italian." The misspelling of the name "Caesar" as "Cessar" on some banking records from Pompeii suggests that pronunciation had begun to change.

It is against this background that I call attention to the rapid and, I suspect, inexorable conflation of the once-distinct English verbs *lie* and *lay. Lie* is an intransitive verb, used correctly in constructions like "*lie* down" and "*lie* around" and "the laundry *lies* on the bed." The present participle is *lying,* the past tense is *lay,* and the past participle is *lain. Lay,* for its part, is a transitive verb, used correctly in constructions like "*lay* plans" and "*lay* the books on the shelf." The present participle is *laying,* the past tense is *laid,* and the past participle is also *laid.*

The two verbs are long-standing rivals, but during the past few decades *lay* has been laying siege to *lie* with growing success. In spoken language the victory of *lay* is virtually complete. "Whenever I smell a cigar now," David Letterman told a reporter for the *Los Angeles Daily News,* "I almost just *lay* down and go to sleep, they smell so good." "Election years are hell for the Fed," a former president of one of the regional Federal Reserve banks told a *Washington Post* columnist. "They just hope they can *lay* low, and not be accused of going in one direction or another until after

Election Day." Speaking about his fellow Democrats after last November's Republican surge, Representative Kweisi Mfume told the *Los Angeles Times,* "Many have just *laid* down and rolled over; they just cannot get over the fact we've lost control of the House." Increasingly, the substitution of *lay* for *lie* and *laid* for *lain* is occurring not only in casual speech but also in printed matter produced by professional writers and editors; you'll quickly collect plenty of examples if you keep an eye out for them. A few months ago an advertisement appeared in these very pages bearing the words "This Christmas give a gift that's been *laying* around for twelve years"—a lapse that elicited irate letters from a number of readers. "If my subscription were not a gift from my mother," one woman wrote, "I would cancel it because of the English in this ad."

The conflation of *lie* and *lay* is an old problem and, admittedly, an understandable one. Among other things, the verbs share a manifestation (*lay*). Moreover, when you *lay* something down, you cause it to *lie*. Also, there was once a reflexive pronominal use of *lay* (as in "Now I *lay* me down to sleep . . ."), which has undoubtedly sown confusion. And *lie* and *lay* as nouns, connoting a configuration of ground, can at times be used interchangeably ("the *lie* or *lay* of the land"). Before the nineteenth century the verbs *lie* and *lay* were sometimes used synonymously, by such writers as Francis Bacon and Laurence Sterne, and the *Oxford English Dictionary* has citations for an intransitive use of *lay* going back to roughly A.D. 1300. Still, the *lie–lay* distinction has been generally in force for the past two centuries, as grammarians and lexicographers pulled English into something approaching a standardized form.

Why is the distinction vanishing? One person I know blames the lyrics of pop and country music: "Lay down Sally." "Lay, lady, lay, lay across my big brass bed." "I could get used to you, oh darlin', you're so fine. I could grow accustomed to your body layin' right next to mine." Lyrics like these obviously do play a role, but something larger is at work. I observed above that in spoken language the victory of *lay* over *lie* has been decisive. Until the invention of movable type and the advent of mass literacy the influence of the spoken word was at least equal to and probably greater than that of the written word when it came to determining the evolution of language. Gutenberg altered the balance of power. With the help of the printing press, language could more easily be tamed, domesticated, made to live by rules across vast areas. The printed word was sovereign for four centuries. It brought standardized English to every continent. But ever since the development, a hundred years ago, of electronic methods of reproducing sound, the spoken word has been roaring back. By comparison with the written word, it has always been sloppy and unruly—a fact of modest consequence in, say, the ninth century, when even the most influential person's voice could reach only a very small audience. Today audiences for words that are spoken (or sung) can easily exceed a billion. Next to this, print is a marginal force. The one place in which the written word is enjoying any sort of renaissance—in communications by means of computer—offers no counterforce whatsoever. As anyone familiar with it can attest, cyberEnglish is characterized by a penchant for grammatical laxity and semantic shorthand.

Our language, then, is embarked upon a period in which we may well be watching it—and hearing it—change faster than it ever has changed before. What is odd is that so many of its professional custodians seem prepared to take this, as one might say, laying down. On the issue of *lie* versus *lay,* for example, the editors of *Merriam-Webster's Dictionary of English Usage* point out in a survey of reference works that the scholarly consensus seems to have shifted from deeming the misuse "illiterate" to deeming it "disputable" to deeming it, in essence, irrelevant. The linguist Dwight Bolinger offers this verdict: "The *lie/lay* distinction is fragile and impractical, and the price of maintaining it is too high." This, of course, is the attitude we have come to expect on all such language issues, though I must confess that some of the ways it surfaces can still take me by surprise. Recently Professor Richard Hogg, the general editor of the *Cambridge History of the English Language,* suggested that the apostrophe "may well just decline of its own accord" and stated outright that he "would not go to the stake" to preserve the distinction between *its* and *it's.*

Language changes. Linguistic rules are arbitrary. I concede all that. It is instructive to note, though, that 1,519 years after the Fall of Rome the University of Newcastle-upon-Tyne has someone on its faculty who could have conversed with an educated citizen of the Roman Empire. In A.D. 3514, I wonder, will there be anyone who could have conversed with me?

TAKING ESSAY EXAMS

You will write many essay exams in college. Professors like to give essay exams to see how students assimilate and understand information from lectures, discussion, and reading. Essay exams also give students a chance to show what they know: to reveal mastery of the secondary material and of what they have heard in lectures and read in texts. A well-written essay bespeaks accomplishment; a poorly developed, wandering, ungrammatical essay suggests not only a lack of understanding but also a lack of preparation and caring. This section is here so that you can think about how to use effective principles of research, reading, and writing to produce strong essay-exam responses— a sample of which you may include in your portfolio as an example of in-class writing, or perhaps as a bonus or free-choice portfolio piece. Writers who succeed in essay exams prepare thoroughly and deliberately.

Studying for Essay Exams

Careful preparation is essential to writing fine essay examinations. These suggestions will help you study efficiently for essay exams.

1. **Start early.** You put yourself at a serious disadvantage if you procrastinate and begin studying only the night before an exam. Studying is a process, just like writing and reading; all require time. Essay exams require you to have mastery over the material—and that rarely comes overnight.
2. **Trade places with the professor** in your imagination. What questions would you ask if you were the professor? What themes have been emphasized in the pro-

fessor's lectures and in the readings? What do your notes reveal about the interests of the professor? What ideas and images surface repeatedly in lecture notes? In your dialogue journal? In your responses to the professor? In your progress reports?

3. **Talk about the exam** with the professor or teaching assistant running your study group. Describe your method for preparing for the examination and ask for advice or feedback. You want to know if you are on the right track. Do *not* ask what is going to be on the examination. The professor will not tell just one person what the exam questions will be, but he or she may tell or possibly hint about the exam to the whole class. Listen carefully and pay attention. Talk too to your classmates; ask how they are preparing for the examination and what they think will be the featured ideas for essay items. Getting many ideas about possible exam questions will help you think more comprehensively about the material.

4. **Write to learn.** Writing notes forces you to process information and helps you remember it. Preparing comparative charts or creating some kind of graphic organizer may also help you conceptualize and remember information. Figure 8.1 shows a section of a chart comparing two modern poets; the student is preparing to write a question on one of the poets (but doesn't know which one) on an American literature examination.

Another strategy for preparing to write essay exams is to write out questions that you think the professor will put on the exam. Then write out practice responses to your own questions. This activity forces you to think comprehensively about the exam material; and even if your questions don't exactly match those the professor asks, you will be dealing with the same basic content. Answering your own questions about the material prepares you to address the ones your professor does ask.

Sitting for Exams

Get plenty of sleep the night before the exam so that you will be alert and clear-headed during the exam itself. Pulling an all-nighter and trying to learn two months' worth of articles and notes in one night may set you up to be fuzzy and forgetful, if not downright sleepy, during the exam.

Take enough supplies to the exam. Wear a watch. Be sure you have more than enough paper or examination books for writing answers and at least three pens with which you feel comfortable writing. Don't use a pencil: pencil smears, looks unprofessional, and can be difficult to read, especially under artificial light.

Be sure you are physically comfortable—fed, comfortably clothed, neither overheated nor too cold—when the exam begins.

When you actually receive the exam, resist the urge to start writing right away. Take five minutes to study the exam questions thoroughly; leave your pen on the desk while you read the test carefully and understand what is expected of you. If you encounter a question you don't know, stay calm: sometimes an answer will come to you as you work on an alternative part of the exam. Most of the time, clues to answers are present in the exam itself.

Author	Relevant Bio	Key Elements of Style	Themes and Subjects	Representative Poems or Works
John Berryman (1914–1972)	John Smith—McAlester, Okla. father committed suicide Columbia, Cambridge threw himself from a bridge in Minneapolis	variety of voices shift from educated language to broad dialect voice like a minstrel	intensely personal verse poetry wounds and is wounded contrary to Eliot Henry—alter ego pungent, many-leveled confessional & neurotic	*His Toy, His Dream, His Rest* (1969)—2nd vol. of Dream Songs—most important book *Dream Songs*—meant to "terrify and comfort"—tone is first wildly humorous, then melancholy. 1950—biography of Stephen Crane "The Ball Poem"—"the epistemology of loss" "Homage to Mistress Bradstreet" "A Professor's Song" *Delusions, Etc.* 1972—last book, debates faith with God Each dream song—18 lines, strict six-line stanzas 1,2,4,5—pentameter 3,6—trimeter irregular syntax, asides, etc.
Robert Lowell (1917–1977)	New England ancestry born in Boston— knew Richard Eberhart Harvard, but transferred to Kenyon to study with John Crowe Ransom greatly disturbed by advent of WWII. converted to Catholicism from traditional Episcopalianism after marriage to Elizabeth Hardwick	gnarled, knotty, unwieldy Jacobean taste for violent passion sometimes a deliberate awkwardness density of detail jagged syntax later tried to break through with a looser meter— early work laden with Christian symbols—not later	connected rise of predatory capitalism to Puritan tradition (Tawney) poetry became very confessional after he dropped the Eliotic voice tortured consciousness	"Colloquy in Black Rock"—humanity of the speaker is parallel to the scene at Black Rock. "The Quaker Graveyard in Nantucket"—evocation of *Moby Dick* and the malevolence behind the surface of life; desperate need to justify God's ways. "To Speak of Woe That is in Marriage"—a poem partly about detachment "Skunk Hour"—a tone of disillusionment. "For the Union Dead"

Figure 8.1 A comparative chart

Writing the Exam

Respond straightforwardly to the questions on the exam. If the question is made up of one or two central or umbrella questions and a series of narrower questions, the professor is probably trying to guide your thinking and the structure of your essay as well. Try to address all parts of the question, and add more detail and information if you have time. Remember: *Show what you know.* If you don't write something down, how will the professor know that you know?

Do what the question asks you to do. If a question asks you to show how poodles and wolves are alike and you explain why poodles have curly hair, you have not answered the question, regardless of the brilliance of your response. Be careful of the verbs in an essay question; if you aren't sure exactly what the question asks you to do, ask for clarification. The verbs that frequently appear on essay exams and explanations of what exam-writers typically intend them to mean are listed in Table 8.1.

Structure your essay to match the structure of the question. Professors value clarity, direct organization, and completeness in essay responses. Creativity and cleverness are admirable, but the bottom line is really this: Can you address the question *as it is written*? Begin your response with a phrase that cues the reader back to the question, that is reminiscent of the question, or (least desirable) that reiterates the question. This signals the professor that you understand the question and plan to deliver what has been asked of you.

Watch the clock. Don't spend disproportionate time on one essay. Force yourself to keep moving and don't allow yourself to become stuck on any part of the exam; it's better to spend your time on what you know. Try to leave ten minutes at the end of the exam period for a quick reading of what you have written. Ten minutes give you time not only to fix as many of the inevitable errors as possible but also to insert points you forgot when you drafted the response. (A note: No professor expects an essay exam to be super-neat or super-correct. That said, however, make your essay as readable as possible.)

Looking at an Exam Answer

The question and answer below are taken from a twenty-minute quiz in a U.S. history survey course (1865 to the present). The question addresses material on the period during the late nineteenth and early twentieth century known as the Gilded Age. Notice how the way the question is framed suggests how students should organize their responses.

> *Question:* Briefly describe agrarian and working-class responses to industrialization in the Gilded Age. The anger, disappointment, and sense of betrayal among some industrial workers and farmers was often expressed in violent deeds—so that some political leaders and intellectuals feared the possibility of class warfare. Why *wasn't* there a social revolution during the late nineteenth century in the United States? Did celebration of traditional American political and economic values defuse the possibility of social upheaval? What then was the significance of the "Free-Labor" ideology? Explain and discuss.

Table 8.1   Verbs most frequently used in essay questions—and their meanings

Verb	Meaning
ANALYZE	Show why or how; present stages of steps in a process, as in *Analyze why the Baltimore Orioles didn't win the World Series.*
ARGUE	Use a logical arrangement of specific facts, ideas, and information to support a point of view or specific thesis, as in *Argue the case for prohibiting smoking in the workplace.*
ARRANGE	Put information in some logical order, whether it be chronological, historical, spatial, numerical, most-to-least-significant, least-to-most-significant, interesting, or meaningful, as in *Arrange the following incidents from eighteenth-century American history and write a rationale for your ordering.*
COMPARE	Show in specific ways and with specific details how two things, events, concepts, ideas, or notions are alike, as in *Compare the French Revolution to the American Revolution.*
CONSIDER	Similar to *discuss* (see below), meaning think about, reflect on, and evaluate an item or idea; present facts and draw conclusions, as in *Consider the implications of gene splicing in the agricultural community.*
CONTRAST	Show how two things, events, concepts, ideas, or notions are different, also in specific ways and with specific details, as in *Contrast deductive learning with inductive learning.*
DESCRIBE	Give details and examples to show that you understand an event, situation, or concept; paint a word picture so that a reader can visualize the item or event or feeling being described, as in *Describe the Impressionist style of painting.*
DISCUSS	Both explain (or tell what you know about the term; see *explain* below) and comment on (provide some reflection or evaluation to accompany the explanation), as in *Discuss the drop in teenage pregnancy rates nationwide.*
EXPLAIN	Tell the meaning, structure, order, or process of something; tell how something happens, works, or operates, as in *Explain how an electronic ignition works.*
SUMMARIZE	Add up information, facts, details to present a succinct statement of their significance and/or importance; generalize and determine significance of something from a collection of specific information, as in *Summarize the significant events in the American suffrage movement during the 1920s.*

Response: In the late nineteenth century, farmers' organizations and industrial working-class unions organized to mount what some historians have called a "counterrevolution" against the monopoly power of Big Business. These farmers and workers argued that the "new industrial order" created by trusts, holding companies, and monopolies had rigged the game—violated the natural economic process of "equal opportunity in the marketplace" and disrupted the natural growth of the American economy. Nevertheless, both farmers and the industrial working class (native and immigrant workers) were basically "conservative" in their political ideology and, like the rest of society, rejected radical (socialist or communist) solutions to their economic problems. This in large part was due to the belief that American political and economic traditions offered the best opportunity for self-improvement, economic and social mobility. Both groups embraced and internalized what some historians have called the "Free-Labor ideology"; that is, the belief that all workers, with hard work, self-determination, and ingenuity, could transform themselves from workers into capitalists or property owners. They could start out like Andrew Carnegie with little in their pockets and through sheer will and energy—"rugged individualism"—and the opportunities in the marketplace transform themselves into industrial magnates or successful entrepreneurs and agribusinessmen. The inclination of the Republican party to favor business over labor and agriculture did not dissuade the farmers and workers from their overall belief that America was a land of opportunity.

CONSIDER . . .

1. Does the response address all the parts of the question? Point out how the answer fits the structure of the question.
2. Indicate at least one instance of specific detail supporting a generalization in the response.
3. How does the respondent show the professor that he/she understands what *Free-Labor ideology* means?

Some Final Advice about Essay Exams

Test taking is a skill perfected through practice, but these tips may smooth your way.

1. **Preparation is vital to success.** You cannot walk into an essay exam cold and expect to perform superbly.
2. **Good, clear writing is part of a sound essay answer.** Writing reflects thought and understanding. If your comprehension of a subject is clear, you can write clearly about it, provided you slow down to think about what you are doing. Also, professors are grateful for lucid, easy-to-follow papers.
3. **Address the question as it is written.** Going off on a tangent to write about something you want to express will likely earn you an F. Write your own question and response if and only if you find that you are totally blank.
4. **Apologies, excuses, and happy faces are best left off essay answers.** These are seen as manipulative by professors, who are usually totally unaffected or even irritated by them.
5. **If you don't perform as well as you hoped, confer with your professor.** Without making excuses, make it plain that you expect to do better in the future and ask for advice about how to do so. Your professor will respect and should respond to this behavior and acceptance of responsibility.

DOCUMENTING AN ESSAY

A research essay begins with a question. How do tropical storms develop into hurricanes? What happens to a check after it is deposited? Why is a ceremonial pipe important to the Sioux—and what is a pipe ceremony like? How are billboards pasted up? If your instructor asks you to write a documented essay, don't let the idea of documenting the essay alarm you, but build on what you know or have already done. Return to the file of subjects you chose not to develop and see whether any of them interests you enough to be worth pursuing through research. If you haven't any such file on hand, you'll want to go through the process of finding a subject you care about and then writing a draft.

Invention Ideas

Sometimes topics are more restricted in research essays; your instructor may set parameters for the assignment or even ask that you write on a specific topic. Although some writers may feel constrained by diminished choices, others may feel more secure. It is still very possible, regardless of how your topic comes to you, to create an original piece, to make the writing and the topic your own. Because invention strategies may differ according to how much liberty you have to construct a topic, this section presents two different approaches to invention for a documented or research essay. Read both and then adapt the advice into something appropriate for your circumstance.

INVENTION: WORKING FROM A TOPIC.   If you are beginning with a topic (which may or may not be assigned), your existing knowledge of the topic may be insufficient to produce good writing. Your first step, then, is to learn as much as you can about the topic. To do this, you will have to begin by reading at significant depth and breadth. You are now reading not only to gather information but to analyze it. (Refer to Chapter 5 for tips on critical reading and analysis.) Take time to absorb the information. You may find that writing a dialogue journal with a colleague will help you uncover a deeper understanding of your topic. Perhaps a series of freewrites will reveal how you are processing the information. Or some time spent webbing or mapping how you see the topic unfolding may prove worthwhile as you search for information, knowledge, and ways to order that knowledge.

When you feel fairly secure about your subject or topic, draft a piece. You are likely to draft an analysis, particularly if your topic is assigned. Once you have a draft, you are ready for the next part of the process.

INVENTION: WORKING FROM A DRAFT.   Here is where good research really begins: with a draft of what a writer knows and has within her or his intellectual command. From your reading or from your experience or observation, you may know a great deal about a subject, enough to construct a draft with general arguments, support, and some details. It's likely, though, that your initial draft won't have quite enough specific and convincing detail and support; that's where the research comes in. Starting with your exploratory draft, ask yourself the tough questions to identify areas where further research and documentation are needed. Look at the following draft passages and the accompanying questions that a writer trying to develop the passages might ask.

Excerpt from a Draft	*Questions for Development*
To become a practicing clinical psychologist, you must study for an advanced degree and then do a long internship.	What kind of degree does a clinical psychologist have? What is the nature of the internship? What exactly do clinical psychologist interns do and where do they do it?
When Socrates was imprisoned and condemned to die, his friend visited him and urged him to escape. But Socrates refused because of a principle from his own teaching: Injustice must never be done, not even in defense of one's own life.	When was Socrates imprisoned—and where? Why? What were his offenses? Who was the friend who urged him to escape—and why did the friend encourage Socrates? What are the implications of Socrates' refusal to flee?
People who buy posters prefer cheerful, colorful scenes, and this preference can, in turn, affect the value of a poster. One of Toulouse-Lautrec's happier posters is worth almost ten times as much as one of his more depressing ones.	Which posters specifically are referred to? How much is each poster worth? What does the writer mean by a *happy* poster? Why are Toulouse-Lautrec's posters valuable? How much are they worth?

To get the answers to the questions raised by your exploratory draft and to develop that draft into a finished and documented essay, you will now likely have to do further investigation and research. Your research strategy may assume any configuration of primary research and secondary research—interviewing; surveying; and/or reading in encyclopedias, books, journals, magazines, or pamphlets. What you learn from research will be folded back into your original draft—to make it full and interesting and informative. It's important to understand these fundamental ideas: Research begins with *your* ideas and *your* writing; research is a vehicle for filling in the inevitable gaps in *your* knowledge; research is a tool for enhancing *your* credibility and making *your* writing more valuable.

Doing Research

When you know what you need to know and can formulate the questions that need answering, you're ready to do research. Consider doing a combination of *primary research* (where you personally gather information and write it down) and *secondary research* (where you go to books and magazines and gather information from what's already been written, from someone else's primary research). See Chapter 7 for help with doing primary research and writing about the results.

INVESTIGATING PRIMARY SOURCES.   Can you think of someone you can interview about your topic? In a college community you are surrounded by experts, and someone who knows something about your subject may be nearer than you think. Do you need to learn something about strip mining? Consult your university or college directory for the department of geology, politely inquire of the person who answers the phone about the name of a professional who might be willing to help you, and set up an interview. Do you need information about the commodities market? Perhaps a professor in the business school can help you. If you're having trouble thinking of someone to interview, ask your instructor to give you some tips. If you have enough time, you can also conduct a survey to gather information for your essay. A survey report is a useful way to add details about local events or populations: If you are writing about eating disorders, for instance, you might conduct a survey among local university students to learn more about the nature of eating disorders at your school. If you are writing about the numbers of guns at the university, conduct a survey to determine how common gun ownership seems to be on your campus. Information gleaned from surveys or interviews is an excellent way to add substance and depth to your writing. Remember, though, that you must *document* your findings from interviews or surveys—so take careful notes and keep all your evidence.

INVESTIGATING SECONDARY SOURCES.   Of course, the library's resources are invaluable for providing specific details and the information you need to make your writing believable as well as interesting. But you need a strategy for approaching the immensity of most university libraries: You need a plan. These suggestions may help you find what you need in a library and save you time as well.

Find the appropriate keywords for your topic. Near almost any card catalog or on-line terminals in a university library, you will find the thick volumes comprising the *Library of Congress Subject Headings.* Use this reference to establish a list of keywords to use in encyclopedia searches, card catalog searches, bibliographic searches, and on-line or computer searches. The *LC Subject Headings* gives you the keyword options used by Library of Congress catalogers to catalog new books, and many indexes are also arranged according to the same keywords. Become familiar with this reference; you will save time if you learn to use it. Look back at Figure 2.2 in Chapter 2 (page 26), which is a sample page from the *LC Subject Headings.*

Looking up *spider* in the *LC Subject Headings,* for example, you would find that there is a spider game and that there exist spider monkeys and spider wasps. You would discover headings for spiderwebs, spider fossils, and a host of specific narrower topics (NT)—specifically, kinds of spiders—as well as for the folklore of spiders (*spiders–folklore*) and the mythology of spiders (*spiders–mythology*).

Once you have a list of keywords with which to look up your subject, pursue a general-to-specific research strategy. *Choose an encyclopedia for an overview and for a beginning bibliography,* literally a book list or list of sources to be consulted. An encyclopedia will give you background, history, and general descriptive information—facts—about your subject. An encyclopedia will also help you achieve perspective on your subject. Most encyclopedias also have, at the end of each reference article, a short list of references or short bibliography you can consult for additional information. It may be helpful to begin with a *general* encyclopedia, like *The Encyclopedia Britannica* or *Encyclopedia Americana*. Or you may find your topic addressed in one of these *subject-specific* encyclopedias:

> *The Guide to American Law* for law-related topics
> *Encyclopedia of Crime and Justice* for crime-related topics
> *Encyclopedia of Art* for art-related topics
> *International Encyclopedia of the Social Sciences* for topics in economics, sociology, anthropology, political science
> *Encyclopedia of Philosophy* for topics related to philosophy
> *McGraw-Hill Encyclopedia of Science and Technology* for topics related to technology
> *Encyclopedia of Computer Science and Technology* for computer-related topics
> *International Encyclopedia of Film* for film-related topics
> *Editorial Research Reports* for information about current topics in the news
> *Cassell's Encyclopedia of World Literature* for literature-related topics

Next, establish a *working bibliography* (a list of books or articles that may be helpful to you as you investigate your topic). It's useful to have at least ten sources in the beginning, but the working bibliography swells and shrinks throughout the research process as you add sources that may be useful and delete ones that don't help you develop the topic. You may find it helpful to keep a five-by-eight-inch card for each item in the working bibliography. Be flexible throughout your research process.

Computer Writing Tip: Keep a working bibliography of Internet sites that you are using, too. It's wise not only to bookmark each site in Netscape but also to print the Uniform Resource Locator (URL) address on a five-by-eight-inch card.

To establish a working bibliography, you may want to look at a *subject-specific bibliography* (or list of books) like one of these:

> *A Bibliography of Philosophical Bibliographies* for topics in philosophy
> *Guide to the Literature of Art History* for art-related topics
> *Harvard List of Books in Psychology* for psychology-related topics
> *MLA International Bibliography* for literature-related topics
> *Science and Engineering Literature* for engineering bibliographies
> *Social Work Education* for social work-related topics

A reference librarian can help you find an appropriate subject-specific bibliography.

Or you may find it useful to refer to a subject-specific index (index of published articles from journals, books, or other documents arranged by subject) like one of these:

> *Art Index* for art-related topics
> *Applied Science and Technology Index* for topics related to technology
> *Biography Index* for citations of biographies
> *Education Index* for education-related topics
> *ERIC Information Center Resources* for education-related topics
> *Film Index Literature* for reviews of films and information on movies
> *Humanities Index* for humanities-related topics

Music Index for music-related topics
Psychological Abstracts for psychology-related topics
Social Sciences Index for topics in the social sciences

Remember: Indexes give you *citations* or places to find specific articles, *not the articles themselves*. You have to use the citation to find the cited articles or books and then read the information. Be sure to write down the entire citation accurately, or you could find yourself on the sixth floor of your university library in the middle of the PN stacks, trying vainly to remember the other numbers and letters in the call number.

Investigate the card catalog or the on-line catalog. Look for books that may contain useful information. You don't have to read books cover to cover: Often you will find exactly the information you need in a particular section or chapter of a book. Remember to use the keywords you gleaned from the *LC Subject Headings*, whether you use the manual catalog or the on-line catalog. If you are searching a card catalog, you may serendipitously come across materials related to your search just by fingering through the cards. If you use an on-line catalog, however, you will find only information matching the parameters of the keywords you use. This is how the *LC Subject Headings* is particularly useful.

Computer Writing Tip: If you have a modem or an Ethernet connection, you can probably access your university library's catalog from your room on or off campus. Check with the folks in your college computer center to find out how.

Use your computer to access resources on the Internet and the World Wide Web. From your dorm room or a computer center on campus or a computer in the reference section of your campus library, you can access the holdings of many libraries across the country and get information from many databases; you can also "chat" with people who may have information you need. On-line information has the advantage of being up to date—often even more so than information in periodicals, whose articles present ideas or research that may be two years old before it is published. Internet research also enables you to search widely, pinpoint the exact information you need, then download and print it relatively quickly. But doing research on the Internet requires caution as well. Even though you may suppose that Internet resources are up to date, it is frequently impossible to determine how recent the information actually is. You must also be wary of the quality of the information you are accessing. There is no quality control in Internet publishing, and literally anyone can be a "publisher." As a researcher, you must be able to evaluate the Internet resources you find and use.

What is the Internet? The Internet is a giant network of computer networks around the world. You can access the Internet in two ways: *host-based mode*, which is text-based; and *direct-access mode*, which enables you to access multimedia information (sound and video) in addition to text. Direct-access mode, gained through mouse clicks instead of typed text, has become significantly more popular than host-based mode.

What is the World Wide Web? The WWW is technically a set of standards that lets many different kinds of computers share information, including multimedia information, across networks. The web uses a document description language called HyperText Transmission Protocol (HTTP); in a multimedia format, it supports many special document features, including "links" to other documents and computer files. At any one web site you'll usually find one major page with links to other pages both inside the document and at other sites. For instance, you can read a page about your university—such as your university's home page—and from the home page be linked to a faculty directory, to the university library, to information about course offerings, to a list of student activities, and more.

There are many tools for exploring the enormous resources of the World Wide Web: Netscape is perhaps the best-known software application for surfing the web. Most university libraries can provide you access to Internet resources; most also provide instruction on the best ways to search the 'net and the web. Indeed, because the Internet changes so rapidly, you should get instruction regularly just to remain current. For starters, though, understand that there are two major kinds of tools for searching the web: *search engines* and *indexes* (also called *subject directories*). Search engines, also known as spiders, robots, or web crawlers, are actually computer software programs that "crawl" from web server to web server gathering information; they search web pages by keyword. The results of a search engine query are directly linked to the keywords you type in. So use a search engine when you have a very specific topic. Some of the best search engines are

Alta Vista	<http://www.altavista.digital.com>,
Excite	<http://www.excite.com> and best of all, the engine of engines,
Metacrawler	<http://www.metacrawler.com/>

Indexes (or subject directories), on the other hand, are lists of web sites compiled by humans. Some indexes are quite small; others are huge, covering hundreds or thousands of subjects. Some indexes have general databases; others are subject-specific. Many can be searched by keyword. Use an index when a topic is new to you and you are looking for an overview. Two well-known indexes are

Yahoo!	http://www.yahoo.com
WWW Virtual Library	http://www.w3.org/pub/DataSources/ bySubject/Overview.html

If you have specific Internet addresses, you'll have to spend less time searching. Just type in the Internet address or Uniform Resource Locator (URL) and tell the application to hook you up. Here's what a URL looks like and what its parts mean:

http://library.lib.binghamton.edu/subjects/education/basiced.html

path and filename on server

Internet address of server

type of resource

In place of "http" you may also encounter one of these, each of which is a different kind of resource:

gopher	wais (wide area information service)
telnet	usenet
ftp	tn3270

Before long you will have a collection of URLs for finding information. You should definitely seek help from your librarian in locating useful URLs, but here are a few places you may want to check out:

■ **Whole Internet Catalog** (from O'Reilly and Associates, an excellent publisher of print Internet information):
   <http://nearnet.gnn.com/wic/newrescat.toc.html>

■ **Publicly Accessible Mailing Lists**—a list of mailing lists, indexed by subject and name; a good way to get information from experts in a particular subject area:
   <http://www.NeoSoft.com/internet.paml>

■ **Federal Web Locator**—from the Villanova Center for Information Law and Policy:
   <http://www.law.vill.edu/fed-agency/fed.webloc.html>

■ **The White House:**
   <http://www.whitehouse.gov>

■ **Aristotle**—a guide to education resources:
   <http://aristotle.isu.edu/menu.html>

■ **Monster Board**—career and job-hunting assistance and information:
   <http://www.monster.com/home.html>

■ **On-line Exhibitions and Images**—a guide to exciting graphics from around the world:
   <http://155.187.10.12/fun/exhibits.html>

A useful book for understanding and exploring the Internet is Geoffrey W. McKim's *Internet Research Companion* (1996). This is a scholar's guide to the Internet, helpful for undergraduate students.

Arrange your working bibliography in clusters. If you have your bibliographical items on separate cards, this task is easy. Put the cards together and then arrange them in "library order" (alphabetically first, then numerically within the same letter configurations) so that you can find the sources quickly: Put the HL 302 books before the HL 310 and LL 815 books, for instance. Using the catalog, find the call numbers for any journals you will need—and arrange them in "library order" too. Following these steps will help you use your working bibliography to locate the information you need quickly once you actually get inside the library.

As when you worked with primary sources, be sure to record all the pertinent information about your sources: complete name of author; name of editor(s), if any; full title; publisher, place of publication, date of publication; volume number, series number; and number of pages. You will need this information later when you document your essay.

EVALUATING SOURCES. Before you begin drafting, take a careful look at your sources: Evaluate them carefully, whether they are Internet sources, books, or journal articles. Here is a guide for examining your sources; if you subject each source to the scrutiny of these questions and use the sources that measure up, you can be relatively certain of having reliable information.

1. **How old is the source?** Use sources that are fewer than ten years old, as a general guideline. Technical and scientific information ages rapidly; historical and literary information, less so. More recent scholarship, if it is legitimate, tends to build on

"On the Internet, nobody knows you're a dog."

and refer to past scholarship. So it is a good bet to use more recent information for citing in particular. You may need to read the scholarly literature further back in time, though, if your paper requires historical knowledge.

2. **What is the reputation of the source?** Trying to divine the reputation of a source can be tricky, but you can sometimes tell a lot from a few indicators. If you are evaluating a book, consider the publishing house: Have you heard the name before? Has the publisher been established in the book industry for a significant time? Your reference librarian can advise you about this if you aren't familiar with a publisher's name; several references about the publishing industry can provide information such as how many books a publisher issues annually, what the editorial interests or contents of the books tend to be, professional awards or honors garnered by the house, and telephone numbers and addresses for contacting the publisher. If you are evaluating a magazine or journal, the same considerations apply. You can learn more about individual journals or magazines in *Ulrich's Guide to Periodicals* or similar

guides in your reference room. In evaluating periodicals, you should also check for names of sponsoring organizations. If a journal is published under the aegis of a reputable professional organization like the Modern Language Association (which publishes *Publications of the Modern Language Association* or *PMLA*, among other periodicals) or the National Council of Teachers of English (which also publishes a host of professional journals), you can be sure that the information contained in the journal has been refereed, or checked by a board of editorial advisors, before it was accepted for publication. And you might also look to see where a journal is housed and who constitutes the editorial staff. If you see, for instance, that a journal is published at an established university and edited by university faculty, it is most likely a reliable journal. You can often check the reputation of writers by looking up their scholarly credentials—and your reference librarian can help you do this too.

3. **How objective and reliable does the source seem?** If a source seems reputable, it is more likely to produce and present reliable information, but you still have to be concerned with the objectivity and accuracy of any source. It is important to ask a few basic questions about any source. Does the information from the source add up? Do the conclusions and arguments match the facts presented? Does the information make sense? Is there a logic to the way it is presented? Is the information checkable? Are sources for the information provided? Does the material seem slanted toward a particular point of view? Does the material promote the view of an organization or association? As a scholar you must at least attempt to be conscious of bias, slant, or downright perversion of information. Scholars don't expect or aim for pure objectivity; rather they seek and promote informed thinking based on a wide variety of accurate information. They seek truth. If you are reading a source about affirmative action policies in college admissions, for example, you should at least be aware of whether the source you are considering supports affirmative action policies (and why) or opposes them (and why). You need to understand the ideology on which information is based.

A NOTE ON EVALUATING INTERNET RESOURCES.   When you evaluate an Internet or web source, you have to be especially alert. There are many bogus sites; Internet publishing is relatively easy and inexpensive and is entirely missing the extensive checks and balances system that operates in most major publishing houses. To assess the reliability of a web site, check out the author: Is her or his name clearly visible? Is there a link to the author's e-mail address or to a legitimate and well-known university's home page or library page? Does the author belong to or represent an organization—and is there additional information about the organization or a link to the organization's web site? You should also be skeptical about the accuracy of a web site: Does the information presented there seem reliable? How do you know? Are sources for the information listed? Does the information have a particular slant or bias? Be alert for loaded words, ones that reveal an author's feelings or attitudes about the subject. It is also prudent to consider the objectivity of a page: What viewpoint is being expressed? What is the purpose of the page (for marketing, for information, for political purposes)? Does the information seem unbiased? Finally, check to see how current the page is, when it was last updated as well as how current the links are.

Drafting: Incorporating Research Findings into Your Writing

Once you find the information you want or need and have confidence in that information, you have the task of incorporating it neatly into your draft—or revising the draft to accommodate the information you uncovered. In some locations you'll add just a word or two; in other cases you'll have to add several sentences, as when you add specific examples to support a generalization or when you add details and statistics to establish a point. You may also add entire chunks or sections of information to your paper—if, for instance, you decide that your draft omits important ideas that your reader should know.

WEAVING IN INFORMATION AND QUOTATIONS.   Add research information to a draft in several ways. When you incorporate what you learn from research, you may summarize, totally assimilating information into your own words. Or you may quote. Most of the time, summarizing is the best strategy, but occasionally a quotation will be just what you need. You can incorporate quotations directly or indirectly. *Direct quotations* are formally introduced to preserve the syntax or word order of the original statement. Here is an example of a direct, formal quotation:

> Randy Wayne Wright says of a small town in Newfoundland: "The whole town seemed to crawl into a shell of shyness. People stared at me from afar, but when I came closer, they ignored me."

Here is the same material quoted indirectly:

> Randy Wayne Wright describes how the "whole town seemed to crawl into a shell of shyness."

In either case, an accompanying note or reference citation would indicate that the quotation came from Randy Wayne Wright, "A Walk in Newfoundland," *Outside*, August, 1993.

Here are some other examples; compare the direct, formal quotations with the indirect, informal quotations. How can you describe the differences?

Direct quotation: "The autopsy conducted the day after Byers died confirmed that his bones and organs were dangerously radioactive," Machlis writes. (Roger M. Machlis, "The Great Radium Scandal," *Scientific American*)

Indirect quotation: Byers's autopsy, done one day after his death, revealed that "his bones and organs were dangerously radioactive."

Direct quotation: Ruthen said, "The consensus among theorists is that certain combinations of strange quarks with others are stable."

Indirect quotation: Ruthen reports that theorists generally agree that "certain combinations of strange quarks with others are stable."

Direct quotation: Joseph Schorr explains: "Print servers—Macs connected to a network designed to receive files for printing from multiple users—
arrange jobs in queues and send them one by one to designated
printers." (Joseph Schorr, "Maximize Your Printer," *Macworld*)

Indirect quotation: Joseph Schorr explains that "print servers—Macs connected to a
network designed to receive files for printing from multiple users—
arrange jobs in queues and send them one by one to designated
printers."

Notice that *direct* quotations are complete, independent clauses and that they are preceded by a comma or colon—punctuation that points to the quotation. Note also that the direct quotation begins with a capital letter to signal its formality. In contrast, *indirect* quotations are generally dependent clauses or phrases, not signaled by punctuation or a capital letter; rather, the quoted material is integrated with the writer's existing syntax, maintaining the integrity of both. The direct quotation is more obvious, distinct, and formal; the indirect quotation is less noticeable, more apt to blend in with the writer's syntax, and relatively informal. Either is correct; both are useful.

Sometimes you may find it necessary or useful to quote a long passage, one longer than four typed lines. Handle this a bit differently than a short passage; rather than use quotation marks, show that a passage is quoted by indenting it one extra tab (or a total of ten spaces) from the left. Leave the spacing within the quotation and the spacing of the right margin alone. Punctuate the introductory material the same as you would if the quotation were not indented. Here's how a long direct quotation might look.

Gibbs explains how Biomuse technology can enable severely paralyzed patients to
operate a computer with these results:

Crystal, an 18-month-old quadriplegic, cannot even breathe on her own. But,
within minutes of wearing a headband, the toddler learned how to move a smiley face around a computer screen with her eyes. Older quadriplegics could use
an eye-tracker in combination with existing word and sentence-completion software to write.

(Quotation from W. Wayt Gibbs, "Body English," *Scientific American*.)

And here's a long indirect quotation; notice how the introductory phrase segues into the quotation and how there is no intervening punctuation:

In *A Natural History of the Senses,* Diane Ackerman says that

pungent odors are absorbed by fats. If you put an onion or cantaloupe in the refrigerator with an open tub of butter, the butter will absorb the odor. Hair also contains fat, which is why it leaves grease stains on pillows and antimacassars. (22)

KNOWING WHEN TO QUOTE.   Your writing sounds most authentic when it comes straight from you, so quote the words of others sparingly. Sometimes writers trying to include a lot of research information fall into the trap of letting the research write the paper by stringing together large blocks of quoted passages. Your research will be a lot more readable if *you* do the work—if you assimilate the information and present it in your own words. A writer does the work so that the reader finds the reading pleasurable. So, rather than quote, you should read, think, and then cast the information in your own words. *Quote less rather than more, and quote only when the original source is especially poignant, clever, or meaningful.*

KNOWING WHEN TO CITE.   Knowing when to cite or to give credit to other writers and researchers is a bit more tricky. You must cite sources when you

- quote any words outright from someone else's work,
- summarize or paraphrase information or ideas,
- refer to an idea from a known source,
- use anything that is not common knowledge.

You do not have to cite information that is common knowledge (George Washington was the first president of the United States, bleach can remove color from clothing, ice melts at temperatures above 32 degrees Fahrenheit). If you can find the information in four or five sources, you can probably consider it common knowledge.

Be careful not to borrow original phrasing, syntax, or wording unless you quote and cite. To use another person's direct words, to borrow ideas, or even to imitate sentence structure without giving credit or documenting is considered *plagiarism*, and you can get in very serious academic trouble if you plagiarize another writer's work.

Citing Sources

When you document your research, you'll be guided by a style sheet or style guide. Most professions have their own style guides. For example, engineering and technology professions use the Institute of Electrical and Electronic Engineers (IEEE) system; scientific and medical professions abide by the Council of Biology Editors (CBE) guidelines. The social sciences and business professions generally follow American Psychological Association (APA) style, and humanities professions typically use Modern Language Association (MLA) style. The most common style reference books are the *MLA* (Modern Language Association) *Handbook for Writers of Research Papers* or the *Publication Manual of the American Psychological Association* (APA), both exemplified in this book. Your instructor will suggest which style guide to use. Read the style guide carefully; you'll find that each guide prescribes distinctive ways to format cover pages, to number pages, to handle citing, to prepare a list of sources. Both APA and MLA style use *parenthetical* citing: That is, when you cite another writer, you do so in abbreviated form in parentheses within the text—not with a footnote number directing the reader to a note at the bottom of the page. Notes are no longer *footnotes*, but citation notes clustered at the end of the paper. Notes are now reserved for information tangential to the text, information related to the text but not closely enough to be included in the body of the text. This may sound complicated at first, but documenting in the text is simple and will speed your drafting.

Here's how a passage from a research essay would look, parenthetically documented in MLA style:

> One theorist explains that "a woman identifies with her mother" (Chodorow 47).

The quoted material is found on page 47 of Chodorow's book, the full citation of which will be found under *Chodorow* on the *Works Cited* page in this documented essay.

In APA style, here's how the parenthetical citing would look:

> One theorist explains that "a woman identifies with her mother" (Chodorow, 1974, p. 47).

Or

> Chodorow explains that a woman identifies with her mother (1974, p. 47).

The quoted material is linked to the *References* page of an APA-style documented essay, where it will appear under *Chodorow*.

Arguing against Sources

Frequently you will use sources to buttress your information, to shore up an argument or a series of points that you have made largely from your opinion. You use the source, in other words, to validate your thinking and to make your argument more credible. But occasionally you will want to argue *against* a source: You may want to dismantle some writer's outdated or wrongheaded argument or simply to present an alternative view. In these instances, be especially careful to follow the guidelines for persuasion (see Chapter 6) and structuring your argument. Also follow some commonsense guidelines. First, don't poke fun. You look small and occasionally even ignorant if you make fun of or ridicule what seems to be a ridiculous argument. It is better to assume a reasoned, measured tone. Second, don't refer to a writer by first name—unless you are indeed very good friends with him or her and want that fact to be known. To do so creates an overly personal tone that tends to distract from the seriousness of your argument. Third, list arguments that you want to refute systematically; then calmly dismantle them, as in this point–counterpoint passage:

> Among her other points, Jean Fraiche maintains that a longer school day will improve test scores because students will have more opportunity to "pursue a subject in depth" (13). She also believes that an extra hour added to each school day "wouldn't strain school budgets significantly" (15). But consider these ideas: A longer school day does not necessarily mean an additional whole period in which to pursue academic interests. Split among a typical seven-period day at most U.S. high schools, one hour minus 4 minutes for passing time, or 56 minutes, would mean only 8 additional minutes per period—hardly enough time to pursue anything meaningfully. Then too, if teachers or students aren't inclined to use the time wisely, the extra hour tacked on to the school

day is just wasted time. Fraiche's point about the strain on school budgets is additionally flawed. Will the utilities allow us to heat and light our schools for free for five hours a week, forty weeks of the year? Will teachers, aides, administrators, and support personnel volunteer to serve an additional 200 hours per academic year? An hour a day doesn't sound economically significant, but add it up over a school year, and it will make a difference. Fraiche's intentions are surely intended as part of a cure for what ails America's schools, but her remedies would just create more dis-ease.

> ⚠ *Remember:* What you read in a book or periodical is not sacrosanct. Scholarship is occasionally flawed because of the logic of its presentation, the inadequacy of the research on which it is based, or omissions or inconsistencies in the writer's thinking. You can disagree in print with scholarship if you have sound arguments.

Preparing a *Works Cited* or *References* Page

Once you complete and document your draft, you're ready to construct the *Works Cited* or *References* page. Regardless of the style guide you use, some features tend to be consistent:

- The list is in alphabetical order according to the author's surname.
- Indentation is key. APA indents the first line of an entry, but MLA uses hanging indentation—all lines of the reference *except* the first line are indented. You can command your word-processing program to do this for you.
- Each item on the list refers to an actual reference or citation in the paper. Do not pad the list with names of references that you may have read or to which you referred but did not cite. Each parenthetical reference in the body of the paper should thus refer to an accompanying full-reference item on the *References* or *Works Cited* page.

DOING AN MLA *WORKS CITED* PAGE.   The MLA entry has three basic parts, each separated by a period: the author's name; the title; the publication data. Figure 8.2 illustrates a few entries so that you can distinguish their parts.

Now here are some examples of some common citations. Remember to consult your style guide directly for specific style information and documentation.

Book by a single author:
> Oakes, James. <u>The Ruling Race.</u> New York: Knopf, 1982.

Book by two or more persons:
> Woodward, Bob, and Carl Bernstein. <u>The Final Days.</u> New York: Simon and Schuster, 1976.

Work in an anthology:
> James, William. "How Two Minds Can Know One Thing." <u>The Writings of William James: A Comprehensive Edition.</u> Ed. John J. McDermott, U of Chicago Press, 1977: 227–31.

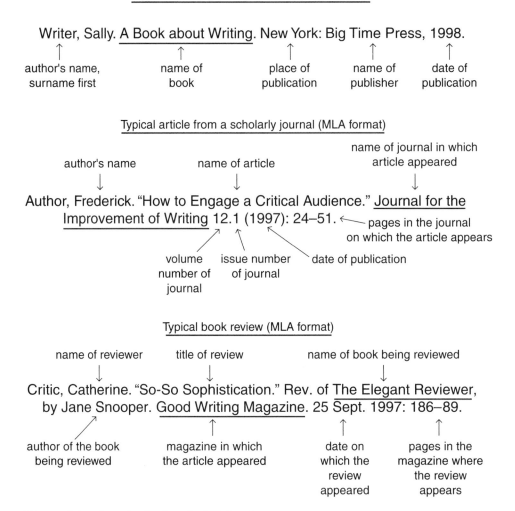

Figure 8.2 Sample citations in MLA style

Republished work:
> Twain, Mark. <u>The Adventures of Huckleberry Finn.</u> 1884. Ed. Henry Nash Smith. Boston: Houghton Mifflin, 1958.

Article in a scholarly journal with continuous pagination:
> Baker, Nancy Westrich. "The Effect of Portfolio-Based Instruction on Composition Students' Final Examination Scores, Course Grades, and Attitudes Toward Writing." <u>Research in the Teaching of English</u> 27 (1993): 155–74.

Article in a scholarly journal that pages each issue separately:
> Simon, Anthony H. "The Battle for Parcel Post." <u>Journal of the American West</u> 13.4 (1974): 79–89.

Article from a weekly or biweekly magazine:
> Beschloss, Michael R. "Clifford Speaks." <u>The New Yorker</u> 6 Sept. 1993: 44–52.

Article from a monthly magazine:
> Stuart, George E. "Etowah: A Southeast Village in 1491." <u>National Geographic</u> Oct. 1991: 54–67.

Article from a daily newspaper:
> Deas, Tommy. "Tide Dusts Off an Old Formation, Then Dusts Green Wave, 31–17." <u>The Tuscaloosa News</u> 5 Sept. 1993: C1.

Review:
> Remnick, David. "Fleeting Bliss." Rev. of <u>Mrs. Ted Bliss,</u> by Stanley Elkin. <u>The New Yorker</u> 25 Sept. 1995: 104–05.

Radio or television program:
> "Case of the Missing Rugrat." <u>Rugrats.</u> Dir. Howard E. Baker. Nickelodeon, 25 Sept. 1995.

Electronic mail:
> Murphy, Anita. "About the PDS Newsletter." E-mail to Michael Melamed. 17 Sept. 1997.

Interview:
> Jordan, Pat. "Conversations with the Dinosaur." Interview with Carlton Fisk. <u>Men's Journal</u> May–June 1993, 116+.

Many kinds of documents create special occasions for citing. Be sure to refer to the MLA handbook for information on citing editorials, letters to the editor, or abstracts; articles on microform or material accessed on a CD–ROM or disk or through a computer service; electronic text; sound recordings or performances; works of art or musical composition; maps, charts, or cartoons. Note also that MLA style abbreviates *University Press* as *UP* (*Purdue UP* for *Purdue University Press*) and uses standard abbreviations for months of the year. Also, a note: if the writer is anonymous, just begin the entry with the title.

WRITING AN APA *REFERENCES* PAGE.   APA style differs considerably from MLA style. In APA style, the author is listed first, then the date (in parentheses), then the title (with only the first word and proper nouns capitalized), then the remainder of the publication data, with each segment separated by commas (a colon separates the place of publication and the publisher). Here are the same examples that were used to illustrate MLA style, now recast into APA style.

Book by a single author:
> Oakes, J. (1982). <u>The ruling race.</u> New York: Knopf.

Book by two or more persons:
> Woodward, B., and Bernstein, C. (1976). <u>The final days.</u> New York: Simon and Schuster.

Work in an anthology:

> James, W. (1977). How two minds can know one thing. In J. McDermott (Ed.), The writings of William James: A comprehensive edition (pp. 227–231). Chicago: University of Chicago Press.

Republished work:

> Twain, M. (1884/1958). The adventures of Huckleberry Finn. Boston: Houghton Mifflin.

Article in a scholarly journal with continuous pagination:

> Baker, N. W. (1993). The effect of portfolio-based instruction on composition students' final examination scores, course grades, and attitudes toward writing. Research in the Teaching of English, 27, 155–174.

Article in a scholarly journal that pages each issue separately:

> Simon, A. H. (1974). The battle for parcel post. Journal of the American West, 13(4), 79–89.

Article from a weekly or biweekly magazine:

> Beschloss, M. R. (1993, September 6). Clifford speaks. The New Yorker, 123, 44–52.

Article from a monthly magazine:

> Stuart, G. E. (1991, October). Etowah: A Southeast village in 1491. National Geographic, 262, 54–67.

Article from a daily newspaper:

> Deas, T. (1993, September 5). Tide dusts off an old formation, then dusts green wave, 31–17. The Tuscaloosa News, p. C1.

Review:

> Remnick, D. (1995, September 25). Fleeting bliss. [Review of the book, Mrs. Ted Bliss]. The New Yorker, 116, 104–105.

Radio or television program:

> Baker, H. (Producer). (1995, September 25). Case of the missing Rugrat. In Rugrats. Nickelodeon.

Electronic mail:

> Murphy, A. (1997, Sept. 17). About the PDS newsletter [E-mail to Michael Melamed].

Interview:

> Jordan, P. (1993, May–June). Conversations with the dinosaur. [Interview with C. Fisk]. Men's Journal, 116+.

For further details about documenting other kinds of sources, see the appropriate style guide. You can find style guides in the reference section of your library.

Finishing and Formatting an MLA-Style Essay

An MLA-style documented essay has no cover page. Instead, the information about you, the writer, is placed on the first page, double-spaced, on the left side, one inch from the top of the page. Include your name, your institutional affiliation (your professor's name and course name), and the date, flush with the left margin and double spaced. Leave a double space and write the title, centered. Leave another double space and begin the text. You can read all about this in greater detail in your style guide. Here's a sample first page, formatted in MLA style.

Paulie 1

Nathan Z. Paulie

Professor Burch

ENG 106, Writing and Literature

23 May 1996

Mark Twain's *Pudd'nhead Wilson:*

'Blood Will Tell' and the Importance of Heredity

Mark Twain's *Pudd'nhead Wilson* is a perplexing novel. It may be argued that Tom Driscoll's white upbringing is his ruination, that the pampering and indulgence he receives at the hands of Roxy and the Driscolls make him self-centered and cruel. Philip S. Foner suggests, however, that Twain seems to follow the "blood will tell" theory in his rationale for Tom's despicable behavior (213). The theme of "politic concealment and exhibition of seminally transmitted virtue" (Berkeley and Eidson, 25)—or "blood will tell"—may indeed be central to Twain's attitude toward his characters in this novel. His use of this theme, whether conscious or unconscious, particularly with the characters of Thomas Driscoll and Valet de Chambre, implies a belief in the importance of heredity and in the ultimate superiority of white culture.

Legends and stories illustrating the "blood will tell" theme have antecedents in medieval tales, legends incidentally reflecting a stratified social system. Twain, of course, read widely in medieval literature; Louis Schleiner argues that he grounded his problematic plots in "aristocratic or chivalric romance and romance epic" (332). She writes that Twain read Malory (rich in the 'blood will tell' motif) in 1884–85, that he tried to read *Canterbury Tales,* and that he probably knew Tasso's *Jerusalem Delivered* and Ariosto's *Orlando Furioso,* as well as Cervantes. Twain's fascination for medieval settings, motifs, and European nobility

The margins of your documented MLA essay should be an even one inch all around—top, bottom, and sides—and the spacing should be double. Check to make sure that spacing is truly double and not space-and-a-half. Number pages, even the first page, in the upper right-hand corner, one-half inch from the top and one inch from the right margin. Put your surname immediately before the page number; this helps your reader keep pages of your essay together.

Computer Writing Tip: Your word-processing program can put your surname and the page number in a header.

In an MLA-style documented essay, all material—even *Works Cited* and *Notes* pages—is double-spaced. For those special pages, center the appropriate title one inch from the top of the page, double-space, and begin listing entries.

The *Notes* pages should contain all your content notes. Content notes contain important information that is related closely to your paper, but not exactly essential to it. Content notes give you an opportunity to present information that might ordinarily violate the coherence of your paper but that is also potentially useful or interesting to the reader. Content notes are like asides, bits of extra information to share with the reader. Here is a sample *Notes* page.

Hinden 26

Notes

[1]In an interview with Harold U. Ribalow, Schaeffer said she believed that Jewish families are characterized by obsessive parent–child relationships (Ribalow 77–92).

[2]For a full description, see "Family Structure and Feminine Personality," 43–66.

[3]Gilbert and Gubar note that sometimes women writers project their rebellious impulses into "mad or monstrous women" to dramatize "their own self-division, their desire both to accept the strictures of patriarchal society and reject them" and that often the "mad double" is "the author's double," created so that women writers "can come to terms with their own uniquely female feelings of fragmentation" (78).

[4]The deaths of the two older boys while Lily, the oldest daughter, survives illustrate the strength and dominance of females, a pronounced theme in the book.

[5]Leslie Tonner points out in the preface to *Nothing But the Best: The Luck of the Jewish Princess* that real Jewish princesses may be spoiled, pampered, overbearing, snotty, and materialistic, but that they also have strength, intelligence,

---

If you have a *Notes* page, put it before the *Works Cited* page. On the *Works Cited* page, list alphabetically all works or references cited in your paper. Again, list only the works referred to directly in your paper: Resist the impulse to pad the *Works Cited* page to make your research efforts appear super-industrious. Your reader can tell whether your research has been sufficient, and that is all you need to worry about: whether you have done enough research to satisfy the reader's questions. Here is a sample MLA-style *Works Cited* page:

Burch 17

Works Cited

Bullough, Robert V., and Andrew D. Gitlin. "Educative Communities and the De-
velopment of the Reflective Practitioner." <u>Issues and Practices in Inquiry-
Oriented Teacher Education.</u> Ed. B. Robert Tabachnick and Kenneth M.
Zeichner. New York: Falmer, 1991. 35–55.

Elbow, Peter. <u>What Is English?</u> New York: MLA and Urbana, IL: NCTE, 1990.

Hoy, Wayne. "The Bureaucratic Socialization of Student Teachers." <u>Journal of
Teacher Education</u> 28.1 (1977): 23–26.

Kagan, Dona. "Professional Growth Among Preservice and Beginning Teachers." <u>Review of Educational Research</u> 62.2 (1992): 129–69.

A few points to remember about preparing an MLA-style documented essay: Number all pages, including *Notes* and *Works Cited* pages, consecutively throughout. Make
sure that margins are consistent. Check to see that the text is followed by the *Notes* page
(if you have any content notes, that is) and that the *Notes* page is followed by *Works Cited.*
You're finished!

Finishing and Formatting an APA-Style Essay

An essay documented in APA style looks a bit different from an MLA-formatted essay.
You should consult the APA publication manual for very specific details. To begin, an
APA-documented essay has a separate title page that looks like this:

Portfolios 1

Running Head: PORTFOLIOS FROM THE INSIDE

Portfolios from the Inside: A Description of What Students Think
C. Beth Burch
Binghamton University, SUNY

Here are some features you should notice about an APA-style paper:

- On the title page, the title of the paper, author's name, and institutional affiliations are centered on the page and done in uppercase and lowercase type.
- The header contains a short title and page number and is found at the upper right-hand corner of every page of the paper.
- The running head—an identifying short title—is specified in all capital letters and placed two lines below the header, flush left. The running head and the header are not the same thing.

Inside, the margins are one inch all around. On the first text page, the title is repeated; then, following a double space, the text of the paper begins. Throughout, the paper is double-spaced. Also, note that in APA style no words are hyphenated and that the lines are not justified (made even on the right-hand side). Underline words that should be typeset in italic, even if your word-processing program does italics. Parenthetical citations, or short references in the text, are done differently than in MLA style: The citation gives the author, date, and page number.

All reference information is presented on the *References* pages (in MLA this is called the *Works Cited* page). Again, the style of citing is a bit different (see page 307), but all entries are presented alphabetically by authors' surnames but with regular, not hanging indentation. APA style emphasizes the date of the citation and tends to seem more scientific and objective, perhaps because authors' given names (and therefore genders) are not revealed. Here is an excerpt from a sample APA *References* page:

Portfolios 31

References

Belanoff, P., & Dickson, M. (Eds.). (1991). Portfolios: Process and product. Portsmouth, NH: Boynton/Cook.

Belanoff, P., & Elbow, P. (1986). Using portfolios to increase collaboration and community in a writing program. Writing Program Administrator 9(3), 27–40.

Elbow, P., & Belanoff, P. (1986). Portfolios as a substitute for proficiency examinations. College Composition and Communication 37, 336–339.

Gardiner, J. K. (1982). On female identity and writing by women. In E. Able (Ed.), Writing and sexual difference (pp. 177–192). Chicago: University of Chicago Press.

Looking at a Documented Essay

Paul Winks, a forestry major, first drafted a paper about a subject familiar to him, the history of white-tailed deer in Indiana. He wanted to explain what he knew about white-tailed deer, but he found that he needed additional information beyond what he had in his personal repertoire; he needed not only background details but also specific information about the numbers of deer. Here is a draft of his research essay. Read it and consider its strengths; think too about where other information would add substance to his essay.

Paul Winks
Professor Burch
English 103
15 April 199-

White-Tailed Deer in Indiana: A History

One chilly fall morning, an old farmer in Vincennes, Indiana shrugged into his coat, picked up his rifle, and slipped out into the dawn. When he fired his gun and the smoke cleared, he had killed the last deer in Indiana. It may not have happened just that way, but it did happen. By the end of 1890, Indiana's native deer herd was gone (Smith 1). Marginal habitat and uncontrolled hunting had proven too much. Yet today, a hundred years later, it is not uncommon to see deer along rural highways, and even in suburban parks. Where did these deer come from, and how are they faring as we approach the twenty-first century?

In 1934, conservationists and state wildlife officials began a stocking program to reintroduce the white-tailed deer to Indiana. Deer from Missouri, Michigan, and Pennsylvania made up the nucleus of the new herd (Smith 1). I wonder how many were in the new herd. Deer had never been plentiful in Indiana, but the Depression had created a perfect habitat for them: abandoned farms, overgrown fields, neglected orchards, and cut-over woodlots. The result was a literal explosion of deer. Deer have a tremendous biotic potential; that is, ability to reproduce and increase their population. An adult doe will produce two fawns per year, three if conditions are favorable, and doe fawns, born in the spring, may breed their first fall (Weeks). The deer population grew so fast that the Indiana Department of Natural Resources (IDNR) was able to conduct a controlled hunt in 1954, only twenty years after deer were first reintroduced (Weeks). Today, there are about 400,000 deer in Indiana (Smith 1). That is good news for some Hoosiers and bad news for others.

The good news is, partly, that deer hunting has become a major part of the program of the IDNR Division of Wildlife. In 1988, 150,580 hunters took to the woods during the three different deer hunting seasons and killed 60,234 deer (Huggler 118). At $13.75 per license, that year's deer hunt represented about $2.7 million to help fund the IDNR's management programs, such as wild turkey release projects and bald eagle restoration. For the hunters, deer season means a chance to get away from the problems of everyday life and, if they are lucky, meat for the table and a trophy for the wall.

Hunters are not the only ones who enjoy the abundance of deer in Indiana. State parks, such as Brown County and Eagle Creek, have become very popular because visitors can almost always see deer during their visits. Birdwatchers, hikers, and sightseers all enjoy catching sight of a doe and her fawns emerging from the woods at dusk.

Not everyone, however, is so happy to have so many deer around. Deer have become a serious pest in some parts of the state. Farmers suffer economic losses when there is an overabundance of deer. Corn, soybeans, and forage crops are preferred food sources for deer when they are available. Foresters and orchard owners suffer losses when their trees' branches are eaten and the bark rubbed off as bucks clean their antlers in the fall. In some counties these losses are large enough that steps have been taken to reduce the deer population through increased hunting opportunities.

Motorists have also suffered from the increased deer population. In 1983, there were 3,739 deer/auto accidents. In 1988, there were 10,214 accidents involving deer (Smith 1). If we assume that the average deductible for automobile insurance policies is $200, the accidents in 1988 cost Hoosier motorists $2,042,800 in deductible payments alone.

What does the future hold for deer in Indiana? An increasing deer herd, coupled with an increasing human population, points toward more costly encounters between deer and people. To minimize the number of deer/human encounters, the IDNR is seeking to reduce the deer herd by 20% over the next two years (Smith 1). The only predators deer in Indiana have today are men with cars and men with guns; so, to accomplish this reduction, certain counties have been designated "Bonus Counties." Hunters in these counties are eligible to apply for special permits which allow them to harvest an antlerless deer, a doe or yearling buck. Hunting is the only way that IDNR officials have to regulate deer numbers. Harvesting bucks only has no effect on deer population growth because one buck can breed many does. Reducing the number of does in a population results in a decrease in the number of deer born in the spring and a net reduction of the population. This may sound like a mass slaughter of deer, but it is interesting to note that even though hunters killed over 60,000 deer last year, that level of hunting is not even adequate to hold deer numbers at their current level (Weeks). It is hoped that with reduction, the deer herd can be held within reasonable limits for the enjoyment of everyone. [Works Cited Omitted]

_____
CONSIDER . . .

1. What sentences early on in Winks's essay suggest his purpose?
2. Can you find a place where Winks could add information to satisfy readers better?
3. Find a place where Winks explains a concept or an idea. Are there other terms that need defining?
4. Is this paper MLA or APA style? You should be able to tell, even without the Works Cited or References pages.

_____

Writers' Group: Rethinking the Documented Essay

The complexity of documenting an essay accurately may mean that your writers' group needs to meet more often and for longer times to ensure that all members can get help with the details of their papers. Writers' groups will want each member to address two major considerations: the content of the text and the mechanics of documentation and presentation. Here are a few questions for you to address in peer sessions.

Content of Text

1. Is my thesis or purpose carried through in this paper? Does it constitute the guiding principle of this paper?
2. Do I have adequate and reliable support for the arguments or points I used to support my thesis or undergird my purpose?
3. Have I presented my evidence in a logical manner?
4. Does my conclusion have a clear relationship to my thesis or to my purpose statement?
5. Are technical terms and concepts adequately explained for the audience?
6. Does any additional information need to be provided?

Mechanics of Documentation

1. Is everything documented that should be documented?
2. Do reference citations fit the style sheet being used? Are they complete?
3. Are all the parts of the documented essay present?

Reflecting on and Presenting the Documented Essay

You may be asked to present your essay to your classmates. If you are, use the oral presentation as an opportunity to get feedback from your listeners. If the audience has a good many questions or needs clarification (if you see puzzled glances or bored stares), you may need to do further research or to weave your research information more smoothly into your essay. Ask your writers' group and/or instructor for help. Your reflection for this piece may be more extensive than for other portfolio pieces, owing to the complicated processes and perhaps the new concepts you have been grappling with. You may also find that you have quite strong feelings about the writing of this paper, feelings you should definitely articulate for the portfolio. When you present this essay in your portfolio, present it just as you would any other essay—being especially meticulous, though, about the cover page and documentation.

PREPARING AN ANNOTATED BIBLIOGRAPHY

Although an *annotated bibliography* sounds very complicated, it is not difficult to prepare. A *bibliography* is literally a *book (biblio) list* or, more specifically, a list of books or references on a given topic. An annotated bibliography, a bibliography with notes, is very useful to a reader trying to select appropriate references or to a scholar surveying the literature (articles and books) on a subject. You might find or write an annotated bibliography of articles and books about, or related to, the subjects of earthquakes in California, compost piles, the writings of Louise Erdrich, or cathedral architecture. In a *selected bibliography* the bibliographer presents merely a selection of readings and not a comprehensive list of available sources. A *selected annotated bibliography* of books and journal articles about Shakespeare's *Midsummer Night's Dream* would, for example, be considerably more brief than a *comprehensive annotated bibliography* on the same subject. (A comprehensive bibliography would attempt to list everything that had ever been published.)

 Writing Task:

Prepare a selected annotated bibliography on a topic that interests you. Include at least ten sources, documented in either MLA or APA style.

Invention Ideas

How should you begin preparing an annotated bibliography? When you determine or are assigned a subject to investigate, first make sure that the subject is adequately narrow. To do even a selected bibliography of books and articles on the Civil War would be a never-ending task, but you might be able to manage a selected bibliography of books and articles about the Civil War uniforms. Look at the list of topics below: Which ones are doable? And which ones would likely be very long-term projects, even for a *selected* bibliography?

Military planes
19th-century immigration
Disney Studios
Moustaches
Articles about O. Henry's "Ransom of Red Chief"
Recycling
Nuclear waste disposal in Pennsylvania
History of Levi's jeans
Harrier jets
Ernest Hemingway
American pottery of the 1930s
Gargoyles in 16th-century France

Drafting the Annotated Bibliography

Once you have a manageable subject, do the reading and research necessary to learn about it. Keep careful citations of articles and books that you plan to use in your annotated bibliography. You may find it useful to use large note cards—four-by-six-inch or five-by-eight-inch cards—for recording information. Not only will you find them easy to track (they don't get lost in your book bag), but you may like the idea of having plenty of room to write notes about a reference. Once you get a critical mass of cards, you can alphabetize them, add your notes, type up what you have written, and—you have a draft. Here's a sample note card:

Front

Baker, Carlos. "Sherwood Anderson's
Winesburg: A Reprise." Virginia Quarterly
Review 48 (1972): 568–79.

Back

In this review of *Winesburg, Ohio,* Carlos Baker
notes that "key terms for recurrent patterns" in
the book are *deprivation, search, release,* and
repressing. This is clearly relevant to readers
interested in a psychological interpretation of
the story.

Each entry in an annotated bibliography has two parts: the *citation* and the *annotation*. The *citation*, usually composed in MLA (Modern Language Association) or APA (American Psychological Association) style, tells the reader where to find the original reference. The *annotation* is a note on or about the reference; it may be a summary or a description or both. It usually mentions key ideas or major points of the reference; and it frequently contains, at least incidentally, your evaluation of the reference. You may, for instance, describe a reference as *helpful, clearly written, disorganized,* or *artfully arranged* and by using such labels cue readers to its usefulness.

You have several choices of arrangements for an annotated bibliography. You may structure your bibliography in a straightforward alphabetical order by surnames of authors. Or if you have numerous citations (say, more than twenty-five or thirty), you may first classify the kinds of references you have accumulated and then alphabetize each group. You might, for example, subdivide your citations into citations for books, journal articles, magazine articles, and interviews. Then label each subdivision with a heading and alphabetize all the entries in that group before you list another group. Find out if your instructor prefers a certain structure or order.

Writers' Group: Revising and Editing the Annotated Bibliography

Your drafting task done, turn to editing and proofreading. You and your writers' group may find it helpful to follow these guidelines:

- **Check each entry for conciseness.** Readers want to know what is in the reference; they typically do not want to read extensive remarks and commentary. Ask yourself, "What does my reader want and need to know?" Then make sure to address that question in each notation. State the main point of the reference. Describe any historical or philosophical perspectives that may be important to your reader. Add evaluation that may be helpful to your reader.

- **Check each entry for accuracy and correct form.** Make sure that names are spelled correctly; that journals' volume numbers and page numbers are cited correctly; and that full titles are used. Make sure that entries conform to the style manual your instructor requests or prefers, down to each comma, period, and space.

- **Check formatting.** You'll want to be sure that each citation and notation fit together. If you indent each notation the same number of spaces as the hanging indents of the citations, the entry will appear physically coherent; it will look as if it fits together on the page. Double-spacing within each entry but triple-spacing between entries may also help readers identify the entire entry visually.

Examining Two Annotated Bibliographies

Here are excerpts from two annotated bibliographies, one done in MLA style (a literary bibliography) and the other in APA style (a bibliography on grammar for teachers).

This first, a bibliography of literary criticism, cites references that comment on a Sherwood Anderson story, "Adventure." The focus of this bibliography is restricted, therefore, to what critics have said—or not said—about this particular story. You'll find a few sample entries here (the original bibliography was fifteen pages) and then an optional passage at the conclusion that summarizes the findings. You may want to add such a summary at the end of your annotated bibliography.

Nena Matz
Professor Burch
Eng 106, Writing and Literature
10 March 1996

Sherwood Anderson's "Adventure":
An Annotated Bibliography of Early Criticism to 1975

Anderson, Sherwood. "Adventure." In The Writer's Art: A Collection of Short Stories. Ed. Wallace Stegner, Richard Scowcroft, and Boris Ilyin. Boston: D.C.
Heath, 1950. 140–45.

In an analysis of the story, Stegner, Scowcroft, and Ilyin focus on Alice's realization that "many people must live and die alone, even in Winesburg." This
awareness, say the editors, is ultimately what the reader must aspire to and
what lends the story universality. The editors note that Alice could in fact be any
woman up to the point of her "adventure," but that then Anderson shifts his
method, no longer including Alice as part of a "general truth." Beginning with her
naked descent into the rainy night, Anderson uses dramatic action and makes
time specific ("one night"); throughout this section of the story, he neither edito-
rializes nor explains as in the earlier part of the story. This sudden shift in technique lends "emotional intensity" to the adventure, claim Stegner and company,
and the subsequent return to the universal "many people" at the end lends
"scope and meaning" to the incident, probably because it has a sudden tele-
scoping effect. The story is negative, claim these critics, yet it asserts a belief in
"positive human conditions" and posits an inarticulable comment on the human
dilemma. Anderson would probably appreciate this insistence on the ultimate in-
effectuality of words.

Asselineau, Roger. "Language and Style in Sherwood Anderson's Winesburg,
Ohio." In Sherwood Anderson, Winesburg, Ohio: Text and Criticism. Ed.
John H. Ferres. New York: Viking, 1966. 345–57.

Asselineau maintains that Anderson did not intend to present a "photographic image of life, nor a faithful record of conversation." Rather he wanted to
"recreate life so that his stories would be the fruit of imagination rather than exact observation." A style that fulfills these criteria allows for the creation of everyday life as well as for the "calm revelation" of the inner life. Such a style can also
lend itself to "heaviness," "awkwardness," and "prolixity," Asselineau notes; he

cites the pointless repetition of "face" in the final six lines of "Adventure" as evidence of careless writing.

Ciancio, Ralph. " 'The Sweetness of the Twisted Apples': Unity of Vision in Winesburg, Ohio." PMLA 87 (1972): 994–1006.

In this full and excellent discussion of Winesburg, Ohio, Ciancio maintains that not all the grotesques are horrible, that some are amusing, others "almost beautiful." (To Anderson, they were probably all beautiful.) Ciancio suggests a comparison between Alice Hindman and Dickens's Miss Havisham in Great Expectations and points out that Alice's room, like that of Miss Havisham, is insular, a refuge as well as a restraint. Ciancio quotes Ihab Hassan's remark that the aim of the grotesque is to perpetuate the victim in the self and uses Alice Hindman as an example of this phenomenon because she pretends to be Ned's wife and dreams of his return for eleven years, thereby thoroughly incapacitating herself emotionally.

Hoffman, Frederick J. Freudianism and the Literary Mind. Baton Rouge: Louisiana State University Press, 1945.

Although Hoffman does not comment on "Adventure," he does offer insights into Anderson's work which may illuminate that story. Hoffman notes that for Anderson's characters, frustration has two sources: "external pressures against an active search for normal happiness—that is, conventionality and 'the morality of the average'—and the timidity and weakness of the individual." The last part of this statement bears examination in relation to Alice Hindman, who seems to be the victim of a heartless lover, a martyr at the altar of love. But Alice's isolation may indeed result, at least partially, from her inability to transfer her feelings from Ned Currie to another man or from her relinquishment of hope, of even trying to live in the world. She is so timid that the fear of a second rejection incapacitates her. . . .

Phillips, William L. "How Sherwood Anderson Wrote Winesburg, Ohio." In Sherwood Anderson, Winesburg, Ohio: Text and Criticism. Ed. John H. Ferres. New York: Viking, 1966. 263–87.

Phillips places "Adventure" in a group of five stories written on the back of nine fragments which were, in turn, all composed evidently from the "same small pile of abandoned manuscript." "Adventure" is the first of the cluster, which includes "The Strength of God," "The Teacher," "Loneliness," and "An Awakening." Phillips also notes physical "connections to the pages of manuscripts on the back of "The Thinker," "Surrender," and "Terror" and dates all these "third group

Matz 3

stories" somewhere between fall, 1915, and winter, 1916. Phillips posits a kind of associational theory for the inspiration for the stories; he postulates that the character Alice Hindman was suggested by Kate Swift's "naked form at prayer."

Schevill, James. <u>Sherwood Anderson: His Life and Work.</u> Denver: U of Denver Press, 1951.

    Schevill sees <u>Winesburg</u> in mythic terms: The town is the "lazy, gentle village of the Christian virtues." Anderson intends, argues Schevill, to "replace the myth of small town Christian virtues with the myth of the grotesques." Section one introduces the secular aspects of the myth. . . .

    Critics and scholars have generally neglected Sherwood Anderson's "Adventure," offering it scant notice in papers on the theme of isolation or cataloguing it as evidence of the motif of sexuality in <u>Winesburg.</u> Indeed, none of the critical treatment of "Adventure" satisfies. Many writers focus on the story as a tale of isolation; Wallace Stegner, Boris Ilyin, Edwin Bowden, Maxwell Geismar, Carol Maresca, and Brian Way underscore the separateness of Alice Hindman. . . . But what is primarily lacking in all the critical works I read is a careful examination of Alice Hindman's character. Anderson supplies a fairly full account of her life, but no scholar seems to question the impact of such events as her niggardly accumulation of money (the combination of the motifs of money and sex are often very instructive, especially in juxtaposition) or the remarriage of her mother. . . . Finally, the larger implications of Alice's "adventure" and her resulting turn toward the wall should be studied: Can Alice be read as a metaphor for the childlike naiveté of America, an America which increasingly turns its gaze inward as the age of mechanization encroaches on an idyllic past? Are we to perceive her in purely individual terms? Is there any significance to Ned's failure in Cleveland, his necessitated move westward to Chicago? These issues explored, we would have a better sense of what Anderson was about in "Adventure," a most unjustly neglected story.

    These materials were not available for examination:

Fertig, Martin J. " 'A Great Deal of Wonder in Me': Inspiration and Transformation in <u>Winesburg, Ohio.</u>" <u>Markham Review</u> 6 (1977): 65–70.

Hilton, Earl. "Sherwood Anderson and 'Heroic Vitalism.' " <u>Northwest Ohio Quarterly</u> 29 (1957): 97–107.

Love, Glen A. "<u>Winesburg, Ohio</u> and the Rhetoric of Silence." <u>American Literature</u> 40 (1968): 38–57.

CONSIDER . . .
---

1. How does Matz remind you that she is reporting what other writers have written about "Adventure"?
2. Explain how Matz has artfully limited the scope of her bibliography.
3. Comment on the extent and usefulness of quotations. Are there too many? Are they helpful?
4. How does Matz address the problem of evaluating references?
5. What is the effect of the closing summary? What does Matz show the reader about her understanding of the material by writing the summary—and also by listing the material "not available"? Why do you think the material was not available?

The next excerpts are from an annotated bibliography of references useful to an English teacher teaching grammar. It's done in APA style, common in the social sciences community. Again, you'll find just part of the bibliography reproduced here, not the entire piece.

Running Head: GRAMMAR READINGS

Annotated Bibliography:
Selected Grammar Readings for Secondary English Teachers
Jeanne L. Hicks
The University of Alabama

Grammar 2

Annotated Bibliography

Broyles, Bill. (1988, Oct.). Let's not have to get going: Eliminating weak verbs. English Journal, 197, 59–60.

Bill Broyles describes an assignment of self-assessment for students that teaches them to limit weak verb usage in writing. He lists six advantages of his assignment, including the fact that it encourages students to employ clauses, phrases, and appositives. Broyles's idea is especially helpful at the beginning of the school year to promote greater confidence and creativity in students' writing.

Dasenbrock, R. W. (1991, Jan.). Do we write the text we read? College English 7, 17.

Dasenbrock's article, a summary of views concerning how readers read texts, focuses on the conflicting views of Stanley Fish and Donald Davidson. Davidson asserts that readers bring past experience to reading, thus bringing interpretive assumptions about the world which change the way individuals relate to a text. Fish believes that because each person reads a text differently, the text itself is different. This article is useful in helping teachers to solidify their understanding of the debate and to help students who may have difficulty interpreting material.

Donovan, J. M. (1990, Jan.). Resurrect the dragon Grammaticus. English Journal 79, 62–65.

Author Jeanne Donovan uses the analogy of a dragon to see if grammar has been "slain and buried" or "tamed to function as servant" in the English classroom. Her survey finds that grammar is, in fact, alive, although research indicates that it is not as useful for improving writing and speaking as the surveyed teachers believe. Donovan presents an outstanding proposal to awaken the dreaded dragon Grammaticus, a proposal that includes discovery, ambiguity, metacognition, and cooperative learning, and she concludes with an example of how her proposal may be enacted.

Flint-Ferguson, J. L., Meyer, J., & Youga, J. (1990, Jan.). Grammar in context: Why and how. English Journal, 79, 66–70.

The premise of this article is that grammar, being often taught, is seldom learned. The main reason for failure in grammar instruction is the fact that traditional instruction is given without a context that is realistic. The authors assert that (a) grammar should be included in an integrated curriculum, and (b) grammar should be focused on writing assignments. The authors provide an excellent example of a unit using Poe's "The Tell-Tale Heart." . . .

CONSIDER . . .

1. How does Hicks's title indicate the focus of her bibliography?
2. Many of Hicks's references come from one source. Do you consider this a strength or weakness of the bibliography?
3. Find one or two places where Hicks evaluates the references she uses. As a reader, do you find the evaluations and descriptions of the articles helpful? Can you suggest ways that Hicks could make the bibliography even more useful?
4. Finally, comment on the formatting of this piece. Suggest one way that Hicks can make the bibliography easier to read and process.

PORTMANTEAU OF WRITING FROM READING AND SECONDARY RESEARCH

This portmanteau section contains more academic writing. First, you'll find articles about paternity leave and about risk factors for coronary artery disease (CAD)—and summaries of those articles. Next are two essay questions and responses for you to evaluate. Two documented essays are the next items for you to consider, and another annotated bibliography on grammar rounds out the portmanteau.

Articles and Summaries

Read "The Politics of Paternity Leave," from *Newsweek*, and "Risk Factors: What Are Your Personal Odds?" from *Esquire*. Evaluate and, if necessary, revise the summary of each article.

The Politics of Paternity Leave

TOM MCMAKIN

Valerie's asleep now, having snacked most of the morning, fussed and finally closed the brightest blue eyes I've ever seen. Quiet moments like these are rare when you are taking care of a 4-month-old. When she sleeps, it's time for me to mix more formula, wipe the counter, call about life insurance and then, if time allows, break open the laptop and sit down to write for a few minutes. Welcome to paternity leave, a spicy stew of belches and smiles, DPT shots, heavy warm diapers and the odd moment of reflection.

The idea that fathers should take time off from work to be with their newborn children is a relatively new one, but it's an idea that is long overdue. Two years ago, time at home with Valerie would not have been possible. But thanks to the Family and Medical Leave Act of 1993, here I am changing my daughter's diapers and enjoying her first gurgles and giggles. Who would have thought it? A bunch of far-away lawmakers passed legislation, and it profoundly affected my life. Their law, PL103–3, requires that companies with more than 25 employees allow them to take up to 12 weeks of uncompensated time off to care for their children. Because of this legislation my life is richer.

Much richer. This bundle of sweet smells I call my daughter has given me the gift of new sight. A trip to the supermarket used to be a dreaded errand; now it is the highlight of my week. Valerie has taught me to look beyond our store's confusion of brands and hype and focus on the colors, shapes and happy chatter that make each visit a carnival of sight and sound. We squeal at the celery, spit heartily at the dairy rack and shrink in terror at the sight of the frozen turkeys. The moving counter by the cash register is a revelation.

A walk downtown has been similarly transformed. Everyone loves a baby. And we love them back for it. People I've never spoken with, but have passed on the street many times before, smile and ask how old she is. To be a baby, I've learned, is to live in a friendly, welcoming world. But it's not just her world; it's mine too. Because of my time home with Valerie, I'm also much more understanding of children and parents. I rush to help a mom with a stubborn car door or a dad whose youngest is on the verge of straying. I smile at mischievous kids, happy to see them speeding off in this direction or that, ruining their parents' best-laid plans.

I have paternity leave to thank for teaching me these and other lessons (never dump formula in cold water—it doesn't mix). I am grateful to my wife and to my employer for encouraging me in my decision to stay home and am grateful to a government that made taking this time possible.

Sadly, when Valerie and I walk downtown and stop at the local coffee shop, we hear people talking about government in two ways, neither of them very good. They say that government is either ineffective or misguided, with most agreeing that it is both. It is not hard to understand why the ranchers and business people clustered around the small Formica tables think this way. In our state of Montana, the public owns 39 percent of all land. That means there are legions of federal, state and local managers running around doing surveys, convening task forces, forming policy and interpreting regulations. With so much at stake and with so many bureaucrats in action, it is inevitable that these well-intentioned civil servants make mistakes. When they do, the mistakes are widely discussed and greatly criticized.

That's a shame. Somewhere in the rush to criticize, we have failed to see the forest for the trees. While Bozo the Clown may run a public agency or two, I cannot escape the fact that my sitting here today trading coos with my daughter is a salute to the possibility inherent in public action. On Feb. 5, 1993, our representatives in Washington decided it was important that families be allowed to spend time together when they most needed it and, more important, that wage earners should not lose their jobs while caring for a dying mother or recuperating from a serious operation or spending time with a newborn. In my book, that bad boy of American culture, Congress, did something right when it passed this law.

The citizenry of this country has expanding and contracting tastes in what it wants its government to do, not unlike the members of the credit union to which I belong. One year we may ask the credit union's management to make sweeping changes, add more services and expand the types of loans it is willing to make. And then that energy runs its course and the membership elects a new board or hires a new manager to trim costs and services. When we ask the credit union to add services, we are not suggesting that credit unions ought to take over the world. By the same token, when we ask it to cut services, we are not saying credit unions are worthless. It's more like riding a horse up a hill: you might go to the left for a while and then to the right, but, even with the zigs and zags, you are still headed in one direction—toward the top.

In this current season of scaling back government—both Republicans and Democrats seem to agree that this is a good thing these days—my hope is we remember that government is capable of doing things and doing them well. I work 40 hours a week because my great-grandfather voted for a reform Congress at the end of the last century. My savings at the credit union are insured because my grandmother voted for FDR. My dad put Eisenhower and a forward-looking Congress in place in the late '50s. As a result, it takes me one hour to travel to Butte and not two, on an interstate-highway system. Government isn't bad in and of itself. It isn't some malevolent Beltway-girdled ogre perched on the banks of the Potomac. It is, rather, an expression of our collective will.

But wait. Valerie is stirring. Little wet slimy hands await. I need to warm a bottle, find a fresh diaper, pad upstairs and quietly make sure she is serious about ending this nap, and finally peek over the side of the crib and drink in that bright, beautiful smile that never fails to remind me why I so like being a dad at home.

Summary of "The Politics of Paternity Leave"

The Family and Medical Leave Act of 1993 granting workers twelve weeks of unpaid family leave and protecting their jobs if they take the leave is something good that Congress has done recently, says Tom McMakin, who currently stays home to care for his four-month-old daughter. McMakin, a resident of Montana, where the federal government is frequently not highly thought of, puts the Family and Medical Leave Act in the company of laws that have provided real social benefits, such as laws that established a forty-hour work week, provided federal insurance for savings accounts, and built the interstate highway system. The federal government isn't a bad institution, he argues; rather it is an expression of "our collective will."

Risk Factors: What Are Your Personal Odds?

DAVID NOONAN

Dr. Timothy Denton knows just about all there is to know about atherosclerosis and the risk factors associated with CAD. He also knows what he likes, and one thing he likes is eating at L'Orangerie, a high-end French establishment just a few blocks from the L.A. hospital where he tends to hundreds of bypass patients each year. Being a male with a cholesterol level of 204 and a family history of premature CAD—his father had bypass surgery at fifty-five—Denton, forty-three, has three of the eight classic risk factors and might be expected to forego the foie gras for carrot sticks and wheat juice. But he practices what he preaches: a practical, realistic approach to the risks of heart disease.

"I would like to work on my cholesterol more," he says, "but to be honest, that would affect the quality of my life." So he tries to strike a balance by maintaining a vigorous exercise routine. He mountain-bikes ten miles through the Hollywood hills each weekday and twenty to thirty miles on Saturday and Sunday. "I ask myself, 'Do I want to be a vegetarian for the rest of my life, or am I willing to take that incremental increase in the chance of a heart attack?'"

It's the kind of informed decision that Denton helps his patients make as well. The key to managing risk factors is understanding exactly what a risk factor is. It's a statistical concept, a number, a possibility, a morning line of sorts. It is anything but a certainty. It's estimated, for instance, that 52 percent of American adults—more than ninety-four million people—have cholesterol levels of 200 or higher. And thirty-seven million of them have levels of 240 and above. Those are incredible numbers. Yet, as Denton points out, "the vast majority of people are not going to get heart disease, although it is the most common cause of death. They're going to get cancer, they're going to get hit by a truck. . . . Yes, you need to be concerned, but it's not like 100 percent of people get heart disease by the age of seventy."

At the same time, the epidemiological evidence supporting the connection between heart disease and the classic risk factors is strong indeed. You have to assess your lifestyle and devise an approach that you can actually live with. "Everybody is different," Denton says, "and everybody has to make his own trade-offs."

The known risk factors for CAD are:

1. **Elevated Cholesterol Level.** Cholesterol level is the batting average of cardiac health—an extremely complex set of biochemical relationships and phenomena reduced to a single three-digit number. A modern American obsession. Under 200 is good; under 180 is even better. One study of 360,000 men monitored over six years showed that men aged thirty-five to fifty-seven with total cholesterol levels over 300 were four times as likely to die from CAD as men with levels under 180. LDL (low-density lipoproteins) and VLDL (very-low-density lipoproteins) are the bad cholesterols associated with atherosclerosis. HDL (high-density lipoproteins) is the good stuff that carries the bad cholesterols to the liver, where they are disposed of. The higher your HDL level, the better. Above 45 is preferred; below 35 is too low.

2. **High Blood Pressure.** The "silent killer" is often exactly that—no symptoms, no warning signs, cause almost always unknown. Hypertension killed more than thirty-five thousand Americans in 1992 and was a factor in the deaths of many more. Uncontrolled high blood pressure triples the risk of CAD. As with smoking, high blood pressure often combines with other risk factors to multiply the danger.

3. **Obesity.** Excess weight puts a strain on the heart, can increase blood pressure and blood-cholesterol level, and contributes to the risk of diabetes. The distribution

of fat on the body may affect one's risk as well. According to the AHA, a waist-to-hip ratio of greater than 1.0 (the waist measurement exceeds the hip measurement) on a man "indicates a significantly increased risk." A woman's waist should not be more than 80 percent of her hip measurement.

4. Diabetes. Seven million adults in the U. S. are known to have diabetes, and as many as seven million more have it but don't know it. It increases a man's risk of developing heart disease two times and a woman's five times. More than 80 percent of diabetics die of some form of heart or blood-vessel disease. Ironically, the symptoms of CAD are not as apparent in diabetics, possibly due to a nerve abnormality that affects their ability to sense pain.

5. Inactivity. One nation, flopped on the couch. According to the Centers for Disease Control, 24 percent of adult Americans are "completely sedentary," while another 54 percent are "inadequately active." Such sloth is associated with lower HDL levels, increased blood pressure, an increase in some clotting factors, and increased body weight. The great thing about getting off your butt is that it has a direct and dramatic impact on two other prime CAD risk factors: cholesterol level and blood pressure. Make that three if you include diabetes.

6. Smoking. Smoking increases blood pressure and heart rate and reduces the amount of oxygen in the blood. Smokers are twice as likely as nonsmokers to have heart attacks and two to four times as likely to suffer sudden cardiac death. Two-pack-a-day smokers triple their risk of heart attack. Smoking also reduces the ratio of HDL to LDL in the blood. Quitting can raise the HDL level 10 percent in a month.

7. Family History. Nothing you can do about this one. But is the heart disease in your family in fact premature? If a close relative had a heart attack at, say, forty-eight, you've definitely got a history. Generally, heart disease that develops after sixty doesn't qualify.

8. Being a Guy. Sorry, dude.

Summary of "Risk Factors: What Are Your Personal Odds?"

Many physicians help their patients make informed decisions about coronary artery disease (CAD) by factoring in the quality of life. Strong evidence supports the connection between heart disease and eight classic risk factors, including blood cholesterol and obesity.

CONSIDER . . .

1. What kinds of sentence structures and strategies does the summary of "Paternity Leave" use to include a lot of details? If you can't think of the terms to describe the structures, provide some examples of where the writer weaves in detail.
2. Revise the summary of "Risk Factors" so that it is fuller and has more details yet still contains only three sentences.

More Essay Questions and Sample Responses

The deceptively simple question below appeared on a linguistics examination. Read it and the response that follows and consider whether the student answered the question—and how well the student was able to show what he knew. Are there sufficient details? What kinds of writing strategies do you suggest for improving the response?

Question: Explain several ways in which the meanings of words come to be altered historically.

Response: One way in which words may change their meanings is to go from a narrow, well-defined meaning to a broader, more general meaning. This is called *generalization.* An example of this is the word *thing,* which has become so broad that it scarcely retains any meaning at all. *Condition, matter,* and *gadget* are similar words.

The opposite of generalization is *specialization,* in which a word goes from a broad meaning to a more specialized narrow one. An example of this is *deer,* which used to mean simply an animal. Today it has become specialized to refer to a certain kind of animal, not usually domestic, the male of the species bearing horns, etc.

Words may also go up or down the scale in meaning. A word with a good connotation or favorable meaning may come to mean something negative or disagreeable. This process is called *degradation;* it is the usual course which words follow in the course of time. An example of this is *lewd,* which formerly meant only *ignorant* but which now carries a connotation of *obscene.*

The opposite of degradation is *elevation,* in which words assume a higher position than was indicated by their original meaning. Such a word is *knight,* which was elevated with the introduction of chivalry.

The question that follows was the only one on a twenty-minute quiz in a survey course in American history. How effectively did the student answer the question? What specific details indicate that the student was well prepared? What writing strategies could be used to craft an even better response?

Question: Was seventeenth- and eighteenth-century colonial America a paternalistic society?

Response: Paternalism describes a social order which is static, hierarchical, consciously elitist, one based on the notion that society is inherently unequal. Paternalism stresses an organic unity based on each person's acceptance of his or her place in this stable, stratified social order. It reflected the practical reality of life in seventeenth- and eighteenth-century England. Since feudal times, land had been a source of economic power and political identity. Because there were more people than there was land, it meant that a small percentage of the English population controlled all the property and enjoyed all the privileges of power and profit, with the rest working the land, tied to it, with few political rights and little political privilege or power. This paternalistic class structure and social ethic made sense in England and was sanctioned by the state, by the Church, and by tradition. However, in seventeenth- and eighteenth-century British North America, there was more land than there were people, creating an opportunity in theory and practice for adult white males to become property owners and enjoy not only the opportunity for economic independence but the political rights and privileges that came with it. In addition, there were no laws that supported a class system in colonial America. Colonial Americans may have tried to make their experiences make sense according to their traditions, but the practical reality of these experiences undermined their inherited traditions and worked against the persistence of paternalism in colonial America.

Two Documented Essays to Review

Now consider the documented essay, "Infidelity: Cheaters Never Win." Although this essay makes some worthwhile points, it would be stronger with some revision and more solid documentation. Consider not only the arguments that the writer makes but the reliability of the sources she cites. Mark at least five places in the text where revision would be useful and suggest what is needed or write five specific suggestions for the writer. Also, help the writer cast this draft in MLA style; tell her exactly how she should format the piece, including the Works Cited list.

Infidelity: Cheaters Never Win
Theresa W.

Infidelity, unfaithfulness, disloyalty. Although this definition is very simple, infidelity is not a simple problem. The problem of infidelity causes many terrible feelings for the people who are affected by it. Infidelity has become a very common subject for talk shows, movies, and newspaper articles because it is damaging to many relationships and marriages. Infidelity happens with both sexes; however, it occurs much more frequently in men. Male infidelity has become a terrible problem habitually practiced by all different types of men—but it may, in some cases, be solved.

Infidelity among men happens more often nowadays. In 1948, Alfred Kinsey reported that fifty percent of American husbands had been unfaithful—and all America was aghast (Botwin 8). Shere Hite's 1980s study of 7239 men found that seventy-two percent of men married two years or more had cheated (10). The problem also occurs in couples not officially married but sharing some sort of relationship and commitment. Actually, the whole problem is very ironic. A man chooses a woman to be his and only his partner, to share intimate moments with him and many private things. This woman is special because she was chosen especially by him. However, in a significant number of relationships, a man will look elsewhere for other short-term companions. (In some instances, the companions could turn out to be long-term.) It seems that in all types of relationships, monogamy has become the exception rather than the rule.

In some societies, polygamy (many partners) is practiced. However, in these cases the marriages are frequently for financial or other reasons—not for emotional bonding. A man in these societies will have many wives with a separate household for each wife, thus allowing the man to father many children. In American society today most women and men believe that marriage is an emotional bond rather than a financial necessity. For this reason, when the bond is broken by an unfaithful husband, it can emotionally destroy the wife.

The effects on women who are the victims of an unfaithful partner may differ in severity, but in most cases the shock and despair are of approximately equal intensity. The woman is devastated and feels rejected. She has placed all her trust and effort in making her marriage a happy one for both of them, her and her husband. Yet her husband felt compelled to destroy his wife's trust. It is no surprise that such devastation is felt. One woman describes this feeling: "My knees were shaking and I couldn't breathe . . . I was a complete and total mess . . . I wasn't angry, I was devastated and betrayed" (Penney 3). This is a common response among women whose husbands have been unfaithful. Trust so violated can never be regained.

If all this pain is caused, then why would a man make his wife or girlfriend suffer? There is not a real answer to this question, but there are probably thousands of reasons and thoughts that go through a man's mind when he has decided to cheat. Also there are many different types of affairs. Dr. Rodney Ball, Ph.D., describes different types of affairs. A man who is obsessed with women is a womanizer who will never be faithful no matter who he marries because he can never get enough women. Another kind of affair, Dr. Ball says, may signal that something is wrong in the marriage; and another type of affair happens sometimes when a man reaches a certain age and all the children have left home. He feels empty because no one is there to interfere with him and his wife. He may also feel that he has not accomplished very much in his life, which is nearly over (Ball 1989). These are very general types of affairs, but real affairs are often much more complex and much more difficult to understand.

The basic reason for infidelity in a man usually stems from some sort of insecurity, which could have started in his childhood. Therefore, virtually any situation could trigger this emptiness or insecurity—anything from a man's father cheating to being away on a trip and being unfamiliar with the area. And even a happily married man might be unfaithful (Botwin 38–56).

What can a woman do to keep her man monogamous? Of course the solutions vary from man to man and situation to situation. Women can make sure that all the needs of a man—both emotional and physical—are met. On one Phil Donahue show, a guest doctor advised women to keep the marriage exciting. He suggested greeting your husband at the door and eating a candlelight dinner, all in the nude. Finally, communication is extremely important. If a man is feeling empty and insecure, he needs someone who cares about him to talk with him and listen to him. A woman can only try everything she knows, and that is all that can be expected. If everything fails or the woman does not want to work that hard, the marriage or relationship should probably end.

Just as there is no guaranteed solution to a man's infidelity, there is no absolute way to detect if a man is cheating until he admits it. However, most experts say to trust your instincts. Any suspicious behavior or sudden change in normal activity can indicate an affair. If a man gets dressed up and adds a little extra cologne to go out bowling with the guys, he could be going not bowling but to meet another woman. Women have to be reasonable, though. Overjealousy will create more problems than are really there—and nobody needs more problems in a relationship.

If indeed a woman finds that her man is cheating, she needs to make some important decisions quickly. Is this marriage worth saving? Are both partners willing to put forth the effort in order to save it? These are just two important decisions that the woman will need to make. Dr. Ball gave his opinion: "I think a marriage can be saved after infidelity has occurred, but it takes a hell of a lot of work!" (Ball 1989). After the woman and her husband make the decision to end or work out the marriage, the long hard battle of recovery begins. Professional help is always available. If both partners are truly dedicated and the infidelity ends, then the marriage will most likely survive.

Hopefully, with a little help, honesty, and dedication, this problem can become extinct.

Works Cited

Ball, Rodney. Personal Interview. 26 Sept. 1989.

Botwin, Carol. <u>Men Who Can't Be Faithful.</u> Warner Books, New York, 1988.

"Infidelity." <u>Donahue.</u> CBS. 16 Nov. 1989.

Penney, Alexandra. <u>How to Keep Your Man Monogamous.</u> Bantam Books, New York, 1989.

Next, read "Color Prejudice within the Black Community," an annotated literary analysis. What is Shoyinka's thesis? How does she support it? What role does the documentation play in supporting her point? Shoyinka also needs some help with MLA style: suggest how she should (1) format her heading; (2) punctuate the title; (3) indicate page numbers; (4) cite more specifically; and (5) punctuate the entries in the Works Cited section.

Color Prejudice within the Black Community
Margaret Shoyinka

Many forces have created prejudice within the black community in the United States. One aspect of this prejudice developed when African-Americans of "lighter" complexion maintained a mentality of superiority regarding the "darker" members of their race. The former was accorded more privilege by the dominant society. There also existed African-Americans of all shades who combatted this prejudice. The upholding and resisting of this bias were examined in much of the material written during the Harlem Renaissance. This paper will examine the issue of color prejudice within the African-American community as represented in *Blake,* "The Wife of His Youth," *Passing,* and *The Autobiography of an Ex-Coloured Man.*

Color prejudice is an ugly result of slavery and the racism that accompanied it. Some scholars argue that because slave owners often placed "light-skinned" slaves in the house and "dark-skinned" slaves in the field, the former developed a superior status. Therefore, under slavery this unfounded color distinction was born. (class notes)

The differentiation between "light" and "dark" African-Americans did not vanish after Emancipation. In fact, many organizations maintaining this prejudice sprouted throughout the United States. Martin Delany portrays the emergence of "Brown Societies" in *Blake or the Huts of America.* In South Carolina thrived the "Brown Society, an organization of mulattos, created by the influence of the whites, for the purpose of preventing pure-blooded Negroes from entering the social circle" (Delany p. 109).

These societies were instruments of racism, formed to perpetuate white supremacy. The theory that the "lighter" you are, the better, placed white at the top of the hierarchical color structure. Delany further illustrates this division in the black community when Henry is threatened by a "mulatto gentleman." The man accusingly asserts, "You are a runaway, and I'll have you taken up!" (Delany p. 111). This biracial individual does not see himself in a position similar to Henry's, even though both suffer at the hands of the same oppressor. Instead, he is blinded by the "special" treatment he receives and is willing to deliver Henry back into slavery.

As Delany critiques the "light-skinned" segment of the black population, he also depicts resistance to these practices. As Henry travels through Washington, D.C., he is aided by another "mulatto" gentleman. Delany mentions that "the kindness received at the hands of this family brought tears of gratitude to the eyes of the recipient, especially when remembering his treatment from the same class in Charleston and Richmond" (p. 118).

Further reflection of the color prejudice amongst black people is found in Charles Chesnutt's "The Wife of His Youth." In this short story the author describes "The Blue Vein societies" existing in northern cities. The protagonist, Mr. Ryder, is a member of the Blue

Veins organization. He declares, "We people of mixed blood are ground between the upper and the nether millstone. Our fate lies between absorption by the white race and extinction in the black" (Chesnutt p. 336). The members of these societies attempt to negate their identity as African-Americans. Their goal is to be embraced by white America and to lead privileged lives. What Mr. Ryder and other subscribers to this theory do not realize is that they can never fully gain the equal opportunity which they crave. Racism will not allow this equality, because it would destabilize the structure set up to keep whites on top. Mr. Ryder can only obtain the title of "clerk" at the company he works for, even though he is an educated person.

Many African-Americans protested these societies. Chesnutt writes that "there were those who had been known to assail it violently as a glaring example of the very prejudice which the colored race had suffered most" (p. 335). Those who combatted these organizations understood that the spread of these societies would hinder the progress of black people in the United States. These discriminatory practices were ways of dividing the black community in order to prevent a united resistance against the common oppressor.

Another novel that sheds light on this division existing in the black community is Nella Larsen's *Passing.* Men and women "light" enough to pass for white often abandoned their black community in search of monetary gain. Absorbing into white society, they often lived in fear of being detected. At one point in the novel, three "passing" women are discussing childbearing. Gertrude Martain reveals the fears she had during her pregnancy. She says, "It's awful the way it skips a generation and then pops out . . . nobody wants a dark child" (Larsen p. 60). Gertrude is referring to the possibility that her child may have acquired black physical characteristics. This is a clear example of equating white with superiority. Gertrude considers her African-American roots as inferior.

Passing also depicts resistance to Gertrude's mentality through the character of Irene Redfield. She also has the ability to "pass," but she chooses not to. When Irene is asked if she thought about "passing," she asserts, "No. Why should I . . . I've everything I want" (Larsen p. 44). Instead of negating her black heritage, she embraces it by marrying a man of "dark" complexion. She does not turn away from the black community as many women in her position did. Irene is a force resisting the divisions in the black community.

Also examining forces contributing to the "light–dark" division in the United States is *The Autobiography of an Ex-Coloured Man*, by James Weldon Johnson. The protagonist in the novel says, "I have seen advertisements in the newspapers for waiters, bellboys, or elevator men which read 'light coloured man wanted.'" (Johnson p. 155). He realizes that there exists more opportunity for "light-skinned" African-Americans in the United States. This demonstrates the external force that ignited the color prejudice inside the black community.

The color division is further sustained in the novel by an African-American doctor who states, "you see those lazy, loafing, good-for-nothing darkies; they're not worth digging graves for; yet they are the ones who create impressions of the race" (Johnson p. 155). This sense of superiority stems from white society granting privileges to the African-American doctor because of his light complexion. He places his "darker" brethren in an inferior role, the same way all blacks were placed by racist whites. By referring to these people as "darkies" he is accepting the idea that black is inferior to white.

The protagonist in Johnson's novel also turns his back on the black community by assimilating into white society. He decides to "pass" after he witnesses a lynching. He claims that he passes because of "shame at being identified with a people that could with impunity be treated worse than animals" (Johnson p. 191). He cuts his ties with the black population because of the way blacks are treated. Yet it would make more sense if he were to reject his connections with white society after seeing members of this race cheering and encouraging the burning of a black man.

Although elitism existed in the African-American community, there also was a strong resistance toward these discriminatory practices. Many people looked down on members of "Brown Societies" and on individuals who chose to "pass" in white society. These biased practices were often criticized by leaders of the black community such as W. E. B. Du Bois and Malcolm X. Each author of the novels cited also fought against these divisive forces by critiquing them in their works.

Works Cited

Boyce Davies, Prof. Carol. "Lecture notes" African-American Literature I, Binghamton University, September 11, 1996.

Chesnutt, Charles W. "The Wife of His Youth" *Black Writers of America.* Barksdale, Richard & Kinnamon. New York: Macmillan Publishing Co., Inc., 1972.

Delany, Martin R. *Blake or the Huts of America.* Boston: Beacon Press, 1970.

Johnson, James Weldon. *The Autobiography of an Ex-Coloured Man.* New York: Hill and Wang Inc., 1960.

Larsen, Nella. *Passing.* New Hampshire: Quicksand, 1928.

Excerpts from Annotated Bibliographies

Finally, evaluate these excerpts from other annotated bibliographies. Pay attention to format: Are you able to discern easily where one entry ends and the next one begins? Pay attention to content: Is the information, description, and evaluation in the entry sufficiently helpful to you as a reader? Pay attention to style: Are the writers consistent and accurate in their use of one style guide? Suggest how the writers can make the bibliographies more readable and useful.

Bibliography Excerpt 1

Barratt, Leslie. "Ten Things That Teachers Should Teach (and Students Should Learn) About Language." <u>Contemporary Education</u> 59.2 (1988): 70–71.

Barratt stresses that students will learn formal English only when their study of grammar is supplemented by relevant practice and reading assignments. If teachers are to point out differences between formal English and that which their students speak, they must be familiar with the rules which govern their students' dialects. Class discussion is encouraged as a way to help students understand the role formal English plays in our society.

Christensen, Linda M. "Teaching Standard English: Whose Standard?" <u>English Journal</u> 79.2 (1990): 36–40.

In the United States, one's grammar is judged by many people to be an indicator of one's class and cultural background. For this reason, teachers are obligated to teach students rules of standard English. Instruction in standard English must not devalue the students' manner of speaking, nor should it make students feel inferior because their native dialect is nonstandard.

Collins, James. "Hegemonic Practice: Literacy and Standard Language in Public Education." <u>Journal of Education</u> 171.2 (1989): 9–33.

Collins addresses literacy as a melting pot of social relationships. He points out that it is difficult to judge degrees of student literacy because literacy has historically been enjoyed by a minority of the world's population. Collins argues that literacy is key to our national unity, and to mobility within our social structure. In this way, public education functions as social mediator.

Bibliography Excerpt 2

Annotated Bibliography

by Jon S.

Hairston, Maxine, and John Ruszkiewicz. *The Scott, Foresman Handbook with Writing Guide.* New York: Harper Collins, 1991.

Hairston and Ruszkiewicz provide a complete and user-friendly grammar guide in their latest entry. Included are useful sections on pronoun agreement, reference, and case; sentence markers; and abbreviations.

"Hollywood Speak." Producer. Ted Turner. *Showbiz Today.* CNN, Atlanta. 28 May 1992.

New language is being created in a crop of summer movies (*Encino Man, Mo'Money Boomerang*) in the hope that the country will be using the new slang. "The key is to get the message across," says Dr. Lillian Glass, speech pathologist. "If you can do it through a funny language or unusual vocabulary, why not?" Examples: grindage = food; fundage = money.

Kahler, Wolfgang. "Unraveling the Particularities and Unusuals of English Sentence Patterns." *Forum* **30 (January, 1992): 25–27.**

Kahler expresses concern about the educational shift to meaning-oriented language teaching activities. Kahler states that "mere manipulation of structural devices does not lead to communicative competence." He examines basic sentence patterns, pattern particulars, and methodology.

Bibliography Excerpt 3

Annotated Bibliography
by David P.

Akmajian, Adrian, Richard A. Demers, and Robert M. Harnish. Linguistics: An Introduction to Language and Communication. 2nd ed. Cambridge, MA: MIT Press, 1984. This text discusses what linguistics is and how it relates to language and communication. Morphology, phonology, syntax, and semantics are all discussed in detail.

Blake, N. F. Traditional English Grammar and Beyond. London: Macmillan, 1988. This book is designed as an introduction to the study of English grammar. The author uses the traditional approaches as his base and incorporates newer ideas from modern linguistics where he deems appropriate.

Bryson, Bill. The Mother Tongue: English and How It Got That Way. New York: William Morrow, 1990. A humorous and at times hysterical romp through the history of the English language. This book is a great introduction to the English language, showing how English acquired many of its oddities and eccentricities including its grammatical rules.

Celce-Murcia, Marianne, and Diane Larsen-Freeman. The Grammar Book: An ESL/EFL Teacher's Course. Rowley, MA: Newbury House, 1983. A valuable resource which discusses in depth the various aspects of English grammar. This volume provides analyses of the parts of speech of English and lists potential problems that ESL/EFL learners face as well as giving teaching suggestions and practice drills.

CONSIDER . . .

1. Comment on the formatting of each excerpt. Which is easiest to read? Which is most visually attractive? Suggest ways to make the bibliographies more readable.
2. Address the content of the bibliographies now. Which provide the best (and most) information?

Now that you have a sense of what annotated bibliographies are and how they may look, you can more readily think about how to format yours. Sharing what you have learned about research with an interested reader is rewarding.

9

Showing
Your Style

When we encounter a natural style, we are always astonished and delighted, for we expected to see an author, and found a man.

—Blaise Pascal

He who has nothing to assert has no style and can have none: he who has something to assert will go as far in power of style as its momentousness and his conviction will carry him.

—George Bernard Shaw

We become what we write.

—Donald Murray

Your style reveals itself in everything you do—and especially in your writing. It is particularly evident in your portfolio, where your writing work is concentrated in one presentation. So it is definitely worth your time to think about your style.

Rhetoricians have been thinking and writing about style for hundreds of years. Plato believed that moral excellence was necessary for artistic excellence: Thus, the artist was obliged to be a moral person. This notion was reiterated in the Renaissance; George Louis Leclerc de Buffon wrote, "Style is the man himself." (In those days women weren't thought of as having the option of being writers, and in all ways it was a "man's world.") Jonathan Swift, eighteenth-century English author of *Gulliver's*

Travels, defined style as "proper words in proper places." In more modern times, some of this thinking lingers. We sometimes act as if we believe that some power mystical and good resides in those who express themselves capably. And power does reside in the ability to express and present yourself effectively and professionally. Writing well, the complex result of good ideas and capable, clear expression, does enhance your image, professional and otherwise.

Style is not a feature merely for tinkering, though. It is rather the entire package of how you express your ideas and how you attempt to address, appeal to, or influence your audience; it is in the *form* of your individual texts as well as in the individual sentences. This chapter presents fourteen lessons for developing your style and some alternatives for you to consider as you work with your writing, for style is always a matter of exercising *your* linguistic options.

STYLE LESSON 1:   Writing Honestly

The most important rule of style is this: Be honest. Write accurately. Don't be fake. Don't worry about grandiose abstractions. Make every word count. And write in your voice with words that feel natural to you.

Is the following excerpt honest? Why? Or why not?

> The automobile is a mechanism fascinating to everyone in all its diverse manifestations and in every conceivable kind of situation or circumstance.

Compare the passage about the automobile to this piece of writing, which expresses a more honest feeling and doesn't seem as if its author is trying too hard to be impressive:

> Everyone loves cars—all kinds of cars. We love Corvettes, Cadillacs, Ferraris, and Fiats. We love Jeep Cherokees, Dodge trucks, and Chevrolet family sedans.

What does the next passage tell you about its author?

> Trout are very strong swimmers. They carry an added quality of being exceptionally perceptive.

The writer can sound more genuine by writing more naturally:

> Trout are very strong swimmers. They are also very perceptive.

And what can you learn about this writer from this passage, which introduces a flashback in a memoir? What seems to be happening in this passage? How can the writer make the events clearer?

> Not yet fully awake, I had to force myself, with ambivalent feelings, to board my bike. The kickstand was then pulled back into position, and the bike, accordingly, proceeded to carry me forward into the future to relive the past. At first, my self-written fate, ascertained by my awakening, could not be halted; I was compelled to move. It was like I was

caught in a steadily swift current, made a prisoner of my own desire, so that I would be able to contemplate what happened so many years ago.

Compare the previous passage to the following brief description of dove hunting by a student writer. Notice the cleanness of language, the use of present tense, the inclusion of a quotation, and the simplicity of purpose; all contribute to the simple art of this passage.

Three or four boys pull up to the river in a pickup, then pull their shotguns out of the back and look at the sky to check the weather. When they reach their favorite hunting spot, a couple of them load their guns and you can hear receivers slamming, the wind blowing, voices murmuring, and boots stomping weeds down for a place to hide. A few stray birds fly by and the voices of hunters yelling out their position to others can be heard. One boy takes a chew, then yells to another, "It's 6:30, prime time, and they're leaving the feed patch." Then after that the guns roar like they were defending their owners.

—Mike Luckett

STYLE LESSON 2: Preferring Verbs

Prefer verbs to nouns. Because nouns tend to sound heavy, substitute verbs for them wherever you can. Compare this—

The intention of this committee is the encouragement of improvement in company morale.

to this:

The committee encourages you to improve company morale.

Compare this—

The USDA made several proposals regarding changes in the minimum marbling requirements and maturity requirements for beef.

to this:

The USDA proposed changing the minimum marbling and maturity requirements for beef.

Compare this—

The hindering of construction caused by erosion is of great significance in heavy rain areas.

to this:

Erosion significantly hinders construction in heavy rain areas.

Rewrite the following sentences with an eye to replacing nouns with verbs. You may need to revise radically, changing or eliminating some words; just try to maintain the meaning of the sentence.

1. A nuclear freeze is a ban on testing, development, and deployment of nuclear weapons and delivery systems.

2. The notion of making radical reductions in current nuclear arsenals has been under consideration by policy-makers for more than two decades.

3. Over the years, the electoral college system has undergone many changes, including the combination of presidential and vice-presidential candidates on the same ticket, the strengthening of political parties, and the introduction of the common man's vote into the selection process.

4. When this country was first founded, there was a need for the electoral college due to the relative lack of education among the masses and the absence of technology to quicken the tabulation of election results.

STYLE LESSON 3: Using Passive Voice Wisely

Use passive voice wisely. In many cases, passive verbs not only require more words than active verbs but communicate less effectively. What is the passive voice? Passive voice is the form of verbs in which the subject is *acted upon* rather than *acting*. In English, passive-voice verbs consist of a form of *be* plus a past participle: *was seen, has been shot, is being added, was dressed.* Compare this—

> It was brought to our attention by the manager that we had not sent out the invoice.

to this:

> The manager told us that we had not sent out the invoice.

Compare this—

> The object that was stepped on by me was a ladybug with lavender spots.

to this:

> I stepped on a ladybug with lavender spots.

Compare this—

> The scheme was conceived by John at four in the morning.

to this:

> John conceived the scheme at four in the morning.

How do you recognize passive voice? Look first for the *be + past participle* structure; then see if the subject is passive; that is, is acted upon. How do you change passive voice to active voice? First remove the *be* verb and adjust the tense of the remaining main verb to the appropriate or original tense. Then determine the agent (located in the *by* phrase, which may have been eliminated). Finally, switch places between the agent and the subject of the sentence. Here it is again:

The door was slammed by the wind.	1. Remove the *be* verb (here, *was*).
The door slammed by the wind.	2. Determine the agent from the *by* phrase (*wind* = the agent). There is a *by* phrase in the sentence, but the sentence could have been complete without it, as *The door was slammed*.
The door slammed the wind.	3. Switch agent and subject; remove the preposition *by*.
The wind slammed the door.	4. This is now *active voice*.

Sometimes, though, passive voice is useful—and preferable to active voice. Use a passive verb to show that the agent (the person who does something or performs an action) is not important or obvious and can thus be omitted from the sentence altogether:

The bridge was built in 1923.   *(No agent is mentioned; we are not concerned with who built the bridge.)*

Many odd cures for cancer were tried in those days.   *(Emphasis is on the cures, not on the researchers or on whoever tried the cures for cancer.)*

All eyes were forward, cameras were hidden, passports were in the windows.   *(Who hid the cameras is not important—or it's obvious: Everyone did!)*

You can use passive voice when you do not want to identify the agent directly (usually for social or political purposes):

Your application for credit has not been approved.   *(No agent is mentioned—so no specific person has to accept responsibility.)*

Your examination was given a failing grade.   *(No agent [or professor] named.)*

A check was refused by the bank for insufficient funds.   *(The bank, an anonymous, institutional agent, is named, but the by phrase containing the agent is buried in midsentence, away from the sentence's points of interest.)*

And you can use passive voice to emphasize a word by placing it at the head of a sentence:

The windows were cleaned thoroughly.   *(Not the door.)*

The dog was given a bath yesterday afternoon.   *(Not the cat or the hamster.)*

This room has been thoroughly examined by the detectives for clues.   *(Not the other rooms.)*

STYLE LESSON 4:   Rethinking Expletives

Eliminate unnecessary expletives (words added or inserted to fill out the sentence or to make it sound smoother). The expletive constructions *there is*, *there are*, and *here are*, which begin many sentences, frequently delay the reader's perception of the subject and sometimes add unnecessary words to the sentence. Compare this—

> There are five dogs in our yard right now.

to this:

> Five dogs are in our yard right now.

Compare this—

> There is much money wasted in this club.

to this:

> Much money is wasted in this club.

Compare this—

> There are notebooks scattered on a long laboratory table near the entrance.

to this:

> Notebooks are scattered on a long laboratory table near the entrance.

Sometimes, however, removing the expletive can create an awkward sentence:

> There is only one reason for staying.

would sound strange as

> Only one reason is for staying.

And, of course, if your rhetorical purpose is to delay the reader from perceiving the subject, expletives are useful.

STYLE LESSON 5:   Being Concise

Find and prune redundancies or repeated ideas. Can you find the redundancies in the following sentences and revise the sentences?

> Don't forget to finish your homework completely.

—is better as

> Don't forget to finish your homework.

> We made our future plans based on the past history of our club-type organization.

—is better as

> We made plans based on the history of our club.

The final outcome of the game was a terrible tragedy: We lost!

—is better as

The outcome of the game was terrible: We lost!

At this point in time the education process and athletic activities are the responsibility of the county governmental systems.

—is better as

Education and athletics are now the responsibility of the county government.

What revisions will make the following passage more readable?

It is easy to understand why special interest laws are so attractive to lawmakers who have to share credit with hundreds of other legislators who pass broadly based laws that benefit everyone but can enjoy the special thanks that special groups can offer for successful advocacy of special laws.

STYLE LESSON 6:   Varying Sentence Length

Vary sentence length. Use some short sentences among longer ones for emphasis. Combine several short, choppy sentences into longer, smoother ones. Compare this—

Dean has had to suffer because of his condition. He has a great deal of optimism. He believes that violence must end. He has hope for the future.

to this:

Although Dean has had to suffer because of his condition, he has a great deal of optimism, for he believes that violence must end. He hopes for the future.

Here is a passage with excellent sentence variety (and some other effective stylistic strategies). Read it carefully to see how it works.

I tried to imagine the work it had taken to turn the sand to fertile soil, the years before a crop could be grown. I looked at the tower and tried to imagine having to fight to protect your own border. I tried to imagine a people who could do both and yet strive for peace enough to leave their homes, their farms, their lives. Here they were.

How does the writer use repetition to achieve coherence and rhythm? What sentences have compound elements? How many "long" (more than seven words) sentences are in this passage? How many short sentences are there?

STYLE LESSON 7:   Understanding Antecedents and Agreement

Be aware of pronouns and their antecedents (words that come before, to which pronouns refer) and of agreement between noun and pronoun, subject and verb. Connect pronouns to the nouns to which they refer; match subjects and verbs (if the subject is plural, so should be the verb). If you begin a sentence or passage in one tense, stick with that tense. Not this—

> Adriano *stepped* out of the car well aware of all the attention he was getting and loving it. I *slip* my shades on, hoping to dampen the embarrassment.

But this—

> Adriano *stepped* out of the car. . . . I *slipped* my shades on, hoping to dampen the embarrassment.

Not this—

> Mr. Perry always called *everyone* by *their* last name.

But one of these—

> Mr. Perry always called *everyone* by *his or her* last name.

or

> Mr. Perry always called *us* by *our* last names.

or

> Mr. Perry always called his *students* by *their* last names.

The pronouns *everyone* and *no one* require a singular verb, strange as it may seem. Not this—

> *No one* raises *their* hand.

But one of these—

> *No one* raises *his or her* hand.

or

> *No one* raises a hand.

Beware especially of that pesky pronoun *it*. *It* can give you—and your readers—trouble because its antecedent is frequently altogether missing from sentences. *It* often becomes shorthand to refer to any idea that was just mentioned—and although this strategy may work in conversation, the unfettered *it* in writing can create true confusion. Consider this sentence:

> As we entered the supermarket aisles, it was like *Alice in Wonderland*.

Does the writer mean that the supermarket itself was like *Alice in Wonderland?* Does the writer mean that the *we* speaking felt as if they had stepped into *Alice in Wonderland?*

The antecedent is missing, so readers have a hard time knowing what the writer intends. Now consider this sentence:

> Both her parents had been slaves. Without hesitation she spoke of it.

This writer probably intends the reader to interpret *it* as *her parents' having been slaves.* Can you think of a way to express the concept more clearly?

Also beware of the general and nondescript *they*, which writers sometimes use when they need an agent but don't know precisely who that agent is or should be. Look at this passage:

> Trout prefer fast-moving streams loaded with rocks and fallen timber. A good way to find a stream close by with these qualities is to go to your local hunting or bait shops. *They* will almost always be able to provide you with topographical maps or general information about the features of the streams in your area; *they* may even give away a hot-spot or two!

Now compare this revision to the original: How has the writer eliminated the vague *they?*

> Trout prefer fast-moving streams loaded with rocks and fallen timber. A good way to find such a stream close by is to ask a clerk at a local hunting or bait shop. Someone working at one of these places can almost always give you a topographical map or information about streams in your area; and the clerk may even give away a hot-spot or two!

STYLE LESSON 8: Eliminating Sentence Fragments and Using Virtual Sentences

Eliminate sentence fragments (partial or incomplete sentences) by connecting them to an existing sentence or by altering the verb to make it *finite* or *complete.*

Consider how the following fragments might be revised to be more successful.

> Choosing makeup is tricky. Like foundation, for example, finding the right color.

This writer is writing about the difficulty of choosing makeup and happens to think specifically about the problem of choosing the right color—but fails to finish the thought on paper. Here is one solution for clarifying this partial sentence:

> Selecting the correct color for your foundation is especially difficult.

Sometimes fragments result when writers ignore—or are unaware of—sentence boundaries. Look at the following excerpt and rethink the sentence boundaries (determined, of course, by the periods). Where should sentences begin and end?

> When you are lost. You have no idea of where you are. In relation to certain geographical features. Therefore, before you even start your trip, it is essential to have a picture of your location. On an imaginary map in your mind.

Although sentence fragments are not acceptable in formal writing because they create an impression of incompetence, *virtual sentences* are often found in published writing and in standard formal English. A *virtual sentence* is virtually, or almost completely, a sentence; that is, it is complete in meaning but not grammatically. You will often find virtual sentences in conversation and description or as emphasis. Here are some examples; the virtual sentences are underlined.

> It would appear that the wolf is either inefficient or not very serious about killing moose. <u>Or that more is going on than we understand.</u>
>
> > —Barry Holstun Lopez, *Of Wolves and Men*

> In fact, there were no sights—more of the same and then more of the same. <u>Shop fronts, garages, warehouses, narrow brick bungalows.</u>
>
> > —Saul Bellow, "Something to Remember Me By"

> <u>The Big Apple. New York City. Home of Central Park, the Empire State Building, Times Square, and Wall Street.</u> New York is one of the most exciting cities in the country, if not the world.
>
> > —Sharon Daley, "Surviving a Day in the Big Apple"

Be judicious with virtual sentences. Place them wisely. And if you think your instructor may disapprove or question your virtual sentences, identify them with an asterisk and an accompanying note at the bottom of the page.

STYLE LESSON 9:   Writing in Standard English

Avoid nonstandard usage. Your reader should not think you uneducated. For example, avoid *alright;* use *all right* instead:

> The situation will turn out *all right.*

Not *alot,* but *a lot:*

> We ate *a lot* of watermelon that summer.

Not *anywheres,* but *anywhere:*

> The treasure could be *anywhere* in a five-mile vicinity.

Not *being that,* but *because:*

> *Because* we were tired, we stopped digging.

Not *busted,* but *broken:*

> Central East's defensive back had a *broken* leg.

Not *can't hardly*, but *can hardly:*

> We *can hardly* believe our good luck.

Not *could care less*, but *couldn't care less:*

> Frank *couldn't care less* about Joseph's money.

Not *could of*, but *could have:*

> I was so embarrassed I *could have* died.

Not *enthused*, but *enthusiastic:*

> All the teachers are *enthusiastic* about the new schedule.

Not *hisself*, but *himself:*

> Brian can't hear *himself* think in the noisy lunchroom.

Not *theirself*, but *themselves:*

> Rock stars frequently love *themselves.*

Not *irregardless*, but *regardless:*

> Friends tell one another the truth *regardless* of circumstances.

Not *off of*, but *off:*

> Get that dog *off* the couch!

Not *the reason is because*, but *the reason is . . . :*

> *The reason* we are late *is that* our alarm clock failed.

> We are late *because* our alarm failed.

Not *should of*, but *should have:*

> The boss *should have* known that the customers were con artists.

STYLE LESSON 10: Avoiding Sexist Language

Avoid sexist language. This means not using exclusively masculine pronouns like *he* and *him* to refer to a nongendered antecedent noun or to an indefinite, nonspecified person. This also means not using words like *man* to refer to all human experience. Why should you avoid sexist language? Sexist language is a language of exclusion, and most writers want to include readers rather than exclude them. Using sexist language marks you as insensitive to changing ideas about gender-equal opportunity; sexist language makes you seem antiquated, stuck in the past. You will find that there are several ways to avoid sounding sexist. For example, instead of this—

> A student can determine his own educational needs.

Use one of these—

> A student can determine his or her own educational needs.
> Students can determine their own educational needs.
> Educational needs can be determined by the individual student.
> Educational needs can be determined by students.

Look to the antecedent (in the original sentence, *student*) and see how you can modify it or how you can rearrange the sentence. Again, revise this—

> Textbooks are full of man's quest for fame and immortality.

to one of these—

> Textbooks are full of the quest for fame and immortality.
> Textbooks are full of the human quest for fame and immortality.
> Textbooks are full of people's quests for fame and immortality.

Instead of this—

> When a person becomes afraid and disoriented, he may do violence.

choose one of these—

> When people become afraid and disoriented, they may do violence.
> People who become afraid and disoriented may do violence.
> When a person becomes afraid and disoriented, s/he may do violence.
> When a person becomes afraid and disoriented, he or she may do violence.

Not this—

> Because they often work long, irregular hours, nurses often neglect their husbands and children.

but one of these—

> Because they often work long, irregular hours, nurses may neglect their spouses and children.
> Because they often work long, irregular hours, nurses may neglect their families.

Not this—

> In an experiment with five boys and five girls, each child followed instructions given by his mother.

but one of these—

> In an experiment with five boys and five girls, each child was given instructions by his or her mother.
>
> In an experiment with five boys and five girls, all children were given instructions by their mothers.

Any time you write one of the following problematic words or phrases, stop yourself. Think about replacing it entirely with a gender-free option:

Problematic words	Better options
chairman	*chair* or *chairperson*
the psychologist . . . he	*psychologists . . . they*
lady doctor	*doctor*
male nurse	*nurse*
mothering	*parenting*
mailman	*postal worker, letter carrier*
foreman	*supervisor, superintendent*

STYLE LESSON 11: Using Parallelism and Balance

Use parallelism. Balance words with words, prepositional phrases with prepositional phrases, participial phrases with participial phrases, clauses with clauses. Here are some effective examples of balance and parallelism:

> The largest concentrations of wolves are in northeastern Minnesota (about one thousand) and on Isle Royale in Lake Superior (about thirty).
>> —Barry Holstun Lopez, *Of Wolves and Men*

Notice the balanced prepositional phrases, both containing numbers, after the geographical locations.

> He has nowhere to go and nobody to love him.
>> —Robert Bergstrom, student writer

Bergstrom balances *no* words (*nowhere* and *nobody*) and infinitive phrases (*to go* and *to love him*).

> Having spent the past year as a prospective customer in this market, having analyzed the hundreds of viewbooks mailed to my door, and having tested my analyses against reality through multitudinous campus visits, I have discovered how to glean the most important information from collegiate brochures.
>> —Heather VanVactor, student writer

VanVactor opens this sentence with three participial phrases, all beginning with *having*. The effect of this strategy is to create layers of detail, a context, for the reader's perception of the main clause, which makes a claim about VanVactor's expertise.

> I hope that events like this one will open the eyes of some and touch the hearts of others.
>
> —Elizabeth Beck, student writer

Beck balances verbs-plus-objects-plus–prepositional phrases to lend a rhythmic quality to the sentence.

STYLE LESSON 12: Introducing Sentences Effectively

Introduce sentences deliberately. Move some participial phrases to the front of the sentence. Open some sentences with nominative absolutes. Start an occasional sentence with an adverb. Here are some examples of effective sentence openers:

> Ascending, assailed by doubts, peering up through the gloom, he thought of turning back but at the first-floor landing compelled himself to knock loudly on the door.
>
> —Bernard Malamud, "The Silver Crown"

Malamud strings together three participial phrases, each longer than the one preceding it, to draw a picture in words of the scene *before* the reader can perceive the action.

> From America letters came.
>
> —Nessa Rapoport, "The Woman Who Lost Her Names"

Rapoport uses a short prepositional phrase and atypical word order to draw the reader's attention.

> Finally, after several months of decorous behavior they meet by chance on the street one evening and get to talking.
>
> —Lynne Sharon Schwartz, "The Melting Pot"

An adverb (*finally*) and a prepositional phrase prepare the reader for the main action of Schwartz's sentence.

> To the right of the path, behind the winter lilacs, the crust of the snow was broken.
>
> —Saul Bellow, "Something to Remember Me By"

Bellow writes directional prepositional phrases (*to the right*, *behind the lilies*) to orient the reader in space.

> Recently, drug abuse has become fashionable in professional sports.
>
> —Gerard Gu, student writer

A simple adverb, *recently*, followed by a comma, draws the reader into the time of Gu's sentence.

> Before you start filing, glance through brochures from schools you haven't definitely crossed off your list.
>
> —Heather VanVactor

VanVactor uses an introductory clause to define a sequence of events she advises her readers to follow.

STYLE LESSON 13: Using Repetition

Use repetition for effect. Repeating a key word or phrase gives it weight and emphasis. A bit of repetition is like cayenne in your stew, though: Don't use too much, or your readers will turn to another delicacy. Here are some examples of writers' using repetition effectively:

> What we think we are surely going to do, we don't do; and what we never intended to do, we may one day notice that we have done, and done, and done.
>
> —Cynthia Ozick, preface to *Art and Ardor*

What verb does Ozick repeat, not only in its participial form but also in its infinitive form? Forms of *do* appear seven times in this sentence. The commas between the *done*s emphasize the number of repetitions because they slow the pace and force readers to pay attention. And beyond this, there is also the repetition of a *what* clause.

Consider this passage now:

> The pestilence, we know now, was not one plague but two simultaneously: bubonic plague, which sent the victim's fever soaring and raised ugly pustules on his armpits or groin and which in many instances did not kill him; and pneumonic plague, which attacked the victim's lungs and was therefore much more contagious and almost invariably fatal.
>
> —John Gardner, *The Life and Times of Chaucer*

Notice how Gardner repeats *plague*, which echoes *pestilence*, at the beginning of each part of the second half of the sentence. Note too how the repetition of *victim* and pronouns to refer to *victim* hold the sentence together. Notice also the balance and the combination of colon and semicolon.

Here is another passage to ponder:

> The symbolism and metaphor of wolf imagery is not vast, but it is potent. It is rooted in the bedrock of the soul. The tradition of the wolf as warrior–hero is older than recorded history. The legends of Romulus and Remus and other wolf children point up another ancient image, that of the benevolent wolf-mother. The deaths of those taken for werewolves burned alive in the Middle Ages represent yet another, focusing

negative feelings about the wolf. As old as these, though not as widespread outside Europe, is the sexual imagery associated with wolves, the Latin *lupa* for *whore* and *female wolf*, the wolf whistle, and the French idiom *elle a vu le loup*. On the walls of a Roman catacomb the story of the compromising of the voluptuous Susanna by two elders is depicted as a sheep crowded by two wolves.

—Barry Holstun Lopez, *Of Wolves and Men*

In this paragraph Lopez gives the writing coherence (makes it stick together and makes it seem all one piece) by repeating the key words *wolf*, its Latin equivalent *lupa*, and its French equivalent *loup*. The French idiom *elle a vu le loup* means *she has seen the wolf*—or lost her virginity. Besides the repetition of *wolf* words, Lopez creates a web of words that evoke old time: *tradition, recorded history, legends, ancient image, Middle Ages, as old as these. Children* and *mother* are also related words. *Sexual, whore, wolf whistle, compromising*, and *voluptuous* also have explicit or implicit sexual connotations.

STYLE LESSON 14: Punctuating Effectively

Punctuate smartly. Use key marks—commas, semicolons, and colons—appropriately.

Use commas to separate two independent clauses joined by a coordinator (*and, but, for, or, nor*, or *so*):

Ira edged a little closer to his cousin, and she laid her head against his shoulder and sighed.

—Michael Chabon, "S Angel"

When the clauses are, however, very short and closely related, you may omit the comma.

It hurt but I managed.

—Allen Hoffman, "Building Blocks"

Use a comma to set off introductory elements; set off a person's name used as a direct address.

Sam, I'm not here to penalize you for saying the wrong thing.

—Adam Schwartz, "Where Is It Written?"

In the summers, Claire likes to work outside.

—Allegra Goodman, "Variant Text"

Set off elements that interrupt a sentence with a pair of punctuation marks: commas, dashes, or parens.

Gans, the father, lay dying in a hospital bed.

—Bernard Malamud, "The Silver Crown"

I look at a photograph of myself as a child—a shiny, starting-to-yellow snapshot—and think, not for the first time, *It all started here.*

> —Daphne Merkin, "Enchantment"

Shivering (this seemed the one cold room in the house), I began to pull off my things, beginning with the winter-wrinkled boots.

> —Saul Bellow, "Something to Remember Me By"

Use a semicolon between independent clauses for effect. If you have several independent clauses in a sentence (a compound-compound sentence), use a semicolon to split the sentence visually. This helps your reader process the information better.

With regard to external frame backpacks, *full-length* means that the sack part of the pack extends from the top to the bottom of the frame; *three-quarter length* means that the sack does not cover the whole pack but leaves space underneath to strap a sleeping bag to the frame.

> —Mark Schlagenhauf, student writer

In a long or complicated sentence, use a semicolon between items in a list when one or more individual items require internal punctuation. The semicolon helps the reader's eye find the beginning of each item being listed.

The lives of the whole Loman family are rife with the pressure to embody that American dream—by traipsing off boldly to unexplored frontiers like Alaska, in the grand tradition of the earliest American settlers; by easing off on moral principles and academic discipline, since it is enough in America simply to be "well liked"; by buying the refrigerator with the largest ads.

> —Elizabeth Foley, student writer

Use a colon to introduce rather formal lists or to signal your reader that an important idea is coming. Be sure that a complete clause or sentence pattern comes *before* the colon.

The special utensils required to brew tea the Chinese way are these: one two-inch-deep bowl about five inches in diameter; one teapot about two inches in diameter and three inches high; several small teacups about three inches in diameter and one inch tall. These very small utensils make the tea special.

> —Craig Hsu, student writer

Sometimes it is appropriate to join two very closely related independent clauses with a colon, especially if the first clause establishes a context for the second clause. You may think of the colon as a herald announcing the coming clause.

I had always loved singing: I had given up the violin, my instrument of eleven years, to take singing.

> —Martina Ott, student writer

PORTMANTEAU OF STYLISH PASSAGES

Here are some passages for you to analyze for style. These passages not only address the style principles from this chapter but present other ideas to help you achieve your style. The *Consider . . .* items after each excerpt direct you to the key stylistic features in the excerpt.

In this first excerpt from his essay "The American Bakery," Max Apple writes about writing:

> Jacob wrestled with angels and I with sentences. There's a big difference, I know. Still, to me they are angels, this crowd of syllables. My great-uncle who came from the Russian army in 1909 straight to the American West told me he never had to really learn English. "I knew Russian," he said. "English was just like it." He bought horses, cattle, land. He lived ninety years and when he died he left me his floor safe, which sits now, all 980 pounds, alongside me in the room where I write. My eight-year-old daughter knows the combination, but there is nothing inside.

CONSIDER . . .

1. What is the effect on the reader of Apple's using the first-person *I* in this excerpt?
2. Find some examples of Apple's use of rhetorical balance.
3. If Apple had not used the quotation from his grandfather, how would this passage sound different?
4. Why do you think Apple included the detail about the safe's weighing 980 pounds?
5. What is the effect of not including a conjunction in the series *horses, cattle, land?*

In *Our Fiery Trial: Abraham Lincoln, John Brown, and the Civil War Era*, Stephen B. Oates opens a chapter about Lincoln and emancipation with this passage:

> He comes to us in the mists of legend as a kind of homespun Socrates, brimming with prairie wit and folk wisdom. He is as honest, upright, God-fearing, generous, and patriotic an American as the Almighty ever created. Impervious to material rewards and social station, the Lincoln of mythology is the Great Commoner, a saintly Rail Splitter who spoke in a deep, fatherly voice about the genius of the plain folk. He comes to us, too, as the Great Emancipator who led the North off to Civil War to free the slaves and afterward offered his fellow Southerners a tender and forgiving hand.
>
> There is a counterlegend of Lincoln—one shared ironically enough by many white Southerners and certain black Americans of our time. This is the legend of Lincoln as bigot, as a white racist who championed segregation, opposed civil and political rights for black people, wanted them all thrown out of the country. This Lincoln is the great ancestor of racist James K. Vardaman of Mississippi, of "Bull"

Connor of Birmingham, of the white citizens' councils, of the Knights of the Ku Klux Klan.

Neither of these views, of course, reveals much about the man who really lived—legends and politicized interpretations seldom do. The real Lincoln was not a saintly emancipator, and he was not an unswerving racist either. To understand him and the liberation of the slaves, one must eschew artificial, arbitrary categories and focus on the man as he lived, on the flesh-and-blood Lincoln, on that flawed and fatalistic individual who struggled with himself and his countrymen over the profound moral paradox of slavery in a nation based on the Declaration of Independence. Only by viewing Lincoln scrupulously in the context of his own time can one understand the painful, ironic, and troubled journey that led him to the Emancipation Proclamation and to the Thirteenth Amendment that made it permanent.

CONSIDER. . . .

1. The first two paragraphs of this passage contrast two views of Lincoln. What specific word signals the contrast?
2. Oates is fond of balancing modifiers and parallel structures. Point out an example.
3. Another strategy that Oates uses well is the *list;* can you find an example?
4. Why do you think that Oates capitalizes such phrases as *Great Commoner, Great Emancipator, Rail Splitter?*
5. How does the final paragraph of this excerpt weave together the contraries of the previous two paragraphs and prepare the reader for the chapter that follows? Can you predict how Oates will present Lincoln?

This next excerpt comes from Martina Ott's profile of her friend Gale, a fellow biology student. Both young women worked at a local wolf park, where ethologists studied the behavior of wolves and their interaction with bison. Notice how this passage from the middle of Ott's profile gives you a sense of how devoted Gale is to her pursuits. (Erich is the director of the park.)

The next morning we find a note tacked to the door: "Gale, take your animals out of the freezer! They've been there for a year now, and if you don't take them, I'll throw them away. —Erich." Gale has been keeping several small dead animals in the refrigerator freezer in the visitors' center; she fears they might get lost in the big walk-in one. Erich apparently opened the freezer and found a small, very dead squirrel staring up at him. Gale looks at me and says, "Well, want to help load up the car?" We go to the freezer and take out her stuff: a swan, a goose, several deer heads, a coyote, several small rodents, rabbits, birds. . . . In her trunk she already has a horse head we took out of one of the pens during cleanup. In her apartment in Cincinnati there is always something being skeletonized, boiling in bleach on the stove.

CONSIDER. . . .

1. Suppose Ott had written this passage in the past tense *(we found a note, Gale looked at me):* How would its effect on you as a reader be different?
2. There is considerable quoting in this passage. Do you think Ott handles the quotations well? Try changing the direct quotations into indirect ones. Which do you prefer? Why?
3. Note Ott's use of the colon to signal a formal list. Is there another way she could have framed the sentence? Why is Ott's version of the sentence effective? What makes it work?
4. What other features make this passage an effective description of Gale?

In this next passage, student writer Sara Ubelhor gives advice for working at a fast-food establishment.

> Working as a cashier, you will have to deal face-to-face with customers. No matter how grumpy customers look, always greet them politely with a smile. Your smiling not only pleases your boss, but your smile may just cheer up the customer who is simply having a bad day. If you are friendly, you may even have some interesting conversations with total strangers. If, however, you are being treated rudely by a customer, you can use subtle methods to get even—methods that will not get you fired. For example, do not go out of your way to offer the crabby customer cream or sugar for coffee as you ordinarily would. Or if a customer unpleasantly demands ketchup instead of asking for it politely, give that person only one or two packets so that returning for more will be necessary. These strategies may sound juvenile, but they provide an important psychological function by reducing your feelings of resentment and frustration.

CONSIDER . . .

1. What is the effect of Ubelhor's writing this in the second person *(you)?* If she had written this piece entirely in third person, how would it sound different?
2. What word signals that Ubelhor is shifting the emphasis of her paragraph to include negative features of being a cashier in a fast-food restaurant?
3. What key word is repeated and referred to several times in this passage?
4. Ubelhor uses passive voice when she writes *if you are being treated rudely.* Why do you think she chose a passive rather than an active verb in this instance?

In this passage, Vic Lasic nears the conclusion of an essay about getting lost. He is writing about how to keep yourself from getting lost and about the need to attend to road signs.

> Even if you know these survival skills, you should still pay close attention to road signs. Road signs contain much information that you have been approximating by using

basic survival skills. Highway identification signs remind you which direction you are headed. The number of the highway even gives you an idea of your direction: Odd-numbered highways run north to south; even-numbered highways run east to west. Three-digit interstate highway numbers mean city bypasses. Some signs tell you the distance to nearby cities. Many signs tell you the correct lanes for exiting to a specific destination. Mileage markers appearing every mile on interstate highways tell you how far the state border is. General information signs tell you of gas stations, places to get food or lodging, and rest areas that are just ahead. Billboards can also inform you of the locations of gasoline stations, restaurants, hotels, or just about anything else, including tourist attractions. Always use road signs to gain as much information about your whereabouts as you can.

CONSIDER . . .

1. Explain how Lasic relates to previous knowledge as he begins this paragraph. What words allude to the material that has gone before?
2. Find the sentence where Lasic uses a colon to split the sentence. Do you consider this an effective stylistic device? Can you think of another way to write the sentence effectively?
3. Lasic uses the verb phrase *tell you* several times. Can you think of an effective substitute? Or do you think he should continue to use the repetition when he revises?
4. Can you find an example of balance and parallelism? Of conscious repetition?

A WRITERS' GROUP PROJECT ON STYLE

Working with the members of your writers' group, read the following paragraph carefully. Then choose one of your paragraphs, preferably a passage of explanation, and read it carefully too. Then compare McPhee's passage with yours by filling in brief responses in the chart that follows. See what you can learn about style—yours and McPhee's.

From "A Textbook Place for Bears"

JOHN MCPHEE

When black bears are ready to den, they sometimes just lie down. They pull a few leaves over themselves, some twigs. They make nests. Others use rock cavities, hollow logs, spaces under fallen trees—or woodchuck holes, renovated expansively. Except in Arctic situations bears have no need to consider weather. Their fur is heavy, and the fat within can be as thick as a mattress. If snow falls on them, it melts. If enough snow falls on them, it forms a cave. Their respiration may go down to five breaths every two minutes, while their heartbeats become commensurately slow, but they do not turn cold, like hibernating chipmunks. There is a difference in ratio of surface to volume. Bears' temperatures drop only ten percent. Once or twice a day, their pulses quicken, multiply—hearts pounding—and the bears come up out of deep sleep into almost sudden consciousness. They just lie there for a time, awake, and then drift again to sleep. They eat nothing for half a year. At the end of winter, they still have at least two-thirds of their fat—to live on in the spare months of spring. Some bears will den almost anywhere. In Pennsylvania, dens have been found beside highways and within twenty-five feet of occupied houses, the owners ignorant that the bears were there.

Looking at Style

	McPhee's Paragraph	Your Paragraph
1. How many total words in this paragraph? Estimate by counting a representative line.		
2. How many sentences?		
3. How many words in the longest sentence?		
4. How many words in the shortest sentence?		
5. What is the length of the average sentence?		
6. List topics or clusters of related images or repeated words.		
7. How many sentences have introductory words, phrases, or clauses?		
8. How many sentences begin with expletives?		
9. How many sentences have interrupting elements?		

Sometimes seeing your style in comparison to someone else's helps you define what makes your style distinctive. Take time now to write a three-sentence reflection describing your insights into your style. When you finish, compare your reflection to those of other writers in your writers' group.

This chapter has presented a few ideas for improving your personal style. Working on style is a lifelong endeavor for a writer, though. Now is a good time to begin!

10 Assembling a Portfolio

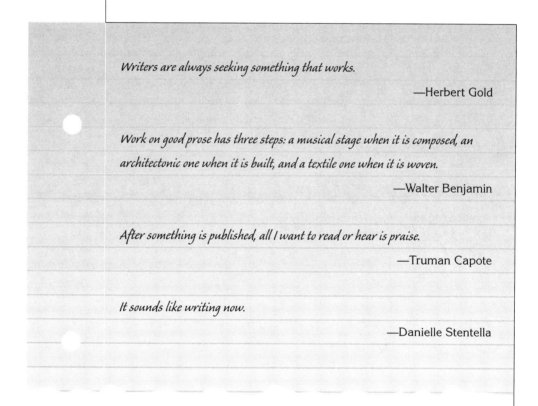

Writers are always seeking something that works.

—Herbert Gold

Work on good prose has three steps: a musical stage when it is composed, an architectonic one when it is built, and a textile one when it is woven.

—Walter Benjamin

After something is published, all I want to read or hear is praise.

—Truman Capote

It sounds like writing now.

—Danielle Stentella

Sooner or later comes that moment of truth when you want to stop revising your pieces of writing and assemble them in a collection for publication or evaluation. When that time comes, you should know

- what you believe to be your soundest and weakest pieces;
- what you consider to be your strengths as a writer—and your weaknesses as well;
- exactly what you are required to put in your portfolio;

- what you may add to your portfolio (optional items); and
- whether there are physical requirements for submitting the portfolio (does it have to be in a certain kind of folder, or do the contents have to be arranged in a particular order?).

These components may vary considerably, depending on what kind of portfolio you are preparing, why you are preparing it, and who is reading it. If you are assembling a portfolio to fulfill a requirement for admission to an honors program (an entrance portfolio) or one to demonstrate that you have acquired skills to leave a program (an exit portfolio), you will choose different specific items and arrange them differently and write about them differently in your reflections. If you are preparing a portfolio to qualify for a job interview, you will likely make different choices than if your portfolio is to be used to demonstrate your qualifications for promotion. Regardless of the kind of portfolio you are preparing, you must review or refresh your memory of portfolio requirements. Read the documentation from your instructor, advisor, or boss, or confer with that person. It is important to know not only what you are required to do but how much leeway you have, for it is often in that extra space or freedom that you may find a way to make your portfolio personal and distinctive. First, though, do what is required.

MANAGING PORTFOLIO REQUIREMENTS

Most portfolio requirements include, besides the writing itself, some kind of *metawriting*, or writing about the writing. Becoming conscious of how and why you make writing decisions is one important outcome of portfolio preparation. This consciousness of self comes from your *selection* of pieces for the portfolio and then from your *reflection* on the writing of these pieces.

Selecting Pieces for Your Portfolio

By now you probably have a feel for what is your best writing. You probably have some favorite essays among those you have written. This predisposition toward certain essays may not, however, be to your advantage; it may cloud the selection process. So, as you choose your essays, try to balance your affection for a piece or its topic with an awareness of its potential effect on your portfolio. How should you choose what to put in your portfolio? First, include what your instructor requires. Insert what you think will show a range of your writing abilities. Put in different kinds of pieces: maybe a narrative or expressive essay, an essay explaining how to do something or how something is done, perhaps a comparison, an interview, an analytic piece, an essay that reviews or evaluates, an opinion piece or an excerpt from your writer's notebook, a summary. Show the breadth of your thinking and writing skills.

Also, consider including work on a variety of topics—unless, of course, you have a topical theme uniting the essays in your portfolio. It is possible to write all your essays on the same broad topic but to explore different aspects of that topic. Your portfolio could be built around the theme of baseball, for instance, and could include a memoir about a particular baseball game in which you made a stupendous error; an advisory essay about how to improve one's batting average; a comparison essay exploring qualities of the world series teams from last year; an explanation of why the original Washington Senators (the Senators of Clark Griffith and Walter Johnson) left Washington, D.C., to become the Minnesota Twins; an analysis of the effect of the designated hitter rule; a survey of how many students in your dorm are baseball fans (and of what teams); an interview with a local baseball hero or coach—and so on.

Another aspect of your choice might be the quality of writing in individual essays. Typically, you'll put your best work in your portfolio, for your course evaluation and grade or possibly your graduation or application to a program may be at stake. You will probably know which work is your best; but if you are having difficulty deciding, ask the advice of your peer group or your instructor. You might also, however, think about including a piece (or pieces) of writing that did not turn out as well as you hoped. If you write a thorough analysis of your effort, you may reveal how much you have grown as a writer; this may be eloquent testimony to your achievement.

Computer Writing Tip: If you are formatting your pieces on the computer, you'll have to consider fonts. *Sans serif* (without the curving edges on the letters) fonts like Helvetica and Geneva are neat and make your text look precise. But many readers find *serif* fonts (Times, for example) easier to read. Whatever you choose, don't mix more than two fonts in one document or three in the entire portfolio. If you include artwork, photographs, or color or graphics, do so sparingly. The point of the portfolio is to showcase your writing, so don't obscure it by drawing attention to the art rather than the writing.

Formatting the Portfolio

Once you select essays for your portfolio, format each piece exactly as you are required to, keeping in mind that the portfolio as a whole makes a statement and thus needs to speak with one voice. That is, you should be consistent with regard to major issues of formatting within the portfolio. If you type one essay, type them all. If you use one-inch margins in one piece, use those margins in all essays. Most instructors require that your drafts be typed, but even if typed pieces are not mandated, consider typing them anyway. Your writing will seem more professional if it is typed, and it will also be more readable. If margin widths are not specified, use standard margins of one inch all around; or you can make the left margin one and a half inches—just be consistent. Number pages in the entire portfolio rather than numbering individual pieces separately.

Considering an Electronic Portfolio

You may want (or even be required) to submit an electronic portfolio—that is, one entirely in a computer file on disk (no paper involved). Although your writing will probably not be significantly different in an electronic portfolio, your presentation will definitely not be the same. With an electronic portfolio, you have to think about distinctive aspects of the presentation. Specifically, the needs of your audience leap to the foreground. If you prepare an electronic portfolio, ask yourself these questions:

- **Can my reader actually read my portfolio?** If you are working in a Macintosh environment and your reader has access only to a PC, your portfolio is not readable. Be sure that you and your reader(s) are working within the same platform (PC or Mac) or in the same environment. This also means ensuring that your word-processing programs are identical or that the file translators preserve formatting of your text. Sometimes a file created in WordPerfect does not, for instance, retain all its fine features when it is translated and read in Word—and vice versa. Spacing, line height, tabs, margins, and fonts may all be affected during translation. Be careful with using exotic fonts; remember that your reader's computer must have those fonts too, or the effect will simply not be the same. The computer reading the file may try to duplicate the unknown font in a less attractive bit-mapped font or may simply read the file in a fairly common font like Times or Helvetica.

  If you exchange portfolios via e-mail over the Internet, you also have to consider the encryption and compression that happens when you attach e-mail files. Talk to a computer consultant at your college about encoding and decoding attached files.

- **Is my portfolio displayed to best advantage?** A computer screen typically does not display an entire page of text, so the whole-page effect of your formatting will be diminished. Consider what will make your pages readable. Helpful are decent margins—so there is ample white space; a readable font—so the reader does not have to squint to make out the words; double-spacing—so the lines don't run together; and appropriate emphatic devices (bolding, italics, underscoring, bullets, indentation), used sparingly and when necessary to emphasize certain concepts or to determine hierarchies in the text (such as lists).

- **Do I take advantage of computer options and features?** To make navigating the portfolio simpler, you will probably want to put discrete items in separate files, but make this decision according to the number of separate elements in your portfolio and its overall length. Vital to your electronic portfolio is a table of contents linked to filenames, sections in the portfolio, or pages in the portfolio and designating the order in which files or sections should be read. Filenames must match or clearly evoke items in the table of contents. If you work in a PC environment, you must have quite succinct filenames; Mac users have more leeway.

Many people have difficulty detecting on-screen errors; to ensure that your portfolio is a clean copy, you might print a hard copy of the entire portfolio while you are editing. To be safe, edit *at least* twice—and make sure you edit at least once on a paper copy. Find errors on the hard copy and make corrections in the files.

Don't forget to label the physical disk that you pass to your reader and to make two backup copies, which you should store in separate locations. If you use a zip drive or if you stuff or compress your portfolio files, be sure that your reader(s) can unzip, unstuff, or otherwise open your files.

If you have a Macintosh, consider presenting the portfolio as a Hypercard stack. Hypercard would configure your portfolio like a huge stack of linked cards, each of which contains a chunk of the portfolio. Your reader could then easily access any essay file from the open table of contents card or any reflection or ancillary piece from an essay card.

And do avail yourself of features like borders, fonts, columns, charts, graphics, and notes—provided your reader's options are compatible. You can even scan in appropriate photos, illustrations, and sound. It might be possible, for instance, for your reader to click a button on an essay and hear your reflective comments. A warning, though: Headers and footers typically don't show on screen (they typically appear only when printed). Use footnotes in a research essay instead of endnotes; scrolling to the end of the essay to read endnotes could annoy the reader. Avoiding conflict with your reader can be simple if you ask yourself, "What is the effect of this textual innovation on my reader? What can possibly go wrong?" and then plan for problems not to happen.

PREPARING METAWRITING

The metawriting is the infrastructure of your portfolio; it reflects, surrounds, and informs your essays. From the metawriting your reader can tell a lot about the writing in the portfolio, so a careful and thorough job with the metawriting will be important to your evaluation. The metawriting shows how thoroughly you understand your writing processes and how thoughtful you are about your writing products. It is very important in demonstrating what and how much you have learned. In this chapter you will find several examples of different forms metawriting may take. They are here as a menu, from which you can pick and choose at will, but you should add individual touches to whatever you include—and you should not skimp on the reflection and metawriting.

Reflecting on Your Writing

You can probably think of several ways to include written reflection within your portfolio. One way is to write an introduction to the entire portfolio: an overview, preface, letter, memo, or formal essay that looks at where you have been and what you have accomplished as a writer during a specified time, perhaps during a course. You may also reflect on your portfolio with a dialogue, poem, or story; some writers like to use these forms to make the reflection piece markedly different from most of the portfolio itself—and to demonstrate their versatility as writers. Regardless of form, the reflective piece often tries to tease out some theme or common strand from the accumulation of work in the portfolio. It frequently comments on each essay, justifying the piece's inclusion or emphasizing its point or illuminating its inception. The reflective piece may present your feelings about particular pieces of writing; it may also present insights into your self, your writing habits, and your strengths and weaknesses as a writer. Here are some questions to consider as you plan the reflective piece (regardless of the form you choose):

- How have I changed as a writer during the time of preparing this portfolio? Has my attitude about writing changed? If so, in what particular ways? Have my writing habits changed? Has my style altered or broadened?
- What have I learned about the act of writing and about myself as a writer? How did I learn this? Is this understanding reflected in any specific places in this portfolio to which I can direct my reader?

■ What piece of writing here is my favorite or my best? Which was the easiest to write? Which gave me the most trouble, and how did I solve the writing problems presented by this essay?

■ What does my reader need to know about each essay in my portfolio? What might my reader like to know about each essay? What have I learned from working on each piece? What special circumstances informed the inception and production of each piece of work?

You may prefer to make your major reflective piece fairly general. If you write a general reflection, you may then choose to write shorter reflections (a few paragraphs, perhaps) to accompany each piece featured in the portfolio. Your writing notebook may be particularly helpful as you reconsider and review what you have thought and written. If you have electronic mail or if you belong to an electronic study group (ESG), you may also capture and print some of your conversations containing comments about writing.

Computer Writing Tip: If you are writing individual reflective pieces to accompany essays, you might format the reflection in bold or italic type of the same font—to link the pieces but simultaneously suggest their different purposes.

Now look at Frank Schefano's major reflective piece, composed as a letter.

1130 River Road NE, Apt 4B
Tuscaloosa, Alabama 35404
December 6, 19——

Dr. C. Beth Burch
Department of Curriculum and Instruction
University of Alabama
Tuscaloosa, Alabama 35487

Dear Dr. Burch:

There was a point in the semester when I approached you because I felt my writing was suffering, perhaps from burnout. You advised me to lay aside my writing completely for one week and maybe this would help. I took the advice, but the next week when I resumed writing I still had difficulty making things work. I felt as if I were forcing words to make an essay fit together. It was at this point I realized something completely new about my writing. I found that I cannot write well when pressured to do so. With this in mind I set out to write future papers as if they were not going to be graded in a class but rather something I was doing for enjoyment. My writing has improved, and I thank you for the role you played in helping me to realize this.

The first essay I chose for the portfolio is the "Writing on Writing" essay. In this essay I was glad to finally put my writing process into words. I believe my style may have changed during the semester, but not very much. Writing this essay was weird, just as it is weird whenever you come to the full realization of anything about yourself. I am just happy that in this case reality was not too shocking.

I put the problem/solution essay in the portfolio because I feel that it addresses a problem that is becoming increasingly dominant in our society. Also, I have personal knowledge about the effects of stress because it adversely affects my diabetes. Every day I do battle with stress, and I am glad to say I'm still winning! I believe that stress is one of the biggest problems in our society, and I wanted to give a little advice on how to cope with it. As a result I believe I have become a more organized person. For the past few years it has been a dream of mine to publish a book on how to deal with stress for people with diabetes. I hope this writing experience was a good start toward fulfilling that dream.

My favorite essay to write was the information essay. I have been building remote control models for thirteen years, so writing this essay was easy; and it was a lot of fun. I only wish that my word processor would format essays into columns like a magazine article, because I wrote this essay as if it was going to be published in a remote control model magazine. In the back of my mind I have a dream to publish this essay, and maybe that dream will come true.

As I wrote in the "Writing on Writing" essay, I like to change things every once in a while. I found myself doing this in the review I wrote of Tom Clancy's novel *The Sum of All Fears.* When I looked at some reviews done by other students, I noticed two things. Some students never indented paragraphs and used single spacing. And one student did indent paragraphs and use double spacing, but he broke up the paragraphs by adding an extra line of spacing between them. I was feeling like an adventurous journalist while writing this essay, so I decided to try something new. I single-spaced and indented the paragraphs and I also added an extra line of spacing between paragraphs; sort of a combination between the two formats mentioned above. Also, I decided to include a small paragraph outlining some of Tom Clancy's credentials for two reasons: First, to make the die-hard Clancy fan drool at the mouth, and second, to further interest anyone who has never read a Clancy novel (truly a miserable person I am sure, ha! ha!). My review of Clancy's novel may sound biased, but you cannot expect anything more from a true Clancy follower. He is my favorite author, and I was delighted to finally review one of his novels.

Many hours of work have been put into compiling this portfolio. I must admit that not all the hours were enjoyable, but the result is that I have had fun and I believe my writing style has improved. Although major aspects of my writing have not changed, I feel the portfolio experience has taught me to refine details that would make my writing easier for someone else to read. I have realized that even if my writing makes sense to me, it may confuse others. Being given the time to revise my essays, I have corrected mistakes and hope this will make my writing more readable to others. This is the first class I have ever taken that uses the portfolio format and I loved it. The pressure of deadlines is eliminated, which allows students to relax and truly develop their writing skills. Each time I revised an essay I became more comfortable with my writing style, and I will take this confidence with me throughout life.

As I worked on the essays this semester I noticed my tone assuming that of a journalist—very straightforward and "to the point." As a result, I often imagined that I was a journalist writing for some magazine or newspaper—hence, the name of my portfolio. This fantasizing really added a lot of fun to the semester and made me feel like a kid again.

May this portfolio be as fun to read as it was to write.

Sincerely,

Frank Schefano III

Frank Schefano III

If you write the reflective piece as a letter, format it correctly. The simplest business-letter form places all major letter parts flush left. It contains a return address segment (street address; town, state, and zip code; date); inside address (name and title of addressee; street address; town, state, and zip code); salutation followed by a colon; body of letter; and complimentary closing. Attend to the proper spacing, too. Allow four lines between the return address and the inside address, two lines between the inside address and the salutation, two lines between the salutation and body of the letter, two lines between the body of the letter and the complimentary closing, and four lines between the complimentary closing and the signature line. *Don't forget to sign your name.*

CONSIDER . . .

1. What kinds of matters regarding his writing does Schefano address?
2. What seems to be Schefano's attitude toward the reader? How would you describe the tone of the piece?
3. Describe Schefano's strategy for addressing individual essays.

Compare now Dee Hughes's preface to her portfolio with Schefano's. Think about how each writer imagines and discusses the portfolio.

Preface

To: Dr. Burch
From: Dee Hughes
Date: December 7, 19———
Subject: Portfolio Introduction

In the preface to *The Prince of Tides,* Pat Conroy wrote, "My wound is geography. It is also my anchorage, my port of call." I think that the papers included in this portfolio reflect my upbringing in the South: my roots in the land, the traditions and the culture. The selections also embody the influence of great people. You can escape many things but you can't deny your roots or the influence of your past on the present.

The first paper in the portfolio, "The Green Snake Fire," recalls a childhood experience that left permanent mental scars on the landscape of my subconscious. When I was developing the essay, I called my mother to get her input. Ironically, she didn't remember the event as well as I did. She did recall using two bottles of Calamine lotion after that vacation, as well as my nightmares, my strategies to fireproof our house, and my intense discomfort when we watched "The Towering Inferno" on television. I didn't receive much help from her in the form of specific details, so in some parts of the paper I had to extrapolate from what I remember about other periods of my childhood. For example, I vividly picture the dolls mentioned in the essay, even now; however, I really don't know if Debbie (the doll) accompanied us to the lake, though I imagine she did.

The primary reason I wrote "The Green Snake Fire" is because of my fascination with psychological imbalances. My sister is a year younger than me, but she can't even recall the vacation, much less the fire. I have always wondered why it affected me and not her.

Before I started the memoir, I wrote another paper about my first date. I discarded that idea after about five drafts. Then I worked on "The Green Snake Fire" from about three different angles. In the first one I used two pages to describe the car ride to Gulf Shores because one of the things I remember most about childhood is travelling with my parents to different locations. I mention this to illustrate the recurring problem that I have with finding a narrow focus for a paper. In fact, with the exception of my difficulty in manipulating verb tenses, I think that finding an appropriate focus was the most difficult part of writing this essay. I also discovered that the topic might bore some readers, as my sister revealed. She also suggested that the idea of a green snake was a little strange, but then, she doesn't remember it.

After I reread the rough draft that I turned in to you, I realized that it was more caricature than characterization. Most of the paragraphs just sketched the events. I didn't notice that when I wrote the first several drafts, because it seemed so clear to me. Your comments helped me to focus on the areas where I did not make myself clear.

In general, I find it difficult to write about myself in an honest way because I always have contradictory feelings on every subject. I'm proud of this essay because I did manage to focus on my own perception of the event rather than relying on the memories of others. Also, after spending many of my formative years writing in the third person, it was difficult to use the word "I." It feels like you are actually taking responsibility for the words you put on paper, which I guess you are.

In contrast, most of the advisory essay proved relatively easy to pen. I used the essay to give advice about preparing a tomato sauce. I spent a lot of time this summer trying out various cookbooks, so it seemed fitting that I use my newly found knowledge in a paper.

Strangely enough, I had a problem finding a focus for this paper. I wanted to segue in and out of the process of cooking, discussing my relationship with my grandmother in the external sections. Draft followed draft and I could not get that structure to work. I couldn't achieve coherence or continuity. I could envision the final product but I couldn't put the words on paper.

The next essay to appear in the portfolio is a review of *The Prince of Tides.* Having read everything Pat Conroy has ever written, having seen every movie based on his books, I felt that I could knowledgeably record my thoughts about the movie as compared to the book. My primary obstacle involved my lack of knowledge about the art of making movies. However, even a novice could see that the heart of the book didn't make it to the screen. *The Prince of Tides* was a fun paper to write, though, which I guess means I enjoyed doing the research for it.

My final essay, "The Salt of the Earth," profiles a dear friend and onetime boyfriend from my home town. Trying to capture the essence of his personality on paper proved to be an impossible task. What an enjoyable trip down memory lane, though. I think you summarized my inspiration for writing this kind of paper best when you suggested that once someone hits a milestone in his or her life, he or she takes time to reflect on the past. In anticipation of graduation I have found myself doing that a lot recently.

I probably spent the most time on this paper. I am the least satisfied with it. I changed the structure so many times that the drafts read like my high school diary. When you have known someone for a lifetime, it's hard to pinpoint those characteristics that most define the person. For example, Timmy possesses a genuinely original and hilarious sense of humor but it was hard to convey that without specific lines of dialogue. I can see that I will have to return to this paper again in the future.

In conclusion, I think the papers in this portfolio reflect my roots in the garden of the South. Each essay discusses a particular event or person that had an impact on me in my youth. I know that in the future I will cherish this collection for the memories it records.

And here is Tara LeMaistre's preface to her portfolio. As you read it, consider the similarities in all these major reflective pieces.

Preface

The four pieces that I have chosen to be in my portfolio are a memoir entitled "The Cold War of 1983," an analysis piece which is actually my personal essay for law school, an advisory piece on how to make albums, and finally two poems that I have written outside of Rhet. 142. All of the pieces I've selected to be a part of my portfolio are bonded by a common element of time. My memoir goes back in time, my analysis attempts to move forward in time, my advisory underlyingly freezes time, and my two poems are simply a reflection of time. I invite all readers to take a journey through my mind courtesy of my portfolio. Please, sit back and enjoy the ride.

My memoir was an easy piece to write, but after it was finished, it was hard to reflect on. When one takes a memory and transcribes it on paper, it is like forcing yourself to deal with all aspects of an incident that you purposely chose to forget. I could easily remember the facts of that miserable year when I was bullied, but when I had to actually conjure up the emotions that I was feeling during that time, I could not do it. When I read my memoir out loud in one of my other classes, that's when all the emotions rushed back to me. When I read the part about trying to commit suicide, I started crying uncontrollably. I guess I finally let out all the tears I was never allowed to cry.

I enjoyed writing the memoir because it made me realize that I had the power of reflection, not simple analysis and documentation. My memoir also revealed to me the power of detail. When I wrote about neon colors and my hair style during that period, it actually made me feel like I was transported back to that time.

My analysis piece was the most difficult piece I have ever written. It is my personal essay for law school analyzing why I should be admitted. I now realize that I write really well under no pressure and restrictions. This essay is required to be handed in by a certain date with a maximum of two pages. So what does my mind do? It purposely can't function until the day before it is due. I would like the reader to note that the personal essay included in my portfolio is not a final draft.

It took a long time for me to figure out what I can advise a person to do. Honestly, I know how to complete a lot of creative projects, but I just thought that making an album would be an easy one to do. This essay would probably be seen in *Better Homes and*

Gardens. It is written for someone who has some type of experience with working with their hands and knows what a glue gun is. Mentioning the album that I made for my mother made the essay take on the persona of an album. You could almost picture on the page a photograph of my mother crying when she finally sees her album. This detail included in the essay makes the piece more special to me.

I thought it was important to include some poetry in my portfolio because it illustrates that I don't just have ability to write prose. I also wanted to include my poetry because my process for writing poetry is totally different from an essay-form paper. What I do is talk into a tape recorder and just say the first thing that comes to my mind. My lines, unlike prose, are very natural and relaxed. I haven't run them through the mill a thousand times. They are my pure thoughts.

I've been thinking about my grandmother lately, so I just wanted to pay a tribute to her by writing a poem for her. My last poem, entitled "To Write a Poem," is about being forced to write when there just isn't any emotion left inside of you. Writing is a very emotional process which takes a lot out of me, and when it is forced it becomes very superficial.

I hope that after having read my portfolio, the reader can gain insight as to what kind of person I am. My writing is like a window to my soul. The beauty of writing is that if you don't like what you see you can easily shut the window.

Tara LeMaistre

CONSIDER . . .

1. What elements in common do these reflections by Schefano, Hughes, and LeMaistre have?
2. What does Hughes's preface do that seems markedly different from Schefano's?
3. Hughes uses a memo form but writes *Preface* at the top center of the page. Suggest how she might revise to eliminate this confusion of form.
4. Explain how Hughes formatted the memo, especially the heading.
5. What have you learned from reading these essays about reflecting on your writing?

Acknowledging Help

To acknowledge those who help you produce your best work is the duty of a writer/scholar. Few of us work in a vacuum. We are surrounded by words and ideas, by information and conversation; we get inspiration from our environments. And we get help in actually producing our work, too. Maybe someone helps us do research in the library or someone allows us to interview him or her. Maybe there are people to whom we tell our ideas and with whom we explore them: roommates, parents, friends, spouses. Maybe some people have read our work and responded honestly to it, offering encouragement and advice. Maybe someone has given us instruction or a splendid example.

All these kindnesses may have factored into our writing—and we ought to acknowledge them, to keep the wheels of courtesy turning.

Here is a collection of acknowledgments, in varying levels of detail and explanation. Read them to see how other writers express this debt—and lend a personal note to their writing as well. First are two professional examples. Patricia Limerick acknowledges those who helped her with her history of the American West, *The Legacy of Conquest*, and Barry Lopez thanks the folks who helped him with his book about wolves, *Of Wolves and Men*.

Acknowledgments

PATRICIA NELSON LIMERICK

I got the idea for this book on June 30, 1981, at a conference in Idaho called "The American West: Colonies in Revolt." During that first day of the conference, government and business officials complained about the current problems of the West, and the prevalent presumption seemed to be that these problems were quite recent in origin and bore little relation to the distant frontier West. I am grateful to Jeanette Germain for initiating the process that brought me to Idaho and to William K. Everson, William Goetzmann, Peter Hassrick, Bruce Johnson, Bud Johns, Annick Smith, and, especially, Alvin Josephy, Richard Harte, and Bob Waite for organizing the event. Those Sun Valley conferences were one of the best things going in Western affairs; I deeply regret their disappearance.

At that conference, after listening to the first day's speakers, I said in my own speech that the West needed someone comparable to C. Vann Woodward to write *The Burden of Western History*. The fact is that there is no one comparable to C. Vann Woodward. But Woodward's example and his encouragement early in the project made the difference between a vision that might have vanished and one that stayed and brought forth at least limited results.

My adviser, Howard Roberts Lamar, not only read the manuscript but made it possible. When I left California for graduate school at Yale, I had no particular interest in the history of my home region. It was about the luckiest thing that ever happened to me: to have Howard Lamar show me what I had missed in my first twenty-one years in the West. As an adviser, Lamar is nearly unrivaled in academic circles for his kindness, good humor, and enthusiasm for widely varying approaches to history. The sound parts of this book are a tribute to his guidance; any tenuous sections are a credit to his tolerance.

Harvard University and the Charles Warren Center gave me a full year of leave in 1983–84. That year gave me not only essential working time but working and thinking conditions as close to heaven as I expect to get. Any time I wanted to test an idea, I had only to step outside my office to see who was around. With Bernard Bailyn, Barbara DeWolfe, Pat Denault, Jon Roberts, Drew McCoy, Don Bellomy, Alan Brinkley, and Helena Wall at hand, the intellectual equivalent of a brisk physical workout was always available. That none of these people found enormous significance in the American West only added to the value of their company, reminding me of what I most hope for in the way of reader response: not agreement, but spirited discussion.

In 1981, James Thomson, Jr., introduced me to his Nieman program at Harvard and transformed a minor interest in journalism and current events into a passion. I am grateful as well to John Seigenthaler and Sid Hurlburt of *USA Today* for allowing me to move from consumer to occasional producer in journalistic matters, for reacquainting me with brevity, and for providing the income supplement that allowed me to stay a jump ahead of library acquisitions.

From the start of this project, Ed Barber and Steve Forman of Norton have been committed and responsive editors. Ed Barber's significance escalated in July of 1984, when I moved to Boulder and we agreed it was time for him to put the pressure on, if this book was to be finished in our lifetimes. He is, the next two years proved, unrelentingly a man of his word. Relieved of the obligation to remind me of deadlines, Steve Forman was an ideal coach, kind and critical without contradiction. I am grateful, as well, to Otto Sonntag for his scrupulous attention to the manuscript.

Alfonso Ortiz, John Echohawk, Roger Echohawk, Karen Easton, and George Phillips helped me by reading chapter 6; Bill Taylor, S.L. Cline, and George Sanchez, by reading chapter 7. Chris Miller, Helena Wall, and Alan Brinkley counseled me on various parts of the text. Peter Decker, Richard White, William Cronon, and Jim O'Brien read nearly the whole manuscript and responded with comments in many ways more interesting than the text they read. Near the end of the project, Ruth Friedman stepped in as proofreader and general manuscript reviewer; her sharpness of eye and vigor of mind came at exactly the right time, when these properties in the author were a bit worn down.

Over the years, I have had the help of a number of talented undergraduates: Yvette Huginnie, Joe Bowen, Paul Fisher, Allison Brown, Gail Bash Butler, Eve Baldwin, Jim Baker, Richard DiNucci, Ann Skartvedt, Dayna Bateman, and Tom Patterson. These people were not only fine research assistants but also great conversationalists and promising scholars (and lawyers, novelists, and banjo players) in their own right.

The Department of History of the University of Colorado at Boulder has a great office staff. Pat Murphy, Sandy Marsh, Veta Hartman, and Rosella Chavez helped ride herd on the manuscript and were my pals during an unsettling two years of falling behind deadlines in a new location. Pat Murphy was nothing short of heroic in her mastery of high technology that still frightens me, in her capacity to follow tangled instructions to add, delete, or transfer, and in her unbroken good humor and enthusiasm for the project. If I had written the words as well as she managed them, this would be an extraordinary book.

For help in finding illustrations, I am indebted to Eleanor Gehres, Augie Mastrogiuseppi, and Kathey Swan of the Western History Collection, Denver Public Library, Jim Lavender-Teliha and Eric Paddock of the Colorado Historical Society, and Stephanie Edwards of the Oregon Historical Society.

Some readers may see my point of view as the product of a 1960s sensibility, formed in the years of student protest. That presumption targets the wrong decade. I have had the happy intergenerational experience of being in complete political agreement with my parents. My sensibility is thus shaped by the 1930s as well as the 1960s; I suspect my point of view is closer to Eleanor Roosevelt's than to Angela Davis's. My parents provided not only the political perspective of this book but also much of the method. As masters of the anecdote drawn from real life, Grant and Patricia Nelson gave me early training both in story selecting and in storytelling; anyone who cares to see how far the apprentice falls short has only to attend an anecdote session with the masters. I would like, also, to take this occasion to acknowledge my good luck in teachers. In high school and college, Lewis Robinson, Robert Bowser, Mike Rose, Laurence Veysey, Michael Cowan, John Dizikes, Jasper Rose, and Page Smith led me to history and to writing; this book is in many ways the outcome of their teaching.

Working on this book has been consuming. I owe a number of apologies to people—especially correspondents—who found me divided in attention over the last few years. My colleagues Fred Anderson, Virginia Anderson, Steve Epstein, Jack Main, and Gloria Main went beyond tolerating the obsession, to accepting and even encouraging it, and thus helped keep me sane.

Though offered the role of quietly self-sacrificing spouse, Jeff Limerick preferred to exercise his customary rights of free speech. Heaven knows, he can talk about history a lot better than I can talk about architecture, and with many hours of conversation about Western affairs, he more than earned his place on the dedication page.

By the nature of this book, I am most in debt to people I have never met—to historians and journalists whose words I have followed closely, but whose faces I have never seen. In the tradition of Western resource exploitation, I have profited greatly from the labor of others. "Thank you" is a mild and inadequate expression for the hard work that produced the material I rely on here.

Life in Boulder, Colorado, at the foot of the Flatirons, reminds you daily that the West is *here* and not "out there." Meanwhile, the interesting weather that blows over those mountains reminds you that the "conquest of nature" remains a bit incomplete. Although I am in no conventional sense an outdoorsperson, I appreciate the reminders.

Boulder, Colorado
November 24, 1986

Acknowledgments

BARRY HOLSTUN LOPEZ

Many people were generous with their time, in interviews and correspondence, and generous with a bed and a meal when the situation arose. I would particularly like to thank Robert Stephenson of Fairbanks, Alaska, with whom I had the pleasure of weeks in the field, and Dave Mech, with whom I stayed in Minnesota and who directed me to a number of valuable people.

I am deeply indebted to the Nunamiut hunters of Anaktuvuk Pass, Alaska, for their ideas; to John Fentress, Department of Psychology, Dalhousie University, Nova

Scotia, for his early encouragement in this project; and to Joseph Brown, Department of Religious Studies, University of Montana, for his direction and encouragement. To Pat Reynolds of the Naval Arctic Research Laboratory, Barrow, Alaska; Dick Coles of the Tyson Research Center, Saint Louis; and the staff of the wolf research facility, Shubenacadie, Nova Scotia, for their hospitality. And to Dale Bush, D.V.M., for his assistance.

The task of research was eased by various librarians and by the staffs of several state historical societies. I would particularly like to thank the interlibrary loan staff at the University of Oregon, Eugene; Minnie Paugh, special collections librarian at Montana State University; the staff of the Montana Historical Society, Helena; the staff of the South Dakota Historical Society, Pierre; and Marylyn Skaudis of Parkville, Minnesota.

Portions of the manuscript were critically reviewed Robert Stephenson, Joseph Brown, and Roger Peters, and I am grateful for their insights.

Some of the ideas here first took shape in conversations with various people. In addition to those already named I would like to thank Dick Showalter, Jenny Ryon, Glynn Riley, Heather Parr, Tim Roper, Sandra Gray, and the late Dave Wallace.

Laurie Graham, my editor at Scribners, and Peter Schults, my agent, were deeply committed to the ideas here and I hope their insistence on clear and elegant expression is evident on these pages.

Sandy, my wife, read this manuscript in progress. Her insights and the range of her vision are remarkable, and I am indebted.

CONSIDER . . .

1. How do both Limerick and Lopez make their work personal through these acknowledgments?
2. How are these acknowledgments alike?
3. Name one way in which these acknowledgment pages differ.

Now examine the acknowledgments from several students' portfolios: acknowledgments by Frank Schefano, Dee Hughes, Jennifer Brackin, and John Sansone.

Acknowledgments

I would like to begin by thanking God for allowing me the faculties to think, write, learn and most of all to dream.

I would like to thank my girlfriend, Mary Dell Corbin, for constantly proofreading my essays and truthfully critiquing them, even when the truth hurt.

I want to thank Dee Hughes and Christy Aldrich, two classmates that honestly gave their opinions of my work during peer reviews.

Also, I want to thank my mother for always being a constant encouragement; without her help I would be nothing.

Finally, I want to thank the human race for just plain being themselves and giving me so many good ideas. I've learned a lot just by sitting back and taking it all in.

To these people I'm greatly indebted, and I share whatever success this portfolio meets with you.

F.S., at my desk

Acknowledgments

As I noted in the preface, my roots and the traditions, the culture, and the people who have shaped my consciousness account for a large part of this collection of essays. My existence began with my parents, two remarkable people. From them I have learned of humility, of the value of perseverance, of the importance of a close, loving family. To them I owe countless thanks and innumerable hugs.

To Leigh, my sister, my fiercest competitor, my dearest friend, I owe a lifetime of devotion and care. Without her insight many of my papers would have collapsed, structurally and logically.

And what can I say about Scott Moore? A thousand lifetimes of dedicated reciprocations would never fulfill my obligation to him. Though we disagree continually about my writing, he is inevitably correct. He sees so clearly those things that I fail to apprehend.

Without the constructive criticism of Frank and Christy, members and astute readers in my peer review group, my essays would have suffered. Additionally, I gained valuable insight into the art of writing by reading their essays.

Three instructors have provided immeasurable aid in constructing and revising my writing. They also instilled within me valuable writing skills and strategies. Dr. Beth Burch's talent as an editor is exceeded only by her gift as an innovative teacher. Everything that "works" about my essays I owe to her. Dr. Ann Henley inspired me to express my thoughts on paper. Her constructive (as opposed to destructive) criticism displayed the marks of a refined motivator, for which I shall always be grateful. Finally, Betty Loomis showed me that brevity means a clear and concise writing style, not lack of thought, and that there exists a limited time and place for passive verbs. God must cast a favorable eye on teachers. No other profession reaps such long-lasting benefits.

I owe my gratitude to the many authors whose books have provided me with pleasure. Once you attempt to write, you learn a profound respect for those who do it well.

Dee Hughes
December, 19——
The University of Alabama

Acknowledgments

There are many people who deserve recognition in this portfolio. My husband, Mark, read over a few drafts contained here, but not many. He has helped with this portfolio in capacities other than editing. He has been the inspiration for many ideas, a constant encourager, and a steadfast rock to lean on when things seemed to spin out of control.

My beautiful daughter, Ashley, was also a great inspiration. Not only an inspiration for stories and ideas, but an inspiration to try again, to keep going, and to be better each time.

Cheryl Walker and Andy Williams were most often my peer-group members. They're great encouragers and criticized not only honestly, but also helpfully. I value their advice and thank them wholeheartedly.

Jenny McWilliams and I shared two classes together this semester. We saw each other every day and most days we spoke to each other again on the phone. Jenny has helped me so much in every class. She has been a great listener, advisor, and empathizer. I am very grateful for all of these qualities in Jenny. I am most thankful for the special friend I have found in her.

Jennifer Brackin

Acknowledgments

I would like to thank the following people for their help and support:

Julie Sansone: My mother, who never let me get down while things were tough.

Barbra King: My English tutor of fourteen years in Tampa. She helped me with my revisions during spring break and has always been there for me.

Maria Castro: My girlfriend, who quietly listened to all of my complaining throughout the semester.

Jeff Gay: My roommate, who listened to each paper ten times to help me come up with ideas.

Sharon Creel: My typist, without whom I would have never had the project completed on time.

John Sansone

CONSIDER . . .

1. How are these acknowledgments different from one another? What kinds of things do you learn about the writers from these personal pages?
2. Compare these students' acknowledgments to those by published writers. Do you see differences in content, style, or level of confidence? Explain.

Adding Other Ingredients to the Portfolio

You may discover other useful items that will make your portfolio more interesting or easier to use. Some students include comments from peer readers/reviewers. Read and evaluate the following comments.

> "I enjoyed this story. Moments of it really brought back reflections of my own childhood. This story should be read by all those who have had a 'Dear Diary.' It is very inspirational."
>
> "Your aunt gave you some very sound advice. I especially liked the part about the three important things you must do when preparing for a blind date."
>
> "As a native of Philadelphia, I was very impressed by the descriptions used."
>
> "I had a hard time getting interested in this piece at first. Is there anything you can do to draw my attention early on in the essay—like maybe the first paragraph?"

What is the effect of adding these comments to a portfolio? Would you like to read fuller comments—or do you prefer brief ones? Do you think these comments are representative of what the peer reviewers said of the writers' work? Which comments do you think were most helpful? Why?

To complete your portfolio and round out the image of you as a writer that the portfolio conveys, you might also add

- illustrations or photographs
- graphs, charts, tables to accompany specific essays
- an index (at the end of the portfolio; the table of contents goes at its beginning)

To make your portfolio different from others' portfolios, you might also try any of these strategies:

- a graphic design as a motif throughout the portfolio
- the strategic use of color
- a theme made explicit through all the contents of the portfolio, as in Dee Hughes's portfolio emphasizing her Southern roots

Computer Writing Tip: Use the *Index* function on your word-processing program to generate an index for your portfolio. Be sure to read the documentation before you begin.

Lisa Liles called her portfolio *Heartstrings* and found a place in the titles of most of her essays for the word *heart*. She added a poem written by her mother, a quotation from Proverbs, and epigraphs from Mark Twain, one of her favorite writers. Dee Hughes named her portfolio *Southern Roots* because after she selected her essays she saw that in some way they all explored her sense of what it means to grow up in the South. She made this theme explicit in her introduction and acknowledgments. Pam Segal called her portfolio *The World at Waltz;* the name, which seemed to reflect her attitude toward her writing, came to her as she was assembling it. And Frank Schefano, who believed in his growth as a writer and for the first time in his life seriously entertained aspirations of writing professionally, titled his portfolio *The Journalist* (Figure 10.1). How can you make your portfolio special?

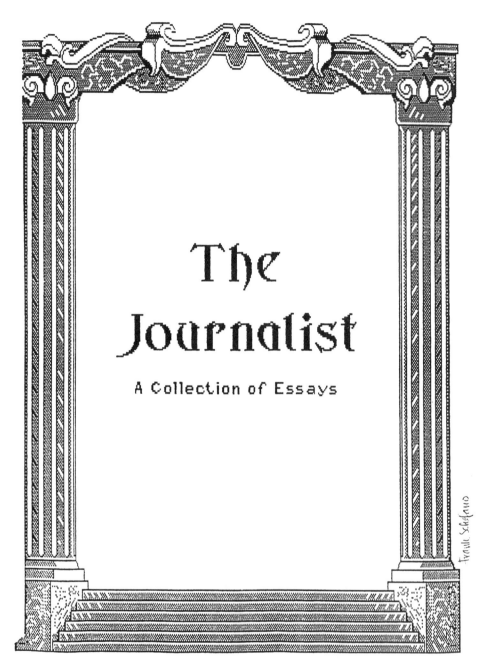

Figure 10.1   Title page from Frank Schefano's portfolio

Listing the Contents of Your Portfolio

Readers will find navigating your portfolio easier if you include a map—a table of contents—for them to follow. You should definitely include a table of contents, regardless of what other metawriting you create. Start by drafting a list of every piece you include in the portfolio. List pieces in the order that you plan to present them; use exact and full titles. Number prefatory pages, also called *front matter* (title page, dedication page [if any], table of contents, introduction or preface, acknowledgments) separately from the body of the portfolio, and use lowercase Roman numerals (i, ii, iii, iv, v, etc.); look at the pagination of this book for an example. Start numbering the body of the portfolio with Arabic numeral *1*. Use Arabic page numbers to number pages of the main text, including the reflective memo, essay, or letter; the essays themselves; explanatory notes; and the index, if you include one. Put drafts alongside essays or in a separate section of the notebook or folder. Some writers keep drafts in separate notebooks within a portfolio, or in separate sections of a portfolio. Others put drafts in a pocket page that follows the final version of an essay. Either way, you may number draft pages or not, as you think best.

Look at Frank Schefano's table of contents, a neatly arranged listing (Figure 10.2). Notice the dot leaders that carry the reader's eye from the listing to the page number. Compare Schefano's table of contents to Jennifer Brackin's (Figure 10.3). How does Brackin help her readers find their way through her portfolio? What does Brackin include that Schefano omits?

Table of Contents

Essays

    Writing on Writing

    "Here's the Way I See It"...1

    Problem/Solution Essay

    "Stress Can Keep a Good Man Down: A Little Advice on
    Coping with Stress" 4

    Information Essay

    "Tips on Preparing to Build a Model Airplane"...........................7

    Review

    "The Sum of All Fears: Clancy's Done It Again!" 11

Acknowledgments 13

Figure 10.2　Table of contents from Frank Schefano's portfolio

Table of Contents

Letter i

Final Essays

Writing about Writing

"The Blank Page" 3

Advisory Essay

"Bath Time" 7

Information Essay

"Look Out! Don't Become a Victim" 11

Review

"Review of The Firm by John Grisham" 14

Rough Drafts

Writing about Writing

Advisory Essay

Information Essay

Review

Acknowledgments iv

Figure 10.3 Table of contents from Jennifer Brackin's portfolio

Computer Writing Tip: In your table of contents, use the *Tab* function to indent rather than the space bar. You will save time and will create more uniform indentations as well. The Tab command also allows you to create dot leaders or dash leaders that link the item with its page number.

Looking at Portfolio Metawriting

Here are some reflective and supplementary pages from Rachel Rosen's portfolio. Consider how her preface prepares you for what lies ahead in the portfolio and helps you know Rosen as a writer and learner, how the acknowledgments show also how she learned and who helped her, and how the table of contents guides you to specific items within the portfolio.

Preface

As I sit and examine my nearly completed portfolio, I ask myself if I will ever come down this road again, writing nontechnical pieces. I am a prelaw student, and my writing usually consists of analyzing philosophers or commenting on Supreme Court decisions. Like everyone, I have no idea what the future holds, but I do hope I can carry some of the editing and rewriting skills I have learned from this portfolio into my major. That is not to say I wouldn't like to continue with writing: I really enjoyed the opportunity to develop a side of me that before was fairly untouched.

The first paper in the portfolio, "Exposed," recalls an experience with my ninth grade English teacher, Mrs. Flynn, which kept me away from the world of writing for a few years. This piece really surprised me—it was the first piece we wrote and, consequently, the first one to end my nonwriting streak. I was shocked at how easily it seemed to leak out of my mind right onto the word processor, as if it was a story I had been longing to tell for a while. Although Mrs. Flynn never reappears in the portfolio, my insecurities about my own writing were a constant hurdle for me to jump.

My advisory piece, "From Twists to Tangles: A Beginner's Guide to Knots," is by far the piece I feel least comfortable with, yet many of my editors enjoyed it the most. Contrary to my bossy (prelaw student, remember?) personality, I felt like it was arrogant and condescending to advise others how to do anything. Choosing a topic such as knots to label myself an expert about was similarly difficult, as was actually figuring out "So how do you do it?"

The memoir "Air Fare" and the editorial "Hanukkah Bushes and Other Such Nonsense" I found very challenging to write. My pit bull–like perfectionist side reared its ugly head and chased me through many rewrites and headaches. I believe these pieces were harder because they are both highly tied to experiences that my parents played a role in, and I wanted the final drafts to be a version I would be proud of giving to them. They both deal with my religion and issues that have developed because of it. My Judaism was a topic that proved so natural (not to say easy) to write about that once I started, I found that many pieces (including those that I omitted from the final cut for this portfolio) would end up exploring a minority/religious/Jewish angle of a situation. Perhaps due to all the struggles with these pieces, they are the two that I like the most also, and would like to see eventually published.

What unites this portfolio? I have found throughout these four works a number of "links." Most notable is my sense of questioning that which surrounds me, including myself. I question traditions around me, how people attack challenges, and how I have dealt with obstacles in my past. Even my ideas for future pieces involve a questioning spirit. I was pleased to discover this, since I consciously value questioning, but wasn't aware it had seeped its way into my subconscious. Furthermore, the sense of inferiority, for various reasons, appears often in my writing. I have heard more than once the words of Eleanor Roosevelt, "Nobody can make you feel inferior without your consent." This I find ignorant; although I am never one to support anyone claiming that they are a victim for whatever reason, I think the emotion of feeling inferior is in a class by itself. It is not an emotion one can straighten their back and walk away from, as Eleanor Roosevelt implies, since it is one of the emotions that cuts right to the bone and hurts deeply. Although I have no feelings of inferiority to anyone anymore, it was an emotion I had some tough wrestling matches with when I was younger.

Writing this portfolio has proved to be an exploration in many senses. As you read it and "explore" what I have to say, may you enjoy the journey, take some ideas with you, and, of course, tread lightly!

Sincerely,

Rachel Rosen
December 10, 19——
Binghamton University

Acknowledgments

To assemble this portfolio has meant undertaking major obstacles: In the course of the semester, I have examined my roots and my sense of self, and I have grappled with the task of examining my goals. Although my goals and my future still hold much uncertainty, this portfolio has really strengthened my belief that my sense of self is highly tied to my upbringing. From this angle, then, my first and foremost "thanks" is to my parents, not only for teaching me about my roots, but also for giving me the encouragement that I often seek when I ask, "So what do you think?"

To my writers' group, consisting of Victor-John Villanueva, Margaret Shoyinka, Pam Segal, Brendan O'Reilly, and Michael Gartell, for not laughing when it could have wounded, for laughing when it healed, and, most of all, for being "brutal."

To my hallmates, consisting of Mary Kate Zebracki, Annie Bucelot, Brian Chase, and Wyatt Bernstein, for their willingness (or smiles under order) at midnight when I dragged them from their own lives to help me sort out mine.

To BMG Music Service, for the background music when I was inspired, and for the foreground music when I wasn't.

Table of Contents

Now you are ready to assemble your portfolio. To get a bit of perspective, remember that the heart of the portfolio is the *writing*, so focus your energies there. Nevertheless, the metawriting, though less important, indicates how you value your writing and how you have come to know yourself as a writer. Take it seriously. But don't forget to have fun creating a portfolio that shows your writing personality.

PORTMANTEAU: A COLLECTION OF PORTFOLIOS

In this Portmanteau section you will first find other examples of metawriting: letters, memos, and essays; tables of contents; and acknowledgment pages. Read them with a critical eye and think about how you would advise the writers to revise. What images of the writers do you get from their materials?

You will also find student portfolios (the drafts have been omitted to save space) by Jessica Fondu and Victor-John Villanueva. A copy of the rubric used to evaluate their portfolios—one developed by their class and their instructor in collaboration—follows each portfolio. Using the rubric, choose a portfolio to evaluate in your writers' group.

For more ideas, turn to the Appendix. The portfolio you will find there is a departure from traditional student ones. It is a course portfolio, assembled by the instructor, who selected and ordered pieces of different genres of students' writing to illustrate the kinds of material generated in her course, reflected on what the class did and how they managed the various genres, and created a table of contents to guide the reader through. When your writers' group considers this Appendix portfolio using the same rubric, ask yourself in addition how well the writing chosen for the portfolio creates a class profile and whether the reflections provide enough insight into the working of the course and the instructor's teaching style.

WRITING PORTFOLIO
Jessica Fondu

Preface

This compilation of pieces is the first completed creative writing project I have produced since high school, and as I reread and collect the contents, I am quite pleased. I feel as if I have travelled halfway across the country, discovering myself again and again, as one discovers new microcosms of worlds in hidden places; beneath damp leaves in a mossy forest, high in the peak of a snow-capped mountain, or among the coral reef of the sea. This *is* a dramatic comparison, but I feel so renewed, so rediscovered by the completion of this project as a whole, and this is the analogy that comes to mind! This does not mean that I am 100% pleased with each individual piece, but the fact that I have written something, after years of futile attempts, is enough to make me smile. All I ever wanted to do was to write.

In second grade, Mr. Goldsholl had us all staple very wide-ruled sheets of paper together into booklets every week and spend about 30 minutes of class time writing stories. Any topic we chose was fair game, and though many of my books contained whimsical stories of beautiful princesses who bore dozens of children (nauseating, I realize), I remember the one "long" story for which I was praised. Entitled "The Prince, the Princess, and the Monster," this fairy tale went along as one would expect, though we had to throw into each sentence a newly ingrained, 25-cent word. Not only did the attractive prince rescue the helpless maiden from the colossal, humongous, atrocious beast, he brought along a pair of scissors and, after brutally stabbing the monster, skinned him and deftly cut out a fashionable coat for the woman, who was quite cold by the time he finally arrived on the scene. Quite gallant, wouldn't you say?

Since that time I just figured I would be a writer, not realizing the amount of time and frustration and patience and rough drafts it would take before I would be fully pleased with something. I do believe that now, finally, I am prepared to rework a draft that holds some promise until I am a medium shade of red!

I begin the portfolio at the very beginning, with the first piece of writing I wrote for class. It actually is entitled, "Tales of a Struggling Writer-to-be . . .", which was what I was in early September. Through this therapeutic piece I practically solved my own problem, and I created my first piece for the portfolio in the process. I suppose I have been too impatient with my work, and now I do know that it takes reworking and reshaping, and lots of patience to produce a suitable piece of writing. It's interesting to me now to read this piece after I have spent the whole semester as a productive writer.

The Memoir piece was one that, in general, gave me a lot of trouble. This final copy is not the original idea I began with, which was mostly about my relationship with my father. I just found it was very difficult to begin, to find a voice for the piece, and to explain what I wanted to say. I had the memory, I drafted several copies, but none of them were the right angle, so I began another idea, which happened to flow smoothly, in the middle of the night. "The Little Yellow House Where Mom Lives" is about my mother, and some memories my brother and I shared when we were very young. Once, my brother and I recalled together the memory of the fight I describe, and we had basically the same memory, though his was from his point of view and mine was my own. The fight had always seemed sort of like a dream to me, and I was amazed to hear my brother give almost exactly the same recount of it that I had known.

I wanted to create happiness out of this memory though, because our family did a lot of laughing throughout the years, despite the underlying sadness. I also wanted to talk about the divorce because I was always the kid who never admitted, even to myself, that this was a difficult thing to handle. It wasn't until some years ago, about 10 years after the divorce, that I began to remember little scenes that weren't as wonderful as I had made myself believe. My brother was always honest about his unhappiness and disappointment, and so this memoir was a release of sorts for me—the first written admission of my fears. And, for my mom, who was always disappointed that my previous stories had "sad" endings for some reason, I wanted to remember our hilarious times in that cozy little house as well.

The Advisory piece was just an enjoyable experience for me. I loved recalling last year's events, when Tom and I lived in England and were able to travel for a month during school vacation. We backpacked all over Europe it seemed, on a very low budget, and had a blast. Last year was my first time being out of the U.S., and my eyes were opened wide during that trip. I knew that I would remember every single detail, and I could have written about it for days and days. I remember the smell of the Paris subway, the biting cold of Amsterdam as we wandered around trying to find the Anne Frank House, and the way I felt so small in Vienna, amidst the towering architecture. It was just a fun piece to do.

"308 Maple Street, Apt 4" was a short story I had begun this summer when I was swimming in memories of my Vermont days, which I will always miss. I began the story in one of the cloth-bound journals I speak of in the Metawriting piece, and this story, like the others, was begun feverishly at midnight and was later tossed into a drawer as a piece of junk. When I filed through some of the journals this September, I found it and thought I would try to revise it.

It is basically a recount of my first year in Vermont with Tom, right after high school. Of course, the memories are now warm and fuzzy, and I would love to go back, but at that time it was extremely difficult. I sometimes forget how I cried for 2 weeks straight when I couldn't find a job and had my first rent due. Tom remembers the "bad vibes" and the struggles our relationship went through that first year. It was not nice. However, it did turn around, and I enjoy remembering the next year, and how our experience worked for us, and made Vermont into a wonderful, fuzzy memory after all.

I include some of my sketches in the portfolio as well. Last spring I made these copies because I was interested in drawing women who seemed to be in quiet contemplation. I was studying art history, and the topic of the time was women and the Muse. I wanted to copy some drawings of women who were the subjects of the art work, but not as sexual or inspirational muses. These women are not taking notice of the viewer, but are lost in their own world of active thinking, instead of passive modelling.

In conclusion, I spent a lot of time rediscovering my writing style this semester and focusing on memories of the past, which are important to me. It is a triumph, of sorts, that I followed through with these pieces to create this portfolio. I enjoyed writing about the past and looking at certain scenes from the different points of view along the way; it has taught me much, about myself as a person and myself as a writer.

Jessica Fondu
December 10, 19———
SUNY Binghamton

Acknowledgments

I would like to thank the members of my writing circle; J.R., for reading the whole thing and editing the finishing touches upon completion, and for letting me read his, which I really enjoyed; Danielle, Tracee, and Pamela. Thanks for all of the interesting comments, for sharing your work with me, and for the all-around pleasant conversation!

A big thanks to Dr. Burch for the encouragement of her comments with regard to my "writing voice." She suggested writing the truth, in plain tones. This is excellent advice for someone who is searching for a "pleasant" way of saying something not so pleasant. The honest result is usually better than the false one, even if it is unpleasant.

I thank my late grandfather, Henry Fondu, who died this past September, and was unable to see me become the writer he wanted me to be. I still remember how he used to call me the future writer of the family, and I remember how much I wanted to be just that—and to please him. Now I want most to please myself with my writing, but I thank Gramps for the incentive, and I hope someday, should anything come out of this dream, that he will somehow know it and be proud.

Tom, I just thank you for being You—as well as the biggest part of my life for close to 5 years, and the best friend I'll ever know. Though I share the intimacies of my everyday life with you, I know I really haven't shared my writing. In truth, I've been afraid of your criticism, too afraid to risk hearing your praise. Thank you for being there to provide the juice for some of these pieces, and for more to come. I look forward to a lifetime of reading your creations and to sharing mine with you. I suppose that means this is the first step! Well, here it goes. . . .

Jessica Fondu
December 10, 19——
SUNY Binghamton

Jessica Fondu   (Sept.) Dec.
Metawriting   Portfolio

Tales of a Struggling Writer-to-Be . . .

There was a time when I jotted down ideas in my notebook and produced short stories for fun. There was a time when I tried some poetry, and wasn't afraid to show it. There was even a time when I wrote for my high school newspaper, and joined a young writers' conference, and wasn't afraid to write. Then something happened.

A few years back, something happened to my writing. It was lost. I felt I had nothing to say. I felt I had no experience worth cultivating. I was embarrassed by my paltry efforts, and I went out with a sad little whimper. I really don't remember exactly when all this occurred. It was an uncomfortable feeling because I still wanted to write, but nothing I wrote was ever satisfying enough.

It is important to me to reclaim a hobby I once loved, and one with which I felt at ease. There are not many places in the public world where I feel at ease. Writing was always an outlet for me. It is, perhaps, the shy person's haven.

I enjoy letter writing nowadays. It is actually where I have transferred most of my writing energies. Many moments of my life are documented on scraps of looseleaf or printed stationery, and have been distributed about the country. The drawback to this is that I have no way to notice the changes in my style as the years go on, and no way to edit any piece of writing. I have tried many times to date the corner of a page in a cloth-bound journal and talk about my daily life. I have tried even to make it creative . . . my latest effort being a journal bought as an "anything goes" type of book. I sketched three pictures and wrote one introduction to a story, and that was as far as I got. Now it is buried in a drawer among two other books of a similar fate.

In my mind, writing should be easy-flowing and cleansing; a way to say, in whatever form, something that needs to be revealed. It's a process that I wish would come as second nature to me, the way I think it must come to writers for whom I have great respect. This is what I have always desired; however, I have not yet put in the effort it requires to be a good writer. Anyone can write. It takes some work and some patience to do it well.

So when I see myself as a writer, I see someone struggling and trying too hard. I don't want it to be a chore. It's high time I sloughed off this encrusting writer's block, and it's time to lighten up and write. Just write.

Jessica Fondu   December
Memoir 3   Portfolio

The Little Yellow House Where Mom Lives

I was sifting through an old mound of photographs, looking to reminisce, when I found it. Nothing special, just an old school portrait of a littler me, in third grade. I remember the cotton dress I was wearing, the only dress I would agree to wear in those strange and finicky years. The white one with colored hearts scattered over the left breast, like my old Raggedy Ann doll whose signature mark was a painted red heart placed on her peachy skin, over the place where we all learn our hearts to be in childhood.

My hair is flying a bit wild in this picture, part of it pulled into a ponytail because of the uncontrollable morning pillow-head; uncontrollable because we were running late that day. I brought the photograph up to the light, and peered into the shadowy eyes. I sifted some more and discovered a portrait of my younger brother from the same year, when he was seven. His eyes looked the same—maybe I hid the sadness a bit better, maybe my half-smile was a little more convincing than his, but in both sets of young eyes was a story of sadness that I hadn't remembered in quite a while.

"Jesus, what a couple of happy campers, huh?" said I to my mom, who came to kneel down and sift beside me.

"Oh yeah, that must have been right after the divorce . . . oh look . . .", but I forgot to listen because I was trying to remember that day.

We were all late. The three of us had overslept—again. Turning in my half-slumber I heard Mom fumble for her clock downstairs in her bedroom where she always left the door open. I heard her soft "Oh shit," and her feet hit the floor. Her tired, low voice floated its way up the echoey stairs into my ears ". . . Jessie. . . ." I heard this overslept-morning-voice many times throughout the next nine years of living in the little yellow house on Glendale Avenue. I don't remember us oversleeping when my dad lived there, but we must have, at least once.

This particular morning was the day school pictures were to be taken. There was no time for a shower, and I was lucky I made it into a dress at all. Already vain at nine years old, I was upset and self-conscious because my hair couldn't be tamed for lack of time. We were in time for pictures that day, but there would be other close calls in the future.

Dumped in the middle of the living room floor, scattered, out of order, and upside down, these old, but not forgotten, photos freeze-framed our past. I noticed a picture of my old bedroom which showed the lamp with the red and white checks on its shade that I used to love. It was to the right of my bed, on the nightstand; the same lamp from that dream I used to have . . . every time I had a fever . . .

The house is shaking. The Norman Rockwell in the hallway is dancing on the wall. My red and white checkered lampshade dances with it, but not to music—no—such noise, such a deafening roar of a noise. Like the visit to Niagara Falls that one time, only louder, and deeper. This noise is in my bones. My lampshade rattles; "stop moving!" I whisper, but it's the house which is trembling. Downstairs in the living room I stand next to Mom. She is staring out the big window into the driveway—and then I see it too. A tire, the biggest monster truck tire in the world, perhaps because I'm so small, is crashing through our window—the one with all the tiny window-panes. The wooden frames splinter and the glass explodes toward us. It is Dad who has rolled it through the window, and he is yelling. The wheel comes toward us, to-ward Mom, as if he meant to do it. The red is everywhere. All red. My ears—this noise is pounding at me—my ears can't stand the noise. . . .

This is the recurring dream that had haunted my sick-in-bed days for years, even once during my teenage years, and always while I was delirious from a fever. It doesn't make sense to me now, no more sense than my two-year-old mind's nightmare of being chased by a giant rolling pin. Nobody ever threw a tire through the window, and the only sound of glass breaking that I can recall was from my mother's fist coming through the kitchen window, that night when Dad locked her out of the house. The night of the quietest fight ever.

My brother and I, playing on the floor, were actually surprised when our father picked up our mother and dropped her outside the front door, without shoes or a jacket, and locked it on her. We hadn't even heard an argument brewing. There was nothing to hear, but the thickness of a dislike so strong it penetrated the air swirled in heavy motions through the room, piercing our child senses, but not our ears. Instinctively she ran to the back door, but we never thought she would punch her fist through the window when she found that locked too. We would have opened it, but were told not to by the only person able to frighten us into immobility, even when it meant helping our own mother. Of course, he did let her in after that. Maybe he even helped her wrap up her bloodied hand, but it took a long, long time for me to shake that fear of the power he had over us from my soul.

We finger through those old photos, my mom and I, and every so often we go back to that wooden drawer of the desk that never closes correctly, and whines on its tracks until you jiggle it just right. Then it will heave a sigh of relief and relax smoothly into its cubby. This is how I feel going back to that little yellow house, whose interior has changed often during twenty years, but which somehow manages to remain the same. After four years of being away, calling other walls "home," I find I am stubborn in fitting back in at first, but if I give it time, I'll always relax and fit smoothly back into this cubby.

I suppose it's where I belong. And this woman kneeling next to me, shifting the gears of her own memory to accompany each photograph; does she know how completely incredible she is, and how much I adore her? Does she realize that while she's criticizing her hairdos and -don'ts of the past, I am seeing a woman who raised two children, and loved them, and showed them all of her strengths, and most of her weaknesses. Above all the frustrations and tantrums and playful threats of running away, glittered the love she gave to us for free, desiring only a fraction of that in return. And I've never laughed so hard as I've laughed with Mom and Dave. That doubled-over laugh that wrenches the stomach muscles and steals the breath from the soul. That laugh which squeezes tears from the corners of the eyes and hurts when it's over, leaving little aftershocks which grow again into the heartiest of guffaws.

This is what I think of when I go back to that dusty pile of memories which draws me up close to Mom, every time.

Jessica Fondu (November) Dec.

Advisory Piece Portfolio

How to Enjoy a Low-Budget European Adventure

OK—you've saved up the money, you've made your decision, and you're ready to go. Maybe you've been studying Spanish, or reviewing your knowledge of English history. Maybe your sketchbook is overflowing with replica paintings of the great French Impressionists, or you're off to find your Irish family roots. Perhaps it's just time for an adventure. . . .

Whatever your reason for travelling, you may be feeling some normal pangs of uncertainty, to balance your excitement. What should you pack? How will you function in another country? What do you do once you're there? It is important to be armed with a plan, even if your plan resembles a slice of Swiss cheese. Holes are inevitable, and necessary, in this personal adventure.

Let me just suggest a few essentials before you leave. . . .

Since this is a low-budget student trip, you will be travelling light. One big hiking pack will suffice, with a small sack for light day trips. The pack need not be new and smelling of plastic; in fact, it will be less tempting to a thief if it is old and frayed and dusty. Well-loved, in other words. You will be encountering hordes of American backpackers as well, throughout the European continent, and you may find yourself feeling altogether "cooler" than they appear, with their brand-new, purple passion-fruit–colored hiking bags with matching boots. (You won't have to search long and wide to make new American friends. They are ubiquitous, but it would be worth your while to meet some non-Americans—there is so much to learn on a train going from point A to point B with someone of another culture.) If you've never owned a backpack, however, you can remedy this situation by rolling your new pack around in the dirt, filling it with rocks or books and hiking around your block with it on your back. Adjust all the straps, make sure it's comfortable, and get acquainted with this most important necessity!

Comfortable shoes are, of course, a must.

You'll also be needing a *Let's Go Europe* book, updated, to help you along with your adventure. These *Let's Go*s come in many single countries for even further detailed information if you are staying in one region, and they are perfect for the needs of travelling students. This book will become your road bible. Before you leave the airplane, the train, the bus, the hostel, this is the object you will be double-checking for. In its pages lie a wealth of information on every cost, address, and "must see" you will need in every European country. You may even find yourself reading passages for fun. Excellent writing is one of its highlights. This book will save you time by having many of your questions already answered (in your own language).

Stapled to its front cover you may want to keep the addresses and phone numbers of any distant relative or friend of the family who lives anywhere you might be going. You will use them. No matter how unknown the person is, if you've ever been offered a bed for the night, you'll need it now. Often, student hostels are overcrowded, cheap hotels are not cheap enough, and the possibility of a hot shower and maybe even breakfast will be greatly appreciated after the exhausting time you'll spend on the road.

The International Student Identity card is another necessity that will be used for discounts on everything from train fares to museum passes. This can be obtained through your university or a travel agent.

A sleeping bag will also come in handy for those below-par hostels that don't offer sheets on the frightening mattresses, and you will be glad you brought it along, though it takes up precious space at the bottom of your pack. And, should you be caught homeless in some foreign country for a night or two, your trusty sleeping bag will again come to the rescue, and you can pretend you're camping in the mountains, even if you're only on a park bench or underneath an awning keeping dry.

The last essential is rather optional. A best friend, or someone whose company you really enjoy, can make this one of the best trips of your life. Even if it is someone you meet up with along the way, you will enjoy the company. Remember, you will be spending perhaps 24 hours a day with this friend, enduring eternal train rides, playing gin rummy even though you hate cards, taking sightseeing tours, taking photos together . . . the works. If you are not all that fond of your companion, you may be pulling your hair out by the second week. If you choose to travel solo, you will most likely come back with a stronger, more assured sense of yourself, and you will know that now you can do anything. So either way, prepare yourself for the weeks that lie ahead.

Now that you've checked off your "haves" and "have nots," it's time to outline your travel route. I would suggest landing in London and making England your first stop, unless you have been overseas before. Although English is spoken, Great Britain is still packed with enough differences to make you spin. As you leave the airport, look right before crossing the street, not left. Being taken out by a taxi cab is not how you'll want to begin your European tour. For the world's convenience (and safety), most London streets are painted with the directions "Look Left" or "Look Right" directly on the pavement. Seems funny enough, but crossing hesitation will affect everyone from time to time.

Taking the Tube, or Underground, will save you money, and it is very easy to use. The old-fashioned black cabs are tempting and very "English," but beware of the cost.

Travelling with travellers checks is a good idea, as every major city contains an American Express office. Unless it's an emergency, exchanging money at change stands will only suck you dry, as the rates are very high and very false, in some cases. Cities such as Amsterdam and Prague are sprinkled with Change Stalls every half block, but the convenience is sometimes not worth the rip-off.

Ferries, from England to France for example, are a good idea, fun, and not too expensive. They give you a chance to see other cities and the coastlines. Trains have a European charm that we don't experience often in America as we crawl through traffic to our vacation destinations, and it's nice to be able to enjoy the scenery and nod off at will.

One thing to remember as you plan your journey is that there is nothing you should feel compelled to see if you are not 100% interested. If you want to spend three weeks smoking pot and stringing beads in Amsterdam, then by all means, go ahead. If you make it to the Van Gogh museum or the Anne Frank House, then you'll enjoy that too, but it's not necessary to see everything each city has to offer. You won't be able to anyway, so be prepared to leave Europe having only skimmed the surface. The Eiffel Tower and the Arc de Triomphe will always be in Paris, so if you prefer to travel the countryside practicing your French with the natives and living on bread and cheese, then you can do Paris another time.

It is quite possible to travel to any country without speaking the language. You may feel more comfortable knowing a handful of phrases, especially "hello," "please," and "thank you," but English is spoken everywhere, if not by everyone. You will find someone to help you if you ask politely. Part of the fun is trying the language too, and once you get over the initial embarrassment of using the strange accent and the wrong words, you'll find it a lot of fun, and you may have better results with the Europeans than if you hadn't tried their language at all. Perhaps someone else will want to practice their English on you as well, so don't be shy. Whip out that dictionary and try a phrase. The worst that will happen is that they'll smile and try to understand you efforts, no matter how pathetic. As a rule, Europeans are generally more polite to foreigners than we Americans are. They may poke fun of you afterwards amongst themselves, but you won't know because you can't understand what they're saying.

The whole point of the trip is for you to experience other ways of life, to learn about yourself, and to succeed in getting from place to place and back home again. Remember to notice the history and the age of some of the buildings. Look for repairs where a building was bombed during World War II. Notice the cobblestone streets that have been scuffed over for hundreds and hundreds of years, by thousands upon thousands of boot soles; the smooth erosion of stone on steps leading to a castle or cathedral first built in 1100. This is the history that America lacks, but you don't need to lug around your history book to make a lesson of it. You will learn by talking to the stranger in the seat next to you on a train going across her country, and you will see it in the eyes of the citizens as they pass you by on their way to work.

Well, it sounds easy enough. Now you just have to go. Remember one last thing—this will be your vacation, and these have been my experiences, so feel free to disregard them all.

Jessica Fondu (Sept.) Dec.

Free Choice Sample Portfolio

308 Maple Street, Apt 4

When they moved into their very first apartment, the young couple felt that they were much more mature than they actually were. Here was a chance to make a home, begin a life together with no permanent strings attached. Strings, they decided, could cause tension; and tension, they were sure they knew, was not a good way to begin a life. It turned out that there would be much tension to follow, but before all this, there was joy.

The young couple selected pot holders and bath towels at a cheap warehouse store, congratulating themselves on finding a good bargain. Those same "irregular" towels would, in time, develop stains from unseen dye in the fabric, and they unravelled almost as quickly as they were sold for the bargain.

The young couple made the rounds to various homes of relatives, collecting unwanted or unused furniture with care and excitement, as one adopts an animal from the pound. They sanded, painted, re-covered kitchen chairs, lined the insides of bureau drawers with clean paper, just as their mothers suggested. They were playing house, and those same mothers watched them with a reserved happiness, intuitively knowing some of what would lie ahead for the young couple, and hoping they would be able to handle the unavoidable vicissitudes of life.

All smiles, the young couple hung their posters on spackle-spotted walls and placed their houseplants in the best patches of sunlight, plants that would be dead and shrivelled in two months' time. They cooked their first meals side by side, marvelling at the good job they thought they did, meals that were, at best, creative. They squatted in beanbag chairs and lifted mismatched utensils to their mouths. They smiled and laughed and rolled along with the comfortable pace of life.

The summer, as it does, stepped aside to autumn, and the weather changed— almost drastically. The sun's heat faded out and the frost took over. And so it became with the young couple. Suddenly, it seemed to them, things began to change. They felt the weight of responsibility heavy in the air. Bad vibes, they dubbed it. One could walk through the door at any given time and be engulfed by bad vibes. They seemed to be coming apart at the seams. Like an old quilt that's been washed and handled too often. Only, unlike the patches of an old quilt, the young couple had not been sewn together for enough length of time to know that, every now and then, it is necessary for some new thread, and some patience, to pull it all together again . . . good as new.

Her mundane job as a waitress was wearing her *joie de vivre* thin. The inconvenient, almost cruel predawn hours were disheartening to a girl of eighteen. This was not what she expected from maturity. He had the burden of difficult college classes and a demanding varsity sport on his shoulders, which were, for a boy of eighteen, not as wide as maybe he'd needed them to be. And so it happened that they found life was not exactly as understanding as they wanted it to be.

As the busy-ness of it all continued, the pet peeves became more petty. The complaints had to take a number—the office was packed. The plants were dying and nobody had time to care. The laundry hadn't been taken care of, again ("but it was my one day off in two weeks"). The dishes were piled high in the sink ("but I have a test in the morning and I haven't read the book yet"). She had no time to argue and he had no energy. The important, late-night discussions which were their only sanity were forced to a premature close. For the alarm clock which now ran their lives would be buzzing unsympathetically in mere hours, and there was no turning it back.

And so, sadly, their lives became a chore, a constant irritation and reminder of the difficulties of responsibility that they had once so longed for. Balancing jobs and schoolwork and housework and checkbooks when they could have been guzzling Bud Lights on the lawn with thirty of their closest "buddies." Screw the laundry, lose the electric bill—who's up for a beer run?

Now doesn't that sound nice.

The problem was, they were nobody else's "buddies" but their own. They had chosen this isolated life, and really it was what suited them best.

Time and practice eventually healed this union of youth. There was a laundry plan, and a changing of attitudes, not to mention a new school term for both, which put them on equal ground (so to speak). The toothbrushes remained side by side at the sink, different toothbrushes, same place. The young couple, renewed, returned to their rightful place, side by side. They allowed time for late-night discussions that would end only when the last syllable of the last barely uttered word escaped the exhausted lips. Sometimes, in the middle of the night, one partner would awaken, just for a soft second—long enough to slip into the warm spot of the sleeping partner, and whisper the one phrase that made it all so worth it. . . .

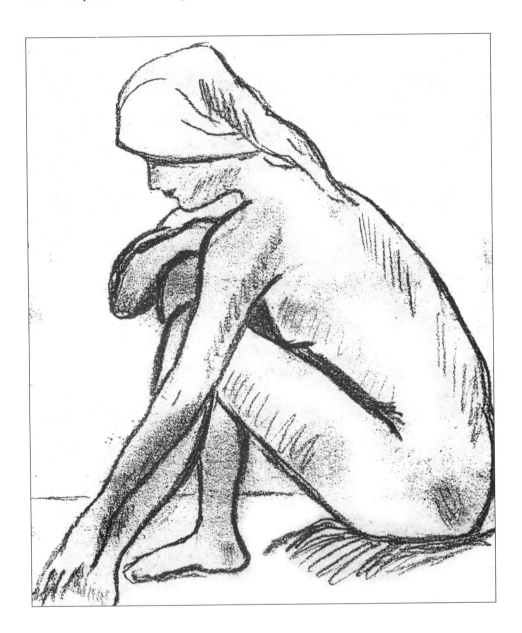

Rubric for Portfolio Evaluation

Portfolio Writer _____   Date _____

                                                  Evaluator _____

A. What's in the portfolio? (75%)

___ Four pieces of writing, including one free choice (write titles below)

   1.

   2.

   3.

   4.

___ Reflective analysis that includes *at least* an introduction to the portfolio

___ Acknowledgments page

___ Other nonrequired features (write titles below)

B. How does this portfolio reflect its author's accomplishment in this class? (25 %)

___ **Creativity**

   How well does the portfolio reveal an unmistakable voice, a clear evocation of a real person? Is the portfolio put together in an interesting, unique, or original way, with at least one surprise?

___ **Polish**

   How professional does the portfolio appear? How clean are the mechanical aspects of the writing and of presentation as well? How neat and organized is the portfolio?

___ **Clarity and Substance**

   How well does the writer make his/her points understood in the context of the audience that has been described? How solid and substantial are the ideas? How well does the writer use details to develop significant and thoughtful pieces of writing?

___ **Improvement**

   What evidence is there of the writer's growth during the time covered by the portfolio? How well does the writer reflect on her/his drafts to make the published versions better? How carefully does the writer consider criticism from readers?

C. What are your responses to and questions about this portfolio? What would you like to tell the writer? Please write your comments here and on the back.

WRITING & DISCOURSE

Portfolio

written & compiled by
Victor-John Villanueva

Contents

Preface

Each individual essay within this portfolio has its own story. They each have their meager beginnings and their eventual conclusions. You will encounter those as you read on. When viewed together, they tell the story of myself as a thinker, as a doer, and, most importantly, as a writer. Writing each of these pieces has made me think of myself and the ways in which this thought can be communicated onto paper. The abstract ideas that I had about the subject at hand took on new meanings during the writing process. Communicating the intangible via physical symbols we call words takes a writer on a journey. Sometimes incredibly gratifying and other times painfully disappointing, these excursions of the mind cause a writer to grow, develop, and learn.

Needless to say, I have learned greatly during this course. Among my newly gained knowledge is the fact that good writing does not spring from a dark mysterious void; it is the result of careful planning, helpful editing, and endless revising. More importantly though, I believe that these pieces have allowed me to go beyond the barriers which have prevented my growth as a writer in the past. At one time words were my barriers and shields which defended me from an unknown adversary. I would hide my true identity behind obscure words and polysyllabic phrases in order to convey thought without incorporating character. Adopting a false persona allowed me freedom to express the ideas in my head, but it simultaneously stunted my artistic growth. The person who is Victor-John Villanueva was not apparent in the pieces of the past. Although remnants of such a style may be found in this collection, I know that my voice is more audible in these pieces than it has ever been. For this self-discovery, I am forever indebted.

Without further ado, I present "Smoke," "Touché," "Uughaaaahaa," an untitled editorial, and their respective reflective stories. The picture that emerges at the end of this collective work is that of an eclectic writer whose style traverses the wide range of emotion and form. Hopefully each piece will provide a glimpse of myself, as I provide a definition of their existence.

....

"Smoke" documents one night during *high* school when the name of the educational institution actually lived up to itself. Recalling the events of that night was not a problem, and neither was the actual writing of the piece. It practically wrote itself. Most of the text of the original draft remains in the final version of the piece. This is probably true because I have always thought about that moment, recollecting from different vantage points. It clearly communicates my ideas and it effectively illustrates my change as a result of the smoke. This piece was not only my favorite one to write, but also turned out to be, in my opinion, the best. It unifies a vivid memory with meaning that came from personal reflection. Easy to write and easy to read, this memoir is a record of one night when casual hanging out was mixed with drugs to form a mind-altering experience.

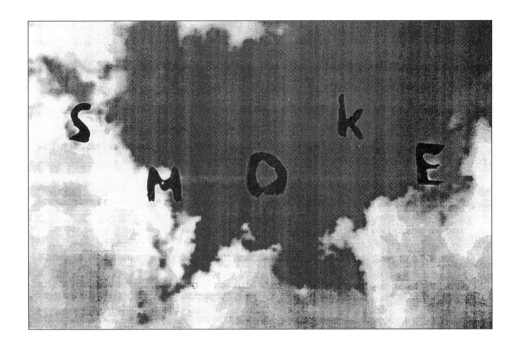

Smoke

"I brought something . . . ," he said.

With eager anticipation, I uttered, "I know what it is."

He Rolled It

I remember that night so clearly. My parents and older sister had gone away (I don't remember where; I guess that the simple fact that they were *gone* was more important than to where they had ventured). I invited Carlos over to spend the night. Too lazy to read a three-hundred-page book, we borrowed the audio version of *The Autobiography of Malcolm X* from the library. Popping it into the cassette player seemed so much easier than actually reading the epiclike saga. Even though I decided to listen rather than read, academia had always been a priority in my life. With a rank at the top of my class, a spotless disciplinary report, and an introverted personality to complement the two, I appeared to be the picture of intelligence, responsibility, and fervor. I never cut school; I was never in detention; I was never unprepared for class. That night, however, my seemingly straight-edged, type A persona was altered as junior year American history took a back seat to an independent study of drugs and behavior.

I Lit It

Malcolm was recording in the bedroom, while we were smoking in the kitchen. With each puff, we slowly smoked away the forbidden villain of those fighting for a partnership for a "Drug Free" America. Suddenly, the "Just Say No" motto was replaced by *Nike*'s "Just Do It."

We Smoked It

Although expectations were high, I wasn't. Feelings of euphoria did not come about from the sudden induction of THC in my system. On the contrary, dormancy was replaced by frenzy; calmness with hyperactivity; potential energy with kinetic. My mind, my hands, my feet—all were in disarray as I tried to satisfy Carlos's sudden pangs of hunger. I was all over the place. As the drug affected my body, I was met by a new state of consciousness. My physical actions meshed with my mental activity as time, space, and meaning were distorted and blurred. With my mind working faster than my hands and vice versa, I attempted to cook four dishes at once, but wound up burning and spilling most of our munchies. The commotion in the kitchen caused us to forget about James Earl Jones's narration of the Malcolm X saga. It was as if one world swept out as a new one pranced in.

Marijuana, Weed, Pot, Buddah—whatever society labeled it did not matter that night. It was more than an illegal drug; it was a source of rebellion. That nickel bag was my ticket into apparent deviancy. Legality became the measure of normality and deviance. I was no longer the pure, unadulterated straight-A student. In my mind, I was transformed. After that night, I looked the same and I acted the same. I was intrinsically the same person, but there was a part of me that couldn't be changed. The changes in my biochemistry, my thought, and my personality that night would not be erased.

Peer pressure didn't make me inhale, and neither did Carlos. I did it. I did it because I wanted to. I wanted to do something for which I did not repeatedly consider the consequences. With my first high, I temporarily broke away from the world of a conscientious, responsible young adult. The THC in my body transported me to a new realm. Although I knew that I'd eventually return to my reality, my excursion was as gratifying as it was hectic.

He Rolled It
I Lit It
We Smoked It

This is all true. It, however, changed me. *It* rolled up my psyche; *It* lit up my nerves; *It* smoked away my innocence. Right versus Wrong, Legal versus Illegal, Normal versus Deviant: These dichotomies no longer hold the meaning that they once did. Malcolm X's story of rebellion, change, and enlightenment was recorded that night on my stereo. This memoir is my record of my rebellion and change. After that point, I began to see things in a new light. The cut-and-dried mundane reality I had known disappeared. That night, I made an irrevocable decision to enter a realm of new possibility as I watched my former self dissipate with the smoke.

I definitely found it more difficult to think of a topic for the advisory piece as opposed to the memoir. "What am I good at?" became the definitive question of the paper. My first attempt at drafting left me with a meager beginning of a paper on how to cram for an exam and still succeed. After trying this, I realized that it was going nowhere. My words were vainly written as I tried to write an instruction manual for something for which everyone has a personal method. On the other hand, fencing requires fundamental basics from which no successful fencer can stray. Having read a good amount of fencing manuals, I decided to add a little twist to my advisory. With that in mind, I made my piece centered around fencing being the renowned "Sport of Princes." Although I had the topic and the novel approach, the actual paper was difficult to write. I did not enjoy meticulously explaining an action that comes so naturally as a result of continued practice. I felt that my writing style was constrained in this piece because I was obligated to describe the fundamental steps of fencing. I was not allowed the freedom that I was in the other pieces, and thus I feel that this may be one of the weaker works within the collection.

Touché

Regarded as the "Sport of Princes," fencing is an activity that demands both physical dedication and mental concentration. You must routinely practice and eventually master the introductory steps before you can be bestowed with the royalties of a prince/princess. Having climbed up the fencing hierarchy by actively participating in several fencing clubs and tournaments, I can instruct the introductory steps of attaining a royal status to any eager apprentice. The foundation of fencing regality is as follows. So, if you're ready, toss aside the rags of serfdom and get "On-Guard!" as we prepare to transform paupers into nobility.

If you are to start to adopt the skills of fencing royalty, the on-guard position is the first step to the kingdom. Combined with back-and-forth movements called advances and retreats, the on-guard position enables the fencer to maneuver with regal grace and stealthy defense.

In order to get on-guard, you must first form a ninety-degree angle with the heels of your feet. Right-handed individuals will have their right foot facing their opponent, while left-handed fencers will find the opposite to be true. Maintaining the ninety-degree angle, take a step forward while keeping the rear foot firmly planted on the ground. Your step should be the length of your two shoulders. At this point, make your trunk and torso the center of gravity for your body. Allow your body to sink at this center so that your knees are bent. It is important to keep the upper body turned so that the exposure of the chest and torso, the target area, toward the opponent is minimal. Next, take the arm corresponding with the rear foot and form a squarelike shape. While facing your opponent, your arm's biceps should be pulled behind your head and parallel to the ground, while your forearm should be perpendicular to the floor. Keep your hand limp near the back of your head. Your other hand will be used to manipulate the weapon.

The foil, epee, and saber are the three weapons that a fencer uses to defend his/her honor. The foil is the smallest of the three weapons, and it is used to train a beginning fencer. Both epee and saber differ from foil in that both weapons and their respective target area are larger. Depending on which weapon is being used, the following advice may change slightly. Having used this method while fencing foil, I am certain that this weapon is best suitable for the following advice.

The weapon arm should be relaxed and loose by the fencer's side when in the on-guard position. While your shoulder is at your side, your forearm will be parallel to the ground. Grasping the weapon, your hand should be palm side up in what is called supinade position. This may feel awkward in the beginning, but it is a small price to pay for the status of royalty. With your heels at a ninety-degree angle, knees bent, shoulder in squarelike formation, and a relaxed weapon arm, you are in the on-guard position. Although it seems to be plenty to remember, as you assume the role of a noble, it will become not only easier but natural. Now that you are on-guard, you must learn how to walk like a noble. Just like everything else, noble footwork is simple to learn, but difficult to master.

A series of advances and retreats is the key to the agility and stealth, which are needed in order to be successful. In order to advance, the back foot is used to propel the front foot forward. As you push off with your back foot, lift the toes of your front foot, thereby starting the lifting of the entire foot. Take a step forward and always land heel first, toe last. As the forward foot moves, the rear foot should follow. When the front foot begins to settle on the ground, the rear foot should be lifted up. Only when the toe of the front foot touches the floor should the rear foot likewise settle. A retreat is the opposite of an advance. Using the front foot to push off from, take a step backward. Make sure that when the rear foot lands on the floor it is done simultaneously to the front foot, landing in a heel–toe step. Walking like a prince/princess demands concentration and effort, but without it the defense of one's honor would not be the same. Now that you look like a noble, it is time to defend your honor from eager usurpers. Learning to lunge is the final step to attaining nobility.

The lunge is the basic attack of a fencer. In order for it to be effective, it must be carefully planned and carried out with ease. Those at the top of the fencing hierarchy have instinctual lunges which prove to be their best method of defense when faced with those hungry for the crown. The lunge must start with the point of the weapon. Once the point is in the desired target area, namely the entire upper body (exclude the arms and head while fencing foil), the arm should be quickly and smoothly extended from the shoulder. The footwork of the lunge follows after the arm extension and should be practiced enough to be natural and instinctive.

After your arm is extended and directed at your opponent, propel the front foot forward with the rear foot, which remains flat on the floor in order to maintain balance and leverage. The rear leg acts like a catapult or a compressed spring as you crouch in the on-guard position. As the rear leg extends, the rear arm is flung backward, palm up, so that it is in line with, and parallel to, the rear leg. When the lunge is complete, your body should be in the following position: the front knee bent directly over the foot's instep, hips below trunk, shoulders level, rear leg extended, and rear foot on the floor. The recovery from the lunge is made by pushing backward with front heel while pulling the body back with the recoiling arm and leg. When the recovery is completed, the on-guard position should be resumed.

Armed with a strong on-guard position, gliding footwork, and a powerful lunge, you are ready to go out into the battlefield and be a defender of the kingdom. Your skills must be used in conjunction to your mental ability. You must now think like a king/queen as you aim for the keys to the kingdom. Now that you are prepared, yell "Touché!" as you defend yourself from dangerous fencers and eager usurpers.

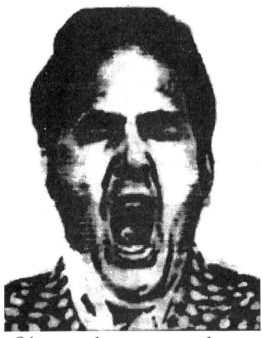

Uughaaaahaa

an onomatopoetic title

During an in-class exercise, I came up with the question, "Why are yawns contagious?" This question became the basis for my analysis piece. Although I had some lingering ideas as to why yawns have their infectious quality, I thought it would be best to do some research and find out what the experts have to say. Surprisingly, my speculation was combined with their speculation, and the result is a purely speculative paper that raises good points. As far as the actual writing of the paper, I found it to be pretty simple. My sentences are sometimes intentionally drawn out and somber. I was aiming at giving them a suggestive power that would make the reader yawn. "Uughaaaahaa" is an interactive analysis which makes the reader learn . . . and *y a w n.*

Uughaaaahaa

Watery eyes, tremulous eardrums, and, of course, a gaping mouth—these are all characteristics of one of the more perplexing aspects of human behavior: The Yawn. Remaining mysterious among the other idiosyncratic bodily functions, the yawn is a phenomenon that manages to confound modern-day scientists. Perhaps one of the most confusing qualities of a yawn is its contagiousness. If I yawn, chances are that you will yawn, and if you yawn, the person next to you will yawn. Although the contagiousness of the yawn is not fully explainable, the following are three theories which provide insight to the open, pitch black, area of the yawn.

The most speculative among the explanations of the yawn's infectiousness is the one I have named the balancing/unbalancing theory. Based on the biological function of a yawn, we must examine a yawn's purpose before delving into the reasoning. "A yawn opens the eustachian tubes, balancing atmospheric pressure between the air-filled ear and the environment" (Provine 119). This biological role of the yawn causes one to hypothesize about the environmental pressure that exists between yourself and your fellow yawner. The question I pose is: If the eustachian tubes open to balance pressure within one person's air-filled inner ear, doesn't that balancing automatically imbalance the pressure of the inner ear adjacent to you, thereby causing that person to yawn? Although this balancing/unbalancing of pressure theory may explain why yawns multiply among people situated closely together, it does not explain why one yawn turns into two (or three for that matter) when one sees another yawn across the room. The second theory attempts to explain this variation of the "catchy yawn."

You are looking around the room. Some people catch your eye, while others do not. They don't grab your attention, until you see one of them open his/her mouth and release a big, satisfying y-a-a-a-w-n. You try to continue without releasing one yourself, but your attempts are futile. Why? The reasoning behind this scenario rests slightly higher on the speculation meter than the previous one, and it manages to provide further explanation.

As we mature, imitation is inevitable. Whether it be the imitation of conformable or nonconformable behavior, humans imitate others in a variety of ways. According to Provine, "Yawn-induced yawning may be an example of such 'imitative' behavior that has survived into adulthood" (120). The logic behind this theory is founded on the tendency in human nature to imitate another's action. It provides insight to the realm of imitation and its possibility of carrying over into the latter stages of life. Moreover, the compulsion to imitate another's yawn provides insight to the more general area of face detection.

The enchanting and mesmerizing capability of viewing a yawn may have its basis in a facial-feature detector in the brain. "The discovery of a perceptual process activated exclusively by visually observed yawns establishes a precedent for a facial feature and/or expression detector in humans" (Provine 211). Linking these two theories together, it becomes possible to view the yawn as a bodily function that automatically triggers a person's facial-feature or expression detector, and in turn causes them to unconsciously initiate a yawn.

The final theory of yawn infectiousness is the most scientifically based among the three. The third theory utilizes the scientific principle of neurobehavior to explain the yawn's hypnotic power: "An observed yawn initiates a complex series of neurobehavioral events that culminates in a yawn in the observer" (Provine 120). According to this theory, there exists an abstract component of the human psyche which is neurobehaviorally stimulated by a yawn. Once stimulated, the person observing the yawn has no other choice but to complete the chain by yawning him/herself. Although this may be the most scientific of the three reasons, the conundrum of the yawn and the confusion that it creates must be recalled.

The yawn and its characteristics have caused many to speculate, but few to conclude. Is its contagiousness the result of an unbalancing/balancing act, or it is an imitative behavior projected into adulthood? On the other hand, can its infectiousness be blamed on the neurobehavioral impulse that is so characteristic of the yawn? Until science finds an explanation for the yawn, those who search will tire and not know the reason why their yawn will make another y a a w n, which will make another y a a a w n, which will make another . . . etc.

Works Cited

Provine, Robert R. "Faces As Releasers of Contagious Yawning: An Approach to Face Detection Using Normal Human Subjects." <u>Bulletin of the Psychonomic Society</u> 27 (1989): 211–14.

———. "Yawning As a Stereotyped Action Pattern and Releasing Stimulus." <u>Ethology</u> (formerly <u>Zeitschrift für Tierpsychlogie</u>) 72 (1986): 109–22.

While trying to invent a topic for the advisory essay, I ran into some trouble. In retrospect, however, I can say that the process was nothing compared to the one that I went through for the final piece in this collection, the editorial. I could not get my opinionated personality to reveal itself in the early stages of the piece. After drafting the beginning to a piece on why major requirements cannot be met in Binghamton University, I abandoned the project. My opinion on the matter was not strong enough to write a full, convincing editorial. The topic on which I finally wrote my paper came to me from a conversation that I had with one of my best friends/best writing critics. His rejoicing over a recent ruling in Hawaii on gay marriage inspired me to write this piece. Once I got the topic, the paper just flowed. My argument was manifested in one sitting and a couple of minor revisions. Pleased with its completed version, I present it to the opposition and count upon their enlightenment.

Editorial

Companionship; Love; Unity. The foundation of marriage lies within the emotions and meanings that these words convey. The foundation and/or justification of marriage is not dependent on the genders of two people. The opponents of same-sex marriage condemn the transformations and reconstructions of the "traditional" bride-and-groom marriage formula. As the new combinations of bride and bride/groom and groom come about, the propaganda and rhetoric surrounding the issue builds. While some argue that the homosexual marriage strips America of its "family values," in reality, same-sex marriage not only upholds the aforementioned foundations of marriage, but also engenders them.

Recent debate over same-sex marriage has been spawned by the lifting of the ban forbidding it in Hawaii. On December 4, 1996, a circuit court judge in Honolulu nullified the ban, deeming it unconstitutional. Such a decision has likewise caused those who disagree with the ruling to voice their opinion. "Robert H. Knight, the director of cultural studies at the conservative Family Research Council in Washington D.C., denounced the ruling as a denial of 'not only the wisdom of generations but the law of nature and nature's God' " (Goldberg A26). Other traditional beliefs include the opinion that a homosexual union is inherently counter to the primary purpose of marriage: The Preservation of the Species. This belief automatically denies the right to marry to those who are infertile and those who have no intention of having children. Moreover, in a world that is overpopulated and stricken with parentless children, the adoptive possibility of gay couples serves a useful purpose. These two voices of opposition are part of the rhetorical arsenal that anti–gay marriage representatives secure. These arguments not only reveal the extent to which opposing arguments are traditionally based, but simultaneously reveal the insecurities and ignorance that plague their reasoning.

Similar to xenophobia, the paranoia of difference is one of the underpinnings of arguments such as Knight's. Questioning and subsequently deeming another's sexual preference as unnatural and ungodly is a self-centered mentality that robs others of their freedom of thought, freedom of expression, and freedom to love. Although Knight's comment attributes wisdom to past generations, it is clear that past generations have decided upon matters which intimately dealt with the fundamental differences that divided a people. If America could be wrong at one point in its warped history, why can't this matter be another wrinkle waiting to be straightened out (no pun intended)? Clearly paralleling the race discrimination that plagued this country a generation ago, gay marriage creates controversy and scandal. The headlines and commotion created by the marriage, however, are created in vain. The marriage being contested and berated is fundamentally the same as the marriage acknowledged by all.

Unnatural? How can it be unnatural to care for another human being, to help another human being, to become one with another human being??? The tenets of marriage are in this case reaffirmed as humans long for the emotion that only another's commitment can bring. Whether the desire is to be with someone of the same sex or of the opposite sex, human emotion transcends the societal construct of marriage; and as such, it should be honored despite superficial differences. Those who claim differently are stuck in a mentality void of understanding. Narrow-minded concepts must be annihilated because they are the *true* destroyers of family values; they tear apart the nation and force people to take sides in the debate. Division originates in this propaganda, while unity is fostered by the love that a man/woman has for a partner. Maintaining a spectrum of emotion that transcends gender reaffirms the emotion and intellect upon which marriage is founded.

A husband, a wife, two point five children, and a home in suburbia—this was once the picture of the American ideal. Today, however, change and evolution are altering the ways love, life, similarity, and difference are viewed in the world. As emotion pushes the concept of marriage to the forefront, we must change and adapt so as to not become stagnant in the era of change in thought. To do so would mean the dismantling of societal structure, human emotion, and family value.

Works Cited

Goldberg, Carey. "Hawaii Judge Ends Gay-Marriage Ban." <u>New York Times,</u> 4 Dec. 1996, natl.ed.: A26.

Cover Page Photo Credits

"Smoke"	Wes Thomson photo from <u>The Stock Market.</u>
"Touché"	Ric Thomson photo from <u>Foil Fencing</u> by Bower.
"Uughaaaahaa"	From "Faces As Yawn Releasers," <u>Bulletin of the Psychonomic Society</u> 27 (1989): 211–14.
Editorial	Artwork by Keith Haring. Copyright The Keith Haring Estate.

Acknowledgments

I give the greatest thanks to my family. Without the strength of my mother, the consideration of my father, and the love of my sister, the person who is conveyed in this portfolio would cease to exist.

For the realization of the freedom and beauty that the English language possesses, I thank all of my former English teachers.

Without Alex Ramirez the "wall of words" that has protected me in the past might still be erect. You are my dearest writing confidant. More importantly, you are a dear friend. Ankthug ouyug!

Lastly, I thank Nereida Rios for staying up with me till 4:30 in the morning while I wrote and typed, and wrote, and typed. . . . I guess that your ghetto computer isn't that bad, huh? :-)

I owe gratitude to a multitude of individuals. To those who are not listed here, THANX.

VJ Villanueva
Binghamton, NY
December 10, 19——

Rubric for Portfolio Evaluation

Portfolio Writer _____   Date _____

                                                 Evaluator _____

A. What's in the portfolio? (75%)

____ Four pieces of writing, including one free choice (write titles below)

1.

2.

3.

4.

____ Reflective analysis that includes *at least* an introduction to the portfolio

____ Acknowledgments page

____ Other nonrequired features (write titles below)

B. How does this portfolio reflect its author's accomplishment in this class? (25 %)

____ **Creativity**

How well does the portfolio reveal an unmistakable voice, a clear evocation of a real person? Is the portfolio put together in an interesting, unique, or original way, with at least one surprise?

____ **Polish**

How professional does the portfolio appear? How clean are the mechanical aspects of the writing and of presentation as well? How neat and organized is the portfolio?

____ **Clarity and Substance**

How well does the writer make his/her points understood in the context of the audience that has been described? How solid and substantial are the ideas? How well does the writer use details to develop significant and thoughtful pieces of writing?

____ **Improvement**

What evidence is there of the writer's growth during the time covered by the portfolio? How well does the writer reflect on her/his drafts to make the published versions better? How carefully does the writer consider criticism from readers?

C. What are your responses to and questions about this portfolio? What would you like to tell the writer? Please write your comments here and on the back.

Dozen:

A Course Portfolio

The Writing of the Students
of C. Beth Burch

3 April 1998

Division of Education
Binghamton University, SUNY
Binghamton NY 13902–6000

Dear Reader:

I am glad that you are reading my course portfolio, *Dozen*, a collection of writing done by student writers in my courses. The portfolio is *Dozen* because, wanting to include fine and varied writing, I could force myself to include no fewer than these dozen pieces. Twelve, a familiar measure, resonates and satisfies. Quilted together, these pieces provide a textured view of how students see and process their worlds through writing. And though these pieces tend toward the external and analytic, they also reveal their writers' interests and ideas, their personalities and preferences.

The portfolio is arranged by genre, from a study of a place to a persuasive piece to more specifically analytical work. Examples of writing from and about research constitute the last four items. Each genre is preceded by a brief commentary and reflection upon the students' writing experiences as I remember and reconstruct them from class artifacts. The reflections address my thoughts about teaching the genre and my observations of students' experiences; I also include students' comments and thinking about their processes, difficulties, triumphs.

You should know that the pieces in this portfolio are not all equally realized; some of them may need another draft; some keener editing; still others, close reading and adjustment. But I include them anyway in the hope that you will consider each piece critically—not negatively, but with a sharp and evaluative eye—to determine how it can become an even stronger piece of writing. We can learn from imperfect models (indeed, whose work is perfect?), and the space of a semester may strain the effort at reflection that is so necessary for thorough and thoughtful revision. I hope you will also consider critically the whole that is here constituted: What do these formal pieces reveal about the purposes and results of the course? What do you believe the students have learned? How can I become a better writing teacher? I welcome your letters and suggestions as part of a dialogue about writing and composing that will help me create not only a better portfolio but better learning and teaching experiences.

Reexamining a quite large collection of student writing to select these pieces has proven worthwhile and instructive. I have reread hundreds of students' essays in the process of choosing these. Because of this rereading, I am more deeply appreciative of the ingenuity of young writers, more respectful of their talent. For this particular rereading, I took more time for thinking—and I was also no longer the evaluator: I was simply on the track of good writing, which I found and present here. Because of this rereading, I am reminded that students write best when they write what they know and care most deeply about. I am refreshed by the variety of experiences chronicled here. And I am buoyed by the remembered intellectual pleasure that comes from teaching and seeing others learn.

This, then, is my course portfolio. Read and enjoy.

Regards,

C. Beth Burch
English Education

Table of Contents
for
Dozen: A Course Portfolio
by C. Beth Burch

ACKNOWLEDGMENTS

In the process of writing a book, strange things happen—and lo! the book that you thought you were writing turns out to be a book you hadn't quite imagined. This is what happened with this book about writing in the portfolio classroom, and this is the kind of situation that occasioned this particular portfolio. Reviewers of the manuscript for *Writing for Your Portfolio* asked for a model portfolio with less personal and more academic writing. I hadn't saved copies of too many complete portfolios, and anyway none quite fit that description. One day I was relaying this dilemma to Pamela Segal, whose work is represented in this book, and lamenting that I wasn't going to be able to satisfy the suggestion (now become in my mind an imperative) that the chapter contain more academic writing. In mid-complaint, it suddenly occurred to me that I could create a *course portfolio;* that is, a portfolio of several students' work, work done in courses that I had designed and taught, rather than a portfolio of writing by just one student in just one course. And that is how the notion of *Dozen* originated.

Thus I am grateful to Pam, who engaged me in the conversation that led to this idea; to the reader/reviewers of this manuscript, whose knowledge of their students' needs occasioned their request for a more analytic and academic portfolio; and to the students whose writing is presented here. For the ideas and for the material in this portfolio, thank you.

STUDY OF A PLACE

Comments and Reflection: The Study of a Place

I almost always present this assignment—to write a study of a place—relatively early in the course because it accustoms students to observing, describing, and writing based on observation and realized mostly through description. These are basic writing skills that are used throughout the course—and, indeed, in most writing courses. A study of a place is actually a variation on the profile essay, a descriptive piece that may be either a travel essay (complete with advice for travelers) or a more meditative piece (one describing a place and examining its significance). In the end, most writings combined both notions; as no genre is "pure," neither were these essays. But one feature of all well-written studies of places is a careful attention to observed as well as remembered detail and to the needs of the reader: useful considerations for all sort of academic writing to come. The supply of good ideas for topics was, well, virtually endless. From thinkpieces written about prospective subjects, listen to the voices of writers considering topics for this assignment:

> I haven't made up my mind yet, though I was thinking about a town in Europe that I visited or maybe North Dakota or an outdoor essay about a city (instead of about wilderness, which everyone expects). I'm thinking I'm beginning to favor "Beulah, North Dakota: What's there to do there?"
>
> —Robert Kmec

I live in Lafayette, Indiana, and I'm thinking about doing a historical tour of that city. I've grown up with two history freaks and have gone to about every historical site and antique shop in this state!

—Mindy Whitmore

I might do something about either Yosemite, Yellowstone, or the Madison, Wisconsin Summer Violin Camp Session. I still have to narrow my choices down a bit, but those three are my strongest ideas presently. I will just pull out a few pictures and letters from the past and will later decide on which one I should choose.

—Young Ro

I think I'll stick to Purdue and this area of town. Maybe places in the Union building, since it has historical background, many food places, and places for activities—bowling, pool, etc. I am not committed entirely to this topic, but I would like to use the Union as a specific part of my topic.

—Angie Chesterman

Not everyone could think of a place to write about at first; Aaron Blanding wrote that he had "absolutely NO IDEA," that he hadn't been anyplace. But as he kept writing and thinking, he also decided to write about Lafayette, Indiana, as the place where the Colt World Series, an international baseball tournament for fifteen- and sixteen-year-olds, is held. Most students did write about a familiar place, one they remembered or still frequented: a summer camp, a favorite place they had visited with their family, a place of historical significance, a place within a place (such as the special barn at a grandmother's house or the trading floor of the Chicago Board of Trade, where one student had been fortunate to spend a morning). The resulting writing was of delicious variety and truly interesting. And although these studies were done with the purpose of informing a reader about the places, I found them nevertheless to reflect their writers' personalities keenly. I have come to realize that that is something I value in writing, something that I think makes writing "good"—that regardless of how objective or impersonal or informative a piece is supposed to be, the voice of its writer somehow makes itself heard, indeed *insists* on being heard.

Rachel Cain's voice is clearly audible in the piece she wrote about her experiences in Recife, Brazil. In a thinkpiece, Rachel considers how she wants to handle her subject:

I feel like writing about Brazil. I don't know what aspect of it or what form exactly this would take, but Brazil is inexhaustibly my favorite subject, because I lived there for several years. Maybe I'll write a report as though for a magazine or a book. I could write about Recife and the people in the Northeast where I lived. Information would be easy to get because it was my mother's job to talk about stuff like that.

The essay that eventually developed from this kernel of an idea not only shows us Recife and gives us a sense of its people but transmits Cain's values about society as well. When you read it, notice especially how the description is colored by personal observation and how the use of the second-person *you* creates an intimacy with the reader. I had a difficult time persuading some of my students that the second person—and even the first person, as in David Koller's paper—were acceptable in a formal essay. They had been taught absolutely not to use anything but third person in writing for "school."

David Koller's piece was closer to home. As a longtime Indiana resident, he had wandered many areas of the state; thus, he chose to write about one of his favorite places, the Indiana Transportation Museum. In some ways, this piece also resembles a review, so you might want to think of it later when you read the review section of this portfolio. Clearly, Koller wants you to understand his expectations for a museum (note his use of the first-person *I*) and how a museumgoer feels when those expectations aren't met—even if the result is somewhat surprising.

Please notice two features of both these essays. Note how Cain and Koller structure their descriptions—the organizing principles employed by each. Also, watch for the way that details are selected and accumulated. I always find it interesting to speculate on what writers leave out, and why.

Now, the studies of places.

Rachel Cain
Advanced Composition
12 January 199—

Recife—As Seen by Bus

You are going on a tour of Recife, a Brazilian city of 2.8 million people. It is midday, and there is no shade where you are standing as you wait for the bus. You are starting your tour in one of Recife's less fortunate neighborhoods, for this is not a tourists' sightseeing tour; it is a tour of the city where you are going to live for the next couple of years. And, as is true with most of the people with whom you will be working, the bus is your only means of transportation. You have been waiting for at least fifteen minutes, and you are beginning to get hot and frustrated. Your guide, standing next to you, is as calm as can be and doesn't seem worried at all about the delay. He sees your distress and tells you that the buses are sometimes late; it's something you have to get used to. Then around the bend you see a bus, blowing dust all over the place and sounding like a train. You notice that the bus sags to one side as if from weight and that people are hanging all over the bus, even out the back entrance. To you, the bus looks way too full to be safe. Yet everyone waiting scoots even closer to the curb in a disorderly attempt at a line; you and two dozen other people want to get on this bus. Finally, it screeches to a halt, throwing everyone inside forward a bit as if to make room for more. All the prospective passengers rush forward, but your guide pulls you out of the moving mass and shakes his head: "There's no way I could get you on that bus!" he tells you. "It takes a lot of pushing and shoving, and I don't think you can take it. We're in no hurry; we'll wait for the next one. It should come soon," he says hopefully. "It might even be empty."

Sure enough, a couple of minutes later, another bus comes along. It is almost empty, but it looks like it might fill up with all the leftover passengers who couldn't get on the previous bus. In the midst of a lot of pushing and shoving, you finally get on—and find yourself in a cagelike contraption until you pay and go through the turnstile. Because you are hot, you find a seat by the window and try to open it to find a breeze. But the window won't budge. It's broken. You look around and notice that many other things are broken: Seats are torn, windows are cracked, the floor is dirty and littered, and everything looks old and considerably used.

At the first stop after you get on, about twenty children get on the bus. Evidently school has just dismissed. The younger children get on through the front door, the older ones in the back. The ones in back crawl in, avoiding the turnstile and avoiding paying. The collector just sits there looking bored. The driver smiles and chats with the children, who are standing up holding on to whatever they can to keep their balance. They all wear scruffy shoes and stained, torn uniforms. Already people are standing up, and now there are even more without seats. Most of the passengers are in very uncomfortable positions, hanging over other people's heads.

At the next stop, an injured man climbs aboard up front. He is helped by a friend who seats him in the first seat, kindly offered by an older man. The friend gets on in back, and your guide tells you that they are probably going to the emergency room to get that cut over the man's brow sewed up. He adds that they obviously couldn't afford a taxi.

Looking out the window, you see that another school has just released its students for the day. This one is different, though; the building to which this bus belongs is larger and prettier, and the students' uniforms are tidy and neat. These students are waiting to be picked up by their parents or chauffeurs. "It's a Catholic school," your guide tells you; "only the rich people go there." At the stop nearest that school, you notice that not one student boards the bus.

Indeed, you now seem to be in a richer section of town. The houses are larger, with high, imposing walls and gates around them; dogs threaten the passersby and protect beautiful, well-kept gardens. You come upon a very large shopping mall with what seem to be hundreds of cars parked in front. In the lot next door, you are shocked to view a huge trash heap crawling with people in rags obviously searching for something. Your guide tells you that they are looking for food and for cardboard and paper to sell for a couple of pennies at a recycling center. You watch as a woman parks her car and gets out to shop, holding a handkerchief to her nose, averting her eyes from the scene.

Another bus goes by. It is much newer and better kept than the one you are on, and it is empty! You ask your guide the reason for the obvious difference in quality of systems. He tells you it's because that nicer bus goes only to the rich sections. Those buses cost a little more, and they make their round of stops more quickly so that the rich don't have to wait. You argue about the injustice of it all, and your guide dryly replies: "That's the way things are. It's life in Recife."

Your bus now approaches the more commercial part of town, nearer downtown. A bustle of people on the streets hurry along in forty different directions. The bus stops in front of a bank. You watch as a beautiful, well-dressed woman steps out of an important-looking car and heads toward the bank entrance. Beside the doors an old woman wearing rags fans herself. She has a young child lying on her lap; her hand is extended toward passersby; she mumbles something unintelligible. She seems to cry out to the rich woman, but the woman doesn't even glance her way; she just goes in, ignoring the beggar. The beggar obviously isn't expecting anything because she continues reaching into the crowd, pleading for some alms.

Your guide tells you that you'll be getting off in two stops. At the second-to-the-last stop, a very pregnant woman gets on the bus through the front door; she carries a baby who can't be more than a year old. A large purse weighs down her shoulder. Without hesitation your guide gets up and offers his seat. Sighing in relief, she thanks him, sitting down beside you. The baby sleeps, resting comfortably in its mother's arms. Then before you know it, your guide calls you to get nearer the door because the next stop is yours. You are glad to get off and feel the fresh breeze. You are eager to see the rest of Recife. You think about how in the past half hour you have experienced much more than a tourist sightseeing excursion could ever show you in a week.

David Koller
Advanced Composition
Dr. Burch
20 January 199—

The Indiana Transportation Museum: A "Hands-On" Museum

As I pulled into the fairgrounds, I smiled at the wide-open grassy areas and well-manicured, curvy drive. "This place must be nice," I thought, as I considered my trip to the Indiana Transportation Museum near Kokomo. I continued down the winding lane, marveling at the beauty of it all. Eventually I came to a fork and spotted an out-of-place, battered sign: "I. T. Museum—Left." Not discouraged by the rickety sign or the growing dumpiness of the road, I continued.

Soon I reached the museum gate and stopped at the chain-link fence. A decrepit woman tramped out of the even more decrepit entrance booth and shouted at my window, "Adults, two bucks; kids, fifty cents." She seemed impatient as I warily checked out my surroundings. Off in the distance, I spotted some beaten-up railway equipment. Reluctantly I paid up.

"Park over there," the lady yelled, as she pointed to a block of five gravel parking spaces. I parked the car after narrowly missing a whimpering, ill-fed dog. As I stepped out of the car, I was startled by a ringing, whistling sound. Looking up, I saw an ancient trolley whiz by at thirty miles an hour, over equally old tracks. "Apparently the state inspectors haven't been here lately," I thought.

Meandering toward the old railway equipment, I met a man whom I had previously met at another railroad museum. After exchanging the usual rail fan pleasantries, I asked him about the Indiana Transportation Museum.

"Well," he started in, "the Museum was begun years ago as a way to preserve Indiana railroading heritage. Basically, it started with the donation of some old, broken-down equipment, and that's how it has continued. Yessir, any time you got some old rail cars, just give 'em to the Museum," he chuckled.

We wandered among the five tracks jammed with old boxcars, gondolas, and cabooses. It was different from any other railroad museum I had ever visited. For one thing, there were no plaques, brochures, or markers. There was no walkway, and the ground was strewn with scrap metal, litter, and other various objects.

It was a whole different perspective, though. My new friend demonstrated how couplers locked and showed me how to open and close a giant boxcar door. We climbed into all the cars, noting all the usually unseen interior details. I was thrilled when I put the brakes on my first caboose and climbed up for a view out the cupola. We traveled a lot of ground and ended at the far end of the museum grounds, where we found a giant building that my friend said was the museum shop.

"Whenever the Museum gets a half-decent piece of equipment, they take it in here and fix it up. Unfortunately, the fixed-up pieces never stay at the museum," he explained; "they go on tour all around the state." As we passed around the shop, I did a double take: There in front of me was a giant hunk of rusted metal. Only at second glance did I realize that this rusting hulk was a neglected model of my favorite locomotive: the 1951 EMD F-7. We spent quite a while crawling all over that engine. The entire locomotive was accessible; engine doors were torn off, and the cab was open. My companion pointed out how the power was transferred from the engine to the various engine-driven mechanisms. We sat in the cab and pretended to be the engineers.

As the day began to get dark, my friend made a suggestion. "You've got to sample the one special attraction of this place, the trolley," he advised. While we walked to the loading dock, I remembered how rickety it had originally looked. These fears melted, though, when I met Rusty, the 80-year-old trolley operator.

"Hop on up here, son," he cried, giving me a hand up the steps. "How'd you like to run this thing yourself?"

With the veteran guidance of Rusty, I tried my hand at operating the trolley. Then with a blast of the horn, we pulled back in near the parking lot, just as the sky was turning black. As I walked away, Rusty yelled after me.

"Hey, son, you come back now. We'll still be here. We're a hands-on museum, you know,"

"Yes," I thought, "you definitely are."

ADVISORY ESSAY: HOW SOMETHING IS MADE OR DONE
Comments and Reflection: The Advisory Essay

Like the study of a place, the advisory piece demands careful attention to detail and to the needs of the reader. The advice must be presented in such a way as to be useful to and usable by the reader; it must be full of explanatory detail and ordered carefully, yet not sound didactic or arrogant. To be credible, the writer must sound confident yet not irritate the reader's sensibilities. I think you will find these features in the pieces included here, essays on how a McDonald's hamburger is made and on how a boomerang is made and flown.

You will notice that the essays, while informative and full of advice, are framed somewhat differently than the other essays of advice in this book (although they are closely related). These pieces describe a process—how something is done—primarily to inform the reader about how the process occurs rather than to help the reader replicate the process. That is, Marty Ryan's essay on how hamburgers are made is written so that you understand the process, not so that you can step behind the McDonald's grill and cook two dozen burgers. Scott Radcliffe's piece on boomerangs tells the reader how to make and fly boomerangs—but his primary purpose is to have you understand those processes rather than for you to sit down and make, then fly, a boomerang. Thus, you will find that these more academic variations on the advisory piece differ subtly from the advisory essays elsewhere in the book. Nevertheless, they are all kin. Ryan's piece follows a step-by-step organization that could be easily transformed into a "first do this, then do this" kind of essay. Radcliffe's piece combines two pieces of advice (making the boomerang and flying the boomerang) with a brief history of the toy/weapon. Studying these more academic advisory pieces may help you structure your academic writing in courses where the professor asks you to write about how something is done: how photosynthesis occurs, how a transitive verb functions in a sentence, how a resolution moves through the United Nations.

My students enjoyed writing advisory pieces, perhaps more than any other kind of writing done during the semester, because these pieces allow them to draw on their expertise to write about something they know well. Some fascinating issues emerged in writers' group. One group explored the notion of audience with regard to this paper and determined that the audience had to be very specifically defined if the writer were presenting fairly technical information. For instance, not everyone will enjoy reading about boomerangs or even care about them; the group decided, then, that writers might want to append a note to these pieces to explain who the anticipated audience was. That note would signal the reader that the writer wasn't trying to appeal to a general audience—an important consideration, the group believed. They didn't want to be perceived as writers who didn't address the needs of their audiences. The notion of audience is directly related to the amount and level of detail, another group decided. If you write about how a lemon pie is made and you use the term *lemon zest* without explanation, you are assuming that your reader has some culinary experience. That puts your advice on an entirely different level than it would be if you thought it necessary to explain the term in the text. John Robertson put the dilemma this way:

> It was hard for me to decide what to exclude in keeping my essay specific and not overwhelming. I hoped that the reader could easily understand everything that I discussed; but the more I think about it, the more I think that background information is lacking. I may have left some important details out and included some not so important facts. On the whole, this paper sort of played tricks with my dancing pen.

See what rhetorical issues you notice as you read these advisory pieces.

Marty Ryan

English 103

Dr. Burch

December 7, 199—

Between the Buns: How a McDonald's Hamburger Is Made

How many times in your life have you eaten a McDonald's hamburger? If you tried to guess how many McDonald's hamburgers you've eaten, what would you guess? 100? 500? 1,000? The odds are that you had eaten at least 100 of these hamburgers by the time you entered high school. The odds are probably even greater that you still don't know how they are made. Here's what you would see if you went to the nearest McDonald's and observed the whole process.

About once a week, when the general supply of food and other restaurant necessities gets low, the manager orders sufficient quantities to fully stock the freezers and supply shelves. A supply truck arrives and delivers frozen goods as well as shelf goods. This is how a frozen hamburger patty, packed neatly in a box with several hundred of its comrades, arrives at McDonald's with most of the other necessities for making hamburgers. From the truck, the frozen burgers are loaded directly into the main storage freezer, located in the back of the restaurant. The buns arrive in separate trucks every few days, wrapped loosely in plastic bags and placed on a stackable rectangular plastic rack. These racks of buns are unloaded from the truck and stacked up about five feet high in a rear storage area near the freezer.

The patties will probably sit in the main freezer for about two weeks until they are moved to a smaller freezer. This freezer is the immediate reserve freezer. It holds nine boxes of patties, and it is very close to the grill. Right next to the grill is a still smaller freezer that holds one box of patties. When this box gets low, another box must be gotten from the reserve freezer. When this is done, the patties are in place and ready to be cooked.

A call for more hamburgers comes from a register worker: "Gimme 12 ham, please."

The grill worker starts into action. He or she takes the crowns (tops) from 12 hamburger buns and places them white side up on a tray and puts them in the bun toaster, which has an automatic timer. The bottoms of the buns are placed white side down on another tray on top of the toaster for later. The grill worker then lays 12 patties on the grill in two rows of six and hits the grill timer button. About ten seconds later, the "sear" light flashes, and the timer beeps loudly until he/she shuts it off. The grill worker then gets the searing tool, a flat, round metal disk with a handle on top, and gives each patty two or three seconds of pressure (this helps the meat cook faster).

Shortly after the meat is seared, the toaster timer will go off, meaning that the crowns have been fully toasted. The bottoms are then placed in a different part of the toaster that does not toast but merely warms. The crowns are placed on the dressing table, which has all the sauces and extra things needed to make a hamburger. Each crown gets one squirt in the center, first from the mustard and then from the ketchup dispenser (the ketchup squirt is considerably larger). On top of the ketchup and mustard goes one pickle slice. Now the grill worker must find out how many of these crowns will become cheeseburgers.

"Cheese on 12 ham!" he or she shouts.

A register worker will quickly survey the bin where the hamburgers and cheeseburgers are kept, decide how many of each are needed, and then tell the grill worker.

"Cheese eight, please."

The grill worker then places a slice of cheese on eight of the crowns. Now the grill timer beeps and the "turn" light flashes. The crew person takes the spatula and turns the hamburger patties, gets the dressed tray of crowns from the dressing table, and sets it beside the grill.

A few seconds later, the grill timer beeps one last time, indicating that the meat is fully cooked. The grill worker sprinkles some chopped onion on each patty and takes them off the grill two at a time with his spatula, placing one on each crown. He or she then gets the bun bottoms from the toaster and slides them on top of the patties. The hamburgers are complete. The worker places them on the counter that separates the grill area from the register area and calls, "Ham up!"

The entire process from the moment the crowns are put in the toaster until the finished burgers are placed on the counter takes about three minutes. From there, a register worker takes the burgers and wraps them, then places them in a bin, where they remain until served or until they get too old, in which case they are thrown away. That is how a McDonald's hamburger is made and how it gets to you.

Scott Radcliffe
English 103
Dr. Burch
December 11, 199—

The Making and Use of the Modern Boomerang

The boomerang has its roots in Australia, where even to this day the Aborigines use them to hunt small animals. These boomerangs, called Kylies, can be up to three feet long and are curved only slightly so they will fly in a straight line up to 250 yards! The boomerangs that most Americans are familiar with are shaped like a V. This type, when thrown correctly, will come back to the thrower. Many people worldwide are boomerang hobbyists, but Americans are especially fond of them. Understanding how boomerangs are made and a bit about how they fly increases the pleasure of flying them for hobby or for fun.

Making a toy boomerang is an easy process that can be completed in a couple of hours. The design of the boomerang is very forgiving, and small errors in construction do not seem to affect its flight terribly. The basic pattern of a boomerang is a banana with a sharp curve in the middle. Its two wings or blades resemble the wings of an airplane; they intersect at about a 90 to 100 degree angle. Each wing has a leading edge (one that leads the boomerang into or cuts into the wind) and a trailing edge (opposite the leading edge). Look at a boomerang wing from the end, and it looks like an elongated teardrop, a shape that creates lift when it passes through the air. Toy or sport boomerangs are made from quarter-inch, five-ply plywood, which has a crisscrossing grain that will withstand rough landings. After a boomerang is shaped and rounded, it is sanded smooth and covered with a protective finish. It is possible to vary the boomerang's appearance simply for style and to vary its basic design for maximum flying time (up to half a minute) or for distance, but most boomerangs look remarkably alike.

The workings of the boomerang have puzzled physicists for years. A Dutch physicist, Felix Hess, spent seven years writing a 555-page report on why the boomerang flies the way it does. The main secret to how the boomerang can fly back to the place where it started is that the two blades are traveling forward through the air at different speeds. Each wing has two velocities that make up its forward velocity: the rotational (the boomerang tumbling in the air, end over end) and the linear (straight line) velocities. Soon after a boom is released by a thrower, it begins its vertical rotation stage. In this stage, a number of forces act on it to make it turn back toward the thrower. The top wing has a forward velocity that is the sum of the linear and rotational velocities. The opposite wing on the bottom has a forward velocity that is the difference of the linear and rotational velocities. This difference of speeds between the two wings creates two different lifts; the top wing with its higher forward velocity has more lift than the bottom wing.

Because of these two different lifts, the boomerang tends to fly in an arc-shaped flight pattern; its gyroscopic properties are working to correct the unbalancing effect created by the unequal lifts.

If you really appreciate boomerangs, you'll also want to learn to throw yours correctly. (Your boomerang will also last longer when it's thrown correctly—fewer crash landings.) When you get ready to throw your boomerang, be sure to consider environmental conditions. About ten miles per hour is the top wind speed under which your boomerang can fly predictably. Make sure you are in a wide-open area without hard surfaces near. Hold the boomerang with the bottom part of the V toward yourself and with one wing pointing away from your body. With an overhand motion, release the boomerang almost vertically and watch it travel gracefully out and up in a large arc, almost like a bobsled turning up an icy bank. Then watch the boomerang travel back to you, flattening out until it flies horizontally, then hovering in for a landing.

To learn more about boomerangs, read one of the many books on the subject at most libraries and bookstores. One boomerang fanatic, author, and expert on boomerangs, a printer from Sydney, Australia, named Frank Donnellan, throws boomerangs out over theater audiences and make flawless catches on stage, all while blindfolded. You don't, however, have to be a fanatic to enjoy boomerangs. You can make one for yourself or purchase one at a toy or hobby store—then spend some relaxing time throwing it in the park!

PERSUASIVE ESSAY
Comments and Reflection: The Persuasive Essay

Isabeau Hallstatt exhibited courage when she wrote this persuasive piece about what is called The Machine, an all-campus superfraternity at The University of Alabama whose membership was constituted of only the top officers of all other Greek organizations on campus. But she believed strongly that what was then happening within the sororities and fraternities was corrupting the nature of Greek life, which she valued; as a sorority member, she presents here the insider's view on fraternity and sorority politics. Thus, she wrote this piece to persuade readers, specifically those in Greek organizations, to act to dismantle The Machine. This is an example of where personal feelings can be an impetus behind one's response to an assignment to write persuasively. When you read this piece, look carefully at the way Hallstatt includes (or does not include) her feelings and emotions on the subject; consider whether you are satisfied with the essay as it is or whether you think it can be improved. Incidentally, Hallstatt changed not only the names of the individuals involved in the events, but the names of the fraternities and sororities as well. What do you think might be her reason?

Finding a subject to write about doesn't come as easily to all students as it did this particular time to Hallstatt. Most everyone found it necessary to work through the problem-finding process (see Chapter 6) more than once and to talk in writers' group quite extensively about manageable and appropriate subjects. Many writers initially wanted to do very ambitious subjects, ones that would require a semester's research to do well. Typically, their groups (or sometimes I) talked them out of such endeavors until everyone found a doable topic that may have required research but didn't require thesis credits. As you read Hallstatt's piece, consider whether her writing here might be further informed by additional research—and if so, what questions the research should address. Here is "When the Walls Come Tumbling Down."

Isabeau Hallstatt
April 23, 199—

When the Walls Come Tumbling Down

Almost anyone vaguely familiar with the University of Alabama has at least heard of The Machine. For years, people outside the Greek system have tried to learn about this covert organization. Some members of the Greek community blatantly deny such a group even exists. Others explain the group by its commonly known definition: The Machine, also known as Theta Nu Epsilon, is a coalition of select fraternities and sororities designed to influence campus politics. A few will even go a step further and say The Machine is merely a political party, representing all students with the best government possible. But there is something no one will say—The Machine is tearing apart the Greek system.

Yes, the long-standing walls of the Greek system at the University are crumbling. Many members of Greek organizations blame people outside the system for the coming destruction. These Greeks claim outsiders are criticizing something they know little or nothing about, these biased criticisms leading to the collapse of the system.

However, I am inside those crumbling walls, and I can say that the Greek system is destroying itself from within. I see Machine members tearing down the walls, doing much more damage than those outside throwing stones. When it comes to criticizing the Greek system, those outside it barely scratch the surface of the problems and corruption that exist. Yes, the Greek system is falling apart, but members have no one to blame but ourselves. We allow The Machine to exist.

The Machine is more than a coalition; it is a corrupt, secret organization in which a few dictate to many the direction of campus politics. The Machine is more than a political party choosing candidates and stands for a platform. The Machine controls virtually every area of campus life. The Machine intends to do much more than influence campus politics: It wants to dominate and control every aspect of this university.

As a member of Theta Alpha Tau sorority at the University for four years, I have witnessed firsthand what this system is about. I know The Machine exists, and it is based on the idea of intimidation and brainwashing. As a senator in the SGA from 1994 through

1996, I was required to attend not only the weekly senate meetings but also a weekly meeting of senators from The Machine, the purpose of which was to design strategies for the upcoming senate meeting. Every Wednesday night during this three-year period, senators from Machine sororities and fraternities met in the basement of the Delta Chi Delta house where the SGA vice president, the person in charge of the student senate, would present the agenda and the business for the upcoming senate meeting. With little or no discussion about the bills, Tom Rowe, an officer in The Machine and a senator, would assign two or three senators to speak about a bill, tell them what they would say about the bill and then tell us all how we were supposed to vote on the bill. The next night at the senate meeting, all would go basically according to the rehearsed plan.

Bills for funding rarely received consideration based on their merit and worth. The few people deciding the fate of the bills, those who were actually members of The Machine, based their decisions on who was sponsoring the bill and who would benefit from its passage. If an independent senator sponsored a bill, it was scrutinized much more than if a Machine senator had sponsored it. Bills sponsored by independent senators usually were substantially cut from the requested amount—if they were passed at all. Bills for organizations not supporting the Greek system or not having many Greeks in membership often met the same fate.

Besides dictating the operation of student government, The Machine chooses the number of non-Greek students selected for membership in many of the University's most prestigious organizations. Membership in Mortar Board, Omicron Delta Kappa and Anderson Society is largely determined by The Machine. Because officers in these organizations and a vast majority of the groups' memberships are either Machine members or members of Greek organizations affiliated with The Machine, selections for these high honors are caught in a vicious circle, with old members recruiting new members based on cooperation with The Machine.

Further, since 1990, The Machine has chosen the Homecoming Queen at the University. Following the election of a black Homecoming Queen in 1989, The Machine began choosing a candidate Machine Greeks were required to support. On the Sunday night before Homecoming week, Machine fraternity members met in the basement of the Delta Chi Delta house with résumés and photographs of the women in Machine sororities who had applied for the title. After reviewing résumés, examining photographs and discussing each candidate's cooperation with The Machine, these members selected one candidate all Machine organizations supported. Signs were posted at all Machine fraternity houses telling members who they were to vote for; fraternity pledges had shifts at polling sites during which they kept a count of who had cast ballots. Machine sorority members did not participate in the Homecoming Queen selection; their non-participation supposedly prevented bias on the part of candidates' sorority sisters. That such a backward, elitist group would concern itself with bias is a frightening irony.

Besides using basic intimidation and brainwashing techniques to get Greeks to support the chosen homecoming candidates, Machine members also penalized those in Greek organizations who did not participate in the election. As with SGA elections, substantial fines were imposed on those who did not vote. Machine members verified each Greek person's participation in the election by checking the election's alpha list, the University's official record of who voted. Other consequences for nonparticipation included social probation for members not voting. With this, the member not voting was restricted from attending social events associated with his or her fraternity or sorority.

Overall, the Machine seeks to eliminate outsiders from having a voice in any aspect of the campus. However, not only does The Machine fail to represent those outside of the Greek community, it fails to represent those it was designed to represent. The Machine generally ignores Greek organizations not associated with what is known as Old Row. Old Row does not necessarily refer to the oldest Greek organizations at the University or to the physical location of the Greek houses; instead it more specifically refers to those sororities and fraternities traditionally with membership from old, Southern money. Old Row sororities and fraternities such as Kappa Gamma, Pi Gamma Theta and Sigma Tau take priority when the Machine is involved. These groups have overwhelming representation in high student government positions and in prestigious campus organizations. For example, prior to the 1992 SGA elections, the past three SGA presidents were also members of Old Row organizations. Despite the fact that every Greek organization pays the same amount of money to be a member of The Machine, only Old Row organizations reap the benefits of dishonesty and corruption.

Yes, The Machine is only one of the causes of the decay of the Greek system. However, it is the *major* problem and the one that must be dealt with before any other problems can be corrected. The Machine is not concerned with improving the University; it is not concerned with quality in campus organizational membership; it is not concerned with promoting harmony and better relations among students here. The Machine is concerned only with promoting the interests of the few in power. And those in power have little ability to dictate how the entire campus should operate. The Machine is destroying the Greek system at the University.

Certainly the collapse of the Greek system at the University of Alabama means very little to people outside it. However, these problems signal problems inherent in much of politics and society today. The Machine at the University should be a warning to everyone: We should all be gravely concerned that such an organization has been able to maintain itself for nearly 100 years; we should all be concerned that these young people are the politicians and businessmen of tomorrow.

Moreover, the collapse of the Greek system means a great deal to those involved in it. The University could lose a substantial part of its tradition if it loses the Greek system. Members of the system should stop ignoring the corruption of this organization.

Certainly those in power are unwilling to relinquish that power, but a vast majority of Greeks are being ignored, along with the students outside the system. Together, these students could make a difference in the influence The Machine has on this campus. We cannot expect human relations in this country to improve if we judge people by the Greek letters, or the lack thereof, across their chest.

Certainly the Greek system, despite controversy and criticism, is not entirely bad. Greek organizations do many projects to serve the campus and community, these efforts often unnoticed by critics. Members of the Greek system who believe the system offers positive aspects to the community and campus should work to eliminate the influence of this corrupt organization. If Greeks are unwilling to work to throttle the Machine's power, then we should all watch out for the crumbling of the Greek system's walls.

[NAMES OF FRATERNITIES AND SORORITIES HAVE BEEN CHANGED IN ORDER TO PROTECT THE IDENTITY OF THE AUTHOR.]

ESSAY EXAMINATION
Comments and Reflection: The Essay Examination

The essay exam included here appeared in the portfolio of one of my students, although it was not written for my course. Our class worked with the writing of essay examinations, but my students didn't take examinations in their writing course—so Samantha Van Buren put a U.S. history exam into her writing portfolio. The exam essay appears, as Van Buren explained, as an example of in-class thinking and writing: writing not reviewed, revised, or rewritten. This kind of writing is useful in a portfolio, for it provides an opportunity for assessing one's strengths in writing under pressure and makes possible a type of reflection different from the reflection one does on a considered and carefully wrought draft.

I found this particular examination, essay, and response interesting on another note, however: It is an excellent example of dialogic writing, where two writers engage in a sort of written conversation on a particular topic. The question that Van Buren addressed was itself a mini-essay, a laying out of background and terrain within which a writer could respond. The history professor wanted to create a context for the students' answers, so the question indeed included considerable exposition or information-presenting. Van Buren's response should be considered then as an entry in a larger conversation. Incidentally, although the length of the question makes it seem intimidating, the professor gave the entire question to students before the examination in a study guide, thus enabling them to become familiar with it and to plan sufficient responses.

As you read, consider how Van Buren's answer addresses the question and whether you are satisfied with the thoroughness of her response. Then read the professor's comments following her answer as the third entry in the dialogue—and as an aid for Van Buren as she plans her writing for the next examination. The bracketed numerals in Samantha's essay are keyed to the numbered responses by the professor.

American Slavery and American Freedom
Samantha Van Buren

The Question:

From the earliest British settlements in the seventeenth century in the American marchland, one thing seemed eminently clear: Liberty was inextricably linked to private property. Economic independence and political identity were inherent in the ownership of property—all property. By late eighteenth- and nineteenth-century America, the role of the government was to protect private property and create an environment for growth and development and economic expansion. Liberty meant opportunity; opportunity for most Americans meant land! Personal interest in the acquisition of property coincided with the national interest in the acquisition of territory, and those interests overlapped in turn with America's sense of mission, its Manifest Destiny. Result: Individuals projected on their newly won liberty in post-Revolutionary America the desire to colonize and exploit the West. This attitude produced an expanding slave empire where white people's liberty rested increasingly on black people's bondage. What is the meaning of this? How were slavery, territorial expansion, and liberty linked in American political thought? Freedom was an integral part of their history almost from the beginning; how could Americans rationalize this incongruity? How could they balance their love of freedom with the continued existence of slavery in their republic? Was it greed, racism, intellectual dishonesty, or something else that allowed Americans to celebrate liberty in a "slave empire"? With this in mind, address the following questions:

a. All New World slave societies had this much in common: Their very being was inconceivable except as a function of capitalist development. New World slavery was itself the servant of the driving force of capitalism. Colonial Virginia was no exception. But was the decision for slavery in Virginia "inevitable"? Was it the product of market forces, class interests, or racism? Which came first—racism or slavery? Did Virginians regard Africans and, later, African Americans as not only racially distinct and culturally different but also inherently inferior?

b. When and why did Virginia become a slave society? Was racism a "natural" part of the decision, or was it ideological; that is, "constructed" or invented for social and political objectives? What then is the significance of Bacon's rebellion in 1676? What were its consequences?

c. What then are the implications for our understanding of racism in the history of American political culture? Is racism transhistorical? Eternal? Static? Or does race become the ideological medium through which people pose and understand basic questions of power and dominance, sovereignty and citizenship, justice and rights?

d. Why did succeeding generations of politicians maintain the political consensus regarding slavery? Why did American politics fail to address this seminal issue? Were there instances prior to the total collapse in 1861 where this agreement to suppress all debate of the slavery issue broke down? What were the consequences? How then was political harmony restored?

e. Why did the election of Lincoln and the Republicans seem to the Southern slave-holders like a fulfillment of the South's greatest fears of a "conspiracy" against their liberties? Finally, what was the "slaveholders' revolution"?

Samantha Van Buren's Response:

Slavery in America first started in Virginia and then spread, driven by the increasingly market culture of American society. It was Bacon's Rebellion of 1676 that spurred on [1] the idea of slavery in Virginia. The Rebellion was an intraclass conflict between "old" and "new" money. As tobacco became more important as a cash crop and the number of indentured servants receiving land increased, [2] the availability of land declined. Bacon wanted a stronger voice in the House of Burgesses regarding Indian land. A coalition of poor people joined behind him, including poor blacks, whites, landless people of all races. The elite [3] attempted to break up this coalition by using the race card. Fearful that they might lose, they tried to appease the poor whites by showing them the benefits of owning black slaves. [4] Slave codes were eventually passed, and the black people of Virginia [5] were to be slaves. This gave the poor whites self-perpetuating labor at a one-time cost. [6] The black landowners were driven away by a created harsh social environment. Thus, slavery and then "racism" were constructed in Virginia to satisfy the class interests of the elite. The decision for slavery was not "inevitable" but rather a clear rational decision based on economics and power. [7]

Racism then came about to "justify" slavery in the eyes of the slaveholders. Racism is not eternal but is created to rationalize power and dominance. Slavery came first and racism followed.

The rational decision of slavery has important consequences for understanding society. It can be used to look at other seemingly irrational decisions in history. Throughout American history, as with the Populist movement in the late nineteenth century, the race card has been used to break up multiracial coalitions. White supremacy is used as a cover for economic and class interests. Ideas of inherent inferiority are constructed to rationalize human bondage or subjugation. The slaves were thought of as inherently inferior only after paternalism had given way to liberalism. [8]

As slavery became more and more important to Southern life, the idea of slaves came to be synonymous with the "rights" of property, which rested upon the notion of liberty; neither the North nor the South wanted to split the newly formed union by debating the issue. Debate over slavery was submerged, and a variety of compromises came about. From the Constitutional Convention came the Three-fifths Compromise and the agreement to end the international slave trade twenty years hence (1808). Each side (North and South) understood this to mean something different. [9] The South figured that in twenty years there would be no need for a slave trade because they would have enough slaves by then. The North thought of this as the first step to ending slavery. Many Northerners also believed that the tobacco industry was declining and that slavery would eventually die out. Each side thought that it was both winning something from the other side and at the same time protecting the unity of America. [10]

The "politics of harmony" were formed, and politicians continued making compromises to avoid the violent nature of the issue. At times, as regarding the tariff issue, things had to come to a head; and indeed the tariff became a "stalking horse" for slavery. The Northerners passed an unfairly high tariff that benefited themselves but crushed the South. The South, fearful that if the North could do this with a tariff then they could do it with slavery as well, reacted. [11] Again, compromises were reached, and the tariff was repealed in an attempt to restore the balance. Other compromises on land issues (those swirling around the Missouri debates [12] and Mexican wars, for instance) brought the issue out, but the two sides tried to maintain a balance to avoid violence. Expanding land meant expanding slavery to the South, and the North felt that making the West slave-free meant a declining number of slaves. [13]

Eventually conflict came to a head as each side began to feel its personal liberty at stake. The North thought that slavery threatened society and America in general. With the election of Lincoln and the Republicans, the South felt that finally the conspiracy to rob them of profits was actually happening. The "slaveholders' revolution," as James Oakes describes it in *The Ruling Race,* was the slaveholders' decision to secede based on the principles of the American Revolution. Freedom = property = slavery—and all equalled liberty. These were American virtues! The slaveholders seceded to preserve their deeply held values of what the Union stood for.

Slavery created out of class interests became the driving force of the Southern market economy. [14] Racism was constructed to defend slavery and thus liberty as liberty was defined as the right to property and opportunity in America. It was rational market economics that compelled the decision and so created an issue so deeply interwoven in people's lives that compromise was used to ignore and submerge it. It was the definition of liberty in America that allowed slavery to continue while at the same time slavery is counter to what is thought of as the American ideal of "all men created equal." Liberty also caused the split of the Union as each side tried to defend its liberty and maintain opportunity for profit and success in the ever increasing and expanding American economy. [15]

The Professor's Responses to Her Answer:

1. Be careful. Did slavery exist in Virginia before 1676? What then was the significance of Bacon's Rebellion? The shift from indenture to slavery?

2. You are essentially correct—but it's even more interesting than this!

3. Why were they the "elite"?

4. They sought to break the coalition by making race the central element, the key to freedom and social and economic mobility.

5. Not all! Be careful. There were free African-Americans. When were the slave codes ratified?

6. I'm not sure what you mean here. Were there immediate benefits to poor white Virginians?

7. You're essentially right, but it doesn't quite emerge as clearly in your essay as you have written it so far. What about other factors? Role of ethnocentrism?

8. Nice transition! Yes! Your insights are provocative, but you need some factual support here to strengthen your argument.

9. Why? It may also be more appropriate to identify them as slaveholding vs. non-slaveholding folks.

10. Security of the Union was the key. They had no desire to be disillusioned regarding their perceptions.

11. No. Not all the South. Just South Carolina. Why?

12. 1820—This is before the tariff debates of 1828–1833.

13. Both the North and South believed that slavery needed new land to survive.

14. Again, while economic issues are important, there are other factors involved as well. Indeed. Slavery and the cotton economy were central to the growth of the American political economy until the 1840s.

15. Samantha, not bad! You have grasped (in some cases, quite elegantly) the essential themes and issues and written a thoughtful and reasonably well-crafted essay. Bravo.

REVIEW

Comments and Reflection: The Review

Emily Eckstein, in reflecting on her review of Purdue's ballet troupe, wrote that as soon as the review assignment was given, she knew the "perfect subject"—the troupe's fall performance. As a dancer and a student of dance, she knew what she expected from a performance; and, more importantly, she knew the vocabulary of dance. She knew the words she needed to describe the performance. This knowledge and the credibility of a specialized vocabulary lend authority to her review, included here.

Reviews present a special challenge to a writing instructor, for writers of reviews must juggle several large considerations. They have to abandon the notion of objectivity, first, and define for themselves what makes a good dance performance or a good movie or a valuable book or CD–ROM. This is difficult for students who have not been allowed to think for themselves or whose informed opinions have never or rarely been sought. The review requires a special voice, too: one of confidence and surety, one that knows what it is talking about. And the review also requires judiciousness. Reviewers must restrain themselves from summarizing and from giving away endings and plot twists. They must somehow explain, interpret, and evaluate without boring the reader or going on too long. This is a rather tall writing order, but it yields a delightful repast of information for the instructor. I have read reviews of cleaning ammonia, hair dryers, mascara, exotic sports cars, VCRs, classic and current movies, pizza (as in the dozens of pizza houses in any college town), and of course books.

I like the way that Eckstein really knows her subject in the review that follows. I would have liked a bit more information though; I wanted a better sense of how many other numbers were on the program and of the theme of the program (if there was one). I wanted to know a bit more about the dancers and choreographers. Were they all students? Did some of the professors/instructors/creative directors dance? What were the credentials of the choreographers? As a university dance group, the troupe must be largely peopled by students. I am curious about the academic roles that may affect the performances. See what you think.

Emily Elizabeth Eckstein

English 104

Dr. Beth Burch

December 13, 199—

Review of Purdue Repertory Dance Company's Fall Concert

Purdue Repertory Dance Company

Fall Concert, November 6

Stewart Center, Experimental Theater

West Lafayette, Indiana

$5.00 general admission

Abstract, cryptic, and only occasionally well executed, the fall concert put on by the Purdue Repertory Dance Company was, to a trained observer, sadly amateur to no fault of the dancers. The concert opened with *Round Riddle* and *Sun Dance,* which was a mistake. *Round Riddle* was intended to convey the artist's ideas about worshipping ideals; however, this intention was not apparent to anyone who merely viewed the piece. The last half of *Round Riddle* deviated sharply from the modern style: The dancers used primarily gymnastics and theatrics for a good three minutes before the dance continued with unrelated and garbled choreography. The three white-clad dancers were only reassembled at the very end in an attempt to recapitulate the first half. Altogether *Round Riddle* was a riddle indeed and too weighty for an opening number. In *Sun Dance,* however, the dancers had no problem with continuity of style. In fact, the dance could probably be cut in half without noticeable damage; Munsey moved in and out of the main body of the dance too quickly and chose music that never changed style. The dancers moved on and offstage and in and out of groups smoothly enough, but once they were together failed to move in tandem. This dance made particularly evident the fact that the cast was not well subgrouped by size or by ability. The one short solo highlighted the one short dancer who even without the spotlight would stand out from her peers. Her jumps were exquisitely timed and her landings were without flaw. The most attractive part of *Sun Dance* was that Munsey used a technique employed frequently in good choreography, individual and pair canon—where one set of steps per subgroup is delayed.

Decision, the next number, was an encoded love story, effectively plucking dramatic moves from ballet and surprising the viewer with a taste of Philip Scott's jumping ability. Despite this, the number was over almost before it began. The story-without-words moved too quickly to be understood with just one viewing, and the complex interplay of romance was encapsulated in only a few intense moments. There were a few fuzzy minutes of indecision before the plot took any definitive direction, which further confused the audience and detracted from what could have been a very good *ballet au moderne.*

On the brighter side, *Card Number 16: Thematic Apperception Test* was an encouraging beacon, drawing thunderous applause and shouts of glee as it closed the best performance of the lot. Regrettably, this number was buried in the program amid inferior performances. The fact that all the dancers involved were professionals in dance was a deciding factor in its huge success. The dancers' technique was superb, as were the costuming and choreography. Although occasionally jerky, the movements did blend into one another fluidly, and the body truly became the canvas of a skilled artist. The costumes—identical modern white gowns with bodysuits as undergarments of either red, blue, or black—provided the individuality of color and the possibility of interchange. The red and blue characters did interact occasionally with the black character, but often with each other. Black seemed indicative of the dancer's role; she was hesitant to join red and blue in movement, and even retreated occasionally, remaining a pensive figure. This allowed a focus on the action on the stage, something unfortunately lacking in other numbers.

In the whole performance, the programming was barely adequate to sequence the individual dances, each about eight minutes long. To complicate matters, the lack of a curtain in the Experimental Theater lent an air of unprofessionalism to the openings and closings, where the dancers simply walked on and off the stage. It always destroys the grand illusion to see a ballerina walk, not plié, not frappé, not jeté. Walk. Something even the clumsiest of us do well. This and many other details I've mentioned highlight the major flaws of the concert, giving me an almost overwhelming desire to demand my money back. Perhaps if it weren't for *Card Number 16: Thematic Apperception Test,* I would.

DOCUMENTED LITERARY ANALYSIS
Comments and Reflection: Documented Literary Analysis

Students tend to find the literary analysis a challenging paper, partly because this kind of writing demands not only that they work with the nuances of a text and write about it, but that they write with authority; and this stance requires taking sometimes tremendous chances and putting an interpretation of a work out there for all to see. That Pamela Segal wrote a paper on Shakespeare's *Richard the Third*, then, is impressive; *Richard the Third* is one of the most entangled of Shakespearean history plays, one that requires an understanding of the historical events represented in the play as well as an ability to work within the drama form. This play is difficult! I was pleased to see what she did with it.

Segal's thesis is that Shakespeare was influenced by the work of Machiavelli, whose thinking was widely known in Elizabethan England, and that the character of Richard follows, to an extent, the principles that Machiavelli articulated in *The Prince*. Segal argues, however, that in the end, Shakespeare wanted to subvert the Machiavellian paradigm: Richard seems Machiavellian but really isn't, she maintains. When she was writing this paper, Segal found that she had first to acquaint her readers with the rudiments of Machiavelli's philosophy in order to set the character of Richard within, then against, that philosophy. Then she had to make her case for Richard as a not-altogether-Machiavellian character by matching Richard's behavior and character against the basic tenets of Machiavellian philosophy.

As I reconsider how we write about literature in our English classes, whether writing or literature classes or both, I understand how critical time is to the process of understanding a text and then writing about it. And I understand, too, how writing about that text seems to open it up for readers/writers—how perhaps we teachers of writing and literature unjustly ask for papers at the end of a course rather than all along or from the first week or so. It would seem more helpful, and more conducive to learning, to write and then to return to the text with the class, then write again, all the while deepening that initial understanding of the text. I will have to think more on this.

Pamela Segal
English 245–08
4/11/9—

Deformed Shadow: Richard the Third As a Machiavellian Prince

In literature, it is common for a character to adopt a certain role but through the course of events deviate from the role tremendously. In the beginning of Shakespeare's *Tragedy of Richard the Third,* Richard takes on the role of a Machiavellian prince, a role which can be determined by examining evidence of Richard's conscience throughout specific scenes. As the play develops, Richard wavers from this role and finally toward the end completely defies it. If we analyze Richard's relationships with Lady Anne,

Buckingham, and the Duchess of York, his transformation becomes apparent. By examining Richard's symmetries and asymmetries with the nature of a Machiavellian prince, we can illuminate his transformation as a character.

Sixteenth-century Italian philosopher Niccolo Machiavelli has generally been described as a social scientist of modern times. His pragmatism and rationalism are the hallmarks of his philosophical studies. Machiavelli is most famous for *The Prince,* in which he attempts to examine politics from a scientific perspective. According to Bronowsky and Mazlish, coauthors of *The Western Intellectual Tradition,* Machiavelli maintains that a ruler must consider certain questions to survive. Machiavelli does not describe a just or honorable way for a ruler to behave or how society should be run. Rather he writes that a ruler must determine how to run a kingdom based on how his society does behave. One of Machiavelli's first points is that morality must be left out of politics. Attention should be placed on "what is" rather than on "what should be."

Richard exemplifies this aspect of a Machiavellian prince. He experiences many moments where he is thinking aloud and his lack of morality is quite obvious. His thoughts are ruthless and coarse. It is as if he speaks and thinks without a conscience. Richard's plans are self-centered and simple; therefore, his approach to politics is scientific. His immoral manner is inherent; he intends to obtain the throne and to discard anyone who threatens this goal. He is not moved by anyone, including his mother, the Duchess of York, or his brother George. No one is able to make Richard soften, not even those whom he is supposedly close to. He does not have to think about being immoral; it comes naturally to him. This makes it easier for his politics to be simple.

Richard's immorality is linked with his tendency to lay blame on others for his physical deformities. He is aware that compared to his brothers, nephews, cousins, and servants, he possesses a strongly unpleasant appearance. From the start of his life, he has been been tainted; his mental pain has blistered his conscience. Through time, the blisters have pussed over to form the indelible scars that he will not let himself forget:

> But I, that am not shap'd for sportive tricks, / Nor made to court an amorous looking-glass; / I that am rudely stamp'd . . . I, that am curtail'd of this fair proportion, / Cheated of feature by dissembling nature, / Deform'd, unfinish'd / . . . Scarce made up /. . . And that so lamely and unfathomable / That dogs bark at me as I halt by them. (1.1.14–23)

Richard's scars motivate him to operate without conscience in his plot to achieve power by removing it from those whom he blames. He feels as if he has been deceived and plans to take the throne, which is justifiably his. Richard strips morality from politics by lunging full force at every obstacle in his way. He plots to kill his brother, George of Clarence, so that the throne will be vacant for his future kingship when King Edward soon dies. Richard knows who is in his way, and his evil pushes him to terminate them: "I am determined to prove a villain / Plots have I laid, inductions dangerous, / By drunken prophecies, libels, and dreams" (1.1.25–27, 30, 32–33).

Machiavelli's view on human nature is that it is inherently evil. Man is moved by the same passions in every generation. Man starts off pure in life but is gradually corrupted by civilization. Similarly, Bronowski and Mazlish label the sixteenth century as an important time for individualism in power; in that era the individual's capability and power were highly respected and given exaggerated significance (35). Richard fits this paradigm precisely.

Doomed from his birth, Richard has become depraved through the influence of society. He lacks confidence and has become unbalanced during his life. His undoubtedly evil manner has been draped over his bent shoulders and has pushed him into a treacherous cycle of malicious lies. He lets people believe he is interested in their well-being when he is really staging an act that is only moving him one step closer to the throne. Although he has plotted Clarence's death, he covers his plan with eloquent words to his brother: He says that "This deep disgrace in brotherhood / Touches me deeper than you can imagine" (1.1.111–12) when he refers to Clarence's concern about a fatal prophecy given to him. After Clarence leaves, Richard sarcastically chants to himself, "Simple plain Clarence, I do love thee so / That I will shortly send thy soul to heaven" (1.1.118–19). Richard's deceitful, villainous nature leads him to kill Clarence and thus to accomplish the first major move in his plan.

From this point onward, Richard begins to fall short of Machiavellian attributes. According to Bronowski and Mazlish, one of Machiavelli's essential points is that "the prince does not hesitate to fool his people and to deceive them. . . . People are easily fooled. It is to the prince's advantage to spread false doctrines among the people" (42). Richard does not fool people but rather manipulates and seduces them into his scheme. People are afraid not to consent with him because of the vile consequences that seem bound to occur. Also, the Machiavellian prince's lies are supposed to preserve the state from treachery and ensure serenity and stability among his people. Yet Richard's lies and his deeds escalate the contempt and horror. England becomes weaker and more decrepit with each plot he concocts. This trend can be examined more thoroughly in Richard's interaction with Lady Anne.

Richard leads Anne through a tangled feast of manipulation. He has killed her husband, Edward Prince of Wales, and Edward's father, King Henry the Sixth. When we are introduced to her, she is in hysterics over Richard's beastly doings. She refers to him as having an "ugly and unnatural aspect" (1.1.23). One of Richard's tactics is that he permits Anne to lash out at him and express her hatred for his wrongdoings. Richard lets Anne spit insults at him only because he knows he can seduce her with his syrupy talk. This incenses Anne even more. It disgusts her to hear him call her an angel and make remarks that he wants to sleep with her. She thinks the only suitable punishment is for him to die. Obsequiously winding Anne down, Richard then spins the situation around, informing her that it was her beauty that caused him to kill Edward so that he, Richard, could be her new husband. He lets her think she is revengeful and proceeds to wrench guilt from her and even is successful in attaining her forgiveness and manipulating her into marrying him. Lady Anne is conscious that she is allowing Richard to seduce her: " 'Tis more than you deserve" (1.2.222). He mocks her for her feebleness and malleability after she leaves for his house in Crosby.

This scene provides a powerful example of Richard's ability to fold Anne into his deformed strategy, and it leaves the audience wary of her future. "Shine out, fair sun, till I have bought a glass, / That I may see my shadow as I pass" (1.2.262–63), says Richard, suggesting that he will soon march by his shadow and surpass his deformities as well. It is not until later, when Anne finds out she will be crowned Richard's royal queen, that she understands the far-reaching effects of his seduction: "My woman's heart / Grossly grew captive to his honey words, / And prov'd the subject of mine own soul's curse" (4.1.78–80).

Another Machiavellian principle is that the prince should not adhere to useless cruelty. Bronowsky and Mazlish add that the prince "does not, like an Oriental tyrant, cut off people's heads if they happen to displease him" (42). Richard does not live by the precept either. He has a close relationship with the Duke of Buckingham throughout most of the play. Buckingham is subservient to Richard and tied into all his plots. Richard moves Buckingham like a pawn until the bitter finale of his hellish scheme, when he demands that Buckingham's head be chopped off, employing useless cruelty with a loyal subject. Buckingham's loyalty to Richard disintegrates because Richard takes advantage of Buckingham's sense of duty. An understanding of Buckingham's true loyalty before he is murdered can be gained by tracing his character during his service to Richard. There are few scenes where Richard orders Buckingham to perform services for him. It can be concluded that either these scenes take place and are not shown or that Buckingham makes decisions on his own that are to Richard's benefit. Both theories suggest that Buckingham has total loyalty for Richard and his plans.

When Prince Edward arrives to claim the throne after Edward the Fourth dies, he wishes to see his mother the Queen and his brother, Duke of York. Hastings tells Edward that the two have taken sanctuary; Buckingham knows that Richard wishes York to be present so he can place the brothers in the Tower. Buckingham reacts fiercely against the Queen: "fie, what an indirect and peevish course / Is this of her! / . . . From her jealous arms pluck him perforce" (3.1.31–32, 36). When the Cardinal tells them it is a sin to defy the holy privilege of sanctuary, Buckingham protects Richard's actions: "You are too senseless-obstinate, my lord, / Too ceremonious and traditional" (3.1.44–45). Whether Buckingham has this reaction because he dislikes Elizabeth and her family or whether he wants Richard to be king, he is still acting in Richard's favor. Buckingham's strong subservience helps Richard appear as if he is not contriving all the plans on his own: Richard looks relatively blameless.

When Buckingham asks Richard what they will do if Lord Hastings does not express full loyalty to Richard, Richard simply spews out, "Chop off his head" (3.1.193). To cover this sudden outburst revealing an evil and quite Machiavellian consequence, Richard quickly lets Buckingham know that he will make him the Earl of Hereford and give him all his deceased brother's property when he is king. Although this bribery provides Buckingham with further incentive to remain on Richard's side, Buckingham is already bound to him. When Richard finally does chop off Hastings's head, it is because Buckingham discloses to him that Hastings is not on their side; they trick Hastings into defining himself as a traitor.

As Richard's plan moves at a heated pace, Buckingham grows extremely obsessed with his role. He instructs Richard in his own plot where he feels it necessary. Buckingham spreads gossip among the citizens that Edward cannot be the real heir to the throne because of his father's promiscuity. In front of an audience of the mayor and the citizens, Buckingham plays Richard's director and leads him inside carrying a prayer book, standing between two clergymen. Buckingham prompts Richard by orating: "We heartily solicit / Your gracious self to take on you the charge / And kingly government of this your land . . . / Your right of birth, your empery, your own" (3.7.130–32, 136). He leaves Richard open spaces in which to recite all the perfect dialogue that leads to his acceptance of the crown. This is where the curtain closes, but on Buckingham the director, not on Richard the actor.

When Buckingham says he needs time to think about Richard's next request—killing the two small princes—Richard interprets it as disloyalty. He requires absolute dominance over every circumstance. It is when Richard stubbornly ignores Buckingham's request for the earldom he was promised that Buckingham flees from his bitter, maniacal cousin: "And is it thus? Repays he my deep service / With such contempt? Made I him king for this? / O, let me think on Hastings, and be gone / To Brecknock while my fearful head is on!" (4.2.119–22).

After Buckingham's undivided faith to Richard's causes, Richard, like an Oriental tyrant, cuts off Buckingham's head to buy time for considering the next move. Buckingham's ghost visits Richard in a dream before he goes to fight Richmond: "The first was I that help'd / thee to the crown; / The last was I that felt thy tyranny. / O, in the battle think on Buckingham, / And die in terror of thy guiltiness!" (5.3.167–70). Although Richard sees Buckingham as a traitor, Richard provokes Buckingham to flee.

Machiavellian philosophy also insists that if a choice must be made, it is better for a prince to be feared than loved. Bronowsky and Mazlish add that a Machiavellian prince "drew a distinction between being feared and being hated" (42). Richard's mother, the Duchess of York, is an excellent representation of this idea. After Clarence is murdered, his children tell the Duchess that Richard informed them that it was the Queen who influenced the king to imprison their father. The Duchess is shocked:

> Ah! That deceit should steal such gentle shape / And with a virtuous visor hide deep vice! / He is my son—ay, and therein my shame; / Yet from my dugs he drew not this deceit. (2.2.27–30)

She is fully aware of how dangerous Richard is; she knows his motives and sees through his act. In a conversation with Elizabeth, she describes him as "false glass" (2.2.53). She cannot believe that it was her womb from which her wretched son was born.

Richard uses similar tactics with his mother as he does with Anne. But instead of the Duchess's growing tired from reprimanding her son, she is even more angry at his apathetic attitude. After Richard becomes king, the Duchess knows that he is responsible for all the murders. She refers to herself as "she that might have intercepted thee, / By strangling thee in her accursed womb, / From all the slaughters, wretch, that thou hast done!" (4.4.137–39). Richard does not want anyone to hear the Duchess's foul words, so he threatens to leave. But she pleads with him to stay and listen to her, to which Richard quickly replies, "And brief, good mother, for I am in haste" (4.4.162). This enrages her, and her intense parting words to Richard before his battle with Richmond predict Richard's fate: "My prayers on the adverse party fight . . . / And promise them success and victory. / Bloody thou art, bloody will be thy end; / Shame serves thy life and doth thy death attend" (4.4.191, 194–96). It is important to recognize that the Duchess of York fears for England. She does not fear Richard himself; rather she fears for the future of her land because of her distrust and deep-rooted hate for Richard.

Machiavelli emphasizes the connection a prince must have with his state. Bronowsky and Mazlish explain that in Machiavelli's time, the word "state" came to mean

> primarily a political standing, which was superior or supreme. . . . Gradually the holders of such a status were able . . . to identify their position with the entire administrative and bureaucratic structure of the community. When this was achieved, the prince and the state, the political theory of the time, became one. (36)

Richard never becomes "one" with the state. He possesses no heart, emotion, or loyalty for England. A ruler can justifiably govern his state and has the power to punish those who are disloyal to him, but first he must commit his own loyalty to the people whom he leads. This is Richard's primary flaw, and it is what leads him to his ultimate failure. Bronowski and Mazlish continue: "A prince must be entitled to do whatever he wants, provided it is for the satisfaction of the community as a whole and not for his own personal aggrandizement" (37). From the start, Richard's intent is to attain power over England. He clings too tightly to his designs and moves too rapidly in his scheme to realize that he will never catch up with his shadow—and this leads to his downfall.

Richard's lack of a conscience in the first half of the play illustrates his resemblance to a Machiavellian prince. Further into the play we learn that Richard has a guilty conscience. After ghosts of those whom Richard has murdered appear to him in a horrifying nightmare, he awakens in a panic. This scene can be labeled as Richard's moment of self-assessment and realization:

> O coward conscience, how dost thou afflict me! . . . / Cold fearful drops stand on my trembling flesh. / What do I fear? Myself? . . . / Is there a murtherer here? No. Yes I am. / Then fly. What, from myself? Great reason why— / Lest I revenge. What, myself upon myself? . . . / O no! Alas, I rather hate myself / For hateful deeds committed by myself. / I am a villain; yet I lie, I am not . . . / There is no creature loves me, / And if I die no soul will pity me. (5.3.179, 181–82, 184–86, 189–91, 200–01)

Richard recognizes that his conscience is cowardly; it betrayed him in the dream. The dream is a significant factor in Richard's downfall.

Richard's role as a Machiavellian prince lasts for a very brief period. The audience has a limited view of his conscience's implications. But throughout the play, Richard's guilt is plied against his conscience. The deviation from his role as a Machiavellian prince is symbolized by a chain of events where he exhibits a series of un-Machiavellian attributes as seen through his relationships with Lady Anne, Buckingham, and the Duchess of York.

Works Cited

Bronowsky, J., and Bruce Mazlish. The Western Intellectual Tradition. New York: Harper & Row, 1975.

Shakespeare, William. The Tragedy of Richard the Third. In The Riverside Shakespeare, 2nd ed. Ed. G. Blakemore Evans. New York: Houghton Mifflin, 1997. 748–804.

INTERVIEW

Comments and Reflection: The Interview

Most of my students have warmed to the interview assignment. Some like it because it gives them an excuse to talk to someone whom they've been curious to meet or to engage in conversation. Others like it because it gives them an opportunity to learn about a subject of interest by talking directly with an expert. Still others like it because the very act of conducting an interview creates a draft with which to work: That task of writing everything down for the first time somehow seems less daunting. I like the interview assignment for all these reasons too, and for another: The interview assignment shows students how to learn. It gives them a tool for gathering their own information, for becoming researchers about topics that they care about. It creates a confidence in the writing voice that makes the text an especial pleasure to read.

Yet the assignment is not without pitfalls. Many a student has found danger along the route. Here, then, is advice from students who had just completed the interview draft and were reflecting on their experiences.

Interviewers should make sure that they are interested in the topic their interviewee is knowledgeable about. If they aren't, then they won't enjoy listening to the interviewee or writing the interview.

—J. D.

I found the interview a little difficult because I interviewed my coach. He felt a little uncomfortable telling me personal and background information. I would advise others to interview someone that they don't know personally. I didn't have as much trouble with the conclusion as I thought I would. You were right; there was one question which just seemed to be the proper ending.

—Allison

I really liked doing the interview, even though I am not Barbara Walters! It was hard to act professional because I wasn't sure how professionals act, but it worked out well anyway. My interviewee was very nice, and it was plain to see that he enjoyed talking about the subject. I wish I could do the interview over because now I think I could do it a lot better! I now know what to do and would like to do more interviewing some time.

I do think, though, that I needed a more definite purpose for my interview, something to center it around. Other than that, the writing of this paper seemed easy!

—Becky

The one thing that helped me before interviewing Mrs. Werbiansky was talking with her daughter first. Her daughter suggested what I should talk with her about and even gave me a couple of questions to ask. She informed me about what happened during the period of time I talked about with Mrs. Werbiansky so I wouldn't go into the interview knowing nothing.

Interviewing takes a lot of organization. First I had to think about whom to interview and what about. Then I had to make arrangements so the interview could take place. And research must be done before going into the interview. Making sure you are prepared is very important. Even if you don't ask all your questions or follow your outline, make sure to go in with questions ahead of time. And don't be afraid to ask questions not on your list. Those might be the ones you use the most in your interview.

—Amy

Conducting an interview and then writing about what is learned from that interview enables writers to escape themselves, even temporarily. This assignment takes writers (and their instructors) out into the world to learn and to write about others, and that engagement is what, as a teacher of writing, I especially like about the interview. Vanessa Peterson interviewed a fellow student whom she had known for some time about his career choice: meteorology. She was curious about the subject and wanted to find out more about it and why her friend Sam was studying it. I find this interview a strong one because Peterson asks good questions. Her questions are engaging, probing, yet attentive to the responses coming from the interviewee, responses accumulating in the course of the interview. She seems comfortable; the prose is informal, and we feel as if we are overhearing a conversation between her and her friend Sam. Peterson presents herself well and does justice to her subject. What do you think works about this interview?

Sam Lashley, Student Meteorologist
Vanessa Peterson

Sam Lashley is studying to be a meteorologist, or atmospheric scientist as he likes to be called, at Purdue University in West Lafayette, Indiana. I have been friends with Sam since high school, yet I still find myself curious about his future profession. When I tell other people he is a meteorologist, I receive either a blank stare or the question, "Really, what's that?"

So I decided to confront Sam with some questions about himself and the meteorology field. My goal was to satisfy my own curiosity and have the answers to "Really, what's that?"

I talked with Sam in his apartment on the eve of one of his weekly lab report due dates. I have a feeling that knowledge he had stored for the lab report found its way into our conversation, because he occasionally slipped in terms like *Sutcliffe's* and *hydrostatic equations*. But the interview was relaxed and friendly, just like his stretched position over a gold beanbag. Our interview began with a clarifying question.

Q: Some people are unfamiliar with the term "meteorologist." Tell me what a meteorologist is and the types of jobs a meteorologist does.
A: We like to be referred to as atmospheric scientists rather than meteorologists. A meteorologist's job can vary depending on the type of field he goes into. A meteorologist who goes into television will generally not deal with as many maps. He will not have nearly the access to the information a meteorologist or atmospheric scientist who goes into the National Weather Service would have.

Q: So is there any difference then between a meteorologist and an atmospheric scientist?
A: There is no difference. We are scientists, and meteorologist is just an old-fashioned term, really.

Q: What are some of the job opportunities for a graduate of meteorology or atmospheric science?
A: The easiest to get into as a straight meteorologist would be the National Weather Service or NOAA Weather Service, which you can find in any major airport around the nation. They give out the forecast that you see on TV or hear over the radio. TV meteorologists need some kind of communication background, and it is a tough job to get into. But the pay is much, much better than a person going into the government or National Weather Service type job.

Q: Are there any private organizations?
A: Many air pollution consulting firms or firms with air pollution problems are employing meteorologists. Public Service Indiana employs eleven meteorologists who will advise them. There are different phenomena in the atmosphere that affect air pollution.

Q: What are the pay scales in that sort of job compared to the National Weather Service?
A: Much higher. The average starting salary is probably ten to twelve thousand dollars higher in a broadcasting or consulting firm than the National Weather Service.

Q: What kind of skills are necessary to be an atmospheric scientist?
A: A lot of physics, calculus, chemistry, and dynamics background. You don't think of the math that goes into meteorology.

Q: So what would you say to a high school senior who is thinking of going into meteorology? What should he/she do?
A: Have a strong math and strong physics background. I'm getting by because I've had to learn it as a college student. I thought I had a strong high school background, but I really did not. Everything we have dealt with so far has been the math and physics of it; very little actual "this is the weather and how it works."

Q: So what would be the best kind of high school student to be a meteorologist?
A: Someone strong in calculus and physics.

Q: Who is your personal hero in the meteorology field?
A: I would have to say Tom Skillings. He is a broadcast personality and one of the few actual meteorologists/atmospheric scientists—whichever you want to call him—who got his degree and then went into broadcasting. He is very popular in the Chicago area. He does things with his computers and graphics on TV that let you actually see the weather systems and how they move. He explains it very well.

Q: When did you realize you wanted to be an atmospheric scientist?

A: Oh, I've always been interested in the weather since I can remember.

Q: Was there any specific weather event that triggered you to the meteorology field?

A: I do remember when I was in the sixth grade, I was about four blocks from home and one of the biggest storms to come through our home town was six miles away and heading straight for us. I saw the damage from that storm and it just made me want to go into meteorology more.

Q: Which weather phenomenon is your favorite?

A: That's a toss-up between tornadoes and hurricanes. Tornadoes, on the small scale, because they are fascinating and unexpected. On the large scale, it would be hurricanes.

Q: So would you be willing to risk your life to experience one of these phenomena?

A: Well, in anything you do you risk your life. It's how you look at it. If you know what you are doing, you can observe a tornado from a safe distance without being in danger. There are very few people in the profession who are killed by weather phenomena. The knowledge is there to observe but be safe.

Q: So you are saying your training will help you avoid danger?

A: Training will definitely help avoid danger. There is always the risk, but training minimizes it.

Q: Where is the best place in the U.S. for studying weather?

A: Anywhere in the world is a good place to study weather. Weather happens everywhere. But if I had to pick a place, it would be in the arctic. It would be so interesting.

Q: Why?

A: It is so cold. The arctics have the lowest amount of moisture, which is hard to believe since it is all ice. Storms can produce a lot of snow there.

Q: How much would you say an average American knows about the weather?

A: I would say the average American knows about a cold front, a warm front, a high pressure, and a low pressure. Most people think that meteorologists sit around looking at satellite pictures and come up with forecasts. There are three different kinds of computer-generated models, and for a twelve-hour forecast, all three could be completely different. A meteorologist has to decide which one is right.

Q: So how would you sum up a meteorologist/atmospheric scientist's job?

A: We are competing against Mother Nature. We are trying to determine what Mother Nature does, and it is hard.

SURVEY

Comments and Reflection: The Survey

The survey report is a natural corollary to the interview report, and I often teach them one immediately after the other. Frequently, I present the survey as a group project. One of the survey reports presented here is the result of a collaborative effort in which four writers joined forces to create and test the questionnaire, conduct the survey, analyze the results, and then write the report. This particular group enjoyed the collaboration, but I can't say that every group has liked working together: Sometimes groups have a difficult time jelling. As a teacher I have some difficulties making and evaluating group assignments because I am aware of the inequities that sometimes occur in groups. I know too that sometimes folks are just so shy or reticent that their voices are lost, even in a relatively small group. And I get really frustrated at the evaluation of group work, regardless of the efforts I make to be fair. I worry that perhaps I haven't acknowledged one student enough or have credited another with too much. That said, though, I also know that group projects have considerable value. In the world beyond college (for college is the world too), considerable collaboration occurs; I collaborate on grant applications and departmental business communications regularly, and I chair one university committee and serve on others. The members of each committee collaborate to conduct much of the university's business. In reality, we do have to work together in the world, and perhaps the classroom is a good place to learn to do that well; that is why I keep encouraging and sometimes requiring collaborative projects. (I am not writing about peer review here, which I think is absolutely necessary to a writing class.)

The collaborative interview report that follows addresses the issue of sports in the midst of academe. Many students participate extensively in sports in high school, only to go to university and withdraw from athletic activity. The writers in this group wanted to know about the lives of those who continued to take part in sports, so they undertook this project. One of the strengths of their questionnaire is that it gathers information from both participants and nonparticipants in sports. About halfway through the document, the questions fork: If the respondent does play sports, he/she continues with one set of questions; if not, he/she answers another set. This strategy allows the writers to draw conclusions from both sides of the population and makes their results more valid. The group's data analysis is fairly convincing, and their use of the graphic to depict partial results is quite helpful to readers who learn visually and have difficulty internalizing the meaning of numbers.

Lisa Connors worked alone on her report, surveying forty female students from her dormitory in an attempt to take the pulse of the female dormitory resident. Connors's report might have turned out quite differently had she surveyed students in another dormitory or at a different university; and she might have had different findings if she had interviewed male students. Wisely, though, she establishes the limits of her survey in the opening paragraph of her survey report, thus shaping the reader's expectations. As long as Connors is explicit about her population and restrains herself from claiming too much for her data, her survey results and report are quite valid.

Here are some excerpts from students' informal in-class letters about conducting surveys and writing reports on the results. Notice that the comments almost always take the form of advice, which the writers felt eminently qualified to give after this experience.

I had a lot of trouble getting back the surveys that I sent out. I don't know whether my dorm mailperson just didn't deliver it or if the people I sent the questionnaires to were just too busy. I would recommend that students send out a lot more questionnaires than they think they need so that they will have enough material to use. I sent out 100 questionnaires, so I would recommend sending out at least 150.

—Freddy

It is very hard to see in the beginning how much information you'll get from all your surveys. I had loads but wish that I had been more specific in my questions. The smart person would devise some system or plan for how to organize and write up the information before issuing the final survey. My topic was very broad; several surveys based on more specific information could have come out of it. This makes me wonder how useful my writing really is. I liked this project and believe that next time I will know better what to do. I learned a lot.

—Anna

I thought it was hard to order the information after we tabulated all the responses. It was a major difficulty to reorganize the questions and answers to produce a usable text.

—Ron

The survey went well for me; I found the assignment to be very self-motivating because I could apply it to something I enjoy. That said, I want to suggest that if possible, anyone administering a survey should stand in the room with the respondents, because that makes the survey seem more important—and you'll have a much better response rate too.

—Jonathan

The survey went fine. The hardest part was tabulating all the results and figuring percentages. After that, it was a relatively simple paper to write because I had worked so much with the information that I believed I knew it.

—Matt

I hope you enjoy these survey reports as much as I have enjoyed rereading and thinking about them.

Sports and Student Life

Survey of Athletics in Students' Lives

This is a survey dealing with the role of athletics in students' lives. We are interested in discovering how athletic participation affects the personal and the academic life of athletes. Please take a couple of minutes to complete this questionnaire. Do not feel obligated to give us your name. When you finish with this questionnaire, please put it in the box marked *Sports Questionnaires* on the information desk in the student union. Thank you for your help!

Please circle the most appropriate response. Write in comments wherever you like.

1. Are you a
   a. Male
   b. Female

2. What is your approximate grade average?
   a. A (3.5 and up)
   b. B (2.49 to 3.5)
   c. C (1.49 to 2.5)
   d. D or below (0 to 1.49)

3. Do you participate in any intramural or varsity sports?
   a. Yes
   b. No

If you answered *No* to the above question, please finish the survey by answering questions 4 and 5. If you answered *Yes* to the above question, skip ahead and answer questions 6–9.

4. For what reasons do you choose not to participate in sports?
   a. Lack of interest in sports
   b. Lack of athletic ability
   c. Work
   d. Too much studying
   e. Other_____

5. What would attract you to participate in a sport? (Please write a brief sentence or two.)

6. What sport(s) do you participate in?

a. Baseball	f. Gymnastics	k. Track
b. Basketball	g. Soccer	l. Volleyball
c. Football	h. Softball	m. Wrestling
d. Cross-country	i. Swimming	n. Other_____
e. Golf	j. Tennis	

7. Does participating in sports reduce the amount of time you spend studying?
   a. Yes
   b. No

8. How would you say that participation in sports has affected your grades?

    a. My grades have gone up considerably.

    b. My grades have gone up a little.

    c. Playing a sport has not affected my grades.

    d. My grades have gone down a little.

    e. My grades have gone down considerably.

9. How do sports help or hurt your social life? (Please write a sentence or two.)

Sports and Student Life

Eric Leland

Janahan Vivekanandan

David Koller

Charles Tong

Sports are an extremely important facet of student life. All throughout the nation, thousands of college students compete interscholastically in athletic events. Here at Purdue University, things are no different. Interested in discovering the relationship between athletics and student life, we surveyed a cross-section of first-year students about their views and attitudes toward athletics.

The survey reached 115 students, 59 of whom were males and 56 of whom were females. Sixty-four percent of those surveyed played sports. Broken down further, 71 percent of the males and 57 percent of the females surveyed played sports. Males seem to have more of an inclination to compete in sports than females because there is a wider variety of sports offered to males than to females. The percentage of people playing in each sport can be seen in the graph below.

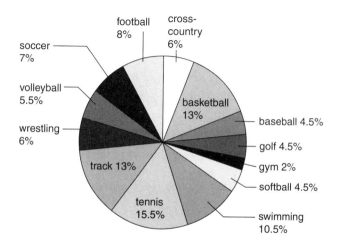

From the graph here, you can see that the most popular sport among students is tennis, followed closely by basketball and track. It is important to note that these three sports are played by both males and females, and thus are more popular. On the other hand, those sports played by only one sex, like soccer and football, seem less popular; but actually the same amount of males as play football play tennis. The percentages of students participating in fall, winter and spring sports are spread fairly evenly at 37 percent, 31 percent, 32 percent, respectively. This shows that the students are playing sports regardless of the weather.

We first decided to find out whether time spent on sports affected schoolwork. Surprisingly, the majority of the athletes think that sports do not reduce the time they spend on studying. Over 60 percent of the athletes said sports do not affect their ability to complete homework and studies. From this it appears that one can balance time spent between sports and schoolwork.

We were also curious to find out how grades are affected as a result of competing—either interscholastically or intramurally—in sports. At first, we thought that the answer was obvious—grades would go down. However, upon reading the survey, we found some surprising results. Twenty-one percent of the female athletes conveyed that their grades have gone up as a result of competing in sports, while an even 50 percent of them thought that their grades have not been affected by participation in sports. Nearly 15 percent of the male athletes thought that their grades rose as a result of playing in sports, whereas 65 percent of the males thought their grades stayed the same. This shows that participation in sports does not have an adverse effect on grades. It seems that athletes have plenty of time to devote to academics.

Next we asked what grade point average athletes currently hold. We found that males who play sports have more A's and B's than males who do not play sports. Eighty percent of the male athletes receive A's or B's, while only 60 percent of the male nonathletes receive A's or B's. Female athletes led the way, with almost 95 percent of them receiving A's or B's, and about 80 percent of the female nonathletes receive A's or B's. Since sports take up a lot of time, this shows that athletes have found a way to manage their time more efficiently and thus have more time to do homework. They are aware of the importance of academic achievement, and thus they don't let sports use all of their time. So much for the stereotype of the Dumb Jock!

We were also interested in how sports affect the social lives of athletes. This question gathered a variety of answers. More than 70 percent of the athletes said that sports improved their social life in some way. The most common response (about 85 percent of the above 70 percent) was that sports help people to meet new friends. One person wrote, "They [sports] help your social life by giving you the opportunity to meet people interested in the same things you are." Another person told us this: "Sports keep me closer to my pals and to babes who play tennis." However, many people had good reasons why sports can hurt social lives. As one person explained, "It [sports] hurts because now you have to spend all your free time studying." Another response was, "There is too much competition, which can ruin friendships." On the whole, it seems that for most people sport is beneficial to social life. Sports help students meet new people in their school as well as in other schools. Although some students think that sports create too much competition, the majority see sports as great exercise and just plain fun.

Although the majority of students play sports, many do not. They have many interesting reasons why they wish not to compete. Thirty percent cite lack of interest as a reason for not competing in athletics, while jobs or homework account for 25 and 24 percent, respectively, as reasons. There are many other reasons why students choose not to participate in sports. One student said, "Competition, rivalry, and the American way make school sports into much larger, more important events than they really are." Generally these people do not have the time or the interest to "waste" their time playing a sport. For example, one person said, "I would rather work and do homework!!" These people seem to care less about sports than other activities. Many of these people would rather earn money than waste it on sports-related expenses.

Ever since professional sports have thought of the idea of randomly selecting athletes for drug testing, many arguments have been made for and against the idea. Many people argue that a random sample of athletes violates their right to privacy and thus is unconstitutional. Others see it as a way to discourage drug use. When we asked our student sample their opinion, here is what happened. About half of the athletes think that random drug testing is a good idea, while only 20 percent think this is a bad idea. Strangely, the nonathletes think the opposite. Forty-five percent believe random drug testing is a bad idea while only 20 percent think this is a good idea. We believe that the athletes must see more of a problem with drugs in sports than nonathletes and would tend to support this kind of antidrug measure. This shows that people directly involved with this serious problem are beginning to search for and support legislation designed to help the drug problem.

Athletes have proved that they are much different than they are often thought of as being. The typical stereotype of athletes is this: Big dumb jocks incapable of intelligent thoughts and reason. They take steroids and hang out in a bad crowd. But we have seen that athletes on the whole are quite capable of receiving good grades and doing intelligent thinking. The majority are not shooting steroids into their bodies; rather, they realize that drugs are devastating to the body and to society. Sports are a beneficial part of students' school lives and their lives of the future.

Roommates: Who's Getting Along and Who's Not

I'm conducting a random and anonymous survey of roommates for my English class. I'm curious about your background and personality and how you're doing in a dorm room situation. If you would take a few seconds to fill out this questionnaire, I would really appreciate it. Thank you for your help.

—Lisa Connors

Please put a check in the appropriate answer space or write in brief responses.

1. What year are you?
_____ first-year
_____ sophomore
_____ junior
_____ senior

2. What state are you from? _____

3. How many brothers and or sisters do you have? _____ brothers and _____ sisters

4. If you are not the only child, where are you, approximately, in the birth order?
_____ only child
_____ oldest child
_____ middle child
_____ youngest child

5. How many children are in your family?
_____ one
_____ two
_____ three
_____ four
_____ more than four (please write how many): _____

6. How do you get along with your parents?
_____ very well
_____ OK
_____ not very well
_____ not at all

7. If you are not an only child, how do you get along with your siblings?
_____ only child
_____ very well
_____ OK

_____ not very well

_____ not at all

8. How would you describe your room at home?

_____ always clean

_____ usually clean

_____ rarely clean

_____ a pigpen

9. Would you prefer to be with

_____ one close friend?

_____ a small group of friends?

_____ a large group of friends?

_____ a party of people?

10. Do you have a steady boyfriend here at Purdue?

_____ yes   _____ no

11. Are you involved in sorority rush?

_____ yes   _____ no

12. Did you know your roommate before you came to Purdue?

_____ yes   _____ no

13. Is your part of the dorm room

_____ always clean?

_____ usually clean?

_____ rarely clean?

_____ a pigpen?

14. Are your and your roommates' interests

_____ the same?

_____ very similar?

_____ somewhat similar?

_____ very different?

15. Do you watch television

_____ all the time (six or more hours a day)?

_____ a little every day (one to two hours)?

_____ very little (15 minutes to an hour)?

_____ not at all?

16. Do you like your music loud?

_____ yes

_____ no

17. When you study, do you need

_____ complete quiet?

_____ some quiet?

_____ background noise?

_____ constant white wall of noise?

18. How often do you and your roommate argue?

_____ always

_____ often

_____ sometimes

_____ never

19. Have you considered changing roommates?

_____ yes

_____ no

Once you complete the survey, seal it in the provided envelope and drop it off in room NE 318; there is an envelope on the door. Thanks again for your help!

....

Lisa Connors

English 103

Dr. Beth Burch

15 November 199—

Roommates: Who's Getting Along and Who's Not

For first-year college students, being in a dorm room situation can be very traumatic. For the first time in their lives, they are forced to live away from home with a total stranger in a very small area. Some roommates become lifelong friends while others become archenemies. What types of people are getting along with their roommates and why? A recent survey tried to answer these questions. Approximately forty first-year girls from a variety of disciplines responded to a questionnaire on their backgrounds, personalities, and personal habits.

According to their responses most of them appeared to fall into clearly opposite categories. Some were sloppy, some clean; some shy, some outgoing; some serious students, some here for fun. Various combinations of these traits seemed to click or not click.

The most successful roommate relationships were between girls with similar interests, habits, and personalities. In most cases, even the most difficult person to get along with had little trouble adjusting to someone similar to herself. For instance, one girl admits to keeping her room like a pigpen, likes the television and stereo on all the time, and prefers parties to studying. Although she might be considered a less than ideal roommate for most people, she gets along with her roommate excellently because they share the same interests.

Unfortunately, everyone is not lucky enough to get a roommate very similar to herself. A surprisingly large number of "middle children" from large families (those with four or more children) get along well with their roommates. This group fits in best with all types of people. These girls generally get along with their parents and siblings, keep a somewhat clean room at home and school, and are flexible about the television and stereo. Being stuck in the middle of a large family has most likely prepared them for any situation they may encounter in a dormitory.

Although many people are happy with their roommates, others are not. Friction seems to occur most often when an introvert and an extrovert are put together. The girls who prefer very small social groups, if any, watch very little television, and like silence for studying have a difficult time adjusting to someone who prefers parties and loud study periods. The source of their friction is obvious: There is no common ground.

Even when they are paired with a roommate with common interests, a shockingly high number (over half) of only children surveyed do not get along with their roommates. Many in this category who admitted to having very similar or somewhat similar interests still did not like their roommates. Apparently many had trouble living with a peer for the first time.

Of course, not everyone can be classified so easily, nor do all the people in these classifications behave as their classifications indicate they might; but nevertheless some clear observations can still be made. Although some people are not getting along with their roommates, worried mothers will be glad to hear that 78% are!

ANNOTATED BIBLIOGRAPHY
Comments and Reflection: The Annotated Bibliography

The annotated bibliography is not a trendy assignment, but I like it. It gives writers a chance to do serious research (mostly among secondary sources); it requires writers to summarize or condense the research in a brief paragraph of explanation; it frequently employs evaluation when the writer judges the usefulness of a given source; and it allows writers to practice using style sheets and scholarly citation without worrying about constructing a research essay. I like the annotated bibliography as a culminating assignment at the end of a course; then the writer can bring to bear his or her entire experience in the course as the bibliography is constructed and annotated. Annotated bibliographies also give writers practice in narrowing topics, for an annotated bibliography with a virtually unrestricted subject will not be helpful and will not give the writer practice in deep research.

Allison Jaffe's bibliography, done in MLA style, presents the results of her inquiries into the work of Latina writers in America. Notice how narrow this topic is; Jaffe didn't look at all the writing by Latina authors, nor did she look at all the Latin American writing done in America. She narrowed her topic—first, to make her research more coherent and meaningful; and second, to make the physical task of doing research simpler. I like the way that Jaffe makes clear the merit of various sources, calling Gloria Anzaldua's essay in *Braided Lives*, for example, a "useful piece for anyone interested in demonstrating the dynamics of language." I also appreciate the way that Jaffe includes a concluding comment that in retrospect articulates her purpose and describes what she includes in the bibliography. It's useful that she connects these books by Latina writers to the larger experience of reading too; as a reader, I believe that she has carefully considered and selected with care the items she includes here. Finally, I am considerably impressed that Jaffe lists the books she found references to but could not find (because someone else had checked them out of the library or because our library does not own them). Her including this list tells me that she worked hard to create a comprehensive bibliography.

And this brings me to the final reason that I enjoy annotated bibliographies: I always learn of new scholarly resources—and knowing about those new books helps me keep my reading current too.

Allison Jaffe

English

Dr. C. Beth Burch

7/7/9—

The American Experience As Seen through the Eyes of Latina Writers: An Annotated Bibliography

Alvarez, Julia. <u>How the Garcia Girls Lost Their Accents.</u> New York: Penguin, 1992.

Alvarez gives her readers a rich look into the lives of the Garcia Family. Revolving mainly around Yo, one of the four Garcia daughters, this book describes the effects of a family uprooted as they struggle to fit in to the new mystifying ways of the Americans. Wonderfully written, <u>How the Garcia Girls Lost Their Accents</u> reveals the difficulty involved in trying to keep old world values and traditions alive in a new country. Alvarez carefully shows us the problems within our melting pot, as Yo struggles for an identity between two opposing cultures.

Anzaldua, Gloria. "How to Tame a Wild Tongue." <u>Braided Lives.</u> Ed. Deborah Appleman and Margaret Reed, Cochairs Editorial Board. St. Paul: Minnesota Humanities Commission, 1991. 94–97.

A great autobiographical piece, "How to Tame a Wild Tongue" is a description of the complexities of the Spanish Language as it integrates with American standard English. The author explains the variety of Spanish dialects which are available in the U.S. She also describes her struggle not to speak the "oppressors' language" (English), even though she is punished for speaking Spanish at school. This is a useful piece for anyone interested in demonstrating the dynamics of language.

Cisneros, Sandra. The House on Mango Street. New York: Vintage Books, 1984.

In The House on Mango Street, the reader looks through the eyes of Esperanza, a young girl growing up in a world she doesn't understand. The book is divided into lovely little vignettes as Cisneros deftly crafts an intimate picture of life in a Latino neighborhood. Characters are vivid and real as Esperanza gives an up-close portrait of each. The House on Mango Street is a wonderful story of a young girl's struggle to find her identity as she examines those around her.

Cofer, Judith Ortiz. The Latin Deli. New York: W. W. Norton, 1993.

The Latin Deli is a collection of poems and short stories, often autobiographical, many of which could prove useful in the high school classroom. "American History" is a lovely short story in which a young girl falls in love for the first time, only to be turned away by the boy's mother due to the color of her skin. "The Story of My Body" is an autobiographical tale which investigates the impact of color in metropolitan and rural settings as the author emerges into womanhood. "Not for Sale" is the story of a sixteen-year-old narrator grappling with her parents' stern Puerto Rican beliefs. These are just a few of the many pieces to choose from, most of which are suitable for the high school audience.

Cofer, Judith Ortiz. "Nada." Daughters of the Fifth Sun. Ed. Bryce Milligan, Mary Guerrero Milligan, and Angela de Hoyos. New York: Riverhead Books, 1995. 44–57.

This is a story of women, their relationships with each other, and their relationships to men. As the story opens, Dona Ernestina learns of her son's death in Vietnam. As she struggles to accept the reality that she has lost both husband and child, she refuses the flag and medals offered to her by the American government. Deciding that trinkets are no replacement for a human being, she quickly begins to abandon all of her possessions, much to the amazement of the other women in the building. This piece describes not only the relationships between these women, but what roles they play in society, and also what role the Vietnam war (or rather the American culture) plays in their lives.

Santiago, Esmeralda. When I Was Puerto Rican. New York: Vintage Books, 1993.

Santiago crafts a wonderful book about a young girl's coming of age in a time of turmoil. As the book opens, Negi and her family are living in near poverty in Macun, Puerto Rico. We quickly learn that her father is not a man to be counted on as he drifts in and out of their lives. After several attempts to leave him, Negi's mother finally decides to take the children to New York to live with their grandmother, where they must cope in a completely different life. This book is not just about acculturation, it is also about the relations between families and the generations within them.

Vasquez, Enedina Casarez. "The House of the Quilts." <u>Daughters of the Fifth Sun.</u> Ed. Bryce Milligan, Mary Guerrero Milligan, and Angela de Hoyos. New York: Riverhead Books, 1995. 67–81.

"The House of the Quilts" is an account of migrant workers in America as seen through the eyes of a young girl. Against the landscape of a dairy farm in Wisconsin, Velasquez carefully delineates the social and economic differences between the narrator's family and the owners of the farm. With great detail she discusses the lives of the six other families they share a house with and the problems which result from living in such close proximity. Altogether, she gives an interesting view of the lives of migrant workers in the 1950s.

Viramontes, Helena Maria. "Growing." <u>Braided Lives.</u> Ed. Deborah Appleman and Margaret Reed, Cochairs Editorial Board. St. Paul: Minnesota Humanities Commission, 1991. 118–24.

This is a story about Naomi, a young girl coming of age in the city. Her parents, although immigrated to the U.S., still uphold the ways of the old country. For this reason, Naomi must have a chaperon, her younger sister, with her everywhere she goes. As Naomi struggles to free herself from her sister's watchful eye, she struggles also to free herself from her childhood. As the story progresses, we learn that maybe she is not quite ready to grow up after all.

Books on Latin American Culture:

De Hoyos, Milligan, and Milligan, eds. <u>Daughters of the Fifth Sun.</u> New York: Riverhead Books, 1995.

This book contains a great collection of short stories and poems. Although I only gave a description of "Nada" and "The House of the Quilts," I encourage everyone to investigate the rest of this rich book. On top of wonderful fiction, there is a thoughtful foreword and an introduction that seeks to explain the plight of the Latin American writer. It is an interesting piece to consider, full of history which helps explain the evolution of these new lyricists.

De Varona, Frank. <u>Latino Literacy: A Complete Guide to Our Hispanic History and Culture.</u> New York: Henry Holt, 1996.

A detailed description and year-by-year account of Hispanic history is given in this comprehensive book. There are several chapters which may prove useful for teachers who intend to study Latin literature or the impact of Latin Americans on American culture. One of these is a chapter devoted to language and gives a list of words which have been incorporated into the American language. Chapters on music and art provide examples of the diverse Latino culture. There is even a chapter devoted to food. A fun book, <u>Latino Literacy</u> really shows how the Latin culture has impacted America.

Shorris, Earl. <u>Latinos: A Biography of the People.</u> New York: Avon, 1992.

This book is a useful tool for discovering the history of a very diverse people. Information about religion and politics is also included in this thoughtful portrait. Several short autobiographical pieces are included, which may be useful in painting a fuller portrait of the people, rather than depending on facts and figures. Most importantly, special attention is paid to just what the Latin experience in America really is.

The goal of this annotated bibliography is to supply a list of female Latina writers who describe what the American experience is. Works include short stories as well as novels which will be useful in teaching grades 9–12. I've also included a couple of books which would be useful for giving a background of Latin American culture to place these stories against.

All of these stories tell of the Latin American experience in America, but they have other links as well. "Nada," "Not for Sale," <u>When I Was Puerto Rican,</u> and <u>How the Garcia Girls Lost Their Accents</u> all deal with the relationships between men and women and with what being Latina means in these relationships. All of the stories deal with parent/child relationships and with how Latin American descent affects these relationships. Most importantly, they all deal with the difficult transition to becoming an American, especially problems with the language. Since it is so difficult for the protagonists to adapt to the American culture, they often are faced with discovering just exactly who they are. Although this dilemma is present in almost all of the works cited, it is shown most clearly in "How to Tame a Wild Tongue," "Growing," "The Story of My Body," and <u>How the Garcia Girls Lost Their Accents.</u>

All in all, I had a hard time putting these books down. They are all entertaining and poetically written (especially <u>The House on Mango Street</u>) and often have a bittersweet ending. They are sure to entrance at least a few young students into the wonderful world of reading, and that's what it is all about.

Books Not Available for Examination:

Carlson, Lori M., ed. <u>Cool Salsa: Bilingual Poems on Growing Up Latino in the U.S.</u> New York: Henry Holt, 1994.

Chavez, Denise. <u>The Last of the Menu Girls.</u> Houston: Arte Publico Press, 1991.

Hinojosa, Maria. <u>Crews: Gang Members Talk to Maria Hinojosa.</u> San Diego: Harcourt Brace, 1995.

Novas, Himilce. <u>Everything You Need to Know about Latino History.</u> New York: Plume Books, 1994.

Thomas, Joyce Carol, ed. <u>A Gathering of Flowers: Stories about Being Young in America.</u> New York: Harper Collins, 1990.

CREDITS